The Prehistory
of Denmark

JØRGEN JENSEN

The Prehistory
of Denmark

METHUEN
LONDON AND NEW YORK

First published in 1982 by
Methuen & Co. Ltd
11 New Fetter Lane, London EC4P 4EE

Published in the USA by
Methuen & Co.
in association with Methuen, Inc.
733 Third Avenue, New York, NY 10017

Phototypeset in Linotron 202 by
Graphicraft Typesetters Hong Kong
Printed in Great Britain at the University Press, Cambridge

British Library Cataloguing in Publication Data

Jensen, Jørgen
The prehistory of Denmark.
1. Denmark–History–to 1241
I. Title
936.3   DL161

ISBN 0-416-34190-X
ISBN 0-416-34200-0 Pbk

Library of Congress Cataloging in Publication Data

Jensen, Jørgen, 1936 July 30–
The prehistory of Denmark.
Translation of: Dansk socialhistorie.   v. 1.
Bibliography: p.
Includes index.
1. Man, Prehistoric–Denmark.   2. Denmark–Antiquities.
I. Title.
GN826.J4613   1982   948.9'01   82-24885
ISBN 0-416-34190-X
ISBN 0-416-34200-0 (pbk.)

To my wife Barbara

Contents

List of Figures

Preface

This book was written to present a general survey of the prehistory of Denmark as it has emerged after the past decade of research. Up to the 1960s Danish archaeology was dominated by a handful of distinguished scholars: Sophus Müller, Johannes Brøndsted, Gudmund Hatt, P.V. Glob, and C.J. Becker. Moreover the discipline was strongly influenced by continental modes of thought, and the chronological problems were still the main focus of research.

However, in Denmark as in other European countries, the 1960s became a period of change. A wave of new theories did away with the old diffusionistic framework. Many scholars spoke of a crisis in the profession. But as elsewhere in the west, the 1960s also marked the beginning of a rich productivity in the field, and today we can speak of at least three contrasting theoretical perspectives in Danish archaeology: positivist, marxist and structuralist. Each one of them has been able to open up fruitful perspectives for future research.

These changes first developed after the publication of the last major survey of Danish archaeology to be translated for readers outside Denmark, Johannes Brøndsted's *Nordische Vorzeit* from 1960–3. It therefore seemed quite clear that both students and teachers in other countries would have need of a general introduction to the perspectives recently opened in Danish archaeology.

It is this need which the present book seeks to meet. To be sure, many of the conclusions are preliminary, because detailed, systematic and up-to-date studies are still required in many fields. Despite this lack, I have written the present book in the hope of providing a synthesis of the 10,000 years of Danish prehistory up to the early state formation of the Viking period.

This work could not have been written without the inspiration of many discussions with colleagues in Denmark and abroad, too numerous to be mentioned here. However, I owe special thanks to Professor Olaf Olsen, State Antiquary and Director of the National Museum of Denmark, who in 1975 encouraged me to write this book; to Professor J. Desmond Clark, University of California, Berkeley, who extended his generous hospitality to me during a stay in Berkeley in 1980; to Professor John Coles, University of Cambridge, who willingly offered advice in the preparation of this English edition; and finally to the Danish Research Council for the Humanities, which supported this project financially.

I also wish to thank my wife, Barbara Bluestone, who did the translation and without whose endless patience, support and linguistic help this work could not have been completed.

Jørgen Jensen 1982
The National Museum, Copenhagen

Introduction

Archaeology in Denmark

It all began in 1807, when the British army bombarded and burned down much of Copenhagen. Denmark found itself in the midst of one of the devastating wars of the Napoleonic period. This period also witnessed another sort of destruction. In the wake of the radical agricultural reforms of the 1780s terrible damage was wrought to thousands of prehistoric monuments in Denmark. New forms of land management led to the cultivation of regions which had not been ploughed for more than a thousand years. A profusion of buried treasures from heathen times was ploughed up from the soil – all while their hiding-places, the prehistoric monuments, were damaged.

In that catastrophic year 1807, this alarming situation led to the formation of a royal antiquities commission. The goal of this commission was primarily to save what could be saved from destruction and also to ascertain what remained of prehistoric monuments in the Danish countryside. With the formulation of this task, a new epoch was born not only in Danish archaeology but also in what later developed into European archaeology. For the first time ever in Europe, archaeology was defined as an independent discipline, focused upon prehistoric artefacts and monuments.

The next major step was taken in 1816, when the commission hired a prosperous young businessman, Christian Jürgensen Thomsen (1788–1865), to arrange its collections of prehistoric finds (Figure 1). Three years later, in 1819, the collections were presented to the public in an exhibition in which the 'antiquities' were arranged into three groups according to their material: stone, bronze and iron.

Up to 1830, C. J. Thomsen slowly developed the idea that this

Figure 1 Christian Jürgensen Thomsen (1788–1865), the creator of the three-period system, the first technological evolutionary model in European prehistory. Drawn in 1846 by the Danish artist Magnus Petersen.

threefold division according to material was also a chronological framework. Thus Thomsen created the three-period system with his Stone, Bronze and Iron Ages, which became the first technological evolutionary model in prehistory.

Thomsen's pioneering work was soon supplemented in many ways, especially by his successor as director of the national collections, Jens Jakob Asmussen Worsaae (1831–85). The years up to Worsaae's death in 1885 saw the founding of the entire institutional and theoretical framework which has prevailed in Danish archaeology almost up to the present. The National Museum in Copenhagen was founded; in addition a central registration of Danish prehistoric monuments, still one of the essential tools for archaeological research, was established in 1873. During these years there flourished in Copenhagen an archaeological milieu, internationally oriented and open to related sciences as well as to amateurs. The same era saw the rise of cultural – historical diffusionism, the theoretical framework for Danish archaeology until the 1960s.

Up to the 1960s, the National Museum in Copenhagen was the focus of most archaeological activity in Denmark. The economic surge of the 1960s, however, also led to changes in the institutional structure of archaeology in Denmark. Some activities were centralized, others de-centralized and taken over by the growing number of local museums directed by professional archaeologists. A similar trend could be observed in the other Scandinavian countries. The 1960s and 1970s also saw the boom of the cities and the rapid growth of motorways, housing projects, pipe-lines, etc., all of which contributed to the widespread destruction of prehistoric monuments. Therefore one of the most significant archaeological events in Denmark during these years was the passing of a series of environmental laws under which all prehistoric monuments are protected. The term 'monument' embraces every trace of prehistoric man, be it grave, settlement or votive find. Protection of all archaeological sites in Denmark is thus ensured by law and has as a result become integrated in the long-range planning for the country as a whole. All observations of archaeological interest must be reported to the National Museum, the director of which is the leader of all antiquarian activities in Denmark.

A wide spectrum of archaeological research, including rescue excava-tions of prehistoric monuments, is carried out by three types of institutions in close co-operation: the National Museum in Copenhagen, the many smaller museums spread throughout the provinces, and the institutes of archaeology at the universities of Århus and Copenhagen.

The National Museum (Figure 2), the most venerable of these part-ners, possesses the most important prehistoric collections in Denmark. This institution is clearly a product of the liberal humanism espoused by the educated classes in the mid- and late nineteenth century. Like a number of other European museums, the National Museum was found-ed upon the vision of a grand all-inclusive universal repository. The First Department of the museum contains the prehistoric collection. Here, as we have mentioned, a unique central registration of all prehistoric finds in Denmark has been conducted since the late nineteenth century. The archives which are now in the process of being computerized include information about more than 125,000 localities. Thus they offer the natural foundation for all archaeological research in Denmark. The National Museum also houses a number of valuable laboratories for such studies as radiocarbon dating, pollen analysis, dendrochronology, etc. Other museums also contribute to the joint effort. About eighty

Figure 2 Prinsens Palæ (Palace of the Crown Prince) in Copenhagen. Built in 1742–4; it is now the main seat of the Danish National Museum.

provincial museums are officially recognized by the Danish state and twenty-two of them are directed by or include one or more university-trained archaeologists on their staff. Efforts to decentralize the system have increased the number of archaeological projects – especially rescue excavations – carried out by the local museums. Impressive archaeological collections are found in Ålborg, Århus, Haderslev and Odense.

The archaeological institutes at the universities of Copenhagen and Århus have flourished since the 1960s. Besides educating archaeologists, a process averaging six years, these institutions now also participate in research projects, often in conjunction with the National Museum or local museums. Although the institutes possess no collections, they do carry out excavations and finance much archaeological research in Denmark.

The work of these various archaeological institutions is co-ordinated by the Ancient Monument Board, established in 1977. This council was created to define guidelines for the research policy for all archaeological activity in Denmark.

The last twenty years have not only brought great changes in the external organization of Danish archaeology. There have been internal upheavals as well. Modern methods and new theoretical concepts have

been introduced, and field work has been revolutionized by mechaniza-
tion. Since the 1960s ambitious excavations of prehistoric settlements
have been successfully completed. Entire village complexes spreading
over several hectares have been uncovered, thus providing insight into
the organization of prehistoric society to an extent which would have
been inconceivable with the limited methods of earlier generations.
These new methods have had a tremendous impact on our knowledge
of, for example, the farming communities of the Iron Age. Nor has the
size of the excavations been the only change. Novel excavation techniques have also entailed a wider application of scientific methods such as
pollen analysis, radiocarbon dating, thermoluminescence dating, dendrochronology, etc. Equally vital developments have occurred in
archaeological theory. Until the 1960s, the theoretical framework of
Danish archaeology was based primarily upon diffusionistic thought
from the nineteenth century. A highly mechanistic concept of cultural
evolution prevailed. Evolution was viewed as a series of static phases
succeeding one another as a result of invasion, climatic change, technological innovation and similar isolated factors.

In the 1960s, however, archaeologists struck out in new directions.
Ecological approaches became ever more integrated into Danish
archaeology. The study of man's environment became as essential as the
study of his tools – somewhat later, social anthropology, particularly as
practised in England and America, exerted a powerful influence. As in
most western countries there was talk of a new archaeology which with
more exact methods sought to determine the relationship between the
various parameters in prehistoric cultural systems.

In the following account, an evolutionary perspective has been
applied to the tremendous period stretching from the last Ice Age to the
Vikings. This account is based upon the course of nature during the
millennia following the last Ice Age. This natural process and the
changes it caused in the resources accessible to man were of prime
significance in determining the size of the population, its exploitation of
the resources, and its social structure. In the next chapter we shall
therefore attempt to trace the intimate bond which existed between man
and his environment from the earliest communities of reindeer hunters
to the late hunter-gatherer communities, the lives of which were
completely transformed by the introduction of agriculture around the
end of the fifth millennium BC.

Denmark, the bridge to the north

Perhaps it was on a winter day 12,000 years ago, at the end of the Ice

Age, when a human being gazed at the Danish landscape for the first time. It was a bare arctic land, sharp in its contours, cold and windy and with only a meagre tundra vegetation – just enough for herds of reindeer to find food here part of the year. These reindeer provided man with his first foothold in the arctic regions so far to the north. In pursuing and hunting these reindeer, man had taken the first step in what was to be 10,000 years of continuous human settlement in southern Scandinavia.

Throughout these many millennia, Denmark served as a bridge between central Europe and the Scandinavian peninsula. This continued to hold true when the land developed its present archipelago nature, about 7000 years ago. Its many islands and its shallow waters functioned as an effective link to the northernmost part of the continent.

The topography of Denmark bears witness to the fact that the land was only partially covered by the ice sheet during the last Ice Age, the Würm-Weichel glaciation. The margin of the enormous expanse of inland ice ran down through the centre of Jutland, dividing the young moraine from the old moraine landscape (Figure 3). West of the ice sheet, the edge of which formed what is today called the Main Stationary Line, there was, during the last Ice Age, an open arctic area. This was an old moraine landscape which had been created during the next-to-last Ice Age. Running water, rain, snow, wind and frost together formed its surface. Today this landscape is characterized by the so-called hill islands, the oldest feature in the Danish terrain. The gently rounded forms of these hill islands contrast greatly with the far bolder relief of the young moraine landscapes east of the Main Stationary Line. The old moraine landscape is devoid of the tunnel valleys, marginal moraine, lakes, hilly areas and undrained depressions which distinguish the young moraine landscape.

A modern traveller to west Jutland will see the hill islands rise up from the vast flatness of the outwash plains. These plains were the deposits of the meltwater rivers, sandy inland deltas created near the ice margin during the last glacial period. The outwash plains are cut by low river valleys; their flat surface is in places disturbed by circular hollows formed by subsidence when masses of dead ice melted. These hollows may be filled by lakes or bogs, those damp places which have meant so much in the prehistory of Denmark because of their remarkable preservative qualities. In north and east Denmark, the modern traveller encounters quite another sort of scenery. Here is the young moraine region with its dramatic relief. Yet in east Denmark as well, the rugged surfaces were gradually smoothed out by millennia of ploughing.

Young moraine landscapes in north and east Denmark are either hilly

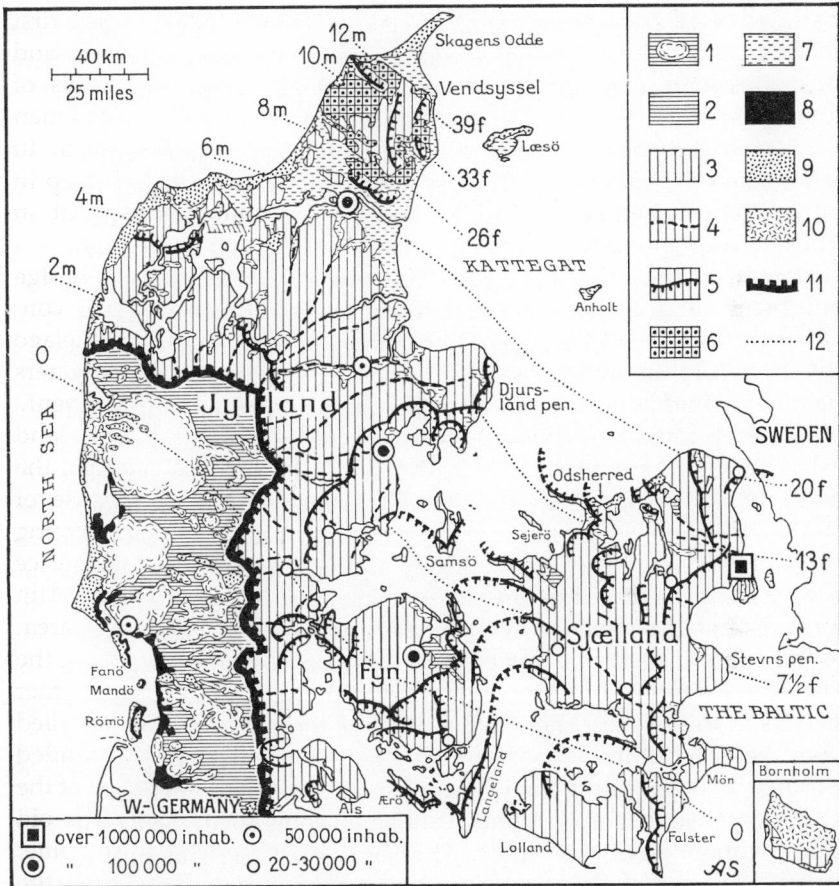

Figure 3 Geomorphological map of Denmark. 1. Old moraine landscape, Riss-Saale glaciation. 2. Outwash plain, meltwater deposits from the Würm-Weichsel glaciation. 3. Young moraine landscape, Würm-Weichsel glaciation. 4. Subglacial valleys with long lakes and bog depressions. 5. Significant marginal zones, in many places forming the glacial series of landscapes: central depressions separated by marginal moraine hills from the distally placed outwash plains. 6. Late-glacial plateau, raised sea floor. 7. Marine foreland. 8. Marsh plain. 9. Dune landscapes. 10. Granite landscape with rocky coasts and joint valleys in Bornholm. 11. Main Stationary Line during the Würm-Weichsel glaciation. 12. Isobases for the relative uplift of land since the Litorina-Tapes transgressions.

or flat. During the last Ice Age, the hill country was created in the border zone of the ice by the accumulation of moraine material. When the ice moved forward, it pressed vast quantities of earlier-deposited material together, sometimes in rampart-shaped ridges. These ridges consist of particles of all sizes, from grains of clay to huge boulders. Today this marginal moraine has become a countryside of rounded hills hundreds of metres long. Here and there are rows of hills stretching kilometre after kilometre.

In contrast to the moraine hills, the moraine flats are normally formed where there is boulder clay. This type of terrain, exemplified by the area bordered by Copenhagen, Roskilde and Køge, is smoothly undulating. The relatively thin layer of moraine soil was left behind on an ice-eroded surface when the ice melted away 10,000 years ago. With their fertile soil and plane surface, the moraine flats are the finest agricultural land in Denmark today. Yet they were not cultivated until late in prehistory, due in part to the difficulties they presented to primitive tilling instruments. Furthermore, the moraine flats had to be laboriously drained before they could be cultivated to the extent they are now.

No matter where one travels in Denmark, the sea is always close at hand. In fact, no spot lies more than 50 kilometres from the shore. The 7000-kilometre-long coastline is marvellously varied. Places such as Møn, on Stevns in eastern Denmark, and Bulbjerg on the North Sea, boast cliff coasts carved in limestone rocks. Most of the other coasts are formed of glacial deposits, boulder clays and sand. Danish shores are usually flat and can be categorized either as beach-ridge shores or marshland shores. The former type evolves where the breaker zone sweeps in to the shoreline. Here a beach is formed of gravel and sand from the beach drift. These very wide flat shores are found along the North Sea, whereas the Baltic shores span only a few metres.

The marshland shore is found at sheltered spots such as the estuarine areas of inner bays and fjords. The south-west coast of Jutland, for example, is bordered by an almost unbroken marsh. Here, at their lowest-lying point, the outwash plains are submerged. Only here do we find a tidal range of any consequence, namely about 2 metres. Further north the tidal amplitude diminishes and in the inner Danish seas it is very slight.

The countryside of today has been moulded by man, chiefly over the past 200 years. Towards the end of the eighteenth century, radical agricultural reforms were carried out in Denmark. Land which had been untilled since the Middle Ages was reclaimed. Thus a sweeping transformation of the landscape was initiated. With it followed the dawning interest of the Romantic era in prehistoric monuments, an interest which led to the creation of Danish archaeology.

PART I

The hunters and gatherers
11,000–4200 BC

A changing environment

After the last Ice Age

During the Pleistocene, northern Europe underwent at least four waves of fierce, cold ice ages. During at least two of the warmer periods which intervened between the ice ages, man appears to have lived in Denmark. The oldest and best documented finds are man-made tools from Vejstrup Forest in Jutland. Through them we can trace the presence of man in Denmark more than 200,000 years back in time.

Unfortunately, our knowledge of the first appearance of man in Scandinavia is so scanty that it would be impossible to attempt to determine his behavioural patterns. Not until after the last Ice Age, the Würm-Weichsel, can we piece together a coherent picture of human evolution in Denmark.

Approximately 13,000 years ago began the climatic change which brought the last Ice Age to a close. During this glacial period, Denmark was completely covered by ice except for the western parts of Jutland. At Hald near Viborg, the edge of the ice made a sharp angle. From here it extended westwards towards Britain. To the south the ice margin extended down through mid-Jutland.

As the ice sheet retreated, vast quantities of meltwater began to flow out to the cold arctic sea, and where the ice had once lain, a barren landscape was now exposed. The most striking feature of the newly revealed land was the pale raw soil. This barren raw soil imparted to the landscape a remarkably light colour due to the fact that the soil contained no humus but much lime. Even where sparse vegetation gradually began to grow, the light colour predominated. Only after an exceedingly slow 'maturation' process lasting thousands of years was the light raw soil converted into dark fertile mould. When the ice disappeared, the land was, from a biological point of view, still young.

The first pioneer flora which spread over the barren earth, thus creating an open tundra, consisted in part of mountain avens (*Dryas octopetala*), which was conspicuous in the landscape with its ivory-white flowers on long stems. Here and there were white carpets of this flower. Dwarf willow (*Salix herbacea*), arctic willow (*Salix polaris*), dwarf birch (*Betula nana*) and sea buckthorn (*Hippophaë rhamnoides*) flourished, along with the now rare Öland rock rose (*Helianthemum oelandicum*) which tinted southern slopes yellow during the short arctic summer (Figure 4). All these immigrated pioneers were hardy and cold-tolerating. Many of them could survive under snow most of the year; all of them managed to blossom and produce seeds during the brief cool summer. These pioneer growths were characterized by their love of light and their preference for calcareous soils. During this period, the summer temperature averaged 8°–9°C.

Around 10,500 BC came one of the first brief warm phases which can so deeply disturb the delicately balanced arctic vegetation. The first Late Glacial warm phase is called the Bølling oscillation. During this short period, a park tundra developed in Denmark with light forests of birch in the warm areas. The open tundra still dominated in the cold north-facing or damp areas. The landscape became green in the summer, but the return of the night frost must have brought bright yellows and reds, followed by winter whiteness.

During the Bølling oscillation, the area which is now Denmark was freed of ice; but the mild temperature was only a brief respite. A new cold thrust around 10,000 BC (the Older Dryas) caused a major recession; the light pioneer forest was obliterated and once more the open tundra prevailed.

Then, several centuries later, a new warm phase known as the Allerød period began. Once more a park tundra grew up with birch (*Betula pubescens*) as the dominant tree. Quaking aspen (*Populis tremula*) and rowan (*Sorbus aucuparia*) also appeared together with juniper (*Juniperus communis*) and bird cherry (*Prunus padus*). The climate was so mild that presumably pine also grew.

During the Allerød period the south-eastern and north-western parts of the country contrasted sharply with one another. South-east Denmark now had a temperate climate with an average July temperature of 13°–14°C. Then around 9000 BC, a last sudden temperature drop (the Late Dryas) was felt over most of Europe north of the Alps. The climate became sub-arctic, the summer temperature sank to about 10°C. The inland ice ceased to thaw on the Scandinavian peninsula, and in Denmark trees very nearly stopped growing. The south was a park tundra, whereas in the north-west a wide open tundra dominated. The flora resembled that found today near the northern pine forest limit.

Animals as well as pioneer plants found their way to Denmark toward the close of the Ice Age. The reindeer was the characteristic tundra animal. In pursuit came its worst enemies: the wolverine and the wolf. Bison and wild horses grazed in the Late Glacial terrain, and there were also lemmings and blue hares. Fish of the Late Glacial waters included perch (*Perca fluviatilis*) and pike (*Esox lucius*).

During such mild periods as the Bølling and the Allerød, animal life grew increasingly varied. It was, from a modern viewpoint, a strangely mixed fauna. Tundra and steppe animals such as the reindeer, wild horse and bison still flourished in the milder environment. Now, however, the open forest vegetation attracted forest animals to the country. The newcomers included the now-extinct Irish elk (*Megaloceros giganteus*) and the common elk. The beaver, the brown bear and the lynx also arrived.

The Late Glacial ice sea was inhospitable to both flora and fauna. During cold periods the sea was frozen in the winter and filled with drift ice in the summer. However, whales and seals made their home in this ice sea. There are traces of the Greenland whale (*Balaena mysticetus*) and the killer whale (*Orcinus orca*); the ringed seal (*Pusa hispida*) and the walrus (*Odobenus rosmarus*) probably also lived in the glacial sea. Fish included the high arctic cod species *Gadus saida*. In warmer periods there was less drift ice. Along with the temperate mollusc fauna, new larger animals such as the rorqual (*Balaen optera physalus*) and the blue whale (*Sibbadus musculus*) also appeared. Arctic birds on the open sea included multitudes of long-tailed ducks (*Pagonetta glacialis*).

The extent of the land during the Late Glacial period is still not entirely known. At first northern Denmark was still heavily weighed down by the ice sheet masses. Northern Jutland consisted of a series of islands and the ice sea extended further eastwards, along the island of Læsø, roughly down to the present north coast of Zealand. The Baltic surface was still frozen. The land now freed from the weight of the ice gradually rose. But during the warmer periods the sea-level rose even faster then the land due to the influx of meltwater. In the end, it was the rise of the land which most influenced Denmark's geography. By the end of the Glacial period the land mass seen in Figure 6 had appeared.

This outline of the development of nature from the Late Glacial period and on through the millennia is based upon more than a century of research. Geological, pollen-botanical and zoological investigations have shed light on the migration of plants and animals to the land uncovered by the melting of the ice. Of especial importance is the relative

Figure 4 An open landscape covered with a hardy and cold-tolerating vegetation
was the scene of the appearance of the first hunting groups to arrive in
Denmark after the last Ice Age. The general impression may have resembled
this landscape from the Tollund bog in central Jutland.

chronology of Danish vegetational history which has been described in
botanist Knud Jessen's division of the pollen diagrams (Figure 5) into
nine zones (i–ix). These zones can today be pinpointed chronologically
by radiocarbon datings. In the main, the great drama of the development of the environment after the last Ice Age has been revealed.
However, it still remains to identify the factors which set this drama into
motion: the development of the climate and the soil, and not least of all
man's influence on nature.

In the Late Glacial landscape just described, the first hunting communities appeared. Man's role during this period resembles that of the
pioneer plants and animals. The lives of the hunting people were totally
shaped by their marginal environment. Nor is it surprising that traces of
the first reindeer hunters are so scarce. This reflects a tiny population,
the size of which was proportional to the resources available. To be sure,
the fauna of Denmark has probably never since been so varied as in the
sunny Late Glacial period. But these resources were subject to extreme

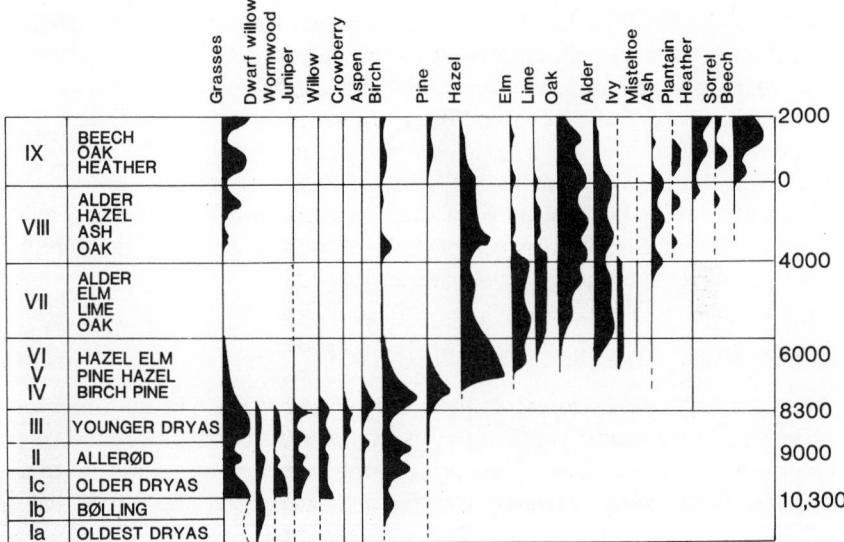

Figure 5 Pollen chart of the vegetational development in Denmark as described by botanist Knud Jessen in his division of the pollen diagrams into nine zones.

seasonal changes which determined both the size of the population and human behaviour. As will be shown, rising average temperatures in the subsequent period eased conditions for the hunting people and altered their existence.

The first continuous forest

Quite suddenly, around 8300 BC, the temperature rose drastically and in a short time the open park tundra was completely transformed. This period is termed the Pre-Boreal. Now a light and open birch forest spread over the terrain. The rapid rise in temperature encouraged the growth of trees such as aspen and birch which here and there had survived the cold period. Pine followed. All these trees were light-demanding pioneers and were the only species which survived long. They had already existed in the warm Allerød period. However, their development was irregular. Shortly after the first steep increase in temperature a brief cold period set in, delaying growth for some centuries. Then once more the temperature rose.

The continuous forest created by the warmer climate totally altered the animal life of the territory. The abundance of big game which had once roamed the open land now disappeared, to be supplanted by more localized species. The hunters' favourite game, the reindeer, vanished, and the aurochs and elk instead made the forest their home. Gradually red deer also became common in the light pioneer forest. Naturally, the presence of these meat-yielding animals strongly influenced the hunters' way of life.

During the Pre-Boreal, the land mass of Denmark looked completely different from today (Figure 6). It was then the northernmost tip of a large continent extending westward all the way to Britain. The climate was still cool, averaging about 15°C in July.

A new forest scene: the Hazel–Pine forest

After the light, open forest of the Birch–Pine period had endured for more than a thousand years, a new and more radical transformation of Denmark occurred about 7000 BC. As the summer temperature continued to rise trees appeared which later dominated the forest: oak

Figure 6 The relationship between land and sea about 8500 BC. A major part of the Scandinavian peninsula is still covered by the inland ice.

(*Quercus*), elm (*Ulmus*), hazel (*Corylus*), aspen (*Populus tremula*) and lime (*Tilia cordata*). Hazel, the first to migrate, now reigned in the forest together with pine. The appearance of hazel marks the beginning of the Boreal period. This tree thrives in the meagre shadow cast by a forest of birch, pine and aspen, where it also receives an ample quantity of sunlight. The underwood must have been rich in nuts, which became a vital supplement to the diet of the forest inhabitants.

In the Boreal hazel–pine forest, the large meat animals such as the aurochs and the elk still abounded. At the same time the red deer, the roe deer and the wild boar also became common. Compared with the wealth of game in the Late Glacial landscape, the forest of the Hazel–Pine period was nearly barren. In the poverty of its bio-mass, the Boreal forest can be compared to a desert or semi-desert. But from an ecological point of view, nature had evolved into a new stage of greater diversity and stability than before. Seasonal fluctuations in the availability of resources became less drastic. A broader spectrum of choice of existence now opened to the inhabitants of the land. The transformed environment had remoulded the life of the hunter communities. Most probably the population gradually increased due in part to a lesser dependence on seasonal variations in the access to food, the presence of large game animals, and the abundance of edible plant foods such as nuts, roots, bulbs, mushrooms, bark, fruits, plant juices, and many more. Although these plant foods have not yet been studied carefully, it is likely that gathering played an ever-increasing role in the life of human societies. In the following, the term 'hunters and gatherers' will refer to the societal form which prevailed from the Pre-Boreal period onward.

During the Boreal, Denmark was still much larger in area than it is today (Figure 7). But in both the Pre-Boreal and Boreal periods, the sea-level rose rapidly. The North Sea flooded over the land bridge between Jutland and Britain. One arm of the sea reached south of Britain, thus creating the Channel. The Baltic was turned into an enormous lake (the Baltic Ice Lake), the outlet of which was a wide river running through what is today the Storebælt. The land mass was at least one-fourth larger than modern Denmark. Today almost all the old coastlines are submerged.

The stable primeval forest

Warmth-loving trees immigrated to Denmark during the Boreal: first came hazel, later elm, ash (*Fraxinus*) and lime. No stable equilibrium among these trees existed. However, the forest slowly evolved toward

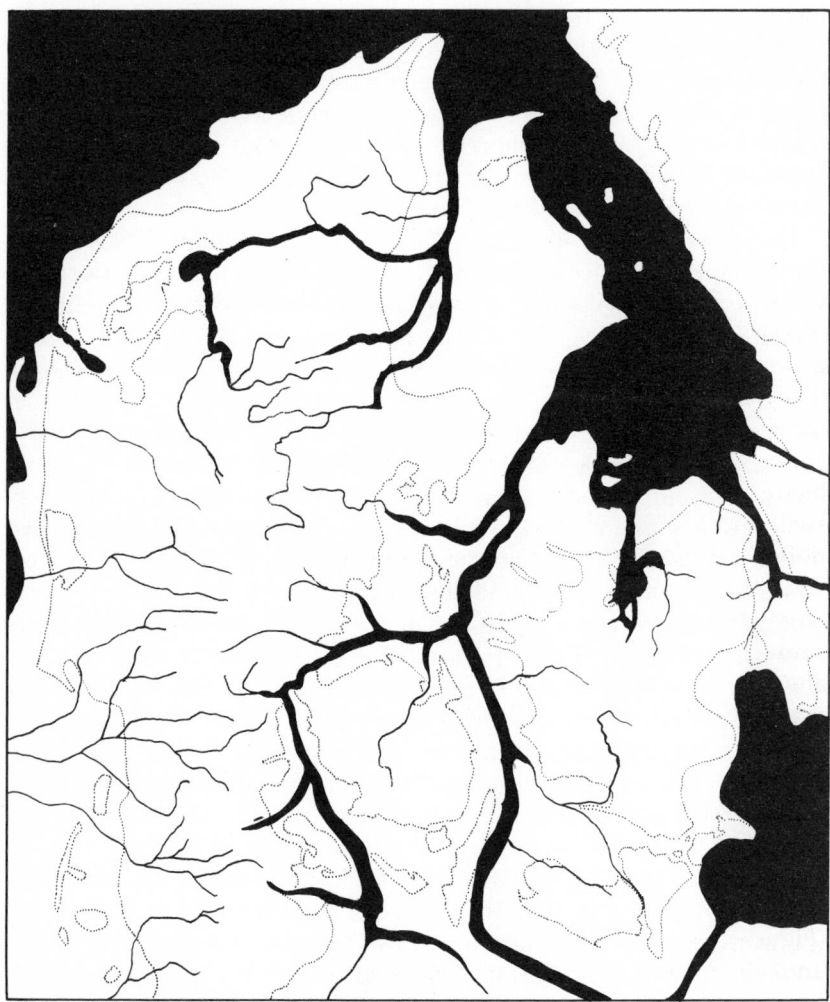

Figure 7 The relationship between land and sea about 7000 BC.

the stable primeval forest of the Post-Glacial warm period. By this is meant that the light-demanding pioneer trees of earlier times were gradually supplanted as shade trees gained ground. This process produced the equilibrium characteristic of a mature ecosystem. This period – the Allerød – saw the culmination of climatic development. Presumably the summer temperature was 2°–3°C higher than today.

At the commencement of the Hazel–Pine period, hazel competed with the pioneer trees and these were, in the long run, doomed.

Increasing warmth encouraged new shade trees to immigrate. Thus the forest moved into the phase of stable development which was to change the existence of its inhabitants so profoundly. By 6000 BC the stable primeval forest seems to have been formed. This stage was achieved at the same time as the climate changed from dry to humid; Denmark acquired an Atlantic oceanic climate. Doubtless the formation of the North Sea played its part in the increased humidity and warmth.

The dense primeval forest covering the land after 6000 BC was especially dominated by the lime, but elm and oak were also highly visible in the forest. The most striking feature of the stable primeval forest was its dense canopy. As undergrowth was relatively sparse, big game was afforded a poor selection of food. Aurochs and elk gradually died out and red deer and roe deer also decreased in number. However, the wild boar, which seeks its food in the moist forest floor, apparently survived undisturbed. In general it seems that the decrease in the bio-mass is sometimes exaggerated. A number of factors indicate that swift and synchronous alternations between dense and sparse vegetation could occur over large areas comprising whole stands of trees. Cyclic regeneration in the forest did not take place in isolation but over large areas covered by a whole stand of trees of the same age which had simultaneously been toppled by a storm. Thus the interior of the forest always included large glades which offered favourable conditions for many of the food plants of the big forest game. On the whole, however, the interior forest shows low productivity and low diversity. It is thus hardly capable of supporting year-round settlements even on a minor scale.

Out by the coasts and around the numerous inland lakes, swampy areas and streams, living conditions were much more favourable. Here the vegetation and fauna were far more richly varied than in the forest (Figure 9). Abundant sunlight provided a basis for fertile plant growth and teeming animal life. In time this situation became even more important for the population of the country.

The far north of the Scandinavian peninsula was still locked by enormous quantities of ice from the Ice Age. To the south, however, the increasing warmth continued to release great quantities of meltwater and the ocean rose. In Denmark this meant that the rise of the sea during the Atlantic period (the Litorina transgression) obliterated the coastline of the Boreal period. The land shrank considerably in size, losing an area equivalent to about one-fourth that of present-day Denmark. But what the land lost in area, it gained in an overwhelmingly long coastline. The Danish coast now consisted of deep fjords, sheltered coves and numberless small islands close to the coast (Figure 8).

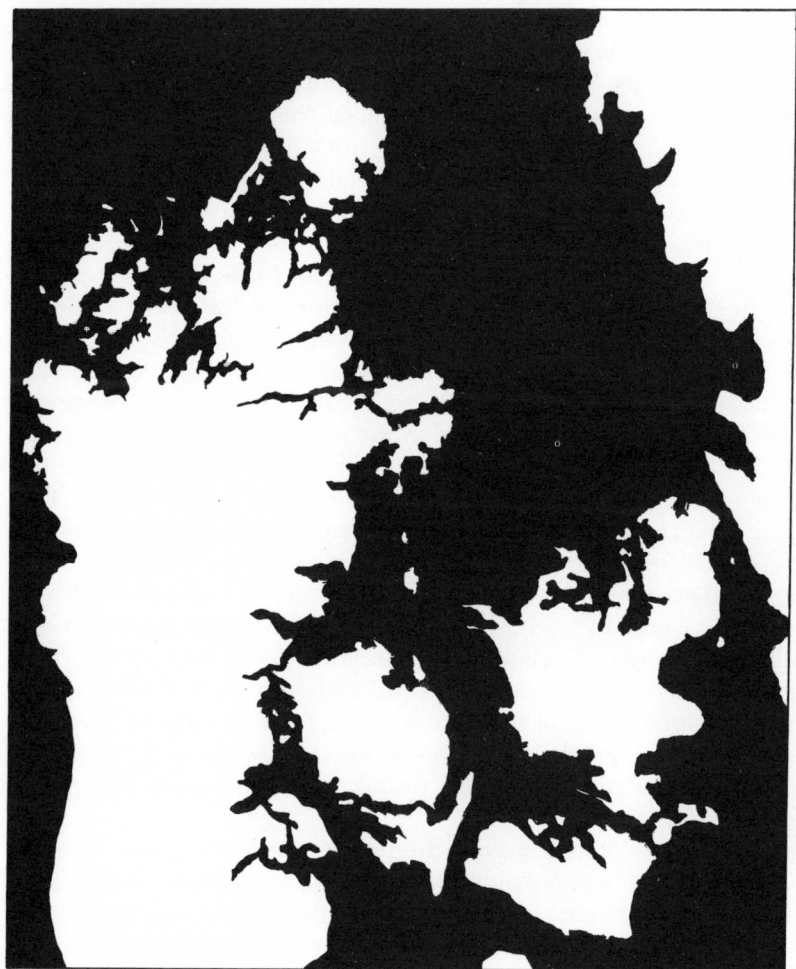

Figure 8 The relationship between land and sea about 4500 BC.

This coastal zone created the setting for a range of resources never before equalled. The high summer temperature, which resulted in a high water temperature, together with the fact that coastal erosion added many minerals to the sea, were among the factors which made the coastal zone so productive biologically.

From the viewpoint of cultural history the rise of the stable climax forest meant a basic change, as yet not entirely clarified, in the ways of adaption of the hunter–gatherer communities. A shift in the population balance may have been the result, and even if in the course of the

Figure 9 In the High Atlantic period, the Danish estuaries
and the areas immediately adjacent provided living
opportunities for the hunter-gatherer communities
almost all year round. This type of landscape can still be
found at some of the smaller Danish islands, here the
island of Ormø in southern Denmark.

Atlantic virgin-forest period man made an apparently subtle adaption to
the new living situation – first and foremost through an intensified
exploitation of the marine zone – it can hardly be doubted that in the
long run the environmental changes provoked a number of profound
technological and social changes. One of the most radical changes in the
living conditions of the prehistoric society began to make itself felt at the
end of the fifth millennium BC: prehistoric society was slowly becoming
agrarian.

Man and the ecosystem

As we have now seen, a number of remarkable environmental changes took place in Denmark in the interval between the close of the Ice Age and the end of the fifth millennium BC. The summer temperature rose from about 9°C to over 18°C – this meant a transition from a sub-arctic to a temperate climate. The summer temperature rose steadily, although it was marked by a number of small fluctuations (Figure 12). The earliest fluctuations had a notable effect on the development of the environment. In a sub-arctic climate even slight fluctuations in the average temperature may result in catastrophic changes of living conditions for both plants and animals.

Through the nearly 7000-year-long period discussed here, the Danish landscape was drastically transformed. It evolved from an open tundra vegetation to a dense stable virgin forest. Ecologically, this transformation can be termed a transition from a young ecosystem to a mature one, and the difference between the two extremes in the development was very great indeed. The young ecosystem, the tundra landscape, was exploited dynamically by a number of animal and plant species which in a short time had spread a large population throughout the area. There were, for example, plants which possessed a tremendously effective ability to spread, rapid growth and early sexual maturity, but also a relatively brief life span. This sort of ecosystem is characterized by rapid growth and high production – but it is unstable and provides poor protection for plants, animals and man. It may be seen as a system which pays high interest from a very small capital. From a biological viewpoint the young ecosystem invests in rapid growth, high production and large quantity.

In contrast, there is the mature ecosystem, which we encounter in the dense stable virgin forest which covered the country around 5000 BC. The mature ecosystem is characterized by so-called equilibrium species. For example, there are plants with a poor and ineffective ability to spread, slow growth and late sexual maturity; but in compensation they can grow very old. The equilibrium species creates a very balanced ecosystem, in which each species has its place, the boundaries of which are determined by the ecological adaptability and competitive capacity of the species. The mature ecosystem is thus characterized by great variation and stability. Due to its uninterrupted development, the mature ecosystem is adapted in all ways to the given physical–chemical conditions. It is therefore tremendously stable and well-protected from disturbances caused by natural forces. The amount of organic material produced in the ecosystem is consumed by the system itself, so that from a human viewpoint the mature ecosystem is not very productive. It invests in itself. In contrast to the young ecosystem, the mature ecosystem might be said to have a large capital but to pay little interest. In return, its range of variation is very wide.

Understanding of the development of early human societies in Denmark must be founded upon knowledge of the natural process sketched above. As will be shown, the development of the prehistoric communities was not controlled by any one factor. The decisive element was the interplay of the many factors, an interplay which was complicated and based upon mutual dependence. From an ecological viewpoint the growth of the human communities can be described as a process in which an ever larger part of the total energy flow of the ecosystem was channelled through the cultural system. To stimulate this development, human societies employed a multitude of means. The result was usually a growing labour input per unit of food gained. It is this development, the increase of the labour input of the prehistoric societies, which we shall now attempt to trace.

2

The hunting population

Fertility and mortality

The palaeodemographic material which we possess from the prehistoric hunter–gatherer communities is still very scanty. From Denmark and south Sweden together, about thirty individuals in all may with certainty be ascribed to the period. Denmark, however, has yielded one particular find which can give some idea of the mortality of the hunter population up to the introduction of agriculture. This is the find from Bøgebakken at Vedbæk, excavated in 1975 (S.E. Albrethsen *et al.*, 1976). Here a little cemetery from the end of the sixth millenium BC was found to contain twenty-two individuals. Four of these were newborn babies and one was about one year old. The ratio between the number of dead infants and dead adults is thus 5:17. However, this hardly gives a correct impression of infant mortality, which was most probably even higher, as the number of children's graves is hardly representative. Other investigations of prehistoric populations (G. Acsádi and J. Nemeskéri, 1970) indicate that an infant mortality of about 35 per cent or more is not uncommon.

At the cemetery in Vedbæk, of the seventeen individuals whose age could be determined, eight died before they attained the age of 20 years. This high figure is hardly surprising. Until late in historical times, mortality in the age group up to 20 years old was 50 to 60 per cent. This means that only about 40 per cent of the living-born individuals survived beyond 20 years of age.

Among these survivors, moreover, there was a great difference between men and women. At Bøgebakken there were nine adult men; five of them were over 40 years of age, one was 25–35 and the age of the others cannot be determined. Of the women, two died around 20 years

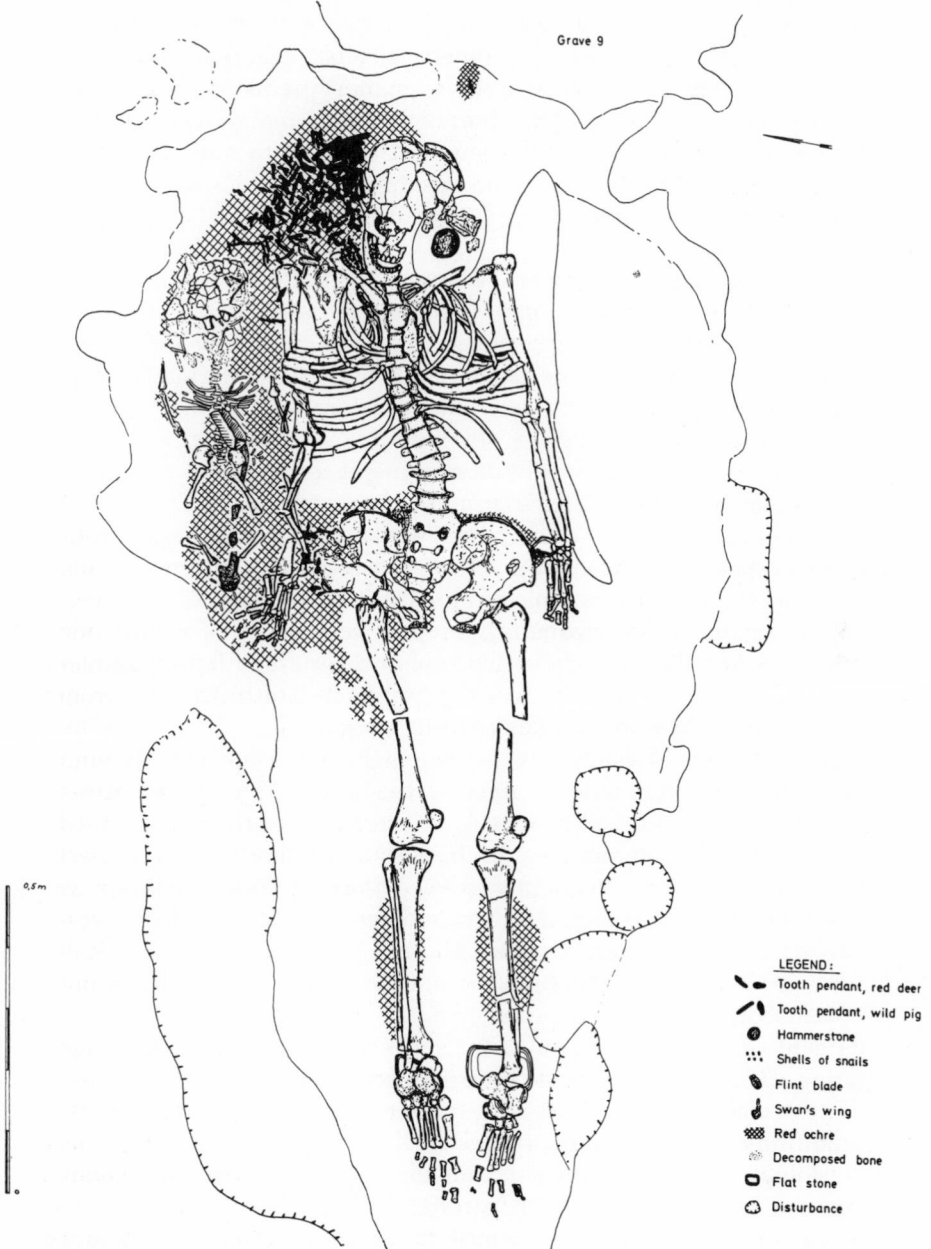

Grave 9

LEGEND:

- Tooth pendant, red deer
- Tooth pendant, wild pig
- Hammerstone
- Shells of snails
- Flint blade
- Swan's wing
- Red ochre
- Decomposed bone
- Flat stone
- Disturbance

0,5 m

Figure 10 Mesolithic grave at Bøgebakken, Vedbæk, northern Zealand. Woman buried with a new-born infant, *c.* 5000 BC.

old, three were over 40 years old, and the ages of two cannot be determined. The two young women probably exemplify the higher female mortality which can be observed in most prehistoric populations. This figure ranges up to 40 per cent higher than that of men and must represent the hard physical burden which childbirth must have been. The cemetery at Bøgebakken illustrates this in a striking way: two of the young women were buried together with their newborn babies (Figure 10).

Although the material from the hunter–gatherer society is slight, it can still give us an impression of the mortality rate. A population with such narrow chances of survival can of course grow only very slowly. Population increases are the result of a complicated interplay of many physiological and culturally determined factors.

While the above-mentioned observations on mortality seem to be representative for prehistoric hunter–gatherer communities, the fertility of the prehistoric population is far more of a puzzle. By fertility is meant the actual reproduction of the population, when the maximum reproductive capacity of a woman is considered together with the physiological and cultural factors which influence the birth rate.

With regard to the maximum reproductive capacity of women very little is known. Present-day societies with a very high fertility can, for example, be encountered in minority groups in North America, where on the average a woman gives birth to ten children. The theoretically possible figure is probably considerably higher. It is, however, impossible to form a well-founded idea of the figures for the prehistoric population. The only alternative is to refer to studies of present-day hunter–gatherer communities. In these communities the average number of children born is frequently reduced to five or six due to prolonged breast-feeding, physiological control and abortion. This figure is further reduced to from three to five children by infanticide and similar culturally determined measures. A natural infant and child mortality further reduced this figure probably by 20–50 per cent. Finally, about 5 per cent of the surviving individuals are believed to have been killed during childhood as a result of warlike activities.

The variables which determine the birth rate in a hunter–gatherer community are thus both physiological and cultural in nature. The physiological control factors are relatively easy to describe. They usually derive from the fact that the strongly seasonally determined food situation easily creates crises which result in less robust children; for example, in these periods children are deprived of sufficient nourishing milk and therefore die more easily. Poor food also leads to more birth abnormalities; fluctuations in the quantity of resources demand more labour, which in turn causes more miscarriages and unsuccessful births. The physiological factors are thus dependent upon the quantity of resources and are clearly a contributing factor in limiting extreme fluctuations of population size.

Meanwhile, many observations indicate that another set of control factors helps prevent population crises in the hunter–gatherer society. In the low-technology society, population growth results first in a certain increase in the quantity of food per individual, in so far as this is possible. This increase takes place because normally a more productive technology will come into function. However, if the population exceeds this demographic optimum, a number of culturally conditioned measures for restricting the birth rate will come into play: infanticide, for example.

However, the demographic optimum most often lies far below the number which the territory is able to carry. An exploitation of only 20–30 per cent of the maximum carrying capacity is not uncommon. It should also be added that this sort of population balance is often maintained by a daily labour input of 2–4 hours per individual. To illustrate this, the hypothetical situation set out in Figure 11a shows how the quantity of resources can fluctuate over an 80-year period within a given region, here exploited by a hunter–gatherer community. Figure 11b shows the total amount of resources within the same area over a similar length of time. It is here evident that the demographic optimum of about fourteen families is a good deal lower than the number of families able to survive by exploiting the maximum carrying capacity of the territory.

In later years, it has frequently been observed that hunter–gatherer communities, at least those in temperate and tropical zones, are adapted to their resource situation, often with a wide margin of safety. With regard to the hunter–gatherer populations in prehistory the temperate areas' abundant production of plant food has often been forgotten – though in fact this production may have given the hunter–gatherer communities the opportunity of adaption with a wide margin of safety. To some degree this sort of adaption may have allowed fluctuations in population size without the danger of destroying the economic system. Such a situation is thought to have existed during most of the Mesolithic period in Denmark. Here, however, a crisis apparently arose about the fifth millennium BC. Probably as a result of this crisis the agrarian economy was introduced.

From a biological point of view, this situation is illustrated in the so-called Liebig's law of minimums. The biologist Justus Liebig (1803–73) postulated that the degree of an organism's growth is determined

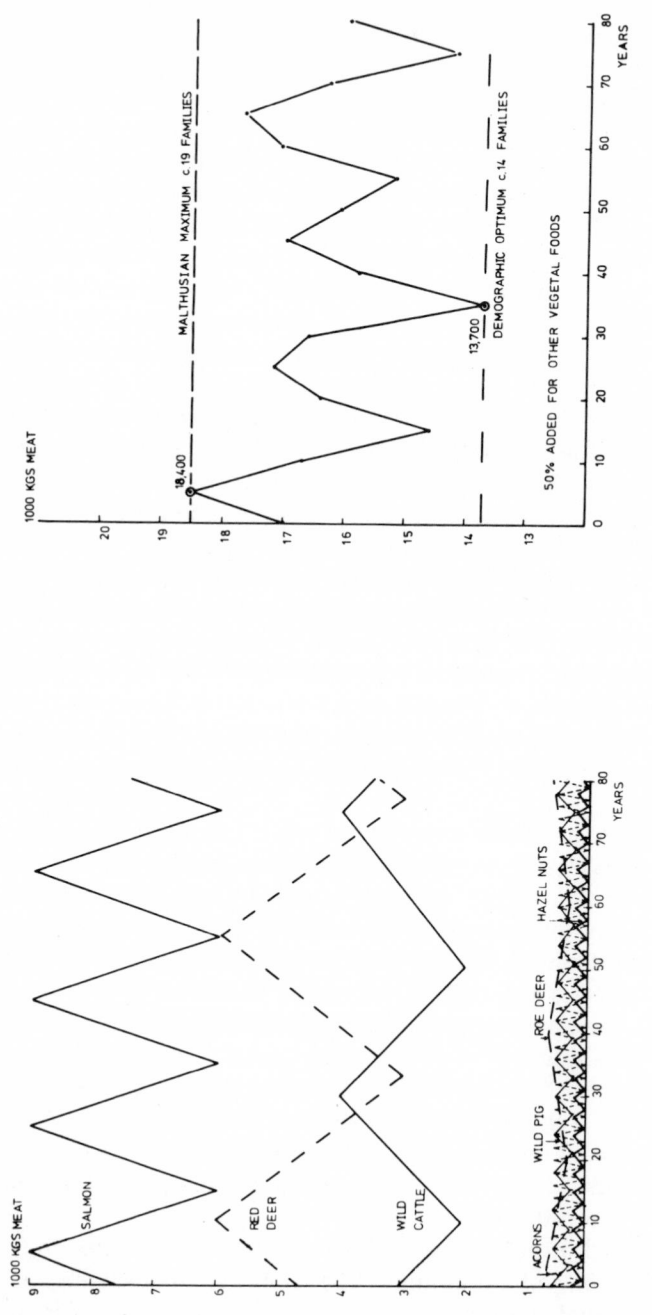

Figure 11 Hypothetical representation of how food resources in a forest area can fluctuate over an 80-year period (left). The graph (right) shows the total amount of resources compared with the demographic optimum capacity.

by the weakest link in the chain of essential life factors: plants, for example, are dependent upon the amount of water, light, nutrients, and so on. Applying this concept to human societies, it is implied that the minimum of food resources, including seasonal variation, determines the population size within a given territory.

Of course, insight into population problems in human society is not achieved by simple analogy with biological laws. The factors which catalyse the control measures must also be clarified. In relation to the hunter–gatherer communities, these measures are far from clear, but it has been indicated that the area per individual, the space between various groups, the amount of food per individual, the distance covered to obtain food and the intervals between the moving of settlements are factors which contribute to trigger off control measures. In particular the amount of labour per individual seems to be of decisive significance in establishing cultural norms for population control. It has been mentioned that the large burden of work placed upon women by most hunter–gatherer societies is one of the most efficient means of preventing uncontrolled population growth. Women's work often includes gathering great amounts of food, fetching water, collecting firewood, taking care of children, preparing food, transporting possessions when the dwelling is moved, and so on. This very burden puts a severe strain on a woman and may provoke, for example, infanticide, sexual withdrawal or miscarriage. Thus the sexual division of labour may very well have had this function in prehistoric hunter–gatherer societies.

How many were there?

We have now listed a number of factors which may have helped maintain the population balance, that is, an adaption to the food situation in Mesolithic Denmark. These remarks have been made because archaeological explanations are often based upon the theories of T.R. Malthus (1766–1834). A frequent assumption is that by itself a population will expand to the maximum which the environment can support. This sort of growth will result in a minimum of resources per individual, which in turn leads to crises resolvable only by war, epidemics, famine or the introduction of a new technology. In contrast to this viewpoint, newer population studies seem to have shown that in hunter–gatherer societies there is often a surplus of resources per individual. The implication is that the population problem can only be understood by studying the means by which the hunter–gatherer communities prevent over-exploitation of their territories.

As shown above, the ecological system in Denmark underwent

profound changes between 11,000 and 4200 BC. These changes were primarily caused by rising summer temperatures and the consequent modifications in fauna and vegetation, as well as the shifting balance between land and sea. The rises of sea-level in the Atlantic period, for example, may very well have resulted in increased population pressure, quite simply because the accessible land area was diminished. The following pages will attempt to illustrate how man responded to these changes. But first it is necessary to consider a few archaeological estimates of the relative population size during the period.

The population curve shown in Figure 12 is partially based on the number of known finds. It is therefore quite hypothetical, as the number of finds is always dependent upon the intensity of research devoted to a given region. The find quantity is also determined by the focus of the study. Thus the population curve shown here can only be regarded as a hypothetical tool based on a combination of demographic, scientific and archaeological evidence.

For the period up to c. 7500 BC, the population curve shows a number of fluctuations separated by long, seemingly empty periods. This can hardly mean that the country was uninhabited in these latter periods, but only that a low population density existed. After 7500 BC, there is a continuous rise in the curve, which culminates around 6500 BC; thereafter the curve is stabilized for a longer period before the last upward swing around 4700 BC, the period preceding the introduction of agriculture.

This graph depicts only relative population development in Denmark. No precise idea of the absolute population size can be gained, although some attempts have been made. One was made by J. Troels-Smith (1955) who compared the Palaeolithic hunters of the Late Glacial to present-day reindeer hunters living in northern Canada (Barren Grounds) in natural conditions resembling those of Late Glacial Denmark. Troels-Smith's line of thought is as follows: the Canadian Eskimos live with a population density of 0.003 per square kilometre – 'if we imagine that a similar number of people lived here in Denmark in the Late Glacial, this would correspond to about 120 people divided into 25–30 families; in other words, Denmark was divided among about 30 active hunters.'

The other alternative was suggested by J.G.D. Clark in 1975. Over the roughly 70,000 km² large area which in Late Glacial times encompassed Scania, Denmark and Schleswig-Holstein, Clark estimates that about 330,000 reindeer could live. He further estimates that to maintain an average family unit 500 reindeer per year are required. That is, that number of reindeer could support a population of about 660 family units

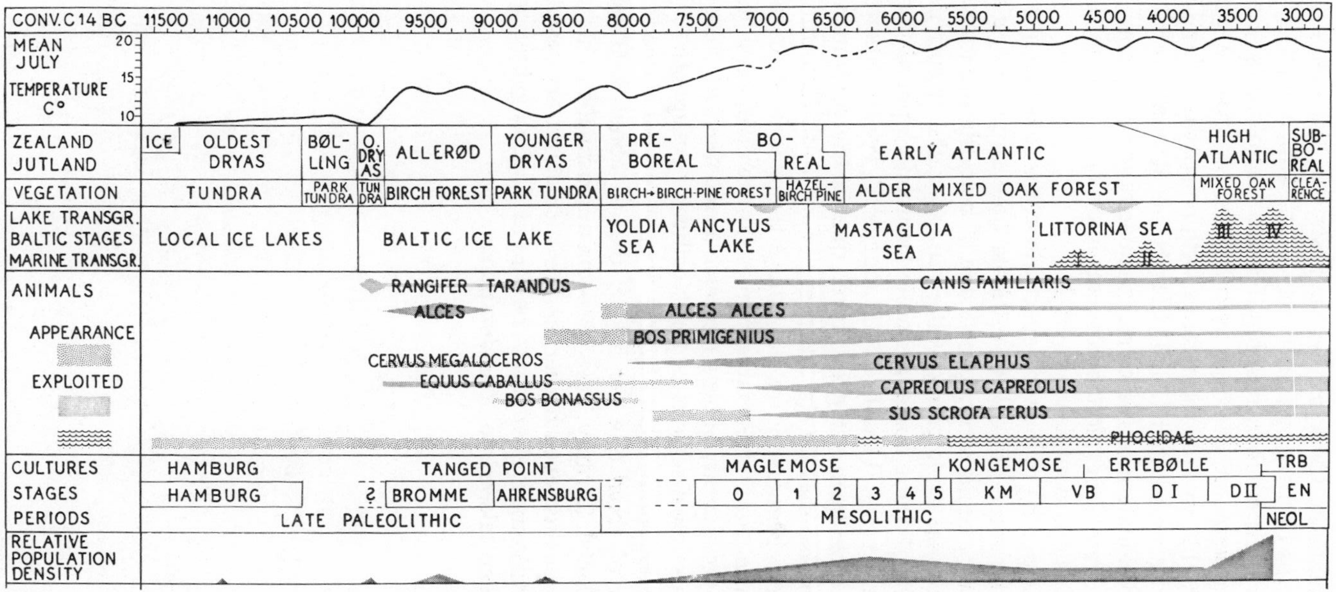

Figure 12 Survey diagram of the Danish Mesolithic period.

or 3300 individuals. Clark further suggests that the reindeer hunters lived in groups of three or four family units, which is to say that the entire area was exploited by roughly 165–220 'micro-bands'. Finding the common denominator of these calculations, we have a population ranging from 120 to 1700 individuals within what is today Denmark. It ought to be noted that J.G.D. Clark's calculations operate with a maximum exploitation of the carrying capacity of the region. As mentioned, this degree of exploitation seems improbable, so the estimate of 1700 individuals is doubtless too high.

With the widening of the food spectrum in the subsequent millennia, it becomes far more difficult to estimate how large a population the Danish territory could carry; knowledge of both the resource situation and the territorial exploitation of the hunter–gatherer societies is still sadly deficient. For the Boreal period in Denmark, a population density of about one per 20–50 km^2 has been suggested. For the Atlantic period the figures have been set even lower due to the presumed gradual decline of the bio-mass in the Atlantic climax forest. Unfortunately, no attempts have been made to determine the extent of the accessible available marine and terrestrial resources. Yet comparison with modern statistics on the quantity of big game such as red deer, roe deer and wild pig in various forest regions in the Northern hemisphere (P. Mellars, 1975) yields noticeably higher figures than suggested above. A population density of about one per 5 km^2, that is, about 8000 individuals within the Danish territory, does not seem unreasonable. This figure can probably be pushed even higher, as the calculations are based only on how much big game is shot yearly; neither fishing nor gathering of plant foods has been taken into consideration.

3

Subsistence and settlement

Mobility and territory

Investigation of man's habitat in south Scandinavia in the interval between the melting of the ice and the beginning of agriculture seems to show that before the High Atlantic period no single ecological zone offered sufficient resources to provide enough food for a year-round population group. Consequently, the hunter–gatherer societies had to exploit not one but several ecological zones. Only in this way could they alleviate the risk of food shortage during the critical months of the year. An understanding of the prehistoric hunter–gatherer communities is therefore dependent upon the extent to which it can be ascertained how the annual territory was used season after season and what size the hunter–gatherer groups had in the various seasons. Knowledge of these conditions is also necessary in understanding not only the material culture but also the organization and structure of the population of Denmark in the millennia under discussion.

Theoretically there are many possible ways of adaption which a hunter–gatherer community can choose. Two of these ways in particular may apply to the Danish territory in the Palaeolithic and Mesolithic periods:

1 The base camps were moved throughout the year according to seasonal and ecological variations leading to the formation of an annual migration circuit.
2 The base camps were permanently placed in proximity to different ecological zones. Thus the inhabitants could exploit several biotopes by sending off smaller foraging units for shorter periods.

As yet our knowledge of the strategy of the hunter-gatherers in the centuries after the melting of the ice is still too limited to allow for firm conclusions. In the long perspective, however, the period up to the introduction of agriculture seems to have witnessed a gradual transition from the first alternative to the second.

In learning how the hunter–gatherer societies adapted to their physical environment the study of territorial conditions of course gains great significance. A hypothetical model has been constructed by J.G.D. Clark (1975) who distinguishes four different types of territory. The first is the territory which is exploited from the single base camp. Of course the extent of this territory cannot be determined generally. If hunting people move on foot alone, their radius will hardly exceed a walk of a couple of hours, about 10 kilometres. However, if boats or other means of transportation such as sledges or skis are used, then naturally the radius is enlarged.

The second type of territory is comprised of the area which is covered by the mobile community in the course of a single annual migration circuit. As already mentioned, before the end of the Mesolithic there was probably no ecological zone in Denmark which had sufficient available resources to secure food for a year-round population group. The hunter–gatherer societies may have moved periodically to exploit the seasonally determined foraging opportunities. This may have held true for much of the Boreal period, for example. Sometimes, such as in a winter with heavy rain or snow, the base camps must have remained at the same site for months. In such periods the group very likely increased in size. At other times of the year, the moves apparently were frequent. The group size may thus have diminished, so that a single nuclear family may have foraged alone.

The third type of territory is somewhat more intangible. It is called the social territory. This concept is based upon the realization that the exchange of goods and probably also of women plays a decisive role in most low-technology societies. Analogy with present-day societies also indicates that this sort of exchange is based upon permanent structured patterns. The exchange of goods often branches out among common descent groups, a circumstance to which we will return later. Archaeologically the social territory may be characterized as the area which the individual settlement group draws upon for raw materials and finished products. The social territory often corresponds to that which most Danish archaeologists term a cultural group.

The last territorial unit, and the most all-encompassing, is called in archaeological terminology a culture, a techno-territory or a techno-complex. This is a group of social territories sharing many common features of subsistence and economy. In the Late Glacial period, for example, most of the north European lowland constitutes a single techno-territory.

As yet the picture of man's first presence in Denmark is very unclear. A very small population leaves only a very scanty archaeological record. At the same time various geological conditions make the archaeological material appear very fragmented. In the following the evaluation of this scanty material will be approached from the viewpoint that the adaption of subsistence to environmental conditions determines the population size, the character of the settlement, the extent of the territorial units, and the relationship between these groups. In other words, the basis upon which the relationship between man and nature is to be studied is the human labour process; in the widest sense of the words, society's means of production. The social structure of the hunter–gatherer society is thus the result of a complicated interplay of factors such as natural food production, population size, and means of production.

Reindeer hunters

The Late Glacial imposed identical ecological conditions upon the vast north European lowland. Common features of the territory included the vegetation, the climate – and above all the reindeer herds which during most of the era provided the major source of protein for the mobile hunting societies which found their subsistence in the open tundra landscape. In warmer periods the number of species of wild animals was most probably changed. The food potential of the hunting communities was thus expanded; yet reindeer hunting remained essential throughout the Late Glacial period.

As a result of this ecological homogeneity many closely related hunting communities can be traced throughout the northern European lowlands in the Late Glacial period. Most likely the society functioned at such a low level of integration that single families and individuals could move over vast areas and at different times could merge into various groups, as known from present-day arctic hunting communities. This may explain the homogeneity which characterizes the material equipment of the Late Glacial society.

In a sub-arctic hunter society, where the main staff of life is reindeer hunting, the need for protein may result in a number of different hunting strategies. These differences are based upon the unique behaviour of the reindeer. Reindeer live in such large herds that they must constantly seek new grasslands. Normally a hunting community including women and children cannot follow the herds for longer periods, as the animals simply move too quickly during their seasonal migrations. This and other hunting problems are resolved by the hunter communities in diverse ways. Often they are only seasonally dependent on reindeer, as the hunting of sea mammals, for instance, may yield an alternative source of food. Elsewhere, fishing in inland waters is the modifying factor. Finally there is the possibility that year-round reindeer hunting remains the primary source of food. The hunting community then covers a wide-ranging annual territory, not by following a single herd, but by moving the camp when supplies run low and furthermore by supplementing the production from more incidental sources. This practice involves great risks for food crises and requires in all cases that the hunter groups be quite small. All of these possibilities must be weighed in the evaluation of the first human colonists which during the Late' Glacial arrived at the territory which is today Denmark.

Probably the oldest bands which moved around in what is today Denmark belonged to what is in archaeological terminology called the Hamburg culture, which most likely had already appeared in the Bølling period. In recent years the hunting strategy of these groups has been re-evaluated to some extent (see, for example, J.G.D. Clark, 1975). The northernmost settlements from the period are found near the Danish-German border. These settlements were once thought to be camps established during the summer hunts for the reindeer herds which grazed near the edge of the ice in the warm season. But this picture may have to be altered. Several factors indicate that the seasonal migrations of the reindeer were actually quite the opposite. In the winter months the snow in the northernmost part of the lowland was not deep. Thus the reindeer herds probably sought the north in the winter. Consequently the excavated settlement sites must be interpreted as settlements from which great quantities of reindeer were hunted in the cold season during their migration northward. At this time of the year, the meat could be frozen, so the hunting peoples could have remained at the same place all winter. With the coming of spring, the southward reindeer migrations were also exploited. Soon afterwards, the camp was abandoned and the hunters moved southwards, probably all the way down to the central German highland regions, where an open vegetation of birch and pine comprised the fringes of the forest.

In the following centuries the traces of the hunter communities' presence in Denmark are scattered and unrelated. First around 9700 BC – in the Allerød period – with the beginning of the so-called tanged-point techno-complex, the finds again become more informative (Figure 13). The warm climate of the Allerød period and the consequent change in the flora and fauna of the land doubtless resulted in changes in the subsistence strategy of the hunting communities: in colder periods reindeer comprised the sole source of food, whereas in the Allerød

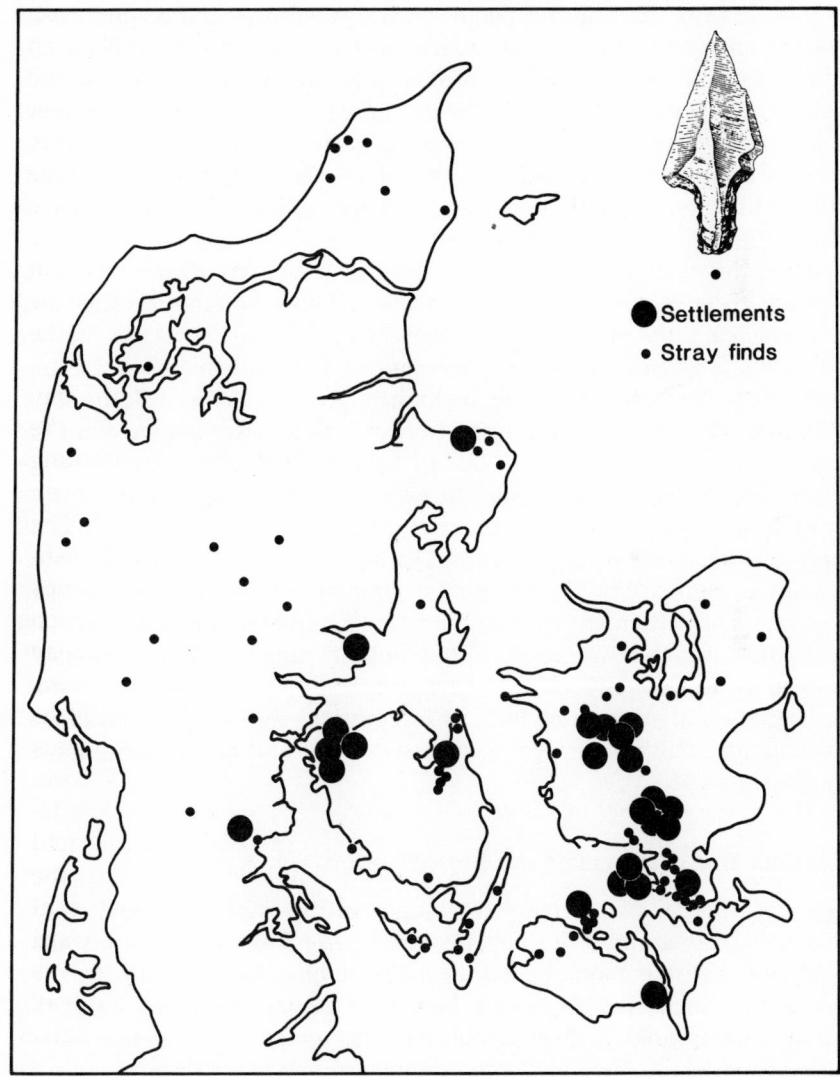

Figure 13 Stray finds and settlements from the tanged-point techno-complex.

period there was a much more varied selection of game – and also of plant foods. Yet the size of the group at the known sites, all of which were seasonal settlements, continued to be quite small. Probably the group consisted of only a single nuclear family. Of course, in certain seasons groups of nuclear families might live together. Perhaps they did so in the coastal zones during the winter.

Exactly how the hunting people in the Allerød period adapted their food strategy to the reindeer herds and at the same time exploited alternative food sources is still unclear. Coastal capture of sea mammals such as seals (through holes in the ice) may be one possibility. Stranded whales may also have turned up now and then, but there is simply no evidence for this as the coastal zone from that era is now submerged. Inland fishing may well have been practised, to judge by the location of the settlement sites in the terrain.

With the final phase of the Late Glacial, the Younger Dryas, the climate grew colder and once again the reindeer became the sole land mammal of any significance. Once again a transformation of the subsistence strategy may be presumed to have taken place, a trans-formation resembling that which characterized the earlier cold periods. It is true that only scattered finds from this period are known from the present-day Danish territory, but in Schleswig-Holstein the finds are more informative. As a whole they give the impression of a hunting culture which by means of seasonal migrations expertly exploited all opportunities for hunting reindeer. Among other things there is unmis-takable evidence of the systematic selection of reindeer bulls as opposed to cows. The settlement sites still indicate a minimal group size, at least from the autumn to the early spring months, when the hunters probably moved up to Denmark. We are here still dealing with a society so open in character, at such a low level of integration, that single families and individuals could move over vast areas – now and again merging into various groups.

Hunters and gatherers of the Boreal period

The Post-Glacial period created changes in the flora and fauna which gradually transformed the lifeways of the first colonists. The resource spectrum became more varied as a result of a warmer climate. The reindeer, which had previously been the primary food source of the hunting communities, disappeared and was replaced by a wide range of animal species. As the newly immigrated animals were for the most part animals accustomed to living in smaller groups and collectively suited to a broader range of local environments in contrast to the migrating flock animals of earlier times, the social behaviour of the hunting people was affected to no small degree.

The archaeological record from the beginning of the Post-Glacial period is still rife with gaps. But from the end of the eighth millennium BC the sources multiply, so that through the seventh millennium a picture of the hunter–gatherer communities emerges with greater clarity. The cultural region in which the hunting peoples in Denmark were integrated expanded in comparison to that of the Late Glacial period. In archaeological literature this territory or techno-complex is termed the Maglemose culture. For nearly 1500 years there was a striking unity in subsistence form and technology over much of the great north European lowland, the area which today includes England, Denmark, central and southern Sweden, northern Germany and parts of northern and western Poland. In all, this region covered about 300,000 km². To be sure, the hunting communities varied in behavioural forms within this vast region. The seasonally determined migrations of the communities were of course intimately related to the meat animals which still comprised the chief source of protein – and in fact the movements of these animals in the terrain were determined in great part by the topography of the country. In this regard there is a clear-cut difference between a lowland region such as Denmark and a region with more distinct surface relief such as England. Yet although certain differences in the seasonal pattern of the hunting peoples are evident, the material is too meagre to permit sweeping generalizations.

The same uncertainty also holds true of attempts to define the annual territory. Most often, the hunter–gatherer communities of the Pre-Boreal and Boreal are depicted as typical inland cultures. But this view may be challenged due to the one-sidedness of the source material. The coastlines of the Pre-Boreal and Boreal (Figure 7) lie mostly beneath the sea today, so traces of any possible coastal settlement sites are necessarily few. Even if the coastal zone in the Pre-Boreal and Boreal period did not offer quite the same biological richness as later during the Atlantic with the rise of the sea level, it is logical to assume that the exploitation of the resources of the coastal zone was also part of the seasonal life pattern of the hunter-gatherer communities, for example during the critical spring months; in fact, seal hunting has been documented. In evaluating the significance of the coastal zone it must be remembered that even in later periods, for while intensive exploitation of the coast has been documented, we find only few traces of coastal hunting at the inland settlement sites.

The accessible evidence of the hunter–gatherer communities' exploitation of the resources, particularly in the seventh millennium BC, shows a broad exploitation of the biological potential of the forest. All species of large meat animals were hunted. Among these, elk and aurochs could yield about 500 kilogrammes of meat. Both of these large meat animals were present from the beginning of the period but gradually played out their role as game in the course of the following millennia in pace with the increasing density of the forest. The plentiful red deer and roe deer were also hunted. In fact, living conditions for these animals improved in the course of the period. The same holds true of the wild pig, which during the period played an ever-larger role as a source of protein. The preferred fur-bearing animals were the beaver, the marten, the fox and the badger. Inland fishing was dominated by the catching of pike, for which fishing spears and lines were used. There is but poor evidence of the gathering of plant foods; the gathering of hazel nuts and a few other fruits and seeds is the only indication of this vital aspect of the subsistence pattern.

Due to the marked lopsidedness of the archaeological record, knowledge of the annual migrations of the hunter-gatherer communities, and consequently of their annual territory in the Pre-Boreal and Boreal, is limited. The best-known aspects are the camps of the summer season, which were made primarily by inland fresh-water streams and lakes. From a number of these localities there are finds of small rectangular huts apparently built of branches rammed in round a floor and pulled together at the top to make a roof. These small huts were inhabited by small groups of people – probably just a single nuclear family. The summer huts were the base camp for many activities such as hunting, fishing and gathering of plant food. To judge from what we know of present-day hunting societies we can presume that gathering was largely carried out by the women.

The settlement sites of the winter months are, in contrast, virtually unknown. A few localities indicate that during the cold period settlement was made on dryer land, although still near fresh water. It is an important observation that the winter settlements seem to have been comprised of larger groups than those of the summer. Winter settlements were apparently based upon the advantages of co-operative hunting.

Little is known of how the hunter–gatherer bands moved between these two settlement types. Presumably exploitation of the coastal zone took place in the late autumn and early spring months; both periods seem to be advantageous for the hunting of sea mammals, as indicated by a few finds. Aside from the more permanent summer and winter settlements, we know of a number of specific activity camps seemingly more transitory in character, such as butchering-places, where big game such as elk and aurochs were quartered before transport back to the base camp. The fishing sites also found were probably connected to the summer settlement. Finally there are some sites which may have functioned as transit camps on the way between the seasonal settlement sites of the coast and the inland sites. The picture is still dim, but it does seem certain that the strategy of the hunter–gatherer communities entailed a mobile settlement pattern and that segments of the bands split off temporarily during certain seasons in order to exploit especially favourable ecological niches of the territory.

The material equipment of the hunter–gatherer communities in this phase shows a varied exploitation of the accessible resources. The hunters used the bones of the aurochs and the elk for making at least fifteen different types of tools; the hides were used for clothing. The tool types include spearheads, which seem to have been widely used in hunting as well as fishing. Fishing hooks are also known. The hunter's bow and arrows attest a highly developed woodworking technique. The bow is accompanied by several different kinds of specialized arrows (Figure 14). Wooden spears and clubs are also known, as well as a number of specialized axes for purposes such as woodworking. Other implements include paddles, which imply the use of boats (probably hollowed-out tree trunks). The boat type is still only known from the fringes of the techno-territory. Aids in hunting may also have included the dog, which already seems to have been domesticated in eastern Europe in the Late Glacial period.

Hunters and gatherers of the Atlantic period

Improved living conditions in the Boreal created the preconditions for a population increase which presumably culminated around the middle of the seventh millennium BC. But because in the following period the dense shady virgin forest gained ever more ground, it is conceivable that a certain impoverishment of the fauna of the forest began during the sixth millennium BC. Both for the elk and the aurochs, but also for the deer species, the density of the forest meant a certain decline in living conditions. During this period the land began to shrink in area (Figure 8) as a result of the rise of the sea-level. Stratigraphical observations have shown that this occurred in four stages, probably separated by intervals in which the sea-level sank slightly. The last two of these four rises were particularly extensive. It is logical to assume that the rises of sea-level gradually encroached upon the territory of the hunter–gatherers, thus resulting in both a greater permanence of settlement and a more severe strain on the resources. For a time the richer and more varied biological environment at the coasts could relieve the growing population pressure, but in the long run the situation was untenable.

If this theory is correct, it may explain some of the changes in the behaviour of the hunter–gatherers during the sixth and fifth millennia BC. As yet the nature of these changes is not clear, but in light of the environmental situation it is understandable that gradually the productive coastal zones were thoroughly exploited. In contrast to the view

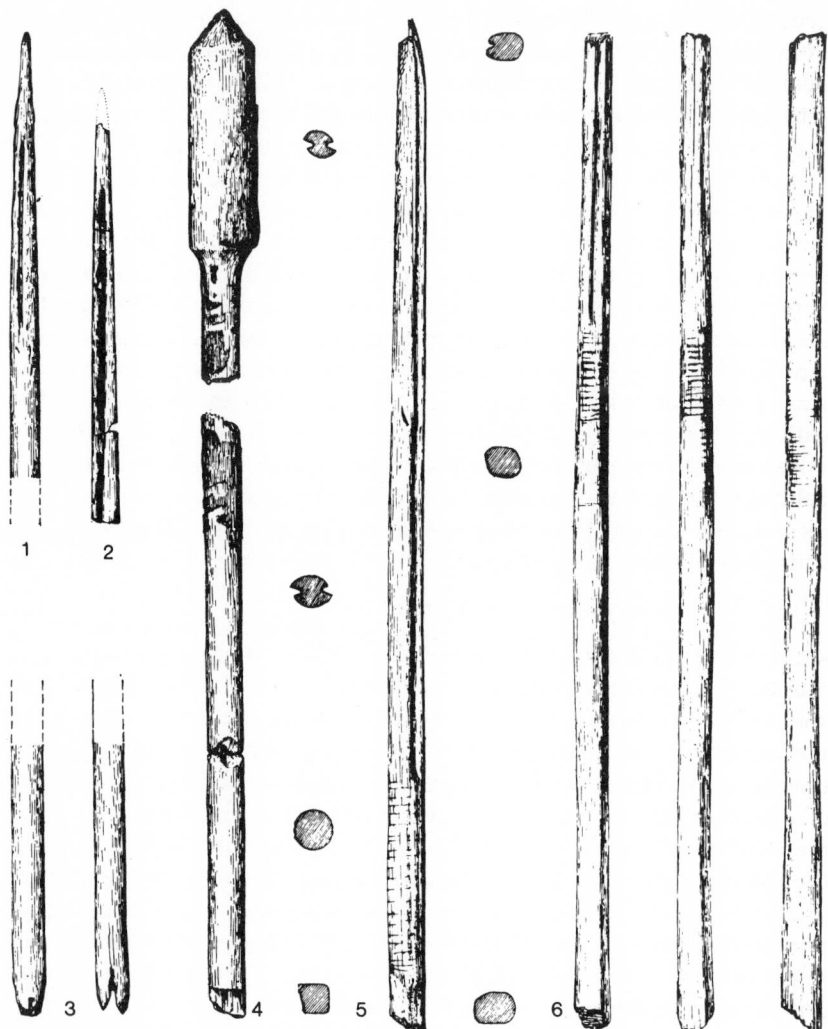

Figure 14 Wooden arrows and spears found at the Maglemosian settlement Holmegård IV, Zealand. Both arrows and spears have furrows intended for insertion of flint microliths.

frequently put forward in older archaeological literature, we must assume that the inland regions were also exploited to some degree. Earlier ideas of the all-dominating role of the coastal zone for the hunter–gatherer communities are due in some degree to a onesidedness favoured by the selection of sites chosen for excavation by earlier generations of archaeologists. Today a great number of settlement sites from the sixth millennium BC are known from both the coast and inland. Zealand especially predominates, whereas not until recently have settlements been revealed on the coasts of Jutland. Inland settlement sites in Jutland have been located but not yet excavated.

In viewing the archaeological record from the sixth millennium BC, a differentiated settlement pattern may be discerned. The topographical location of the settlement sites shows that the population still exploited several ecological zones. Inland, the hunting of big game such as elk, aurochs, red deer, roe deer and boar dominated. By the coasts, sea mammals such as the seal and the porpoise were sought. At the same time fishing for piked dogfish and cod in particular was carried on, along with extensive bird hunting. But there is still no evidence of the gathering of plant products.

As the finds from the sixth millennium BC, the so-called Kongemose culture, were not distinguished in the archaeological record until fairly recently, details of the settlement pattern of the hunter–gatherer communities are very little known. No clear idea of the seasonal patterns of the bands and consequently of the extent of their annual territory can yet be obtained. Only two types of seasonal settlements are known, and strikingly enough both seem to have been summer settlements. The first type is encountered in the coastal regions, usually near sheltered coves and on islands in calm inland shallows, not surprisingly in exactly those resource areas which were characterized by the greatest biological production. The finds clearly imply an intensive exploitation of marine resources; among other things, fishing and hunting of sea mammals and coastal birds are here for the first time supplemented by the intensive gathering of shellfish. The second settlement type is found inland. Here the topographical location of the settlement sites corresponds precisely to the summer settlements made in the seventh millennium BC by inland fresh-water systems. The biological production here is second in line after the coastal estuaries. In some cases the settlement sites quite obviously seem to indicate a more intensive settlement than previously; apparently they also include a larger group size. But as yet no coherent picture of the seasonal pattern can be formed – the source material is far too scanty and incidental.

It can thus be very difficult to evaluate the presumed changes in the behaviour of the hunter–gatherer communities in the sixth millennium BC. The changes in the forest scene, the rising of the sea-level and the increased biological abundance at the coast most likely led to a transformation of the subsistence strategy of the bands and their social organization. But these changes first clearly show themselves in the archaeological record after the transformation had already occurred, when the communities seem to have sought a new equilibrium. This seems to have happened in the course of the fifth millennium BC.

The hunter–gatherer society which in this epoch exploited the potential of the country is termed in archaeological literature the 'Ertebølle culture'. The traces of Ertebølle settlements are known to a degree which indicates that population pressure had grown in the course of the fifth millennium BC. The cause of this may possibly be sought in the tendency towards a more sedentary settlement pattern which was the result of the increased coastal biological production in the High Atlantic period. In general the rise of the sea also resulted in a diminishing of the land area and consequently in an increase in population size per square kilometre.

However comprehensive the source material may be, it cannot be arranged into a complete picture of the subsistence strategy of the hunter–gatherer communities. One reason is that topographically conditioned variations in the quantity of game which have not yet been determined probably affected the behaviour of the different bands. Another explanation takes into consideration the topographically conditioned differences in preservation conditions for organic material. In fact, the presence of organic material is decisive for the understanding of the character of the individual settlement, its period of function and the extent of hunting and gathering.

Just as in the sixth millennium BC, the fifth millennium BC witnessed an intensive exploitation of both the coast and inland. The decisive factor is that in the course of the period there seems to have been a gradual transition to a more sedentary settlement pattern, that is, an exploitation of the same localities over longer periods of the year. Naturally enough, this happened particularly in the coastal zone, where the biological production was greatest. Here too arose the situation which destroyed the traditional regulation of population size and in the end led to intensified manipulation of the environment and hence a transition to food production.

To understand this development and to be able to describe the tolerance of the Ertebølle subsistence system, it is necessary to illuminate the various resource areas which were at the disposal of the hunter–gatherer cultures: the estuaries, the fresh-water systems of the inland, the islands off the coast, the exposed mainland coasts, the forest interior, and so on. Ecological studies here have shown that the resource regions can be arranged in a qualitative ranking with respect to their relative degree of productivity, diversity, seasonality and overall stability (C. Paludan-Müller, 1978).

At the top of the ranking order there are the estuaries, the average annual carrying capacity of which is higher than anywhere else. In fact, along with tropical rain-forests and coral reefs, estuaries rank as the most productive category of ecosystems in terms of primary production. In the High Atlantic period the Danish estuaries and the areas immediately adjacent must have provided living opportunities for the hunter–gatherer communities almost all year round.

Next in rank come the fresh-water systems of the inland areas. They too are characterized by high productivity and high diversity, but also by a higher degree of seasonality than the estuaries. It has therefore been concluded that they were exploited mainly from mid-spring to mid-autumn. However, a more restricted and specialized exploitation may have taken place during the rest of the year.

Next in line come the outer peninsulas and the narrow straits of the coasts as well as the small islands which were so numerous in Denmark during the Atlantic period. Here there is a more complex pattern of fluctuation of resources, often with several interrupted bulk occurrences of food resources during the year.

Finally, at the bottom of the scale of productivity we find the exposed mainland coasts and the closed forest of the inland areas. At neither of these environments can any allocation of settlements be expected beyond the level of occasional short-term camps.

Thus the settlements in the estuaries are of primary interest and this group also includes a very large portion of the well-known settlement sites from the High Atlantic period. In north-east Zealand, for example, a large number of settlements are concentrated in the four fjord regions by Villingebæk, Nivå, Vedbæk and Klampenborg. A fifth settlement concentration is found on the island of Amager. From these five settlement concentrations, with transportation ranges rarely exceeding 10 kilometres, it was possible to control a territory of about 600 km^2 with a coastline of about 170 kilometres.

The large coastal settlements are frequently distinguished by considerable layers of shells, the striking remains of an intensive food-gathering. The gathering of molluscs played a major role especially in the Limfjord regions, along the east coast of Jutland, and in the northern parts of Funen and Zealand. The gathering was carried out together with a wide-ranging exploitation of both the terrestrial and the marine fauna.

In the inland forests, red deer, roe deer and wild pig were hunted along with a broad selection of fur-bearing animals. Marine mammals, fish, molluscs and a plentiful variety of birds were hunted and gathered on the open sea and by the coast.

Few of the settlement sites have been carefully studied. However, a number of investigations of one of the classic coastal settlement sites, Mejlgaard on Djursland, resulted in the hypothesis that the shell mound was used by a community of approximately forty people on a prolonged seasonal or mobile-cum-sedentary basis; that it was repeatedly occupied from year to year; and that it was dependent on a diversity of resources, among which both the molluscs and the non-molluscan marine resources contributed at least as much to the site economy as the terrestrial resources.

Unfortunately our knowledge of the large coastal settlements suffers from many gaps. The remains of dwellings are very meagre and little is known as to how long the various settlements were in function. If the large coastal settlements do in fact represent the transition to a more sedentary settlement form – and there is much to indicate that this is the case – then they must have played a role in the transformation of the population situation. In a settlement pattern with a large annual territory and short-term stays at the individual settlement sites, the number of infants to be transported will always be low. But when the annual territory and hence also migratory distances are diminished, so that the women, at least, remain longer in one place, then improved living conditions are created for children and population growth is encouraged. It may be concluded that the altered circumstances in the fifth millennium BC led the hunter–gatherer communities towards a changed strategy. But in the long run this strategy may have destroyed the equilibrium of the subsistence system and resulted in an increasing population pressure, which around the close of the fifth millennium BC impelled the inhabitants of Denmark to introduce an agrarian economy.

Whereas the large coastal settlements probably represented a more permanent settlement form, the small seasonal camps were still established on the coast. These were intended to exploit only certain resources. Late autumn settlements have been found which were intended to exploit the migrations of sea mammals such as the grey seal (*Halichoeru grypus*). While awaiting the favourable migration of seals, other food, such as cod, could be caught. This fish (*Gadus morrhua*) may have been subsequently dried and stored as a food reserve.

Not surprisingly, inland seasonal camps are also known from both the summer and winter seasons. Most often these were founded on islets or by the shores of inland fresh-water systems. In some cases the local fauna was exploited to the fullest – in other cases hunting was focused on just a few species such as boar and fur-bearing animals. Finds of the bones of sea mammals at inland settlement sites demonstrate that the inhabitants had contact with the coast, although details of the migrations of the hunter–gatherer bands cannot be known. The role of gathering is indicated by finds of an abundance of seeds and fruits, but the extent to which their presence is coincidental is still unclear. The great variation of edible plants, herbs, bulbs, fruits, berries, nuts, bark, shoots, as well as insects and small animals, which the Atlantic forest offered in the summer, doubtless constituted a vital percentage of the food, though how much cannot be known.

The material equipment of the late hunter–gatherer communities was not great but in relation to earlier times it is clear that more effective hunting methods were being sought. The fish trap was an example of this (Figure 15). The trap is a labour-saving device used for both coastal and fresh-water fishing. Net fishing now also appears as well as the

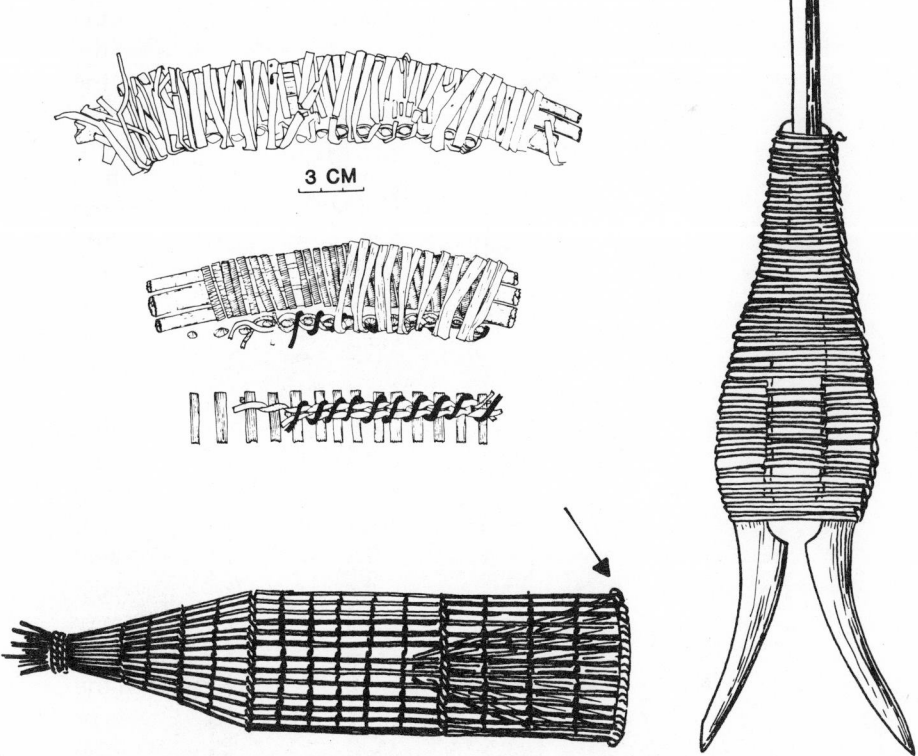

Figure 15 Mesolithic fishing implements. Left top: fragments of fish trap from Maglemosegårds Vænge, Zealand; bottom: reconstruction. Right: Fishing spear found at a submerged Mesolithic settlement off the island of Ærø, southern Denmark.

capture of fur-bearing animals in traps. An important innovation is the use of pottery which was included in the equipment of the hunter–gatherer communities about 4700–4600 BC. The pottery technique was

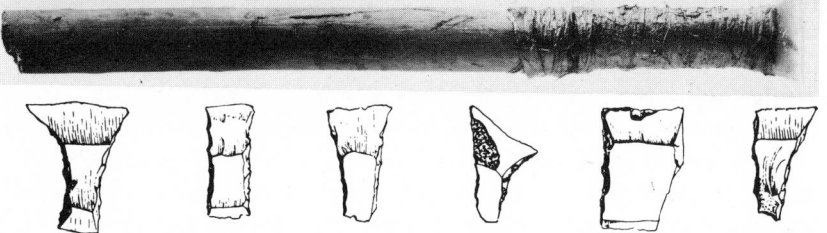

Figure 16 During the Atlantic period a large selection of arrow types was used by the Ertebølle hunters. The most common type had a transverse arrowhead, as seen on an arrow found in a bog in Ejsing parish, Jutland (above). Below: typical Ertebølle transverse arrowheads made of flint.

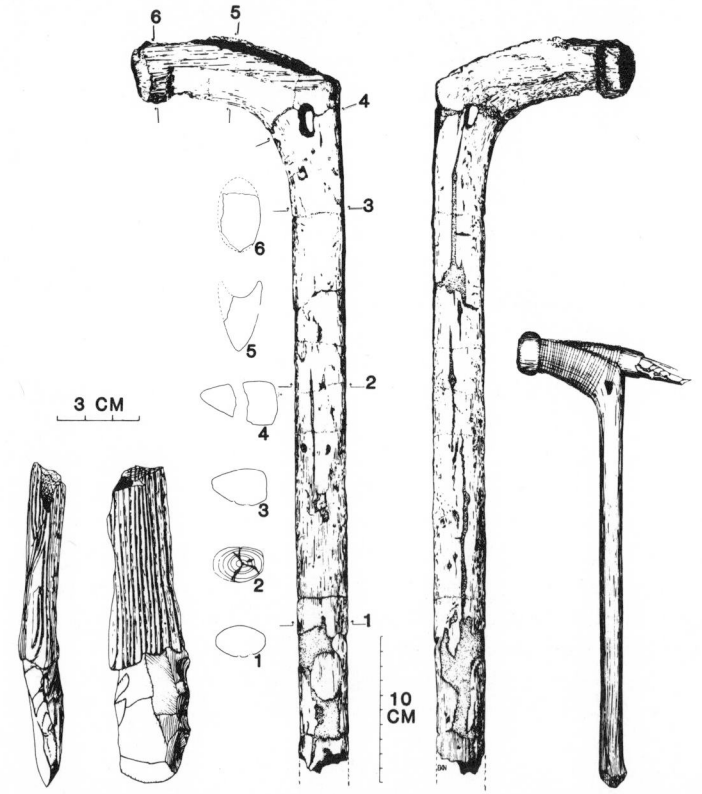

Figure 17 Axe shaft found at a Mesolithic settlement, Maglemosegårds Vænge, Zealand, and axe head found at Kolding Fjord, Jutland. Right: reconstruction.

used for the production of blubber lamps and of containers for the preparation and storage of food.

This increased need to preserve food ought to be viewed in connection with the introduction of the agrarian economy from the south. In the period around 4700 BC there were agrarian cultures in northern Germany and Poland, not far distant from Denmark. It is likely that the hunter–gatherers' familiarity with, for example, pottery technique may be ascribed to contact with the agrarian cultures in the south.

The material equipment also included harpoons, fish hooks, bows, and arrows (Figure 16), boomerangs, wooden spears, and clubs, together with a large selection of special axe types (Figure 17). Finds of paddles (Figure 18) indicate that just as in the foregoing period, boats were used not only for inland sailing but also, to judge by the fauna, for hunting on the open sea. Finally, it should be remembered that nets, pit traps, poison, and many other devices do not leave visible traces. The dog is still the only domesticated animal which has been documented.

A population crisis at the end of the fifth millennium BC?

The still rather fragmentary picture of the economy of the hunter–gatherer communities in the fifth millennium BC leaves us with many unanswered questions. These questions are mostly related to the profound transformation of the subsistence strategy of the prehistoric population which set in at the end of the fifth millennium BC with the beginning of agriculture.

In the period after 6000 BC the altered environmental situation must have created a number of marked consequences for the hunter–gatherer communities either in the form of an altered demographic situation and/or as changes in the subsistence and settlement pattern. The first possibility is difficult to evaluate, but again the population size may have stagnated in the course of the sixth and the beginning of the fifth millennia BC. But after this, there again seems to have been a rise, in fact a striking one. This increase may have been indirectly triggered by an environmental transformation caused by the rising sea-level in the Atlantic period. If this is the case, and if the population balance had been shifted, then it is not surprising that during the fifth millennium BC the hunter–gatherer communities apparently exceeded the tolerance of their subsistence system. With the introduction of technological innovations they began an intensified manipulation of their environment.

The decisive factor in this process is the greater permanence of settlement observable especially in the period after 4700 BC. After this time we can expect to find proof that the inhabitants of the country

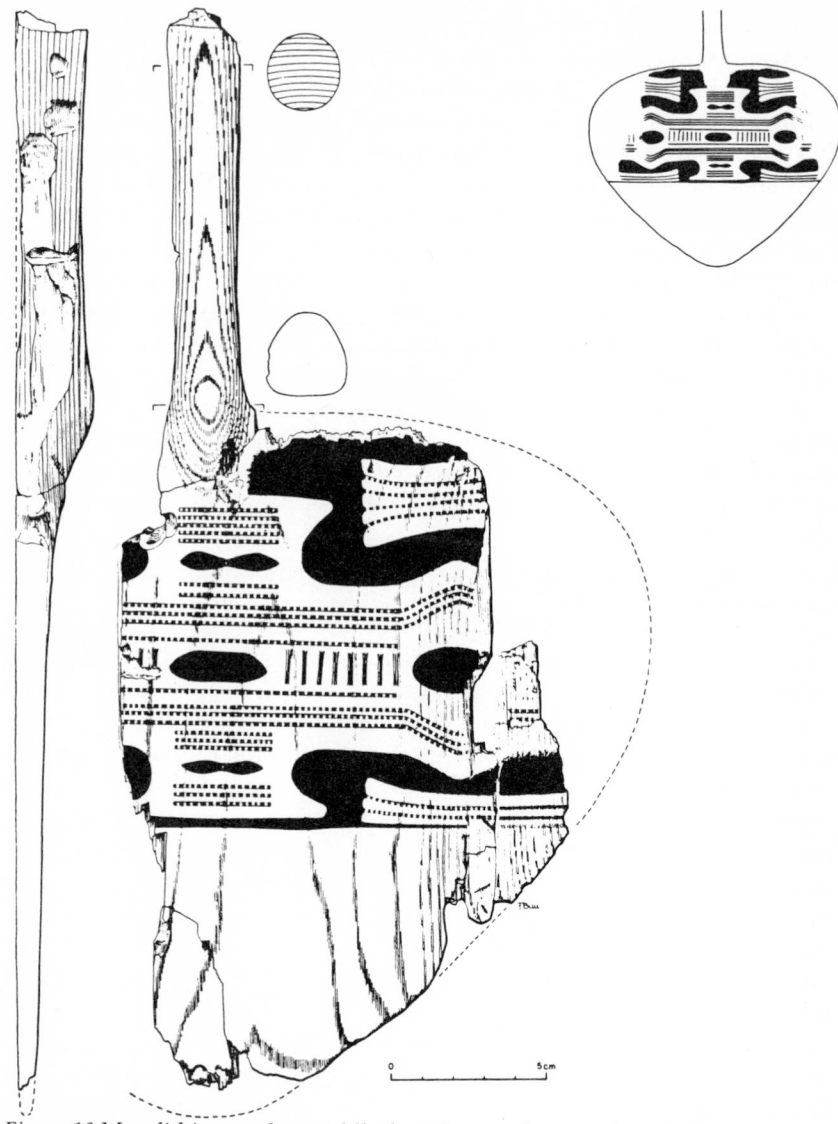

Figure 18 Mesolithic wooden paddle found at a submerged Ertebølle settlement
at Tybrind Vig in Lille Bælt.

began to employ new supplementary subsistence forms – namely a sort
of agrarian economy.

The first indirect traces of the presence of agriculture, according to
radiocarbon dates, come from about 4200 BC. At this time, the archaeological finds yield for the first time the thin-walled pottery which is

thought to represent the earliest agrarian cultures, the so-called 'Funnel-Necked Beaker culture.' The direct traces of agriculture, impressions of grain in pottery, cereal pollen, and bones of domesticated animals, however, first turn up at a slightly later point in time, namely around 3900–3800 BC. Already prior to 4200 BC, however, the prehistoric inhabitants seem to have established contact with the agrarian cultures which flourished just a few hundred kilometres south of what is now Denmark. Knowledge of pottery-making, which may have been sought due to increased demands for storing food, turns up around 4700 BC. The tempering, shaping and firing of clay are accomplishments which clearly derive from foreign impulses, more specifically from the contemporaneous cultures in north-west Germany.

The material equipment of the late hunter–gatherer society also includes features which point to a connection with the agrarian cultures in north-west Germany. Certain new tool types, especially those made of bone and antler, seem best explained by this postulated contact. Similarly, there are features in the technological development which placed new demands upon tools. As a case in point, certain changes in flint techniques indicate a more advanced woodcutting technique. It is not unlikely that future research will demonstrate even more profound influences from the southern agrarian cultures in the period 4700 –4200BC.

Still, the hypotheses about the rise of agriculture in Denmark are very tentative. One possible explanation is presented in L.R. Binford's comprehensive Post-Pleistocene theory (L.R. Binford, 1968a). According to this theory, the Post-Glacial formation of certain rich environments where sedentarism became possible destroyed the traditional regulation of the population size, so that population growth was triggered off, and surplus population budded off and resettled in less favourable areas.

Danish archaeologists have long been aware of the fact that the estuarine resource space of the High Atlantic period in Denmark provided just such a rich environment where sedentarism may have been possible. This theory has recently been formulated thus (C. Paludan-Müller, 1978):

With the beginning of the High Atlantic period (c. 5000 BC) the carrying capacity of the estuaries increased considerably so as to permit permanent residence within the same area for the first time. Constraints on the reproduction of the population occupying the estuarine resource space became insufficient or non-existent. Around the middle of the fifth millennium BC the estuarine areas began acting as 'propulsive areas' in the sense that they began to produce a population surplus. The budding-off of the surplus population resulted in an increasing exploitation of the inland fresh waters and the seaward islands on a seasonal basis. After some time, however, the natural optimal carrying capacity for food gatherers in the inner fresh waters and the seaward islands had been achieved. This situation necessitated an increase in the carrying capacity of the area as a whole, which meant a more effective human manipulation of the environment in order to boost the productivity of organisms of economic significance.

The only ecosystem which would lend itself to this sort of manipulation was the climax forest. And the best place to manipulate the climax forest would be inland. A site here could encompass more forest within its home range than at an estuarine site, where population density figures would already range near the 'social carrying capacity', or at an island site, where there would be little forest to manipulate.

The manipulation could entail, for example, that the large trees were ringed in order to create clearings in the forest in which could grow edible plants such as hazel and eagle fern. These clearings were also good browsing areas for game. The next step in the manipulative process inland would be the introduction of more efficiently controlled resource species such as domesticated cattle and eventually domesticated plants.

This sort of model can explain some of the changes which occur in man's bio-environment in Denmark during the fifth millennium BC and the beginning of the fourth millennium BC, changes which gradually led to a semi-agrarian economy.

But it must be emphasized that this theory is built on a shaky foundation. First and foremost, it lacks the detailed chronological framework within which the data of the settlement finds can be grouped. Not until we have many more radiocarbon dates than we have today will we be able to test the validity of the theory. Until then, the centuries which witnessed the transition to a semi-agrarian economy are still among the most poorly illuminated centuries in Danish prehistory.

Economy of the hunters and gatherers

After this description of environmental development since the last Ice Age, demographic changes and the evidence of the archaeological record regarding subsistence and settlement patterns, it is logical to seek a synthesis of the economy of the hunter–gatherers. Economy is here defined as that part of social life which includes production, distribution and consumption of goods and services. Our present focus will be on production.

Flexibility and mobility, the main characteristics of the hunter–gatherer communities, were evident in the description of the interplay of the natural food situation, the population size and the means of production of the bands. By means of production we mean a process in which both man and nature participate, a process in which man on his own initiative establishes, regulates and controls his metabolism with nature.

The previous sections described the factors which constitute and determine this process. These factors are: 1) the labour input, which depends upon the population density and the quantity of resources; 2) the labour object, that is nature, the finished products of which are appropriated by society; and 3) the tools of production, that is, the material equipment or capital of the hunter–gatherer communities.

The tools of production fall into two categories: capital goods and consumer goods. The first category includes mainly the hunting implements of the hunter–gatherer communities, from their bows and arrows to the boats from which hunting took place. These capital goods were quite modest, as befits the virtual inability of the hunter–gatherer communities to accumulate capital.

In the prehistoric hunter–gatherer communities, production consisted of goods which could not be conserved. There are very few exceptions to this rule prior to the beginning of agriculture. A general conclusion is that the hunter–gatherer communities have a very poor ability to save, that is, to postpone consumption. This inability to accumulate capital means that improvements of the production apparatus can only to a slight extent be based upon this ability.

As a general rule, the hunter–gatherer communities' difficulty in postponing consumption prevents their economy from becoming dynamic. As a result, very little economic growth can occur. This is one of the basic reasons why the societal form survived relatively unchanged through the millennia following the melting of the ice from Denmark and up to the beginning of food production around 4200 BC. In other words, this means that we can determine how the production tools in the hunter–gatherer communities can be termed aids in appropriating the finished products of nature. In this way the resources strongly influence the very type of organization and labour practices of the hunter–gatherer communities. For example, we have seen how the type of food resources and the forms of technology by which the biota are exploited are the most important determinants of local group size and composition. In sum: the labour form made possible by the environment as well as by the population size determined the economic and social organization of the hunter–gatherer society.

4
Social structure of the hunters and gatherers

The archaeological record which can illuminate the social structure of the early hunter–gatherer society in Denmark is very slender indeed. Comparisons with present-day hunter–gatherer societies can to some degree expand our ideas of the societal forms in Denmark before the introduction of agriculture, but such comparisons will always be problematic; present-day hunters and gatherers are usually dependent upon other societal forms or have been forced into marginal areas, thereby experiencing a modification of their original culture features.

The patrilocal or patrilineal band has been considered the most 'typical' form of social organization before the beginning of agriculture. As often pointed out, the band society seems to have existed under extremely varied natural conditions everywhere on earth. It seems to be the most effective social organizational form in regions with low population density. It is also thought to be the oldest form because it can be adapted to areas with widely differing natural conditions.

A band society is comprised of a number of small, usually mobile groups. Each group is self-sufficient and the subsistence form is generally hunting and gathering. The only known division of labour is based upon age and sex. As a rule, the society is egalitarian in its social organization, that is, there is no regulated inequality in the access to economic resources and to social status positions. Consequently there are no specialized political positions. In the individual hunter–gatherer group social authority is normally in the hands of the oldest male members of the group.

A number of features of the band society are regarded by evolutionistic anthropology as being quite ancient in the history of human societies. The first feature of interest here is the group division and the rules controlling the relationships among the various social groups. More theoretical speculations as to why man, like many primates, lives in groups, will not be examined here. The need for food and shelter and the fact that the sexual behaviour of most primates is not seasonal have been suggested to explain why man primarily lives in groups all year round.

In establishing the most elementary rules of group behaviour, social anthropology has emphasized the role which sharing must have played for the earliest forms of society. Why this mutuality arose is not clear. In the hundreds of thousands of years which it has taken mankind to spread out over the earth, the exchange of women has been one of the earliest features. The French anthropologist Claude Lévi-Strauss, for example, has described how in primitive society a woman is often regarded as a gift, and how a man and his group are the recipients of this gift. This sort of mutual exchange between human groups transforms simple couple relationship to 'marriage alliances', as the exchange involves one or another relative stability in the couple relationship. It is also frequently observed that in present-day hunter–gatherer societies monogamy is the dominant form of common life. Thus monogamy is not the late form of marriage implied in many older evolutionary theories.

The nuclear family was probably also stabilized by the division of labour between the sexes. In a hunter–gatherer society hunting usually requires that men can roam far and wide, whereas at any given time there will always be women who are prevented from doing so. The monogamous relationship thus provides many economic advantages. The men participate in the hunt, which in a society with poor technological equipment frequently demands the collaboration of several men, whereas women, due to pregnancies and child-care, are less mobile and hunt small animals, gather plant food and carry out more localized activities such as food preparation, childbirth and child-care. As pointed out above, this division of labour also favours population control.

The advantages of marriage rules are also obvious for the group or society as a whole. Marriage outside the group, exogamy, has a vital function in the eyes of society: it establishes ties among groups and thus diminishes the potential for conflict. The exchange of men is rare in a hunter–gatherer society because collective hunting is more effective if a man belongs to the territory. A woman, on the other hand, can more easily transfer to another group without weakening her original group. The men's permanent sense of belonging to the group can thus in a low-technology society be of crucial importance for co-operation and group solidarity.

Of course, this description can only offer generalities on the societal basis for the hunter–gatherer communities which existed in Denmark from the melting of the ice to the beginning of agriculture. The intention here has been to demonstrate that social organization can hardly be based upon the nuclear family, because this family was presumably created by society and not vice versa. This line of thought bears a number of structural consequences for the hunter–gatherer societies. If exogamy was the basis for couple relationship and the woman usually followed the man, then every group included married women from another group and at the same time gave away some of its own marriageable women. In this way the individual band was integrated into a larger whole, namely the group of bands which comprised the social territory. These bands were related by genealogical ties and probably also by forms of co-operation such as the exchange of goods. The social structure thus comprised of the following groups: 1) nuclear families; 2) extended families consisting of more or less permanent associations of adult males and their nuclear families; and 3) the territorial society, the group of bands which constituted the social territory.

Of the groups listed, the nuclear family made up of father, mother, offspring, and perhaps elderly relatives, was the most cohesive unit in the hunter–gatherer society. The division of labour based upon age and sex which exists within the nuclear family is the only essential one in the hunter–gatherer society. This means that in periods the nuclear family could forage alone if the resource situation allowed. It is precisely this flexibility which seems to be discernible in, for example, the settlement pattern of the Boreal period.

This leads us to the size of the hunter–gatherer communities, which seems to vary over a relatively narrow range. Groups of up to eight or ten men are very common, that is, the community will often be comprised of about thirty or forty persons. In fact, this is the group size estimated for the coastal settlements of the Atlantic period. The social territory of a group of genealogically related communities rarely exceeds one thousand persons. But it is important to bear in mind that we are not dealing here with a tribe in the sense which the word acquires later in the discussion of the first agricultural communities.

If, as suggested above, not only the size but also the topographic distribution of the communities is directly related to the quantity, seasonality and stability of the food resources, a number of general features of this form of organization are given. These features are: low population density, geographic mobility, flexible group structure and small group size. Wherever hunting, for example, demands the co-operation of many people and the game captured can feed everyone at one time, the group size will normally be large. In other periods, however, the food situation can compel the nuclear family to obtain its food alone. This seems to have been the case in periods of the annual cycle in the Boreal and perhaps also in the Atlantic period. These variables are noted to emphasize that the nuclear families which comprise the extended band do not necessarily live together all the time, or even much of the time, in order to be perceived as such. To judge by our knowledge of present-day band societies, we know that such factors as shared mythology, common ceremonies and kinship relationships may integrate nuclear families in periods of wide geographical distribution.

Finally, it should be mentioned that the annual territory exploited by the hunter–gatherer community is not necessarily enclosed by boundaries. One of the chief functions of marriage outside the group seems to be that it opens the group for territorial exploitation so that larger variations of natural resources can be utilized by related groups.

Naturally this description can only serve as a hypothetical framework for understanding the prehistoric hunter–gatherer society. However, as we have mentioned, the most striking feature of the subsistence form and settlement pattern in the period after the melting of the ice from Denmark is the flexibility of the group size. The summer camps of the Boreal period, for instance, seem to reflect a seasonally conditioned division into nuclear families and a correspondingly large group size in the winter period. This sort of strategy seems best explained by the ecological situation in which the hunter–gatherer communities existed.

It is considerably more difficult to explain the settlement concentrations of the Atlantic period – for example in the Zealand fjords. Do they represent a larger group formation which moved around together in the fjord region – or were they several scattered contemporary settlements? Both strategies had advantages but only future research will be able to answer the question. There is yet another related question: did the hunter–gatherer communities during the High Atlantic develop higher forms of social integration than the band society? Did the hunting societies at the end of the fifth millennium BC operate on a tribal level such as has been suggested for other areas of Europe (R.B. Lee, 1968)?

In any case, the archaeological finds from the period predating the introduction of agriculture do not indicate specialized forms of labour. We can thus hardly expect to find social organization forms beyond the egalitarian. In this connection it is important to remember that egalitarian does not necessarily mean that all members of a social unit are equal. In modern egalitarian societies it may be seen that a prestige position achieved through recognized status, such as that of a good hunter, cannot be transferred by inheritance or in any other way. Just because a man is a good hunter, his sons are not necessarily good hunters. The egalitarian social forms thus restrict social inequalities to a minimum.

In summary it may be said that the momentary character of the labour processes, the hunter–gatherer communities' lack of ability to postpone consumption and accumulate capital, the limiting of division of labour to age and sex – all of these factors place the early hunter–gatherer society at the level of social organization labelled the band society. With the apparent restructuring of the subsistence strategy in the course of the fifth millennium BC, a new situation must have been created. The more sedentary settlement pattern and the presumed change in productivity may have created higher forms of integration. The problem is as yet unresolved and demands first and foremost many new finds from the important transitional phase between the late hunter–gatherer society and the semi-agrarian society of the fourth millennium BC.

5
Finds and interpretations

Most of our knowledge about the Palaeolithic and Mesolithic cultures during the Late and Post-Glacial period up to about 4200 BC derives from excavated settlements of the hunter–gatherer communities. As yet the archaeological record includes very few grave finds.

The study of the settlements of the hunter–gatherer communities in Denmark is seriously hindered by the inconsistency with which the source material has been analysed. To analyse finds from a Palaeolithic or Mesolithic settlement, the collaboration of many scientific disciplines is demanded. Unfortunately, many of the principal settlements of the period are accessible only in the form of preliminary reports. These include such noteworthy finds *as Holmegård* (C.J. Becker, 1945); *Åmosen* (K. Andersen, 1951); and *Kongemosen* (S. Jørgensen, 1956). Other finds, such as the important settlement of *Lundby* on Zealand, excavated in 1928–31, have never even been published. Yet another lack is that the archaeological record is so little representative. As a case in point, study of the settlement pattern of the hunter–gatherer communities has made it evident that many of the known settlements must have functioned as a base camp for specific activity camps, in which the hunter–gatherer communities carried out strictly seasonal activities. This group of finds is badly under-represented in the archaeological record.

Little of the source material which has turned up in the past hundred years can fulfil the demands of modern archaeological research. However, since the 1940s improved excavation methods have remedied many problems. We can hope that the detailed regional investigations now in progress will be able to shed some light on the representativeness of older source material. In this connection investigations now underway in the Øresund region, i.e. north-eastern Zealand and western Scania, are particularly significant. Nowhere else in Europe do we have such a rich and varied concentration of Mesolithic settlements representing a long uninterrupted coastal settlement.

The first excavation of a Mesolithic settlement on the Zealand side of the Øresund took place in 1912. Since then a number of excavations have been made here, but the enormous potential of the area first became evident with the start of the so-called Vedbæk project in 1975 (E. Brinch Petersen, 1979; K. Aaris-Sørensen, 1980b). This project includes investigation of the unique Mesolithic cemetery Bøgebakken (E. Brinch Petersen, 1976b).

The goal of the Vedbæk project is to study cultural and environmental changes by a Stone Age fjord during the Atlantic period. Here, the collaboration of archaeologists and researchers from many branches of natural science has, among other things, revealed the influence which changes in the water-level of the Litorina sea had on such factors as the location of the settlements, their preservation, their tool kits and their chronology. Thus the project can also help evaluate the representativeness of the finds made earlier. A similar project is underway on the east coast of Jutland (S.H. Andersen, 1976).

Older archaeological literature describes many significant excavations. However, there are but few published reports on settlements from the Palaeolithic, that is settlements which predate the transition between K. Jessen's pollen zones III and IV (T. Mathiassen, 1946; S.H. Andersen, 1972). Yet we can anticipate an increase in the archaeological record (for example, see A. Fischer, 1978).

The most important works on the Mesolithic Maglemose culture include, in chronological order from the Pre-Boreal period up to the transition to the Kongemose culture of the Atlantic period: *Klosterlund* (E. Brinch Petersen, 1966); *Holmegård vi* (C.J. Becker, 1945); *Sønder Hadsund* (E. Brinch Petersen, 1966); *Verup* (K. Andersen, 1960); *Mullerup* (G.F.L. Sarauw, 1903); *Ulkestrup* (K. Andersen, 1951); *Holmegård v* (C.J. Becker, 1945); *Sværdborg i* (K. Friis Johansen, 1919); *Stallerupholm* (R.E. Blankholm and S.H. Andersen, 1967); *Ulkestrup ii* (K. Andersen, 1951); *Sværdborg ii* (E. Brinch Petersen, 1971); *Holmegård i-ii* (H.C. Broholm, 1924); *Sværdborg i* (B. Bille Henriksen, 1976).

The subsequent Kongemose culture yields very few finds; these include *Kongemosen* (S. Jørgensen, 1956); *Vedbæk Boldbaner* (T. Mathiassen, 1946); and *Brovst* and *Øster Jølby* (S.H. Andersen, 1969).

From the last part of the period, the Ertebølle culture, there is an abundance of sites. These sites often show traces of repeated settlements, the youngest of which have been interpreted as specific activity camps for the first farming communities (J. Skårup, 1973). Among the most noteworthy of these are: *Dyrholm* and *Kolind* (T. Mathiassen, 1942); *Norslund* (S.H. Andersen and C. Malmros, 1965); *Ertebølle* (A.P. Madsen, 1900); *Mejlgård* (H. Hellmuth Andersen, 1960; G.N. Bailey, 1978); *Sølager* (J. Skårup, 1973); *Aggersund* (S.H. Andersen 1978); *Bloksbjerg* (E. Wester-by, 1927); *Ølby Lyng* (E. Brinch Petersen, 1970a); and *Ring Kloster* (S.H. Andersen, 1974).

Grave finds from the Mesolithic period in Denmark have until recently been very rare (H. Norling-Christensen, 1945; U.L. Hansen, 1972a; E. Brinch Petersen, 1976b). The excavations at Bøgebakken near Vedbæk have augmented the material considerably and also provided us with insight into Mesolithic anthropology (S.E. Albrethsen *et al.*, 1976). All the Danish finds have recently been published in conjunction with other European Mesolithic finds (R.R. Newell *et al.*, 1979).

Familiarity with environmental history is a necessary prerequisite for understanding the development of the hunter–gatherer communities, especially in a territory such as Denmark where ecological changes are most clearly marked. Thus a close collaboration with the natural sciences has been maintained in Danish archaeology since the mid-nineteenth century, when the early settlements in Denmark were first studied. In particular, the results of the so-called 'kitchen-midden commission' (published by A.P. Madsen in 1900) served as a forerunner for modern research. A history of investigation can be found in E. Brinch Petersen (1973).

Studies of the Late and Post-Glacial vegetational history of Denmark and south Sweden have been summarized by J. Iversen (1973) and B.E. Berglund (1966 a and b). Detailed knowledge of the various phases of vegetational history derives first and foremost from K. Jessen's zone classification (1935, 1937, 1938); later modifications were made by J. Iversen (1941) and S. Jørgensen (1963). Climatic history was recon-structed (Figure 12) on the basis of evidence of the immigration of animals and plants; see, for example, studies by J. Iversen (1954, 1973) and B.E. Berglund (1966 a and b, 1968, 1969), whereas the relationship between the land and the sea has been illuminated by studies of J. Iversen (1937), K. Jessen (1938) and J. Troels-Smith (1942). Of particular importance are recent Swedish investigations which correlate datings for the Litorina transgressions (changes of the ocean level) with pollen evidence and radiocarbon datings (B.E. Berglund, 1971b).

From the abundant literature on Late and Post-Glacial fauna, only the most important works will be cited. A useful overview of the animal species represented at the Palaeolithic and Mesolithic settlements is provided by E. Brinch Petersen (1973); whereas C. Paludan-Müller (1978) has produced a summary of the food potential of the various biotopes in the Atlantic period. Of particular relevance for the study of faunal conditions are, furthermore, works of M. Degerbøl (1933), U. Møhl (1970), B. Løppenthin (1967), M. Degerbøl and B. Fredskild (1970) and K. Aaris-Sørensen (1980 a and b). See also D.A. Sturdy's important study (1975).

Unfortunately few detailed statistics have been compiled on the quantitative relationship of the various animal species represented at the settlements; however, see important studies by C.G.J. Petersen (1922), J.L. Bay-Petersen (1978), K. Aaris-Sørensen (1980 a and b) and E. Brinch Petersen (1970a). The problems concerning the representativeness of the faunal remains are well illustrated in a study on the Mejlgård shell mound by G.N. Bailey (1978). Piecing together a complete picture of the diet of the hunter–gatherer communities is also difficult due to problems in demonstrating the extent of gathering of plant products (R.W. Dennell, 1979). Perhaps in the future, isotopic analysis of prehistoric bones will bring us closer to illuminating these problems (A.B. Brown, 1974). For a discussion, see Boaz and Hampel (1978).

In recent years there has been a growing tendency to take an ecological approach to the study of the Palaeolithic and Mesolithic societies; see, for example, works by E. Brinch Petersen (1973) and C. Paludan-Müller (1978). Stimulating works from the field of social anthropology which have influenced Danish archaeologists include publications of R.B. Lee and I. DeVore (1968) and A. Leeds and A.P. Vayda (1965).

Another major trend in newer archaeological research is the interest in demographic factors. A survey of the development of this field has been published by Philip E.L. Smith (1970). Publications which have had relevance for Danish conditions include Brian Spooner (1972), Brian Hayden (1972) and P.R. Ehrlich and J.P. Holdren (1971). As a consequence of the interest in demography in recent years, attention has been focused on the significance of the carrying capacity of the various ecological zones. This concern may be found in several more recent studies, for example C. Paludan-Müller (1978). An estimate of the relative population size in Denmark during the Late and Post-Glacial periods has been attempted by E. Brinch Petersen (1973), whereas the absolute population size has been estimated by J. Troels-Smith (1955, 1960a) and J.G.D. Clark (1975).

An important part of Danish Mesolithic archaeology has been concentrated on chronological studies. Over the years, many attempts have been made to establish a functional chronological framework (E. Brinch Petersen, 1973). These attempts have sometimes resulted in most complicated schemes (Figure 19). The relatively new radiocarbon dates

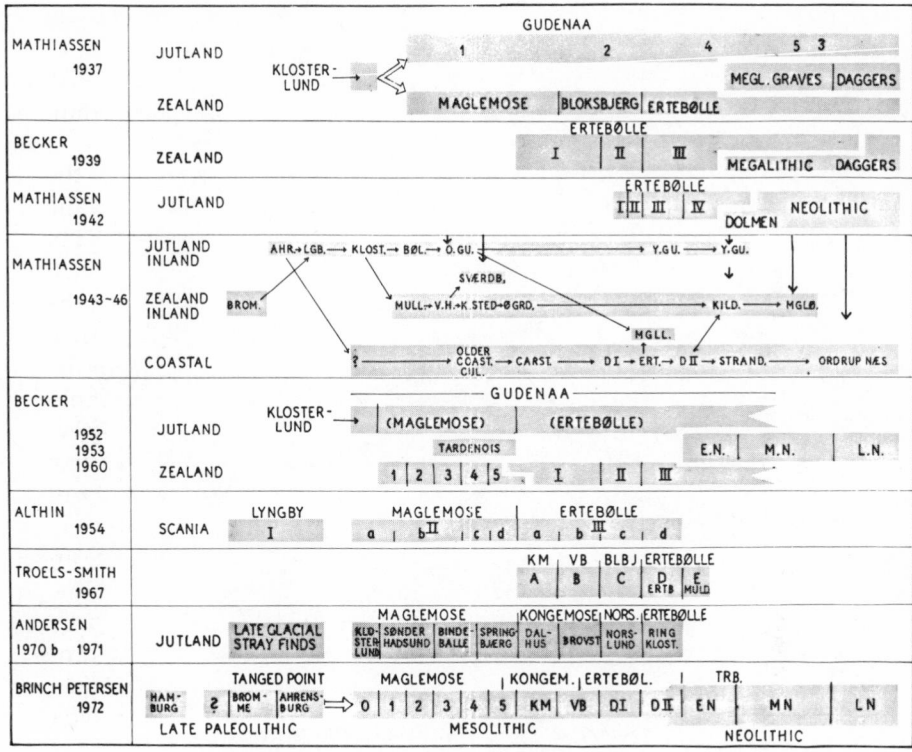

Figure 19 Danish Mesolithic chronology, research history.

have contributed to an altered and partially simplified conception (Figure 20). The radiocarbon dates used below are based on a number of corrections of older conventional dates. These so-called calibrated radiocarbon datings have in recent years led to a radical re-evaluation of north European prehistory (C. Renfrew, 1973b). Among other things, the introduction of agriculture to Denmark has been pushed back 1700 years earlier than the date which scholars only twenty years ago accepted.

From the period between the close of the Ice Age and the introduction of agriculture there are now (1981) more than one hundred radiocarbon datings of the Danish Mesolithic period at our disposal (Figure 20). Together with improved archaeological methods, these datings help create a firmer basis for chronological discussions. Most significantly, the postulate of the complete or partial contemporaneity of a number of 'cultures' has been rejected. For example, the term 'Gudenå culture' (T. Mathiassen, 1937) has been abandoned (S.H. Andersen, 1971). Instead,

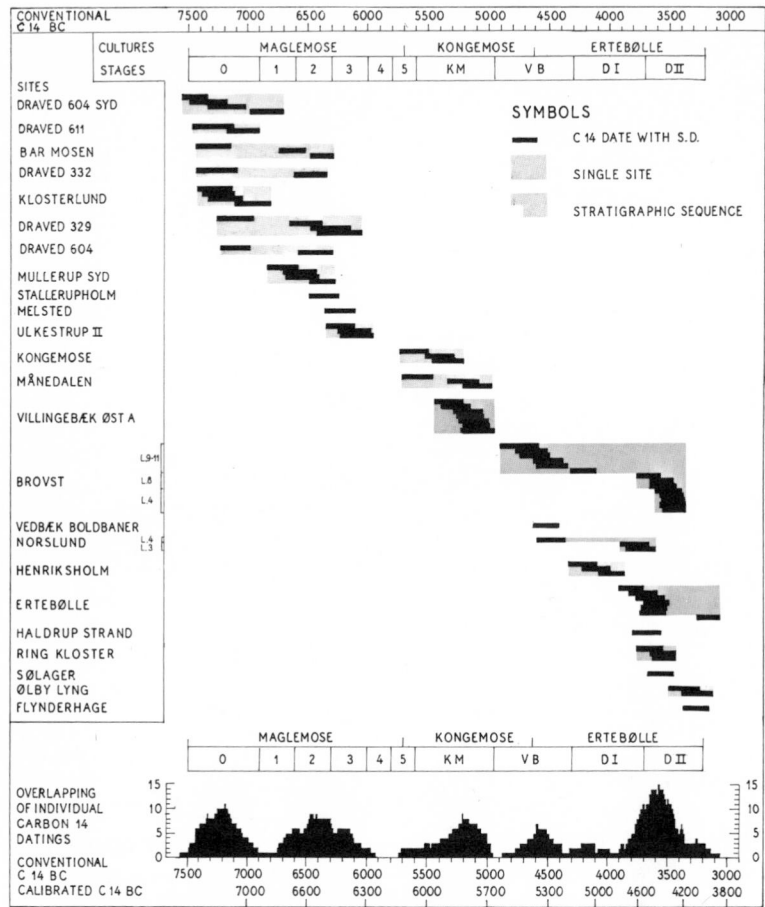

Figure 20 Radiocarbon dates of the Danish Mesolithic period.

a unilinear cultural development has been proposed (E. Brinch Petersen, 1973; S.H. Andersen, 1971; A. Fischer, 1978) in which the various phases succeed one another in a simple chronological progression.

General surveys of the period as a whole are relatively rare; one of them, published by J.G.D. Clark in 1975, offers a number of astute observations pertaining especially to the early part of the period. For the Late Glacial period (the Palaeolithic) there is a popular summary by J. Troels-Smith, 1955. For many years, the few Danish Palaeolithic stray finds could only be illuminated through a number of excavated settlements from northern Germany (A. Rust, 1937, 1943). After excavation of the Palaeolithic Bromme site on Zealand (T. Mathiassen, 1946a), the

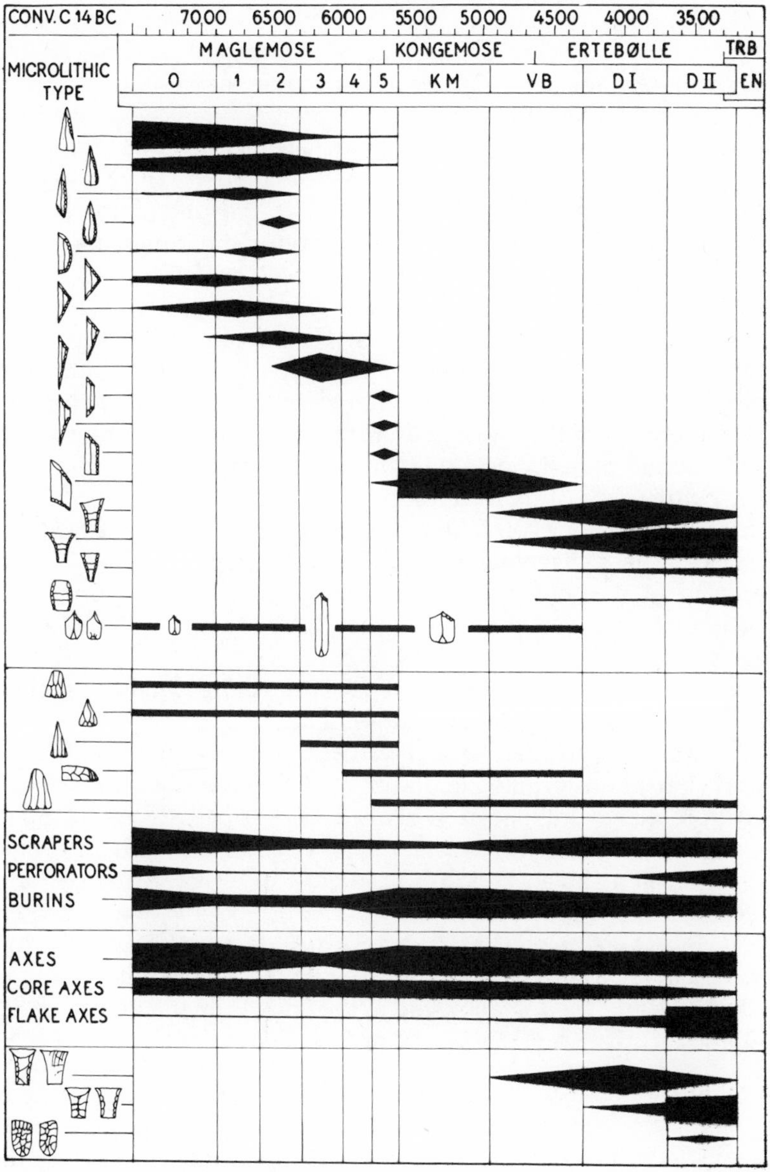

Figure 21 Chronological sequence of microliths and other lithic types during the Mesolithic period in Denmark.

Danish material has also been augmented (S.H. Andersen, 1970); equally important finds have been made in Scania (B. Salmonsson,

1964). Noteworthy contributions to the discussion also include works of E. Brinch Petersen (1970b), C.J. Becker (1971c) and A. Fischer (1978).

With the more ample archaeological record from the Pre-Boreal period and thereafter (the Mesolithic period), a clearer picture is also drawn of the individual cultural phases. From an archaeological viewpoint, each stage is defined through the composition of its tool kit. The Mesolithic Maglemose culture is characterized by various microlithic points and triangles, whereas the rhombic arrowhead typifies the Kongemose, and the transverse arrowhead the Ertebølle (Figure 21). A cultural designation thus defined can consequently only be taken as a functional unit for the archaeologist. The border between two 'cultures' will logically have to be drawn where the new microlithic type appears in numbers exceeding 50 per cent of the total microlithic tool kit (E. Brinch Petersen, 1973). On the basis of the successive transformations of tool types, the entire Mesolithic period, including the Maglemose, Kongemose and Ertebølle cultures, can be divided into ten chronological stages. However, there is no obvious correlation between archaeological and vegetational stages. The archaeological cultural terms refer exclusively to the development of the tool tradition. In so doing, the often very rigid approach of earlier Mesolithic archaeology has been radically modified (E. Brinch Petersen, 1973).

The methodological views described have been employed in a number of vital new works. For the Maglemose culture, reference is made to publications of E. Brinch Petersen (1966, 1971), R.E. Blankholm and S.H. Andersen (1967) and B. Bille Henriksen (1976). Finds from the Kongemose culture have only been described to a small degree – S.H. Andersen (1969b) and S. Jørgensen (1956, 1961) – whereas the Ertebølle culture has been a subject of growing interest in recent years; see, for example, works of J. Troels-Smith (1953, 1960a, 1966, 1967), C.J. Becker (1954), E.. Brinch Petersen (1970a) and S.H. Andersen (1973, 1974). An important part of the debate has dealt with the finds from the final Ertebølle phase and their relationship to the finds from the first farming communities (C. Paludan-Müller, 1978).

PART II

The first farmers
c. 4200–2800 BC

The introduction of farming in Denmark

Introduction

In the period after *c*. 4200 BC it is possible to observe a number of decisive changes in the economy of the prehistoric population in Denmark: the first signs of a new subsistence form, agriculture, now appear. The early archaeological evidence for the incipient food production is very sparse, but after the middle of the fourth millennium BC the innovations appear in their full range. This radical transformation of the economic structure of prehistoric society seems, as already mentioned, to be very complicated and is still far from clarified. Formerly the process was considered in Danish archaeology to have occurred quite suddenly and to have manifested itself as an economically, technologically, chronologically and demographically distinct transition. Nowadays, there is much to indicate that a far more complex view of this vital transitional phase must be employed. One fact, however, is indisputable: the incipient food production, meaning stock-rearing and grain-cultivation, gradually came to exercise a profound influence on all areas of the population's mode of living. Yet we must remember that early farming hardly revealed itself immediately as a great blessing to its first practitioners. There is good reason to presume that at first farming was only a modest supplement to normal activities. Most of the food probably still had to be obtained by hunting and gathering.

In a social regard, the new economy which distinguished early food production gradually caused a transition from one type of society to another. The band society, which had been the hunter–gatherers' organizational form, was very likely replaced by a more complex social pattern. Probably new societal forms now grew forth within a tribal mode of organization. The reason for this was that the new agrarian economy could not operate under the social and religious structure of earlier Mesolithic societies. In the beginning the agrarian economy probably diminished the pressure on the resources which had created it, resulting in a loosened social organization. Agriculture, however, probably also destroyed the traditional regulation of the population size so that a population growth was triggered off. Consequently more or less marked changes had to occur in the economic and social structures, allowing increased densities of population and precipitating changes in the settlement pattern. At present the archaeological evidence of this transition is meagre, but as will be described below, a number of observations indicate sweeping transformations in the course of the fourth millennium BC.

To understand the background for this lengthy course of development a number of factors must be clarified. On the whole very few of the material prerequisites for the beginning of agriculture in Denmark can be discerned in the period predating 4200 BC. A multitude of elements in the new cultural form had to be introduced from abroad. Such elements included domesticated animals, cultivated cereal types, and vital aspects of the technology inherent in the new subsistence form. Certainly, there had been contact between the late hunter–gatherer communities and the agrarian communities to the south – but this contact alone cannot explain the introduction of an agrarian economy about 4200 BC. So it is necessary to consider some possible causes of the origin of agriculture and its dissemination throughout Europe.

It is also important to emphasize that the prehistoric population could hardly have chosen the new subsistence strategy voluntarily. Compared with the existence of the hunter–gatherers, the introduction of stock-rearing and cereal cultivation meant that prehistoric man had to furnish a greater input of labour. An agrarian-based economy offered greater potential for growth than an economy based solely on hunting, fishing and food-gathering; but in return agriculture demanded a higher labour input per unit of food gained. This changed subsistence strategy may be viewed as the hunter–gatherers' response to a falling living standard. This view is justified by the fact that a low-technology society normally strives to employ the subsistence strategy which can nourish the population at the cost of a minimal input of labour. Meanwhile, it is possible that, as already mentioned, near the close of the fifth millennium BC a resource crisis threatened the Danish prehistoric population. This crisis may have hastened the introduction of domesticated plants and animals into the prehistoric society. Finally, it is important to emphasize that inherent in the transition to a subsistence form mainly based upon domesticated animals and cereal cultivation were hitherto unknown possibilities for economic and demographic growth. The root of this growth lay in the relative flexibility of the resources. Precisely for this reason, agriculture as a means of subsistence entails a constant demand for technological innovation. The factors named here will be described in more detail below.

The moving frontier

In recent decades, investigations of the origins of agriculture in the Middle East have shown that the understanding of this revolutionary step in the history of mankind must be sought in a study of the lifeways and adaptions of the inhabitants of the area during the Pleistocene. Many modern investigations seem to indicate that the introduction of agriculture was the result of a certain hunting and food-gathering strategy developed by hunters and gatherers by the late Pleistocene – and that the catalyst for change was a demographic one.

At the heart of modern research lie questions such as: what made agriculture advantageous and what helped stimulate changes in the early domesticates in the Middle East? A variety of hypotheses have been formulated to explain these developments. One of the most frequently cited hypotheses (K.V. Flannery, 1969) suggests that population growth in certain areas of the Zagros Mountains had begun already 20,000 years ago due to the so-called broad spectrum revolution. This change consisted of a significant broadening of the subsistence base to include ever greater amounts of fish, crabs, shellfish, birds and possibly plant food. Reliance on a broad range of food sources encouraged a sedentary settlement pattern which in turn stimulated population growth. This caused the surplus population to move into more marginal environments, taking with them wild forms of sheep, goats, wheat and barley.

The marginal zone hypothesis cannot be fully tested with data from the archaeological record in the Near East. But no matter how one explains the origin of the agricultural economy there is hardly any doubt that it arose as a result of a growing strain on the resources in the region of origin. The critical point seems to have been reached when a society of hunters and food-gatherers attained the population level on which resource scarcity forced the population to supplement gathering with, for example, cultivation of plants, and hunting with animal husbandry. In the beginning these new strategies were relatively restricted in relation to the traditional mode of obtaining food. But in time they increased, as the new strategies which provided an opportunity for an increase in the food production stimulated a population growth at the same time.

Many thousands of years intervened between the rise of agriculture in the Middle East and the first signs of agriculture in southern Scandinavia. Between these two events the dissemination of agriculture followed paths which over the past few decades archaeological research has been able to determine with a good deal of certainty. The process seems to have been characterized by a pattern of rapid spread and relatively low population density, as the surplus population of the farming communities had apparently expanded to ecological niches resembling the original territory as much as possible. Radiocarbon dates reveal that in the seventh and sixth millennia the agrarian economy spread from Anatolia to the Balkan peninsula and hence via the lower and middle Danube to central Europe.

The first European farming societies on the Balkan peninsula branched out by means of the network of fertile river valleys on the peninsula. From the Balkan peninsula the moving frontier continued via the loess regions along the lower and middle Danube. This final spreading in the loess plains of Europe betokens the transition from a frontal to an axially orientated distribution pattern. From north-west Hungary, there was a spread via the loess-covered areas up to the upper Danube, the lower Rhine and the lower Oder. These regions were then covered by a light open mixed oak forest and comprised a relatively unexploited ecological niche. The composition of the forest doubtless determined the farmers' choice of arable land.

The distribution of the early agrarian societies has been described as a wave of advance which progressed with an average speed of about one kilometre each year. Settlements were always made in regions with high agricultural potential. Probably the rise in temperature in the Atlantic period also favoured the spread – in any case, it can be observed that the great spread out over Europe began in the seventh millennium, that is, at the beginning of the Atlantic period. In the fifth millennium BC the wave of advance had reached the earlier ice-locked regions on the north European lowland. Then the colonization shifted in character, as the agrarian culture now confronted regions with soil types which were either unexploitable or less productive. Archaeological terminology distinguishes between a central European so-called 'Linear Pottery culture', associated with the loess regions, and a north European 'Funnel-Necked Beaker culture'.

Whereas the spread of the 'Linear Pottery culture' could be described as a wave of advance, which seemed to force the surplus population forward in an axial distribution pattern, another explanation must probably be sought for the rise of the agrarian economy within the great lowland region of northern Europe. The consistent preference earlier shown for certain soil types within the 'Linear Pottery culture' does not exist in north-west Germany and southern Scandinavia. The neolithization of this area has therefore been termed a secondary phenomenon as it apparently had a different background from the early neolithization of central Europe. This background has already been touched upon above. To delve further into the problem, we shall now seek to illuminate the environmental conditions which characterized Denmark at the end of the fifth millennium BC.

The farming communities and their environment

The High Atlantic period was the warmest of the great Post-Pleistocene periods. In the fifth millennium BC, in the last phase of the Atlantic, the rise in temperature in Denmark culminated. The climate was now warm and moist: the summer temperature was at least 2°, more probably 3°, higher than today. This favourable climate continued into the succeeding period, during which the agrarian communities began in earnest to make their mark on the environment.

The fifth millennium BC also witnessed the culmination of the Litorina transgression, possibly resulting in a shift in the population equilibrium. If this is the case, it may explain why at the end of the High Atlantic period the first signs of a true agricultural economy can be observed in Denmark. From this time, the relationship between the prehistoric society and its environment acquired a completely new dimension: man's manipulation of the fauna and the vegetation now became a vital factor. However, the influence of a primitive agricultural system on the forest is difficult to identify in the beginning. Consequently, up to the middle of the fourth millennium BC, the changes observed are difficult to interpret.

The natural environment which was the scene of the first farming communities in Denmark was above all dominated by the climax forest. Through the foregoing millennia, the vegetation had tended towards a climax stage. The stable virgin forest had formed and conditioned the development potential of the newly established subsistence strategy. The agrarian economy demanded new forms of labour, the most important of which was forest clearance.

The forest which confronted the first farming society represented a climax stage in the great ecological succession. It was a stable virgin forest; when trees died, new trees of the same type grew up in their place; no longer did forests of pioneer trees encroach. The virgin forest of the Sub-Boreal period covered all of Denmark, interrupted only by the many lakes and swampy areas. The lime seems to have been the predominant forest tree. On poor dry sandy soil such as that in west Jutland, oak rivalled the lime. Elm too was common, although it suffered a decline around 3800 BC. This decline will later be examined more carefully. The role of the ash was not large, but it did grow around the beginning of the fourth millennium BC. By the shores of streams and lakes the alder was the leading tree.

Within the various landscapes, the composition of this dark, shady virgin forest was naturally varied. On high, well-watered ground the lime predominated. On moister ground there was a more varied forest – a mixed oak forest. Here lime, elm and ash grew, with the oak as the predominant tree. In the moist swampy regions the alder reigned, whereas birch alone was found near the moist deep peat bogs.

The interior of the virgin forest was murky. Tree trunks were far more massive than is normal for modern forests. The underbrush-vegetation on the forest floor was scanty as a result of the dense canopy, and the forest floor was full of mouldering wood.

The small farming communities which arose around 4000 BC seem primarily to have been located on the border between high well-watered ground and low ground where the moist forest floor could provide nourishment for domesticated pigs. On the high ground small clearings were established by burning the forest, the heat of which released nutrients in the upper few centimetres of the forest soil. However, ash had only a slight effect as a fertilizer. The burning also rinsed the forest floor of competing growths and weed-like vegetation. All of these results bettered growing conditions for cereal.

The stationary condition which characterized the forest meant that the amount of humus mineralized each year corresponded to the amount formed by the dead organic materials which were left. This process is most noticeable on soil which is rich in nutrients and it increases with the rising temperature. In short, the mould production of the Atlantic climax forest must have been great, a factor which benefited agriculture tremendously.

This process was a link in a much greater cycle, the course of which has been described in conjunction with the environmental development in the Post-Pleistocene. A similar cycle can also be shown to have existed between the glaciations. The cycle commences with a glacial period, in which solifluction prevents the formation of a stable plant growth. Then comes the formation of a soil rich in lime and minerals which is neutral or slightly sour, and at some places soil exhaustion begins. This stage corresponds to the climax forest in the climatic optimum of the Atlantic period. At last, when the temperature again begins to drop, comes an increased exhaustion of the soil with an increasing degree of sourness and podsolization as a consequence (J. Iversen, 1969).

As evident, there was a large production of mould in the dense climax forest during the transition between the High Atlantic and the Sub-Boreal periods. The natural deterioration of the soil was as yet slight but the impact of man hastened it considerably synchronous with the earliest agrarian cultures. The spread of agriculture in Denmark thus rapidly became an irreversible process.

The extensive swiddening practised by the first farmers destroyed large areas of forest. As we will see later, the exhausted fields were abandoned after a brief period of cultivation. Thus more ways for exhausting the soil were created. In particular the light forest with scrub pasture here and there which resulted from cattle grazing must have suffered rapid soil deterioration, a condition which is also familiar from more recent times (S.T. Andersen, 1979). On hilly terrain the destruction of the natural vegetation could also be accompanied by soil erosion when the mould was no longer anchored by the roots of the plants.

So there is good reason to believe that the mould of the forest floor which must have existed when agriculture was introduced degenerated badly quite early. This factor, in addition to the negative effect of ard ploughing see pp. 99 ff, 143 ff, and 222 ff) and the lack of manuring, seems to have had a decisive impact on the future course of agriculture. We will return to these circumstances later.

The evidence of pollen analysis

An understanding of this process and of the existence of the first farming society in the dense climax forest is first and foremost conveyed by the natural sciences and in particular by pollen analysis. This discipline determines the quantitative relationship of the pollen of various plants. By analysing samples from all layers in a number of bogs, it has been possible to establish a relative chronology for the vegetational development in southern Scandinavia. This development is marked by a number of expansion stages caused by the intrusion of the farming communities into nature. Four stages have been identified. The first stage began during the fourth millennium BC and represents the 'landnam' of the first farmer. After some centuries, this first human intrusion into the forest is supplanted by a new expansion period which set in somewhat after the beginning of the third millennium BC at approximately the same time as the so-called 'Single Grave culture'. In the centuries predating the birth of Christ an increase in human activity is again apparent, but dwindles somewhat about 400–500 AD. A last expansion phase begins in the Viking period – and again lessens in the late Middle Ages (Figure 22).

Of these four expansion stages which have been determined on a very general basis, our interest is focused primarily on the first stage. Often this first landnam phase is divided into two parts: an A-landnam corresponding to the so-called elm fall, marked by a drastic fall in the pollen curve of the elm at the transition to the Sub-Boreal; and a B-landnam, which very clearly shows the effect on the vegetational

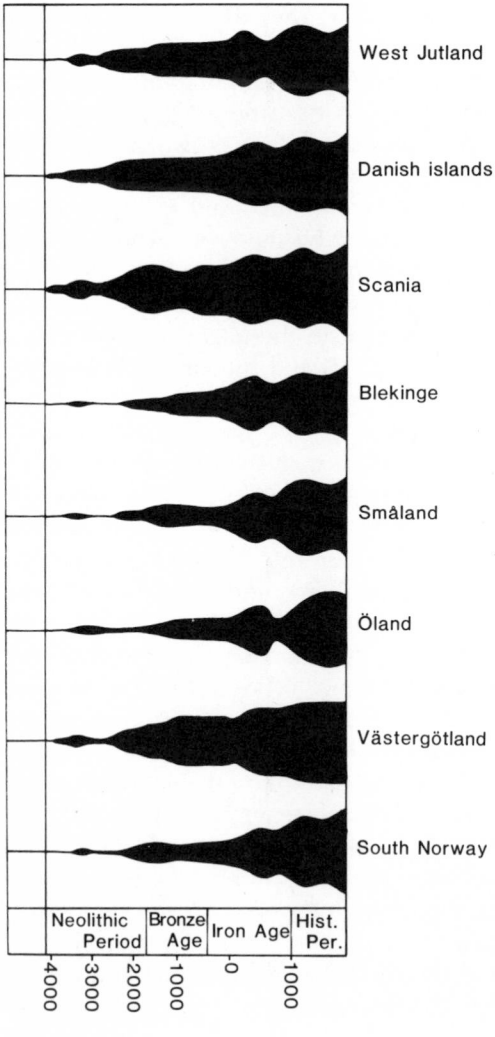

West Jutland

Danish islands

Scania

Blekinge

Småland

Öland

Västergötland

South Norway

Neolithic Period	Bronze Age	Iron Age	Hist. Per.

4000 · 3000 · 2000 · 1000 · 0 · 1000

Figure 22 Survey diagram illustrating human influence on the vegetation in eight areas of south Scandinavia. The chart attempts to illustrate the four general expansion stages of farming and stock-raising during the prehistoric period. 1. The early Neolithic 'landnam' (*c.* 4000–3200 BC). 2. The late Neolithic and early Bronze Age expansion (*c.* 2800–1000 BC). 3. The expansion of the early Iron Age (*c.* 200 BC–400 AD). 4. The expansion of the Viking period (*c.* 800–1000 AD).

development of the primitive swidden farming of the early farming communities.

The elm fall or the A-landnam is the first change in the vegetational development which may be attributed to human activity. Whether this holds true, however, is very uncertain. On the border between the Atlantic and the Sub-Boreal, the pollen curve of the elm falls noticeably. A corresponding fall can in fact be observed over all of north-western Europe. The elm fall has been explained climatically with regard to the so-called elm disease which has also ravaged Europe and North America in our century.

However, a number of scholars have persuasively argued that the elm fall is the result of primitive agriculture. It has been pointed out that in a deciduous forest region such as Denmark, primitive stock-raising must be based upon leaf fodder. Ecologically the elm fall can be perfectly well explained as the result of a primitive agricultural economy with husbandry. But it is difficult to integrate this theory with the conclusions which can be drawn from archaeological investigations of contemporary settlements. Whether or not the elm fall was the result of the encroachment of the first farming communities in the forest is a question which must hang in abeyance. In the meantime the existence of the farming communities prior to the elm fall may be traced in other ways. Finds of pottery assignable to the first agrarian communities have been radio-carbon-dated to the period immediately preceding the elm fall.

Around 3200 BC – here and there even earlier – that is, one thousand years after the first archaeological evidence of the slow advance of the agricultural economy, we find a number of vegetational changes – the B-landnam – which quite clearly can be ascribed to an agrarian culture. The specifics of these changes will not be discussed here. However, it may be mentioned that in the detailed pollen diagrams, this landnam phase may be divided into three stages. The first stage corresponds to the forest clearance of the agrarian communities. This clearance has been interpreted as having entailed a swiddening or burning-off of the trees and bushes growing on the land intended for cultivation. After a fairly brief period of cultivation follows another stage which, according to the pollen analysts, is the result of cattle grazing on the abandoned fields. The third stage represents the regeneration of the forest after the cessation of cattle grazing. After a certain development this phase ends with the forest strangling all other plant species in its growing density.

Early agriculture had but a limited effect on the dense virgin forest. Throughout the fourth millennium BC Denmark was still dominated by dense forest and underbrush. Not until the third millennium BC did the scrub pastures gradually grow in importance.

7

Population growth and food production

The growth potential of the agrarian society

The beginning of agriculture has often been claimed to be one of the most revolutionary steps in the history of mankind. The beginning of food production is said to have created the potential for economic and demographic growth of previously unequalled extent. However, it is not until recently that Danish archaeologists have delved more deeply into these problems. Whilst the modern world is increasingly confronted with population problems, prehistoric archaeology has sought to gain insight into the societal mechanisms which lead to population growth.

In older research the problem could be defined fairly simply. Population growth was frequently regarded as the direct result of technological innovation. Today there is a more pronounced tendency to see population pressure as an independent variable affecting other cultural and environmental factors, a view which requires a re-evaluation of many archaeological hypotheses.

An attempt has been made above to demonstrate that the cause of agriculture in southern Scandinavia should possibly be sought in the demographic situation. An attempt will now be made to determine whether this basic viewpoint can also be maintained in relation to further agricultural development in Danish prehistory. It may be asked whether this hypothesis can explain the expansion stages indicated, for example, by pollen analysis.

As suggested earlier, we must presume that seasonal fluctuations in the amount of resources were of crucial importance in establishing the optimal population size of the hunter–gatherer communities. The population size had to be adapted to the resources in the poorest seasons and to fluctuations in the resources over the years. With the introduction of the agrarian economy the effect of such fluctuations is diminished by such innovations as the development of methods of preserving and storing. Above all, however, agrarian societies are characterized by the emphasis they place on resources with a high potential for expansion. Animal husbandry combined with plant cultivation entails just such a potential. Each of the two subsistence strategies has its own characteristics. The holding of domestic animals is less productive than plant cultivation, as animals rank more highly in the food chain than plants. But domesticated animals are mobile, and herds can be led to where there is a sufficiency of food. However, a significant expansion of stock-holding demands drastic changes in the ecosystem. Obtaining a larger grazing area in a terrain of virgin forest, for example, demands an enormous investment of labour. Cereal cultivation also demands a considerable investment of labour. The cultivated area can be enlarged fairly easily although it requires an increase in regular labour to care for the fields. In return even quite small technological changes often deeply affect the yield. In conjunction the two subsistence forms have a high potential for expansion, depending of course upon the possibilities for an increased investment of labour.

Thus there exists a wide difference between societies based wholly or partially on agriculture and all other societal forms. In agrarian society demographic control is not so crucial as in the hunter–gatherer society due to this growth potential. But at the same time this growth potential is accompanied by a constant demand for technological innovation. It is the nature of this innovation which we shall now attempt to illuminate.

A theory of agricultural development under population pressure

The Danish economist Esther Boserup's studies of present-day low-technological societies have had tremendous significance for the understanding of the development of early agriculture in Denmark. Her point of departure is the fact that in a primitive agriculture much of the arable land must lie fallow most of the time to regain its fertility.

To begin with slash-and-burn farming, which is the most economical agricultural system in a sparsely populated area, a series of stages can be observed. These stages occur as the fallow period is increasingly shortened as a consequence of the intensified harvesting necessitated by growing population pressure. To counteract a fall in the yield, farmers are continually forced to employ new means. The introduction of the plough to Denmark during the third millennium BC and perhaps even earlier thus represents the next stage in the process. The technology of the agrarian society must of necessity be modified in each new developmental stage to ensure a sufficiently high yield.

However, the development of the agrarian society demands an ever growing investment of labour, that is the growth of the population results in an increased labour input per food unit gained. Production rises but the product per labour unit falls. It is this fall in productivity which sheds doubt on older theories which instead viewed population increase as the direct result of technological innovations. Contrary to this viewpoint, Esther Boserup claims that an agrarian population does not naturally increase its labour input voluntarily, even if this input is very small, as in the earliest agriculture. Growing population pressure provoked by the tendency toward sedentarism can, however, force the agrarian society to increase its labour input. Harder and more efficient work also raises effectiveness in other areas, greater population density allows more specialized divisions of labour, and the process is thus set in motion.

As we have said, Esther Boserup points out that with a low population density an extensive agriculture based upon slash-and-burn is the most economic agricultural system, as regards the investment of labour. This system has various consequences. First of all, farming with long fallow periods demands but little preparation of the soil because cultivation only occurs for a short length of time. Nor is it necessary to maintain fertility by fertilizing during the cultivation period; it is hardly worth the effort to clear tree trunks out of the way. Therefore the use of a plough is unnecessary and the cultivated area can be abandoned when the weeds begin to compete seriously with the cultivated species, and when the nutrients released by the swiddening diminish. In short, a relatively small labour input is sufficient to ensure a good yield. However, slash-and-burn farming demands large areas per family when the fallow areas are taken into consideration. Slash-and-burn cannot therefore be maintained when the population exceeds a certain point when there would no longer be enough land to continue with the long fallow periods.

As remarked above, the population increase gradually necessitates an abandonment of slash-and-burn and the introduction of agricultural systems which exploit the area more effectively. In return, there is a lower yield per working hour; more work is required. In Denmark, the first step in this direction seems to have occurred at the end of the fourth millennium and throughout the third millennium BC. Traces of ard-ploughing are more frequent in this period; animal husbandry continues to expand. Both of these changes demand an increased labour input: the draught animals must be fed, fodder must be gathered, the fields must be cleared, weeded and enclosed; therefore the various amounts of invested labour rise. It is not possible to trace this process in detail by means of the archaeological record. The process probably occurred at a different pace in various regions. After the introduction of ard-ploughing, however, the expansion of productivity seems to have occurred primarily by means of the raising of domestic animals. This situation will be examined later.

The hypothesis suggested here is on several counts an extension of the views proposed above regarding the development of the hunter–gatherer communities up to *c.* 4200 BC. Here too an attempt has been made to show how the continued effort to adapt to the food situation entailed the use of a number of culturally conditioned means to control population size. The incipient food production around 4200 BC has been seen in the same perspective and explained as the response of the population to a falling living standard. This sort of explanation makes it possible to reject the invasion hypotheses which formerly played an exaggerated role in European archaeological literature. To explain the rise of agricultural economy by simply suggesting a massive invasion of foreign peoples is in reality no explanation at all, as the economic analysis which provides an understanding of the dynamics of further cultural development is thereby often neglected. In the same way the hypothesis of the 'filtering in' of foreign ethnic groups and their assimilation with the local population cannot be supported on chronological grounds. Determining the primary catalyst in the set of factors which led to the introduction of agriculture demands a deeper understanding of the complicated interrelationship of the food situation, the population size and society's means of production. With the introduction of the agricultural economy, the population size once more fell far below the limit imposed by the previous subsistence form. For more than a thousand years, the population grew again, until a new maximum was reached – a development which will be treated in the following chapters.

Fertility and mortality in the early agrarian society

In the discussion of demographic conditions in the hunter–gatherer communities, reference was made to a number of more general results which in part pertained to the prehistoric population's chances of survival. Many of these results were obtained by comparison with present-day low-technology societies. With the beginning of the agricultural economy around 4200 BC, we have more concrete evidence regarding the individual's chances of survival. A number of results from early Swiss agrarian communities, for example, confirm the statistics mentioned above; moreover, they seem to have validity for the Danish situation.

A survival chart for individuals from a number of contemporaneous Swiss farming communities is shown in Figure 23. The extremely high mortality in the younger age groups is clearly evident – indeed it is probably even higher, because the skeletons of infants cannot be well preserved. The survival chart shows that after 13 years only about 40–45

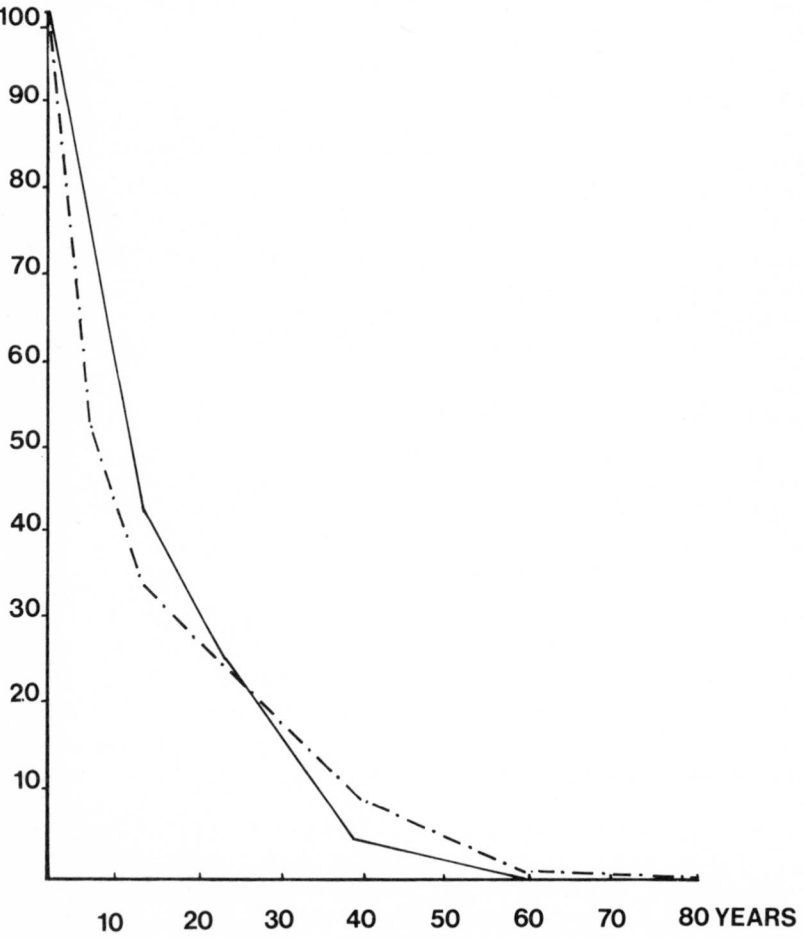

Figure 23 A survival chart from a number of Swiss Neolithic communities. The height of the curve above the horizontal axis indicates how large a percentage of a generation survived in each age group.

per cent of the living-born individuals are still alive. After 22 years, more than 70 per cent of the individuals are dead – the average life expectancy for living-born individuals is between 20 and 25 years. This implies that only about 30 per cent of those born attained adulthood.

The distribution of the two sexes also shows some striking features, in particular men's distinctly better chances of survival. In general only very few changes in mortality can be expected in the course of prehistory. Swedish investigations of the medieval population in Jämt-land in Sweden (N.-G. Gejvall, 1960) show a noteworthy correspondence with the observations in Figure 23. Infant mortality for the first year of life of over 30 per cent does not seem to have been uncommon. Similarly, observations of the high mortality in the young age groups and women's poor chances of survival in comparison to those of men seem to be applicable to all prehistoric periods (G. Acsádi and J. Nemeskéri, 1970).

These factors naturally had great significance for the composition of the individual populations. The farming communities must have possessed a sizeable surplus of men. The number of individuals in the younger age groups was only slightly larger than the number in the mature age groups. Population growth must have occurred extremely slowly, and even though 'over-population' is a relative phenomenon, it seems only to a limited extent applicable as an explanatory basis in the hypotheses of invasions with which earlier archaeology operated.

Regarding the health conditions of the prehistoric population after the introduction of agricultural economy, only a few factors will be mentioned here. The wide-spectred subsistence strategy which characterized the early farming communities would hardly have caused any major changes. Growing dependence upon cereal food, which came to characterize the farming communities, may in periods have been accompanied by a lack of proteins and fat. It is very possible that vitamin deficiency, especially in the vitamin groups A, B and D, and the consequent deficiency diseases existed in the population after c. 4200 BC. In fact, rachitis has been identified on skeletons from the the Neolithic period in Denmark. Despite the fact that food could now be produced in hitherto unimagined quantities, deficiency diseases and food crises may paradoxically have been the result of the introduction of agriculture. This situation will be studied more closely in the following chapter.

8

Subsistence and settlement

Introduction

The first expansion of agriculture in Denmark extended over a period of about 1500 years. In archaeological literature this period is referred to by the rather unfortunate name, 'the Funnel-Necked Beaker culture'. After the latest calibrated radiocarbon dates this period is believed to have begun about 4200 BC, which is 1700 years earlier than was believed just twenty years ago.

In the same way, various hypotheses regarding the period have had to be modified. It was formerly thought that several hundred years after the introduction of agriculture a new ethnic group, the so-called 'Single Grave people', invaded Denmark. The oldest agrarian population of the country was hence thought to have lived alongside this new ethnic element until the two groups merged after some centuries. Again, radiocarbon datings have modified earlier theories. The parallelism alluded to between the two population groups has not been confirmed by either archaeological or scientific studies. A more logical hypothesis is that in the course of the third millennium BC, especially after *c*. 2800 BC, a number of profound economic and social changes occurred within the agrarian communities. In the archaeological literature this new developmental stage is termed the 'Single Grave culture'. The entire problem is still under debate and will be described more thoroughly in the next chapter.

Through nearly 1500 years the first agricultural culture evolved relatively undisturbed in Denmark. The archaeological remains which can provide information on the trends of the period are, to be sure, quite abundant in the latter half, when a series of environmental, cultural and organizational factors favoured a rapid growth of the agricultural communities. In general, however, one gains the impression of great continuity in societal development during the whole period.

Land use of the early farming communities

The subsistence form practised in the fourth millennium BC in Denmark is rather obscure. This is because the settlement pattern of the first agrarian communities is still a neglected area of research. Up to the present, very few settlements have been studied for the purpose of gaining an overall picture of the nature of a settlement site. The same neglect holds true of ecological studies, which could, among other things, describe the relationship of the settlement to the biological zones exploitable by an individual village. Knowledge of the geographic distribution of the early farming communities also leaves much to be desired. In this regard, however, a single valuable study has been made, based upon the preserved and protected grave monuments (J. Bekmose, 1978).

The point of departure for this latter investigation consisted of the protected megalith graves from the end of the fourth millennium BC, the well-known dolmens and passage graves. Of these, only the rectangular type of dolmen without passage can be dated to the earliest farming communities, whereas there is a growing body of information dating most other types to a period of only a few centuries around 3200 BC.

By means of a statistical study it was concluded that the preserved megalith structures could be presumed to constitute a representative sample. The monuments should therefore prove useful as a basis for conclusions regarding the geographic distribution of the agrarian communities, the selection of settlement areas within the arable regions of the country, and the relative population situation of the period.

The point of departure is naturally the extent of the country in the period under discussion. North of a line which runs diagonally from Nissum Bredning in the west of Jutland to northern Falster in the east of Denmark, the land was then considerably lower than today. The fjords of northern Zealand were considerably wider, Djursland was divided by the now dry Kolind fjord, and northern Jutland was broken up into numerous islands. South of the line, however, the land was higher. Tåsinge, Ærø and Falster comprised one island. This also held true of Lolland and Falster, just as the islands of the Wadden Sea were connected with southern Jutland.

On the map of Denmark, Figure 24, which shows the present-day coastline of the country, the spatial distribution of the dolmens in long barrows is illustrated through a trend-surface analysis. The dolmens in

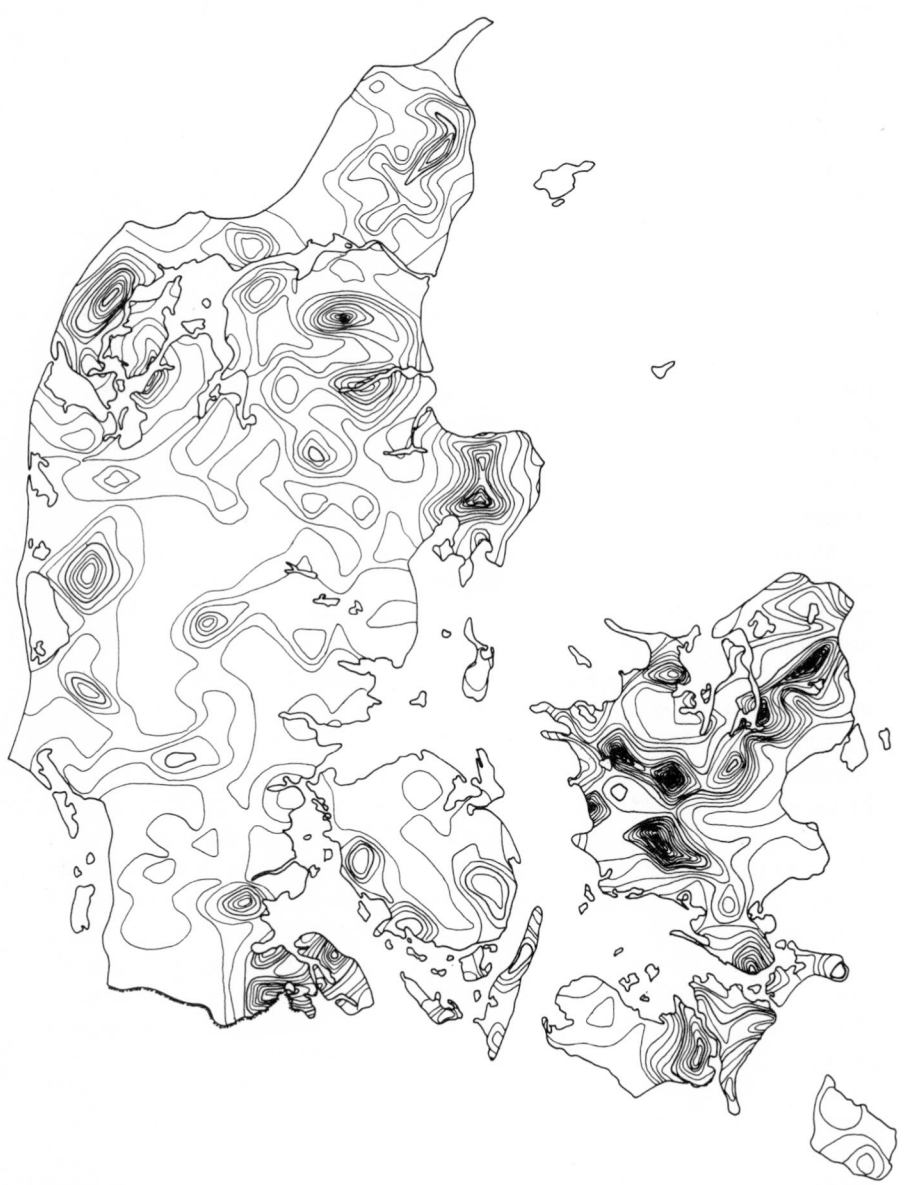

Figure 24 The spatial distribution of Neolithic dolmens in long barrows, illustrated by a trend surface analysis.

long barrows are a group of monuments which is spread throughout the country, although there are areas which are strikingly poor in finds in central, western and eastern Jutland. The same holds true of Funen, just as there are small areas which are poor in finds on western Lolland and eastern Zealand. The geography of the Atlantic period naturally plays a role for the understanding of the distribution pattern, but as a whole concentrations can be observed around what was once a series of archipelago-like coastal regions. The concentrations lie in northern Zealand, on Lolland, Falster, southern Zealand and eastern Funen with connection to the eastern part of south Jutland. Finally there are concentrations on Djursland, in Himmerland and in the western Limfjord area together with a less noteworthy one by Ringkøbing fjord.

In general it can be observed that the early agrarian communities showed a preference for high-lying well-drained ground. But the distribution of the settlements can hardly be explained on this basis alone. The relationship with the archipelago regions of the time and their multitude of various biological zones must have been just as decisive. As will later be seen, this corresponds to the wide-spectred subsistence strategy practised by the early farming communities.

The map on which the geographic distribution of the dolmens in long barrows is plotted helps provide an idea of the basic pattern in the geographic distribution of the early agrarian communities. Supplementing this picture with, for example, the distribution of the dolmens in round barrows, few important exceptions can be noted. To be sure, the dolmens in round barrows have a more limited distribution than dolmens in long barrows but still many of the groupings which characterize the distribution of long dolmens are present. In the main, the passage graves also correspond to the map in Figure 24. The passage graves, however, are primarily an east Danish phenomenon and are often associated with the distribution areas of dolmens.

The great significance ascribed to the megalithic monuments such as dolmens and passage graves is due to the role which they must have played in the territorial patterns of the agrarian communities. If it is presumed that as a result of swidden agriculture settlement was moved at regular intervals within a defined territory, then the great stone graves in contrast must have been among the few permanent elements in the existence of the farming communities. This view has been expressed by Colin Renfrew (1976) as follows: that for the individual community the grave monument was not merely the grave of the forefathers; it was also a permanent symbol of continuity in the possession of the surrounding territory.

This situation will be studied more closely later. Here it will only be suggested that the distribution of the large stone graves seems to indicate the settlement pattern of the farming communities. This pattern is not necessarily completely valid, as the stone graves are not the sole grave form of the epoch. The picture which can be glimpsed about 1000 years after the first traces of an agrarian economy appear are settlements which, particularly in southern Denmark, were established with a certain preference for the heavy soils, primarily of glacial clay, and – of perhaps even greater importance – situated around a number of archipelago-like coastal regions where the variation of resources was especially great.

Within the individual settlement areas, development assumed a number of forms. The correspondence between the multitude of biological zones and benign soils seems to have provided the south Danish settlements in particular with the opportunity for great expansion at the beginning of the third millennium BC. Here, in fact, new settlement concentrations arose, for example on northern Funen, where a new archipelago settlement appeared. In northern and central Jutland development seems to have stagnated to a certain degree after an initial establishment phase; demographic concentrations similar to those seen in southern Denmark never seem to have been achieved.

We have now considered the overall picture of the settlement of the farming communities as it appeared in the final centuries of the fourth millennium BC. This is the period during which the megalith constructions were erected, called in archaeological terminology the end of the Early Neolithic and the beginning of the Middle Neolithic. Unfortunately it is very difficult to determine the long-term trends in the development of the settlement. This is due chiefly to the fact that the archaeological sources which illuminate the so-called Single Grave culture, the period after 2800 BC, occur scattered and by chance. Not even the intensive regional surveys carried out by the Danish National Museum in the 1940s and 1950s can provide any unambiguous picture. However, some long-term tendencies can be glimpsed.

The intensive regional surveys mentioned were carried out both in north-west Zealand and in north-west Jutland. In the former area, where the quality of the soil is quite homogeneous, settlement in the first millennium of the existence of the farming communities shows a relatively even spreading over the entire area. For instance, the central parts of Zealand were also the location of a relatively intensive exploitation. The regions near the coast, however, seem to have had the largest population concentration. It also appears that the exploitation of the inland diminished somewhat after c. 3000 BC. An expansion of the settlement in the coastal regions and a certain thinning out in the inland regions seem evident. This marked tendency continued with growing force in the succeeding millennia.

The explanation for this situation should hardly be sought in a decreasing population. In fact, quite the opposite may have been the case. The shift was presumably related to changes in the agricultural system. Whereas the earliest slash-and-burn agriculture probably compelled the farming communities to a high degree of mobility, the gradual introduction of the plough and perhaps especially the expansion of stock-raising observable in the course of the period may thus have favoured a more sedentary settlement pattern. The farming communities may thus have preferred different types of soil and especially vegetation than previously. The dense virgin forest in the interior of the island may no longer have been so attractive. Instead growth gradually took place in a terrain where more intensive settlement had created a more open vegetation and thus better conditions for an expansion of animal husbandry.

This tendency may also be evident in the other area which has been thoroughly studied, the north-western part of Jutland. The settlement here shows in the first phases an even distribution over the moraine regions along the southern part of the Limfjord. The sandy regions of the outwash plains in the south, on the other hand, show a far more scattered settlement. As on Zealand, the farming communities seem at first to have sought the dense forest areas which were necessary for swidden agriculture. But in time the lighter soils seem to have been preferred rather than the heavy moraine soil. This tendency gained great impetus in the following millennia, and at the same time the open forest vegetation on the present-day heathy plains were to an increasing degree taken over for settlement. Again it can be presumed that the development from swidden agriculture to an agriculture with growing emphasis on cattle was the reason for the shift in settlement. In these areas of Jutland a major change in the settlement pattern seems to have taken place around 2800 BC. The attempts of the communities to expand production, especially by increasing stock-breeding, may well have been directed toward the more open vegetation forms in preference to the dense forest areas on the heavy moraine ground.

These two examples perhaps describe the beginning of the settlement type which can be distinctly observed in the second millennium BC: in Jutland, settlement seems to be concentrated with growing intensity on the lighter, although not the very lightest, soils whereas the dense forests growing, for example, on the moraine soil of eastern Jutland seem to have been avoided. On Zealand the moraine areas in the interior of the island seem to have been gradually abandoned. Instead, settlement was concentrated in the regions near the coast where a relatively large population gradually created a countryside with a quite open forest. The extensive swidden agriculture accompanied by a mobile settlement pattern seems to have been gradually replaced by a more sedentary settlement pattern. The prerequisite for this may have been the growing importance of the plough and the increase in stock-rearing, with the consequent greater need for grazing areas. As yet this process cannot be followed in detail, but it became distinct in the course of the second millennium BC.

Settlement

The picture which can be drawn of the settlement pattern of the early farming communities on the macro-level seems also to be repeated on the micro-level. The very wide-spectred subsistence strategy practised by the farming communities through the fourth millennium BC explains why settlement took place especially in areas with a great environmental variation. The same pattern is also evident in more restricted settlement areas and in the study of individual settlement sites. Here it is also seen that every single community adapted itself in all details to the ecological niche in which it existed. For example, the composition of the livestock was determined by the specific ecological advantages offered by the environment. Access to grazing areas, to fresh water, to hunting, and so on, seems to have deeply influenced the character of the individual settlement site.

The study of the first farming communities' settlement pattern in Denmark is, however, still in its infancy. As yet very few settlement sites have been excavated, so it has not been possible to gain an impression of, for example, the house-types – and consequently of the size of the individual settlement. The structures which were once considered typical of the dwelling form of the farming communities, the so-called longhouses from Barkær in Jutland, have been proved in recent studies to be enormous grave structures, probably long barrows. Intensive investigations of small defined areas are also very few. Yet a single newer investigation made within a 1600 km² area on the east coast of Jutland (T. Madsen, 1978a) has yielded significant results which can serve as a guide for future research.

The area investigated in this latter study (Figure 25) is a tremendously varied hilly moraine landscape traversed by numerous wide valleys with lakes and streams at their bottom. During the marine transgression in the fourth millennium BC the inhabitable area was somewhat smaller than it is today; it was also more emphatically divided

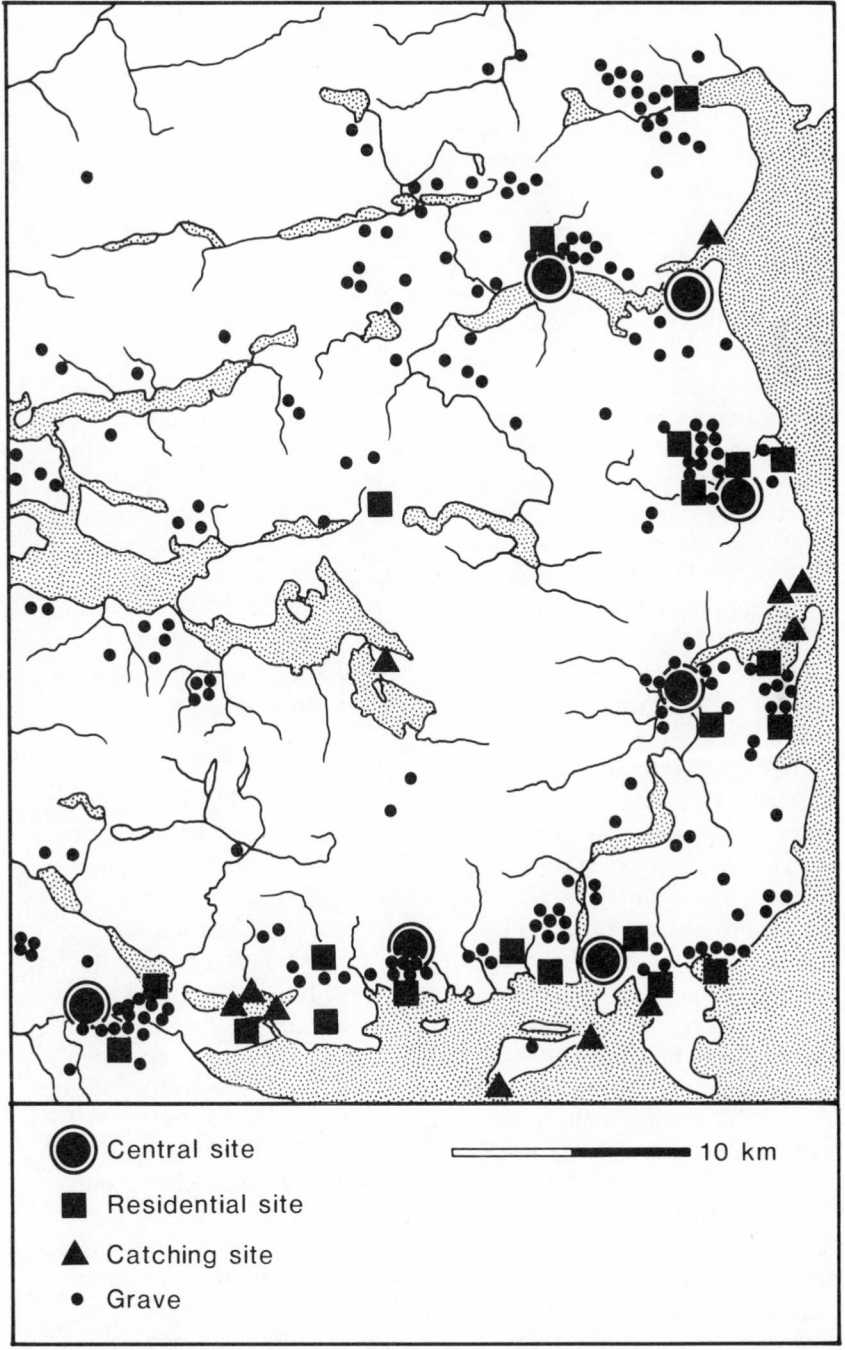

Figure 25 Settlement pattern of Neolithic communities in a hilly moraine landscape in the central part of eastern Jutland. The megalith graves, central sites, and settlements are mostly clustered around the swampy valleys a few kilometres behind the coastline.

by watercourses. First, the settlements of the region and the graves (megalith graves and so-called earth graves) were plotted and a distinct pattern thus emerged. Of particular note are the small clusters of megalith graves and settlement sites which, just a few kilometres behind the coastline, are concentrated around the moist valleys which at that time were quite marked. On the high moraine ground between the valleys and in the interior there are practically no traces of either settlements or graves. In the interior of the land the traces of the early farming communities are concentrated chiefly around lakes and the stream system to which they are associated. Distribution here seems to have occurred mainly where the large water systems lead inland. A typical feature of the settlement pattern is thus the intimate connection to the river valleys with their lake- and bog-basins, together with the fact that the most pronounced concentrations are all near the coast. Quite clearly the preferred areas were those with a large variation of resources and a location close to the low-lying areas with a high water-table and open water (sea, lakes or major watercourses).

Through analysis of the settlements of the region it has been possible to distinguish a number of different categories, namely the so-called maintenance sites, specific activity camps and so-called central sites, of which the latter were shared by an undetermined number of communities.

The so-called maintenance sites comprise the most poorly illuminated aspect of the settlement pattern. This is partially due to the fact that many of the sites which were earlier thought to be maintenance sites have instead proved to be central sites, i.e. causewayed camps, and thus to have had a different function in the settlement pattern from that presumed earlier. Other sites, such as the well-known Barkær on Djursland, have, as already mentioned, proved to be grave complexes, the timber constructions of which may have had a certain resemblance to the dwellings of the farming communities, although they did not serve as actual dwellings. What is left is a group of sites, each of which was probably the centre of agricultural activities within its individual territory. Their location often seems to be on the border between high, well-drained ground and low-lying moist land. This location has been explained as a response to the wish to exploit the high-lying ground for swidden agriculture and the moist damp forest regions for pig-raising. It also seems incontestable that these sites were moved at intervals when necessitated by the resource situation. This corresponds well to the picture of swidden agriculture suggested by pollen analysis.

Moreover, there are vague indications that the size of these maintenance sites increased in time. At the beginning of the fourth millennium BC they seem to have been quite small, perhaps serving only a single extended family. Over the centuries however, they grew in size, which may be the beginning of the more sedentary settlement pattern which is the prerequisite for the changes of subsistence which occurred in the course of the third millennium BC.

Near the maintenance sites are the hunting places, a site category which has recently been acknowledged as part of the settlement pattern. These are small sites of seemingly very temporary character. Very frequently the same localities were used over and over again; often the Neolithic settlement layer lies directly on top of a Mesolithic one. This continuity in the use of the hunting sites supports the thesis that the transition from the hunting society of the fifth millennium to the agrarian society of the fourth millennium BC occurred very gradually. This means that at first farming was only a modest supplement to the traditional subsistence activities. A major proportion of food probably still had to be obtained by hunting and gathering.

The hunting sites are located in both coastal and inland areas, sometimes on small isolated islands. Seal hunting may have been the purpose of some of these brief stays. Other sites lie near narrow passages in the fjords where the shifting tides created enormous shell banks and where net fishing could be carried out with favourable results. It was earlier thought that the significance of the hunting places diminished in the course of the fourth millennium BC. But this can hardly be the case. Judging by the archaeological record, hunting and gathering seem to have continued as a significant part of the subsistence pattern of the farming communities for a very long time.

Thus it is possible to discern a detailed pattern for the exploitation of the natural resources. The general impression which emerges shows a very wide-spectred subsistence strategy in which hunting, fishing and food-gathering were practised in conjunction with primitive swidden agriculture. Not until sometime in the third millennium BC did this pattern start changing as cattle-raising was gradually given primary emphasis.

The central sites or causewayed camps are the last category of settlements within the Neolithic settlement pattern. These peculiar complexes have been known to Danish archaeology for very few years. But already a great number of finds have been made, and there is no doubt that in Denmark the causewayed camps are an integral part of the settlement pattern of the farming communities. As yet, only the localities Sarup on Funen and Toftum in east Jutland have been the subjects of larger investigations. The size of the complexes seems to have been impressive. The cultural traces at Sarup (Figure 26) cover an

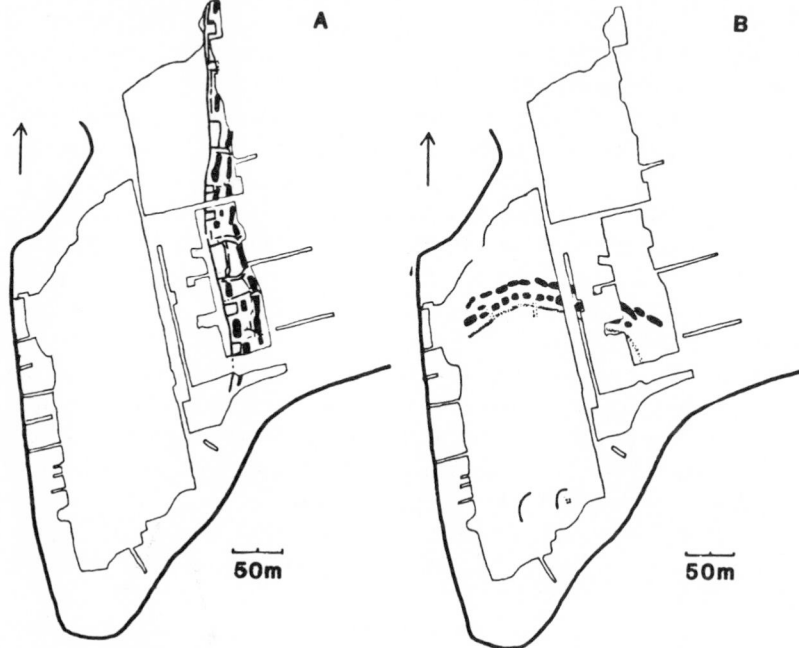

Figure 26 The two phases of the Sarup complex. A: The first phase radiocarbon-dated to about 3250 BC (calibrated). B: The second phase radiocarbon-dated to about 3150 BC (calibrated).

area of about 4 hectares, and at Toftum (Figure 27) about 3 hectares.

A common feature of these sites is that they are often located on small promontories surrounded on three sides by watercourses and meadows. The overall appearance of the complexes is not yet known but they are frequently enclosed by palisades and rows of short ditches interrupted by earthen bridges.

The Sarup complex (Figure 26) is, as already mentioned, one of the most thoroughly studied complexes. It contains traces of construction from a long period of the Neolithic, but the most important settlement phases are those from the final 200–300 years of the fourth millennium BC. From the first of these phases, radiocarbon-dated to *c.* 3250 BC, there is a palisade ditch at least 250 metres long and 1 metre deep, in which there once stood a fence consisting of oak posts 3–4 metres long. Next to this palisade fence, there was a series of outbuildings, each 6 × 7 metres, flanking a larger outbuilding measuring 7 × 20 metres. Between and in front of these there were moat-like depressions and at the extreme east there was yet another moat with numerous earthen bridges. At one place in the palisade fence there was an entrance enclosed by posts.

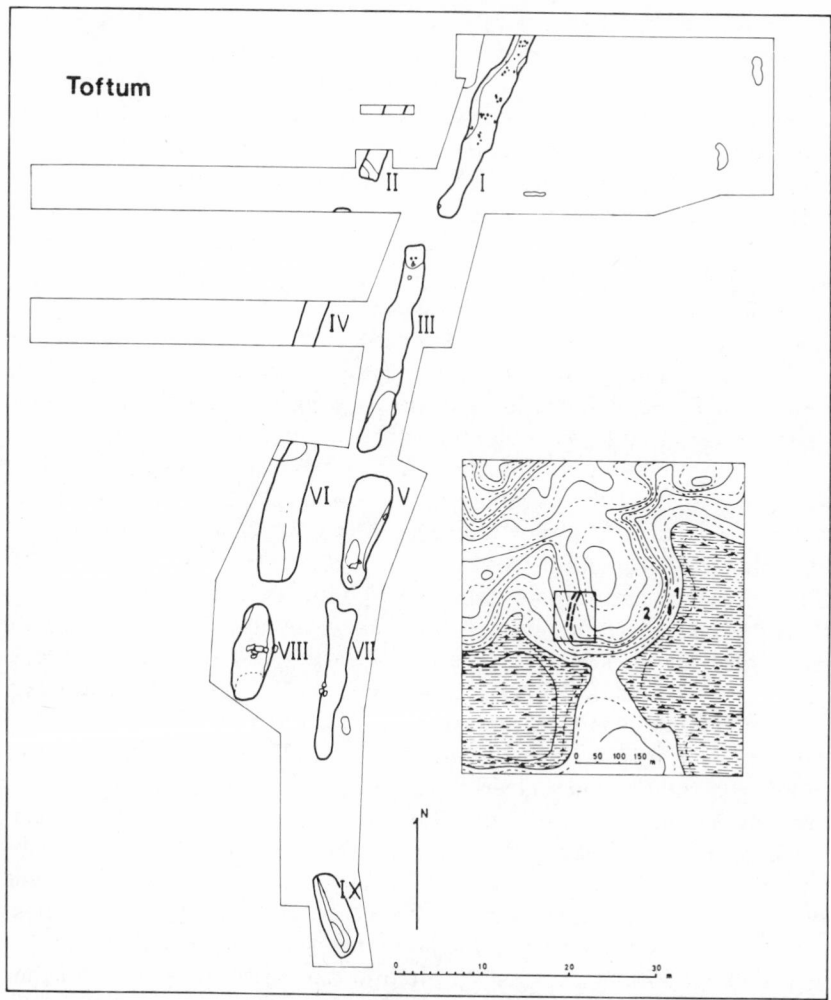

Figure 27 Plan of excavations at Toftum, a Neolithic central site in eastern Jutland. Insert: contour map of the locality (contour intervals 2.5 metres).

The bottoms of the so-called moats contained intact clay vessels, fragmented human skeletons and traces of fire. The moats had been filled in manually very quickly, possibly even the same year that they were dug. In the areas enclosed by the palisade, finds have been made of unbroken clay vessels, some of which contained grain. From a similar, as yet unexcavated, causewayed camp at Årupgård in Jutland there is still another find of a clay vessel containing numerous pieces of amber and metal.

About one hundred years later, another palisade structure was erected at Sarup, radiocarbon-dated to about 3150 BC. However, this structure was only half as large as the older one and consisted of a double row of moats 1 metre deep, together with a palisade fence. In the area thus enclosed, pits have been found with whole clay vessels or flint axes, all of which indicate that this complex, just as the one a century earlier, served a ritual purpose.

Here and there in central and north Europe, similar complexes from about the same period are quite common. The determination of their function, however, is not yet conclusive. They have been interpreted as temporary defence structures and as cattle folds, in which the separation and marking of calves and the winter slaughter were carried out. But it is more probable that these huge enclosures were meeting-places which served social as well as economic and ritual purposes.

This interpretation is confirmed in part by calculations of the labour necessary to erect the complex (N.H. Andersen, 1980). The palisade fence of the Sarup complex required at least 1800 oak logs 3–4 metres long and about 42 centimetres thick, in all about 800 cubic metres of oak. If the chopping and transportation of each log took three working days, then the palisade fence would have taken about 5400 man-days. The digging of about 5000 cubic metres of earth from the moat required about 2500 man-days. Thus the complex as a whole took 7900 man-days. As the complex was used only for a very short time, probably only a single season, its erection may have required 110 men working for three months, a figure which clearly indicates that the complex must have been the result of a co-ordinated effort by several settlement units.

A locational analysis in the south-western part of Funen, where the Sarup complex lies, has shown the existence here of 108 identifiable and probably contemporaneous megalith graves. These graves clearly lie in clusters, as confirmed by statistical analysis. With the help of the so-called Theissen polygons, an attempt has been made to define the territories which belong to the individual clusters of megalith graves (N.H. Andersen, 1980). It appears that there were probably sixteen nearly identical territories or settlement units (Figure 28). There is still uncertainty as to how the individual households were situated within the settlement units, as the habitation sites are still only known in very few cases. But there is reason to believe that the various households lived scattered, gradually moving as the soil became exhausted. Precisely such a dispersed settlement and the labour tasks related to the farming economy would have created the need for an integration of the various settlement units. The central sites of the type to which the Sarup complex belongs seem to be an expression of this integration.

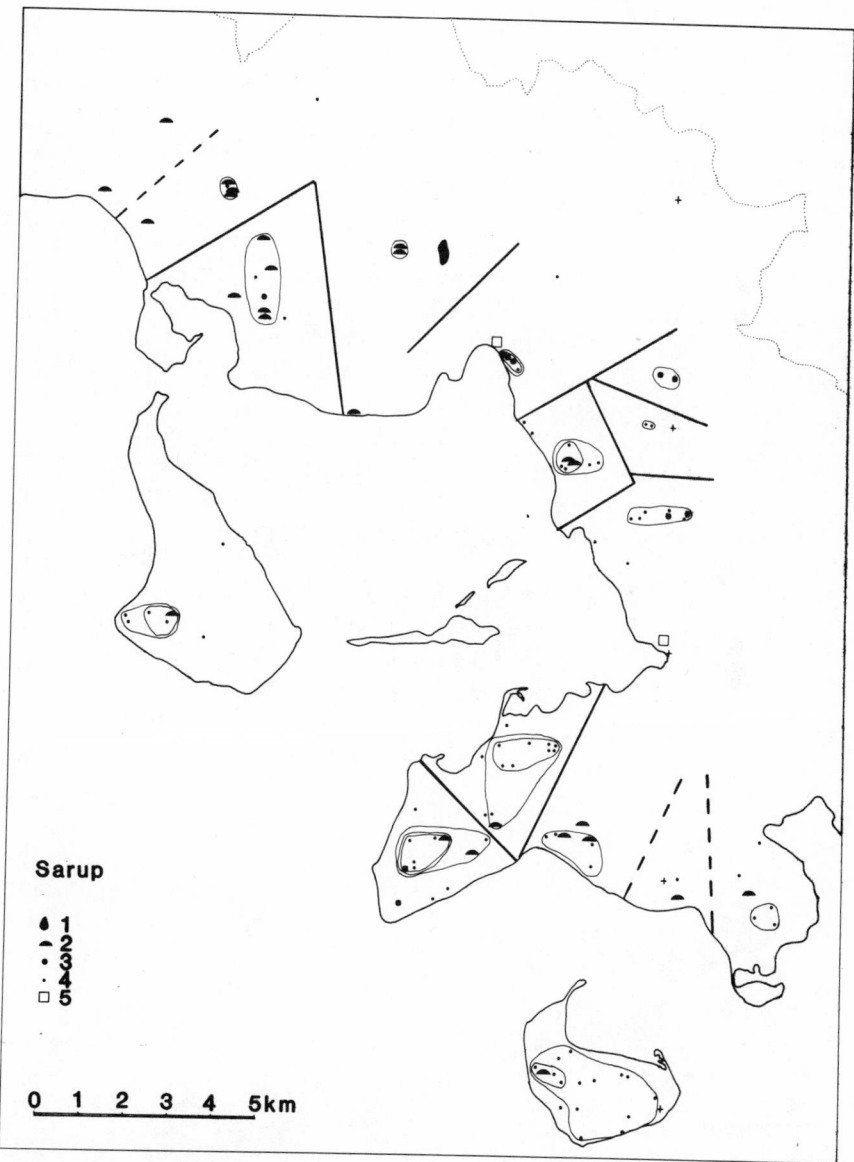

Figure 28 Hypothetical division into territories of the settlements around the Sarup complex. 1. Central site. 2. Long dolmen. 3. Round dolmen. 4. Single megalith grave. 5. Settlement site.

Subsistence patterns

After the prehistoric population had begun to exploit the soil produc-
tively around 4200 BC, there arose labour tasks which demanded an
investment of human labour to a hitherto unequalled degree. Pollen
analysis can provide an impression of the impact which forest clearance
had on the vegetation and can thus lead to conclusions from which the
main features of the new production form can be deduced. The first
stage is obscure, but in the course of the fourth millennium a picture
emerges of a swidden agriculture based upon the burning-off of the
forest. The traces of this extensive subsistence form seem particularly
apparent in the pollen diagrams from the end of the fourth millennium
BC but may go back even further in time.

As mentioned above, the landnam phase typically appears in three
stages in the pollen diagrams. The first stage represents the forest
clearance. The second stage shows cattle grazing on the abandoned
land, and the third stage shows how the high forest returned, although
in a changed form. At the end of this phase, the dense virgin forest
again closed in. We do not know how large the cleared area was. One
can only imagine how clearance was carried out in the early spring as a
collective effort. It has been calculated that with the techniques available, chopping with polished flint axes (Figure 29), an area of about 1
hectare could be cleared by five men in less than fourteen days.

In burning, the heat released nutrients in the upper centimetres of the

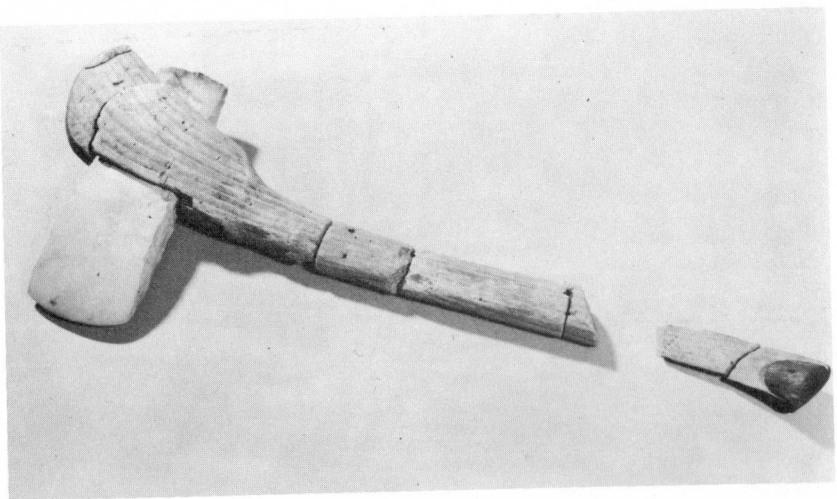

Figure 29 Thin-butted flint axe with a haft made of ash, found in a bog at
Sigerslev, eastern Zealand.

soil and at the same time cleared the soil of competing plants. Weeding the crops was therefore hardly necessary.

It seems that monocultures were raised, but as yet very little is known about the relative proportions of grain types raised. But it is possible that wheat types dominated through the fourth millennium, whereas in the course of the third millennium there was a certain shift to barley, which remained the leading grain type throughout the rest of pre-history.

The methods of cultivation are shrouded in uncertainty. It has been suggested that grain was raised near the settlement on small areas tilled with a spade-like tool. This supposition appears likely, but it should also be added that this cultivation form was probably mainly associated with swidden agriculture. It has already been described how population growth and probably also the increasing exhaustion of the soil quite early led to a gradual decrease of the slash-and-burn technique and a transition to a more sedentary agriculture based on ard-ploughing.

The oldest traces of ploughing in Denmark date from the end of the fourth millennium BC (see figure 36); throughout the third millennium and thereafter they become ever more frequent. The significance of this development will be described in the following chapter. Here we can only list some of the observations which have been made with imitative experiments in ard-ploughing (H.O. Hansen, 1969).

In ard-ploughing, the soil is loosened but not at all (or only very slightly) turned. The ard can be used to plough down grain, but it cannot be used to plough down weeds, a plant growth which otherwise could be transformed to humus.

Another negative effect of ard-ploughing results from the fact that the furrows are narrow and quite shallow. This yields an insufficient airing of the soil and a poor water balance. This effect is unfortunate, as plant roots use oxygen and eliminate carbon dioxide. If the soil is not sufficiently porous, plant growth is hindered by the accumulated carbon dioxide and living conditions are poor for worms and micro-organisms.

This situation inevitably leads to soil exhaustion. New mould formation occurs only to a very slight degree and erosion becomes an active factor in soil exhaustion. These negative effects were not counteracted until the introduction of manuring. It must therefore be concluded that the ard was not a particularly suitable implement – indeed it contributed to the soil exhaustion which in the course of the third millennium must have considerably weakened the subsistence economy of the farming communities (S. Nielsen, 1980).

With regard to the size of the crops there is naturally also a scarcity of information. Imitative experiments have been able to show that with slash-and-burn quite large yields can be achieved – probably as high as thirteen-fold. But these yields must have been very brief, lasting probably only a couple of years. Ard-ploughing produced a considerably lower yield – at the most from twofold to fourfold. This helps to explain why in the long run an expansion of productivity could not be achieved by cultivation but instead had to take place via expansion of stock-raising.

Aside from the cultivation of small fields close to the settlements, a considerable amount of labour must have gone into gathering the leafy fodder consumed by the cattle during the winter months. Elm and ash were very valuable as fodder. This also held true of the leaves of other sorts of trees, especially of the lime, which was a favourite of cattle.

As yet our knowledge of the domestic animals in the first farming communities is relatively limited, but from the latter half of the period, around 3200 BC, evidence from a number of the large settlements in general seems to show that a settlement adapted itself in all details to the ecological niche in which it was located. If a village lay near suitable pastures, perhaps near the coast, then this situation would be reflected in an emphasis on sheep-raising.

However, the dominant activity at the sites was the raising of pigs, which doubtless provided the major source of protein. This situation is easy to understand when it is considered that the pig is, in fact, biologically adapted to areas of dense leafy forests where the production of mast is ample and where it can thrive with a minimum of care. Pigs demand practically no investment of human labour, in buildings for example. Furthermore, pigherds can easily be adapted to human needs if other sources of food fail.

Sheep and goats also played an important role. Their ratio was probably about 5:1. As mentioned, the holding of sheep increased in relation to the proximity to natural pastures such as shore meadows. Like pigs, sheep offer a number of easily achieved economic advantages. Sheep place far fewer demands on the investment of human labour than do cattle. Moreover, sheep can eat grass throughout the growth period and require relatively little investment of labour in the form of gathering winter fodder. Sheep meat is also well-suited for wind-drying and thus constitutes a major meat reserve in lean seasons. The holding of sheep in the early farming communities seems to have been intended for meat production. A few mature goats were probably kept at the settlements – mainly to ensure supplies of dairy products.

The role of cattle-raising in the early farming economy is not yet particularly well illuminated. Cattle herds consisted of mature breeding cows and a few bulls. Steers were raised for meat and heifers to renew the stock of breeding animals. No traces have been observed of the use of bullocks, which bears out the assumption of the minor role of the plough in early agriculture. The slaughtering age was normally 3–4 years, which may indicate that the gathering of winter fodder was not such a burdensome investment of labour; had it been burdensome, slaughtering would have been carried out earlier. The relatively mild and short winters in the fourth and third millennia BC must have been favourable for cattle-raising.

Yet the role of stock-raising in the early agrarian economy raises a number of important problems. The herd could hardly have produced dairy products to any significant degree. But whereas the raising of meat cattle probably entailed a multitude of economic advantages, it should also be kept in mind that cattle require more labour than other domestic animals. The herd could be radically expanded only if increased pasture

Figure 30 Early Neolithic flint mine at Hov, northern Jutland.

was obtained and this land had to be taken primarily from the forest. It is therefore natural that the significance of cattle-raising was relatively slight during the fourth millennium BC. But it is also noteworthy that already in the beginning of the third millennium BC a change can be glimpsed: stock-raising seems to increase in importance as the once so wide-spectred subsistence strategy seems to narrow. It is conceivable that we have here one of the leading factors in the process which in coming centuries caused such profound modifications in the economic subsistence situation of the agrarian communities.

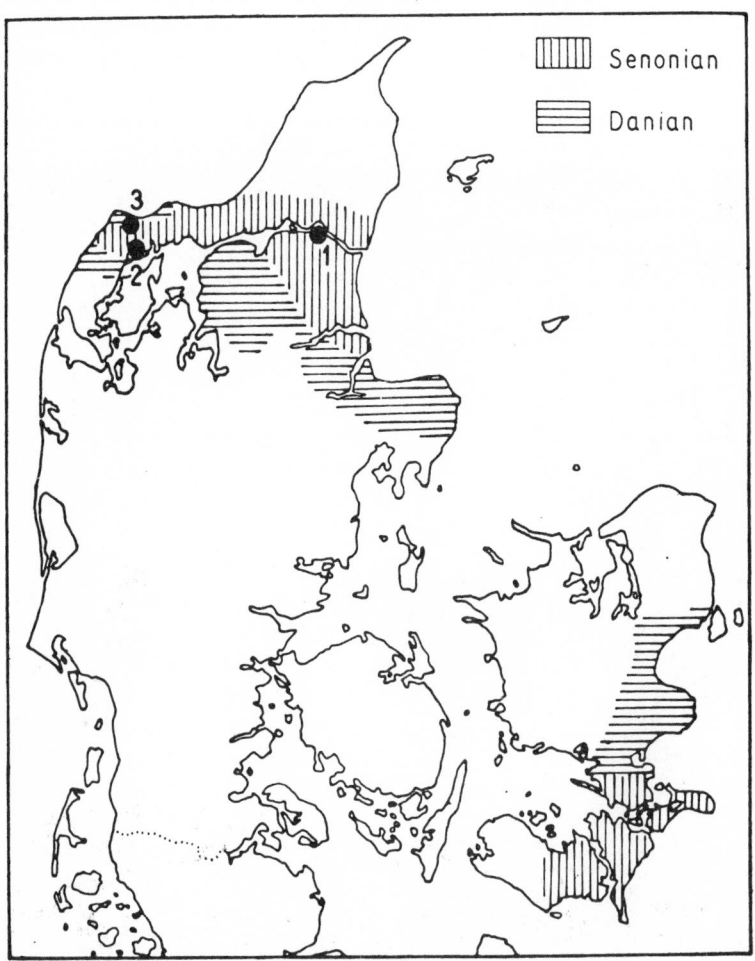

Figure 31 Situation of Danish chalk and limestone deposits with Neolithic flint mines indicated: 1. Alborg. 2. Hov. 3. Bjerre.

Although food production in the early agrarian communities is relatively clear, very little is known about other types of production. In the foreground there is the flint-mining industry at such places as the great hilly areas of northern Jutland, where cretaceous limestone and with it the coveted black or grey Senon flint is found nearly up at the surface. At Sennels, north of Thisted, numerous flint mines have been excavated (Figures 30 and 31). The shafts are shaped like inverted cones, roughly 4–5 metres wide at the surface of the earth. At Sennels the flint is deposited in horizontal layers 3–4 metres deep in the limestone. The mining of the flint took place from galleries hewn out from the bottom of the shaft with deer-antler picks 3–5 metres into the limestone. The abandoned shafts were filled up with chalk from the functioning mines next to the emptied ones.

At the flint-chopping sites between the shafts the flint-smith carried out the initial shaping of the fresh flint; the 'crust' was removed and the flint pieces were made into half-finished goods which were given a final fashioning elsewhere.

Another raw material which played an important part in the economy of the early Neolithic communities was amber. As today, amber in prehistory was found everywhere in Denmark. The North Sea coast of Jutland yielded the greatest quantities. But the coasts of the Kattegat – and in the east of the Baltic – also furnish rich amber finds. Outside Denmark, amber can be found along the German, Dutch and English coasts of the North Sea. And to the east, amber can be found along the Baltic coasts over to the largest amber deposits in the world, in Samland.

In the fourth and early third millennia BC the circulation of amber was confined to the Baltic zone, which included Denmark. Not until later did it spread further south, a story that will be related in the following chapters. In the early agrarian society, however, amber, together with axes made of the coveted Senon flint, seems to have been part of a special group of particularly valuable goods which played a dominant role in the social and political life of the farming communities. The exchange of these goods, probably in ceremonial rituals, seems to have played a central role in social competition. At the same time, both amber and flint were probably necessary for binding and maintaining social relations, just as they very likely also had a sort of fly-wheel effect which served to hold an even wider exchange of goods in motion.

The circulation of goods

The distribution of flint and amber is probably one of the earliest and most striking examples of the production and circulation of goods which increasingly contributed to socio-economic development throughout prehistory. It has long been acknowledged that there was a close relationship between the organization and control of exchange and the development of ranking in prehistoric societies. With this in mind, it is interesting to see that in the course of the fourth millennium BC the archaeological finds in Denmark show an increase in the appearance of non-utilitarian objects such as oversized flint axes, metal ornaments and great quantities of amber (K. Randsborg, 1979).

Regarding amber, there are a number of interesting aspects in the geographic distribution. Far into the fourth millennium its distribution is a simple fall-off pattern with the largest concentrations in the western parts of the country, which also contained the largest natural deposits. In the latter half of the fourth millennium and in the third millennium BC, however, this pattern was disturbed. Instead there were now a number of concentrations at some distance from the richest source areas. Amber concentrations now lay primarily in the rich and economi-cally expansive megalith settlements in eastern Denmark, where amber to a great degree was included in grave-goods. Thus there is much to indicate that amber was increasingly regarded as a material with symbolic value and as such was included in ranked contexts in Den-mark. Outside Denmark, or rather outside the Baltic zone, the circula-tion of amber was still very limited.

A pattern which is similar in many ways can also be observed in the distribution of the thin-butted flint axes. The differences are probably to be ascribed to the fact that this material possessed great utilitarian value besides its symbolic value. This is manifest in the fact that it is not possible to divide the flint axes into two groups, one with technological functions and one with social functions. The types form a sequence ranging from small axes, 15–20 centimetres long, to the imposing oversized 'ceremonial axes' almost 50 centimetres long (Figure 32).

A similar phenomenon can be observed in a more modern context. In an interesting study of the significance of stone axes as prestige symbols in a tribal society in the highland of New Guinea (F. Højlund, 1979), it has been shown how the various axe types had several different potential functions which could be activated in the proper social connection. One and the same axe type could be for the prosperous man primarily a work tool, whereas for the less prosperous man, who did not own special ceremonial axes, it could also possess a ceremonial value.

F. Højlund's study is also a model example of the role which the production and distribution of valuable objects can have for the repro-duction of a tribal society. Among the tribal societies in New Guinea's highland the most important prerequisite for power and position was

Figure 32 Thin-butted ceremonial flint axes of the Neolithic period.

not the control of the land. Instead it was the direct control of people and thereby of their labour. This control was exercised by control of the exchange of valuable objects which were indispensable for binding and maintaining social relationships. A common factor in the exchange of valuable objects was that they primarily took place between neighbouring clans which were bound to one another by marriage alliances. In the highland there was no developed social stratification by which birth or descent gave a person right to a defined position. Instead the manipulation of the exchange of particularly valuable objects with symbolic worth provided the opportunity for the rise of so-called Big Men. By creating a situation of dependency, for example by investing in the bride price required of young men, a Big Man could build a group of 'satellites' around him, bound by personal bonds of dependency, who could provide support in discussions or armed combat.

The production and distribution of the valuable objects also seems in a wider sense to have had significance for the reproductive basis of the highland societies. Groups which controlled many valuable objects were able to marry more women into their group than they gave away to other groups. Thus on a regional plan centres were created with many polygamous marriages and a periphery arose in which there was a lack of women and a surplus of unmarried men. By incorporating both marriageable women and unmarried (or exiled) men from the peripheral groups, the centres increased their control over the labour force. In this way further expansion was made possible – perhaps tending towards a higher degree of political stratification similar to the true chiefdoms in, for example, Polynesia.

Of course, the example described here cannot be transferred directly to the situation in Denmark in the fourth millennium BC. But it can help describe the relationship which always exists between the circulation of valuable objects and the incipient development of ranking in a society at the tribal level of integration. In Denmark this sort of accelerated circulation and concurrent accumulation of wealth in, for example, the funerary cult can be observed. The circulation of symbolic objects, metal ornaments, ceremonial weapons, and so on, thus seems to have had a sort of fly-wheel effect on the establishment of social relations – and on the increased hierarchization within the early agrarian society.

In a more narrow utilitarian perspective, the exchange of goods may also have had the function of preventing sorely needed raw materials such as flint from being underexploited due to lack of direct connections between the areas of production and consumption. In fact, something of the sort has been observed in the highlands of New Guinea (Rappaport, 1968) and may also have been valid during the Neolithic in Denmark with the country's geographically concentrated flint-mine industry. In such a situation, valuable objects such as items of adornment often become trade goods because they may be exchanged for essential raw materials. They may thus stimulate production and at the same time have a fly-wheel effect on the whole system of circulating goods.

The valuable objects could also have functioned in other ways, for example in establishing social relations. Possibly they aided in organizing a labour force of a size which a single society by itself could not muster. The erection of the presumed central sites may be viewed with this in mind.

Economy of the farming communities

After the discussion of the subsistence and settlement pattern of the early farming communities, the main economic trends in the period *c.* 4200–2800 BC will be briefly summarized. A characteristic difference in relation to the hunter–gatherer communities in the foregoing period was that the spontaneous nature of work was now disappearing. In the farming communities most natural products were gathered in the form of a harvest. So to some degree the direct connection between labour and consumption which previously characterized the subsistence form was now ended. At the same time many new forms of work were introduced: forest clearance, fencing of fields, sowing, weeding, harvesting, and storing of supplies. These tasks demanded the co-ordinated labour of many people within a relatively limited period of time. The new tasks also demanded a linking of the labour processes over longer periods, thus causing the disappearance of the spontaneous character of work; instead the typical annual cycle of the farming society appeared.

Beyond these general features the development of the early agrarian society was marked by a number of unique features in the means of production. The early agrarian society may be said to have regulated its balance with nature by a broad-spectred production form. By this is meant a production form which, in contrast to more intensive agricultural forms, sought to ensure the survival of society by including as many forms of production as possible. Each form was to require minimal labour. The composition of the animal husbandry, the extensive practice of slash-and-burn and the continued importance of hunting and gathering were on the whole a manifestation of this. This subsistence form can reasonably be termed a semi-agrarian culture. Towards the end of the period a shift in the subsistence pattern seems to have taken place. The result is an increased emphasis on stock-raising, possibly caused by the growing population pressure.

This shift became ever more distinct in the following millennia. This tendency points to one of the most decisive differences between the hunter–gatherer societies and the organizational form of the agrarian communities. Whereas the hunter–gatherer society probably exercised strict demographic control, the agrarian society apparently slackened control due to its potential for economic expansion. In agrarian society there is a constant need for technological innovation to solve the problems posed by a growing population. At the same time this expansion potential is accompanied by a growing risk of resource crises, because the population more easily reaches the maximum limit which the resources set for growth.

Frequently European archaeologists have sought to explain such crises by proposing the invasion of foreign ethnic groups; the so-called Single Grave culture is an example of this. However, another explanation is also possible: the change in the settlement pattern which can be observed in the course of the third millennium BC may be explained as the farming communities' attempt to heighten productivity, among other things on the basis of increased population pressure. However this may be, the transition of the prehistoric society to an agrarian economy around 4200 BC gradually created unprecedented opportunities for economic growth.

Social patterns in the early
farming communities

As shown above, the early agrarian communities in Denmark ensured their survival via a broad-spectred subsistence form which, in the beginning at least, can be termed semi-agrarian. The procural of food was for a good part based on a true agricultural economy, but beside this, other subsistence forms such as hunting, fishing and gathering were also practised. The presence of the agricultural economy in this broad spectrum – and its potential for economic and demographic growth, its greater complexity regarding labour processes and the increased demands for co-operation – created the basis for an economic and social development of prehistoric society which distinguished it from earlier stages of development.

There can hardly be any doubt that with the beginning of the fourth millennium BC, the formation of more complex societal forms in Denmark was in full swing. Already quite early, the increased productivity evident in food production and the consequent rise in population density led the agrarian society up to the socio-cultural integration level which is called the tribal society (E.R. Service, 1971). Quite soon, as can be seen from the increased circulation of goods, the tribal society evolved into a ranked society (M.H. Fried, 1960) (Figure 37).

The term 'development of ranking' implies that society develops limitations on the access to status. The reason for viewing the circulation of coveted valuable objects such as flint axes, amber, ornaments and tools of metal and the like as a possible cause of such a system is that this circulation is always dependent upon economic or other external factors.

The application of the term 'tribal society' in Service's sense of the word to the early farming agrarian society in Denmark is somewhat more problematic. The term has been hotly debated and several scholars have claimed that the phenomenon exists only on the fringes of more developed cultural systems, for example as a response to neighbouring militaristic states (M.H. Fried, 1968). With reference to Danish Neolithic society the term is used only to distinguish it from the Mesolithic egalitarian band society. Thus the term is used to characterize society with an incipient ranking, at a stage in which leadership is still very weakly developed and there is a low degree of political integration.

From a socio-economic point of view, the tribal societies known from anthropological literature vary widely. This is due quite simply to the fact that as the labour processes are very divergent they pose different demands to the structure of society. Among the common features of tribal societies which distinguish them from the band society is the fact that the settlement groups as well as the general population density are greater than in the hunter–gatherer communities; moreover, productivity is proportionately larger. The continuous or regularly recurring use of settlement areas results in a stronger territorial binding. In turn, this binding, together with the linking of the labour processes over longer periods (the production cycle) creates a greater stability in the social structure. Political differentiation in the tribal society, however, has not reached the point at which political control is institutionalized. Nor has social and economic specialization attained the stage in which there may be professional religious groups such as priesthoods, although there are religious specialists. Nor has economic specialization become more than part-time.

To be sure, all conclusions regarding socio-economic development from the end of the fifth millennium BC and far into the third millennium BC still rest upon a fragile foundation. Earlier Danish archaeologists viewed the appearance of the megalith graves at the end of the fourth millennium as one of the major climaxes in the Neolithic development. The megalith graves were associated with a complex worship of the dead in contrast to what was thought to precede it: the practice of simple inhumation to dispose of the deceased. The underlying opinion was that both stages represented an egalitarian society and the megalith graves were perceived as burial places for families or the inhabitants of entire villages. But recent investigations of such structures as the early Neolithic grave forms and revised views of the Neolithic chronology have led to new interpretations.

The evaluation of the socio-economic development is based partly on studies of the exchange of goods, partly on the study of the graves and so-called central sites of the agrarian society. There seems to be no doubt that the construction of the graves and their contents in some way reveal the social position of the buried person. However, interpretation of these circumstances is seriously hindered by the frequent lack of skeletal remains, so that the age and sex of the dead person can rarely be determined. Yet in cases where the grave equipment consists of more than pottery for food, there are indications of a heavy overrepresentation of male graves in relation to female graves.

Another difficulty is our ignorance of the burial customs of the early farming communities. The picture which has emerged after recent investigations is as follows: already from their formation, the farming communities practised complicated funerary rites which were no doubt related to an ancestor cult. The oldest grave monuments are complicated long barrows with a great diversity of timber structures. These graves could contain one or more persons.

Around the middle of the fourth millennium the first megalith graves (small rectangular dolmens) were erected on Zealand. From here they slowly spread to the rest of the country, where several different types evolved. The majority of the dolmens known were built in a relatively brief period during the last centuries of the fourth millennium BC. At the same time, the building of the great passage graves began.

The tradition of building 'non-megalith' graves, the so-called 'earth graves', in the meantime continued in both eastern and western Denmark. There are signs that the so-called 'mortuary houses' which came into use at the transition from the fourth to the third millennia BC were simply an offshoot of the long barrow timber structures of the earliest farming communities.

None of these complicated burial forms can be termed true communal graves in the sense of continuous use over an extended period. To be sure, both the early and the late graves can contain several people, but as we shall later see, this is hardly evidence of a so-called communal grave tradition. Presumably the graves were originally erected to contain people who had attained a certain rank and hence were buried with material goods and with elaborate ceremony.

Not until quite late in the Neolithic did the grave customs change. As described below, many of the great megalith monuments were now used for repeated burials, or for the deposition of bones. Even so, this is not sufficient reason to speak of a true communal grave form.

As yet, the earliest grave forms of the agrarian society are relatively little known. One of the most thoroughly studied structures is a long barrow at Bygholm Nørremark in Jutland (P. Rønne, 1979), which will here be discussed in more detail as an example of the burial customs of the period.

The structure (Figure 33) was slightly trapezoidal in form, 60 metres long and surrounded by a post-bedding trench. In the eastern end there

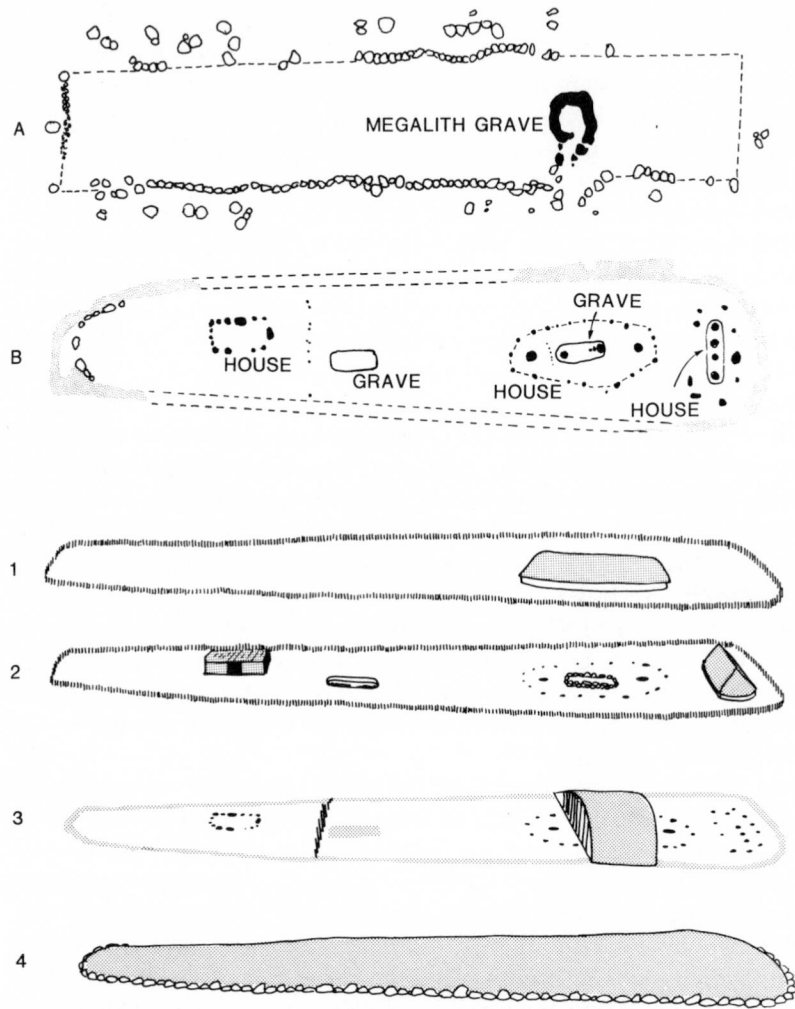

Figure 33 Long barrow at Bygholm Nørremark in eastern Jutland. A. Plan of long dolmen with barrow containing a megalith grave. B. Plan of non-megalithic grave complex found under A. Numbers 1–4 illustrate the four different stages in the construction of the non-megalithic long barrow.

was a façade with traces of an elaborate timber construction. Immediately west of the façade there were traces of two 'houses', one of them with a grave, which probably consisted originally of a wooden coffin. All that was left of the corpse was a greasy black substance together with some tooth-enamel, which was enough to identify the dead as only

13–15 years old. An amber bead by the waist of the dead had probably been mounted on a belt. Near the chest there was an arrowhead, perhaps the cause of death.

Further to the west in the structure lay yet another grave, which contained four people. The dead lay in pairs, two with heads to the east, two to the west. There were no grave goods, neither ornaments, pottery, weapons nor tools.

Finally, furthest to the west there was a little square post-built building. Transverse rows of poles were observed at three places within the enclosure.

Somewhat later than this grave complex there was an extension of the barrow and the construction of a megalith grave in the now 80-metre-long barrow.

The course of events in this imposing and complicated burial can be reconstructed something like this: a young high-ranking individual, possibly killed by an arrow, was laid on his death bier in a house surrounded by a large trapezoidal enclosure. After the corpse had lain there for some time, the mortuary house was torn down and at the site the clothed corpse was placed in a stone-set wooden coffin. Another house, open at one side, was erected; here a ceremonial meal was held. At the same time something similar was taking place in the west part of the enclosed area. Here a grave for four dead adults was dug and a little ritual house was built. After a certain period the space was cleared of enclosures and houses and the earthen barrow was built. This was carried out in stages, as the barrow form was determined by the transverse rows of poles. The intervals between these were filled with soil and a stone-setting was placed around the foot of the barrow.

This grave type, the long barrow with timber structures, is found with many variations – especially in the west of Denmark. As already mentioned, the timber structures from Barkær, once interpreted as longhouses, should most likely be ascribed to this grave type. In fact, this type has parallels over a far greater area, namely over all the northern European lowland, including England. Even with all the variations, they are apparently the result of structurally similar solutions to religious, ritual and socio-political problems common to the Neolithic societies in the great northern European techno-complex of the fourth millennium BC (T. Madsen, 1979a).

A multitude of details in this early Neolithic burial practice anticipates later practices in the megalith graves. Both earth graves and megalith graves were built sequentially into the same barrows – and the megalith graves are not necessarily the latest. 'Purification' fires have also been burnt in both grave types, and similarly the great quantities of pottery found by the façades of the long barrows indicate that rituals took place here just as by the entrance to the megalith graves. The similarities between the form of the earth graves and that of the megalith graves can be demonstrated on many other counts.

These similarities have cast doubt upon earlier ideas of the megalith graves as expressions of a communal burial custom practised by an egalitarian society, and representing a continuous use over an extended period. Newer investigations seem to confirm this doubt. Instead, the picture now emerges of a burial practice, common for both the earth graves and the dolmens, in which individuals or a few together were buried simultaneously with elaborate ceremonies, including lengthy stays or great funeral feasts at the site.

Not until the construction of the so-called passage graves do essential changes seem to have occurred. The lack of small bones among the often large mass of bones found in the passage graves indicate that the dead were skeletalized before deposition in the passage graves. That is, the grave cult called for the deposition of bones in the passage graves and not for proper burials (S. Thorsen, 1980). These depositions should correspond to the high incidence of secondary burials which took place synchronously in the dolmens due to the easier accessibility of these grave monuments. It is also probable that there is a connection with the burials in the so-called stone-heap graves in Jutland. Here excavations have demonstrated that skeletalization of the dead may have occurred prior to actual deposition in the earth.

Finally, finds of fragmented human skeletons in the great ceremonial central sites of the Sarup type can also be fitted into the new hypothesis of the burial customs of Neolithic society. The central sites may have been where the skeletalization of the dead took place before the deposition in the large permanent grave monuments. This new interpretation is still based upon very slight evidence and requires further proof.

The description of the early farming communities in Denmark drew tentatively upon two concepts derived from ethnographic studies: ranked societies and tribal organization. These two concepts have been used here as a kind of heuristic tool. This has been done in the belief that there exists a relationship between the nature and disposition of the archaeological record on one hand and the organization of prehistoric society on the other. The problem, however, is that this relationship is not direct – and that in Danish archaeology the attempts to clarify this relationship have to date been few and uncertain.

As shown, however, interpretations of the archaeological record often entail theories of the social structure of prehistoric society. The earlier assumption of the appearance of a communal burial custom in agrarian society around the end of the fourth millennium BC was an example of this. An attempt has therefore been made to show how many newer investigations of the burial practice in the early farming communities have been able to change that assumption. Today, then, we must presume that already from the beginning of the fourth millennium BC, and possibly even earlier, society tended toward a non-egalitarian ranked society, probably within a tribal form of organization. The large labour-demanding grave structures intended for a minority of people, the imposing central sites which were presumably ceremonial, and finally the network of connections which disseminated prestige goods such as axes, amber and metal – all of this indicates that the process was already well underway quite early in the existence of the farming communities.

With the transition to an agricultural economy, prehistoric society had to face a set of problems which could not be solved within the organizational form of the band society. One of these problems must have been that the numerous new settlement groups were all expanding and therefore could only to a slight degree form an economically integrated society. And in fact it is a frequent observation that tribal societies often live in a permanent state of war. Conflicts in tribal society have a clear tendency to develop into feuds – and feuds tend to continue indefinitely, as regular warfare and the conquering of enemy territory is seldom possible. Psychological warfare, involving practices such as head-hunting, cannibalism and massacres, therefore often typify societies organized on the tribal level. The existence of central sites, traces of cannibalism, the use of such objects as battle-axes for status symbols, all known from Neolithic Denmark, are therefore important elements in the definition of the societal form of the early farming communities. It is also important to investigate how tribal societies can be expected to respond to problems of the sort described.

In order to stabilize potential dangerous relationships among the local groups, tribal society often establishes various institutions: clans, age groups, religious or military societies comprising larger or smaller segments of the settlement group. Concretely, there may be communal religious ceremonies at the great central sites, exchange of gifts, and so on. Such institutions may create a certain integration among the various local groups. But this integration is seldom long-lasting. Frequently the institutions listed only come into play if an external crisis threatens. If the crisis is averted, there is often a reversion to the relatively closed local community.

However weak this form of organization may appear, it does signify a considerable rise of the integration level in comparison with the organizational form of the hunter–gatherer society. This sort of integration, which can be brought into play at any time, does not normally exist in the band society.

Of course, these institutions are very difficult to trace in the archaeological record. But they can explain in theory how the early farming communities functioned in the first thousand years of their existence. At the same time they can also provide a clue to why the development, with its growing population pressure in the following millennia, tended towards a more hierarchical form of organization with a stabilizing of certain status functions as a consequence.

10

Finds and interpretations

The archaeological record which illuminates the first farming communities ranges over a number of main areas, the chief of which are settlements and graves. There also exists an important material of primary ritual deposits in bogs together with a number of significant traces of flint mining in the early agrarian society.

Settlement finds from the prehistory of Denmark have of late been the object of renewed interest. New excavation methods are being used to uncover enormous excavation surfaces because the more limited investigations of earlier times proved insufficient in relation to the framework of problems proposed by modern archaeological research. But on the whole, the comprehensive investigations of recent years have been concentrated on finds from the later periods of prehistory (the Bronze and Iron Ages). So with few exceptions the study of the settlement pattern of the early farming communities in Denmark must be based upon old and often inadequate investigations (Figure 34). Among the localities studied in recent years are *Stengade* on Langeland (J. Skårup, 1975) together with a number of smaller excavations (E. Johansen, 1975; and K. Davidsen, 1978). Important older investigations include *Troldebjerg, Blandebjerg,* and *Lindø* (J. Winther, 1926–8, 1935, 1943), *Bundsø* (T. Mathiassen, 1939), and *Klintebakken* (H. Berg, 1951).

None of these older investigations could incontestably determine house remains. To be sure, the Troldebjerg settlement is believed by several scholars to have consisted of about twenty-five house sites, both large longhouses and horseshoe-shaped huts. The character of the large complex at Troldebjerg, which is about 250 metres long and 100 metres wide, is still a puzzle. Its topographical situation greatly resembles the large central sites of the Sarup type. Meanwhile, new excavations will be able to shed light upon the function of the complex.

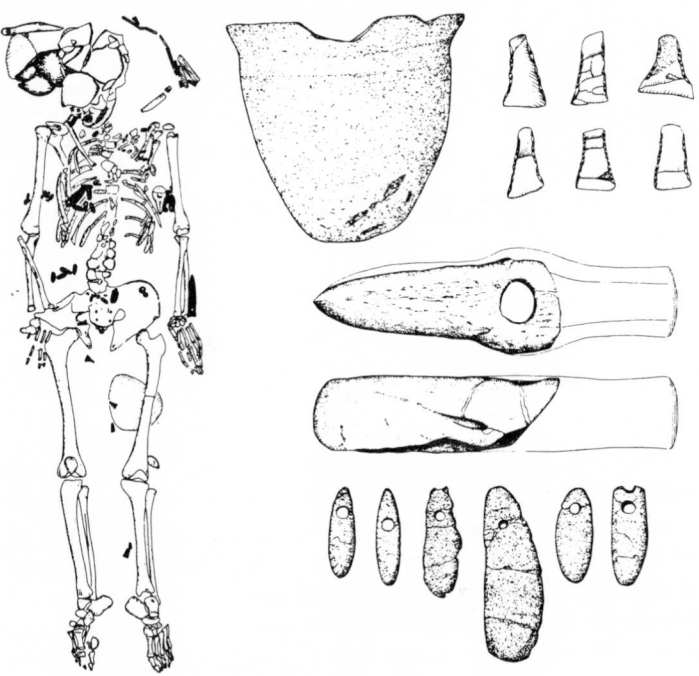

Figure 34 Early Neolithic so-called earth grave with transverse arrowheads, battle axe, amber pendants, and clay vessel found at Dragsholm, Zealand.

Like Troldebjerg, the settlement sites Klintebakken, Blandebjerg and Lindø lie on the island of Langeland in southern Denmark. All these settlement sites are characterized by thick cultural layers, although no house sites have been determined with certainty. On the Lindø settlement, however, there were a couple of rectangular structures which have been interpreted as house remains.

The Bundsø settlement site lies on the island of Als, also in southern Denmark. Thick cultural layers and extensive stone pavings attest a considerable settlement, but not even here has it been possible to identify the nature of the place more precisely. Probably it is a central site of the Sarup type. All the sites mentioned are of great importance for the Neolithic chronology. Each one has yielded finds which represent brief stages in the middle Neolithic development.

In archaeological literature, a particularly dominating role has been played by *Barkær* on Djursland (P.V. Glob, 1949). However, the find has never been published in its entirety, and it must be noted that it has recently been reinterpreted and is now regarded by its excavator as a grave complex (P.V. Glob, 1975). The same interpretation has also been suggested for the Langeland locality *Stengade* (P.V. Glob, 1975).

There are also unique problems associated with the small settlements which have recently been identified as seasonal hunting places for the first agriculturists. This is the case with *Hesselø, Sølager*, and a number of other smaller sites which were all published in 1973 (J. Skårup). Of particular interest in this connection is *Muldbjerg* on Zealand. No proper report on this important and very carefully excavated site has yet been published (Troels-Smith, 1957b, 1959a). The settlement site, which has been completely excavated, lies on a little island in the large Åmose bog. The centre of the settlement was a large hut, 7 × 3 metres, with a bark floor. The finds of pottery in particular date the site to the earliest phase of the Neolithic. Apparently this was one of the small specific activity camps established in conjunction with the large all-year-round settlements.

Excavations of the large presumed central sites can be expected to shed new light on the settlement pattern of the early farming communities. The most comprehensive investigations have been in *Sarup* on southern Funen (N.H. Andersen, 1974, 1975, 1976). *Toftum* near Horsens (T. Madsen, 1977, 1978a) can also be expected to gain great significance. Excavations at these places correspond in many respects to the work at *Büdelsdorf* by the Eider River (H. Hingst, 1971) – but it is still too early to undertake an overall evaluation of this important group of finds.

The total number of settlements from the first phase of the farming society is as yet quite small. Most of the excavations have only studied parts of the settlement areas, so there is still much doubt with regard to the structure of the village complexes, the house types and the settlement pattern in the wide sense. Comprehensive study of this important source area is sorely needed.

Grave finds from the early farming communities also comprise a rather inaccessible find group. General surveys are few (J. Brøndsted, 1957) and often outdated (C.A. Nordman, 1917 a and b).

Of the many grave types, the so-called megalith graves, dolmens and passage graves have long been studied. Regarding the dolmens, there is a 1941 survey with the majority of the finds (K. Thorvildsen), whereas a classification of the numerous construction forms was attempted by E. Aner in 1963 – see further C.J. Becker (1947). Of the more important special studies, there is only room to mention the works of H. Berg of 1951 and 1956, together with S. Thorsen's study of 1980. This latter article demonstrates certain similarities between the dolmens and the early Neolithic earth graves.

Gaps are also apparent in the material on the passage graves, aside from older partially outdated publications by C.A. Nordman (1917 a and b) and G. Rosenberg (1929). Special investigations have been published by such scholars as K. Ebbesen (1975), E. Jørgensen (1977a), P. Kjærum (1957, 1969), K. Thorvildsen (1946), and M. Ørsnes (1956). A number of more general evaluations are presented in works by P. Kjærum (1967) and L. Kaelas (1967). Dating is carefully treated in H. Berg's work of 1951. A number of important Swedish investigations relevant to the Danish situation are found in publications by A. Bagge and L. Kaelas (1950) together with M. Strömberg (1968, 1971b).

The group of non-megalith graves also forms a rather obscure picture (Figure 33). The grave type was first identified by K. Friis Johansen in 1917. A comprehensive up-to-date survey of the early Neolithic structures was published by Torsten Madsen (1979a). This important work discusses newer excavations by E. Jørgensen (1977b), Preben Rønne (1979), David Liversage (1970), Bjørn Stürup (1965), C. Fischer (1975), P.V. Glob (1975), and O. Faber (1976). Views of the relationship of the early Neolithic grave structures throughout the northern European lowland have been offered by S. Piggott (1966) and K. Jazdzewski (1973). The 'unchambered' long barrows from Bygholm Nørregaard described in detail here (see pp. 111 ff) have been excavated and published in a preliminary report by Preben Rønne (1979).

The works mentioned above all treat early finds, whereas U.L. Hansen (1972b) has described a number of late variations of the type. In yet another unresolved relationship to the 'non-megalith graves' are the so-called 'stone packing graves', a grave type first identified in the 1950s (C.J. Becker, 1959; E. Jørgensen, 1977a; T. Madsen, 1975). Since then, about 500 structures have been excavated, but this number is simply the result of a goal-oriented research effort (see E. Jørgensen, 1977a). Almost all the structures are found in a belt stretching from the Ringkøbing region to the west part of Himmerland, but it is not insignificant that research activity has been primarily concentrated in the areas where the graves were first found in abundance. The possibility cannot therefore be ignored that the original distribution covered a larger part of the country.

A still puzzling manifestation of the ritual practices of the early farming communities consists of the so-called 'cult houses' (Figure 35) – a type of structure which has first been demonstrated within the last generation (P. Kjærum, 1967). Reports on cult houses have been published by C.J. Becker (1969), O. Marseen (1960) and P. Kjærum (1955).

The ritual practice of the first agrarian society with special focus upon

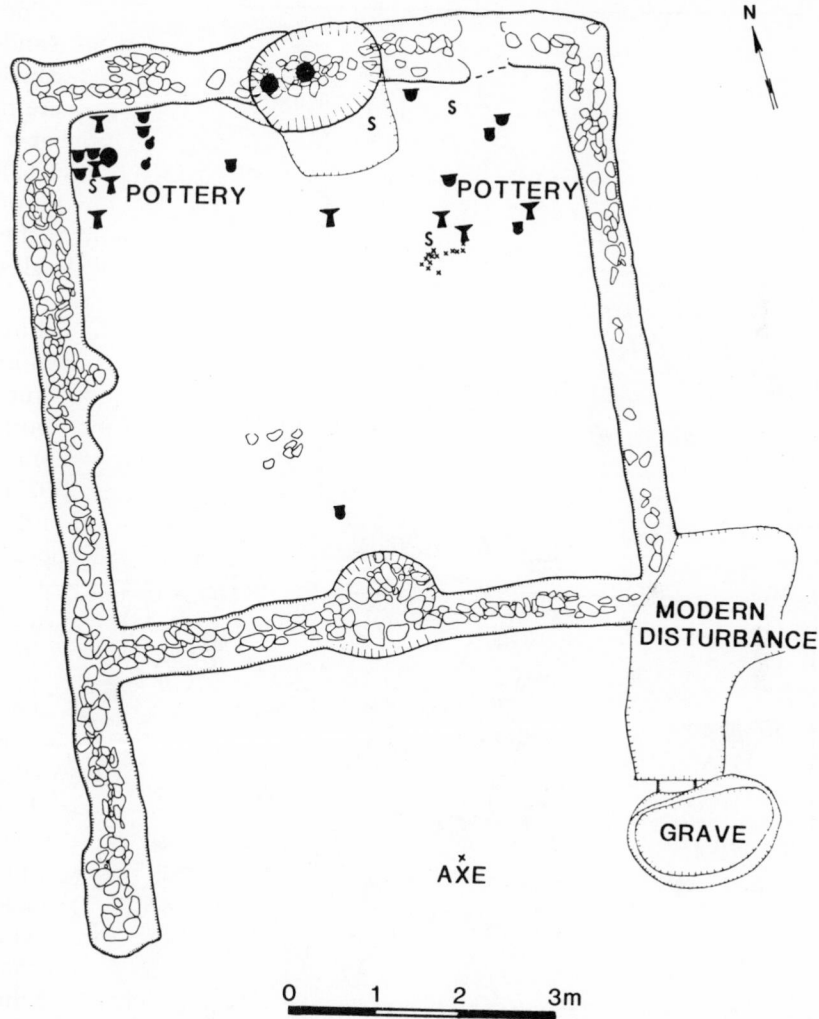

Figure 35 Plan of so-called cult-house, excavated at Herrup, northern Jutland.

the deposits in moist ground is illuminated by one comprehensive work, C.J. Becker's thesis of 1947. The important material of votive finds, that is deposits of valuable objects, especially flint axes, has in recent years been the object of increased interest. A valuable survey of a part of the finds was published by P.O. Nielsen (1977b). Here the find group was perceived as an expression of the development of ranking in the farming communities described above.

Problems related to the origin of agriculture in the Middle East have,

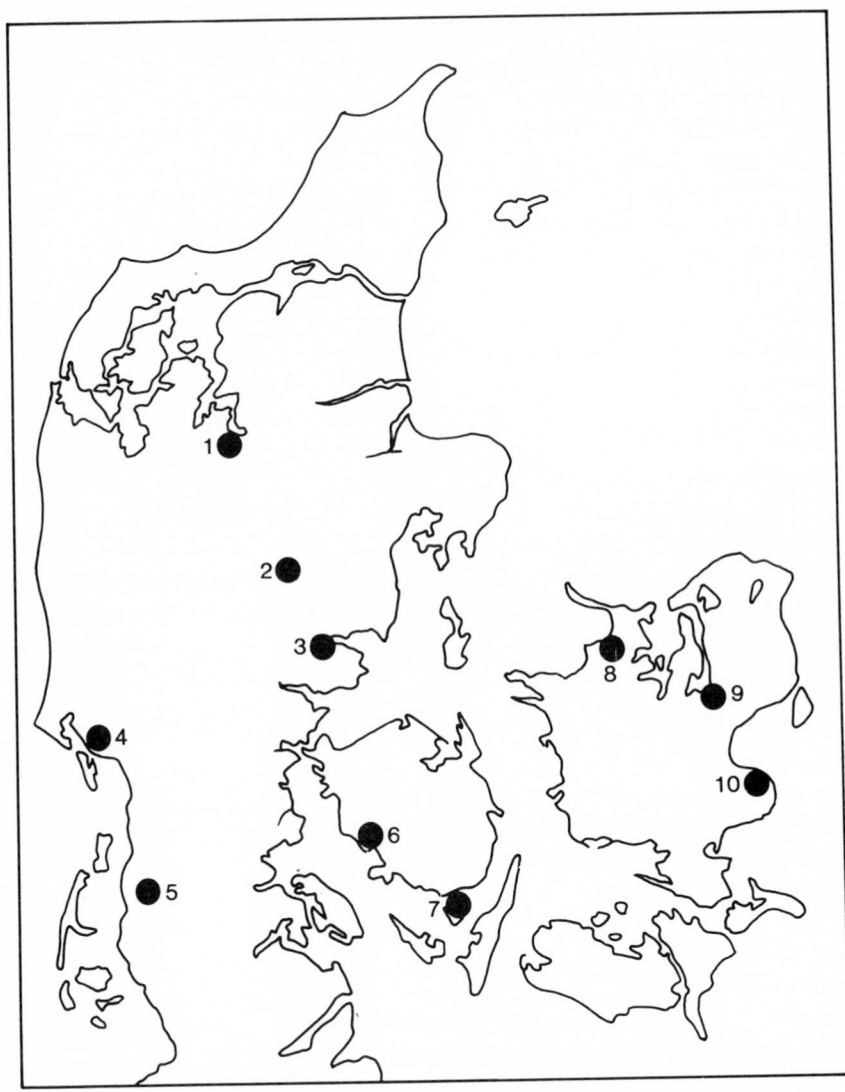

Figure 36 Plough marks found under graves from the Funnel-Necked Beaker culture. 1. Skibshøj, Viborg county. 2. Brendekroggård, Skanderborg county. 3. Præstehøj, Vejle county. 4. Nygård, Ribe county. 5. Steneng, Ribe county. 6. Snave, Svendborg county. 7. Capeshøj, Svendborg county. 8. Blomster-vænget, Holbæk county. 9. Himmelev, Copenhagen county. 10. Fuglebæks-banken, Præstø county.

since Gordon Childe's work in the 1930s, been the object of lively debate. From the abundance of recent literature, only a few works shall be mentioned which described the 'neolithization' on the basis of demographic views, namely K.V. Flannery and F. Hole (1969); a survey of the total material has been published by Charles L. Redman (1978). An interesting attempt to examine the validity of this demographic explanation has been carried out in the USA (Michael J. Harner, 1970). On the basis of a very comprehensive ethnographic material, a model has been set up which suggests that the transition to food production normally occurs in a hunter–gatherer society when it has exploited its resources to the limit of population density. Some social and demographic consequences of this have also been the subject of studies (R. Sussmann, 1972) whose results fully bear out the views expressed above. Related theories may be found in the works of S. Struever (1971) and B. Spooner (1972).

With regard to works on the neolithization of Europe, archaeological literature is very extensive. One example of a newer survey is by H. Müller-Karpe (1968). The ecological and demographic factors behind the dispersion of the farming economy, however, have only been studied to a minor degree. Exceptions to this include works of A.J. Ammermann and L.L. Cavalli-Sforza (1973), A.P. Phillips (1973) and A.G. Sherratt (1972).

Literature treating the first agriculture in Denmark is very extensive and presents extremely divergent interpretations of the archaeological record. A good deal of the literature is devoted to chronological studies, which naturally enough hold an important position in research. However, in later years chronological studies have been enriched with a new dimension through the development of scientific methods. Only twenty years ago, estimates based upon conventional archaeological methods set the beginning of agriculture in Denmark at about 2500 BC. With the first radiocarbon dates, this limit was moved to about 3000 BC. New finds pushed the beginning of agriculture back 300 years more in time. However, calibrations of the radiocarbon dates have set the beginning of agriculture in Denmark to about 4200 BC – that is about 1700 years further back in time than had been imagined just twenty years ago (H. Tauber, 1972). These calibrated radiocarbon dates from the basis of the present work (H.E. Suess, 1970).

Not until recently has Danish archaeology adjusted itself to the new and surprising set of dates. Danish archaeologists have traditionally presented two alternative interpretations: agriculture has been thought to have arisen either as the result of the invasion of a foreign ethnic element (C.J. Becker, 1947) or else as a consequence of a number of modifications in the subsistence strategy of the local hunter–gatherer population (J. Troels-Smith, 1960a, 1966; H. Schwabedissen, 1968). New archaeological arguments (J. Skårup, 1973; S.H. Andersen, 1973) have to some degree brought new elements to this debate, but at the same time the calibrated radiocarbon dates have revealed the paucity of the archaeological record, especially from the first centuries after the introduction of the farming economy in Denmark. This deficiency is also noticeable in newer works which seek to view the process on the basis of theories derived from L.R. Binford's Post-Pleistocene Adaption theory (C. Paludan-Müller, 1978).

The specific chronology within the early and middle Neolithic period has hitherto been based upon two artefact groups: pottery and axe types (C.J. Becker, 1947, 1954, 1957a). On this basis, the period has been divided into two main phases, early and middle Neolithic time (EN = Early Neolithic, MN A = Middle Neolithic Funnel-Necked Beaker Culture). In 1947 C.J. Becker divided the Early Neolithic into phases A, B and C, each of which represented successive stages in a chronological development. This derivative system is still practical for the general categorization of the site inventories, but newer radiocarbon dates have shown that A, B and so-called non-megalithic C pottery are generally contemporaneous (T. Madsen, 1979a).

In conclusion the following can be said about the neolithization in Denmark: the first traces of the early Neolithic farming communities turn up around 4200 BC. In the early period, till about 3600 BC, sites containing A, B and non-megalithic C pottery occur. The A-sites are mainly known in east Denmark, whereas the B-sites are more evenly spread. Non-megalithic C-sites especially are concentrated in Jutland. At the time when megalithic C pottery turns up on the Danish islands, the non-megalithic C pottery continues in Jutland. The megalithic C pottery gradually spread all over Denmark (K. Ebbesen and D. Mahler, 1979) and at the beginning of the MN A, c. 3200 BC, only faint traces of the non-megalithic styles are still present in northern Jutland (T. Madsen, 1979a). The suggestion by Jan Lichardus (1976) that the B pottery is the earliest stage of the agrarian culture in Denmark seems unfounded.

The Middle Neolithic period (MN A) is divided into phases I–V on the basis of the pottery from a number of the largest settlement finds of the period (C.J. Becker, 1947, 1954). The flint axes too have been used to support the division mentioned (C.J. Becker, 1959). Here, however, newer studies (P.O. Nielsen, 1977a) seem to indicate that this find group is not well suited for the purpose. The thick-butted flint axes from the Middle Neolithic range in fact over a far longer period of time, MN A and MN B, than earlier assumed.

Recent contributions to the chronological discussion also include works of K. Ebbesen (1979) and K. Davidsen (1975). The problems related to the end of the period and the transition to the so-called Single Grave culture (C.J. Becker, 1967a; K. Davidsen, 1975; C. Malmros and H. Tauber, 1975; P.O. Nielsen, 1977 a and b) will be discussed in more detail in the following section.

One noteworthy problem deals with the so-called Pitted Ware culture (C.J. Becker, 1950a). This has often been interpreted as an independent ethnic group which appeared in Denmark during the Middle Neolithic. But the Danish finds from the Pitted Ware culture may represent nothing other than specific activity camps founded by the agrarian communities. This problem demands new investigations and will not be examined here (S. Nielsen, 1979).

The profile of the natural environment in which the first farming society arose is based primarily upon the studies which were carried out in Denmark by scholars such as K. Jessen and J. Iversen. A summary of the results of pollen analysts was presented in 1967 by J. Iversen who concluded:

> By and large, the great developmental drama of the vegetation after the Ice Age is now known. What remains is to distinguish the factors which set this whole drama and its various phases into motion – climatic fluctuations, the development of the soil, and in the later millennia not least of all the many kinds of human influence during prehistoric and historic times.

This ecological analysis is still in its infancy and depends upon the continued co-operation of a great many disciplines – including prehistoric archaeology. Many of the results so far have been obtained through this sort of collaboration carried out in Draved Forest near Løgum Kloster in Jutland. Here, a series of practical experiments has led to a widened understanding of such factors as the influence of early agriculture upon the forest (J. Iversen, 1967; A. Steensberg, 1979; S. Jørgensen, 1953; A. Andersen, 1966). Danish pollen analysts have concentrated particularly on an interpretation of the local pollen diagrams, whereas in Sweden (B.E. Berglund, 1969) the attempt has been made to synthesize the many detailed investigations into a comprehensive picture of the vegetational history of southern Scandinavia. This total picture is still rife with uncertainty but there is reason to anticipate great progress in this field.

With regard to the relationship between food production and demographic development, archaeological studies are still in their infancy. Inspiration for new sorts of questions derives first of all from the works of Esther Boserup, which have in later years played a growing role in archaeological literature (P.E.L. Smith, 1970). Debate as to the application of these theories in historic and prehistoric research is still very lively (the Boserup Symposium, 1972; G.L. Cowgill, 1975).

The anthropological material which forms the foundation for conclusions regarding Danish conditions has been published by K. Brøste and J.B. Jørgensen (1956). The above-named studies of Swiss examples were made by W. Scheffrahn (1967). Surveys of the subject are found in such works as H.V. Vallois (1960), as well as G. Acsádi and J. Nemeskéri (1970).

Studies of the economic structure underlying the earliest farming communities are based upon a very slender source material. Generalizations about the settlement pattern have been made by T. Mathiassen in 1948 and 1959 in two studies; the result of these studies have only to a small degree been exploited in Danish archaeology. A number of weaknesses in the classification of the registered finds have contributed to this. Surveys of the subsistence strategy of the early farming communities have been carried out by J. Troels-Smith (1953, 1960) and by C.J. Becker (1954); see also works by K. Jessen (1951) and G. Jørgensen (1976, 1977). An important sketch for the understanding of the role of domesticated animals in the Middle Neolithic has been published by C.F.W. Higham (1969). For a more general survey, see M. Degerbøl's study from 1933.

As yet, no exhaustive study exists of the plough marks from the Stone Age through the Bronze Age, although this would be most helpful. Therefore the history of the use of the plough (ard) can only be followed sporadically through the Neolithic. The earliest plough marks hitherto date from the fourth millennium BC and were revealed during excavation of a long barrow in Steneng, southern Jutland (O. Voss, 1966). With regard to details of the farming techniques in the first phase of the Neolithic, general reference is made to the work of J. Iversen of 1967 and A. Steensberg of 1979. An important survey of a number of pedological problems is provided by S. Nielsen (1980).

Investigations of the role of hunting and gathering in the Danish Neolithic are quite new. This particular aspect of the economy of the farming communities is the topic of J. Skårup's study of 1973. Studies of flint-mining in the Neolithic have been generally treated by C.J. Becker (1951, 1958), whereas a number of more theoretical considerations on the exchange of goods, seen against a European background, were presented by A.G. Sherratt in 1976.

Attempts to determine organizational aspects of the early food-producing communities in Denmark are rare (K. Randsborg, 1975). The relating of the development of prehistoric society to concepts derived from ethnographic literature relies mainly upon works of Morton H. Fried (1960, 1967) and Elman R. Service (1966, 1971, 1975). Here there are two different models of societal organization. The first (M.H. Fried) focuses on the vertical relations between members of a society by describing ways in which societies differentiate their members. Fried distinguishes four different types of society: egalitarian, ranked and stratified societies, together with states. The second model (E.R. Service) describes the development of community organization in terms of a growing socio-cultural integration. Service also distinguishes four different types of society: band societies, tribes, chiefdoms and states (Figure 37).

The two models are not parallel, but they are both useful heuristic tools for studies of social evolution in primitive societies. They have therefore in recent years achieved an ever wider applicability. For example, they have been used by Charles L. Redman (1978) to describe

Morton Fried's terminology	Elman Service's terminology
State society	State organisation
Stratified society	
Ranked society	Chiefdom organisation
Egalitarian society	Tribal organisation
	Band organisation

Figure 37 Terminology used by Elman R. Service (1971) and Morton H. Fried (1967).

the development from early farming to urban society in the Near East. As in Redman's work the two models are in the present work contrasted with one another and moreover are related to the development of the prehistoric communities in southern Scandinavia.

The earliest agrarian communities in Denmark are here assigned to the level which in E.R. Service's model is called the tribe. This refers to a society whose political and economic organization is based on local production organized along lines of kinship. The tribal society distinguishes itself from the band society in its having developed a higher degree of integration. This was achieved by the help of factors such as sodalities which cross-cut local groups, clans, age groups, secret societies, and so on – all phenomena which are practically impossible to distinguish in the archaeological record.

The description of early Danish agrarian society as a tribal society is due above all to the assumption that the growth of the agricultural economy must have confronted society with necessary tasks which could hardly have been solved on a band level of organization. This holds true first and foremost of the subsistence form, but also of some of the socio-cultural phenomena described: the construction of the large labour-demanding grave monuments and the central sites, for example. Some of these phenomena are also viewed as a manifestation of the incipient ranking of society. In relation to M.H. Fried's model, the early farming communities are therefore placed at the transition between the egalitarian and the ranked type of society. This development seems to have commenced quite early in the Neolithic. Once more the question arises of whether the hunter–gatherer society of the Atlantic period managed to develop higher forms of integration than the band society (see p. 57).

No definitive answer can yet be given, but as pointed out, the relating of the archaeological record to the more theoretically oriented models of community organization will have an important heuristic function in future research on the introduction of agriculture in southern Scandinavia. Thus an alternative can be created to earlier research, which has hitherto unsuccessfully sought to explain this revolution on the basis of ethnic concepts and invasion theories.

PART III

Towards a new era
2800–500 BC

11

A changing environment

Farming communities in transition

The third and second millennia BC seem to have witnessed three major developments. First, farming communities gradually abandoned their wide-spectred subsistence strategy for the development of trans-humance, a process with parallels over most of northern Europe (C.F.W. Higham, 1967). Second, the growth of non-egalitarian ranked societies accelerated, ending with the emergence of so-called chiefdoms. The most impressive result of this development was the ambitious barrow-building of the second millennium BC. Third, interregional contacts grew in intensity. The archaeological record reflects this phenomenon in the widespread distribution of metal objects, which also reveal the presence of complex sumptuary rules within the developing chiefdoms.

These three developments took place in a period which in many respects is highly problematic as regards the archaeological record. This holds true for the first four or five centuries of the period, the era of the so-called Single Grave culture. However, much of the problem stems from the invasion hypothesis so dear to earlier generations of European archaeologists. A hypothetical invasion of the so-called Single Grave people was proposed to explain the onesidedness of the archaeological record, namely the fact that the majority of finds from the period were made in west Denmark.

In recent years, however, calibrated radiocarbon dates have toppled this early theory. No longer can the Single Grave culture be considered a foreign ethnic group partially overlapping the so-called Funnel-Necked Beaker culture; we now know that the latter phenomenon quite simply succeeded the former. What actually did happen during the third millennium BC was probably a radical change in the subsistence strategy of the early farming communities. None the less, the period covering approximately 2800–2400 BC is still one of the most obscure in the prehistory of Denmark.

Following the end of the Single Grave culture around 2400 BC, our picture again begins to come into focus. The centuries up to c. 1800 BC comprise the Late Neolithic period. During this time, the farming communities expanded rapidly. The changes in the subsistence pattern which had taken place in the foregoing centuries now emerged clearly. Man's impact on the ecosystem became considerable.

Economic and technological breakthroughs took place from the beginning of the second millennium BC. In particular, the new metal technology was a catalyst for economic development in the farming communities. Thus, from about 1800 BC, we can speak of a Danish or 'Nordic' Bronze Age. We can trace up to c. 500 BC an agrarian society ever more dependent on interregional contacts. Denmark now became an integral part of a large area consisting of southern Scandinavia, northern Germany and Poland. This vast cultural region was loosely held together by shifting exchange systems determined by the productive capacity of each area.

The changing land

During the fourth millennium BC the first farming communities of Denmark made their mark on the virgin forest. But as yet the impact of man on the vegetation was slight. The Danish landscape was still dominated by shady forest and scrub. Only in the more densely populated areas which were formed during the fourth millennium BC was the landscape gradually becoming more open.

As the land was exploited more and more, this picture began to change drastically. In the third millennium BC light forest and scrub could be seen throughout Denmark as a landscape with extensive pastures was created. Widespread grazing, severe exhaustion of the soil, the spread of a new settlement pattern and the increasing use of the ard for ploughing were factors which in the long run affected the entire ecosystem. The result was the creation of a landscape with gradual transition between light forest, scrub pasture and extensive grass pasture (Figure 38). According to the pollen spectra, this type of landscape existed not only in Denmark but over much of the north European lowland.

This development was based on a new ecological situation which necessitated new types of land management. In eastern Denmark the changes may have been introduced even earlier. In any case, Denmark

Figure 38 The typical Danish Bronze-Age landscape was characterized by light forest, scrub pasture, and extensive grass pasture.

seems to have been the scene of an agricultural expansion from the middle of the third millennium BC. Pollen diagrams for that time show, for example, far-reaching forest clearance on Djursland in eastern Jutland. Forest clearance and cattle grazing were now more prevalent than ever. As cattle retarded the regeneration of the lime forest and hazel groves, there were now spacious grass pastures nearly devoid of hazel scrub. This trend continued into the second and first millennia BC. Man's impact on the Danish countryside had become evident indeed.

However, few details are known of the settlement pattern and its ecological background during the third millennium BC. Pollen analyses are unfortunately few in number. Yet all over southern Scandinavia they show the same general pattern, namely a lively agricultural expansion beginning with the so-called Single Grave culture, shortly before the middle of the third millennium BC and persisting throughout the next thousand years.

There were many regional variations. In central Jutland the light sandy soils were preferred because their original open forest vegetation must have been especially well-suited for extensive grazing. In eastern Jutland, however, the boulder clay soils were still quite unsettled. Here lay rich potential for settlement expansion. Yet this potential was not exploited until the last few centuries BC. On the poor sandy soils in west Jutland, deterioration must already have been quite advanced due to human interference. Already at the beginning of the second millennium BC barrows were built on deserted arable land which heavy grazing had converted to poor pasture. In fact, at some places burial mounds were erected on heathland, a vegetation form directly resulting from human exploitation. Already here was the genesis of the process culminating in the last centuries BC when the lightest soils in westernmost Denmark had exhausted their potential for population increase.

The changing climate

Ever since the introduction of farming in Denmark, climatic shifts had affected the subsistence strategy of the agrarian communities and with it the shifting frontier between the forest and the man-made landscape. A long-standing assumption of climatologists has been that from 2800 BC up to the beginning of the Sub-Atlantic period around 600–500 BC the climate was warm and dry with an average summer temperature slightly higher than it is today. The long-term development, however, showed a falling trend towards that of the present-day climate. Around 600–500 BC a drastic change to a cooler and more humid climate marked the close of the Post-Glacial warm period.

In general this picture is still valid. But recent investigations have proved that the process was more complicated. No doubt the average temperature showed a slight decrease during the period 2800–500 BC, but this course was irregular, as it was disturbed by a series of fluctuations. Many opinions held by older generations of archaeologists about the climatic change at the transition from the Sub-Boreal to the Sub-Atlantic period around 600 BC must therefore be revised.

For many years archaeologists, supported by climatological evidence, have claimed that the climatic change around 600 BC (observable in peat bogs as a boundary horizon, the so-called RY III) had a catastrophic impact on the agrarian societies in northern Europe. Perhaps there is a connection between climate and changes in land management in this period. Even so, the catastrophe theory ought to be rejected. On the contrary, the archaeological record indicates that around the middle of the first millennium BC agrarian societies were expanding to a degree hitherto unequalled in the prehistory of northern Europe.

Knowledge of climatic development in the last five or six millennia stems primarily from intensive research on the north European raised bogs. Valuable studies have been made in Sweden in particular. But even in Denmark, where peat digging has unfortunately obliterated the majority of raised bogs, vital information has been gleaned.

The raised bog has been compared to a huge sponge saturated with rainwater. It possesses a completely independent aquatic balance as it is not affected by the ground-water level under the bog. The moisture of the raised bog is obtained exclusively from the atmosphere, so that the growth rate and structure of the peat reflect climatic conditions at the time of its formation. Thus a raised bog can act as a self-registering climatograph for millennia. In dry warm conditions, a dark-brown nearly structureless peat is formed. A cool damp climate results in a light, somewhat decomposed peat of well-preserved sphagnum shoots. The boundary between dark and light peat is called a recurrence level or boundary horizon.

The stratification of the peat bog thus registers general long-term trends in the climate. One boundary horizon in particular has been singled out, the one which marks the dividing line between the Sub-Boreal and the Sub-Atlantic periods, about 600 BC. Recently, however, it has been demonstrated that the boundary horizons in different bogs are not always comparable. Furthermore it appears that the climatic development in the past five or six millennia has had a fluctuation course. New studies based on radiocarbon dates indicate possible cyclical climatic variations lasting about 260 years (B. Aaby, 1974). This periodicity, though, is not general, as in some cases there is a double distance between the registrations of climatic changes (Figure 39). Whether this is due to faulty observation or to an actual absence of change is not entirely certain. Similarly, not all climatic oscillations produce equally noticeable effects in various raised bogs.

Nor is it entirely clear what the boundary horizons signify. To be sure, they demonstrate a transition to a moister environment. But increased moisture can be caused both by reduced evaporation, i.e. a fall in temperature, and by increased precipitation. It is difficult to distinguish between the two causes. Nevertheless, there is biological evidence of a falling trend in the summer temperature from the fourth to the first millennia BC. Consequently Danish scientists have been inclined to

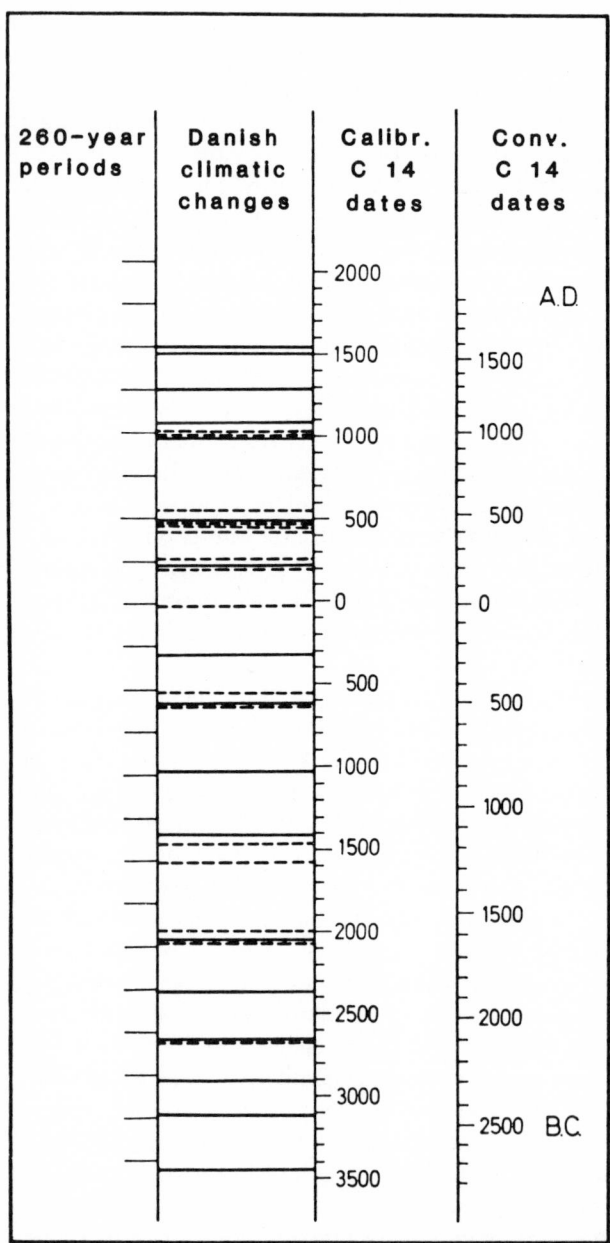

Figure 39 Observed climatic changes in Denmark during the last 5500 years. The radiocarbon dates seem to indicate cyclical variations lasting about 260 years.

regard the major cause of the formation of the boundary horizons as being a wave-like fall in temperature.

For the period spanning 2800–500 BC, this means that changes to moister and colder conditions must have occurred around the beginning of the period, c. 2700 BC. The next oscillation came around 2350 BC, followed by yet another one around 2100 BC. At this stage a hiatus occurred and subsequent climatic changes are registered around 1600 BC, 1400 BC, and 1050 BC. A final change, noted around 600–500 BC, is identical with the so-called classic boundary horizon (RY III) which was earlier credited with the catastrophic significance of having led to the breakdown of Bronze Age society and the rise of Iron Age society.

Today we must acknowledge that climatic changes were far more frequent than has earlier been assumed. Consequently it has become impossible to demonstrate a clear correlation between changes in climatic conditions and changes in the subsistence strategy of agrarian societies of the past.

12

Subsistence and settlement

Towards a new settlement pattern

During the third millennium BC a series of changes in Denmark resulted in a settlement pattern which lasted about 2500 years. Unfortunately the archaeological record reflecting this period is rife with problems. The first difficulty concerns the time span, *c.* 2800–2400 BC, the time of the Single Grave culture. Most of the archaeological finds from that period were excavated in the west of Denmark, in Jutland. On the islands in eastern Denmark, finds are rare.

This unbalanced find distribution has long been used as one of the strongest arguments in favour of the theory of an invasion of the so-called Single Grave people at the beginning of the third millennium BC. This invasion theory postulated that an ethnic group called the Single Grave people settled on the light sandy soils of western Jutland, whereas the original agrarian population still resided on the moraine soils in the east. The Single Grave people were thought to have spread gradually onto these heavier soils in east Denmark, so that by the end of the third millennium BC they were supposed to have established themselves as an 'upper class' in relation to the subjugated 'Funnel-Beaker people'.

Today the entire invasion theory has collapsed under the weighty evidence of modern radiocarbon dating. Consequently recent research has been concentrated on the archaeological record from eastern Denmark. Surprisingly, it has been demonstrated that contrary to earlier theories there was a continuous settlement here from the fourth millennium far into the third millennium BC, that is into a period once thought to be devoid of archaeological remains (P.O. Nielsen, 1977a). For example, it has been shown that the large megalith graves on the

Danish islands were still in use after *c*. 2800 BC. At the same time a remarkable quantity of sacrificial deposits, flint axes for example, were being deposited in lakes and bogs (P.O. Nielsen 1977b). Thus, in contrast to earlier hypotheses, eastern Denmark is far from lacking in finds during the Single Grave period (2800–2400 BC). Even so, it is still impossible to explain the peculiar difference in find quantity between west and east Denmark. One likely cause is the intensive cultivation of later epochs which obliterated earlier remains. Subsequent periods of prehistory, such as the final half of the first millennium BC, also exhibit a similar dearth of finds in eastern Denmark.

Meanwhile, a comparison between the settlement areas of the first farming communities (Figure 27) and the settlement areas which developed towards the end of the third millennium BC testifies to significant changes in the settlement pattern in the intervening period. This may be demonstrated by the map, Figure 40, which conveys some idea of the major settlement features during the Late Neolithic period (2400–1800 BC). The tendencies observed become even more evident in a comparison between the map in Figure 40 and the maps showing settlement in the Bronze Age (1800–500 BC) (Figures 41 and 42). The maps are based upon the distribution of approximately 4000 Bronze Age graves and there is reason to believe that the number of graves within a reasonably large area reflects the relative population density. The overall picture emerging from Figure 42 clearly shows the main settlement features resulting from the changes which occurred in the third millennium BC. At the same time it appears that this new pattern remained virtually unchanged from the Late Neolithic period down to the Iron Age, *c*. 500 BC.

In Jutland, the most striking fact is that settlement apparently avoided the heavy moraine soils of the eastern region as well as the light sandy soils in the west. Population concentrations can be observed in central Vendsyssel, western Himmerland, the westernmost part of the Limfjord, and further south along the ridge of Jutland with extensions toward the west coast. The picture is somewhat blurred regarding the island of Funen, but on Zealand there is a clear-cut tendency to avoid the centre of the island. This tendency is already evident from the start of the third millennium BC. Sizeable concentrations of population existed in the north-west and west of Zealand, in the region surrounding the Isefjord and Roskilde fjord, and in the south on the islands of Møn and Falster.

In the course of nearly 2000 years, as shown by the maps, only small changes occurred either as an expansion of settlement or as an increased tendency to form clusters. These shifts probably resulted in changes of

Figure 40 Distribution of the late Neolithic flint daggers, type I–V (*cf.* fig. 55) from *c.* 2400–1800 BC.

Figure 41 Distribution of grave finds from the Early Bronze Age mapped by parishes. The various signatures indicate the number of graves found within each parish.

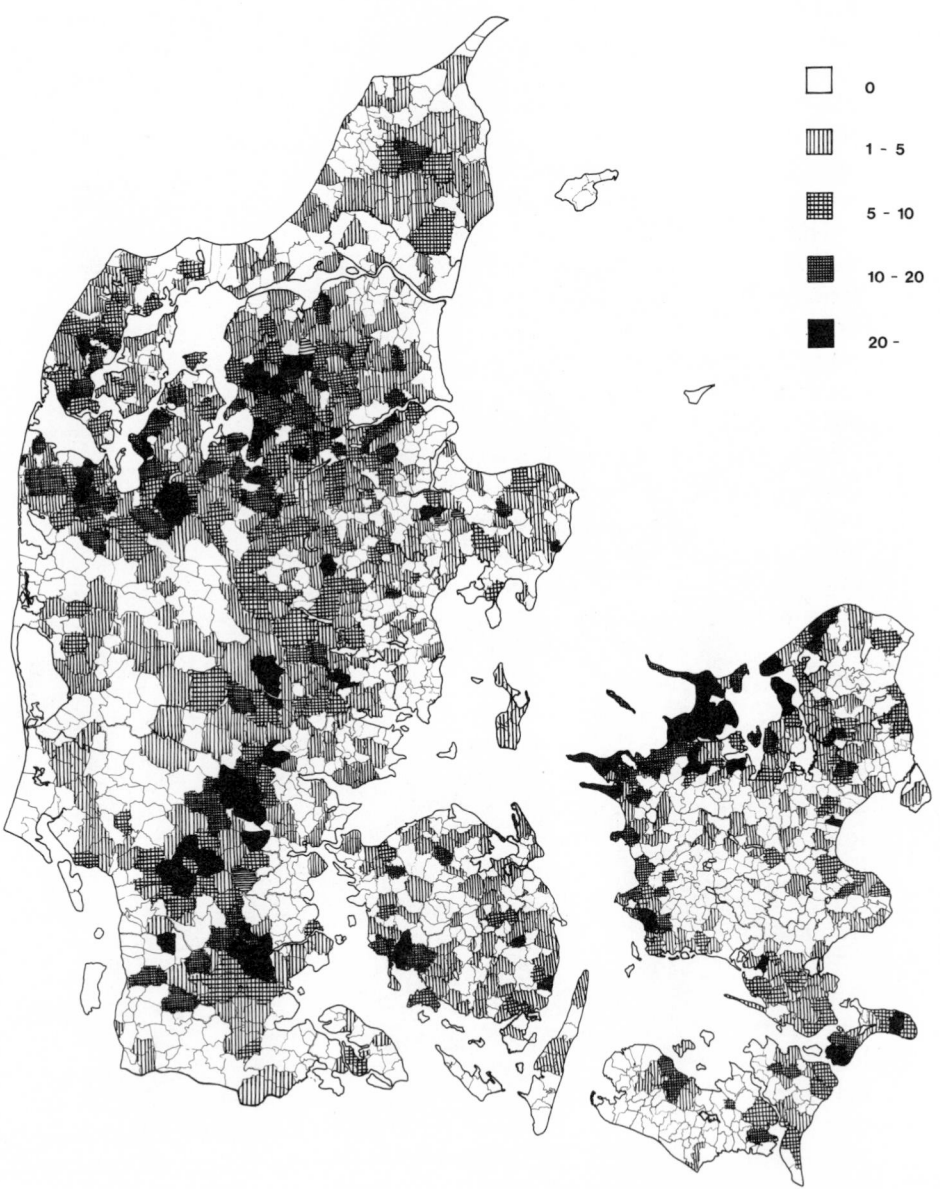

Figure 42 Distribution of grave finds from the Late Bronze Age mapped by parishes. The various signatures indicate the number of graves found within each parish.

socio-economic conditions, a supposition that is supported by the archaeological record. In the long run, however, increased settlement in west Jutland during the first millennium BC is more important. The expanding settlement westward prefigured the expansion which we can observe during the first centuries of the Iron Age, after 500 BC. Perhaps the more abundant precipitation of the first millennium BC improved agricultural conditions in west Jutland for a few centuries. On the whole, though, settlement was strikingly stationary from 2400–500 BC.

The cause of the change in settlement pattern during the third millennium BC has already been touched upon. Apparently the subsistence pattern of the earliest farming communities was a wide-spectred one which demanded a certain mobility. As a result of population pressure, many modifications were introduced during the third millennium BC. The wide-spectred subsistence strategy seems to have been abandoned; instead ard-ploughing became more accepted and greater emphasis was given to stock-raising. As a matter of fact, there seems to have been a similar trend in many areas of central and northern Europe in the same period (A.G. Sherratt, 1980). Here too the dramatic invasion theories of earlier generations have been abandoned of late. Instead, interest has been focused on evidence of technological innovations, intensified forest clearance and expansion of grasslands. These observations point to the development of new subsistence strategies by the farming communities.

To elucidate this process we shall briefly examine some of the few fragments of pedological evidence from early times. It has already been shown how the extensive swidden agriculture practised by the first farmers washed iron and mineral nutrients out of the upper layers of the forest floor, thus exhausting the soil. How long this process took cannot be known. But there is much to indicate that the natural forest mould from the beginning of the Sub-Boreal period, during which agriculture was introduced, deteriorated rapidly.

Prehistoric cultivation horizons confirm this swift degeneration. Buried soils may be found, for example, beneath Bronze Age barrows. Not only do these buried soils, through pollen analysis, testify to the local vegetation when the barrow was built; they can also inform us about the pedogenetic stage of development of the soil, its content of mineral nutrients and its ability to supply plants with water. Compared with modern soil at the same sites, buried soils are storehouses of information which until recently have hardly been exploited (S. Nielsen, 1980).

The emerging impression of agriculture in Denmark up to the beginning of the Iron Age is that of a farming system which hastened the deterioration of the ecological system and contributed to the rapid spread of the heathland, especially in western Jutland.

The buried soil underlying Bronze Age barrows nearly always consists of a poor, very thin layer of mould in which cereal crops, for example, would hardly have produced more than threefold, or at the utmost fourfold. With the technology available to the farming communities, only a very modest layer of mould could be formed. This situation was not bettered until the introduction of manuring during the Iron Age.

Naturally the physical composition of the subsoil was an essential factor in forming the mould layer resulting from continuous cultivation. The heavy boulder clay in east Denmark, for example, resulted in a better mould layer than the light sandy soil of west Denmark. But the present-day layer of mould cannot directly provide information on cultivation at a certain site thousands of years ago. The mould layer in a modern ploughed field is primarily the result of modern methods of cultivation. Therefore, recent studies (K. Kristiansen, 1978a; K. Randsborg, 1974a and b) which have attempted to relate the distribution of wealth in the Bronze Age to measurements of modern soil quality must be taken with a grain of salt. At the most, they can provide very rough generalizations about the varying conditions of farming in various parts of prehistoric Denmark.

On the whole, we can assume that the lightest soils in west Jutland can hardly have been suitable for cereal cultivation until late in prehistory. Thus we have no impressions of grain in the pottery of the so-called Single Grave culture in these regions. Here the major type of subsistence was probably the raising of sheep and cattle.

Even elsewhere in Denmark, where the mould was richer, cereal cultivation played only a modest role in the subsistence strategy. A threefold harvest was probably common; even in the Middle Ages yields in northern Europe were rarely higher. In addition, fields must have been quite small owing to the input of work required. So even on the good lands of east Denmark, stock-breeding, supplemented with food-gathering from marine and other sources, must have constituted the most important part of the subsistence pattern.

These factors help explain the settlement pattern which emerged during the third and second millennia BC. The land which the farming communities selected for settlement was usually what is today considered soil of medium quality. Four thousand years ago this meant areas with a rather open forest vegetation which could easily be exploited for cattle grazing. What we today consider high-quality soils, such as those in east Jutland, would not have been especially attractive due to their far denser forest vegetation. This preference for lighter soils, for areas

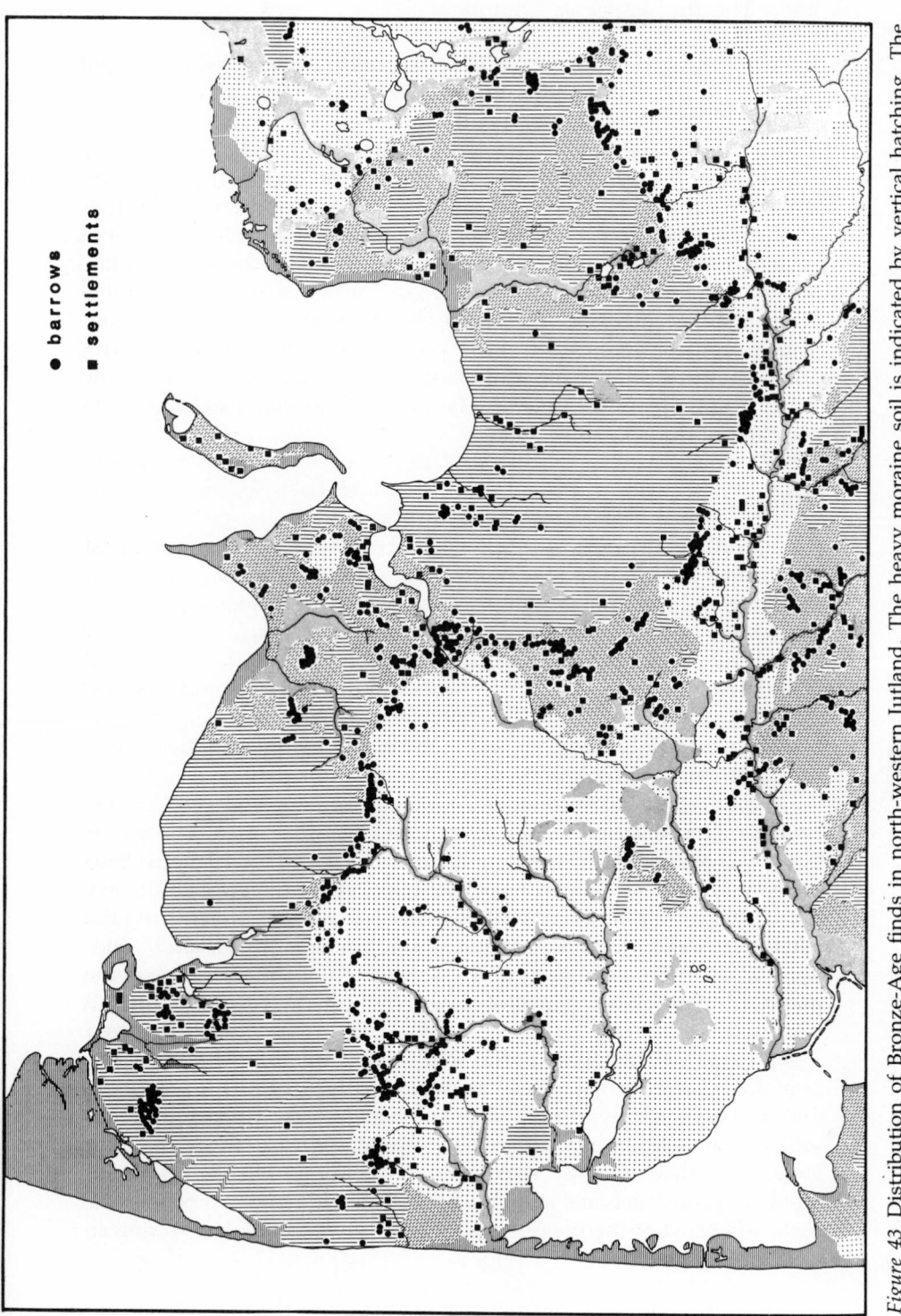

Figure 43 Distribution of Bronze-Age finds in north-western Jutland. The heavy moraine soil is indicated by vertical hatching. The dotted areas indicate the sandy soils of the outwash plains.

which were open oak woodlands with heathy clearings, is for example reflected in the distribution of Bronze Age finds in north-west Jutland (Figure 43) (K. Kristiansen, 1978a).

Often this pattern was adapted to local conditions. In north-west Zealand, which was one of the most populous settled areas from the third to the first millennia BC, topography played a more crucial role than in north-west Jutland. So far, no pollen analyses have been made in this region, but the distribution of the finds together with the topographical situation indicates that large areas were covered with an open forest with abundant grasslands and denser forest in the uninhabited regions. This type of pasture is extremely productive when grazed by cattle. Furthermore the clay soil stimulated reproduction of the vegetation better here than in west Jutland. Marine resources may also have been a vital alternative source of food.

Villages and farmsteads

Recent Jutland excavations, especially those in the western part of the peninsula, have unearthed numerous settlements from the Late Neolithic and the Bronze Age. Large-scale excavations have uncovered whole village complexes consisting of up to fifty houses. The earliest sites date from the beginning of the Neolithic (c. 2400 BC). Unfortunately, the settlement type of the Single Grave culture from the middle of the third millennium BC remains a puzzle. Yet there are hints that the type of settlement which can be glimpsed at the end of the third millennium BC may reach further back in time, in fact to the Single Grave culture.

The excavated sites reveal that around 2400 BC settlements consisted of small clusters of farmsteads, each housing a single family. The typical house is a relatively short rectangular construction, 12 to 20 metres long and 6 or 7 metres wide with a partially sunken floor (Figure 44). The roof is supported by a single row of posts. This house type seems to have been built some centuries into the second millennium BC, after which new types of houses appeared. A common architectural tradition prevailed throughout much of southern Scandinavia and northern Germany.

Sometime in the middle of the second millennium BC the archaeological record shows that a new, well-defined type of house was introduced. Large sturdy three-aisled longhouses now appeared at the settlements. These houses were always oriented east–west, and their roofs were supported by two rows of interior posts (Figure 45). A number of constructional modifications were made in this type over the centuries. Most of the buildings were spacious, frequently covering an

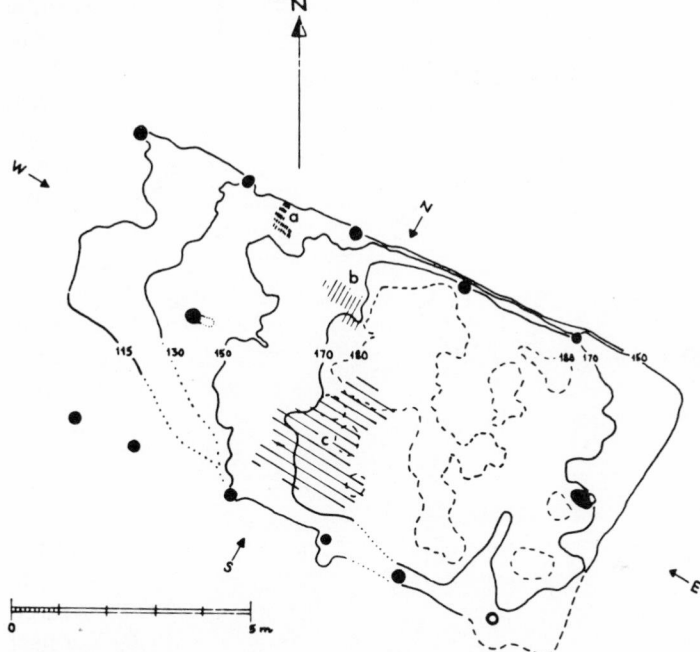

Figure 44 House site of the Late Neolithic period found at Myrhøj,
    western Jutland.

area of 60–150 m². Some houses actually measure up to 250 m².
Variations in size may be related to the differences in wealth observed in
contemporaneous graves.

The large houses of the second and first millennia BC are most often
bisected by two entrances (Figure 46). The west half was the dwelling
area, but the function of the east end is still a puzzle. In some cases,
boxes for large animals have been discovered. But if the east end was a
stall, then the livestock must have been positioned in a way somewhat
different from the position in the Iron Age houses. Together with the
longhouses, smaller storehouses have also been found. These are
normally from 6 to 7 metres in length and 3 or 4 metres in width.

The origin of the three-aisled longhouses is unclear. In the second
millennium BC they may be found side by side with another house type
with turf walls. Certain similarities do exist between the house types,
but as yet the turf-built houses are sparsely documented in the
archaeological record and their function is still obscure.

Architecture followed the same general pattern throughout Denmark
in the second and first millennia BC. In fact, congruence in building

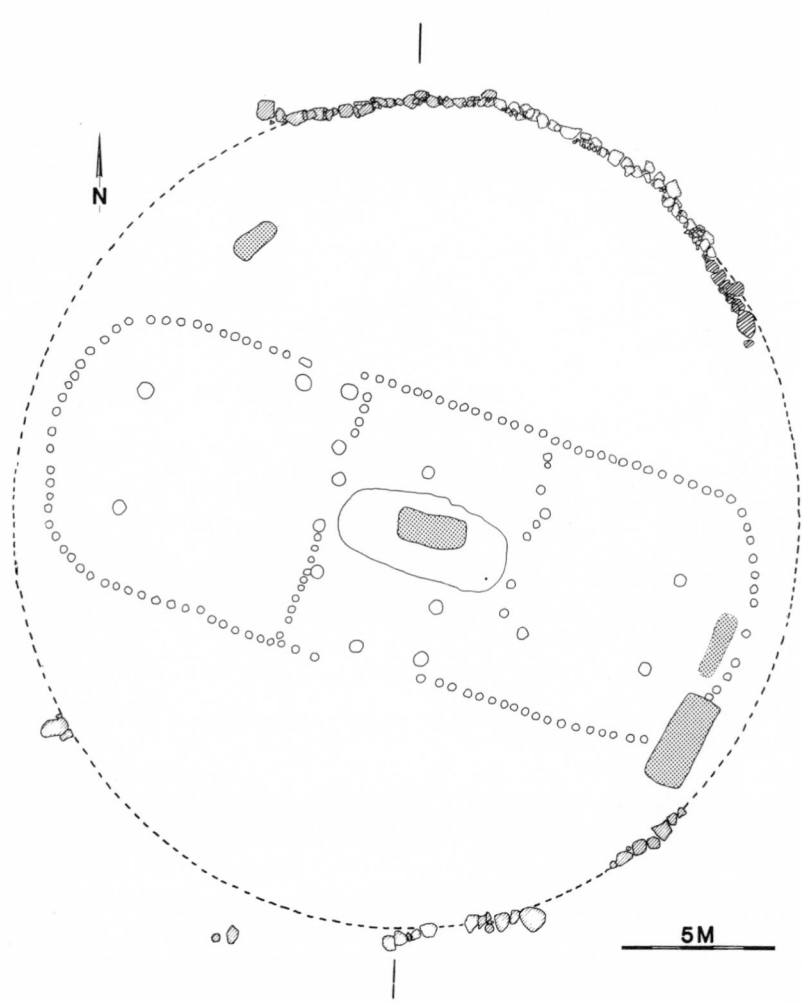

N

5 M

Figure 45 House site of the Early Bronze Age, Montelius period II, found under a
   Bronze-Age barrow at Trappendal, southern Jutland.

traditions stretched even further. From around the middle of the second
millennium BC houses based upon the same constructional principles as
those in Jutland can be traced in the lowland region south of the North
Sea, all the way down to the mouth of the Rhine. The structures are
three-aisled longhouses and, like the Danish ones, are usually divided
into two parts, of which one is for dwelling. The other half can
sometimes be identified as a stall from finds of stall partitions. Dutch
longhouses from the second millennium BC could shelter up to thirty

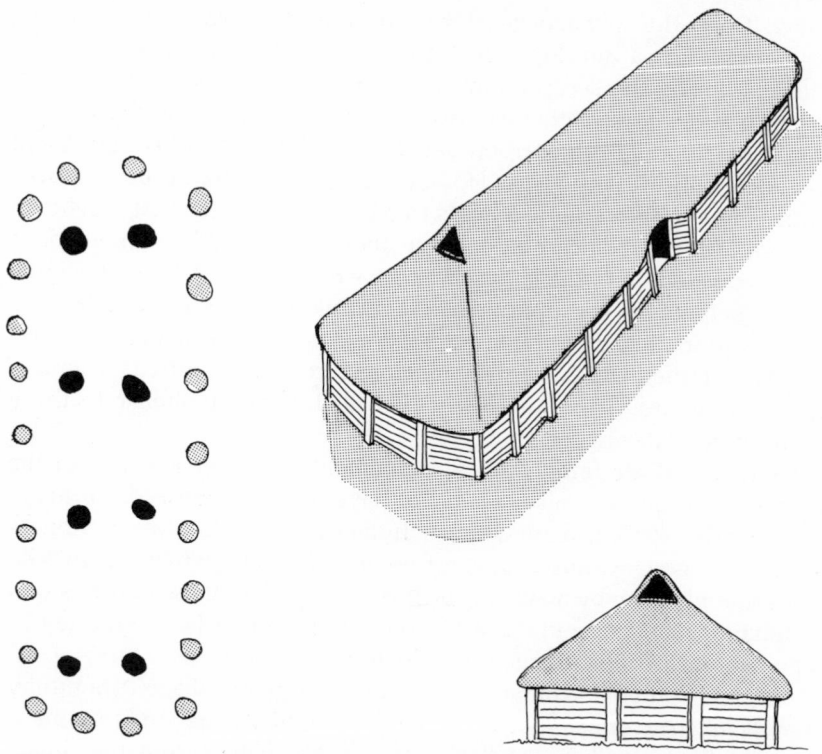

Figure 46 Reconstruction of a typical three-aisled longhouse of the Late Bronze Age. Reconstructed after a house site found at Hovergårde, western Jutland.

head of livestock. Together with the oblong houses, storehouses are often found. Although this type is most common in Holland, it has, as already mentioned, also turned up in Jutland. Radio-carbon dates prove the Dutch houses to be contemporary with the oldest Danish three-aisled houses.

In Denmark and abroad, these structures raise the question of whether the settlements consisted of large and small clusters of independent households or whether they were single farmsteads. This subject has long been debated in Danish archaeology (S. Müller, 1904). In Denmark the question remains unanswered despite the more than one hundred house sites which have been unearthed during the last decade. The crux of the problem is the impossibility of determining how many houses stood at the same site at the same time. No doubt settlements of the Bronze Age differed from those at the end of the first millennium BC. But just what are those differences and how general are they? Does the archaeological record indicate a contraction of the settlement, i.e. a development from individual farmsteads to regular villages during the second and first millennia BC in Denmark?

The oldest-known settlement from the period in question is Myrhøj in northern Jutland, radiocarbon-dated to *c.* 2400 BC. This settlement included only three houses. However there may still be unexcavated houses on the site. This also holds true of another settlement, Egehøj in eastern Jutland, radiocarbon-dated to about 1800 BC. Of the three house sites excavated here, the largest was 19 × 6 metres. But again the limits of the settlement are unknown. At Vadgård in northern Jutland, a settlement radiocarbon-dated to 1350–1200 BC, excavations have revealed a rather large, partially enclosed complex centred around a sacred structure. This can clearly be called a village similar to those encountered later in the Iron Age.

Some of the late finds, such as settlements from the first half of the first millennium BC, also seem to have been comprised of many households. At Spjald in western Jutland, about thirty-three houses were excavated, within an area of about 350 × 70 metres (Figure 47). Even though it can by no means be proved that all of these houses stood simultaneously, the multitude of house sites cannot be interpreted as representing various stages in the existence of one or more farmsteads. The Spjald settlement must have formed a regular village community even if its structure cannot be defined. A similar situation is found at several other localities. At Bjerg, only 7 kilometres from the Spjald settlement, about fifty-five house sites were found, divided into two main groups. Again it is impossible to ascertain the size or structure of

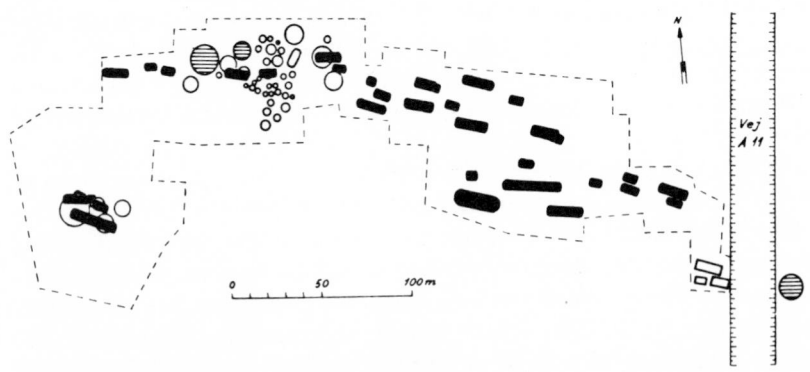

Figure 47 Simplified plan of the Late Bronze-Age settlement at Spjald, western Jutland. The house sites of the Late Bronze Age are indicated in black, later graves and house sites with open contours.

the community at any given stage of its existence. Nor can it be directly compared to the Iron Age village at Grøntoft (Figure 65), only a few centuries younger. Nonetheless there is reason to believe that both individual farmsteads and more extensive village communities existed in western Jutland during the early first millennium BC. The same situation prevailed through the latter half of the millennium, into the early Iron Age.

In east Denmark, only a few house sites have been excavated. Very little is therefore known of the site structure. Refuse layers several metres thick found at the settlement Voldtofte on Funen may indicate that large long-lived villages existed here during the first millennium BC.

But what exactly is a village? In Denmark the village has been the most widespread settlement form for centuries, from the Viking Age up to the agricultural reforms at the end of the eighteenth century. Throughout Danish history, village communities which were collectively supervised possessed formal and informal bodies which administered the rules of husbandry, protected local customs, and enforced peace and order. A village was thus a nuclear settlement forming a system comprised of elements of economic, social and cultural character. However, the definition of a village in historical times is not applicable to prehistory. Here a more simple definition of a village must suffice: a topographical unit comprised of a cluster of three or more independent households. Other features, such as the social, economic and cultural forms of co-operation are of secondary importance. Of course, various forms of co-operation existed in prehistoric villages. But the nature of these forms is unknown and therefore cannot be included in the archaeological definition of a village.

Towards more productive agricultural forms

Throughout the third millennium BC the farming communities in Denmark had slowly abandoned their wide-spectred subsistence strategy. An altered ecological situation and growing population pressure had little by little forced them into new types of land management based upon more extensive stock-raising and a different use of the arable land. Ard-ploughing was now widespread (Figure 48). No doubt these innovations swelled the agricultural output of the farming communities in Denmark. There were, however, serious restraints such as the necessity of a higher input of labour required for working the land. Expansion of the cultivated area was thus strictly limited. Consequently, expansion of pasture and cattle holdings offered the best ways of augmenting agricultural income. This development cannot be closely stu-

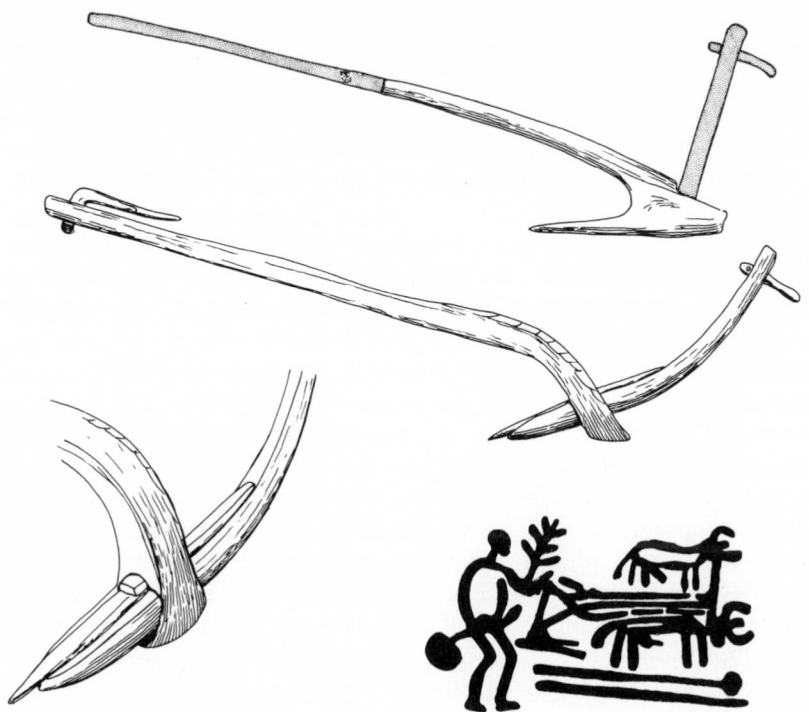

Figure 48 The two different ard types of the Bronze Age. Above: crook ard found at Hvorslev, Viborg county. Below: bow ard found at Døstrup, Ålborg county. Bottom: Bronze Age rock carving with ploughing scene from Listleby, Bohuslän, Sweden.

died from the third to the first millennia BC but its results are obvious in the Late Bronze Age (1000–500 BC).

Regarding the earliest periods, up to the start of the Bronze Age, most theories on the subsistence strategy of the farming communities were once based upon the hypothetical invasion of the Single Grave people, who were seen as nomadic pastoralists. However, the archaeological record from that period presents unmistakable evidence of both stock-breeding and cereal cultivation. The latter is documented by grain impressions in pottery and finds of ard furrows, as well as finds of querns and harvest implements at the settlements. In a few cases, finds of animal bones shed some light on the role of animal husbandry. Pollen diagrams display the effects of man's ever more profound impact on vegetation caused primarily by expansive cattle grazing. In the culturally related areas outside Denmark, the archaeological record reflects the same trend. Furthermore, during the Early Bronze Age (1800–1000 BC) archaeological evidence of the subsistence strategy of the farming communities is scarce. But it is important that aside from countless finds of ard furrows under barrows, the oldest ards themselves, radiocarbon-dated to about 1500 BC, are being discovered in Danish bogs.

During the Late Bronze Age (1000–500 BC) the archaeological record becomes more informative. Hundreds of settlements are known from that period, and almost everywhere they display the same basic features: the primary meat producer, at least on the more benign lands, was the ox. The horse also supplied a good deal of meat, often about as much as sheep and pigs, although the prevalence of these latter animals varies greatly according to physical and biological conditions in the various regions. On the second-rate lands in western Denmark, sheep were probably the most important livestock. The meagre archaeological record cannot yet indicate how the farming communities exploited the various ecological zones. Similarly the age distribution of the cattle does not testify to the overwintering strategy employed by the farming communities. Some finds indicate that winter slaughtering was considerable but no generalizations can be drawn.

Cereal cultivation during the late Bronze Age is noteworthy for the decreasing importance of wheat, especially of emmer. Barley, particularly naked barley, increased correspondingly in importance. When this cropping change occurred is not clear. It seems that the role played by barley had already increased in the third millennium BC. Another improvement which apparently did not take place until the first millennium BC was the introduction of oats and millet. Other cultivated plants included peas (*Pisum*), bean (*Vicia faba*) and perhaps also the oil plant gold of pleasure (*Camelina sativa*).

The role of hunting and food-gathering in the farming communities of the third to the first millennia BC is still very poorly documented in the archaeological record (Figure 49). There are indications that throughout the period marine resources were still exploited. Seasonal camps from the early first millennium BC show that in certain coastal regions fishing, especially for cod, haddock and flounder, supplemented agricultural incomes. The gathering of marine molluscs and the hunting of sea mammals apparently also played a certain role in the subsistence economy.

No matter how minute the changes that the farming communities underwent from the third to the first millennia BC, they all contributed to an altered subsistence strategy. Increased population pressure was probably the prime cause of this process, during which the farming communities gradually abandoned their wide-spectred subsistence pattern. Agriculture became more labour-intensive, leading to heightened

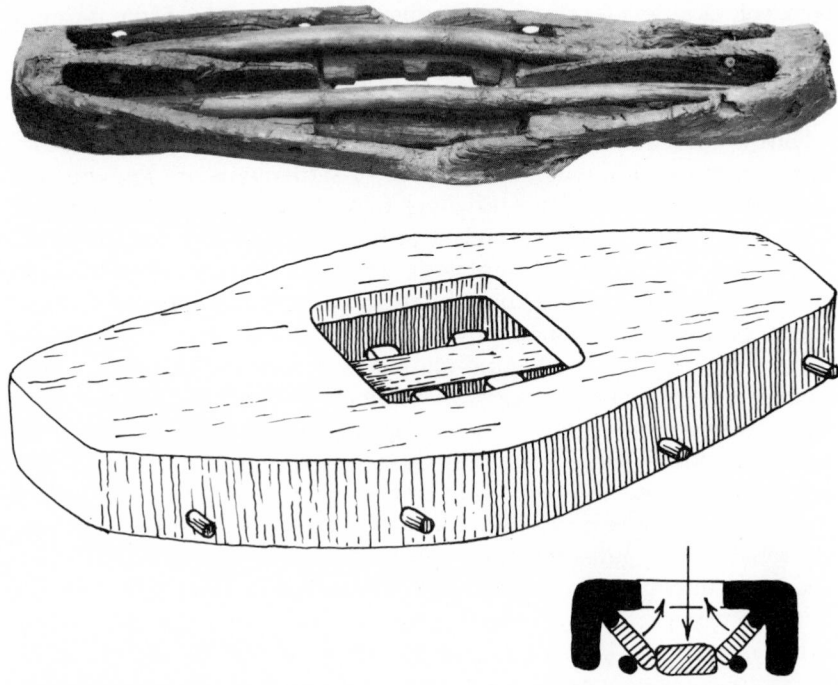

Figure 49 Wooden animal trap from the Bronze Age found in a bog, Nisset Nørremose, Viborg county. Two massive oak flaps are held by a beechwood spring. The merest pressure on the trap would release it.

exploitation of the settled area, a lower degree of mobility of the individual communities, greater emphasis on ard ploughing and a rise in the importance of animal husbandry. Although this development can only be traced sporadically in the archaeological record, it does constitute an alternative to the conventional invasion hypotheses of continental archaeology. However, the greatest limitation of the archaeological record is that most settlements are found on the second-rate soils of Jutland. The paucity of settlement finds on more benign soils calls the representativeness of the Jutland finds into question. Similarly it is most unfortunate that the subsistence strategy of the farming communities first comes into focus in the last thousand years of the period, when the strategy had already been transformed.

In any case, there seem to have been few major technological innovations during the third and second millennia BC. The introduction of metal technology around 2000 BC does not seem to have altered the subsistence strategy to any great degree. Metal was in demand not so

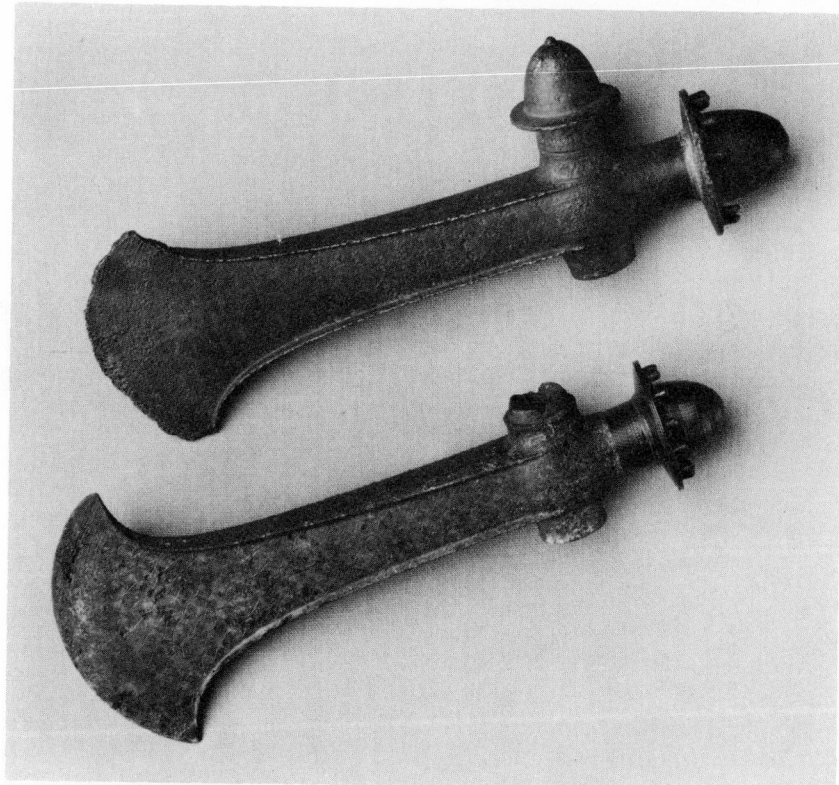

Figure 50 Ceremonial bronze axes, each weighing *c.* 7 kilos, found together at Egebak, Hjørring county.

much for its utilitarian merits as for its symbolic value as an indicator of status and wealth (Figure 50). Thus its effect on the socio-economic development of the farming communities was secondary. As will presently be shown, its importance lay in the reproduction of the social structure.

The exchange of goods and raw materials

In the hunter–gatherer societies of the Palaeolithic and Mesolithic periods, the exchange of certain raw materials already played an important role in defining social territories. Later, in the fourth millennium BC, when the first farming communities developed, the exchange of goods and raw materials became increasingly significant. During the following millennia a close correlation between exchange and the

development of ranking can be observed within the individual settlement areas in Denmark.

In all so-called primitive societies, goods and services are distributed
via institutional forms which may vary enormously. They may also be
incomprehensible from the viewpoint of modern economics. Economic
transactions are difficult to isolate in societies which have not yet
developed a market economy. It is a well-known fact that in such
societies an economic transaction is always the manifestation of an
underlying social relation such as friendship, kinship and political or
religious obligations. This implies that the exchange of goods and
services in a primitive society is normally a brief episode in a more
comprehensive social relationship. The study of the exchange of goods
is thus vital to the understanding of social organization in prehistoric
societies.

Already with the incipient development of ranked societies in Denmark in the course of the fourth millennium BC, a large-scale exchange of
goods took place. Flint from northern Jutland was distributed over large
areas of southern Scandinavia. Far-reaching exchange of amber also
began. In the most prosperous settlement regions, both amber and flint
played a prominent part in ranked contexts.

Around 2000 BC the exchange systems flourished. Amber turns up at
this time in central European finds. Just before the middle of the second
millennium BC its expansion culminated. Baltic amber now appeared as
far south as the Mediterranean in the Mycenaean shaft graves.

Concurrently metal objects circulated widely among the farming
communities in the north European lowland. Obviously some kind of
relationship bound the simultaneous development of metal technology,
the increased exchange of raw materials, and changes in societal
organization.

In Denmark the transformation around 2000 BC has often been
explained by the postulated invasion of the Single Grave people several
centuries earlier. It was thought that at the end of the third millennium
BC the two presumed ethnic groups merged so that the Single Grave
people formed an 'aristocratic warrior class' which owned the means of
production and controlled the interregional exchange (J. Brøndsted,
1957). Meanwhile a 'peasant class', the Funnel-Necked Beaker people,
were thought to have created the economic surplus by which the
supposed warrior class acquired imported metal. Thus the period
around 2000 BC was considered crucial in leading to a kind of 'feudal'
Bronze Age society.

This theory, which was modelled on the Viking period 3000
years later, was founded on the belief that history develops cyclically.

Consequently Bronze Age society was attributed with institutional forms which were in fact foreign to its social structure. Recently, though, many Danish archaeologists have sought other paths. The new concepts employed may lead to a more realistic evaluation of the processes underlying the exchange systems of the third to the first millennia BC.

Concepts of exchange

The theoretical framework used here to describe the basic principles of distribution in primitive society was proposed by economist Karl Polanyi. His three basic concepts of economic life are 1) reciprocity, in which goods and services are exchanged between equal partners without the use of money; 2) redistribution, in which goods and services are brought to a centre from which they are redistributed; and 3) market economy, in which the exchange of goods is regulated by prices varying according to supply and demand. Often these principles exist simultaneously in the same system. The dominant principle is determined by the level of production in the individual society.

Older studies discussing the exchange of goods in the Danish Bronze Age often employ concepts more or less directly derived from a market economy. This is due to the explanation models which have been used to describe socio-economic development in the Bronze Age. The use of concepts originating in later historical periods ignores the fact that a market economy is always related to economic specialization and regional divisions of labour which again are stimulated by the demands of urban centres. As with reciprocity and redistribution, a market economy can be described as a means of distributing surplus. But in contrast to the other exchange forms, the market principle is a brief profit-controlled and socially non-obligating form of exchange. Furthermore it is often (but not always) connected with the centralized authority which lies in the formation of the state. In fact, one of the primary functions of centralized authority is to ensure unhindered transportation within the territory.

This latter function has often been ignored in Scandinavian literature on prehistoric trade. Where administration is weak, unhindered transportation can hardly be relied upon. Moreover, the presence of 'markets' or 'market-places' does not necessarily mean that the market principle has been in function. Reciprocity and redistribution may just as well have created these centres of trade.

The extent to which goods were exchanged during the third to the first millennia BC is still little known. However, it seems likely that foodstuffs were inconsequential both as internal and as external ex-change. The bulk of goods exchanged probably consisted of objects such as raw materials, craft products and foreign prestige goods which were needed for cementing social relations and competitions between different descent groups.

The relationship between the production and circulation of goods on the one hand and prehistoric socio-economic development on the other hand can best be understood by a more general theory dealing with so-called prestige-goods economies. Several modern studies have pointed out a number of socio-economic consequences of control over access to resources obtained through external trade (M.D. Sahlins, 1963, 1965, 1968, 1974; R.A. Rappaport, 1968; K. Ekholm, 1972; J. Friedman and M.J. Rowlands, 1978; S. Frankenstein and M.J. Rowlands, 1978). Neolithic flint and amber trade has been examined in the light of just such a model. This model helps explain some of the typical features of the development in northern Europe from the fourth millennium BC onward.

The earliest stage in this process has already been discussed (see p. 103 ff). Here we saw how an incipient control of the exchange of raw materials and prestige goods could have demographic consequences resulting within a larger area in a differential growth in size and dominance of the various groups. In the long run, this could lead to the emergence of chiefdoms. This is probably what happened at the end of the third millennium BC in several regions of the north European lowland.

At this stage the élite of the emergent chiefdoms may have reinforced their control over the circulation of goods by limiting the use of domestic goods and replacing them with foreign wealth objects. The growing circulation of bronze weapons, ornaments and implements, along with the expanding amber trade from the beginning of the second millennium BC, is here seen in this light. Most probably the numerous wealth objects (Figures 51 and 52) reflect complex sumptuary rules in north European Bronze Age society. A redistributive economic system was now evolving, causing domestic goods to be filtered up through the system in the form of tribute. These goods were used by the élite for external exchanges by which foreign prestige goods or craft products were attained. The foreign goods were then redistributed, serving as bride wealth, funerary goods, status insignias, etc.

Accelerating attempts to regulate the circulation of wealth objects were also manifest in the growth of specialist skills such as metal-casting. Specialized workshops made it easier for the élite to control production of status symbols. This probably explains the existence of highly skilled

Figure 51 Wealth objects, weapons, and ornaments from the Early Bronze Age, Montelius period II.

Figure 52 Wealth objects, weapons, and ornaments from the Early Bronze Age, Montelius period III.

bronze craftsmanship in Denmark around the mid-second millennium BC.

According to the more general theory an equilibrium may occur at this stage. And in fact this does seem to be the case in southern Scandinavia in the second millennium BC. Despite fluctuations in the quantity of bronze coming into Denmark, this equilibrium presumably prevailed over the next thousand years. Around 500 BC, however, the influx of foreign prestige goods shrank remarkably. Some sort of crisis must have shaken the formerly so stable exchange system.

The case of amber

The exchange of amber is a revealing example of the magnitude which the exchange of goods could attain during the Neolithic and Bronze Age of northern Europe. The concept of an 'amber trade' as well as of 'amber routes' is one of the oldest notions of European archaeology and has played a tremendous part in the diffusionist theories of earlier generations. In recent years, however, the analytical work of the American chemist Curt W. Beck has clarified a number of hitherto unsolved problems related to the distribution of the so-called Baltic amber. Using infra-red spectroscopy, Beck has demonstrated that a great deal of the amber from central and southern Europe in the Bronze Age and the early Iron Age is of 'Baltic' origin. By 'Baltic amber' is meant amber derived from natural deposits extending from Britain in the west to the Soviet Union in the east. Although more precise origins cannot be pinpointed, the results unequivocally show that central and south European amber was not local but had a northern origin. The archaeological record confirms that from the end of the third millennium BC north European amber was disseminated ever further southwards by means of a vast network.

As already mentioned, amber distribution before 2000 BC was restricted to more closed exchange systems along the North Sea and the Baltic. However, the launching of bronze technology in northern Europe (around 2000 BC) radically altered this situation. Baltic amber now turned up as an indicator of wealth in rich burials far from its origin: in Brittany, southern Britain, central Germany and Poland. At the same time amber finds vanish from the Baltic zone. Through subsequent millennia the graves and sacrificial deposits of Denmark, southern Sweden and the coastal regions along the southern part of the Baltic contain remarkably little amber.

There are many indications that this shift in the distribution pattern was linked to the flourishing metal import in the north. Throughout the second and most of the first millennia BC bronze objects in northern Europe were prized first and foremost as prestige indicators. The usefulness of metal was clearly secondary. As will later be shown, analysis of the quantity of imported metal in Danish Bronze Age graves clearly proves the simultaneous rise of ranking within the agrarian communities. Nevertheless throughout the Baltic zone, amber seems to only a very minor degree to have been used in a ranked context. Instead it was channelled into the far-reaching network of trade relations by which the coveted metal was obtained.

Amber which was gathered along the coasts was treasured in the north. Minute quantities of amber may be found in otherwise richly equipped graves from the second millennium BC. Magical powers were attributed to amber, as is often shown by its find context. Outside the Baltic zone, amber appears chiefly in the wealthiest graves. Thus along with other treasures, amber spread by means of the élite. This sort of exchange, which was probably carried out via prestige chains, most logically explains the distribution pattern around the mid-second millennium BC. At this time the quantity of amber in central and southern Europe reached a peak, and concurrently there seems to have been a culmination of wealth over much of the Baltic zone.

South of the Baltic, amber can be traced, often in conjunction with glass beads, in rich graves from Mecklenburg and downwards to southern Germany, eastern France and the mouth of the Rhône. Perhaps this latter area controlled the final distribution to such élite as those buried in the Mycenaean shaft graves, the amber beads of which have been identified by infra-red spectroscopy as Baltic.

These hypothetical prestige chains traversed Europe to the Mediterranean, where contact may have been established with freelance traders from the Mycenaean cultural area (C. Renfrew, 1972). Thus the wide distribution not only of amber but also of many other prestige goods can be explained. Most likely such exchanges took place among centres prospering from control of foreign goods.

This was probably also the case at the end of the eighth century BC and up to the fifth century BC. A strong socio-economic development within central Europe bolstered distribution. The prestige-goods economy which evolved around the north Balkan and central European chiefdoms in the early Iron Age must have played a critical role in maintaining a vast trade network. However, turmoil in the Mediterranean area at the end of the fifth century BC caused profound disturbances within the central European chiefdoms, which depended heavily upon the influx of foreign prestige goods (S. Frankenstein and M.J. Rowlands, 1978). And as a result of this unrest, the flow of amber from the north dried up. Not until central European urban manufacturing centres arose at the end of the second century BC did conditions for large-scale trading of amber again develop.

External and internal exchange up to 500 BC

Our overall view of the exchange of goods in the so-called Single Grave period is still indistinct, due in part to the striking imbalance of the archaeological record. Even so, we know that amber and flint were widely distributed in this period as elements in a status-motivated exchange manifest above all in male graves and to a lesser degree in female graves.

After 2400 BC, in the Late Neolithic, the exchange of goods was intensified. Status symbols in the male graves were now daggers and spears. These weapons bear witness to far-reaching contacts from southern Scandinavia northwards. Probably, the hundreds of daggers as well as sickles and other flint implements found along the Norwegian west coast were produced in northern Jutland. The most distant outposts of this diffusion are in the Swedish Norrland. However, the greatest abundance of items appears in Denmark. This corresponds to the demand created by the rise of ranking in the late Neolithic communities.

Around 2000 BC metal objects went into circulation and slowly supplanted flint in the exchange system. Metal weapons and implements from western and central Europe in particular increased. Prestige objects from the central and upper Danube region were channelled through the extensive exchange system all the way up to Denmark. Throughout the second millennium and up to about 500 BC, this great net of contacts ensured an ample influx of metal objects to southern Scandinavia. Subsequently trade was disrupted, as will be seen in the next chapter.

Metal objects were apparently exchanged in the form of finished goods; the Danish finds include no metal ingots. However, metal objects were only some of the goods used for exchange. Other commodities probably included leather wares, wax (for bronze-casting), honey, salt, textiles and many other things. But only objects of bronze, gold and pottery are preserved in the archaeological record.

A remarkable feature of the exchange system is that the majority of central European metal objects belonged to the man's sphere. Weapons and tools are clearly predominant (Figure 53). Women's ornaments rarely seem to have been exchanged. The man's sphere probably also encompassed the important group of beaten bronze cups and buckets.

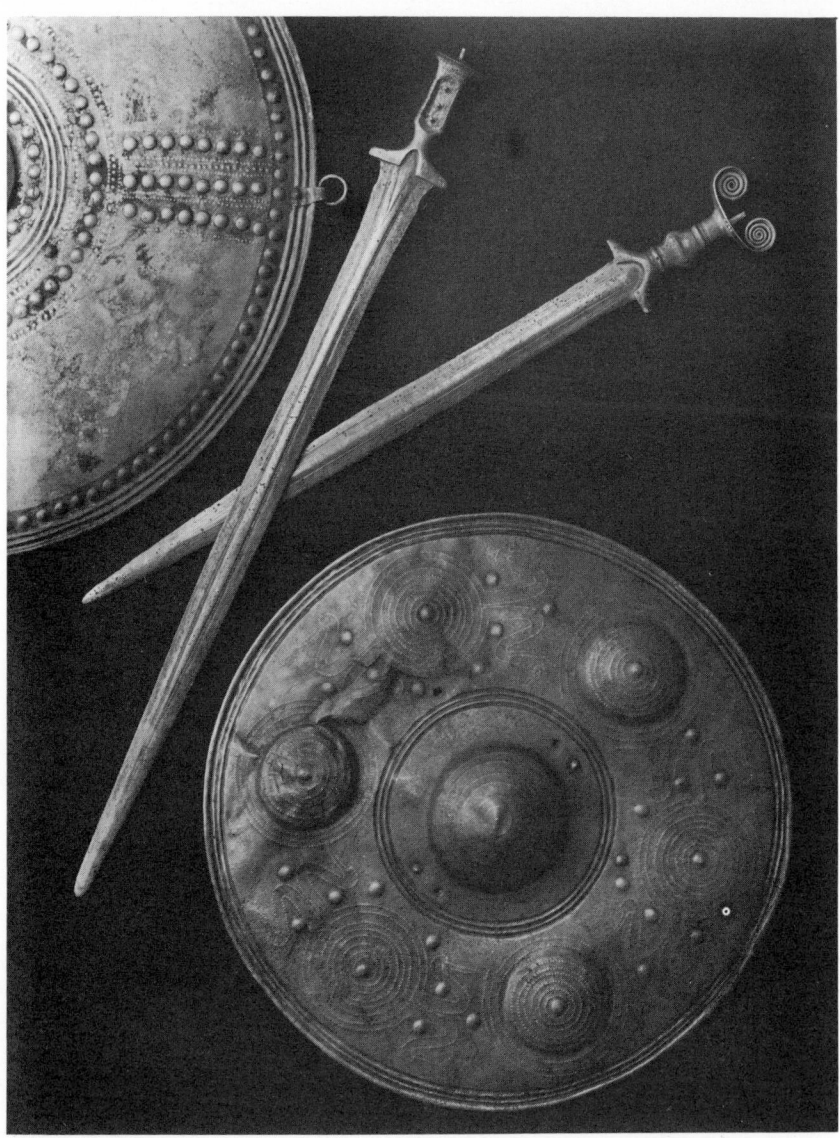

Figure 53 Imported central European bronze shields and swords from the Late Bronze Age. The shield to the left is from Sørup, Ålborg county, the one to the right is of unknown provenance. The sword to the left is from Sønderup, Sorø county, the one to the right from Østerå, Vejle county.

Like other foreign goods, these ought to be interpreted as prestige objects used by the élite. The cups and buckets were probably drinking equipment which functioned in ritual contexts (Figure 54). Although they are primarily found in the so-called votive finds in peat bogs, in certain cases they also figure in the graves of people with high social status.

However, the bronze objects produced outside southern Scandinavia and parts of northern Germany constitute but a limited part of the overall exchange of goods. Far more intensive was the exchange of local so-called Nordic bronzes: weapons, implements and ornaments made in the north of bronze from central Europe. From the beginning of the second millennium BC a uniform art style – which especially characterized the specialized bronze workshops – bound the southern Scandinavian–northern German area. Within this social territory a lively exchange of status objects, craft products and probably also raw materials took place. But in contrast to the circulation of foreign goods, this geographically restricted exchange also embraced objects from both the male and the female sphere. Women's ornaments were scattered

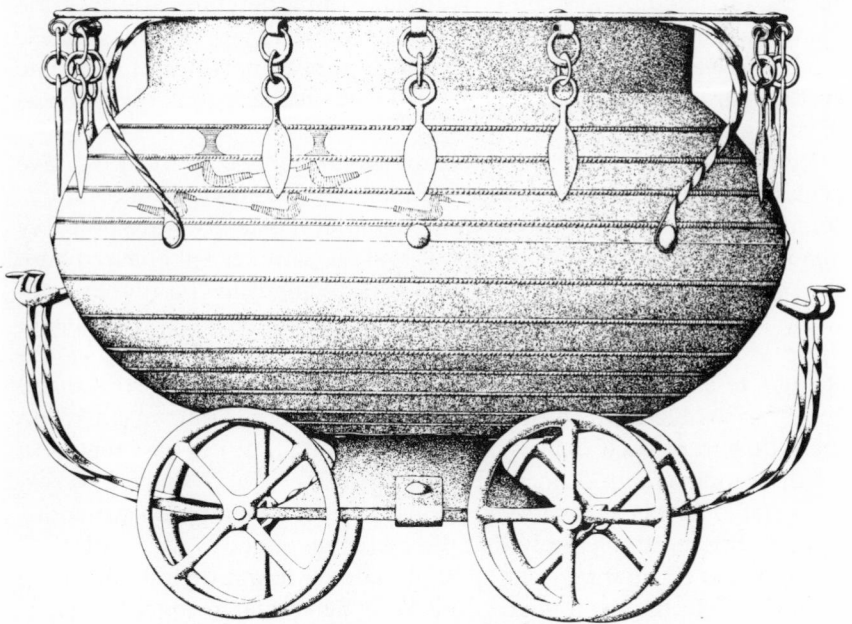

Figure 54 Wheeled bronze cauldron, probably meant for ritual purposes, found in a richly equipped Early Bronze Age grave (Montelius period III) at Skallerup, southern Zealand.

throughout the aforementioned region as widely as, for example, weapons.

Notwithstanding the abundance of evidence for the exchange of goods and raw materials between 2800–500 BC, we are still left with innumerable unsolved problems. However, detailed studies of the provenance of metal objects and the composition of, for example, the votive finds – the so-called hoards – have definitely refuted most older theories of the Bronze Age 'long-distance trade'. The context in which foreign goods are found in Denmark clearly opposes the idea of direct transport via traders from central Europe to the Baltic area. Similarly, older theories of the amber trade and related hypothetical long-distance trade routes crossing the European continent must be rejected. As yet, only few exchange centres have been located. However, several combined archaeological and topographical studies carried out in Denmark have given encouraging results. A survey on the island of Funen has revealed an impressive concentration of wealth in the late Bronze Age. Immense and richly furnished barrows in the Voldtofte region (H. Thrane, 1976) clearly betoken a political and economic centre which must have played a key role in the exchange of prestige goods around 800 BC. A contemporary centre is found in Brandenburg, south of the Baltic, in the Seddin region (H. Wüstemann, 1974). Doubtless these localities were vital nodes in the north European network of exchange systems through which goods travelled vast distances, linking the élites of the agrarian societies.

Diverse ways of interpreting the exchange of goods up to 500 BC have been proposed. Different degrees of hierarchization within the various communities – as yet of unknown geographical extent – were probably manifest in a redistributive economic system. This system ensured both the production of specialized products (as evident in the fine bronzework) and the continuous circulation of goods and services. Externally, these societies practised manifold forms of reciprocity, such as exchange, to cement relationships. Kinship alliances, bride purchase and similar exchange forms observed by the upper social strata may explain the diffusion of such objects as bronzes throughout the vast region of south Scandinavia and north Germany.

As stable as this system seems to have been, geographical variations through the centuries imply that the exchange of goods was controlled by centres of fluctuating political importance. Around the middle of the second millennium BC foreign goods were by and large concentrated in west Denmark. Most of the imports derived from south Germany. The prominent nodal centre in the exchange network encompassed the areas around the mouth of the Elbe and Schleswig-Holstein. From here, foreign goods travelled primarily to western Denmark and to a lesser degree to Zealand. Gold too is mainly found in the west. This implies that the goods carried to Denmark from Schleswig-Holstein came via the Weser region with the Lüneburg area as an important station towards southern Germany.

This pattern endured up to the end of the second millennium BC. Slowly it was replaced by a new pattern, according to which a centre in Mecklenburg controlled the influx of prestige goods from Europe. Much of this influx was still channelled to Denmark, but gradually an alternative network to east Denmark and south Sweden was building up. This eastward shift culminated around 1000 BC when connections from east Denmark over the Baltic to the mouth of the Oder River can be distinctly seen in the archaeological record. These connections also seem to have conducted quantities of southern European gold into Denmark.

The centres south of the Baltic have not yet been localized, although Mecklenburg and the regions south of the knee of the Elbe are known to have been crucial nodes in the network. From here, central European goods were also channelled to west Denmark.

Centuries later the same centres still functioned and the eastern parts of Denmark continued to receive most of the central European prestige goods. A more western-oriented exchange system with contacts to Jutland seems to have existed concurrently, although it was of minor economic significance compared to the eastern network. As late as the mid-first millennium BC both of these networks seem to have been intact, but new connections were established to the Polish Baltic regions. However, at that time the northward flow of metal objects was drying up and around 500 BC it seems to have ceased entirely.

Fluctuations in the import of bronze are also reflected in the circulation time of the prestige goods. Variations in circulation time can be observed from wear analysis of the bronzes (K. Kristiansen, 1978b) and in external supplies. This situation is particularly obvious around the middle of the first millennium BC, when socio-economic changes swept central Europe as a result of contact with Mediterranean civilizations which tapped the central and northern European exchange network for certain goods. These changes will be examined in the next chapter.

13

Social patterns from 2800 to 500 BC

During the fourth millennium BC, the growing complexity in production and the consequent need for co-ordination laid the foundations for a rudimentary form of ranking in the early farming communities of Denmark. These tendencies emerged distinctly at the end of the fourth and the beginning of the third millennia BC. Obviously there was now a decided emphasis on vertical relations within the communities. Through the following millennia, this emphasis became more pronounced as a result of attempts at augmenting productivity. There were severe restraints on these attempts. As the socio-economic system permitted only a slight differentiation of production, the agrarian society from 2800 to 500 BC was fairly static.

As shown in the foregoing chapter on the settlement and subsistence pattern during this period, the archaeological record – particularly that from the third millennium BC in Denmark – suffers from many critical gaps. None the less there is reason to presume that single households merged into more complex village communities as early as the third millennium BC. Throughout the period we find impressive monuments which must have demanded large-scale co-operation within the village communities. The most striking examples are the thousands of Bronze Age barrows. These barrows must have mobilized an enormous amount of labour, organized by the élite of the farming communities. In contrast to the large central sites from the fourth millennium BC this sort of mobilization indicates a more person-oriented cult. This corresponds to our impression of socio-economic development, at least from the second millennium BC.

The archaeological record from the period 2800–500 BC indicates that there existed a far-reaching exchange system ever more firmly based upon a redistributive economy within the various local regions. Thus it has been presumed that the various communities gradually became so thoroughly integrated that they developed into chiefdoms, a more complex form of the ranked type of tribal society from previous centuries. Chiefdoms are typified by 'specialization and redistribution; they are no longer merely adjunctive to a few particular endeavours, but continuously characterize a large part of the activity of the society' (E.R. Service, 1971).

Chiefdoms, however, are still recognized by the variations in rank which are the primary means to social integration. At the top of the hierarchy is the chieftain. His role is to redistribute: to plan, organize and deploy public labour and to be responsible for system-preserving religious functions. The chieftain's authority ensures integration among the various groups. Descent in relation to the chieftain normally decides the relative position of individuals and kin groups within the community.

It is also significant that even in the developed ranked society which seems to have existed in Denmark throughout the Bronze Age, social control must have been based upon enculturation and internalized sanction. Late in the existence of the prehistoric chiefdoms, during the Iron Age, mechanisms for adjudicating and enforcing more formal rules of social control were developed. This, then, is the social and political framework of the chiefdom level of organization to which Danish society belonged from about 2800 to 500 BC. A parallel development apparently took place throughout much of northern and central Europe.

Concerning the archaeological evidence of the settlement and subsistence patterns from 2800 to 500 BC, only a few conclusions can be drawn regarding the social organization of the farming communities. The grave finds, though, can provide more detailed insight into the social sphere. As mentioned, the graves can to some extent help determine the relative population density within the various regions of the country. The question which arises is, how representative are the graves as reflectors of social stratification? Danish archaeological literature often suggests that the graves of the Bronze Age in particular compose a representative sample of the entire population. This claim has been challenged in recent years but final conclusions are difficult to draw because skeletons are rarely preserved. In most graves, the sex of the deceased can be identified by the accompanying artefacts, although some small objects are common to both sexes. Between 2800 and 500 BC, male graves outnumbered female graves; children's graves are very rare. Obviously, then, the graves cannot be representative of the population as a whole. For the so-called Single Grave culture (2800–2400 BC), 75 per cent of the approximately 500 graves known in Denmark are male graves, to judge by the grave-goods. The Late Neolithic period (2400–1800 BC) also seems to exhibit a dominance of male graves. Unfortunately no usable calculations for this period have been made. But for the subsequent period, the Early Bronze Age (up to *c.* 1000 BC), detailed studies do exist. Out of a total of roughly 1000 graves, female graves are only half as common as male graves; children's graves are almost non-existent. The number of female graves and their contents seems to be based upon the relative population size and is thus decided by regional and chronological conditions. In the second half of the Bronze Age (1000–500 BC) identification is hindered by the introduction of cremation and the general paucity of grave goods. Very few analyses of cremated bones from the urn graves of the Late Bronze Age have been made.

We can therefore conclude that the grave finds hardly constitute a representative sample of the general population but are defined by various cultural norms, most of them related to the social status of the dead. A formalized grave cult can betoken the cause of death, place of death, age, sex, social position, group membership, and so on. More general social anthropological studies of societies which have not reached the state level (L.R. Binford, 1971) have shown that there is often a connection between the degree of social complexity and the quantity of symbolizing factors. There is therefore good reason to suppose that essential features of the social organization would be reflected in the Danish graves from about 2800 to 500 BC.

As yet, very few studies have been made of the distribution of wealth and status symbols in the graves of that period. The four centuries of the so-called Single Grave culture are further obscured by the very uneven geographic distribution of the grave finds. It is known that polished flint axes are replaced by battle axes as status symbols. Battle axes now appear in about half of the known graves. Around 2400 BC the flint dagger replaced the battle axe as the male status symbol (Figure 55).

Around 1800 BC the farming communities gradually began to integrate imported metal into their grave rites. It thus becomes possible to make quantitative evaluations of the distribution of mortuary wealth. Recent studies within this field have offered promising results for the Early Bronze Age (1800–1000 BC) (K. Randsborg, 1973, 1974b and c).

These studies have been based upon the assumption that the amount of metal in the graves of the period can be taken as an index for social stratification. Gold and bronze objects from about 1000 Danish Bronze Age graves were weighed and the ratio in value between the two metals was determined by various quantitative experiments to about 1:100. As an example, Figure 59 shows the distribution of bronze within the groups of male and female graves in the Bronze Age period II, i.e. two or

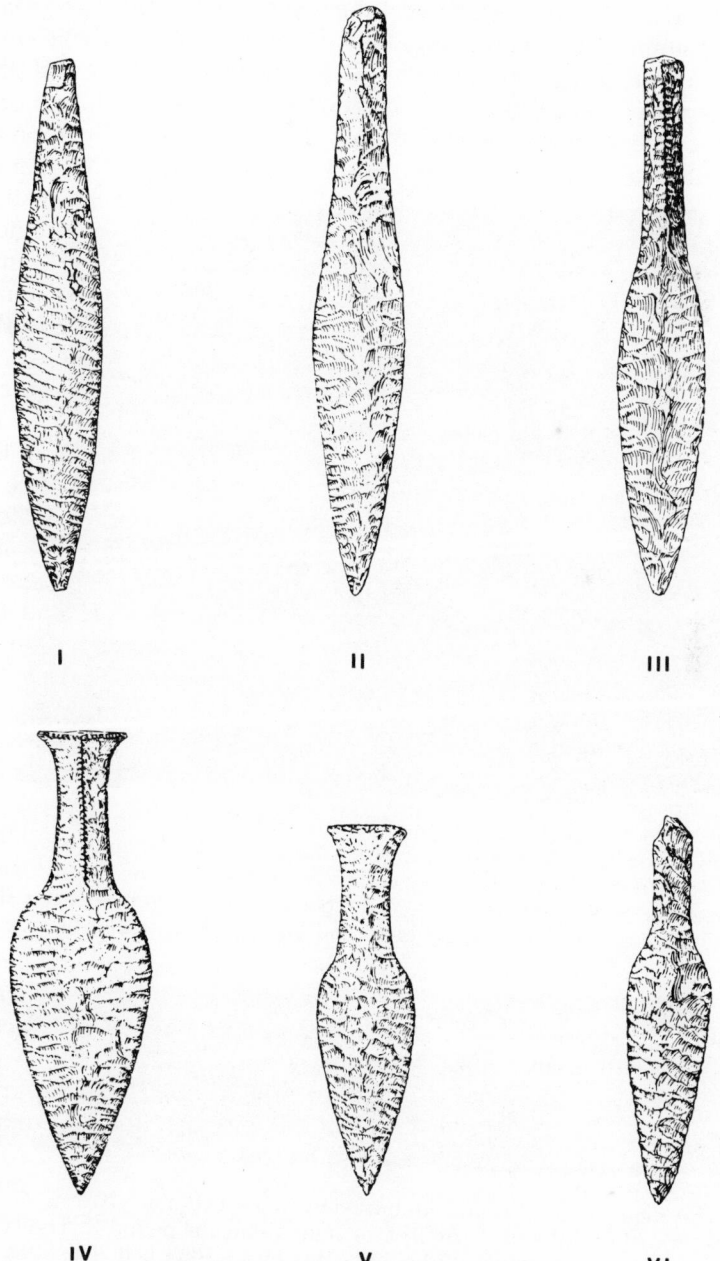

I II III

IV V VI

Figure 55 Typology of the Danish flint daggers. Types I–V are Late Neolithic; type VI belongs exclusively to the Early Bronze Age.

three centuries around the mid-second millennium BC. Male graves are seen to be abundant and more elaborate than female graves (Figures 56 and 57). In both groups, poor graves predominate. From these observations a series of conclusions have been drawn.

In the course of the second millennium BC a society emerged in which

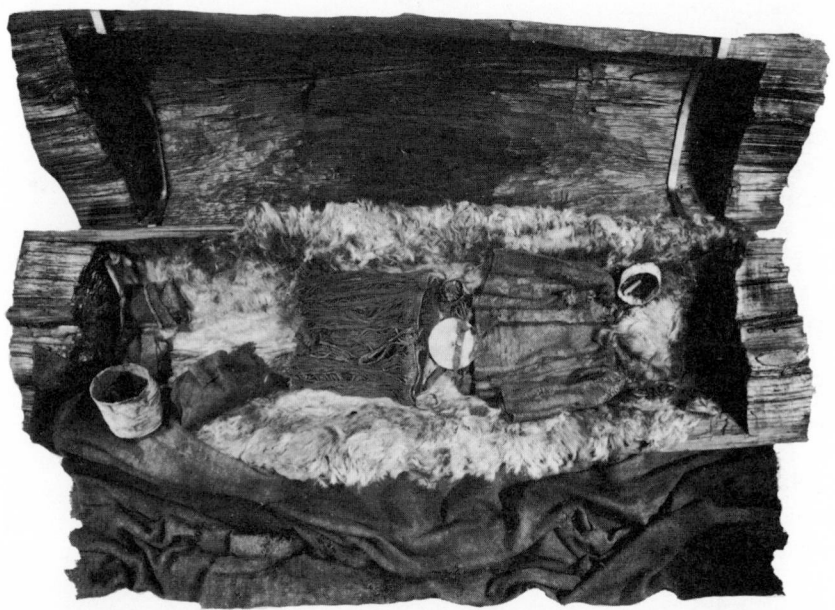

Figure 56 A woman, about 18–20 years old, buried in an oak coffin in a barrow at Egtved, Jutland. Early Bronze Age, Montelius period II. The body was found fully dressed on a cowhide in the coffin. A shirt with elbow-length sleeves covered the upper part of the woman's body. She also wore a string skirt. Before the coffin was closed the body had been covered with a blanket.

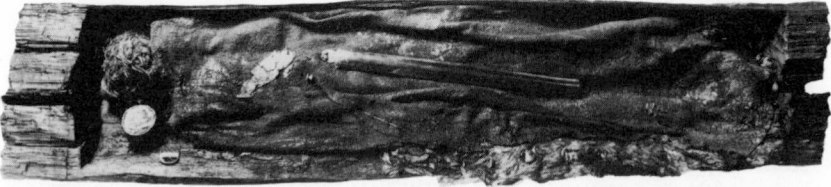

Figure 57 A man, about 20 years old, buried in an oak coffin in a barrow, Borum Eshøj, in eastern Jutland. Early Bronze Age, Montelius period II. The young man was dressed in a loincloth held together by a leather belt. The body had been laid on a cowhide and covered with a woollen cloak. A sword scabbard containing only a little bronze dagger was found on the cloak.

wealth and status were distributed unequally. The graves hold both men and women from the upper stratum of society who, in contrast to the 'commoners', were buried with mortuary gifts of costly metal objects and, at least as regards the men, with wealth objects which can be interpreted as symbols of permanent status positions. It is also possible to observe great but graded distinctions in wealth and status in the graves of both men and women. The graves of high-ranking men contain the personal equipment of the dead, their magnificent weapons and sometimes their work axes. The poorer male graves contain merely a knife each. Gold objects appear chiefly in the rich graves, which also frequently contain objects of symbolic character and which thus can be interpreted as signs of authority. Such objects include folding stools (Figure 58), wooden bowls, staves and badges with metal mountings, and similar objects which are virtually absent from the poorer graves. In the graves of high-ranking women, these presumed symbols of authority are very rare – here high social position is betokened by heavy bronze ornaments and daggers.

The male–female status relationship is implied by the quantitative distribution of the graves. There are usually only half as many high-status female graves as graves containing men of similar rank (Figure 59). In general, the men are clearly superior as regards status positions. Yet the social hierarchy as a whole shows no sharp contrasts. The gap between rich and poor in the agrarian society was hardly wide. It is possible to link the high-status women to the richer half of the men

Figure 58 Folding stool, probably a status symbol, found in
   an oak-coffin grave at Guldhøj, southern Jutland.

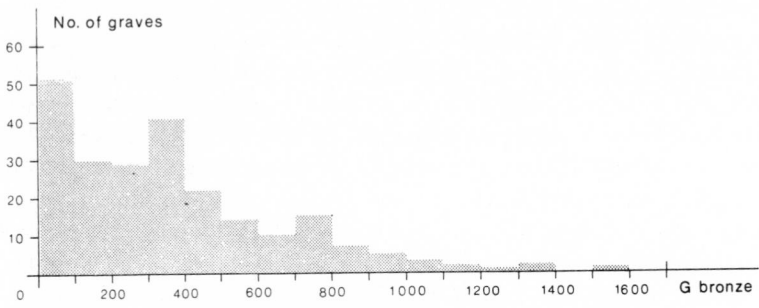

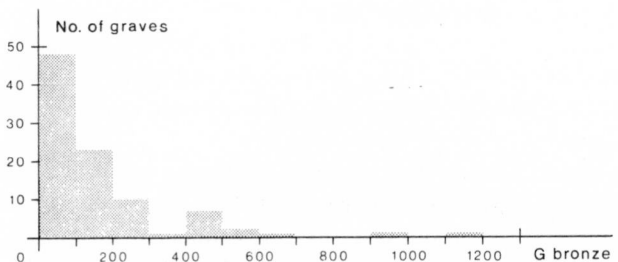

Figure 59 Histogram indicating the amounts of bronze found in men's graves (above) and women's graves (below) during period II (Montelius) of the Early Bronze Age.

represented in the barrows (Figure 60). Consequently the rest of the high-ranking men must have been related to 'commoners', to women whose status was not indicated by the mortuary rituals. The system has therefore been interpreted as a graduated system characteristic of the kinship-based chiefdoms.

Towards the end of the second millennium BC, a new mortuary practice can be discerned. Status symbols are now rarely invested in the graves. Instead the metal objects are laid in sacrificial deposits, the so-called 'hoards'. This shift coincides by and large with a transition from inhumation graves to cremation. Throughout the first millennium BC graves are not particularly helpful as indicators of social ranking. However, the graves still give a profile of the relative population density in various parts of Denmark (Figure 42).

Over the first millennium BC, as the graves decreased in value as indicators of social inequality, the hoards instead took over the role as investments of objects denoting the social status of the owner(s). These objects were chiefly massive bronze ornaments and weapons. The plentiful group of such finds may thus be considered the remains of a

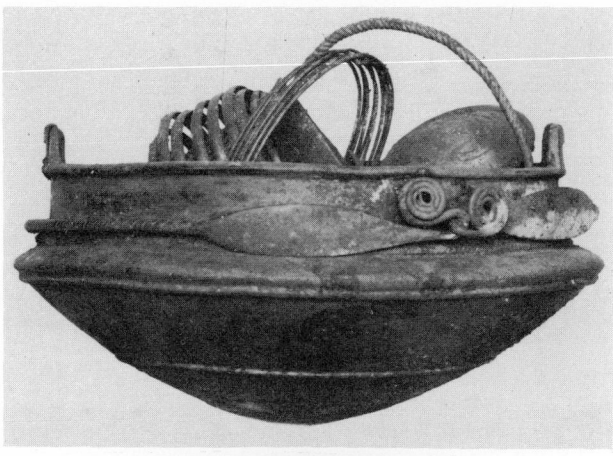

Figure 60 The hoards from the Late Bronze Age are most often found in wetlands such as bogs or meadows. A hoard may consist of one or two complete sets of women's ornaments, as was the case in this period V hoard which was found at Kertinge Mark on the island of Funen.

so-called social production withdrawal system (W.L. Rathje, 1975), in which the social élite transformed wealth into prestige by forcing large quantities of precious metal out of circulation – quite simply by depositing the metal at remote spots, never to be retrieved. The underlying idea must have been that the withdrawal of wealth served to legitimize the hierarchical order and authority of the élite.

Sacrificial deposits constitute one of the richest find groups from the period. This group includes primarily ornaments, tools and weapons. Deposits might consist of complete sets of women's ornaments or of several identical objects such as swords. The find group also includes countless single bronze objects which, like the composite finds, are often found in swampy areas or by large stones.

It is not easy to categorize the sacrificial deposits according to their content. All conceivable combinations of objects are found. The crucial factor for deposition seems to have been the value of the metal. Deposits were usually made on the fringes of a settlement, for example in the swampy lands separating the territories of the villages. With the decline of bronze imports to the north about 500 BC, the amount of bronze deposited dwindles, but sacrificial deposits were still made by the farming communities up to the birth of Christ.

The importance of sacrificial finds in the first half of the first millennium BC seems to be based on a cult focused on authority positions. Along with the personal possessions earlier deposited in the graves, sacrificial deposits now often included ritual objects which must have been related to the élite's practice of rituals: lurs, drinking sets with golden bowls and religious symbols such as figurines.

Throughout the second and most of the first millennia BC, religious symbolism was surprisingly uniform, as was, no doubt, the mythology which integrated each farming community. This homogeneity applied both geographically and chronologically. Many mythological motifs of the north European Bronze Age, such as the ship, the chariot of the sun, the fish and the horse (Figure 61), survived largely unchanged for more than a thousand years. Their dissemination throughout the north European lowland exemplifies the lively communication which existed from region to region.

The investment of wealth in mortuary rituals diminished during the first millennium BC. This decline, along with the predominant custom of cremation, makes it necessary for us to develop new methods to demonstrate social stratification in Bronze Age Denmark. In any case, it is certain that great social inequality still existed, as·seen both by the sacrificial deposits and here and there also by the grave finds. Towards the close of the period, around 800 BC, a sizeable population concentration can be observed, on southern Funen for example. The population density here apparently necessitated advanced social stratification. Rich graves increased in number; some of the most imposing barrows of the period are also found here. To erect Lusehøj, the largest barrow in the

Figure 61 Ship motifs engraved on razors from the Late Bronze Age, Montelius periods IV–V.

Voldtofte area, about 3200 cubic metres of turf were required, which meant that 7 hectares of land had to be stripped. These monuments were erected over graves in which the social status of the dead was displayed by a rich equipment of wagons and drinking vessels – status symbols similar in character to those known from the hoards.

Through studies of the investment of wealth in graves and hoards, a picture emerges of the social organization from 2800 to 500 BC. These studies have uncovered the evolutionary potential of the farming communities along with some of the systematic variability in the operative cultural, biological and physical factors. Here and there are indications of a connection between population growth and increased social stratification. Social inequalities seem to have kept pace with population density, as a consequence of the demands created by the expansion and distribution of production. Similarly, the ratio between male and female status seems to have depended upon the same factors. As a working hypothesis it may be presumed that the position of a man was affected by the size of the male-dominated stock-raising, whereas a woman's status was related to the extent of field work. The archaeological record has provided some indications in this direction but more thorough studies are required as proof.

Although the archaeological record is meagre, it still confirms a relationship among the operative cultural, biological and physical factors. From an economic viewpoint, the bond between increased production and enhanced authority indicates that, as already suggested, redistributive and reciprocal economic patterns dominated in the settlement units. Analyses of the exchange system, mortuary rituals and sacrificial deposits make it probable that at the end of the third millennium BC the farming communities attained the chiefdom level of socio-cultural integration. A leading characteristic of the chiefdoms was that they were founded upon the so-called social production withdrawal system, in which the élite demonstrated its status by a tremendous mobilization of labour, such as that invested in the mortuary practices and by a correspondingly large consumption of exotic materials such as gold and bronze in the grave cult and sacrificial rites.

As regards religious practices, society at this time presumably witnessed the introduction of permanent religious positions. In a chiefdom society, these priestly offices are often passed down in a family line just as secular offices are; in fact, the 'priest' and the 'chieftain' are often one and the same person. Judging by both sacrificial deposits and graves, this situation is likely to have endured over more than one thousand years of the Bronze Age.

So far, the evolution of agrarian society from the third to the first millennia BC has been revealed in brief glimpses only. The most striking feature is that the communities seem to have been so static. Yet there is some evidence that, particularly from the end of the second millennium BC, larger concentrations of population developed in certain regions of Denmark, where the emphasis on vertical social relations also increased. One example is from south-western Funen around 800 BC, where the concentration of wealth and population was manifest in the erection of some of the most remarkable structures of the period. It is, however, peculiar that these concentrations were so short-lived. Several generations later they seem to have been dissolved. Apparently the area still offered potential for an expansion of settlement.

14
Finds and interpretations

The archaeological record covering the period *c*. 2800–500 BC falls into three categories: 1) settlements; 2) graves; and 3) sacrificial finds and hoards. In addition there are a number of other categories of finds such as roads, flint mines, etc.

Settlements. Of the above-named find categories, that of settlements at present constitutes the major area of concentration. Danish archaeology has a long tradition of settlement excavations. Already in the 1920s large-scale excavations of prehistoric villages had been carried out. At that time the primary goal was to excavate house sites so as to ascertain the function and construction of the individual house. But after the Second World War new methods were developed, such as the mechanical uncoverage of larger areas. Village communities could now be studied in their entirety.

However, settlement excavations have mainly been devoted to single prehistoric periods. The Iron Age in particular has been the focus of numerous large projects, whereas Bronze Age villages were first excavated in the 1960s. From the so-called Single Grave period and the Late Neolithic, about 2800–1800 BC, very few settlement sites have been excavated. The same holds true of the Early Bronze Age, about 1800–1000 BC. Starting from the Late Bronze Age, *c*. 1000–500 BC, enough excavations have been made to create a more distinct impression of the settlement structure in the farming communities.

The chronological imbalance of the Danish material is supplemented by a geographical one. Most of the excavations have been made on the light sandy soils of west Denmark. Here modern agricultural activity began rather late. Thus this is the region offering the best opportunities for making relatively undisturbed finds. In eastern Denmark there is still a dearth of settlement finds from most periods.

But serious dangers threaten. To be sure, all prehistoric monuments in Denmark are protected by the law for the protection of nature, ancient monuments and sites, which permits the temporary halt of constructional work for the purpose of carrying out archaeological investigations. But settlements especially are endangered by modern types of agricultural machines. Formerly the normal ploughing depth of a tractor-pulled plough was about 30–40 centimetres. The same layer of mould was turned year after year, and the plough did not reach layers which might contain undisturbed traces of prehistoric activity. But since the 1960s many farmers have introduced new types of ploughs which cut far deeper, thus disturbing the previously untouched layer of virgin soil. As a result, a multitude of settlement finds have been reported, far more than archaeologists have the capacity to investigate. This technological development is one of the factors which has compelled archaeologists to employ more efficient methods of excavation.

In many cases settlements have been localized from the air, as the rather homogeneous Danish countryside is well suited for air reconnaissance. But most frequently settlements are recognized when dark soil, charcoal and potsherds are brought up to the surface by ploughing. A trial excavation is then often initiated, and if promising results are obtained a major excavation may be launched. A tractor shovel scrapes off the upper layer of dark ploughed mould, thus uncovering a large area of light subsoil which the plough could not reach. Often up to 2000 m^2 can be excavated in a week. In some places settlement traces covering up to 100,000 m^2 have been investigated.

It is important to realize that the vestiges of a typical prehistoric settlement in Denmark consist merely of the bottom layers of the settlement. Preserved pavings, floors and hearths are rare. All such house traces have usually been removed by ploughing long before. Potsherds and other objects from the settlement are very few, as they have also been destroyed by ploughing. The 'finds' are thus merely vague dark discolourations in the subsoil which represent the bottom of the pits into which the house posts were rammed. Even so, these bare traces are often sufficient to permit determination of the size, shape and basic constructional details of a house.

The earliest settlement studies were carried out as early as the turn of the century (S. Müller, 1904). Bronze Age settlement studies were taken up at the end of the 1960s on the basis of earlier excavations (J. Jensen, 1967a) and newer investigations (H. Thrane, 1971, 1973b; C.J. Becker, 1968c and e, 1976; B. Stjernqvist, 1969). Even so, no definite conclusions were reached as to the settlement form of the era. More recently a goal-oriented research initiative has improved this picture. (C.J. Becker, 1980b).

For the period *c*. 2800–2400 BC, the so-called Single Grave period (MN B), the results are, as already mentioned, still meagre. Yet unpublished studies hint at a kinship with the settlement form of the Late Neolithic period (LN) which succeeded it. As for the era 2400–1800 BC, reference ought to be made first of all to the *Myrhøj* excavation (J. Årup Jensen, 1972) which includes what appears to have been the leading house type of the period (compare for example M. Strömberg, 1971). This construction type is also found in the Early Bronze Age (N.A. Boas, 1980). Knowledge of the settlement pattern in this period has been augmented mainly by the excavation of the large village complex *Vadgård* by the Limfjord (E. Lomborg, 1973b, 1977).

In the course of the Early Bronze Age new house types gained ground. The three-aisled longhouse turns up as early as the middle of the second millennium BC (S.W. Andersen, 1981). Throughout the rest of the period, this house type predominates in what has become a large group of excavated village complexes. Among these, special mention ought to be made of the as yet unpublished finds from *Fragtrup* (J. Jensen, 1970), as well as the excavations in *Ristoft* (C.J. Becker, 1968e), *Spjald, Bjerg, Kærholm* (C.J. Becker, 1972a and b, 1976, 1980b) and *Hovergårde* (J. Jensen, 1971) – all of which are from northern and western Jutland. Similar village complexes are at present being studied in east Denmark; these include the excavations at *Skamlebæk* on Sejrø Bay (E. Lomborg, 1977) and excavations of three-aisled longhouses at Jersie on east Zealand (unpublished). See furthermore the excavations of a house site under a Bronze Age barrow at Trappendal, east Jutland (S.W. Andersen, 1981).

The settlement excavations raise many questions pertaining chiefly to the total extent of the settlements and to houses the number of which functioned synchronously. The latter question results from the frequently poor conditions for dating the various house construction. As a rule the only basis for dating is a relative dating based on construction details of the house types.

Graves: The so-called Single Grave culture from roughly 2800–2400 BC is represented at Danish museums by nearly 1000 grave finds, mainly from Jutland. A good part of these graves were found as a result of one of the most goal-oriented research projects ever carried out in Danish archaeology. The grave form of the period was first recognized in the 1880s, and by the time the first general survey was published in 1898 (S. Müller) over 300 barrows had been investigated. In the following years the number of finds continued to rise. A general survey of the 'single graves' in Jutland was published by P.V. Glob in 1944, whereas the finds from the Danish islands had already been presented in 1936 (C.J.

Becker). Finds south of the Danish border were published by K.W. Struve in 1955. Recent decades have produced only stray publications of new source material (see, for example, H. Andersen, 1952; S.E. Albrethsen and J. Street Jensen, 1964; H.J. Madsen 1970; H. Thrane, 1967a). One of the most serious problems in connection with the graves of the period is that the skeletal remains were poorly preserved. Determination of the sex of the deceased therefore depends most often upon the grave-goods. Noteworthy new theories on their function as prestige objects have been suggested by F. Højlund (1974).

From the period c. 2400–1800 BC, the Late Neolithic, about 1000 graves are known. A very great part of these contained flint daggers. This period displays a wide range of burial customs. Graves in barrows dominate in west Denmark, where about 300 finds are known. In east Denmark stone cists and graves without barrows predominate, as somewhat over 100 finds of this group have been made. Moreover, secondary burials in the grave structures of earlier periods are very common, with about 300 cases known. The Late Neolithic graves have hardly been studied systematically at all. However, the majority of the known finds are registered in E. Lomborg's work (1973a) on the Late Neolithic flint daggers. Nor has the anthropological material been systematically studied. As a comparison with the presumed overrepresentation of men in graves from the preceding period, a single example from the Late Neolithic will be mentioned, a stone cist from Gerdrup on Zealand (D. Liversage, 1964). The sixteen individuals buried included five children of indeterminable sex. Of the rest, eight were men and three were women – which is to say that this Late Neolithic find also shows a clear overrepresentation of men.

From the Bronze Age, c. 1800–500 BC, about 4000 graves are known. More than 1000 of these date from the Early Bronze Age. Most of these early graves are inhumation graves, whereas the graves from the Late Bronze Age are all cremation graves. Most of the Bronze Age graves were registered, although frequently unsatisfactorily, by H.C. Broholm in 1943–9. Since 1973, an impressive and ambitious project has been underway, namely the complete publication of the finds of the Early Bronze Age (E. Aner and K. Kersten). This work, which includes very fine graphic illustrations, so far covers the Danish islands. For the Late Bronze Age, a valuable supplement to H.C. Broholm's catalogues was published by E. Baudou in 1960. But as yet no exhaustive publication of the graves of the Late Bronze Age exists. One of the reasons for this lack is that the numerous graves which contain only pottery still cannot be dated with certainty. Determinations of the age and sex of the buried individuals have thus only occasionally been attempted (N.-J. Gejvall,

1968). A vast material which has not yet been studied is kept at the National Museum in Copenhagen.

Sacrificial finds and hoards. During the first millennium of agriculture in Denmark the number of ritual bog finds is considerable (C.J. Becker, 1947). But in the following period this group of finds plays an even greater role. In particular the deposits of precious flint and bronze objects become numerous. The finds from the first two phases of the period, however, have not yet been treated comprehensively, due in part to a number of dating problems. A catalogue of a large part of the hoards from the Late Neolithic period may, however, be found in E. Lomborg's work (1973a).

Bronze Age sacrificial finds and hoards are covered in a catalogue in H.C. Broholm's survey from 1943–9 as well as in the publications of E. Aner and K. Kersten from 1973. Important supplements may also be found in E. Baudou's work of 1960. For the Late Bronze Age a catalogue has been published on a number of the single finds from Danish bogs which should probably be interpreted along the same lines as the large hoards (J. Jensen, 1972). For an important source criticism of the find group, see K. Kristiansen (1974), who has proved that the known finds constitute a representative sample of the original find quantity.

Miscellaneous finds. This group does not include many finds from the period 2800–500 BC. Yet there are interesting traces of an extensive flint-mining industry from the Late Neolithic (C.J. Becker, 1951) near Aalborg. From the Bronze Age there is a presumed ritual site at Boeslunde, which in older literature (H. Kjær, 1928b) was considered to be one of the few central sites from that era. However, recent excavations have not been able to substantiate this theory.

Of the three phases which constitute the period from 2800–500 BC, the first phase, the so-called Single Grave culture, is the most problematic. Before the calibrated radiocarbon dates cast serious doubt upon traditional views (H. Tauber, 1972), some of the finds from the Single Grave period were thought to be partially contemporary with the finds from the late Funnel-Necked Beaker culture (see for example C.J. Becker, 1954). On the basis of topographical observations, S. Müller in 1898 suggested that some time after the 'invasion' of the first farming culture there occurred yet another invasion of a foreign ethnic group, the 'Single Grave culture'. This postulate was still accepted in P.V. Glob's work (1944) on the Single Grave culture and in fact even today it thrives in archaeological literature. Even though a number of earlier theories were radically modified during the 1950s (C.J. Becker, 1959) very few scholars challenged the invasion hypothesis (M.P. Malmer, 1962). But radiocarbon datings (Figure 62) from the 1970s (H. Tauber, 1972) have since

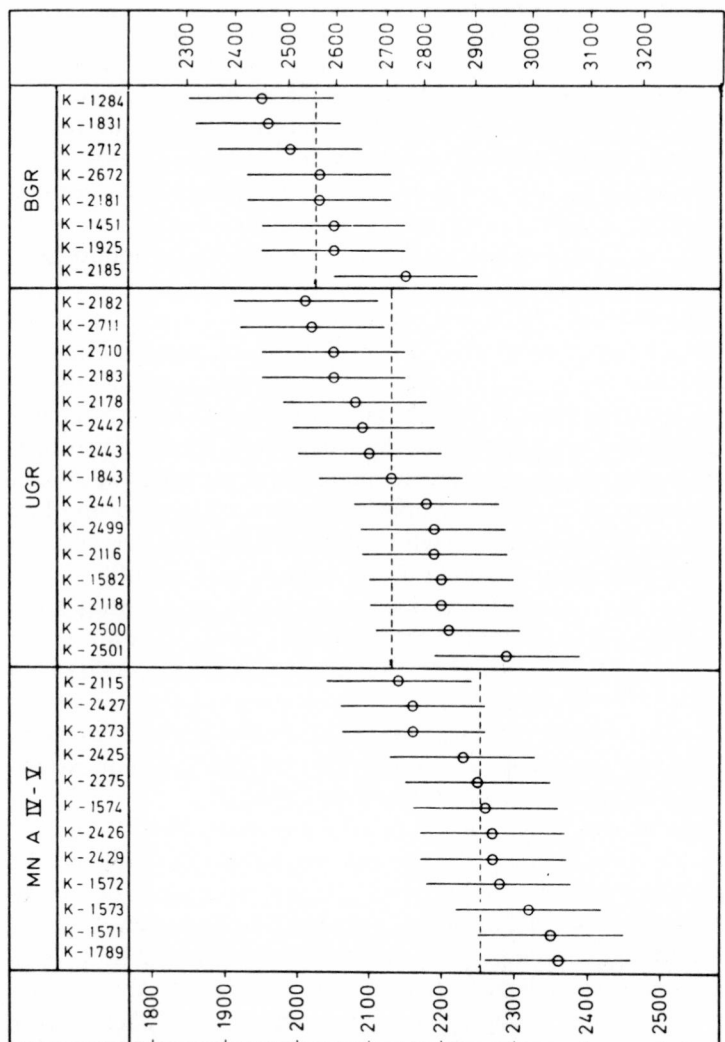

Figure 62 Danish radiocarbon dates of the two last phases of the Funnel-Necked
Beaker culture (MN A IV–V) and the two first phases of the Single Grave culture
(MN B I–II = UGR and BGR). Even though there are minor overlappings of the
datings, the average value of the samples indicates that the late finds from the
Funnel-Necked Beaker culture must be dated earlier than 2700 BC, whereas the
early finds from the Single Grave culture seem to belong to a later era. Below:
conventional radiocarbon datings. Above: calibrated radiocarbon datings.

made it clear that the late finds from the so-called Funnel-Necked Beaker culture must be dated earlier than 2700 BC, whereas the finds from the so-called Single Grave culture mainly date from a later era (C. Malmros and H. Tauber, 1975; K. Davidsen, 1975; H. Rostholm, 1977). The minor overlapping of the datings seems to be due to the usual margin of error of the method, ± 100 years. For this reason in part, it is logical to reject the invasion hypothesis and instead to view the difference between the two find complexes as the result of a chronological development. Due to the slight chronological overlapping, the division line between the two phases, which are called Middle Neolithic A (MN A) and Middle Neolithic B (MN B), is here drawn at about 2800 BC. A renewed critical evaluation of the archaeological record (see for instance N. Sterum, 1978) and the inclusion of settlement excavations are the prerequisites for maintaining the interpretation suggested. Such analyses have begun to appear in recent years (see for example P.O. Nielsen, 1977a).

The Late Neolithic period, 2400–1800 BC, presents a somewhat more favourable set of circumstances. A comprehensive evaluation of the problems of the period was formulated in 1964 (C.J. Becker); since then E. Lomborg's works of 1973a and 1975 have been able to shed light on a number of chronological problems in particular (see also T. Madsen, 1978b). E. Lomborg's results can also substantiate the idea of a unilinear development throughout the third millennium BC.

As we have shown, the two later phases have been somewhat neglected in newer Danish archaeology. The Bronze Age, on the other hand, has been the focus of considerable research activity. The division of the Bronze Age into six periods is based upon the work of O. Montelius in 1885 (see furthermore B. Gräslund, 1974b). This division is still used, although with certain modifications (E. Lomborg, 1968; K. Randsborg, 1968, 1972; G. Jacob-Friesen, 1967). Studies of the relationship between the chronology system of northern Europe and that of central Europe have been undertaken by the three scholars named as well as by H. Thrane (1975) and J. Jensen (1972). General surveys of the approximately 1300-year-long span of the Bronze Age have been published by J. Brøndsted (1958) and H.C. Broholm (1943–9) as well as in a more popular form by J. Jensen (1979a). With regard to the Late Bronze Age, mention ought to be made of E. Baudou's 1960 study.

It holds true of all three phases that until late in the 1960s the archaeological record was restricted almost exclusively to grave finds as well as votive and sacrificial finds. Therefore most conclusions dealing with economic, social, religious and political content have been based on a most lopsided foundation. In the past decade excavations, especially settlement excavations, and new working methods in archaeology and related fields have been able to shed light upon the gradual transformation of agrarian society from *c*. 2800–500 BC.

Yet insight into the ecological situation in this period is still limited. The most comprehensive survey of the environmental situation is that of J. Iversen of 1973. A number of older detailed investigations of the vegetation beneath barrows in Jutland was published in 1939 (H.C. Broholm); and a significant *landnam* on Djursland in the third millennium BC was pointed out in 1942 (T. Mathiassen). A recent attempt to combine investigations in the natural sciences with the archaeological record may be found in a study by K. Kristiansen (1978a), which treats the period *c*. 1500–500 BC. A key source here was that of tax evaluations of the quality of the arable land. For a discussion of the applicability of this method, see S. Nielsen (1980). Both works betoken an important step forward in the attempt to combine such fields as pedology and pollen analysis with the archaeological record.

Knowledge of climatic development in the Post-Glacial period is based upon R. Sernander's (1910) classical investigations of the Swedish bogs. In a number of late works by such scholars as E. Granlund, Sernander's interpretation of prehistoric climatic development has been modified. Important surveys of the archaeological and scientific problems have been published by T. Bergeron in 1956 as well as by G. Sörbom in 1966. Investigations in recent decades of the boundary horizons in Danish raised bogs, chiefly in Draved bog in south-west Jutland, have yielded noteworthy results which have been described in a preliminary report published by B. Aaby in 1974. For a more general survey, see for instance the work of R. Claiborne from 1970.

Formerly, the geographical distribution of the finds from the period 2800–500 BC was surprisingly little studied. However, a number of essential detailed studies were terminated in 1948 and 1959 with the publication of T. Mathiassen's works on the prehistoric settlement of north-west Jutland and north-west Zealand. Unfortunately a number of source problems of a technical nature (see H. Thrane, 1973b) weakened T. Mathiassen's conclusions with regard to the Single Grave culture and the Late Neolithic. For the Single Grave culture finds in Jutland, the major source remains P.V. Glob's study of 1944; but the finds from east Denmark have not been treated as a whole since 1936 (C.J. Becker). Discussions of the peculiar imbalance of the distribution picture may be found in the 1962 study of M.P. Malmer. The map in Figure 40 showing the settled areas in the Late Neolithic was made by combining the distribution maps for flint daggers from the work of E. Lomborg (1973a). Maps 41–2 showing the distribution of Bronze Age finds are based upon the present author's own registration of grave finds in the National Museum as well as in the majority of the Danish local museums, carried out from 1965–72. As already mentioned, an evaluation of the problem has been published by K. Kristiansen (1978a). For settlement studies in a north European perspective, see such works as those of C.F.W. Higham (1967) and A. Fleming (1972).

Only twenty years ago, Danish archaeologists had very vague ideas of the settlement pattern of the farming communities in the period 2800–500 BC. However, the ambitious settlement excavations of recent years have, as we have already pointed out, changed this situation dramatically. To be sure, the archaeological record is still diffuse, and in particular we lack finds from the Single Grave culture. On the other hand, settlements from the Late Neolithic and Bronze Age have become more numerous during the later years. Evaluation of the settlement pattern of the Bronze Age in particular has, since S. Müller's classic work of 1904, been dominated by the discussion on the extent to which settlement consisted of single farmsteads or of regular village complexes (J. Jensen, 1967a). After the first extensive excavations of Bronze Age settlements in Jutland at the end of the 1960s, the question was once again raised (C.J. Becker, 1968e). It was presumed that the village as a settlement form first arose in the period following 500 BC. Now that a richer source material has been revealed, the picture is more distinct. For the Early Bronze Age (E. Lomborg, 1973b) as well as the Late Bronze Age (C. J. Becker, 1972a, 1976, 1980b) it seems fully justifiable to speak of true villages, by which term is meant no more than a cluster of contemporaneous households, consisting of at least two or three farmsteads.

Problems related to the exchange system of prehistoric society have traditionally been granted an important position in archaeological literature. In general, however, efforts have been bent to the determination of 'trade routes'. Not until recently has it been possible to observe attempts to achieve an understanding of the underlying economic institutions (B. Stjernqvist, 1966). Yet within the economic sector of social anthropology, such studies have long played a major role based on the works of Karl Polanyi from the end of the 1950s. Characteristic manifestations of the discussion generated by Polanyi's works include works of G. Dalton (1961, 1965, 1967, 1969), M.D. Sahlins (1965, 1974) and H.K. Schneider (1974). In later years there has been a noticeable tendency to apply the theories of social anthropology to archaeology (see for example T. Earle and J. Ericson, 1977). In a series of newer Scandinavian surveys (C.-A. Moberg and U. Olsson, 1973; K. Lunden, 1972; J. Jensen et al., 1978) there are brief introductions to the ideas of

Karl Polanyi. These ideas have also been hotly debated within Norwegian archaeology (K. Odner, 1974).

In older archaeological literature, the relatively undefined phenomenon 'trade' has often been presumed to have been the catalyst for social changes in prehistoric society, especially after the appearance of metal technology. This holds true of the hypothesis suggested by J. Brøndsted (1958) with regard to cultural development in the period after c. 2000 BC. Brøndsted believed that the economic and social background for Bronze Age culture evinced distinct analogies with cultural conditions in the Viking Age. In recent studies on phenomena such as the exchange of goods and the supply of raw materials, wholly new views (described above) have been suggested with regard to the evaluation of the character of the exchange systems and their significance for general cultural development (C. Renfrew, 1975).

In Scandinavia, a number of comprehensive studies have shed light on various aspects of the exchange of goods, although most authors have limited themselves to speaking of 'cultural connections' in general. For the Late Neolithic, special mention should be made of works of E. Lomborg (1973a) and J.J. Butler (1963); for the Early Bronze Age, works of C.J. Becker (1964b), E. Lomborg (1960), K. Randsborg (1967, 1968, 1970, 1972) and H. Thrane (1975); for the Late Bronze Age, works of H. Thrane (1975) and J. Jensen (1965, 1966a, 1969, 1972). Only some of these works (H. Thrane, 1975) present a more theoretical discussion of trade and the exchange of goods in prehistoric society.

In connection with the exchange of goods in the Bronze Age, theories on amber trade have traditionally played a large role. These theories were based upon the 1925 work of de Navarro, in which 'trade routes' of amber across Europe were postulated. However, a number of publications in the 1960s have raised doubts about de Navarro's interpretation of the dissemination of amber (J. Jensen, 1965, 1968; B. Stjernqvist, 1966). In later years the results of C.W. Beck's analyses (1965, 1970, 1975, 1978) have brought a sorely needed clarity to many questions of provenance. Newer investigations of the guidelines sketched above have recently been published (J. Jensen, 1982).

For the period 2800–500 BC, archaeological literature includes only scattered attempts at a comprehensive evaluation of the economic and social development of the farming communities. As pointed out, the older writings postulated an invasion of the Single Grave people as a prerequisite for the formation of a class-divided Bronze Age society; see for instance J.E. Forssander (1936) and J. Brøndsted (1958). Under the influence of social anthropology and with the corroboration of radiocarbon datings, the modern archaeology has begun to seek alternative explanations for the development of the subsistence economy up to the beginning of the Iron Age (see S. Welinder, 1977; K. Kristiansen, 1978a). In this way, a more precise impression of social development can be achieved. Understanding of the early Bronze Age society has been enhanced by the works of K. Randsborg, but as yet there is a dearth of revised interpretations for both the early and the late phases. But however slight the results so far achieved by such methods as quantitative analysis (K. Randsborg, 1974a and b), they do indicate a fruitful direction.

PART IV

The chiefdoms of the Iron Age
500 BC–800 AD

15

Environmental changes

The development of the open, man-made landscape

Momentous changes took place in Denmark from the middle of the first millennium BC. Around 500 BC the widespread prestige-goods economy of which Denmark had been a part for nearly 2000 years seems to have suffered a considerable set-back. Perhaps this crisis was only transitory, for in the next few centuries there emerged a new agrarian society with a considerable potential for expansion. Everywhere in Denmark around the time of the birth of Christ, there are unmistakable indications of economic growth. This first stage culminated in the third and fourth centuries with the appearance of villages consisting of large farmsteads with a differentiated economy providing opportunities for vital secondary occupations. Agriculture now achieved a productivity hitherto unequalled in prehistoric Denmark. The stage was set for sweeping socio-economic changes which in future centuries would lead the archaic chiefdoms to pre-feudalism.

To grasp these fundamental transformations of agrarian society, we must understand the ecological milieu in which they took place. The few centuries just before the birth of Christ witnessed a profound change in the environment. In many places agriculture had completely stripped the land of forest (Figure 63). Instead there were vast stretches of grassland, small cultivated areas and unpopulated swampy areas. The population gradually increased and so did the destruction of the ancient dense forests, especially those found on heavy moraine soils. Slowly but surely the settlement pattern which had endured for over 2000 years was transformed.

Pollen diagrams sketch the general outline of this process. As already mentioned, the diagrams from *c.* 200 BC to the fifth century AD show how

Figure 63 The landscape of the Early Iron Age in Denmark was characterized by open grassland, small cultivated areas around the settlements, and between the latter vast stretches of unpopulated swampy areas. This type of landscape can still be found in isolated parts of Denmark, as shown here at Røsnæs, western Zealand.

human activity increased throughout most of south Scandinavia. This impression accords with the expansion of settlement onto the heavy soils which earlier agrarian communities had exploited only slightly. From the fifth century BC a sort of stagnation persisted up to a new expansion, the extensive *landnam* of the Viking Age in the eighth century. This presumed stagnation cannot be fully explained. Around the mid-first millennium AD the population of Europe declined markedly, but whether this also held true of south Scandinavia is not certain. In the sixth century the Justinian bubonic plague ravaged much of the continent. According to some calculations, it reduced the population by one-third or one-half (J.C. Russel, 1968). Although there is no concrete evidence of the plague in northern Europe, it may help explain certain symptoms of decline in the sixth century especially. We do not know whether these symptoms were general for south Scandinavia or even whether they were contemporaneous at the various places where they have been observed. Local conditions may very well affect, for example, the picture we have from the pollen diagrams.

Man came to have a profound impact on the composition of the forest. The lime tree had been menaced by the agricultural forms practised in

Denmark since the fourth millennium BC, which instead favoured mast trees and hazel. In the last millennium of prehistory, the lime forest suffered nearly everywhere in Denmark.

This process had several causes. The drop in summer temperature from the climatic maximum of the Atlantic period had weakened the ability of the lime to compete with other forest trees by lowering its resistance to winter cold. On the meagre soils, the deterioration of the soil had also undermined the lime in relation to the beech and the oak. Last but not least, population pressure, especially in the centuries just before and after the birth of Christ, along with the resulting expansion of settlement, set its unmistakable stamp on the forest. For example, the village communities used enormous amounts of wood as building timber and as fuel (also for iron extraction). In the lighter, more open forest where the cattle browsed and on abandoned agricultural land – especially high-lying well-drained soil – conditions for the beech were now bettered. This may particularly be seen in the boulder clay regions in east Jutland and on the islands. On the meagre soil of west Jutland, the beech was scarce up to the end of prehistory. Heavy moraine soils and a high water-table also hindered the immigration of the beech. This held true of places on south-east Zealand and on Lolland, where the oak forest still prevailed.

Together with these changes in the composition of the forest on the benign soils of east Jutland and on the islands, there was a change in the vegetation profile in west Denmark. During the Late Neolithic and Bronze Age, the farming communities preferred relatively light soils. On these soils, agriculture could be expanded by deforestation, which required a minimum of labour. In the centuries just before the birth of Christ, settlement continued to expand on the light soils in west Jutland, which still must have boasted great expanses of light open oak forest. But now the deterioration of the soil became sadly evident. The destruction of the forest caused by cattle grazing and unrestrained forest clearance washed the nutrients out of the soil. Erosion caused by the dry spring wind helped destroy the thin layer of mould on the many fields where trees and all other shelter had been chopped down. These factors, coupled with increased moisture, stimulated the spread of heather. Around the time of the birth of Christ further expansion became impossible.

Even if there is no reason to propose dramatic catastrophe theories to explain the many abandoned 'celtic fields' of western Jutland in the early Iron Age, we cannot doubt that agrarian conditions in these regions took a turn for the worse in the period preceding the birth of Christ. This development is sometimes described as a radical change in the settlement pattern. The fact is that the potential of the poor lands for population expansion had been gradually exhausted and that from now on agricultural expansion chiefly occurred in regions with better soil. South of the Danish–German border, a parallel process is evident. Here in the south, a new biotope was taken over for settlement: the marsh on the coast of the North Sea came into use as grasslands. The overall settlement picture which characterizes the closing centuries of prehistory and the beginning of historical times was thus slowly taking shape in the first centuries after the birth of Christ.

At the same time a new landscape type was being created: the hay meadows. In the pollen diagrams this man-made landscape type is manifest as a decline in the pollen of the alder. A likely interpretation of this phenomenon is that alder in the damp areas had been chopped down when the areas were converted to moist hay meadows. The use of meadows must have been a vital prerequisite for the overwintering of the cattle, an observation which is borne out by the way villages were situated in the countryside.

The development of the climate during the Iron Age

As has been stated, recent investigations of Danish raised bogs have shown that the climate has fluctuated over the past 5500 years and that these fluctuations have lasted about 260 years. New light is thus shed on the relationship between culture and climate. Climatic changes in the final phase of prehistory can be pinpointed with great accuracy. A trend toward increased precipitation and lower summer temperature set in around 600 BC, just before the transition to the Iron Age. The next fluctuation took place around 300 BC, and yet another one took place just before the birth of Christ. In the first millennium AD there are fluctuations around 200 and 500. A last fluctuation follows around 1000 AD. According to the presumed periodicity, we would expect a change around the close of the Germanic Iron Age, in the eighth century, but no evidence of this change has yet been found.

Comparison of these climatic fluctuations with the archaeological record shows surprisingly little analogy. As was the case in the period 2800–500 BC, there is no clear parallel with changes in the development of the agrarian communities in the final centuries of prehistory. This problem is especially perplexing at the beginning of the period, where the climatic fluctuation around 600 BC was earlier ascribed a considerable impact on the environmental situation of the agrarian communities. The centuries following this fluctuation have been described thus: 'The first centuries must have been hard and severe, with crop failure and famine when the flooded fields were unusable and the cattle froze' (J. Brøndsted, 1960). Yet new studies show that at that very time, around the mid-first century BC, the agrarian communities actually expanded, at least in Jutland. Early research was often based upon a very shaky foundation. Intense research in connection with major excavations, particularly in Jutland and on Funen, have led to a more detailed view of the relationship between climatic development and the lifeways of prehistoric man. Future work must evaluate the extent to which the archaeological record can inform us about the settlement and subsistence patterns of prehistoric man.

16

Subsistence and settlement

Expansion of the farming communities

In the five centuries preceding the birth of Christ, a wave of settlement expansion swept over Denmark. The introduction of new types of land management created in the course of a few centuries countless changes in the old settlement pattern which had endured for almost 2000 years. This expansion trend continued up to about the middle of the first millennium AD, after which a stagnation apparently set in. Then, in the seventh and eighth centuries AD, the process again accelerated. During the last centuries of prehistory, socio-economic conditions slowly created the foundation for a development which achieved its full flowering in medieval feudal society.

Indications of this lengthy process must be sought first and foremost in the new methods of production of the agrarian communities. Therefore the archaeological record which tells about the geographic expansion of settlement both on the macro- and the micro-levels, the structure of the village communities and land management itself will be a principal focus of interest.

Archaeologists are, however, badly hindered in determining the geographical extent of settlement in the period from 500 BC to 800 AD. Few regions in Denmark have been systematically researched, so the representativeness of the archaeological record is quite uncertain. By far the majority of maps show only a more or less accidentally found material, grave finds especially. At the same time, these grave finds may represent the most widely differing historical realities, manifested by changing burial customs through the thirteen centuries of the period.

In some periods, the geographical distribution of the grave finds does seem to reflect the prevalent political and social patterns. This holds true of Zealand in the first four centuries AD. In other regions, for example on Funen, the distribution of the graves in the same period provides a better impression of the general extent and continuity of settlement, based very much on the dominant burial customs. In other periods, for example from 500–800 AD, the archaeological record is inexplicably slight. Modern archaeologists are grappling with some of these problems. As the results are preliminary, the problems will only be sketched here.

On Funen, the island in the centre of Denmark, intensive research has resulted in a most informative archaeological record. Both general and more regional surveys have been carried out. One major problem is that the quantity of finds varies considerably throughout the centuries. There is a scarcity of both graves and settlements from 500–200 BC, i.e. periods I–II of the Pre-Roman Iron Age. Thereafter the finds increase considerably in number up to the fifth century AD. More than 500 localities are known from a period lasting 600 years. Following this, the quantity is sharply reduced, with the exception of certain find categories, namely the gold finds. Not until the tenth century is there again an increase in quantity.

If the Funen finds from c. 200 BC to 400 AD are divided into three phases, each lasting 200 years, then we see that the finds from all three periods are geographically distributed in a similar way. This consistency and the congruity between the geographical extent of the graves and the settlements indicate that the finds are in fact representative for the demographic pattern on the island as a whole.

The most interesting results so far derive from studies of agrarian settlement development within narrowly defined regions. A little area on north-east Funen encompassing just a few parishes has been the scene of systematic excavations, aerial photography and field reconnaissance studies. The intention has been to illuminate the relationship between the prehistoric and the medieval settlement in order to see whether or not there had been a gap in the continuity.

The investigations were carried out on two levels. On one level, excavations were undertaken in a number of medieval villages; on the other level, attempts were made to define the resource territories within which the prehistoric settlements functioned in the centuries prior to the Middle Ages. Similar investigations have also been made in Jutland and north-west Germany. Identification of these resource territories is vitally important for the understanding of the settlement pattern throughout the Iron Age and the Middle Ages. In most cases, the resource territories were bordered by streams, meadows or swampy areas. The size of the territories varies greatly, depending upon the available resources. Within the investigation area on Funen, the maximum size of the individual resource territories did not exceed 2 km^2.

The preliminary investigations have given the interesting result that the medieval villages which still exist must have been founded in the period *c.* 1000–1200 AD: traces of older settlements were not found within the villages proper. Consequently a change in the settlement pattern seems to have occurred during the transition from prehistory to the Middle Ages. The prehistoric villages, however, are often found at a distance not exceeding 400–500 metres from the medieval villages. Thus, underlying the settlement pattern of the late Viking Age and the Middle Ages there is an older, completely different, pattern. Moreover, scattered observations from both Jutland and Zealand seem to indicate a similar discontinuity. The explanation may be that at the transition between the Late Iron Age and the Middle Ages, land management underwent a transformation. This may explain why in historical times the location of the villages within the individual resource territories were so different from the location of the prehistoric villages.

Everywhere in western Europe from the ninth up to the thirteenth centuries AD, agrarian communities accelerated in productivity. The same tendency also took place in Denmark, though slightly later. In fact, the increased productivity may explain the observed shift in the settlement pattern in Denmark between *c.* 1000 and 1200 AD. The prime cause of the production increase seems to have been the introduction of a new type of land management, the three-field system (E.P. Christensen, 1979). By this is meant a system according to which crops succeeded one another in a regular sequence interrupted by equally regular fallow periods. One-third of the land was thus left fallow while the rest was apportioned into winter and spring fields. Rye or wheat was sown on the winter fields; oats or barley on the spring fields. The three-field system also made use of the heavy-wheel plough. All these factors helped transform agriculture from an archaic type dominated by animal husbandry to a different type dominated by a more intensive cultivation of cereals such as is known from historical sources in the Middle Ages. The location requirements for a medieval village thus differed radically from those of a prehistoric village with its demand for productive grazing areas, especially meadows.

Thus medieval villages in Denmark cannot be traced further back in time than *c.* 1000–1200 AD. However, there are indications that during the final millennium of prehistory, far into the Viking Age, there existed continuous but *mobile* settlements within the naturally restricted resource areas to which later villages were also related. Here and there we can observe how Iron Age villages were oriented with easy access to meadowland. This location implies that Iron Age agriculture laid great emphasis on animal husbandry.

In much of Jutland and adjacent regions of northern Germany, at least up to the sixth century, a similar placing of settlements with regard for pastures seems to have been common. It is a shame, however, that the archaeological record on Funen from about 400 AD up to the Viking Age is so poor. Even so the preliminary investigations help suggest the following hypothesis: that in the Pre-Roman and Roman Iron Age, Funen and other parts of the country experienced a period of explosive population growth. From a Bronze Age foundation, settlement expanded steadily and achieved a temporary climax in the first two or three centuries AD. Agriculture in this period was typified by extensive stock-breeding with relatively little emphasis on cultivation of cereals. Thereafter settlement may have contracted, possibly in connection with a restructuring of the settlement pattern, although no clear reason for this can be given. During the Viking Age, another expansion took place. Throughout the Iron Age each village was moved about at certain intervals within its naturally delimited resource territory, but a territorial continuity may be presumed to have persisted up to the Viking Age and later periods. However, an actual continuity of place, that is a habitation at one and the same spot, does not seem to have emerged until sometime during the Viking Age and the early Middle Ages.

As only very few Iron Age settlements have been excavated on Funen, little is known about whether or not the break between prehistory and the Middle Ages signifies a more general change in the settlement form, for example from individual farmsteads to villages. However, it is more than likely that throughout the Iron Age settlement on Funen was chiefly organized into village communities. The changes around 1000–1200 AD can probably be ascribed to a restructuring of the village society which took place in connection with the introduction of new forms of land management.

Bornholm, the little Danish island in the Baltic, has also been studied in this regard. Here the size and geographical distribution of the Iron Age cemeteries indicate that up to about 400 AD the island was characterized by village settlement. Thereafter the individual farmstead became dominant and remained so through the Middle Ages and up to modern times. But conditions on Bornholm are quite unique; culturally the island most closely resembles the other Baltic islands of Gotland and Öland.

For Zealand and the surrounding islands, the picture is far more vague. Very few finds are known from the first 500 years of the period. The find quantity rises considerably from 0–400 AD. In the first two centuries AD there is a preponderance of finds in the south, on the neighbouring islands Lolland-Falster and Møn. Zealand shows a more even distribution. In relation to the Bronze Age, a settlement expansion is evident. The central part of the island was now put under the plough. In the third and fourth centuries this tendency continued, but now the focal point was the southern half of Zealand. The finds cluster around Stevns, in fact where the construction of the road network also reached a high point (H. Nielsen and V. Hansen, 1977). In the following centuries the find quantity again falls sharply; the concentrations are dissolved and, as was the case on Funen, it also becomes impossible on Zealand to determine which changes of the general settlement pattern took place in the centuries immediately preceding the Viking Age.

How representative, then, is the picture drawn by the Zealand finds? For the period from 500 BC to 0 absolutely no conclusions can be drawn; there are simply too few finds. The centuries after the birth of Christ, however, provide some basis for speculation. But here we must note a number of problems which partially derive from the fact that the distribution of wealth in the graves in the east Danish regions seems to represent the social and political groupings of the population far more clearly than on Funen. The cause is the predominant burial customs. In particular, the distribution of precious imported goods reflects quite clearly the location of the economic centres. In the first and second centuries AD the focal point was on Lolland. In the third and fourth centuries AD this focus was shifted northwards to east Zealand and the surrounding islands. In these key centuries just after the birth of Christ we must follow an uncharted route.

Since the end of the last century it has been commonly accepted that Danish place-names may be classified according to their suffixes and that certain chronological facts may be deduced from this. Place-names with the endings -inge, -lev, -løse and -sted (for example Sengeløse, Herlev and Alsted) have been thought to comprise the earliest group, the origin of which goes back even further than the Viking Age. These villages were assumed to be the remains of the old settlement pattern prior to the changes in land management in the Viking period and the Middle Ages. Other types of names, for example those ending in -by and -torp, were thought to form a more recent group, mainly from the Viking Age, and still others were thought to stem from the early Middle Ages (H.V. Clausen, 1916). Although many complex theories about prehistoric settlement have been based on these ideas, the reliability of the place-names has been exaggerated. The last couple of generations have evaluated this source group far more realistically.

On Funen, the place-name question has justifiably faded into the background after evidence from the recent field surveys. For Zealand the use of the oldest name types (names ending in -inge, -lev, -løse and -sted) is also problematic, as type identification of the individual names can be very uncertain. A number of statistical calculations of the archaeological find distribution both on Zealand and on Funen, however, ought to dissuade us from completely denying the value of the place-names as a source of settlement history (H. Nielsen, 1978, 1979). These statistics have shown that there is quite a clear tendency for grave finds from the Roman Iron Age to be concentrated around present-day villages bearing old place-names (with the exception of -inge). To judge from observations from Funen, which, to be sure, were made on another basis than those from Zealand, we can presume a continuity of settlement – not a continuity within the existing villages but perhaps rather a continuity within the resource territories related to place-names of the old type.

This could lead to the assumption that continuous, that is mostly deforested, settlement areas existed in the Iron Age in north-west and west Zealand and east and south Zealand. The central part of the island and the Roskilde–Copenhagen area, called 'the heath', may be presumed to have formed unified settlement areas. Despite our ignorance, we do know that we are here dealing with a situation quite different from that of the Bronze Age.

As on Funen, this situation may be seen as the result of the agricultural expansion which must have been in full swing in the centuries just after the birth of Christ. At a later phase in this process, which still parallels conditions on Funen, there apparently was a certain contraction of settlement after 400 AD, although regional continuity around localities with names of the old type was maintained up to the Viking Age.

In Jutland as well, the settlement pattern in the closing millennium of prehistory is tremendously difficult to sketch. The point of departure must be the settlement map, Figure 42, which shows the cultivated areas up to about 500 BC. This picture seems to have persisted right down to the final two centuries BC, although in the west there is an increase of settlement. Somewhat prior to the birth of Christ, expanding settlement is encountered all over the peninsula. In the first centuries of the Iron Age the lighter soils seem to have been the preferred object of increased exploitation but gradually the heavy moraine soils were also taken over. This expansion is most evident in northern Jutland and in the coastal regions by the Danish–German border.

In north-west Jutland, intensive surveys in the 1940s (T. Mathiassen, 1948) emphasized the same tendencies. Iron Age settlement spread both on the lighter soils and especially on the heavy moraine lands.

This circumstance can be most clearly observed in the fertile moraine areas around the west Limfjord. Here investigations in recent years have demonstrated a surprisingly intensive exploitation of the heavier soils from around the birth of Christ and several centuries afterwards. In many areas there are villages every two or three kilometres (Figure 68), a clear illustration of the agricultural expansion which took place around the beginning of our era – the period in which the open Danish cultural landscape truly took form.

As for the size of the population in the final millennium of prehistory, it has not yet been possible to make realistic calculations. However, estimates can be made for thirteenth-century Denmark (including Scania), the population of which is believed to have been about one million. For the period around 1645 AD, that is after the population crises of the late Middle Ages, the same area is believed to have been inhabited by about 800,000 people (E. Ladewig Petersen, 1980). As far as may be concluded from the population growth in western Europe in the centuries around the Viking Age, the population of Denmark towards the end of the Viking Age could hardly have exceeded 700,000. This implies that, in view of the explosive growth of the Viking Age, we can hardly figure on more than about 500,000 inhabitants in all of Denmark in the closing phase of the Iron Age.

Villages and farmsteads around the birth of Christ

Among the many changes which the agrarian society underwent during the Iron Age, some of the most important took place in the structure of the villages. Two observations in particular are of crucial importance for the understanding of the settlement pattern. One of them is that prehistoric settlement was mobile in character, that is the villages were moved at certain intervals, possibly with a long-range tendency to remain for increasingly longer periods at the same place. The other major observation is that the villages were moved within well-defined resource territories.

These two observations have now made it possible to bring a hitherto unachievable chronological dimension into the study of the development of village societies in Denmark. Intensive investigations of various resource areas have thus made it possible to trace individual village communities through as many as 900 years. The great expense of excavations, of course, sets limits for how detailed a picture can be drawn.

The greater or lesser mobility of the village communities in the Iron

Age was first revealed in connection with the extensive excavations at Grøntoft in west Jutland. These excavations traced the existence of a single 'wandering village' through about 300 years within one and the same resource territory. The history of the village lasts from *c.* 500 BC to some time in the third century BC. The number of building phases is not certain, as it has not been easy to define the limits of the resource territory. It is possible that the many excavated houses may have belonged to two neighbouring villages.

The houses of the Grøntoft village are of the three-aisled construction which is found at all of the Danish Iron Age settlements (Figure 64). This construction has roots far back in time, to the middle of the second millennium BC (see p. 146 ff). Around 500 BC it evolved into a rectangular house shape, unvaryingly oriented east–west and with a roof supported by two parallel rows of interior posts. At Iron Age settlements, the length of the houses may vary from just a few metres to twenty metres. The construction dictated that the width was nearly always 5–6 metres. Entrances were found in both of the long sides of the house. The walls of the houses might be timber, either massive or light, with wattle and clay daubing. Massive earthen and turf walls are also known. The houses were often divided into two sections: the east end sheltered cattle; the

Figure 64 Reconstruction of the typical three-aisled Early Iron-Age house at the Historical Archaeological Experimental Centre at Lejre, outside of Copenhagen.

west end with the hearth was for human dwelling. The dwelling section often had a clay floor while the byre may have had a stone-paved gutter and stall partitions.

In three hundred years, the Grøntoft society 'consumed' about 250 of these longhouses. At all stages, the village economy strongly emphasized animal husbandry. However, houses without stalls did exist. When the houses had been used for perhaps only one generation, they were torn down and moved to another site within the village territory. The old sites were ploughed over and the soil was again tilled. The constant moving shifted the original field boundaries marked by balks as well. The balks (forming so-called Celtic fields) which could be observed at the excavations thus stem from many phases of cultivation, possibly separated by fallow periods.

It is difficult to distinguish the various phases of the wandering village and to determine the size of the settlement site at any given time. Yet it is possible to note, for example, that around the third century BC the village was fenced in, probably to protect the houses from the cattle (Figure 65). At that time the village consisted of twelve buildings, as follows: five larger farmsteads, each housing 8–18 heads of cattle; two smaller farmsteads, each with 3–4 heads of cattle; and three longhouses (farmsteads) apparently lacking cattle in a byre; and finally a couple of storehouses.

In total, the third-century BC village must have contained about 8–10 households with somewhat more than fifty individuals. In addition there were about 70–80 heads of larger cattle. In estimating these sizes, we must remember that Grøntoft was a community which in agricultural terms existed on marginal soil. In fact, there is evidence that the village in some cases cultivated moor land. It is also noteworthy that the varying sizes of the households may indicate graduated differences in the distribution of wealth.

Grøntoft in western Jutland is so far the only wandering village in Denmark which has been traced from as early as 500 BC. Nowhere else has a community from the middle of the first millennium BC been studied so thoroughly. Later, in the centuries around the birth of Christ, other finds are known. The mobile village from this period is best documented in the excavations made in the 1970s of Hodde in southwestern Jutland.

In Hodde, the main lines of the history of the mobile village community can be traced through five centuries. All the successive villages lie on the eastern edge of a little hill island at intervals of 300–400 metres. To the north, west and south the hill island is bordered by river valleys. On the east side, where the settlements lie, there are large open stretches of

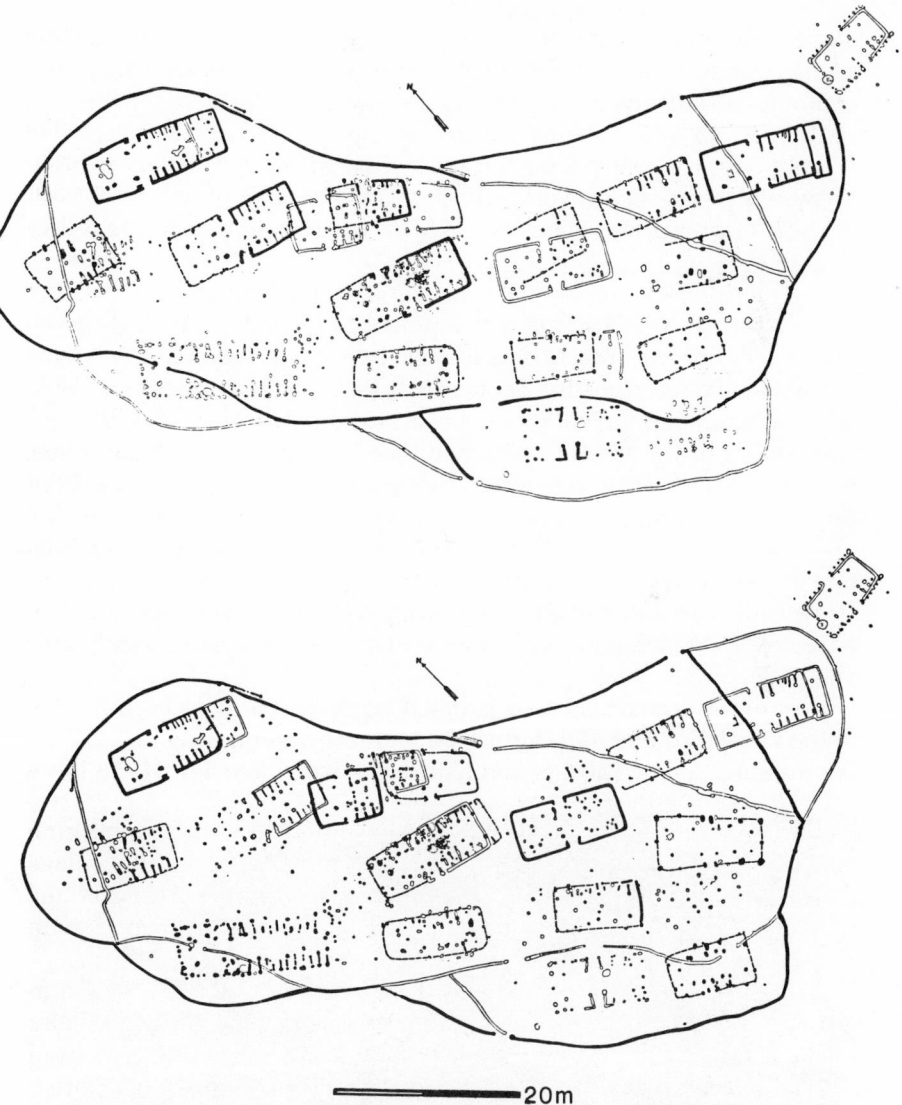

Figure 65 Two phases of the Pre-Roman Iron-Age village at Grøntoft, Jutland. Above: oldest phase with 13 farmhouses. Below: the younger phase with 12 farmhouses and with a partly rebuilt surrounding palisade.

meadow. The settlements are located within this well-defined resource territory in such a way that on one side the land of the hill island could be used for agriculture, while the other side with the large meadows could serve as pasture. In all, three successive villages have been found, along with a cemetery which seems to represent a fourth, as yet undiscovered, village. When this last village is revealed, we will have a continuous settlement with its resource territory dating from the first century BC up to the fourth century AD.

Only one of these village societies, the earliest one, has been fully excavated so far. The village, which covered an area of roughly 11,000 m², was encircled by a fence and had an open commons in the centre (Figure 66).

The many fences of the village, along with stratigraphical observations, allow us to follow the development of the village through many stages. The earliest stage seems to have been the erection of the largest farmstead and its enclosure. Soon after the enclosure was built, the large fence surrounding the village area was erected, thus indicating that the later extent of the village had already been planned. Gradually other farmsteads were constructed until the enclosed area contained a total of fifty-three buildings, which can be separated into twenty-seven units. A unit invariably consisted of one longhouse either alone or together with one or two smaller houses. Twenty-two of the twenty-seven units are farmsteads with a byre at one end of the longhouse, while the remaining have no byre. The house type is identical to those of other contemporary villages.

Most of the farmsteads were situated along the north and south sides of the village, so that each farmstead had its own entrance through the surrounding fence. Most individual farms had room for 14–16 large

Figure 66 Reconstruction of the Iron Age village at Hodde from the 1st century BC. The village, which covered an area *c.* 11,000 m², is characterized by the open commons in the centre. The enclosed area contained a total of 53 buildings.

animals. Some could house more; the oldest farmstead had the greatest capacity, up to 28 large animals. At its most populous, the village housed about 200 people and 300–500 head of cattle. An unequal distribution of wealth, a very marked emphasis on animal husbandry and a seemingly slight occupational differentiation comprise the chief characteristics of this village. Another striking feature is the large open area (the commons) in the centre. Here the animals were probably herded at night during the season when they grazed outside. The noteworthy fact is that the open area seems to have been communal. The excavator describes the village thus: the independently fenced-in farmsteads correspond in principle to the medieval type of farmstead and the open space in the middle can be compared to the commons, which was shared by all the inhabitants (S. Hvass, 1976).

In the final years of the community, at least six farmsteads were torn down until at last the entire village was destroyed by fire.

The subsistence of the village can be deduced from its location in the terrain: on the boundary between field and meadow. This location is typical for most of the known Iron Age villages and probably implies that animal husbandry was the primary subsistence factor. Grazing and abundant water were basic needs which dictated the location and structure of the village.

As already remarked, the size of the palisade indicates that the gradual construction of new farmsteads seems to have been planned already at the founding of the village. In the same way, farmsteads were torn down in the late years of the village's existence – seemingly they were moved to a succeeding settlement only 400 metres away. By and large the village seems to have been moved in stages – and it seems that the life-span of the village was four or five generations, between 100 and 150 years. This was longer than the village community in Grøntoft, which existed three or four hundred years earlier. This tendency became more pronounced through the centuries.

We have noted that the successive Hodde villages have been localized up to the fourth century AD. Trial excavations in the village from the third and fourth centuries AD have shown that the house type here varies from that of the older villages. Now large multi-functional farmsteads completely dominated. An identical development took place in contemporary villages throughout western Denmark.

Excavation of the village community at Hodde has yielded the first glimpse of the settlement pattern within a single resource territory in the Early Iron Age. The constant moving may be ascribed to aspect of land management or there may have been other causes. In several places it can be documented that the abandoned village sites were taken over for cereal cultivation and naturally the soil quality was far higher at sites where a village had existed for several centuries. Still it is hard to believe that this rather limited gain was the sole cause of moving. As yet no other explanation can be suggested.

Other finds from Jutland show that Hodde was not unique. Østerbølle in northern Jutland includes house sites of large longhouses as well as smaller houses lacking byres, which form a village plan with a central commons similar to Hodde.

Information on the mobility of Iron Age village society can also be gleaned elsewhere in Denmark, for example in the low marsh regions by the North Sea in the south of Jutland (S. Jensen, 1980). Here the villages lie clustered along the edge of the so-called 'Geest' out to the low marshes in the west (Figure 67). The location of the villages is most telling. The primary location factor was the large marsh meadows, which were suited for cattle-grazing and for hay-making. The inland villages, which were considerably more scattered than the villages in the west, also existed on their large herds of cattle, as indicated by their proximity to the largest meadow areas.

None of the settlements in this south-west Jutland region date back more than a century before the birth of Christ. This holds true for the entire coastal region to the south and much of the German marsh. The marshes by the North Sea could probably not have been exploited as pasture prior to this. Thus this region is most indisputable evidence of the explosive expansion of settlement which took place in the centuries around the birth of Christ.

Here and there along this coast it has been possible to find villages which 'wandered' for centuries within one and the same resource territory. At Drengsted, for example, a rather small area was found to contain a series of settlements, some with cemeteries dating from the first century BC to the fifth century AD.

At Dankirke in south-west Jutland, a small area was found to contain several settlements with their cemeteries dating from the first century BC to the fifth century AD. Considering the existence of stray finds from as yet undiscovered settlements in the Dankirke region, there may be said to have been a continuity of settlement up to c. 700 AD, a period of 800 or 900 years.

So far the basic pattern seems to have been identical, whether in Grøntoft, Hodde, Drengsted or Dankirke. Over the centuries, mobile village communities based upon large herds of cattle moved around within narrowly defined resource territories. Part of the basic pattern also seems to be that in time the villages developed larger farmstead units and that secondary occupations gained in importance. This

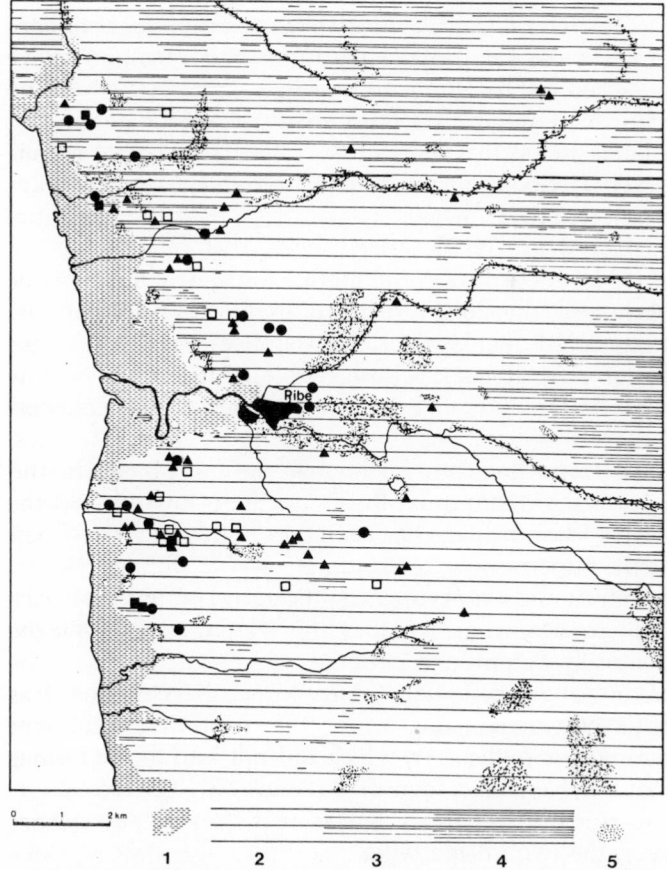

Figure 67 Distribution of the Iron Age settlements in the Ribe area in south-west
   Jutland. 1: Marshlands. 2: Sandy soil. 3: Clayey sandy soil. 4: Sandy clayey
   soil. 5: Meadows and bogs. Triangles: Pre-Roman and Early Roman Iron Age.
   Circles: Late Roman Iron Age, Germanic Iron Age and Viking period. Squares:
   Early and Late Iron Age. Open squares: undated Iron Age finds.

development truly accelerated in the third and fourth centuries AD. In
this connection it may be asked what degree of economic differentiation
existed among the villages as a whole in the centuries just before and
after the birth of Christ? Only one area of the country offers an
archaeological record sufficiently complete to answer this question. This
is the north-westernmost part of Jutland in the Thy region, the area of
Denmark in which the greatest number of settlements have been found.
It is also an area in which the settlement pattern seems to have been less
mobile than hitherto seen.

Within an area of barely 500 km², by the western part of the Limfjord, there is a dense network of approximately forty-six contemporaneous villages from the period just before the birth of Christ and up to the third century AD (Figure 68). Judging by the density of settlement in the terrain, it must be assumed that most of the villages from that period have been discovered. About 70 per cent of the villages lie only 2.5 kilometres from one another.

Most of the villages are characterized by a sort of city mound consisting of refuse layers up to several metres thick. The thickness of these layers is primarily due to the regional architectural tradition of using turf walls up to 1.5 metres thick. New houses were repeatedly built on the sites of older houses, whose rubble or turf walls formed thick refuse layers. Thus, settlement did not move about but remained at the same site.

At Grøntoft and Hodde we can distinguish several phases in the history of a single village community. But in northern Jutland, matters are quite otherwise. Here no village has been thoroughly excavated. Yet even the relatively superficial investigations carried out at Hurup, Vestervig, Mariesminde and Ginnerup are sufficiently comprehensive to permit an attempt to determine whether the lay-out of the villages reveals an economically determined pattern.

Within the area investigated, a total of thirty-three village mounds has been revealed with settlement lasting two or three centuries; at thirteen localities, less permanent settlements which did not lead to the formation of village mounds have been identified (Figure 68). The location in relation to the terrain and soil does not seem to reveal any crucial difference between the two village types.

As yet, the limits of the resource territories in which the various settlements were situated have not been determined. However, various observations may be interpreted to indicate a subsistence differentiation underlying the settlement pattern in the 500 km² area. All the villages seem to have included two house types: a short and a long one. The longhouse type combined byre and dwelling under one roof, whereas the short one lacked a byre. These latter houses were used solely for dwelling and working. The ratio between the two house types seems to vary widely from village to village. In the west part of the region, the short type predominated, but in the east part, the opposite holds true. The difference has been explained as one of subsistence economy. In the west, there was an emphasis on sheep-breeding, possibly supplemented by fishing, whereas in the east, cattle breeding and cereal cultivation were practised to a greater degree.

A related pattern can be glimpsed in the large village Nørre Fjand by

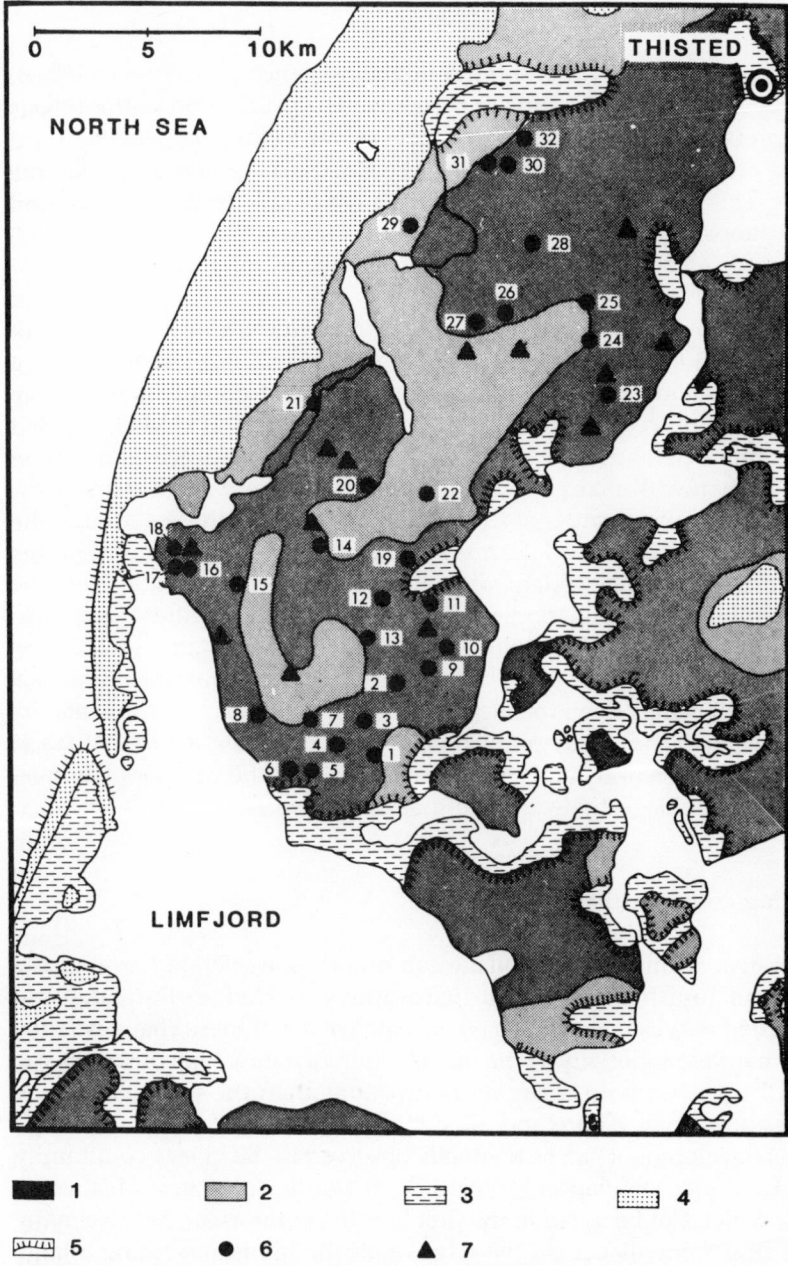

Figure 68 Early Iron Age settlements in the Thy region, north-western Jutland. 1: young moraine landscapes, predominantly clayey soil. 2: young moraine landscapes, predominantly sandy soil. 3: marine foreland. 4: dune landscapes. 5: raised coastlines from the Stone Age. 6: village mounds from the Early Iron Age. 7: ordinary settlements from the Early Iron Age.

Ringkøbing in west Jutland. Here the subsistence pattern was dominated by fjord fishing and sheep-breeding. The production of this village was probably integrated into a larger, as yet unknown, whole.

The economic differentiation in the villages as a whole was still very slight. This is also the case with various crafts practised in the villages. Excavations in Hodde, however, indicate that smithing was a part-time speciality, and the same observation has been made for other Early Iron-Age settlements.

We can thus conclude that up to the first two centuries AD the village communities still showed very little sign of economic differentiation. On the other hand, many of the villages evidence an unequal internal distribution of wealth. The clearest example of this is in Hodde, where a social hierarchy appears with the farmstead of an apparently high-ranking man with many head of cattle at the top and small farmsteads, apparently lacking cattle, at the bottom; in between these extremes are the many medium-sized farmsteads. Naturally the functions of the village demanded a certain degree of co-operation. Aside from the apparently planned periodic moves of the village, there are such indications as the large open 'commons' in the Hodde village, the locations of the farmsteads in relation to this commons, and the extensive fencing. Even the farmsteads of the élite may be explained by the fact that the demographic and economic subsistence situation necessitated positions of authority to administer the co-operative functions of the village by leading and assigning work.

Farming communities in transition

The transformation of the village communities accelerated around the third and fourth centuries AD. Excavations in Hodde, Dankirke and Drengsted in west Denmark have revealed some of these changes. They were manifest especially in the introduction of a new type of farmstead, much larger and with many more functions than the farmsteads from the centuries just before and after the birth of Christ.

This development can be distinctly observed in the village community recently under excavation at Vorbasse in southern Jutland. This settlement, which can be dated to the first to fifth centuries AD, lies like many other Iron Age villages on the edge of a little hill island facing a large meadow area.

The history of the village goes back to the first century AD. Here some enclosed farmsteads were constructed, each consisting of an east–west oriented longhouse with a small rectangular house. The cemetery of this little hamlet is not far away and the graves indicate that the settlement originally consisted of three households.

In the second century AD, the settlement was moved 600 metres to the east, where it evolved into a village settlement covering an area of about 150 × 150 metres. This settlement, as yet known only from trial excavations, still existed at the beginning of the third century AD. The village was then moved back to the site of the original farmsteads. But now the farm type was completely different. To be sure, it still consisted of a single longhouse together with one or two small houses, all standing on an enclosed plot. But the longhouses were now far longer than those of the first century AD. The plot of the farmstead had also been enlarged a good deal. The village still consisted of individual farmsteads separated from one another by sturdy fences. There seems to have been no preconceived plan.

Yet such a plan does seem to have arisen in connection with a regulation of the settlement in the fourth century AD (Figure 69). The old farmsteads were torn down and this time three enclosed farmsteads were erected at a distance of about 100 metres from each other, apparently with an eye to further building. And indeed this expectation was realized. The spaces between the three farmsteads were soon filled in, thus making a row of farmsteads 350 metres long.

Somewhat to the east, yet another row of farmsteads was built, this one 250 metres long; furthest to the east there were still two more farmsteads with a total length of 125 metres. One of these latter farmsteads was the largest in the village. It is noteworthy that it was erected at the spot where a century earlier another very large farmstead had stood. The enclosed area of the new farmstead was 74 × 54 metres, i.e. almost 4000 m². It was thus much larger than the other farms in the village, which averaged about 2000 m². Comparison of this average size with the size of the enclosed areas of the farmsteads 300–400 years earlier in the village of Hodde show that the area of the farmsteads had grown considerably (Figure 70). Their enclosed plots had almost quadrupled. There can be no doubt that the explosive growth of the farmsteads is to be ascribed to an increase in production.

In this phase, there are also indications that secondary occupations began to play a larger role. Indications have been found that a specialized production of, for example, quernstones took place in the village. There are also traces of iron production: furnaces and a smithy were found in one of the small houses belonging to the largest farmstead.

In the fourth century AD, the village was comprised of twenty large farmsteads with a total area of 400 × 250 metres. This was the apex of its development – already a century later, in the fifth century AD, the

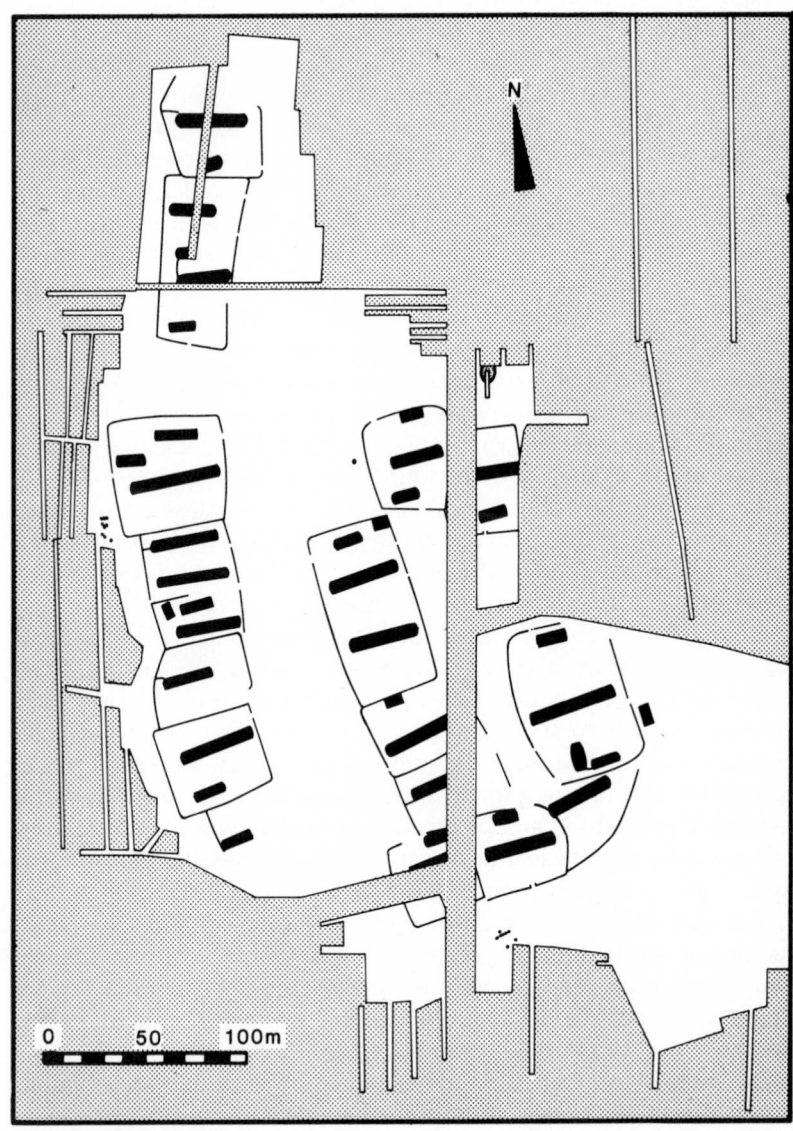

Figure 69 The Vorbasse settlement in the 4th century AD. During this period the
village contained about 20 farmsteads. On average, the fence round the
farmsteads enclosed an area of *c.* 2000 m².

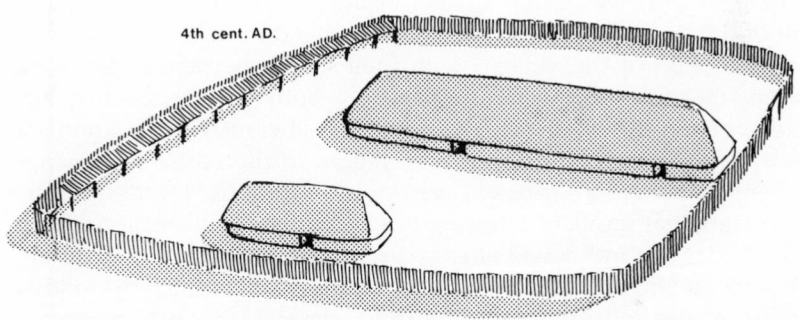

Figure 70 During the first centuries AD the enclosed plot of the typical Danish
farmstead grew considerably in size. Above: a farmstead from the Hodde
settlement, 1st century AD. Below: a farmstead from the Vorbasse settlement,
4th century AD.

signs of decline are obvious. This final phase of the existence of the
village shows that many of the farmsteads from the fourth century AD
continued to exist but that they shrank as the cattle population diminished. Other farmsteads were torn down or moved and now at last the
settlement clustered around an open area, 150 × 120 metres, maybe a
commons as at the 400-years older Hodde village. In the final phase of
the Vorbasse village, the largest farmstead from the fourth century AD,
which had been rebuilt, still existed. This farm seems to have constituted a sort of core for the settlement during approximately 200 years.

A novel feature of this closing phase of the village was that each of the
individual farmsteads now possessed their own small workshops,
so-called pithouses, mostly situated at the edge of the large open central
area. The presence of these small workshops may indicate that the
secondary occupations had now truly been integrated into the subsistence pattern. This feature clearly presages the settlements of the eighth
century and later.

The village was torn down at some point in the fifth century, and its
further fate cannot be traced. As traces of later cultivation can be seen in

the area, we know that an Iron Age community still existed here and that the land was tilled. But a regular settlement at the site cannot be ascertained again until the eighth century AD. And this time it was a thriving Viking settlement.

The Vorbasse village is the youngest link so far known in the evolution of a settlement pattern which can now be followed through more than 1000 years of the Iron Age. Going back in time, the kinship with earlier settlement traditions is unmistakable. This may be seen by a comparison with the Hodde village, nearly 400 years older. The placement of the two villages in relation to fields and meadows is the same. The orientation of the villages with their length perpendicular to the adjacent meadows was also the same. In both villages, animal husbandry apparently was the chief occupation. Obviously the location and plan of the village were chosen with regard to the access to grazing.

In both Hodde and Vorbasse, we can trace from the founding of the village a gradual influx of farmsteads – and in both villages it has been revealed that this influx had already been planned from the beginning. Both settlements lasted for one or two centuries, after which the gradual vacating of the settlement was initiated. Besides an open commons, both villages contained enclosed farmsteads, which constituted independent economic units. The Vorbasse settlement shows that in the course of time the central farmstead building, the longhouse, underwent major changes – as did the enclosed plot and its buildings (Figure 71). In Hodde the length of the longhouse is between 12 and 16 metres. In Vorbasse the average length is over 30 metres. This development of the longhouse can in fact be traced elsewhere in Denmark and abroad.

With this house type, which apparently evolved around the third century AD, a more differentiated division of functions than earlier becomes evident. Figure 72, for example, shows a 38-metre-long farmstead from Vorbasse with roughly 200 m² under one roof. Comparisons with related farmsteads found outside Denmark make it likely that the house was divided into five rooms. The westernmost room was the living room and here too food was prepared. The function of Room 2 is unknown but doubtless it was also for dwelling. Room 3 was the entrance room, probably used for the storage of tools and implements. Room 4 was a byre and Room 5 was probably used as a barn, threshing floor or the like. The question remains whether the size of the house can be taken to mean that the number of persons in each household had been increased. That is not unlikely in view of the fact that in time the secondary occupations also seemed to have increased in importance. This development is manifest in the building of the so-called pithouses. These houses were workshops with various functions: weaving, smi-

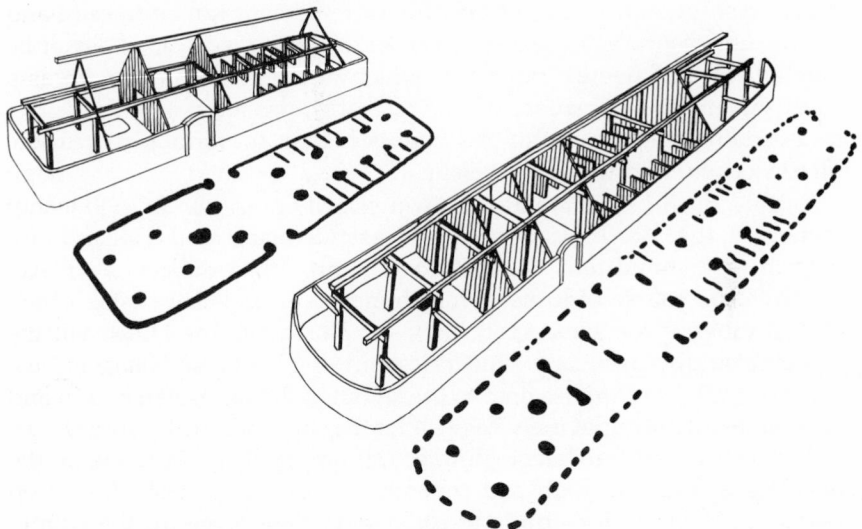

Figure 71 Schematic representation of the constructional and functional changes of the three-aisled Iron Age longhouse from the 1st century AD to the 4th century AD.

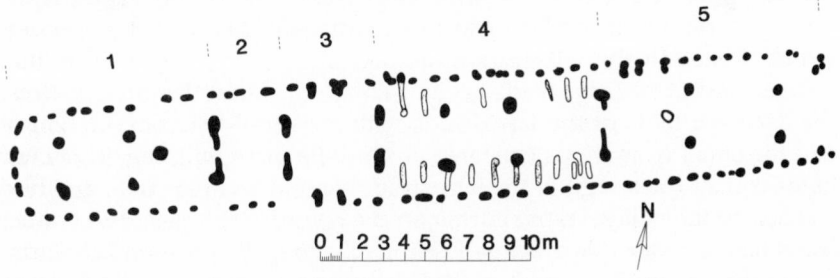

Figure 72 Thirty-eight-metre-long farmstead from the Vorbasse settlement. In contrast to earlier house types, the farmstead has now been divided up into five different rooms indicating a more differentiated function of the house.

thing, pottery-making and other specialized production probably took place here. In general, the village seems to be a forerunner of the farmsteads consisting of separate buildings, each with its own function, as known from the great farms of the Viking Age and on into the Middle Ages.

Villages such as Vorbasse seem to have been common, at least in west Denmark. Similar complexes have been found here and there in south-west Jutland. In Drengsted, where settlement can be traced back to the first century BC, excavations have been made of about fifty longhouses and twenty pithouses which are contemporary with the latest settlement in Vorbasse. In the case of Drengsted it is not possible to ascertain whether or not the houses belong to various successive phases of one and the same village.

Villages of this type are also known elsewhere in the large lowland region by the North Sea, in north-west Germany and Holland. In Flögeln (P. Schmid and W.H. Zimmermann, 1976) there is a village which in the course of three or four hundred years was re-established several times at the same spot, just as in Vorbasse. The Dutch village Wijster also displays many similarities with the Vorbasse village (W.A. van Es, 1967). This applies both to the layout of the farmstead and to the general restructuring of the village about the third or fourth century AD.

After c. 500 AD the archaeological record completely fails us, and as yet no villages from the sixth and seventh centuries have been found in Denmark. We can pick up the thread again in the course of the eighth century, after which further evolution leads to the great village complexes of the Viking Age. This unfortunate gap in the archaeological record makes it impossible to demonstrate a direct connection between the settlement pattern of the fifth century and that of the Viking Age. Yet it is certain that the leap was not a large one. Many of the features which existed in the villages around 500 AD may be recognized in the villages and great farmsteads of the Viking era. These features include the enclosed plots of the farmsteads with a centrally placed longhouse and the small workshops clustered around the main building. This also holds true of the layout of the farmsteads around an open area, and the location of the village in the terrain on the boundary of meadows which could be used for cattle grazing. Presumably no really profound changes in agrarian technology took place in the two or three hundred years from which no settlements have been found. However, it is significant that in the eighth century, along with the village societies, there were now settlements such as Ribe and Hedeby which evolved into more townlike structures in the course of the ninth century.

A general survey of agrarian development up to the Viking Age thus suffers from a number of gaps. But if one were to outline the presumed course of development, it must be assumed that the features which characterize village society up to about 500 AD endured without significant disturbances. Throughout the roughly 1300 years of the Iron Age, agricultural productivity slowly rose; the greatest step occurred around the third or fourth century AD, to judge by the appearance of the village societies (Figure 73). At the same time, the differentiation of production

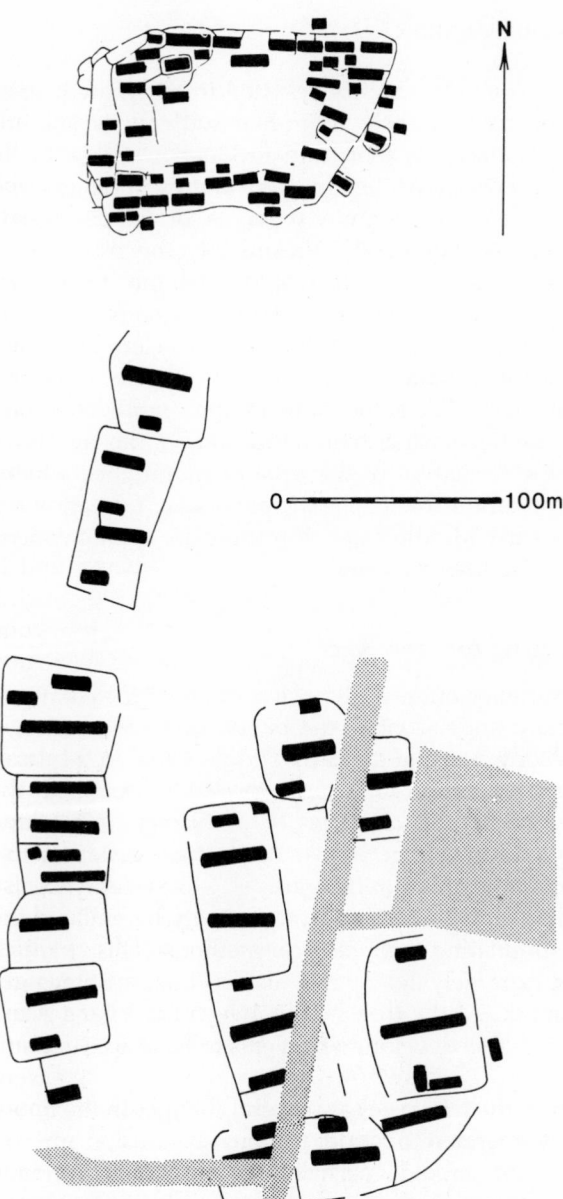

N

0 ━━━━━━━━━━100m

Figure 73 Total view of the layout of the Hodde village
(above) and the Vorbasse village (below). The difference in size between the two complexes is probably
an indication of the growth of agricultural productivity which took place during the 3rd and 4th
centuries AD.

commenced, which in the eighth century resulted in the growth of a population of craftsmen; concurrently town-like settlements started developing. In Ribe such traces as tools and production refuse have been found from several workshops: beadmakers and metalcasters are seen to have worked here. There are also signs of a specialized production of combs and leather goods. Presumably the production exceeded that which the local population could consume; thus it is indirect evidence of a growing circulation of domestic goods.

At many places in southern Scandinavia and northern Germany, this incipient differentiation of occupation set in from the second to fourth centuries AD. However, not until some time in the eighth century, stimulated in part by an increasing hierarchization in the agrarian society, did it lead to the formation of the urban communities which would later play so important a role in the incipient state formation of the Viking Age and the early Middle Ages. But these are events which lie beyond the range of the present work.

Subsistence patterns during the Iron Age

A study of the village societies offers a glimpse of some of the changes which the agrarian society underwent in the period up to the agricultural expansion of the Viking Age and the early Middle Ages. At this late time another agricultural revolution took place, probably provoked by the population growth in the last centuries of prehistory. What lay ahead of this seemingly radical change was an agricultural system with roots all the way back to the third millennium BC – a system which through the Iron Age had slowly increased productivity by embracing ever more production-stimulating technological methods. This change seems to have occurred extremely slowly and also at different times in various regions in Denmark. At the threshold between the Viking Age and the early Middle Ages, this development seems to have accelerated in earnest.

The thirteen centuries of the Iron Age saw several changes in the type of cultivation, apparently intended to hinder ruinous soil erosion and to improve the quality of the mould, partially by use of manuring. Moreover these changes meant that an ever-larger number of animals were kept indoors in the winter, a tendency which may have begun already in the second millennium BC, but which first gained a foothold around 500 BC.

We have earlier seen how it was quite late before the prehistoric agricultural system managed to create a reasonably good layer of mould on the tilled fields. Aside from the natural washing-out of the soil, ard-ploughing and an extensive erosion exhausted the soil, especially the lighter soils. Not only has soil erosion often been observed at archaeological excavations but it also frequently appears in Danish raised bogs. Here there is such a large fall-out of soil particles that it must point to an explosive intensification of agriculture in the centuries around the birth of Christ. This observation corresponds to both pollen-analytical evidence and to the archaeological record.

Soil erosion must have been a serious problem for this expanding agriculture. The means by which the Iron Age farmers attempted to solve this problem may be apparent in the so-called Celtic fields, the remains of the prehistoric field systems. Many of these Celtic fields are known in Denmark. The majority of them are found in the western part of the country, where they were preserved thanks to the less intensive cultivation of historical times. But the balks of the Celtic fields are also known from eastern Denmark, especially Zealand and Bornholm. Here they are usually found in forests, where they were protected from cultivation in more recent times.

The Celtic fields were probably first established around the middle of the first millennium BC. How long they were in use is another question; probably only up to the mid-first millennium AD. Most frequently the Celtic fields are situated on moraine formations, especially in lighter sand-mixed soils. But as the Jutland examples have shown, also heathy areas were cultivated in the Iron Age, resulting in the formation of Celtic fields. The field systems are often naturally delimited by meadows and bogs.

The Celtic fields are bordered by low balks up to 1 metre high. The balks enclose small fields averaging between 1000 and 3000 m^2 and form a net-like pattern in the terrain. It has been suggested that the balks were covered with a hedge-like vegetation intended to shelter the fields from wind erosion. Experience has shown that this sort of net-like system of wind-breaks provides good protection against wind erosion regardless of the wind direction.

Unfortunately, there is no certain pollen-analytical evidence that the balks were in fact covered with these hedges. Hawthorn, which would be a natural form of vegetation, produces very little pollen and is therefore difficult to discern. Yet at one single spot, namely the Pre-Roman Iron Age village in Grøntoft in west Jutland, a vegetation layer found under one of the balks included the pollen of nearby scrub – a dense underbrush – of birch, alder and hazel. Perhaps these are the vestiges of a hedge-like vegetation. The hedges would then help explain the rise of the balks, as the live underbrush would have intercepted the uppermost eroded layer of soil in untilled periods. This helps explain the high content of phosphate sometimes observed in the balks. Other factors such as the moving of soil by ploughing and the removal of stones from the fields undoubtedly also contributed to the growth of the balks.

In sum, it is possible that the balks were formed as a result of several factors; soil erosion before the hedges were sufficiently high; ploughing when the field was under cultivation; soil erosion when the field lay fallow; and wind action through holes in the hedge made by grazing cattle (W. Groenmann-van Waateringe, 1979).

It is thus likely that the Celtic fields are the remains of small cultivated plots, the enclosed character of which was emphasized by a hedge-like vegetation. Most probably, after a field had been cultivated for a period, cattle were allowed to graze on it. The cattle were protected behind the hedge and at the same time the small fields were naturally manured so they could be used later for cereal cultivation.

This continuous use of the land, however, raises the question to what extent manuring was practised on Iron Age fields in order to maintain soil fertility. The introduction of manuring is a major turning-point in agrarian history, as manuring can hinder or at least significantly diminish exhaustion of the soil. As a result, the mould layer will slowly increase in thickness.

It would seem logical that the introduction of manuring would have resulted from the keeping of cattle indoors. When a byre was mucked out, the beneficial influence of the manure on plant growth would have been obvious. And indeed some early Iron Age houses have yielded traces of mucking out. In the Celtic field systems preserved at Grøntoft from the centuries just preceding the birth of Christ, there are also indications of manuring. Similar observations have been made in Holland. Here, however, it has been concluded that fields were some-times fertilized with peat. Still other similar observations have been made on the island of Sild just south of the Danish border (H.J. Kroll, 1975).

There are thus a number of indications that manuring was practised quite early in the Iron Age. We cannot know its extent, but there is reason to believe that the technique was widespread a couple of centuries after the birth of Christ. At this time there begins to be in the archaeological record a striking lack of the rubbish pits always pre-viously found at prehistoric settlements. We can now assume that the refuse was simply collected at dung heaps near the farmsteads.

The tilling of the fields has been to some degree illuminated by finds of ard furrows and ard parts. Ard types, more developed than the simple hook ards, were in use as early as 700 BC (Figure 74). But there is

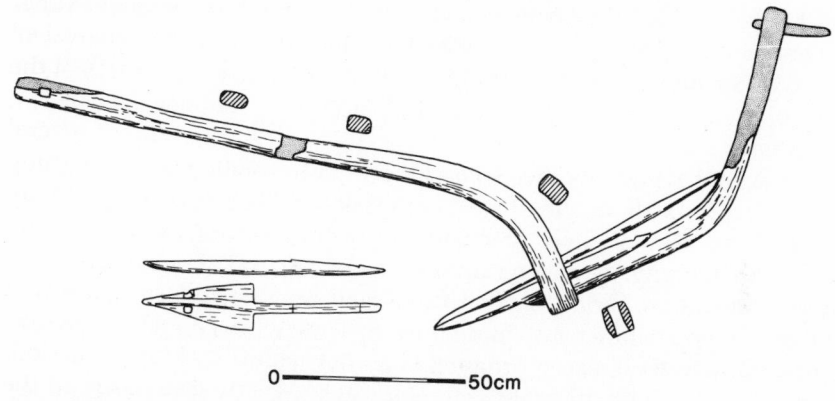

Figure 74 Iron Age ard found at Donneruplund, Vejle county.

also reason to believe that the ard was still in use as late as in the Viking period. However, recent finds just south of the Danish border indicate that more advanced plough types were in use as early as the first century BC (K.R. Schultz-Klinken, 1976). There is still some uncertainty about the interpretation of these finds, and it is usually thought that the mouldboard plough was first used in western Europe after the sixth century AD. The heavy wheel plough with a mouldboard first achieved importance in Denmark with the agricultural revolution during the early Middle Ages.

However, it is not certain that the earliest mouldboard plough was wheel-driven. Thus it cannot be denied that more advanced plough types which could turn the soil may have come to Denmark during the Iron Age. But when this transition would have occurred is completely indeterminable. We must still assume that the rather ineffective ard with its very limited effect on mould formation (see p. 99) was the most widespread ploughing implement during the Iron Age.

As for the composition of the crops, there seem to have been no changes between c. 500 BC and 800 AD. Since the third millennium BC field husbandry must have been based primarily on barley. Only small amounts of other grains were raised. In the first millennium BC wheat suffered a drastic decline, due probably to the climatic worsening which gradually made an impact. At the same time oats were introduced, though only to a small degree, as a cultivated plant. Rye could also be seen on the tilled fields in the period around the birth of Christ, but it was hardly a true cultivated plant in Denmark; the cultivation of rye seems to have been mainly confined to the region south of present-day Denmark. In Holland, rye is known from settlements from the fifth and sixth centuries AD. In Denmark, it was first widely cultivated in the course of the Viking Age. Thus it may be presumed that, together with the introduction of the wheel plough and the three-field system, rye was part of the agricultural revolution which occurred just after the close of prehistory.

We do not know whether some kind of crop rotation was practised on Iron Age fields or whether there existed a fixed cultivation/fallow cycle. This sort of land management would be difficult to prove pollen-analytically, as pollen samples yield a mixture of pollen from the entire cultivation period. Actual three-field farming, which decreased the risk of crop failure by dividing the crops into winter crops and spring crops and which increased production by shortening the fallow periods, is not known until the eighth or ninth centuries in western Europe. Therefore it cannot even be considered for the early Iron Age in Denmark.

Although we lack knowledge of a number of essential technological factors we can conclude that around the birth of Christ, agriculture was not very productive. In the second and third centuries AD productivity began to rise due to the expansion of animal husbandry, but the greatest leap forward seems to have taken place from the ninth to thirteenth centuries, just as elsewhere in Europe. This increase seems to have resulted from the introduction of a new form of land management, namely the three-field system with the technological advances which accompanied it (E.P. Christensen, 1979).

A clear indication of the low productivity of agriculture around the birth of Christ is the extensive gathering of the seeds of wild plants. This gathering must have been practised outside the cultivated areas, on fallow and harvested fields. Prehistoric man has probably always supplemented his diet with the seeds of wild plants. For the centuries around the birth of Christ, it must still be presumed that a very considerable percentage of the vegetable food was made up of the seeds of wild plants. It must be remembered that agriculture demanded time-consuming labour for weeding the fields, and not until the harrow and more advanced plough types came into use was this labour gradually diminished.

Thus, far into the first millennium AD, agriculture was not very productive. A large investment of labour resulted in a relatively small yield, and even though a number of innovative agricultural methods were introduced, the effects were minimal. A threefold or fourfold harvest was probably the maximum attained. (S. Nielsen, 1980). Only the expansion of animal husbandry could make a notable increase in productivity.

This assumption finds partial corroboration in the excavated villages and can moreover be illustrated by some of the calculations which have been made regarding the average yield of a farmstead in the centuries around the birth of Christ. If a household kept 8–9 large head of cattle and 10–12 head of young cattle and calves over the winter, then the annual yield would have been about 500 kilogrammes of meat. Adding to this the dairy products from the milch cows as well as meat from a number of smaller domesticated animals such as pigs and sheep, the total amount of food would hardly have sufficed to cover more than half of the calorie requirements of a family of 7–8 people (including children and the elderly). The remainder had to be supplied by vegetable food. But here too there were serious limitations. With a yield of threefold or fourfold, a cultivated area of about 3 hectares could produce exactly enough to supply the remaining calorie requirements. However this condition is only fulfilled if there is a three-field system. With a two-field system the area would have had to be considerably greater. But here the labour capacity set a natural limitation. Imitative experiments have shown that it takes 8–9 days to plough and about 10 days to harvest one hectare with a hand sickle. In addition there is a considerable labour input in the form of weeding the cultivated area. Thus an average family could hardly have kept more than about 3 hectares under plough.

In view of the cultivation methods employed it is not possible to expect that the amount of vegetable foods could have been increased to any great degree. Only an expansion of the cattle population could have efficiently ensured a yield increase. This situation first changed during the Viking Age and the early Middle Ages, when the prehistoric farming based mainly on animal husbandry was transformed to a farming based on cereal cultivation as a result of a series of technological changes. The result was an expansion of the cultivated area and a corresponding decrease in the size of the grazing areas.

In the above, an attempt has been made to describe some of the main tendencies of the agrarian communities through the Iron Age. In the fifth and sixth centuries AD there was undeniably a connection with the economic and demographic decline which much of the European continent suffered at that time. In the seventh century, in central Europe, this development changed course; the population now expanded considerably; a strong economic boom took place. Denmark too showed signs of increased growth. But still the ancient tradition of animal husbandry seems to have persisted as late as the Viking Age. Technological improvements must have made their mark during the Iron Age. But as long as our knowledge of land management from 500–800 AD is so poor, it must suffice to note that from the eighth century the size of the village complexes and the growing differentiation of subsistence forms indirectly bear witness to the fact that activity had not stagnated in the intervening period.

Iron

The development of secondary occupations is one of the factors which most clearly illustrates the growth of the productivity of the farming communities through the last millennium of the Iron Age. Of particular importance in this connection is the refinement of the craft of smithing and of the complicated technology required for iron extraction.

The gradual advance of iron technology from central Europe can be illustrated with a distribution map of iron objects from the archaeological finds prior to c. 500 BC (Figure 75). The finds are seen to be concentrated along the central Elbe and the central and lower Oder. Further to the north, that is in northernmost Germany and Denmark, the finds are still quite scarce. To be sure, finds of iron do not necessarily indicate the existence of smithing based upon local iron extraction. A look at the nature of the iron finds from the seventh and sixth centuries BC shows that in fact most of them are small objects such as ornamental pins or toilet articles such as razors, tweezers and the like. Proper tools of iron are quite rare, as also holds true of smithing slags. A true iron production probably took place only in Saxony and Silesia, which were regions bordering directly on the iron-producing central European zone.

It is therefore surprising that in Denmark traces are found of smithing and possibly of local iron extraction shortly after 500 BC. Yet this does in fact seem to be the case, although interpretation of the finds is still being debated.

The precondition for this production was – aside from the capacity to produce charcoal – the bog iron ore which could be extracted in bogs and along streams. Bog iron is plentiful in Denmark, namely in south and west Jutland. Here iron is found as an impure ore which is usually blue-black. Bog iron ore from Jutland seems to have been exploited as early as the fifth century BC and until as late as the seventeenth century AD. In any case this seems to be the conclusion which can be drawn from the most recent finds.

In 1976–7, a settlement, probably from the fifth or fourth century BC, was excavated at Bruneborg in the eastern part of central Jutland. Less than one kilometre from the settlement there is a natural deposit of bog iron ore, and from here the raw material was transported to the settlement, where it has been found in abundance, both in its raw state and as roasted granulated ore. One particularly significant find was that

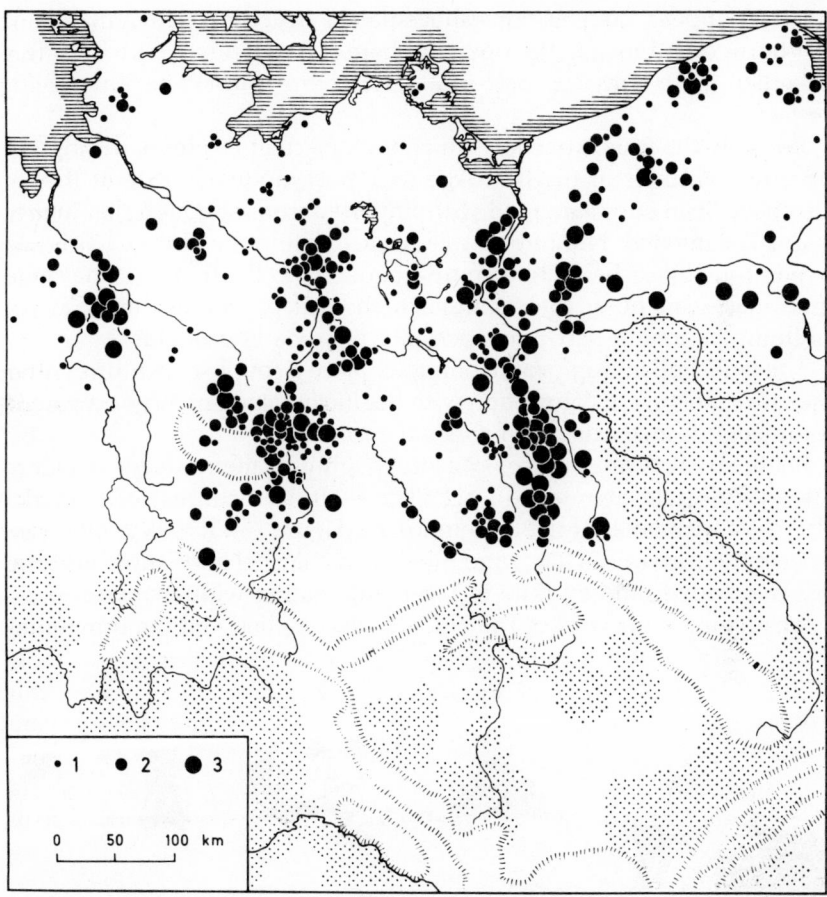

Figure 75 Distribution of iron objects during the 8th – 6th centuries BC in the north European lowland, i.e. period V–VI of the Nordic Bronze Age. The dotted areas show the central European Iron Age Hallstatt culture. 1: 1 object. 2: 2–4 objects. 3: 5 or more objects.

of a smithy in a pit. This contained the forge and other remnants from the fashioning of the iron. The smithing slags were of a type also known from Viking Age settlements; this attests to a smithing technique nearly 1500 years old. Doubtless, smithing took place at the site. But it is somewhat more uncertain whether iron extraction also took place. Iron smelting furnaces have not been found, but worked bog iron has. There are indications that iron extraction may have been carried out in a type of furnace known from other finds from around the birth of Christ. Such furnaces appear today as horseshoe-shaped structures with a mantle of red-burnt clay. Outside the opening there is frequently a pit with slags. Whether these furnaces had a superstructure cannot be known for certain.

Probably the iron extraction which took place in Denmark during the first five centuries of the Iron Age was most modest in extent. It may also have been supplemented with imported iron, although this theory is unsubstantiated. Not until the centuries around the birth of Christ do larger iron objects begin to turn up frequently in the finds. At the same time it is seen how, for example in the village Hodde, the craft of smithing became a part-time speciality in some households.

The landslide in iron production took place a couple of centuries after the birth of Christ in connection with the introduction of more advanced technological methods, such as shaft furnaces.

Shaft furnaces are built over a pit roughly ¾ metre deep, which is intended to hold the melted slags. The shaft itself consists of a conical clay shaft with holes at the bottom for air (Figure 76). It took a long time to heat the furnaces. They were filled with charcoal and straw, and the ore was added little by little in layers alternating with charcoal.

At a temperature of about 1200°C, the slag melted and ran down into

Figure 76 Schematic representation of the stages of prehistoric iron production. 1: extraction of ore. 2: ore piled in a heap for drying. 3: crushing of ore into suitable sizes for the furnace. 4: construction of the furnace. 5: the furnace is preheated and filled with ore and charcoal. 6: when the iron has been reduced from ore, the shaft is broken down and the bloom, a lump of iron and slag, is removed. 7: the bloom is repeatedly heated up in a smithing pit. 8: the bloom is cleansed of as much slag as possible.

the pit. The iron formed in the shaft had a very low content of carbon, less than 2 per cent. It was therefore like a spongey mass which often stuck to the sides of the furnace. When the slag had run down into the pit and the oxidation had ceased, the bloom was broken out of the shaft, which could then be moved to a new slag pit and re-used.

Furnaces of this type are found from the period after *c.* 200 AD at many of the large settlements. They are often situated in groups of eight or ten, and always at some distance from the dwelling area due to the danger of fire. In some villages such as Drengsted in southern Jutland, finds have been made of up to 200 shaft furnaces, some of which contained slags weighing 500 kilogrammes.

Iron production on this scale by far exceeded the needs of the village. Production must have been intended for a larger local area. Moreover, it must have diverted a good deal of labour from food production.

The expansion of iron production seems to have taken place concurrently with the striking restructuring of the village communities – and there is reason to believe that iron extraction was not the only craft which achieved this degree of specialization. Thus the incipient differentiation of production must have been a noteworthy feature during the two or three centuries after the birth of Christ.

17

The development of the economic institutions

Exchange systems

Since the second millennium BC, a developing prestige-goods economy had linked the agrarian societies in Denmark to an extensive network of exchange systems. By means of this network, which covered large parts of the European continent, Denmark was for 1500 years supplied with central European bronze, which was used in domestic circulation to indicate status. For the reproduction of social formations in the Bronze Age, this prestige-goods economy doubtless had decisive importance. But then, in the seventh and sixth centuries BC, metal supplies from central Europe diminished greatly. The reasons for this are unknown but a certain degree of contraction of the interregional trade must have been the result. Then, in the last couple of centuries BC, the exchange of goods rose again; once more northern Europe was bound closely to the more highly developed economic systems in central and southern Europe.

At first contacts were established mainly with the Roman civilization, but later also with its offshoots: the early feudal states which evolved in western Europe from the sixth century AD and later. The prestige-goods economy first culminated a couple of centuries after the birth of Christ. Until then it had developed from rather small local political structures but in time it led to more extensive political unifications, which were reflected in increasingly hierarchical formations. Competition among centres at the local level, disruptions and changes of the trade routes were recurring phenomena and resulted through the centuries in repeated shiftings of the foci of trade and consequently also of the political centres. This occurred synchronously with numerous attempts to unify ever larger local regions. At the threshold to the Viking Age this process had come so far that it resulted in the formation of the first centres with an urban character, that is, with a developed craft specialization. In this way the preconditions were created for the market trade which was to evolve in the coming centuries.

This process is an example of a general phenomenon which social anthropology has discovered in many societies in similar structural positions. In later years the theory has also been applied within the study of prehistoric societies in Denmark (L. Hedager, 1978b and c). At the core of this theory is the assumption that every low-technology society produces a surplus of goods and labour. The purpose of this surplus production is the maintenance of social relations. In this way a circulation of goods arises which most often takes place in connection with events of social or ritual character.

It is important to bear in mind that at this stage of development land and foodstuffs are virtually never included in the circulation. This seems to be a general phenomenon. As pointed out by Maurice Godelier, by excluding from competition problems related to the means of production (land) and the means of existence, the primitive society ensures the physical existence of its members; and by allowing competition for goods which are difficult to obtain it ensures its own existence as a society.

Control of the exchange of goods implies, as we have seen, control over the access to those foreign goods and wealth objects which indicate status and are thus determinant for the development of political power. An internal system arises, based upon redistribution, in which tribute in the form of domestic surplus is passed up through the system to the dominant chief. At the same time wealth objects, often acquired through external trade, are passed down through the same system through a variety of social transactions. These transactions serve to maintain the social reproduction of the involved parties. A differential access to prestige goods thus creates contacts among the political leaders of the local centres, thus creating a network of exchange connections through which goods can be transported over great distances.

Up to about 500 BC this prestige-goods system had functioned in northern Europe without major disturbances. Since the second millennium BC it had given rise to numerous specialized workshops which produced prestige and status items on the basis of, for example, imported bronze and gold. These items were included in a so-called social production withdrawal system (W.L. Rathje, 1975), in which wealth objects are withdrawn from circulation by the élite and through various ritual transactions are converted into status. In the beginning this is achieved by depositing the wealth objects in the graves, later mainly by depositing them in sacrificial hoards in, for example, wet lands or other inaccessible areas.

To understand the further course of events it is necessary to distinguish some general features of the prestige-goods economy. First of all, changes easily occur in the network of exchange if the economic system is linked to another system based on more complicated principles. The adversary will often tend to play the local competing centres against one another. The result will be a number of shifting foci for trade and consequently also for political power. In this way a continuous and conflicting process of evolution and devolution is created. This is apparently what happened in the relationship between the central European centres and their Mediterranean trade partners in the seventh to fifth centuries BC (S. Frankenstein and M.J. Rowlands, 1978). For northern Europe this situation seems to have resulted in the drying up of the flow of bronze from around 600 BC.

The system is also very vulnerable to economic changes within the foreign regions upon which it depends for the supply of valuable goods. This was the case for long periods of the Iron Age, when the northern European areas were bound to economic systems, such as the Roman civilization, which maintained a considerable production for exchange. Changes of production within these core centres normally have a marked effect in the economically less-developed regions.

It is characteristic of production within a core centre that at some point it will change over to mass-produced goods which experience has shown to be particularly popular in the peripheral 'barbarian' areas. The mass production of drinking equipment in the Roman provinces in the centuries after the birth of Christ is one of the most well-known examples of this. Such a production will often create a group of middlemen traders (C. Renfrew, 1975) who take charge of the primary distribution of the products. In the so-called buffer zone outside of the Roman Limes there was probably a group of such middleman traders in the centuries AD.

Finally, there also exists a natural connection between the increasing demand for the exploitation of the resources in the local centres and the ability of social formations to reproduce themselves. If conditions are continually deteriorating, then hierarchization becomes problematic and a sort of devolution can be anticipated, creating a situation with a more competitive economy in which all available surplus is channelled into the horizontal circuits. This cycle can only be broken by a new growth of productivity and this is probably what occurred in the centuries around the birth of Christ in Denmark.

Exchange until 800 AD

The period around 600 BC was a turning point in the history of Europe. Along the Mediterranean coasts political and economic activity began to accelerate, and in the areas north of the Alps a more intensive interaction with the Mediterranean city states led to profound changes in social formations. In the north Alpine zone there now arose a number of economic centres of shifting political importance. These centres, each of which must have been the seat of a paramount, seem to have been surrounded by a system of vassal sub-centres, which through tribute contributed to a centralized production at the paramount centres of such things as bronze and iron objects. Interregional trade seems to have been controlled from these paramount centres. At the same time a redistribution of status objects to the sub-centres seems to have taken place from here. The course of events in central Europe in the sixth and fifth centuries BC is thus an exemplary model of the significance which the control of the exchange of goods may have for political and social reproduction in a chiefdom society.

The city states and colonies of the Mediterranean showed great interest in the central European area, most likely because they wished to attain access to its resources. For this purpose, connections were established to the far-reaching exchange network which for many centuries had existed on the continent. By means of this network raw materials such as iron, copper, salt, amber, wool, hides and presumably also slaves could be obtained and sold on the domestic market. In exchange, the Mediterranean world supplied exotic goods such as bronze objects and other luxury items which entered into circulation north of the Alps, where they were used to indicate political rank.

Baltic amber was one of the raw materials which in these centuries became a part of the widespread exchange. Already in the eighth century BC great quantities of amber had begun to flow to the Mediterranean world via eastern contacts. Unfortunately it is not yet possible to ascertain whether the amber came from the entire Baltic zone, including Denmark, or whether only a single area, namely the eastern part of the Baltic, contributed to the exchange of goods. The latter alternative is the most likely one. For amber seems to have been channelled southward by way of connections which lay further to the east than those which brought bronze to Scandinavia.

The influx of amber to the regions around Caput Adriae culminated in the seventh and sixth centuries BC. In northern and central Italy, a flourishing amber industry now arose, the refined craft products of which in several cases were re-exported to central Europe. Fluctuations in the influx of amber reflect the effect which the increasingly antagonistic relations among the Mediterranean city-states had on contact between the north and the south. In the mid-fifth century, concurrent with the growing crisis in the Mediterranean, the influx of amber stagnated. At the same time central Europe also suffered a period of political instability, thus reflecting the region's heavy dependency upon the more highly developed economic systems in the south.

Exactly what significance these events had for socio-economic development in northern Europe is not entirely clear. In any case, the interaction between the north European and the central European sectors of the exchange system through the seventh and sixth centuries was diminished. The central European surplus production of metal was now channelled southwards instead of northwards, and from the fifth century BC very few central European goods circulated in northern Europe.

For an area like Denmark, which was utterly dependent upon imported metal, this state of affairs had a profound impact. The scarcity of wealth objects must have made it difficult to maintain the earlier hierarchization, and this situation lasted until the first century BC. The extravagant sacrificial rites by which the élite had previously converted surplus into status were modified. Certainly, status symbols continued to be sacrificially deposited in Danish peat bogs, but now the sacrifices consisted almost exclusively of single sets of neck-rings, pins, brooches or other accessories of local fabrication. The metal quantities which went into making these objects come nowhere near the enormous quantities of metal which had been withdrawn from circulation in the first half of the first millennium BC. The few central and southern European wealth objects which did manage to reach Denmark in the period after 500 BC often remained in circulation all the way up to the first century BC. One example of this long circulation is a series of Campanian and Etruscan bronze products (P.J. Riis, 1959) from the fifth to third centuries BC which have been found in Danish graves from the first century BC. These wealth objects must have circulated for three or four hundred years.

About a century before the birth of Christ, new currents were felt. These changes coincided with the development of the town-like settlements, oppidae, which since the second century BC had been established in a wide zone across central Europe from France in the west to Czechoslovakia in the east. After the foregoing centuries of thorough decentralization with division into numerous small chiefdoms, central Europe now moved toward larger unifications, perhaps incipient state formations. There are many similarities between the oppidum civilization and the settlements with an urban character which had arisen about 400 years earlier as a result of the contact between the central Europeans and the Mediterranean city-states. The central European oppidae, like their predecessors in the sixth and fifth centuries BC, were with their specialized production placed in nodal points for trade. Their rise seems to have been catalysed by the desire of the Mediterranean people to gain access to central European resources such as iron. However, the Roman civilization was a considerably more stable trading partner than the Mediterranean city-states of the sixth and fifth centuries BC. At the same time, the central European oppidae civilization represents a more advanced economic stage of development which contained the first seeds of a market economy. As a result, in less than a century, a far-reaching trade network was re-established throughout northern and central Europe.

The first indications of this new situation in Denmark date from the

Figure 77 The Gundestrup cauldron, probably 1st century BC. The cauldron has often been considered a product from a northern Gaulish workshop. However, in light of recent research on silverworks from the Thracian Black Sea region it seems more likely that the cauldron was made in south-east Europe.

first century BC. Once more wealth objects were deposited in the earth as a part of ritual sacrifices. This held true of such objects as precious cauldrons, which had originated in central or south-east Europe. The Gundestrup silver cauldron, most probably the work of a south-east European artisan, perhaps a Thracian, is one of the best-known examples (Figure 77). Another piece, the Brå cauldron, came from a central European workshop in the third century BC, but may not have been buried until the first century BC. At the same time this socio-economic development also curtailed the circulation time of foreign wealth objects, which were now deposited in the graves. The wealth objects included wagons of central European origin (Figure 78) and drinking equipment from the Mediterranean region.

These finds, which plainly indicate an intensified exchange of goods, continued after the birth of Christ, when Roman luxury wares were now dispersed over the entire northern part of the continent as a result of the intimate interaction of at least three different economic systems: the Roman system, that of the buffer zone just beyond the Limes, and that of the rest of northern Europe. In order to understand this exchange we must re-examine the exchange of goods in northern and central Europe. Various analyses (L. Hedager, 1978c) have in recent years been able to clarify the situation further. By measuring the distance from the Roman border, the Limes (Figure 79), at which finds were made of imported

Figure 78 The Dejbjerg wagon from the Pre-Roman Iron Age, found in a bog near Ringkøbing, western Jutland.

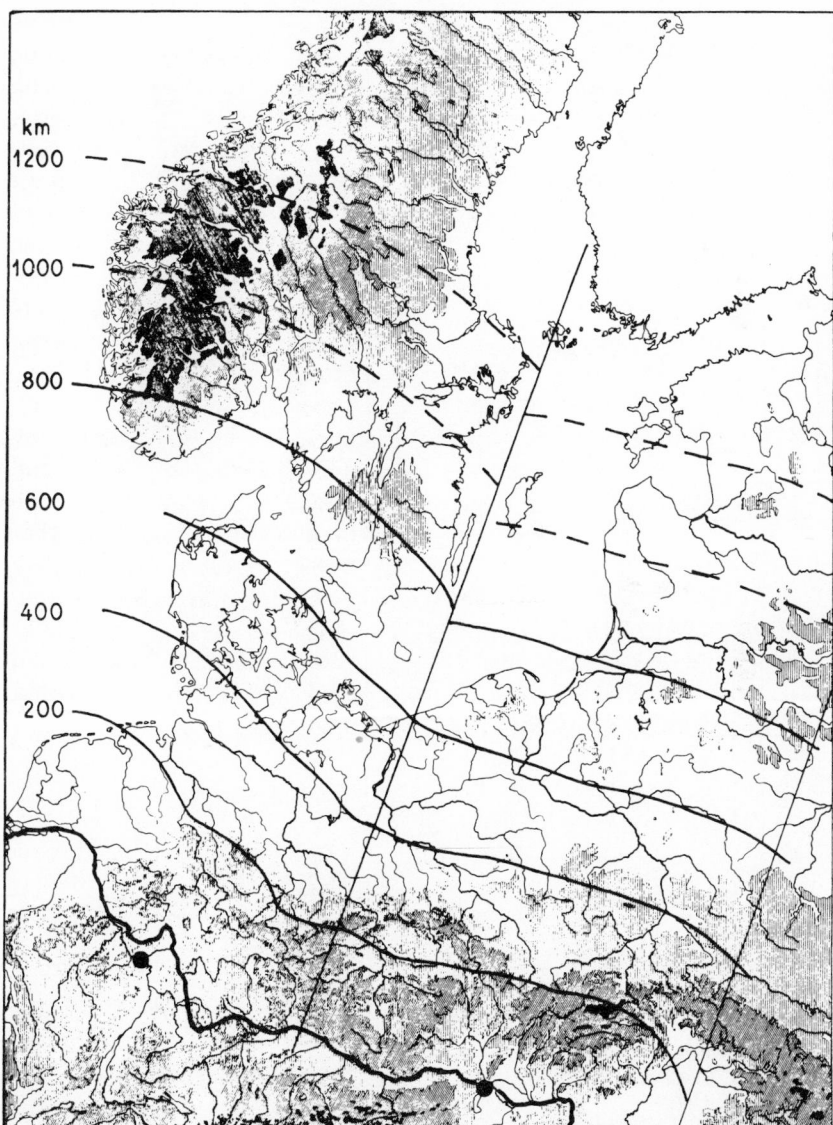

Figure 79 Europe north of the Limes, divided into 200-kilometre units along a borderline separating the area into an eastern and a western part.

Roman objects such as goods made of bronze, glass and silver, or weapons, pottery and brooches, an unmistakable trend emerges as illustrated in Figure 80. The histograms reveal that for one group of objects, the number of finds increases proportionally with the distance

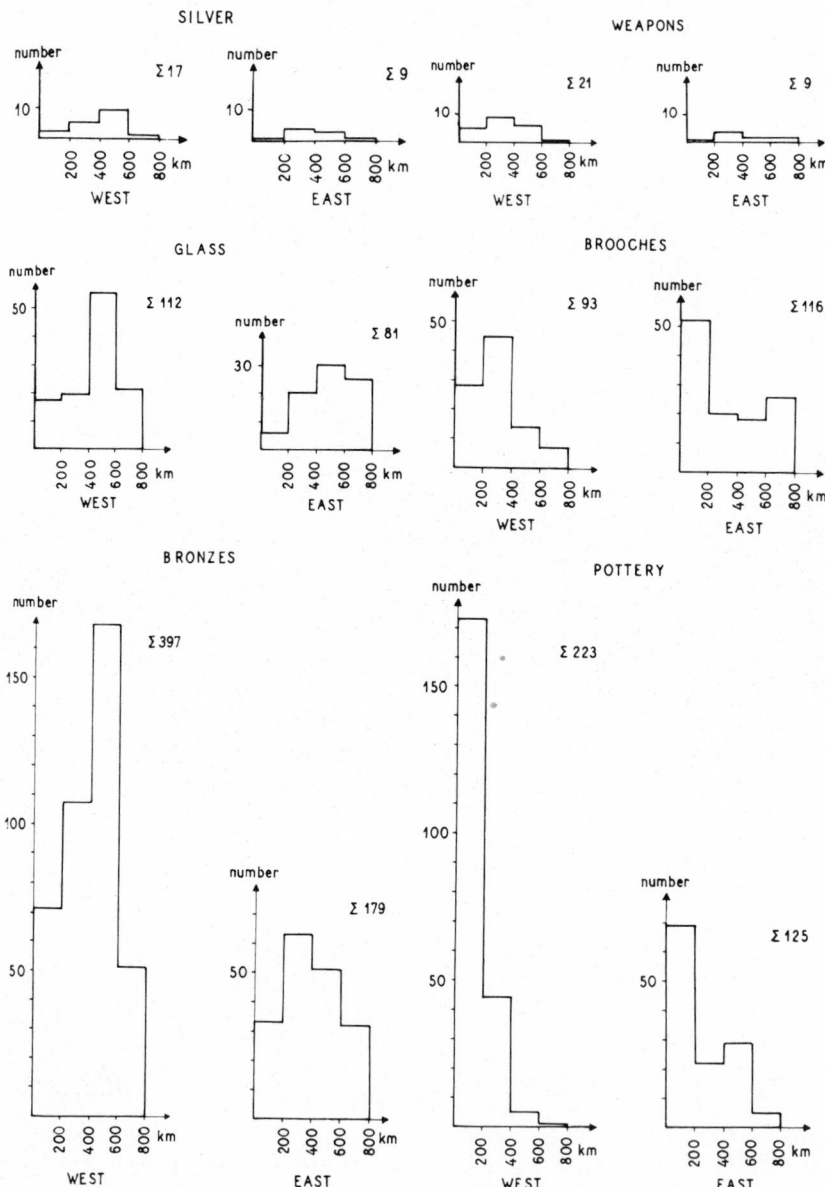

Figure 80 Shortest distance to the western and the eastern Roman border for finds of Roman imports such as silver, weapons, glass, brooches, bronzes, and pottery measured within 200-kilometre intervals.

from the Roman border, but for another group of objects, the number of finds decreases. The objects which increase in number with the distance from the Roman border (up to 600 kilometres) are luxury goods such as bronze, glass and probably also silver and weapons. Objects which decrease in number relative to the distance from the boundary are everyday articles such as pottery and brooches.

This general pattern endured from the first to the fourth centuries AD, although there were some exceptions. Through the first and second centuries AD, for example, there is an extremely large concentration of luxury goods in the zone just beyond the eastern Limes, reflecting the economic importance of the Marcomannian kingdom. After this 'king-dom' lost its political importance, the distribution pattern of the luxury goods again reverted to normal. In the long run, the distribution pattern was quite stable. It may be described thus: just beyond the Limes there was a zone, about 200 kilometres wide, in which Roman luxury goods were rarely deposited as grave-goods. Instead Roman everyday articles were in common use. This may be attributed to two factors: first, the economic trend toward a market economy was more advanced here than further up north, probably because this was the region of the late Celtic oppidae, who had created a more commercially oriented exchange system. Second, the élite of this region had probably been removed from the political system and replaced by Roman influence (L. Hedager, 1978c).

Beyond this 200-kilometre-wide buffer zone, however, there existed a prestige-goods economy based upon a very ancient tradition. Here great quantities of Roman luxury goods functioned in an extremely different context based on a far-flung net of connections among political centres involved in a continuous process of evolution and devolution. No market economy was found here, as may be seen by the finds of Roman coins which indicate monetary functions decreasing in relation to the growing distance from the Roman border (J. Wielowiejski, 1970).

No unambiguous description of this situation can be gleaned from the written sources. However, Tacitus' *Germania*, written at the end of the first century AD, does present a picture of a number of societies seemingly on the chiefdom level of social integration. Judging from Tacitus' rather vague information, the economy of the Germanic chief-doms was characterized primarily by reciprocity and redistribution; no true market economy is mentioned. Within the individual local com-munities the functions of the chieftain included the collection of surplus (cattle are named in several connections) and the subsequent redistribu-tion of this surplus to the warriors. A circulation of prestige objects within the élite stratum seems to have played an essential role, often in connection with various social transactions. Tacitus furthermore mentions that drinking rituals of religious, social and political significance were common among the Germanic people. This may explain the enormous circulation of Roman drinking equipment which took place in the centuries following the birth of Christ. Yet another striking feature of the economic functions is that cattle seem to have functioned as special-purpose money, which could be used for paying a fine or a bride price. This description complements the picture presented here of the northern European chiefdoms in the period around the birth of Christ.

The distribution of Roman goods has been interpreted thus: beyond the Roman Limes there were three different zones. In the first zone, the buffer zone which lay 0–200 kilometres from the border, the transports of Roman luxury goods from the border and the northern provinces were organized. The men delegated to take charge of the transports also acquired everyday necessities of Roman origin such as brooches, which were distributed mainly in zone 1 and only rarely in zone 2 and beyond. This may indicate that the further transport to zone 3, of which Denmark was a part, was organized from zone 2, which was an area lying 200–400 kilometres from the Roman border. In any case, this seems to have held true in the western regions. In the eastern regions, the zone 1 middlemen may have traded in both zones 2 and 3, that is up to 600 kilometres from the Limes. The various zones thus represent areas with political and economic centres among which the exchange of goods was carried on.

Of course, only brief glimpses of this exchange of goods can be obtained, for the archaeological record reveals very little about which categories of goods were traded. The most popular goods were drinking equipment of glass and bronze, and weapons. Archaeological and written sources also attest to amber, wine, coins and the silver goblets which were sometimes included in the drinking equipment. Finally, linguistic evidence indicates that wagons, articles of clothing, geese, soap and hides were also traded. In Figure 81 the three postulated economic systems are presented horizontally and the various categories of goods vertically.

The picture drawn by newer research thus shows a complicated network of connections through which various goods were transported over vast distances. Long-distance 'trade routes' in the conventional sense, however, did not develop until sometime during the second and third centuries AD. This fact refutes the once-so-common theories of a trans-European amber route from the eastern Baltic to the northern Adriatic. Pliny's remarks on a journey made by a Roman horseman to the Baltic regions (Pliny's *Natural History* 37:45) have often been used to

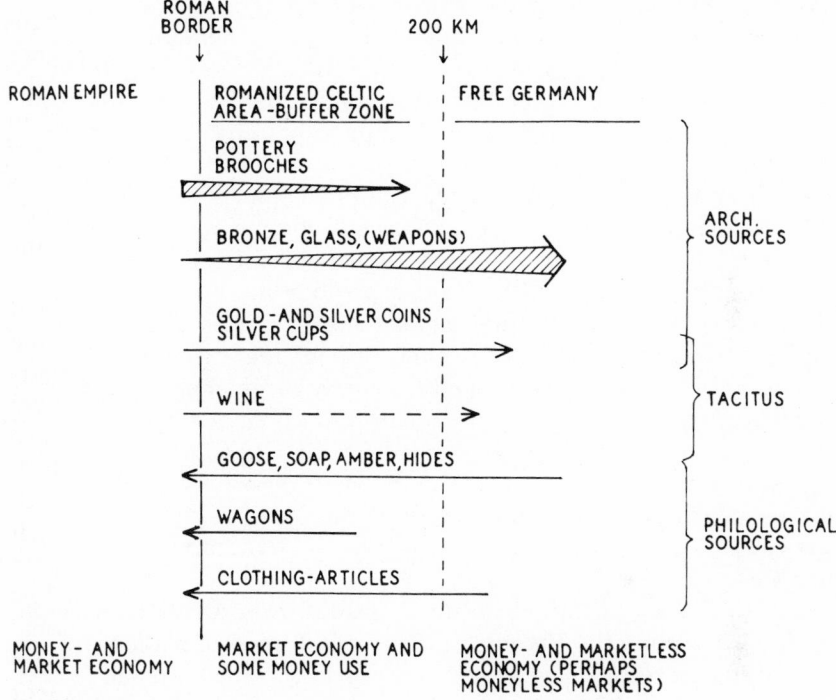

Figure 81 Schematic representation of commodities included in the exchange between the Roman Empire, the buffer zone, and *Germania Libera*.

prove the existence of a long-distance trade route. But in all probability the journey was a never-repeated event and amber, like all other wares, was transported via a long-established network of connections from north to south.

After the amber influx to the south had been considerably curtailed as a result of the economic instability of the Mediterranean region in the fifth century BC, there was again a rise in the first century BC. The reason for this was clearly the renewed growth of settlements of urban character in central Europe, which in turn depended upon intensified interaction with the Mediterranean area. The Celtic oppidum Staré Hradisko in Moravia, for example, was an important place of collection for Baltic amber in the first century BC (C.W. Beck, 1978). Throughout the next two centuries, amber continued to flow by way of the European exchange network to the south, to Carnuntum in Pannonnia, whence the transports continued to Aquileia by the Caput Adriae, the heart of the Roman amber industry. Both the archaeological and the written evidence indicate that Baltic amber was brought to Pannonnia by Germanic middlemen and continued to be brought here until the end of the second century AD, when the eastern contacts were disrupted by the Marcomannian wars. After this time, amber transports to the south declined considerably. Instead, in the third and fourth centuries, amber experienced a renaissance in northern Europe. Here its distribution pattern and its presence in richly equipped graves indicate that exchange among the élite of society was still the means of diffusion.

The many Roman luxury goods which reached Denmark in the centuries after the birth of Christ were spread primarily to the élite in the densely populated agricultural regions along the east coast of Jutland and on the Danish islands. Around 200 AD the exchange of goods intensified. This took place together with a burgeoning mercantilism, particularly in Gaul and lower Germania. At the same time, the Roman production of wealth objects intended for the Germanic regions developed into mass production. Up to the sixth century AD multitudes of Roman provincial and Frankish mass-produced wares circulated among the élite in southern Scandinavia; in time, a large import of gold also followed.

One of the regions in which this trend can most easily be observed is eastern Denmark. Recent fieldwork and re-examinations of the archaeological record have revealed the changes which Roman imports underwent around 200 AD. These changes can be illustrated with the aid of histograms (Figure 82), which show the proportionate wealth in the graves of the region and the distribution of the Roman imports in relation to this. Figure 82 shows how in the first two centuries after the birth of Christ the imports in east Denmark are concentrated within a rather small segment of the Iron Age population. The Roman luxury goods are found in relatively few graves and almost exclusively in graves which, also on the basis of locally produced grave-goods, must be described as very rich. The majority of the graves are far more modestly furnished. This situation more closely resembles the one which we described for the chiefdom societies of the second millennium BC than the situation in the following centuries. For at the end of the second century AD this situation changed drastically (Figure 83). At this time Roman import not only increased in quantity, but was also distributed far more widely among the total number of graves. This observation can thus indicate an increased hierarchization, which may in turn be related to a new distribution pattern of the graves in Denmark (L. Hedager, 1978b).

Figure 82 shows the distribution of the grave finds of Roman imports in east Denmark during respectively the early and late Roman periods.

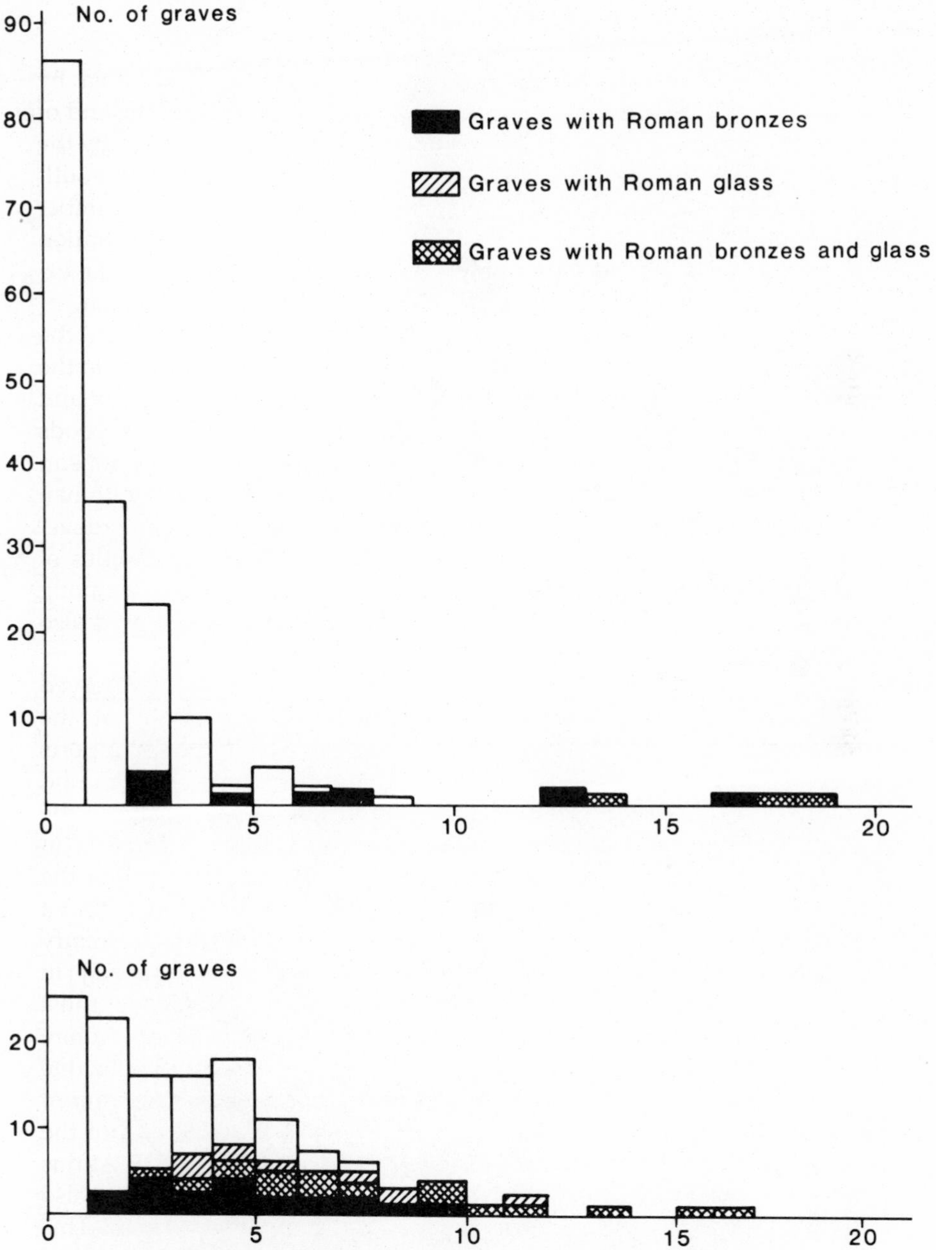

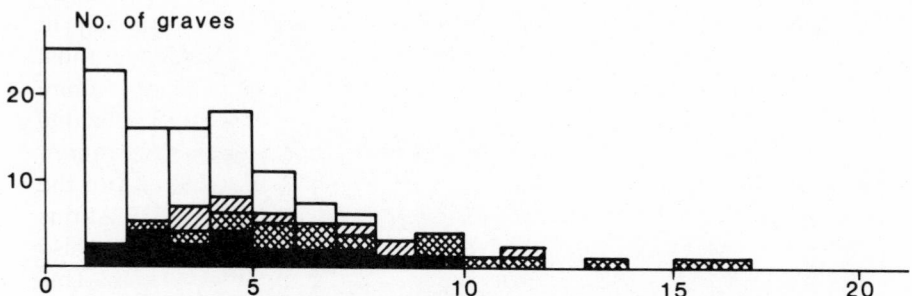

Figure 82 Histogram indicating the proportions of wealth in graves in eastern Denmark during the early Roman Iron Age (above) and the late Roman Iron Age (below). During the early Roman Iron Age the wealth objects were concentrated within a rather small segment of the Iron-Age population. During the later period this situation changed drastically: the Roman imports were now distributed far more evenly among the total number of graves.

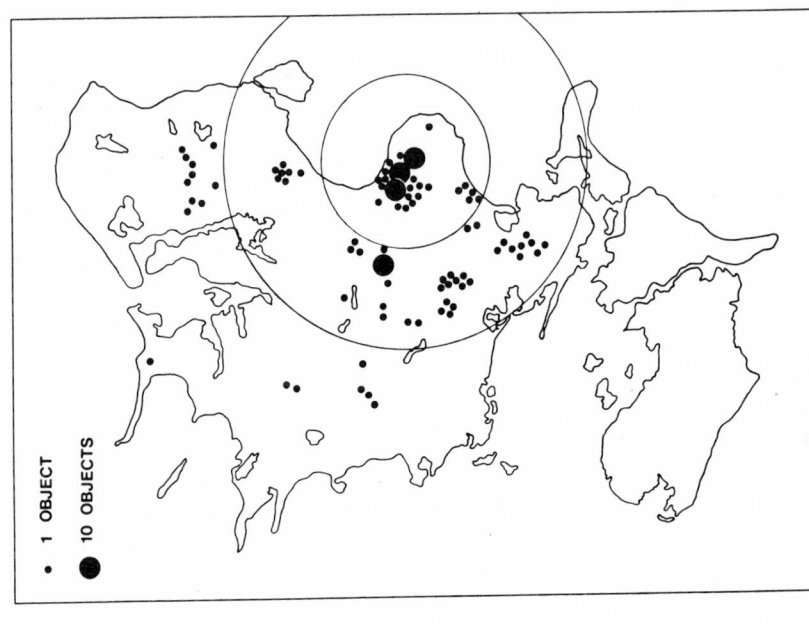

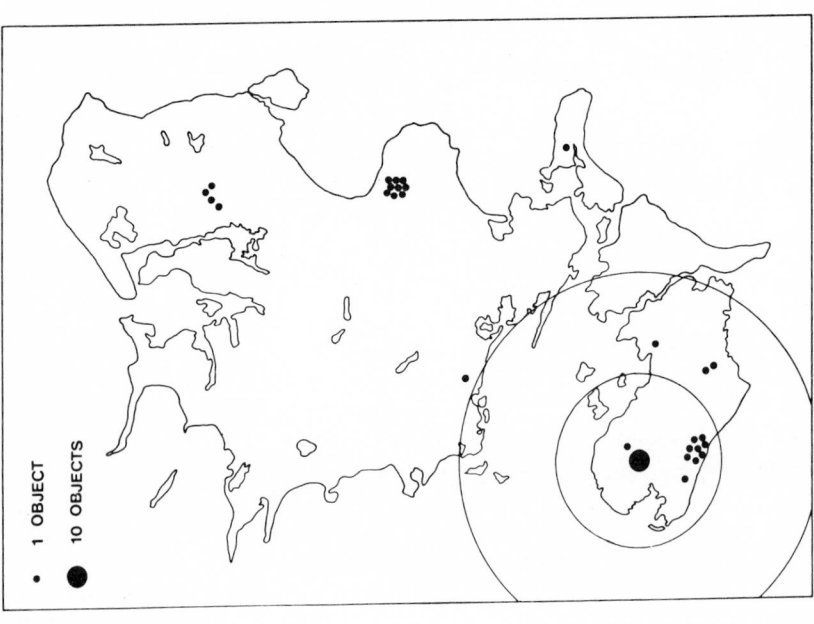

Figure 83 Distribution of grave finds with Roman imports in eastern Denmark. Left: early Roman Iron Age. Right: late Roman Iron Age.

In the early period, most rich graves are found in the south, on the island of Lolland, clustered around the famous Hoby grave, which included the two unique Augustean silver skyphoi (Figure 84). On Zealand the finds are more scattered, although a little concentration of Roman imports does exist in the Stevns region. In the late period, there are no rich graves on Lolland; instead we see a major concentration on east Zealand, where most of the Roman import goods, which had greatly increased in number, are also found.

Figure 84 Augustean grave goods from the famous Hoby grave on the island of Lolland, 1st century AD.

These observations have been interpreted to mean that in the early period, in the first two centuries AD, an exchange system prevailed in which the Roman luxury goods circulated within a very small segment of society and were manifest in the so-called princely graves of the Lübsow type (H.-J. Eggers, 1950). These graves are known everywhere in northern Europe beyond the buffer zone bordering up to the Limes. In the late period, a change set in as a result of the increased hierarchization of society in northern Europe. In Denmark the richest graves were now concentrated on Stevns, Zealand. The sub-centres forming a semi-circle around this centre were not quite as wealthy, but there is evidence of a high concentration of prosperity, including Roman luxury goods. Outside this semi-circle, the sum of wealth is far lower. The distribution and composition of the finds thus indicate that the exchange of goods on Zealand and the surrounding islands was controlled from a centre in eastern Zealand and that this centre exercised control over the long-distance trade.

What we observe here may be an example of a so-called administered trade (K. Polanyi, 1963). By this is meant an exchange based upon tractate relations among the parties concerned. In this way, the extent, composition, quality and prices of the goods exchanged were established. This was thus not a case of a market-created determination of price. The exchange of goods does not generate profit beyond the mutual advantage which both parties derive from it. According to Karl Polanyi, this form of exchange first appeared in Europe, specifically in Greece, about the beginning of the first millennium BC. In central Europe, the epoch of the fortified settlements of urban character in the sixth and fifth centuries BC was probably a manifestation of the same situation. In the Baltic area, including Denmark, administered trade seems to have appeared first with the establishment of economically and politically strong chiefdoms in eastern Denmark just before 200 AD.

According to the general theory we have proposed concerning the connection between the control of external trade and social hierarchization, a development such as the one evident here is not necessarily related to an intensification of subsistence pursuits, for example the introduction of new crop complexes in order to increase surplus. In Denmark, however, administered trade and more hierarchical social patterns arose concurrently with an increase of production, as shown above in the description of the village communities. However, the nature of the relationship between production increase and contemporaneous socio-economic changes in Denmark is still a puzzle.

As already mentioned, a prestige-goods economy in general and administered trade in particular involve very few categories of goods.

These rarely include foodstuffs, because with the weak communication lines it would simply be too risky to depend upon external supplies. Instead, trade will include types of goods necessary for the élite to maintain a certain standard of living. We cannot know to what degree they were distinguished from the rest of the community, but to judge by excavations of village communities from the second and third centuries AD, we may presume that the élite of the Iron Age society were still commoners who tilled their own fields and owned few slaves, if any.

The origin of the presumed administered trade in east Denmark around 200 BC is rather indistinct. It has been related to such goods as hides, which on archaeological grounds have been considered important export articles from the Baltic islands Öland and Gotland (U.E. Hagberg, 1967). In this case Zealand would have played the middleman role in an exchange system which, on one hand, brought Roman luxury goods to southern Scandinavia, and, on the other hand, supplied the Roman army with basic necessities.

As described in the general model, these centralizations of political power based upon control of the exchange of goods cannot have been very stable. Throughout the Roman Iron Age, northern Europe witnessed the continuous evolution and devolution of such centres. Around the fourth century AD the importance of eastern Zealand diminished. Later, other centres arose, for example by the coast of south-west Jutland and on Funen.

In the large settlement Dankirke in south-west Jutland described above, there is an abundance of luxury goods which can best be explained by an exchange of goods at the site, managed by a local magnate. For example, the majority of the glass finds, found at the west end of a house which had burnt down, probably comprised a stock of trade goods. Finds of leaden scale weights in the refuse layers of the same house also indicate trade. The majority of the rich import finds in Dankirke are somewhat later than those of eastern Denmark, being from the fourth and fifth centuries AD.

As in eastern Denmark, however, no indisputable reason can be indicated for the trade at Dankirke. Agricultural productivity was relatively high and a large cattle population must have belonged to the settlements of south-west Jutland. But it is equally important to observe the strong growth of secondary occupations in this era. In Drengsted, not far from Dankirke, traces have been found of a large production of iron. The place included nearly 200 shaft furnaces, so production must have exceeded the local consumption by far. Thus this find attests to an increased domestic exchange probably encompassing many categories of goods.

In the following centuries, the archaeological record fails badly. Future analyses of the only rich find category, the gold finds, will assuredly lead us to new centres for the exchange of goods. It cannot be doubted that south-east Funen in the fifth and sixth centuries AD played an important role in controlling the external exchange of goods. But by and large, our knowledge of the final phase of prehistory, the seventh and eighth centuries AD, is very meagre indeed.

For these last centuries before the beginning of the Viking Age, various attempts have been made to trace the long-distance trade routes on the basis of the very few and scattered finds. Some years ago (C.J. Becker, 1953) a route was drawn through the Limfjord, over the Kattegat and further to the eastern part of the Baltic. The decisive role in the exchange of goods within the Danish territory was thus thought to have been played by northern Jutland. However, recent investigations have indicated that instead it was southern Jutland which functioned as a centre for mercantile contacts between western Europe and the Baltic. New coin finds from Dankirke, excavations in the earliest Ribe and finally the finds from the Hedeby area all indicate that in the eighth century, and perhaps even earlier, power concentrations in southern Jutland administered trade across the Jutland peninsula. A contemporary centre also seems evident in the easternmost part of Denmark, namely on the island of Bornholm (C.J. Becker, 1975).

In this connection, one frequently overlooked aspect of trade ought to be pointed out: its parasites. For in fact insight into the role of trade parasites can provide us with valuable background for the later Viking expeditions. At the end of the eighth century, written sources began to report Viking raids, and Charlemagne, even before his coronation by the Pope in 800 AD, issued orders to guard the coasts of Friesland and the Channel. These actions must have been responses to the growing trade activity which had taken place especially in the seventh and eighth centuries AD. These earliest Viking raids do not yet seem to have been part of any planned military activity. Rather they must have been incidental cases of ordinary piracy.

This early stage also saw the development of that all-important prerequisite for piracy: the ship. From the fourth century AD and onward we have sporadic traces of the development of a vessel with a fixed construction: a double-pointed hull with a very curved keel and curved bow and stern, clinker-laid deck ribs placed symmetrically across the bottom and a thwart or cross-beam for each rib. The earliest known stage of this development was the Nydam boat from around 400 AD (Figure 85). This boat was 23 metres long and could be rowed by thirty men. The next stage was the Gredstedbro ship, found in southern

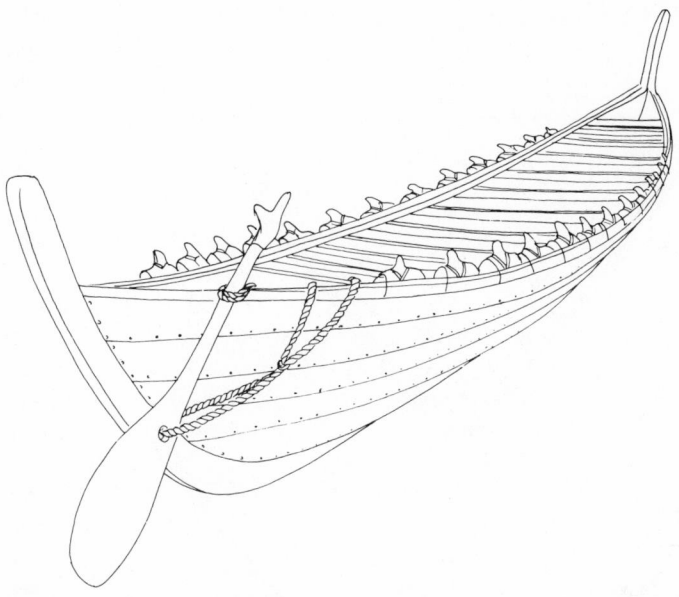

Figure 85 The Nydam boat, *c*. 400 AD, from the large sacrifical weapon find
  excavated at Nydam bog, southern Jutland.

Jutland near Ribe (O. Crumlin-Petersen, 1967). A radiocarbon dating
shows that this ship was built around 600–650 AD, with a 100-year
margin to each side. The Gredstedbro ship displayed both older and
newer features (Figure 86). For example, like the Nydam boat it has a
keel scarf, whereas the ribs were fastened with wooden treenails just as
on the later Viking ships from Skuldelev. In general, the overall picture
best corresponds to the 26-metre-long ship from Sutton Hoo in Suffolk
in England. The Gredstedbro ship was probably built as a rowing vessel;
in any case, the keel was not extended to make the keel of a proper
sailing ship. In the seventh and eighth centuries these Scandinavian
ships adopted the mast and sails of the vessels of western Europe. Thus
there evolved a ship which was quick and manoeuvrable, eminently
well suited for piracy and military raids.

Yet there is reason to emphasize that both in this era and in the first
centuries of the Viking Age, piracy reflected the still unsteady basis of
the trade connections. Regular trade involving the frequent transportation of goods begets a specialized piracy. However, if trade is less than
regular, the piracy which accompanies it will be entirely different and
extremely versatile.

The maximal versatile trade parasite carries on his activities part-

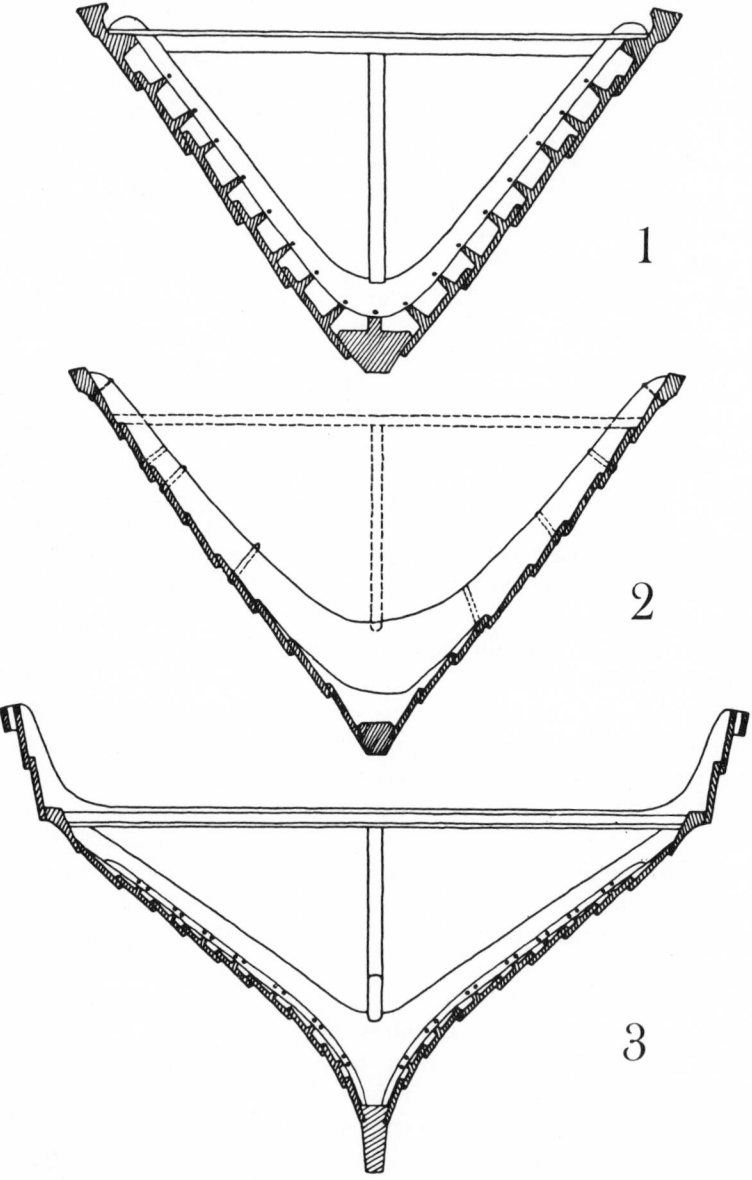

Figure 86 Cross-sections of: 1. the Nydam boat. 2. the Gredstedbro ship. 3. the Oseberg ship.

time, for example in connection with farming. He will steal from all forms of subsistence, both on land and at sea and over as large a geographical area as the means of transportation allows. (K. Lunden, 1972)

This definition applies to the early Viking raids which, indirectly, can attest to a growing but as yet quite limited trade activity.

The same impression also emerges of the earliest settlements of urban character in Denmark and adjacent regions: in Ribe and Hedeby close to the modern Danish–German border. Discussion about these and similar settlements has often been diverted because of historians' wish to frame practical definitions of a town. These definitions, especially those based upon the administrative functions of the town formations, can be of great operative significance in the study of medieval towns. But for the earlier north European settlements of urban character, they are often meaningless. It is far more important to ascertain which types of trade characterized the Iron Age communities up to the beginning of the Viking Age.

In the eighth century, the stage called administered trade had probably not yet been passed. Great emphasis should therefore be placed upon the security required for trade in the period before a general pacification of the regions involved had been achieved. Administered trade seeks to fulfil these security requirements in what Polanyi calls a port of trade. By this is meant a site that offers security to the foreign trader, facilities of anchorage and debarkation, storage and agreement on the goods to be traded. The locality is protected by the local political authority, who ensures his own vital interests in administering the exchange of goods. This exchange is therefore characterized by administrative decisions and cannot, as stressed above, be considered an actual market trade. The potential importance of the port of trade as an administrative centre for the surrounding region is thus of minor importance, which is one of the reasons why the so-called ports of trade are frequently moved. This may explain a statement in the Frankish Annals that in the year 808 AD the Danish king Godfred compelled the merchants of the Slavic town of Reric, as well as those Wismar in northern Germany, to move to his own 'portus' Slesvig, just south of the modern Danish–German border.

The conclusion of the above must be that the long-distance trade was the basis for the earliest trading centres of urban character such as Hedeby and Ribe. However, it could not create any permanent integration of a larger area. This development first took place during the Viking Age and the early Middle Ages. However, through the last 500 years before the Viking Age it may be seen how the growth of secondary occupations led to an increased domestic exchange of goods. From the eighth century there are remains at several large villages by the Limfjord (Bejsebakken, Lindholm Høje and Aggersborg) of workshops and production which attest to a far-reaching occupational differentiation and a growing productivity. Gradually some·of the preconditions were created for the market economy which later came to supplant the archaic prestige-goods economy. This development had still not culminated at the beginning of the Viking Age. Not until the tenth and eleventh centuries can coin finds, for example, show how a market economy was slowly emerging in the urban centres, even as the exchange of goods outside these centres was probably still being carried out according to ancient economic patterns.

18
Political and social development

Economy and social development

One of the first written sources which sheds a faint light upon Denmark dates from the threshold to the Viking Age. In the year 808, the Frankish Annals (*Annales Regni Francorum*) reported on the Danish king Godfred and his plundering of the Slavic town Reric by the Baltic. Moreover the annals relate that King Godfred had the southern boundary of his kingdom fortified against the land of the Saxons by erecting an earth-work at the place where even today the Danish–German border runs. Unfortunately the annals tell nothing about the size of Godfred's kingdom. But judging by the role allotted him by the Frankish chronic-lers, it may be concluded that Godfred represented no insignificant political and military power, probably controlling all of southern Den-mark, if not more.

The question which arises here is, what sort of political power concentrations existed prior to the mention of King Godfred's realm around the year 800 AD? More specifically, one may enquire whether the political situation manifest in King Godfred's strategy regarding Charle-magne's Frankish empire, for example his fortification of the border, was the result of a brief spontaneous situation provoked by external pressure, or whether it was the result of a situation which had existed for centuries?

From a historian's viewpoint, based on the few written sources which have survived, the first-named alternative has often been accepted. The written sources are taken to imply that the extensive political power concentrations of the Viking Age were of relatively recent date. But from the archaeologist's point of view, matters appear quite different. The description presented here of the economic and demographic development of the agrarian society indicates that throughout the Iron Age in Denmark attempts were being made to unify ever-larger regions under one central authority.

Little insight into this process can be obtained from the more general theories on the evolution of social stratification and community organization. To be sure, Iron Age Denmark included societies on the chiefdom level of socio-cultural integration. Nor can there be any doubt that here and there in Denmark in the course of the Iron Age there arose stratified societies, in which some members had unhindered access to the strategic resources, whereas other members were denied or restricted access to the same fundamental resources. This conclusion may be drawn because we know the preliminary end product of this process, namely the state formation of the Viking Age and the early Middle Ages.

The term 'state' as applied here implies an autonomous, political unit equipped with a centralized political power, which has the authority for example to collect taxes, conscript men for war or work, and to issue and enforce laws. The state is thus regarded as a collection of specialized institutions and agencies, some formal and others informal, which maintain an order of stratification (M.H. Fried, 1967). The development of a market economy and the presence of urban centres are also considered decisive traits. If one accepts this definition, then a true state formation in Danish territory first appeared in the course of the late Viking Age and the early Middle Ages. On the other hand, if one chooses a more structural definition, which regards the state as a political instrument basing its function on a legitimate power, then it is probable that already before the Viking Age, Iron Age society developed a complexity which in many respects contained state-like elements (see for example L. Hedager, 1978b).

The definitions of such evolutionary categories as bands, tribes, chiefdoms and states are valuable mainly as heuristic tools. Yet in fact they are nothing more than lists of static traits of different levels of societal organization. They tell very little about the dynamics of social reproduction, that is, about the conditions which caused the system to develop from one social form to another. It is therefore important to describe the Iron Age as a period whose particular structure emerged and was transformed throughout the period.

Yet this approach is rarely encountered in north European archaeology. One of the reasons for this is that many of the evolutionary concepts being used by archaeologists have been developed by the study of the so-called 'early civilizations'. These were formations which depended upon the productive capacity of the very large areas from which they acquired their raw materials. Research has often concentrated upon the core areas of these civilizations, often more or less neglecting the special structural properties which characterize the peripheral areas. However, in recent years important studies have been able to describe how the interaction between, for example, the Mediterranean city-states and the areas north of the Alps in the centuries prior to the birth of Christ led to a commercialization of the latter area before the emergence of any centralized state control (S. Frankenstein and M.J. Rowlands, 1978). They have also pointed out that the particular form assumed by these tribal societies was directly determined by the role which they played within a larger geographical division of labour centred round the Mediterranean world.

This approach, which ought not be confused with more conventional diffusionistic approaches, can prove most fruitful in clarifying the later feudal development in medieval Europe. This is the reason why the present work has so strongly emphasized the importance of identifying the forms of exchange which functioned in Denmark up to the beginning of the Viking Age.

Political and economic power concentrations

Up to the middle of the first millennium BC, the agrarian communities in Denmark had been closely integrated with a far-reaching European exchange network system, which had brought a multitude of prestige goods to the country. These exotic wares became part of the chiefdom's consumption of status symbols and were thus vital for social reproduction. When the influx of these goods ceased around 500 BC, the hierarchization which until then had prevailed in the chiefdoms was hindered, and we must presume that the following centuries were marked by some form of devolution (K. Kristiansen, 1978a). The segmentary hierarchy must have been weakened; the chieftain's control of production must have been modified so that the earliest Iron Age societies developed a decentralized structure. The same phenomenon seems to appear everywhere in the vast north European lowland region. It may therefore logically be associated with the political and economic instability from which central and southern Europe suffered at this time.

For the first three or four centuries of the Iron Age, this basic pattern seems to have dominated. However, the archaeological record for the period shows a considerable population pressure, which led to expanded settlement and the intensification of subsistence pursuits. Excavations of village communities in particular confirm this impression. They show communities whose population fluctuated between fifty and several hundred inhabitants, considerably higher numbers than in the previous period. These statistics are confirmed by the excavated cemeteries which display only faint differences in the distribution of wealth. Objects which can be interpreted as indicators of differential ranking are by and large known only from the sacrificial deposits, particularly in the bogs. Specialized workshops which produced these insignia, for example complicated types of neck-rings (Figure 87), must therefore have continued to exist, just as a more restricted exchange must have been carried out, especially with the areas along the southern borders of the Baltic.

As one might expect in an era highlighted by devolution, population pressure and territorial expansion, traces of warfare are also found. The Hjortspring find from the island of Als in southern Denmark is the most prominent example of this. This find, which dates from around the third and second centuries BC, is the oldest sacrificial weapon find known in Denmark. A vessel, or rather a war canoe, 16 metres long, consisting of five wide boards, one at the bottom and two at each side, had been deposited in a very small bog (Figure 88). Along with the boat, a great

Figure 87 Neck ring from the Pre-Roman Iron Age found in a bog at Væt, Randers county.

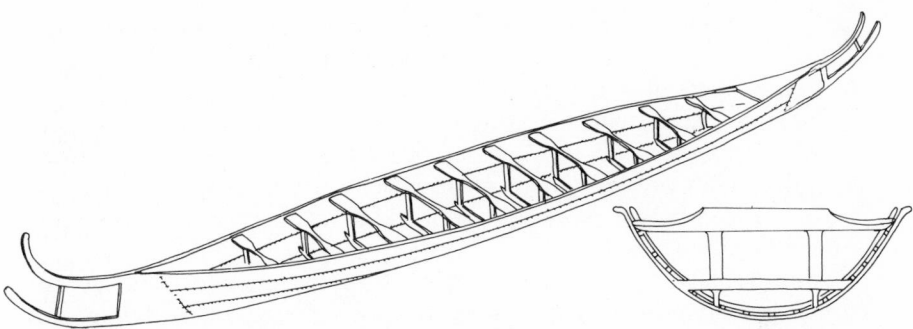

Figure 88 The Hjortspring boat from the Pre-Roman Iron Age, period II, found in a bog on the island of Als, southern Denmark.

number of iron and wooden weapons were also deposited: swords, spears, shields, knives and chain-mail. The boat, which did not carry a sail, could accommodate a crew of 22–24 men. This find must be interpreted in the same way as the sacrificial weapon hoards deposited three or four hundred years later as the possessions of a defeated army, deliberately destroyed by the victor.

Not until the first century BC can a change in the socio-economic situation be discussed. The local prerequisites for this included an intensification of the subsistence pursuits which had taken place through the preceding five centuries, as well as the population pressure which is for instance manifest in the first century BC in the village of Hodde (see p. 206ff), whose relatively light soil supported a population of about 200 with a proportionately large cattle population. The increased strain on the resources can also be observed in the pollen diagrams and in the settlement expansion which concurrently commenced in the boulder clay areas.

Everywhere in the north European lowland, there are contemporaneous indications that a hierarchization of society had been re-established. It is logical to see this process in the light of the evolving commercialization in the north Alpine zone with the concurrent growth of the oppida civilization. Once again, central and northern Europe joined the system which the Mediterranean civilization drew upon for raw materials and probably also for slaves. One sign of the re-establishment of a far-reaching exchange network is that once more Baltic amber came into circulation and flowed abundantly to the Mediterranean area.

Again it became possible to accumulate foreign prestige goods, and consequently in the first century BC we find in Denmark a group of richly equipped graves which are distinguished from the more modestly furnished majority of graves. Social status was now indicated ever more strongly in the funeral rites. A similar development can be observed over large parts of northern Germany and Poland.

The male graves with weapons are especially striking. Here we find swords, lances, shields and knives. Sometimes the grave furnishings include foreign prestige goods such as central European chariots and Mediterranean bronze works, some of which had been in circulation for several hundred years.

Unfortunately, analyses have not yet been undertaken either of the proportion of these rich graves to the poor graves, or of the spatial distribution of the graves. In some cases the graves of the élite were established at special places, separate from the more modestly furnished graves. This holds true of the richest cemetery of the period, Langå on the island of Funen, where a small group of very rich graves was found at some distance from a large cemetery with approximately 100 modestly equipped graves. The Langå cemetery lies in a region of eastern Funen which was strategically placed for communications with both eastern and western Denmark and which at the same time lay central in relation to Funen as well as the surrounding islands of Langeland, Ærø, and Tåsinge. Through the following centuries in Denmark, this centre remained one of the leading economic, demographic and strategic centres in southern Denmark. Here, in the centuries after the birth of Christ, we also find Møllegårdsmarken, the largest Iron Age cemetery in Denmark with more than 2000 graves, only 6–7 kilometres from Langå. Other centres of wealth may be observed in southern and northern Jutland, although these are not yet so evident in the archaeological record as the centre on Funen.

Alongside this demonstration of high status in the graves, a number of very costly votive deposits also were made, including more or less fragmented bronze cauldrons of central European origin. The most striking of the cauldron finds is the huge silver cauldron from Gundestrup. The village communities also display distinct signs of increased hierarchization. The magnate's farmstead in Hodde is an example of this, as regards both the size and the quality of the finds, especially pottery.

The contemporaneous features here include both an intensified exchange of goods over all the north European region and an increased hierarchization of the communities provoked both by an increased demographic pressure and by an increased control of the growing production by the leaders.

These tendencies continued in the centuries after the birth of Christ. Everywhere in Denmark, but especially in the areas with good agricultural soil, the grave finds continue to show a distinct hierarchization. This is seen above all by the presence of Roman imports, most of which were made in southern Italy. Later the predominant goods were the mass-produced glass and bronze goods from the provincial Roman work-shops in lower Germania and Gaul. A special role seems to have been played by the prestigious drinking equipment. Just as in the earlier centuries, it was probably used for drinking rituals by the élite.

As mentioned earlier, the acquisition of foreign luxury goods seems to have been dependent upon high status – and in the first two centuries AD exchange still seems to have taken place within a relatively small segment of society. At this time there clearly existed in Denmark societies organized on the chiefdom level of socio-cultural integration, but the distribution pattern of such things as foreign prestige goods indicates that we are still dealing with rather small local political structures.

About 200 AD, this picture slowly began to change. One of the reasons for this change may have been the appearance of an administered trade. This can be most clearly observed in eastern Denmark, where the number of burials of high-ranking persons increased strikingly. Often these rich graves are found singly or clustered in small groups. They were kept separate from the cemeteries which contained the burials of the lower strata, in itself an indication of a rather hierarchical organiza-tional form. Of utmost importance, of course, is the distribution of status symbols which was controlled by the political centres. The new pattern can best be discerned in the Stevns area on eastern Zealand. Here, a close correlation is seen between the increased influx of Roman imports and political development (L. Hedager, 1978b and c). A centre with a great accumulation of wealth now arose on Stevns, where the graves show a degree of hierarchization hitherto unknown. Round the centre there was a group of dependent sub-centres, probably with vassal chiefs, which received a considerable part of the trade goods. There seems to have been a development of several specialized functions in the power apparatus, a situation which persisted at least up to the fourth century AD, when Roman imports disappeared from eastern Denmark and instead appeared in western Denmark. Throughout this period there probably existed a political centre controlling all of Zealand and the surrounding islands. Less developed centres, also marked by growing hierarchization, can be seen elsewhere in the country. There is much to indicate that Funen and its surrounding islands comprised a unified whole. In Jutland, the situation is as yet quite murky, as analyses of the grave finds and their contents of, in particular, weapons and wealth symbols have not yet been undertaken.

As may be expected, this evolution is not stable geographically. A direct consequence of the spatial shifts in centres and the conflicts which they occasioned may be seen in the so-called weapon-sacrificial finds which range from the centuries before the birth of Christ up to the seventh century AD. The majority were deposited between 200–400 AD.

The sacrificial deposits of weapons in bogs constitute the largest find group from the Iron Age. A total of nineteen large and small finds from Denmark are known (Figure 89), with ten in Jutland, four on Funen, four on Zealand and Lolland, and one on Bornholm. The weapon sacrifices were always deposited on a meadow or bog surface or cast out from the shore of a small lake. These were clearly not abandoned battlefields, because the objects were often arranged in bundles or packed together in cloth. The areas must have been sacred, as indicated by the fact that the site where the objects were placed was sometimes marked off with poles or wattle.

The weapon sacrifices might include more than just weapons; there might be clothing, personal items, tools, agricultural implements, wagons or boats. Very often, the objects bear traces of fighting and of consequent destruction for the unmistakable purpose of rendering them unusable. This clearly indicates a ritual background for the deposits, a

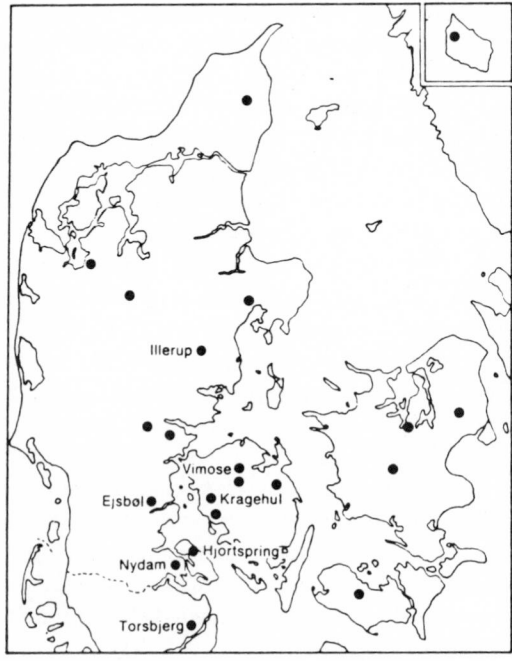

Figure 89 Distribution of the sacrifical deposits of weapons in bogs.

situation corroborated in Caesar's *Gallic Wars*, which describes similar sacrificial customs in Gaul.

Some of the weapon finds include deposits from a number of battles. The find from Illerup in eastern Jutland, for instance, is comprised of at least three sacrifices of war booty. In Ejsbøl in southern Jutland, finds were made of the arms of a large defeated army, along with a couple of smaller deposits. The number of objects found shows that about 200 men had participated in the conflict, and that about 60 foot soldiers and 9 horsemen were killed (Figure 90). Such forces may imply that major power concentrations existed, at least in conflict situations when the élite could gather a considerable force of dependants around them.

More detailed analyses of the contents of the weapon-sacrifice finds will undoubtedly be able to determine the origin of the warriors who fought. Until then it must suffice to associate generally the weapon-sacrifice finds and the military conflicts which they represent with the development of rival centres of political power which arose in Denmark in the centuries following 200 AD. More specifically, the weapon-sacrifice finds have been related to the formation of a political centre in eastern Denmark which up to about 400 AD attempted to extend its power

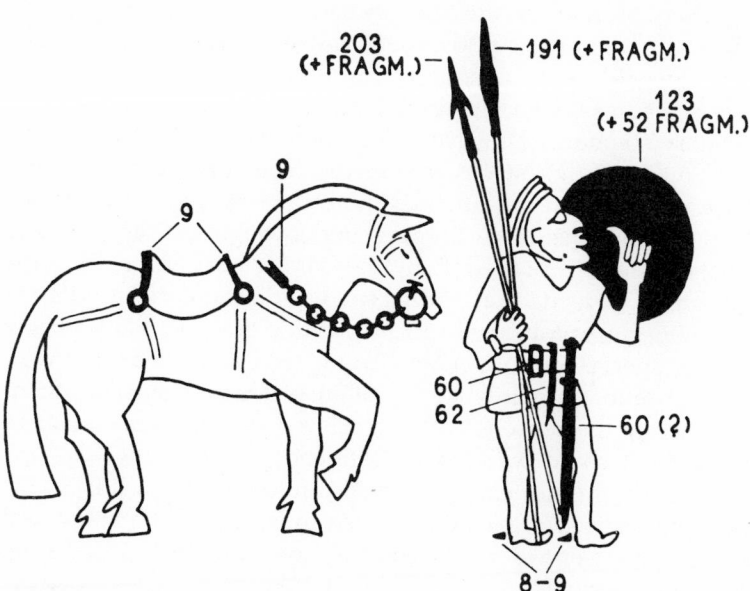

Figure 90 The number of objects found in the sacrificial weapon find at Ejsbøl, southern Jutland, shows that about 200 men had participated in the battle which took place before the sacrifice.

further to the west, 'an attempt which seems to have failed' (L. Hedager, 1978b).

Thus from the second and third centuries AD a number of small 'kingdoms' with shifting political power and vaguely defined territories seem to have existed in Denmark. This development took place along with the growing differentiation in the power apparatus, which can be discerned in the grave finds, and with the appearance of larger farmsteads, as evident in the settlement finds. At the same time the archaeological record shows a considerable population growth and an increasing distance between the top and the bottom in the social system.

One serious impediment to the tracing of this development is the fact that the years from the fifth to the eighth centuries AD comprise one of the most curious periods in the prehistory of Denmark: most of the find groups are very meagre and the archaeological record does not allow for much interpretation.

To be sure, from the fifth and sixth centuries AD there is an overwhelming number of gold finds, many of which may be interpreted as status symbols. The distribution of the gold finds also shows that in southern Denmark, probably on Funen, there existed a centre which played a decisive role in the distribution of the wealth symbols. Analyses of this important find group, however, have not yet been published. The gold finds are of great interest in other respects as well. They have sometimes been regarded as the manifestation of a general gold monetary standard. However, this interpretation contradicts the conclusions hitherto suggested regarding the development of the economic institutions. Instead, an analysis more than 50 years old, by the Norwegian archaeologist A.W. Brøgger, of the weights of the gold may still be valid. Brøgger proved that the Danish gold rings, like the Norwegian ones, were made according to a weight standard based upon the Roman libra corresponding to 12 øre and that the gold had probably functioned as special-purpose money used, for example, to pay wergeld, a compensation primarily for the killing of a man. Indirectly, then, gold may indicate the presence of a formalized legal system similar to contemporary Germanic law on the continent.

With a number of other exotic materials, gold can also testify to the existence of specialized workshops, which must have been associated with the economic centres whose surplus was converted to prestige symbols. From around 400 AD and up to the Viking Age, we may speak of a special Nordic style. The knowledge of this style rapidly spread throughout Scandinavia, probably via wandering craftsmen, of whom there is evidence beginning in the fifth century AD. The political and social unrest in Gaul at this time is assuredly the explanation of this phenomenon.

Yet for the seventh and eighth centuries, it is still impossible for us to define the political and administrative centres which must have existed in Denmark. Newer studies of the development of the Nordic style plainly show that in this last era before the Viking Age, Denmark was not isolated, as earlier archaeologists often believed it to have been. On the contrary, seventh- and eighth-century Denmark was an integral part of a larger cultural region extending from an Anglo-continental region in the Channel region via the Dutch–Frisian coastal areas to Denmark and thence to the Baltic areas. This eastward contact may have many causes. One of them is probably that administered trade took place between political and economic centres.

One of these centres most likely lay in southern Denmark. Here, by the modern Danish–German border, are the remains of the gigantic fortification structure called the Danevirke. The first building phase of this fortification is in historical sources attributed to King Godfred, from the period around 800 AD. However, the newest radiocarbon and dendrochronological datings of the building timber in the north rampart and the oldest part of the main rampart of the Danevirke have shown that the wood was felled in 737 AD, three generations before King Godfred. Thus at this time there existed a political power capable of erecting this 7-kilometre-long rampart with a 2-metre-high, vertical front palisade and a moat about 1.5 metres deep (Figure 91).

We do not know how much of Denmark was united under this

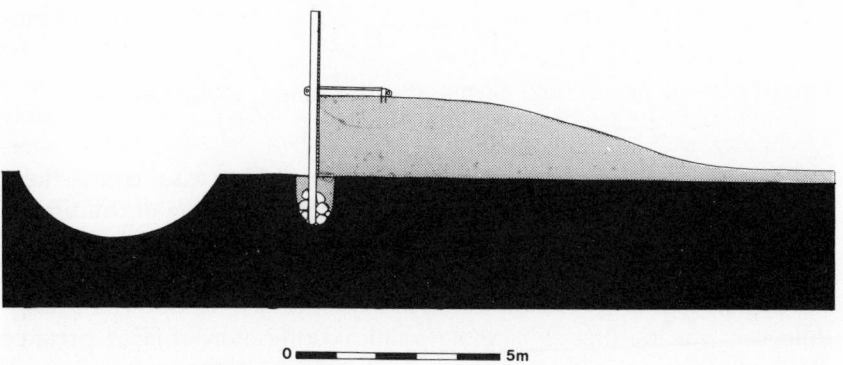

0 ▬▬ ▭ ▬▬ 5m

Figure 91 Cross-section through the oldest part of the rampart at Danevirke. Dendrochronological analysis has shown that the wood included in the construction was felled in 737 AD.

political power. The Frankish Annals from 782 mention a Danish king named Sigfred. It is not unreasonable to extend this royal power some decades back in time and regard one of Sigfred's and Godfred's predecessors as the builder of the first rampart.

In this context reference has been made to a Frankish report written about 800 AD which deals with the Frisian missionary Willibrord. This missionary died in 739 AD after having visited 'the very wild people of the Danes' where a certain King Ongendus – or Angantyr – ruled. It is not inconceivable that this king may have ordered the earliest building of the Danevirke.

Elsewhere in Denmark, there are also impressive constructions most likely carried out by a royal power early in the eighth century. For example, there is the several-kilometre-long Kanhave canal, which bisects the island of Samsø at its most narrow part (Figure 92). A navy based in the Stavns Fjord, into which the canal runs, would have been able to control navigation on both sides of this strategically placed island. The sides of the canal were secured with a plank construction formed by oblique oak planks – and these planks were recently radiocarbon-dated to roughly the same period as the earliest part of the rampart at Danevirke.

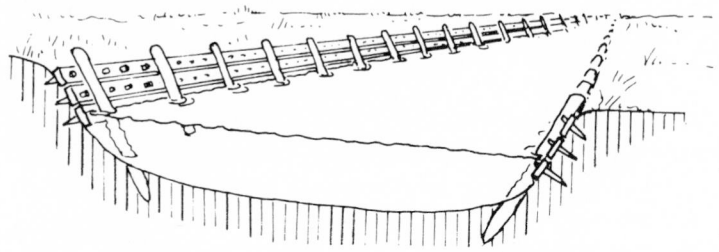

Figure 92 The Kanhave canal on the island of Samsø, constructed in the 8th century AD.

Of course, on this slight basis it is not possible to trace connections from the fifth and sixth centuries AD up to the beginning of the Viking Age, when for the first time the written sources inform us about extensive concentrations of power on Danish territory. But, as shown, the archaeological record indicates that around 800 AD Godfred's kingdom was not the first substantial political unification of large parts of Denmark. The social, political, demographic and economic preconditions for this sort of concentration of power seem to have been present even earlier.

Processes towards the early Danish state

Up to the beginning of the Viking Age, which marked the end of the prehistoric epoch, Danish society was transformed profoundly. The preconditions for this change may be traced sporadically through the Iron Age and it seems clear that the rise of cultural activity which took place in Viking Age Denmark was not created by Viking raids and expanding trade alone. The centuries preceding the Viking Age must have witnessed major changes in the power structure of the society, meaning a development of the relationships of dependency and exploitation.

From a Danish point of view, there are many structural similarities with developments in several neighbouring areas. In England, for example, in the sixth to eighth centuries AD there is sufficient evidence to reveal the existence of many competing kingdoms which were sometimes integrated within larger 'empires' or overlordships. There are several instances in which kings who were firmly incorporated into the kinship system either became monarchs who attained a singular power or were subjected to one (R. Hodges, 1978). An example of the first alternative is that of King Offa, who in the eighth century called himself *rex totius Anglorum patriae*. This may be compared with the Danish king, Harald Bluetooth, who in the tenth century called himself 'he who won all of Denmark and Norway'.

These structural similarities in the pre-Viking Age have been somewhat neglected by Danish historians. Instead the period around 800 AD has been viewed as a sort of cultural breach and has been explained more or less as a direct result of the growth of long-distance trade. In this way the Viking Age has come to appear as a period which decisively broke with the continuity extending far back through prehistoric society. This situation can also be explained by the fact that traditional historians have rarely applied the concepts of social and economic anthropology as well as the evidence of the archaeological record from the Viking period. Therefore the concept of state formation – the phenomenon which definitively terminated archaic Danish society – has not received as much attention from historians as it deserves.

Even though the completion of the process of state formation in Denmark lies beyond the range of the present work, it has been possible to indicate the rise of a number of state-like traits, particularly from the third to the eighth centuries AD. This has been done by depicting some of the main features of socio-economic development, which indeed contributed to the creation of these elements. One of the important prerequisites for this was the attempt to distinguish the economic institutions underlying the exchange of goods in the Iron Age society. The course of development sketched here, contemporary with the commercial flourishing in the Roman provinces around 200 AD, extended an archaic prestige-goods economy to include a so-called administered trade. The origin of administered trade must be presumed to have been social competition and the need of a relatively small social group to maintain a certain standard of living. This implies that through most of the Iron Age, long-distance trade must have been motivated by status. It was directed only towards a relatively small population group at the top of society.

At the same time, an attempt has also been made to demonstrate how throughout the final centuries of prehistory social competition caused a growing accumulation of political and economic power within various parts of the country. This process created the basis for the port-of-trade localities associated with administrated trade, here regarded as preliminary phases of the more town-like settlements which arose in the course of the Viking Age and the early Middle Ages.

What remains to be explained is the relation between this trade activity and the increase of production which seems to have taken effect in Iron Age society from around 200 AD. As mentioned earlier, primitive trade lacks that combination of external and internal trade which is necessary for maintaining a balance in the more complex market economy. This is most likely the reason why the development of secondary occupations occurred at a relatively slow pace through the Iron Age. Nor does the development of the economic means of exchange seem to have exceeded the special-purpose money stage before the eighth century at the earliest. The relatively modest extent of trade activity is also confirmed by the present interpretation of the first Viking expeditions about the eighth century as simply the expression of a very versatile sort of piracy.

To explain this process there is every reason to pay heed to the transformations of not only the primary but also the secondary occupations which took place within the village communities in the period after c. 200 AD. Above, the Vorbasse village was used to exemplify this: it presents a clear-cut picture of an expanding agrarian society. The growing size of the farm plots, the appearance of large multi-functional farmsteads, the undeniable traces of co-operative labour, the numerous workshop buildings and many other features hint that through the latter part of the Iron Age a considerable development of productivity took place as well as an increase in the circulation of domestic goods. As yet, we lack knowledge of a great many details in this process, but there is hope that new archaeological excavation methods can before long fill in the gaps.

None the less the present archaeological record can suggest a number of features of the social organization in the societies which existed from c. 500 BC and up to the beginning of the Viking Age. These societies have been termed chiefdoms, by which is meant hierarchical societies whose internal relations were based upon redistribution and whose central authorities were responsible for political, ritual and economic functions. At the same time it has also been proved that at times there was also considerable social competition among these societies – competition which in periods resulted in armed conflicts. Evidence of this is probably provided by the great sacrificial weapon finds from southern Denmark.

Attempts to enlarge this very rudimentary picture of social and political organization in Iron Age Denmark seen in retrospect from the Viking Age are strikingly rare in Danish archaeology and history. This of course is attributable to the problematic nature of the sources pertaining to the social history of the Viking Age. This holds true above all of the legendary history of the Scandinavians, which has been called 'the morning world of half-remembered dreams' (G. Jones, 1968).

Modern Danish historians have to a great extent rejected the evidence of legendary history with regard to social structure. And it is quite true that these written sources, most of which were recorded in the twelfth century and later, offer a very distorted and idealized picture especially of the uppermost social levels, the élite. At the same time they ignore social relations existing within the remaining sector of society. More-over, many of the concrete episodes in the early literature can be traced to continental history, in particular the events in the struggles between the Goths and the Huns in the Migration period, celebrated in Germanic heroic poetry. Thus these events cannot be regarded as episodes in Danish history.

Furthermore the other sources related to the social history of the Viking Age, the runic stones, the laws and the archaeological sources, reveal only the most general social categories. These can perhaps help reconstruct the basic features of society but not much more.

One of the most frequently encountered assumptions about social relations in the Viking Age is that the most important boundaries were the ones dividing the ruling caste, the aristocracy, from the free peasants, peasant proprietors, smallholders, or whatever they may be called, on one side – and the free peasants from the slaves on the other side. The free men are often thought to have been the backbone of society, and the slaves (the thralls) to have been inferior and to have lacked rights in relation to the free men. This simplified picture has often been projected back in time onto earlier periods, namely the Iron Age society, as it developed after the birth of Christ. This viewpoint may be found in the works both of historians (E. Arup, 1925) and of archaeologists (G. Hatt, 1937).

This assumption, however, has been modified in the present description of the structure of the Iron Age society. In this connection it is also interesting that newer research into the early law texts has shown that there existed a complex hierarchy of status positions ranging from the slaves to the aristocracy. The concept of 'the free peasants' as a 'class' with common legal and political rights must have been maintained for ideological reasons.

On the basis of the archaeological finds the present work attempts to present a more subtle view of society in the Iron and Viking Ages in describing the societies as hierarchical systems in which the social position of the individual was determined by his position in the family. This position determined the rights to which the individual was entitled and the functions he had to exercise. At the top of the system were the leading families, and at the bottom were the slaves – at least from the end of the seventh century, when the written sources suggest that Denmark was a slave society. Between the top and the bottom it seems that, particularly from the second and third centuries AD, an ever greater differentiation of status positions may be observed.

A closely related phenomenon is the development of political power concentrations which can be followed through the centuries of the Iron Age. There seems to be both a strengthening of the positions of authority in the various communities and an integration in over-lordships or smaller 'kingdoms' comprising, for example, areas the size of Zealand.

As yet it is difficult to say anything about the nature of situations in which the authority of the ruling families was mobilized. With regard to the latter problem, however, the picture can be enlarged on a number of points. For example, it may be seen that as late as the Viking Age the exercise of ritual practice was not carried out by a professional priesthood. The celebration of the communal cult was not a profession in itself but was carried out by the élite of society. It is logical to conclude that the priesthood of the 'big men' (the Godi institution) had roots in a sacred chiefdom system which extended very far back into prehistory. It has also been stressed above that in the chiefdoms sacred as well as secular offices were inherited, often within the same family line, just as priest and chief were often one and the same person.

The authority of the chieftains was also foremost in a number of cases related to the exercise of the economic functions. This held true, for example, in connection with the development of society's exchange of goods, not only the local redistribution and gift trade but also the administered trade, which can already be glimpsed in the second and third centuries. Typically, the chieftain's role in this connection is also intimately related to political, military and social contexts.

It has been suggested above that the appearance of the warrior graves around the birth of Christ may indicate the beginnings of the 'hird' system which later in the Viking period had such a marked effect. However, it is important to remember that the dependent peasants whom the magnates could gather by virtue of the redistributive economic system could hardly have comprised any special warrior class. Economically the warriors were probably still commoners in that they tilled their own fields and owned few, if any, slaves.

This same observation may be applied to the rest of the population, which can hardly be said to have constituted a 'middle class', that is a broad spectrum of equal families. A characteristic trait of all chiefdoms is the thorough inequality among individuals as well as groups. Individuals and groups each had their own position in society, determined by their genealogical relationship to the chief. Thus there were families of high descent and those of low descent. This is the most likely explanation for the graduated distribution of wealth evident both within Iron Age village communities and in the grave finds. This sort of graduated distribution of wealth can in fact be traced as far back as the second millennium BC.

A hierarchical structure of society in the sense described here makes it difficult to use the word 'class' in the sense which it later acquired. In a chiefdom inequality is primarily social and to a much smaller degree economic. Families themselves are split up and can theoretically form a graduated rank order from the top to the bottom of society. One exception to this is the slaves, if there are any. For the reasons named it is logical to reserve the term 'class' for true state formations.

There are two groups whose relationship to the local communities cannot be determined: the merchants and the craftsmen, both probably foreigners originally. Itinerant free craftsmen must have existed in prehistoric Danish society, certainly from the fifth century AD and perhaps even earlier. Their impact must have been considerable in disseminating styles of metal-crafting, especially the so-called Nordic animal styles from the period c. 400–800 AD. With the incipient growth of secondary occupations during the third and fourth centuries, it may be presumed that the importance and size of the craftsmen group had increased. Yet its status in relation to what must have been a rather closed kinship society cannot be known.

This same lack of factual insight also undermines our ideas about those active in trade. It does seem that a group of middlemen traders must already have existed from the third century, when administered trade seems to have commenced. From the beginning they seem to have been foreigners, but it cannot be denied that local part-time traders gradually participated in the exchange of goods. At the beginning of the Viking Age Carolingian law mentions guilds consisting of itinerant merchants, but the question remains whether this sort of institutional form would also apply to Danish conditions. With the picture sketched here of the development of trade in prehistoric Denmark, it seems doubtful whether the origin of the Danish guilds known from a later period can be traced further back in time than the close of the Viking Age.

The last population group to be touched upon is that of slaves (thralls). According to the written sources, slavery probably existed in Denmark from around the seventh century. As late as the thirteenth century, Denmark was a slave society in the widest sense of the phrase. But there is no way of determining how far back in time this institution extended. Apparently, a slave system can arise under such widely varying conditions that it is impossible to postulate one from any particular stage in the general socio-economic course of development. In addition, the archaeological sources up to the Viking Age offer not the slightest indication of the origin of the system or its existence.

In describing the prehistoric society as a kinship-oriented society, it ought to be added that to all appearances the kinship system was patrilinear, though with a certain tendency to bilaterality. This is evidenced both by the runic stones from the early Viking Age and by the Danish words for inheritance, as shown by Aksel E. Christensen. In the early medieval laws the tendency toward bilaterality is emphasized very clearly. The genesis of this tendency towards bilaterality cannot be determined, although it does seem to be of very ancient date. In this regard the studies quoted on page 170ff on the distribution of wealth in men's and women's graves from the second millennium BC are thought-provoking indeed. In any case, the bilateral tendencies must have augmented the opportunities for creating kinship alliances – also over large geographic areas. As it has been pointed out (K. Odner, 1973), the kinship system created ideal conditions for a rapid transference of cultural features. The homogeneity of cultural development over much of Scandinavia in the late Iron Age perhaps ought to be viewed on just this background.

About 800 AD the prehistoric era in Denmark drew to a close. The archaic chiefdom society had then set a course which during the Viking

Age and the early Middle Ages would lead to the birth of a class society
on Danish territory. Some of the foundations for this development have
been depicted in this work. To be sure, the gaps in the archaeological
record have been sadly apparent. But the long perspective of prehistory
and the knowledge which we possess today about other forms of society
do make it possible to achieve something of a holistic view. Through this

Figure 93 King Gorm's runic stone, here a painted copy photographed in the
garden of the National Museum. With its runic inscription this stone symbol-
izes the formation of the Danish state and the close of Danish prehistory.

we have been able to follow the development of the ancient Danish society up to the point at which the kinship society was slowly losing the basis of its existence due to new relationships of dependency and exploitation. This change was far from complete at the beginning of the Viking Age. Several hundred years were to pass before socio-economic conditions created the ecclesiastical and royal hierarchy which marked the mature state formation and with it the rise of the class society.

In this period the term 'Denmark' first appears in the written sources. Around 890 King Alfred the Great of England had made an Anglo-Saxon translation of Orosius' *History of the World*. To this work he added a geographic description of northern Europe, including two travel accounts: one by the Norwegian Ottar (Othere), one by the Englishman Wulfstan. The former had travelled from the North Cape to the Schlei by the present-day Danish–German border; the latter had journeyed along the southern coast of the Baltic.

The work of Ottar relates that when he sailed from Sciringesheal (Skiringsal in Vestfold, Norway) he had Denemearc on the port side. Wulfstan writes that when he sailed eastwards in the Baltic he had Weonodland (Venderland) on the starboard side, and on the port side he had Langaland, Læland, Falster and Sconeg (Scania): 'All this land belongs to Dene mearcan'.

Less than one century later, we find the name Denmark on two Danish runic stones, namely the stones which King Gorm and King Harald Bluetooth erected in Jelling, Jutland (Figure 93). One of the stones is inscribed, 'King Gorm made this memorial to his wife Thyra, amender (*or* glory *or* adornment) of Denmark'. On the other stone is written, 'King Harald had this memorial made in memory of Gorm his father and Thyra his mother, that Harald who won for himself Denmark and Norway and made the Danes Christian'. The two inscriptions confirm one another – and they relate with all clarity that the throne of Denmark was now hereditary, that Christianity had become a powerful factor, and that the last step had been taken out of prehistory and towards the early feudal state.

19
Finds and interpretations

The archaeological record which elucidates the last major epoch of Danish prehistory, the Iron Age, consists first of all of grave finds and settlement finds. The latter also include a great many traces of prehistoric field systems. Aside from these finds, there are many others which are, however, difficult to classify systematically. For example, the group of finds from wetlands, primarily bogs and meadowlands, is very extensive. The interpretation of these finds is often problematic but their source value lies in the indications they give us of a wide spectrum of civil and military activities in prehistoric society: religious practices, transportation, army organization, and so on. A final group comprises valuable objects often made of gold or silver, the so-called hoards, a source group which is particularly significant in the Late Iron Age.

Settlements from the Iron Age are known in great number, ranging from finds of a few refuse pits to entire villages covering many hectares. The majority of these finds date from the Early Iron Age. From the Late Iron Age, after approximately 400 AD, only few settlement finds are known, a fact which has not yet been satisfactorily explained.

The study of Iron Age settlements has in recent years grown rapidly. This is mainly due to new excavation methods – the uncovering of large surfaces by machines – which have opened new perspectives in the study of settlement finds. Whereas older excavation methods allowed only limited parts of the settlement area to be uncovered, it is today possible to uncover far larger areas and thereby gain an impression of the settlement structure as a whole. It is obvious that mechanical uncovery is possible only in cases where later ploughing has destroyed all traces of floors, hearths, remains of burnt buildings, etc. The large uncovered surfaces normally reveal only traces of holes from posts, hearths and refuse pits in the otherwise undisturbed subsoil. The original surface layer from prehistory will in most cases be completely ploughed away. Examples of such extensive excavations of whole villages from the Iron Age are Grøntoft and Hodde from the centuries before Christ, and Vorbasse, also in Jutland, from the fourth and fifth centuries AD.

One major problem in the study of Iron Age settlements is the uneven distribution of the finds. Almost all the finds come from Jutland and many are in fact from parts of the country which must have been marginal areas during the Iron Age. Thus our impression of the Iron Age settlement pattern on the heavy soils in the eastern areas of Denmark is based upon a very flimsy foundation. However there are indications that the development of house types in eastern Denmark by and large followed the same lines as in the western part. The house type of the Late Bronze Age, the three-aisled longhouse, has now been identified on both Funen and Zealand. The further development of this house type, the longhouse of the Early Iron Age, is also known on *Funen* (Sarup, N.H. Andersen unpublished), *Lolland* (Naglesti, K.H. Snedker, 1959) and *Bornholm* (Dalshøj, O. Klindt-Jensen, 1957). Thus there is little reason to expect major differences between eastern and western Denmark as regards house construction (see also C.J. Becker, 1980b).

As we have mentioned before, the majority of settlement finds in Jutland date from the Early Iron Age. Up till about 200 AD the number of finds is quite impressive; later, the finds become more scattered. From the early period, which lasted about 700 years, well over one hundred find localities are known, some of the most important of which are: *Borremose* (J. Brøndsted, 1960), *Ginderup* (G. Hatt, 1935; H. Kjær, 1928a), *Grønheden* (P. Friis and P. Lysdahl Jensen, 1966), *Grøntoft* (C.J. Becker, 1965, 1968a, b and c, 1971b), *Gørding* (H. Andersen, 1951), *Hodde* (S. Hvass, 1973, 1975, 1976, 1977b), *Holmsland* (G. Hatt, 1953), *Hurup* (A.K. Rasmussen, 1968), *Kjærsing* (N. Thomsen, 1953), *Mariesminde* (G. Hatt, 1960), *Myrthue* (N. Thomsen, 1964), *Nørre Fjand* (G. Hatt, 1960), *Over-bygård* (J. Lund, 1976a and b), *Sjælborg* (N. Thomsen, 1959), *Skærbæk* and *Østerbølle* (G. Hatt, 1938). A locational analysis of the numerous settlement mounds in Thy was published by S. Jensen (1976a).

In connection with many Early Iron Age settlements, there are also the so-called Celtic fields, a source group which in 1949 was treated as a whole by Gudmund Hatt (see also M. Müller-Wille, 1965; J.A. Brongers, 1976; R. Bradley, 1978). A number of new observations made since Hatt's studies have also been published by V. Nielsen (1970a and b) and C.J. Becker (1971). Of special importance are the observations made by the latter of the relationship between the Celtic fields and mobile settlements.

Only a few of the Late Iron Age settlements will be named. One of the most interesting of the early settlements is the large village at *Vorbasse* (S. Hvass, 1977a, 1978, 1980). From southern Jutland there are also finds from *Esbjerg* (H.C. Vorting, 1973), *Oksbøl* (G. Hatt, 1958), *Dankirke* (E. Thorvildsen, 1972) and *Drengsted* (O. Voss, 1976). All of these have only been partially excavated. See also S. Jensen (1980).

The production of iron at the Iron Age settlements has not yet been studied comprehensively. Various technological aspects have been treated by O. Voss (1962, 1971), who suggests that a local iron production began relatively late in Denmark, namely in the period around the birth of Christ (see also M. Strömberg, 1981). This conclusion seems to be contradicted by settlement finds with traces of iron production from as early as the fifth or fourth centuries BC (J.A. Jacobsen, 1979). For iron production at the settlements of south-west Jutland and the rise of secondary occupations, see S. Jensen (1980).

To date, all the important settlements from the last few centuries preceding the Viking Age are available only in the form of preliminary reports. This holds true of *Bejsebakken* (M. Ørsnes, 1974), *Lindholm høje* (T. Ramskou, 1976) and *Aggersborg* (C.G. Schultz, 1949). In *Ribe* (M. Bencard, 1973, 1974) the investigations have not yet been completed. A comprehensive report on many years of excavation in *Hedeby* was published in 1972 by H. Jankuhn.

Grave finds from the first five centuries of the period, the Pre-Roman Iron Age, are to a fairly large degree available in print. The finds from southern and central Jutland were published by C.J. Becker in 1961; those from Funen were published by E. Albrectsen in 1954 with supplements in 1973. The finds from northern Jutland and the strikingly few finds east of the Storebaelt, however, have not yet been discussed as a whole in any publication. Important supplements to this find group include works of C.J. Becker (1957b, 1962), O. Klindt-Jensen (1950, 1957), and E. Jørgensen (1968). The latter treats the important group of weapon graves from the last century BC. See also J.L. Nielsen (1975).

From the four centuries of the Roman Iron Age there are a great number of finds distributed in both eastern and western Denmark. Yet this abundant source material has been little studied. Johannes Brøndsted's major work on Danish prehistory offers a general outline which can give some impression of the wealth of material, but there are very few systematic, topographical publications. First and foremost there is E. Albrectsen's publication of all the finds from Funen (1956, 1968, 1971) – including the noteworthy site *Møllegårdsmarken* with its 2000 and more graves. A catalogue of the abundant material from Århus county was commenced in 1954 (H. Norling-Christensen) but never completed. A catalogue of the grave finds from the Early Roman Iron Age on Zealand has been published by D. Liversage (1980) while the finds from the Late Roman Iron Age in the same area have been published by L. Hedager (1980). From Bornholm there are significant but rather out-dated surveys by E. Vedel (1886, 1897) from the close of the last century; see also K.A. Larsen's general outline from 1949.

Thus an impression of the find material of the period must be pieced together from treatises large and small, and written from widely differing selective viewpoints. The most thoroughly studied group is that of the graves containing imported goods, treated by H.-J. Eggers in 1951. A number of popular works which convey a general impression of the topographically widely varying grave forms include the following. For northern Jutland there are two important works, P. Friis (1963) and P.V. Glob (1937). Both of these discuss the grave forms of the region, which probably reveal a rather pronounced social stratification. From central Jutland, there are studies of the numerous so-called pottery graves in Århus and Randers counties (C. Neergaard, 1928). Unfortunately this significant material is found only in preliminary excavation reports. From south Jutland there is a detailed publication of the rich double grave from *Dollerup* (O. Voss and M. Ørsnes-Christensen, 1948), together with a complete catalogue of the cemetery *Over Jersdal* (F. Tischler, 1955); see also works by H. Neumann (1953) and E. Lomborg (1964).

The material from Zealand and the surrounding islands is also relatively little published. Here, emphasis has been placed upon the richly equipped inhumation graves whose contents provide an idea of the pronounced social stratification which existed in the Roman Iron Age. This holds true, for example, of *Borritshoved* (H. Norling-Christensen, 1952), *Himlingøje* (H. Norling-Christensen, 1951; U. L. Hansen, 1978), *Hoby* (K. Friis Johansen, 1923), *Juellinge* (S. Müller, 1911), *Nordrup* (H. Petersen, 1890), *Læbrogård, Kildemarksvej* and *Skyttemarksvej* in Næstved as well as *Nesteløgård* (H.C. Broholm, 1954), *Udby* (M.B. Mackeprang, 1944), *Uggerløse* (H. Thrane, 1967) and *Harpelev* (U.L. Hansen, 1976).

The grave finds from the last period of the Iron Age, the Germanic Iron Age, are strikingly few in number. The reason for the meagreness of this source group cannot be determined. However, the first centuries of the period are represented by a fairly large material; see for example publications by H. Norling-Christensen (1956) and E. Albrectsen (1973). This odd find situation is particularly evident in the final two centuries of the period, when rather more than half of the known finds come from the small island of Bornholm. But the few grave finds known from elsewhere in Denmark contain rich equipment which bears witness to an advanced social stratification (M. Ørsnes, 1956b; C.J. Becker, 1953, 1955). A catalogue of all the finds containing metal was published by M. Ørsnes in 1966.

Bog finds from the Iron Age constitute a very extensive find group which includes both the so-called sacrificial-weapon finds and a number of deposits of a more civil nature. The group of sacrificial-weapon finds presents a number of special problems. The majority of these finds were excavated in the nineteenth century and published with admirable rapidity. However, these early excavations employed methods which in certain respects hinder modern interpretation of the finds. Two large excavations in recent times, *Ejsbøl* near Haderslev and *Illerup* near Skanderborg, both in eastern Jutland, have since augmented the material. However, it has become apparent that not all of the finds can be interpreted on the basis of the same model. Both military and civil sacrificial rites, often repeated over a considerable length of time, have been identified at every single site. In the *Illerup* river valley (H. Andersen, 1956; J. Ilkjær, 1973, 1975b, 1977) there seem to have been three sacrifices of equipment from a conquered army, two of which took place about 200 AD, the third about 400 AD. In *Ejsbøl* bog (M. Ørsnes, 1963, 1968) there seems to have been an impressive sacrificial deposit in the fourth century, while in *Vimose* (C. Engelhardt, 1869; J. Ilkjær, 1975a) a large deposit was apparently made in the third century. The *Nydam* find (C. Engelhardt, 1865) possibly contains two or three major sacrificial deposits made in the fourth or fifth centuries. *Kragehul* (C. Engelhardt, 1867) is a single deposit from the beginning of the fifth century, while the *Thorsbjerg* find (C. Engelhardt, 1863; K. Raddatz, 1957) is of a more complex character. Here the deposits can be traced continuously from about the birth of Christ up to the fifth century. This find also contains a large number of civilian objects and ought perhaps be interpreted as sacrificial acts repeatedly carried out in a sacred area over a very long period. Yet it must be emphasized that all the other bog finds also have quite a wide chronological distribution.

The *Hjortspring* find (G. Rosenberg, 1937) is unique. To be sure it is the result of one single sacrificial act, but chronologically it dates from about the third or second centuries BC – that is, far earlier than most other weapon sacrifices.

Regarding the civil finds, comprising a very heterogeneous group mainly of pottery, the majority of the finds date from the period from *c.* 100 BC to 400 AD (C.J. Becker, 1968b, 1971a). Moreover two other important find groups of another type can be distinguished, namely one consisting of wheels and other wagon parts, yokes and whole or fragmented parts of ploughs (P.V. Glob, 1951a; G. Kunwald, 1970), and another consisting of human skeletal parts and so-called bog corpses (P.V. Glob, 1965).

This remarkable group of finds derives mainly from raised bogs in northern and eastern Denmark. In all, more than 160 finds are known (A. Dieck, 1965); however, few of these are preserved. The best-known finds are the bog corpses from *Tollund* (Figure 94), *Elling, Grauballe* and *Borremose* (C. Fischer, 1979). Newer radiocarbon datings seem to show that the bog corpses date primarily from the period from *c.* 750 BC to 100 AD, the closing phase of the Bronze Age and the Pre-Roman Iron Age. The find group has formed the basis for important studies of Iron Age

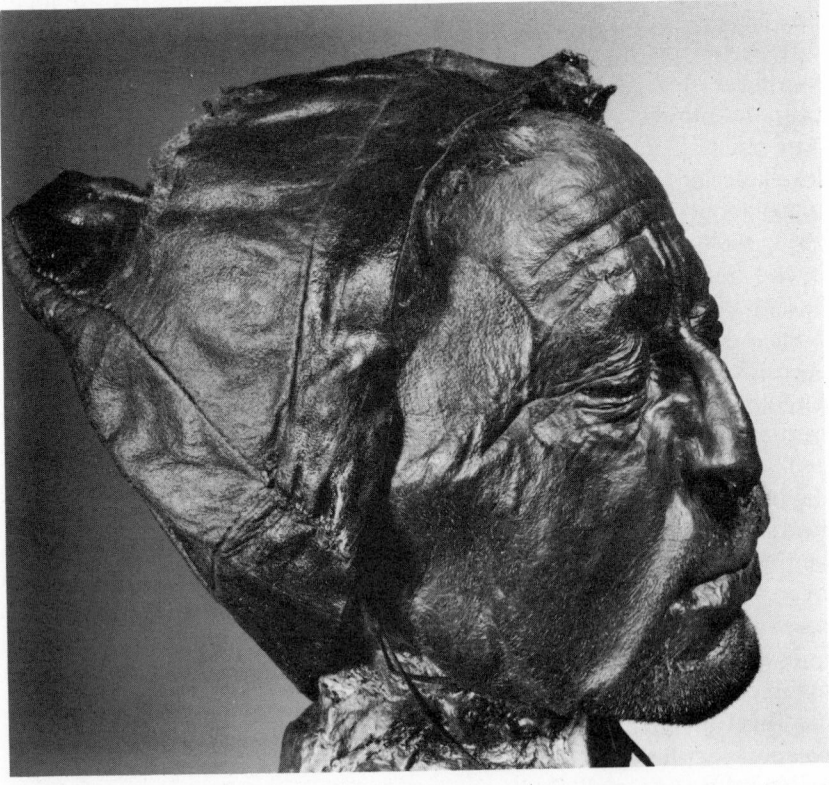

Figure 94 The Tollund Man, a bog corpse found near Silkeborg, central Jutland. The corpse has been radiocarbon-dated to 220 AD. (calibrated) i.e. the Roman Iron Age.

diet (H. Helbæk, 1958) including carbon-13 analyses which show that marine food played only a slight role in the diet (H. Tauber, 1979).

The finds from the wetlands include the roads, which have been particularly well studied on Zealand (H. Nielsen and V. Hansen, 1977). Traces have been found of an extensive and well-maintained road network, which reached its maximum on east Zealand in the late Roman Iron Age.

One last group of finds is that of the hoards, a term covering the group of deposits of valuables, especially of gold, which are known from the fifth and sixth centuries in Denmark. The majority of these finds were published in catalogue form by H. Geisslinger in 1967. A more limited topographical survey exists for the finds from Funen (E. Albrectsen, 1960). Within the hoards the so-called bracteates constitute a significant role. The bracteates were published as a whole by M.B. Mackeprang in 1952. Important analyses of selected hoards have been made by O. Voss (1954) and E. Munksgaard (1953, 1955).

In Danish archaeology the time span, c. 500 BC to 800 AD, is divided into three periods: the Pre-Roman Iron Age (500 BC to 0), the Roman Iron Age (0–400 AD) and the Germanic Iron Age (400–800 AD). In the other Scandinavian countries the term Germanic Iron Age is not used. In Norway and Sweden the period from c. 400–550 is often called the Migration Period, while the span of time c. 550–800 is called in Norway the Merovingian Period and in Sweden the Vendel Period or the late Migration Period. The historical development of the archaeological systems of chronology has been outlined by Bo Gräslund (1974b).

The archaeological datings of the finds from the Pre-Roman Iron Age are in Denmark based upon the three phases into which this age was divided by C.J. Becker in 1961. The basis for this division was primarily a typological classification of the pottery.

For the Roman Iron Age a similar chronological system is still lacking. In 1874 Sophus Müller divided the period into an early and late phase, later termed by Oscar Montelius periods IV and V. From 1897 more detailed datings became possible on the basis of Oscar Almgren's classification of the so-called fibulae. A chronological analysis of the imported Roman objects in Germania Libera, including Denmark, was published in 1951 (H.-J. Eggers). Together with Oscar Almgren's fibula typology, this latter analysis still forms the backbone of the chronological systems. According to the chronology of imports, the Early Roman Iron Age can be divided into phases B 1 and B 2, while the Late Roman Iron Age can be divided into phases C 1, C 2 and C 3 (see also E. Albrectsen, 1968, 1971).

The borderline up to the following period, the early Germanic Iron

Age, has been discussed a good deal – see for example works by H. Norling-Christensen (1949, 1956), O. Voss (1954), U.L. Hansen (1969) and S. Jensen (1978, 1979). The subsequent centuries are divided on the basis of a number of stylistic criteria. The transition between the early and the late Germanic Iron Age is dated to about 550 AD, and from this period till the beginning of the Viking Age three stylistic phases are distinguished: phase 1, c. 550–650; phase 2, c. 650–725; and phase 3, c. 735–800 AD (M. Ørsnes, 1966).

The datings of the Iron Age finds is thus based upon an extremely diversified basis depending, of course, on the variations of the archaeological record within the individual periods.

Very few general outlines have been published of the cultural –historical development through the thirteen centuries of the Iron Age up to the Viking Age. One basic work is volume III (Iron Age) of Johannes Brøndsted's *Danmarks oldtid*, published both in a Danish and a German revised edition in 1960. Later, more popular books (J. Brøndsted, 1977; L. Hvass, 1980) have to a certain extent added new aspects to the picture as a whole.

An up-to-date summary in English of the natural history of Denmark till the Viking Age was published by J. Iversen in 1973. In Sweden, attempts have been made to incorporate observations about vegetational history, and in particular man's influence on the ecosystem, in a more general scheme comprising all of southern Scandinavia (B.E. Berglund, 1969). Yet many problems remain unsolved, especially certain stagnation phenomena observed about the middle of the first millennium AD (see for example E. Nylén, 1962), which have been linked by some scholars to the Justinian bubonic plague (B. Gräslund, 1973). In much archaeological literature, however, the main interest has been focused upon the climatic change at the beginning of the Iron Age; see for example works by G. Sörbom (1966) and T. Bergeron (1956). In 1961, the Danish finds were compared with the evidence of natural history known to date (C.J. Becker, 1961). It was claimed that older theories of crop failure and famine in the first part of the Iron Age were not confirmed by the archaeological record. This viewpoint has since been further strengthened, for example, by modification of R. Sernander's (1910) dramatic theory of climatic deterioration. Thus, as mentioned above, investigations of Danish raised bogs show that over the last 5500 years a series of cyclical climatic variations can be observed (B. Aaby, 1974) whose rhythm correlates very little with changes in the subsistence and settlement patterns of the agrarian societies.

There have been only few studies made of the settlement form of the agrarian societies, and especially of their choice of arable land in the period from 500 BC to 800 AD. T. Mathiassen's major landscape studies from 1948–59, which for the Iron Age are quite insufficient, were up to the 1960s (along with E. Albrectsen's investigations of the finds from Funen) the only systematic attempts. In 1970 and 1974 E. Albrectsen presented a summary of his views on the development of settlement on Funen, with special regard to the relationship between settlement and the earliest place-name types, which are thought to date back to the early Iron Age. A similar evaluation was attempted in 1969 by A.E. Christensen for Denmark as a whole. The basis for the comparisons was, among other things, H.V. Clausen's maps of the oldest place-name types from 1916.

All older research on the subject was strongly influenced by the theory of a systematic regulation of settlement at some unspecified time in the Late Iron Age. This theory originated in a history of Denmark written by Erik Arup in 1925 and has since appeared intermittently in archaeological literature. One example is G. Hatt's work of 1937, where the difference between the village types of the Early Iron Age and the Middle Ages was explained as a result of a state initiative about the middle of the first millennium AD. This theory has also played a large role in the works of A.E. Christensen (1969) and E. Albrectsen (1974).

For a new evaluation of the problems linked to the development of agrarian settlement, the evidence of the so-called mobile village has had great significance. In Denmark this phenomenon was discovered for the first time in connection with the extensive excavations made in Grøntoft, in west Jutland (C.J. Becker, 1965, 1968a, 1971b, 1976, 1980b), at the same time as similar observations were made south of the border, in Germany (R. Schindler, 1957).

On the basis of this and other new observations, good progress has been made in the course of the 1970s, both by the ambitious excavations at Hodde and Vorbasse (S. Hvass, 1973, 1975, 1976, 1977a and b, 1978, 1980) and by a major research project carried out on Funen (T.G. Jeppesen, 1978, 1981; E.P. Christensen, 1979). The problem has also been studied in other regions of Denmark, sometimes in connection with place-name studies (see for example H. Nielsen, 1978, 1979) and in connection with the more permanent settlement form in northern Jutland (S. Jensen, 1976a).

In summary, Danish archaeologists have now abandoned the theory that a 'regulated' village arose sometime during the Late Iron Age. Instead, interest is now focused on the limited territories within which the villages seem to have been moved periodically throughout the Iron Age. From c. 1000–1200 AD a new settlement pattern seems to have arisen as a result of the introduction of the three-field system (E.P.

Christensen, 1979). Yet some of the elements of economic co-operation known from the village societies in historic times must already have existed in the village societies of the Early Iron Age.

In this connection the question of the subsistence form and productivity of the agrarian societies is of great importance. Calculations of the average yield in an Early Iron Age household have been made by W. Abel (1967) and in several areas there are helpful analyses of the quantity and type of animal as well as plant foods (see works of C.F.W. Higham, 1968; H. Helbæk, 1958). To aid understanding of the technology of the agrarian society there is also a rather comprehensive material (P.V. Glob, 1951a; A. Steensberg, 1943, 1973, 1974; M. Müller-Wille, 1965, 1977; H.O. Hansen, 1969). But in general our knowledge covers only the village society of the Early Iron Age. Whatever technological innovations lay behind, for example, the large farm complexes which came into use at various places in southern Scandinavia at the end of the Early Iron Age (B. Myhre, 1975), we have little knowledge of them. The scarcity of settlement finds has so far prevented more wide-reaching conclusions.

The problems concerned with the exchange of goods in agrarian societies have in the present work been formulated on the basis of viewpoints deriving from economic anthropology, especially from the works of K. Polanyi (1957, 1963, 1968), G. Dalton (1961, 1965, 1967, 1969), M. Nash, (1966), M.D. Sahlins (1958, 1963, 1965, 1968, 1974), and H.K. Schneider (1974). Scandinavian archaeologists have until now refrained from allowing terms from economic anthropology to enter into archaeological syntheses. Yet there are exceptions, such as the Norwegian Knut Odner's work of 1973 (compare his 1974 work), in which the cultural development in western Norway in the Migration Period has been explained on the basis of such aspects as redistribution and reciprocal economic patterns. In later years, however, there has been increasing interest in the theories of Karl Polanyi relating to the nature of early trading places (K. Polanyi, 1978). One work (K. Lunden, 1972) provides a deeper analysis of the possibilities of employing the concepts of economic anthropology in the study of the Viking Age and the early Middle Ages. A brief introduction to the theories of K. Polanyi in particular has been published by C.-A. Moberg and U. Olsson (1973).

Of the extensive literature on the exchange of goods in the Early Iron Age, mention will be made only of works of H.-J. Eggers (1951) and G. Ekholm (1956, 1958). For more restricted areas in connection with a postulated administered trade, see works such as those of U.E. Hagberg (1967) and W. Slomann (1959, 1968). A number of important recent studies, U.L. Hansen (1976, 1978b, 1980) and L. Hedager (1978a, b and

c, 1980) have shed light upon the vigorous socio-economic development in eastern Denmark in the Late Roman Iron Age. L. Hedager's
studies deal with the theoretical framework established by scholars such
as J. Friedman and M.J. Rowlands (1978), a framework of decisive
importance for the understanding of the rise of the first state-like
elements in Denmark from around 200 AD. There is an abundance of
literature on later trade activity, including works by C.J. Becker (1953,
1955) H. Jankuhn (1953), J. Werner (1961) and D. Ellmers (1972). These
latter studies discuss various aspects of the exchange of goods from the
middle of the first millennium AD.

In the attempt to describe the social integration level in the final phase
of Danish prehistory, the Iron Age, reference has been made several
times to evolutionistic social anthropology, including the works of
Morton H. Fried (1960), Marshall D. Sahlins (1968) and Elman R. Service
(1971, 1975). On the basis of these scholars' theories of social development, Iron Age society is described as having consisted of chiefdoms,
that is kinship-oriented societies, which were non-egalitarian in their
social organization and which in time absorbed ever more state-like
elements. Chiefdoms of this character gradually seem to have developed
ever more numerous positions of authority and a growing degree of
centralized leadership. These societies were typified by unequal access
to control of goods and production. Social differences based primarily
upon rank existed, but there were no clear-cut socio-economic or
political classes.

The presumed culmination of this process was the formation of a true
state, the class society. This differed from even the highly developed
chiefdoms in that it was integrated by means of institutional forms
which employed the legalized use of power. A state constitutes itself
legally by explicitly declaring in what way and under what circumstances it may employ power, and at the same time it forbids others to
employ power by legal interference in conflicts between individuals and
groups in society.

In sum, the course of development through the final millennium of
Danish prehistory saw the transition from an archaic chiefdom society to
a true state formation. At the beginning of the Viking Age in Denmark,
this transition was still not complete. The conditions necessary for
elucidating the details of this development in its various stages do not
yet exist in the archaeological record. This is due not only to a source
material often full of gaps but also to the fact that essential analyses
of the Iron Age finds remain to be made. In recent years sporadic
attempts have been made in north European archaeology to develop
such analytical forms, for example, in the works of M. Gebühr (1974), R.

Köhler (1975) and W. Schlüter (1970). These works indicate some of the
more fruitful directions which will, hopefully, be taken in Danish
archaeological research in the future.

Bibliography

The following bibliography includes all the works referred to in the text. A good part of the literature has been published in Danish with an English or German summary. This holds true of all articles from the leading Danish journals such as *Årbøger for nordisk oldkyndighed og historie, Kuml* and *Antikvariske Studier* as well as the major series of monographs such as *Nordiske Fortidsminder, Nationalmuseets Skrifter* and *Jysk arkæologisk selskabs skrifter*. The joint Scandinavian journal *Acta Archaeologica* publishes its articles exclusively in English, German or French. The magazine *Skalk* is a popular little newsletter, written in Danish and issued six times annually, which presents brief reports on the most recent finds and excavations. A complete bibliography of Scandinavian literature on prehistory and the Middle Ages, *Nordic Archaeological Abstracts (NAA)* has been published since 1976 with one annual issue.

Aaby, B. (1974) 'Cykliske klimavariationer i de sidste 7500 år påvist ved undersøgelser af højmoser og marine transgressioner,' *Danmarks geologiske undersøgelser, Årbog 1974*, 91–107.

Aaris-Sørensen, K. (1980a) 'Depauperation of the Mammalian Fauna of the Island of Zealand during the Atlantic Period,' *Vidensk. Medd. dansk naturhist. Foren.*, 142, 131–8.

Aaris-Sørensen, K. (1980b) 'Atlantic Fish, Reptile, and Bird Remains from the Mesolithic Settlement at Vedbæk, North Zealand,' *Vidensk. Medd. dansk naturhist. Foren.*, 142, 139–49.

Aaris-Sørensen, K. (1980c) 'The Subfossil Wolf, Canis lupus L., in Denmark,' *Vidensk. Medd. dansk naturhist. Foren.*, 142, 131–8.

Abel, W. (1967) 'Geschichte der deutschen Landwirtschaft vom frühen

Mittelalter bis zum 19. Jahrhundert,' *Deutsche Agrargeschichte*, II, Stuttgart.

Acsádi, G. and Nemeskéri, J. (1970) *History of Human Life Span and Mortality*, Budapest.

Albrectsen, E. (1946) 'Fyns bebyggelse i den ældre jernalder,' *Årbøger for nordisk oldkyndighed og historie*, 1–72.

Albrectsen, E. (1951a) 'Fyns bebyggelse i oldtiden,' *Fynske årbøger*.

Albrectsen, E. (1951b) 'Ein Gräberfeld der jüngeren Eisenzeit auf Fünen,' *Acta Archaeologica*, XXI, 234–53.

Albrectsen, E. (1954) *Fynske jernaldergrave*, I, Odense.

Albrectsen, E. (1956) *Fynske jernaldergrave*, II, Odense.

Albrectsen, E. (1960) 'Fynske guldfund,' *Fynske Studier*, III, Odense.

Albrectsen, E. (1968) *Fynske jernaldergrave*, III, Odense.

Albrectsen, E. (1970) 'Den ældre jernalders bebyggelse på Fyn,' *Kuml*, 123–44.

Albrectsen, E. (1971) *Fynske jernaldergrave*, IV, Odense.

Albrectsen, E. (1973) *Fynske jernaldergrave*, V, Odense.

Albrectsen, E. (1974) 'Fyn i oldtiden,' *Odense University Studies in History and Social Science*, XX.

Albrethsen, S.E. (1976) 'De levede og døde ... for 7000 år siden,' *Nationalmuseets arbejdsmark*, 5–23.

Albrethsen, S.E. and Street-Jensen, J. (1964) 'En højgruppe i Vojens,' *Årbøger for nordiske oldkyndighed og historie*, 1–31.

Albrethsen, S.E. *et al.* (1976) 'Excavation of a Mesolithic Cemetery at Vedbæk, Denmark,' *Acta Archaeologica*, XLVII, 1–28.

Almgren, O. (1897) *Studien über nordeuropäische Fibelformen*. Stockholm.

Althin, C.A. (1954) 'The Chronology of the Stone Age Settlement in Scania, Sweden: The Mesolithic Settlement,' *Acta Archaeologica Lundensia*, I.

Ammermann, A.J. and Cavalli-Sforza, L.L. (1973) 'A Population Model for the Diffusion of Early Farming in Europe,' in Renfrew, C. (ed.) *The Explanation of Culture Change: Models in Prehistory*, London.

Andersen, A. (1966) 'Geologi og arkæologi i Draved mose,' *Meddelelser fra Dansk Geologisk Forening*, XVI, 255–8.

Andersen, H. (1951) 'Et landsbyhus på Gørding hede,' *Kuml*, 40–64.

Andersen, H. (1952) 'Fra tomten af en sløjfet høj,' *Kuml*, 144–86.

Andersen, H. (1956) 'Afsked med ådalen,' *Kuml*, 7–23.

Andersen, H. Hellmuth (1960) 'Køkkenmøddingen ved Mejlgård,' *Kuml*, 25–35.

Andersen, H. Hellmuth (1976) 'Danevirke,' *Jysk arkæologisk selskabs skrifter*, XIII.

Andersen, K. (1951) 'Hytter fra Maglemosetid: Danmarks ældste boliger,' *Nationalmuseeets arbejdsmark*, 69–76.

Andersen, K. (1960) 'Verupbopladsen: En Magelmoseboplads i Åmosen,' *Årbøger for nordisk oldkyndighed og historie*, 118–51.

Andersen, Niels H. (1974) 'Sarup: Et befæstet neolitisk anlæg på Sydvestfyn,' *Kuml*, 109–20.

Andersen, Niels H. (1975) 'Die neolitische Befestigungsanlage in Sarup auf Fünen,' *Archäologisches Korrespondenzblatt*, v, 11–14.

Andersen, Niels H. (1976) 'Keramikgruber fra to bebyggelsesfaser,' *Kuml*, 11–46.

Andersen, Niels H. (1980) 'Sarup: Befæstede neolitiske anlæg og deres baggrund,' *Kuml*, 63–103.

Andersen, Steen Wulff (1981) 'Huset under højen,' *Skalk*, 1981, 2.

Andersen, Søren H. and C. Malmros (1965) 'Norslund: En kystboplads fra ældre stenalder,' *Kuml*, 35–114.

Andersen, Søren H. (1969a) 'Flintægdolken fra Flynderhage,' *Kuml*, 91–5.

Andersen, Søren H. (1969b) 'Brovst: En kystboplads fra ældre stenalder,' *Kuml*, 67–90.

Andersen, Søren H. (1970) 'Senglaciale bopladser ved Bro,' *Fynske Minder*, 85–100.

Andersen, Søren H. (1971) 'Gudenåkulturen,' *Holstebro museums årsskrift*, 14–32.

Andersen, Søren H. (1972) 'Bro: En senglacial boplads på Fyn,' *Kuml*, 7–60.

Andersen, Søren H. (1973) 'Overgangen fra ældre til yngre stenalder i Sydskandinavien set fra en mesolitisk synsvinkel,' *Tromsø museums skrifter*, xiv.

Andersen, Søren H. (1974) 'Ringkloster, en jysk indlandsplads med Ertebøllekultur,' *Kuml*, 11–108.

Andersen, Søren H. (1976) 'Norsminde Fjord undersøgelsen,' *Skrifter fra Institut for historie og samfundsvidenskab, Odense Universitet*, xvii, 18–61.

Andersen, Søren H. (1978) 'Aggersund: En Ertebølleplads ved Limfjorden,' *Kuml*, 7–75.

Andersen, S. Th. (1974) 'The Eemian Freshwater Deposits at Egernsund, South Jutland and the Eemian Landscape Development in Denmark,' *Danmarks Geologiske Undersøgelse, Årbog*.

Andersen, S. Th. (1979) 'Brown Earth and Podzol: Soil Genesis Illuminated by Microfossil Analysis,' *Boreas*, viii, 59ff.

Aner, E. (1963) 'Die Stellung der Dolmen Schleswig-Holsteins in der nordischen Megalithkultur,' *Offa*, xx, 9–38.

Aner, E. and Kersten, K. (1973ff) *Die Funde der älteren Bronzezeit in Dänemark, Schleswig-Holstein und Niedersachsen*, 1 (1973), 2 (1976), 3

(1977), 4 (1978), 5 (1979). Series in progress.

Arup, E. (1925) *Danmarks Historie, I: Land og Folk til 1282,* Copenhagen.

Bagge, A. and Kaelas, L. (1950) *Die Funde aus Dolmen und Ganggräbern in Schonen, Schweden,* Lund.

Bailey, G.N. (1978) 'Shell Middens as Indicators of Postglacial Economies: A Territorial Perspective,' in Mellars, P. (ed.) *The Early Postglacial Settlement of Northern Europe,* London.

Bantelmann, A. (1955) *Tofting, eine vorgeschichtliche Warft an der Eidermündung,* Neumünster.

Bantelmann, A. (1975) *Die frühgeschichtliche Marschensiedlung beim Elisenhof in Eiderstedt,* Frankfurt/M.

Bath, B.H. Slicher van (1963) *The Agrarian History of Western Europe, AD 500–1850,* London.

Baudou, E. (1960) *Die regionale und chronologische Einteilung der jüngeren Bronzezeit im Nordischem Kreis,* Stockholm.

Bay-Petersen, J.L. (1978) 'Animal Exploitation in Mesolithic Denmark,' in Mellars, P. (ed.) *The Early Postglacial Settlement of Northern Europe,* 115–45, London.

Beck, Curt W. (1965) 'Infrared Spectra of Amber and the Chemical Identification of Baltic Amber,' *Archaeometry,* VIII, 96–109.

Beck, Curt W. (1970) 'Amber in Archaeology,' *Archaeology,* XXIII, 1, 7–11.

Beck, Curt W. *et al.* (1975) 'Die Herkunft der Bernsteinfunde vom Hagenauer Forst,' *Bericht der Staatlichen Denkmalpflege im Saarland,* XXII, 5–17.

Beck, Curt, W. *et al.* (1978) 'The Chemical Identification of Baltic Amber at the Celtic Oppidum Staré Hradisko in Moravia,' *Journal of Archaeological Science,* V, 343–54.

Becker, C.J. (1936) 'Enkeltgravskulturen på de danske øer,' *Årbøger for nordisk oldkyndighed og historie,* 145–231.

Becker, C.J. (1945) 'En 8000-årig stenalderboplads i Holmegårds mose,' *Nationalmuseets arbejdsmark,* 61–72.

Becker, C.J. (1947) 'Mosefundne lerkar fra yngre stenalder,' *Årbøger for nordisk oldkyndighed og historie,* 1–318

Becker, C.J. (1950a) 'Den grubekeramiske kultur i Danmark,' *Årbøger for nordisk oldkyndighed og historie,* 153–274.

Becker, C.J. (1950b) 'Die Maglemosekulter in Dänemark: Neue Funde und Ergebnisse,' *Actes de la IIIe Session, Zürich,* 180–3.

Becker, C.J. (1951) 'Late Neolithic Flint Mines at Aalborg,' *Acta Archaeologica,* XXII, 135–53.

Becker, C.J. (1953) 'Zwei Frauengräber des 7.Jahrhundert aus Nørre Sandegård, Bornholm,' *Acta Archaeologica,* XXIV, 127–55.

Becker, C.J. (1954) 'Die mittelneolitischen Kulturen in Südskandinavien,' *Acta Archaeologica*, xxv, 49–150.

Becker, C.J. (1955) 'Smykkefundet ved Ørby,' *Nationalmuseets arbejdsmark*, 26–34.

Becker, C.J. (1957a) 'Den tyknakkede flintøkse,' *Årbøger for nordisk oldkyndighed og historie*, 1–27.

Becker, C.J. (1957b) 'Førromersk jernaldergrav fra Try skole i Vendsyssel,' *Kuml*, 49–67.

Becker, C.J. (1958) '4000 årig flintminedrift i Thy,' *Nationalmuseets arbejdsmark*, 77–82.

Becker, C.J. (1959) 'Stendyngegrave fra mellemneolitisk tid,' *Årbøger for nordisk oldkyndighed og historie*, 1–90.

Becker, C.J. (1961) *Førromersk jernalder i Syd- og Midtjylland*, Copenhagen.

Becker, C.J. (1962) 'Das eisenzeitliche Gräberfeld Nörre Sandegård auf Bornholm,' *Germania*, xl, 317–30.

Becker, C.J. (1964a) 'Sen-neolitikum i Norden: Aktuelle problemer,' *Tor*, 121–34.

Becker, C.J. (1964b) 'Neue Hortfunde aus Dänemark mit frühbronzezeitlichen Lanzenspitzen,' *Acta Archaeologica*, xxxv, 115–52.

Becker, C.J. (1965) 'Ein früheisenzeitliches Dorf bei Gröntoft, Westjütland: Vorbericht über die Ausgrabungen 1961–63,' *Acta Archaeologica*, xxxvi, 209–22.

Becker, C.J. (1967a) 'The Interrelationship of the TRB and the Battle-axe Culture in Denmark,' *Palaeohistoria*, xii, 33–40.

Becker, C.J. (1967b) 'Gådefulde jyske stenaldergrave,' *Nationalmuseets arbejdsmark*, 19–30.

Becker, C.J. (1968a) 'Zum Problem der ältesten eisenzeitlichen Dörfer in Jütland,' *Studien zur europäischen Vor- und Frühgeschichte*, 74–83.

Becker, C.J. (1968b) 'Zur Frage der eisenzeitlichen Moorgefässe in Dänemark,' *Vorgeschichtliche Heiligtümer und Opferplätze in Mittel- und Nordeuropa: Bericht über ein Symposium in Reinhausen bei Göttingen*, 119–66.

Becker, C.J. (1968c) 'Haus und Siedlung der jüngsten Bronzezeit und älteren Eisenzeit in Jütland,' *Die Kunde*, xix, 152–4.

Becker, C.J. (1968d) 'Das zweite früheisenzeitliche Dorf bei Grøntoft, Westjütland. 2. Vorbericht: Die Ausgrabungen 1964–66,' *Acta Archaeologica* xxxix, 235–55.

Becker, C.J. (1968e) 'Bronzealderhuse i Vestjylland,' *Nationalmuseets arbejdsmark*, 79–88.

Becker, C.J. (1969) 'Grav eller tempel?,' *Nationalmuseets arbejdsmark*, 17–28.

Becker, C.J. (1971a) '"Mosepotter" fra Danmarks jernalder: Problemer omkring mosefundne lerkar og deres datering,' *Årbøger for nordisk oldkyndighed og historie*, 5–60.

Becker, C.J. (1971b) 'Früheisenzeitliche Dörfer bei Gröntoft, Westjütland. 3. Vorbericht: Die Ausgrabungen 1967–68,' *Acta Archaeologica*, XLII, 79–110.

Becker; C.J. (1971c) 'Late Palaeolithic Finds from Denmark,' *Proceedings of the Prehistoric Society*, XXXVII, 131–9.

Becker, C.J. (1972a) 'Hal og hus i yngre bronzealder,' *Nationalmuseets arbejdsmark*, 5–16.

Becker, C.J. (1972b) 'Ein Hausgrundriss der späten Bronzezeit aus Westjütland,' *Bonner Hefte zur Vorgeschichte*, III, 13–17.

Becker, C.J. (1973) 'Studien zu neolitischen Flintbeilen,' *Acta Archaeologica*, XLIV, 125–86.

Becker, C.J. (1974) 'Jernalder-landsbyen i Jylland: Aktuelle problemer omkring dens oprindelse,' *Kuml*, 294–6.

Becker, C.J. (1975) 'Hovedlinier i Bornholms oldtidshistorie,' *Bornholmske samlinger*, 1–41.

Becker, C.J. (1976) 'Bosættelsesproblemer i bronze- og jernalder,' *Skrifter fra Institut for historie og samfundsvidenskab, Odense Universitet*, XVII, 70–83.

Becker, C.J. (1980a) 'Hvad sker der i dansk arkæologi? Grundvidenskaben i dag,' *Det kgl. danske videnskabernes selskabs pjeceserie*, Copenhagen.

Becker, C.J. (1980b) 'Bebyggelsesformer i Danmarks yngre bronzealder,' in Thrane, H. (ed.) *Bronzealderbebyggelse i Norden, Skrifter fra Historisk Institut, Odense Universitet*, XXVIII.

Behrens, H. and Schlette, F. (1969) 'Die neolitischen Becherkulturen im Gebiet der DDR und ihre europäische Beziehungen,' *Veröffentlichungen d. Landesmus. f. Vorgeschichte in Halle*, XXIV.

Behrens, H. (1973) 'Die jungsteinzeit im Mittelelbe-Saale-Gebiet,' *Veröffentlichungen d. Landesmus. f. Vorgeschichte in Halle*, XXVII.

Bekmose, J. (1978) 'Megalitgrave og megalitbygder,' *Antikvariske studier*, I, 47–64.

Bencard, M. (1973) 'Ribes vikingetid: En foreløbig redegørelse for udgravningerne 1972–73,' *Mark og Montre*, 28–48.

Bencard, M. (1974) 'Ribes ældste udvikling,' *Mark og Montre*, 20–7.

Berg, H. (1951) 'Tre langelandske megalitgrave,' *Meddelelser fra Langelands Museum*.

Berg, H. (1956) 'Langdolmen bei Pæregård,' *Acta Archaeologica*, XXVII.

Bergeron, T. (1956) 'Fimbulvinter,' *Fornvännen*, 1–18.

Berglund, B.E. (1966a) 'Late-Quaternary Vegetation in Eastern Blekinge, Southeastern Sweden: A Pollen-Analytical Study, Late Glacial

Time.' *Opera Botanica*, XII, 1.

Berglund, B.E. (1966b) 'Late-Quaternary Vegetation in Eastern Blekinge, Southeastern Sweden: A Pollen-analytical study, Post-Glacial Time,' *Opera Botanica*, XII, 2.

Berglund, B.E. (1968) 'Vegetationsudviklingen i Norden efter istiden,' *Sveriges Naturs Årsbok*, 31–53.

Berglund, B.E. (1969) 'Vegetation and Human Influence in South Scandinavia during Prehistoric Times,' *Oikos*, XII, 9–28.

Berglund, B.E. (1971a) 'Late Glacial Stratigraphy and Chronology in South Sweden in the Light of Biostratigraphic Studies on Mt. Kullen,' *GFF*, XCIII, 11–45.

Berglund, B.E. (1971b) 'Litorina Transgressions in Blekinge, South Sweden,' *GFF*, XCIII, 625–52.

Binford, L.R. (1962) 'Archaeology as Anthropology,' *American Antiquity*, XXVIII, 217–25.

Binford, L.R. (1968a) 'Post-Pleistocene Adaptions,' in Binford, S.R. and Binford, L.R. (eds) *New Perspectives in Archaeology*, Chicago.

Binford, L.R. (1968b) 'Archaeological Perspectives,' in Binford, S.R. and Binford, L.R. (eds) *New Perspectives in Archaeology*, Chicago.

Binford, L.R. (1971) 'Mortuary Practices: Their Study and Their Potential,' in Brown, J.E. (ed.) *Approaches to the Social Dimensions of Mortuary Practices*, Memoirs of the Society for American Archaeology, XXV.

Blankholm, R.E. and Andersen, S.H. (1967) 'Stallerupholm: Et bidrag til belysning af Maglemosekulturen i Østjylland,' *Kuml*, 61–115.

Boas, N.A. (1980) 'Egehøjbopladsen fra ældste bronzealder,' in Thrane, H. (ed.) *Bronzealderbebyggelse i Norden*, Skrifter fra Historisk Institut, Odense Universitet, XXVIII.

Boaz, N.T. and Hampel, J. (1978) 'Strontium Content of Fossil Enamel and Diet in Early Hominids,' *Journal of Paleontology*, LII, 4, 928–33.

Boserup, E. (1965) *The Conditions of Agricultural Growth*, London.

Boserup, E. (1972) Boserup symposium (see *Peasant Studies Newsletter: History, Politics, and Economy of Traditional Societies*, I, 2, 34–65, Pittsburg.

Boye, V. (1896) *Fund af egekister fra bronzealderen i Danmark*, Copenhagen.

Bradley, R. (1978) 'Prehistoric Field Systems in Britain and North-West Europe: A Review on Some Recent Work'. *World Archaeology*, IX, 265–80.

Broholm, H.C. (1924) 'Nye Fund fra den ældste stenalder. Holmegård og Sværdborg fundene'. *Årbøger for nordisk oldkyndighed og historie*, 1–144.

Broholm, H.C. (1943–9) *Danmarks Bronzealder*, I–IV.

Broholm, H.C. (1954) 'Fra yngre romertid i Sydsjælland'. *Nationalmuseets arbejdsmark*, 95–107.

Broholm, H.C. and Hald, M. (1939) 'Skrydstrupfundet'. *Nordiske Fortidsminder,* III, 2.

Broholm, H.C. and Rasmussen, J.P. (1931) 'Ein steinzeitlicher Hausgrund bei Strandegård'. *Acta Archaeologica,* II.

Brongers, J.A. (1976) 'Air Photography and Celtic Field Research in the Netherlands'. *Nederlandse Oudheden,* VI.

Brown, A.B. (1974) 'Bone Strontium as a Dietary Indicator in Human Skeletal Populations'. *University of Wyoming, Contributions to Geology,* XIII, 47–8.

Bruce-Mitford, R. (1972) *The Sutton Hoo Ship Burial,* London.

Brøgger, A.W. (1921) 'Ertog og Øre'. *Videnskapselskapets skrifter,* II, 3.

Brøndsted, J. (1934) 'Ein nordjütisches Steingrab aus römischer Zeit'. *Acta Archaeologica,* V, 167–75.

Brøndsted, J. (1957) *Danmarks oldtid I. Stenalderen,* Copenhagen.

Brøndsted, J. (1958) *Danmarks oldtid II. Bronzealderen,* Copenhagen.

Brøndsted, J. (1960a) *Danmarks oldtid III. Jernalderen,* Copenhagen.

Brøndsted, J. (1960b) *Nordische Vorzeit I. Steinzeit,* Neumünster.

Brøndsted, J. (1962) *Nordische Vorzeit II. Bronzezeit,* Neumünster.

Brøndsted, J. (1963) *Nordische Vorzeit III. Eisenzeit,* Neumünster.

Brøndsted, J. (1977) *Danmarks historie indtil år 600.* Politikens Danmarkshistorie, 2nd rev. edn, Copenhagen.

Brøste, K. and J.B. Jørgensen (1956) *Prehistoric Man in Denmark. A study in physical anthropology,* I-II, Copenhagen.

Burgess, C. and Miket, R. (eds) (1976) 'Settlement and Economy in the Third and Second Millennia BC'. *British Archaeological Reports,* XXXIII.

Butler, J.J. (1963) 'Bronze Age Connections across the North Sea'. *Palaeohistoria,* IX.

Caneiro, R.L. (1970) 'A Theory of the Origin of the State', *Science,* CLXIX.

Childe, V. Gordon (1935) *New Light on the Most Ancient Near East,* London.

Christensen, Aksel E. (1966) 'Mellem vikingetid og valdemarstid'. *Historisk Tidsskrift.*

Christensen, Aksel E. (1969) *Vikingetidens Danmark,* Copenhagen.

Christensen, E. Porsmose (1979) 'Bebyggelse, kulturlandskab og driftsmåder på overgangen mellem yngre jernalder og ældre middelalder,' *Skrifter fra Historisk Institut, Odense Universitet,* XXVII.

Claiborne, R. (1970) *Climate, Man, and History,* New York.

Clark, J.G.D. (1936) *The Mesolithic Settlement of Northern Europe,* Cambridge.

Clark, J.G.D. (1954) *Excavations at Starr Carr,* Cambridge.

Clark, J.D.G. (1972) 'Starr Carr: A Case Study in Bioarchaeology,' *Module*, x, 1–42.

Clark, J.G.D. (1975) *The Earlier Stone Age Settlement of Scandinavia*, Cambridge.

Clarke, David (1972) *Models in Archaeology*, London.

Clarke, David (1976) 'Mesolithic Europe: The Economic Basis,' in Sieveking, G. de G. (ed.) *Problems in Economic and Social Archaeology*, 449–81, London.

Clason, A.T. (1971) 'Die Jagd und Haustiere der mitteldeutschen Schnurkeramik,' *Jahresschrift für mittledeutsche Vorgeschichte*, LV, 105–12.

Clausen, H.V. (1916) 'Studier over Danmarks oldtidsbebyggelse,' *Årbøger for nordisk oldkyndighed og historie*, 1–226.

Coles, John M. (1976) 'Forest Farmers: Some Archaeological, Historical and Experimental Evidence Relating to the Prehistory of Europe,' *Dissertationes Archaeologicae Gandenses*, XVI, 59–66.

Cowgill, G.L. (1975) 'On Causes and Consequences of Ancient and Modern Population Changes,' *American Anthropologist*, LXXVII, 505–25.

Crumlin-Petersen, O. (1967) 'Gredstedbro-skibet,' *Mark og Montre*, 11–15.

Dalton, G. (1961) 'Economic Theory and Primitive Society,' *American Anthropologist*, LXIII, 1–25.

Dalton, G. (1965) 'Primitive Money,' *American Anthropologist*, LXVII, 44–65.

Dalton, G. (1967) 'Tribal and Peasant Economies,' *Readings in Economic Anthropology*, Garden City, N.Y.

Dalton, G. (1969) 'Theoretical Issues in Economic Anthropology,' *Current Anthropology*, x, 70–3.

Davidsen, K. (1972) 'Valbykeramik und Kugelamphorenkultur,' *Offa*, XXIX, 133ff.

Davidsen, K. (1974) ''Tragtbægerkulturens slutfase: Nye C-14 datering-en *Kuml*, 165–78.

Davidsen, K. (1975) 'Relativ kronologi i mellemneolitisk tid,' *Årbøger for nordisk oldkyndighed og historie*, 42–77.

Davidsen, K. (1978) 'The Final TRB Culture in Denmark: A Settlement Study,' *Arkæologiske Studier*, V.

Dayton, J.E. (1971) 'The Problem of Tin in the Ancient World,' *World Archaeology*, III, 49–70.

Degerbøl, M. (1933) *Danmarks pattedyr i fortiden*, Sammenligning med recente former, Copenhagen.

Degerbøl, M. and Fredskild, B. (1970) *The Urus and Neolithic Domesticated Cattle in Denmark*, Copenhagen.

Dennell, R.W. (1979) 'Prehistoric Diet and Nutrition: Some Food for Thought,' *World Archaeology*, XI, 121–35.

Dieck, A. (1965) *Die europäischen Moorleichenfunde*, Neumünster.

Donath, P. and Ullrich, H. (1971) 'Einwohnerzahlen und Siedlungsgrösse der Merowingerzeit,' *Zeitschrift für Archäologie*, V, 234–65.

Earle, T. and Ericson, J. (1977) *Exchange Systems in Prehistory*, London.

Ebbesen, K. (1975) 'Die jüngere Trichterbecherkultur auf den dänischen Inseln,' *Arkæologiske Studier*, II.

Ebbesen, K. (1978) 'Tragtbægerkultur i Nordjylland,' *Nordiske Fortidsminder*, ser. B, V.

Ebbesen, K. and Mahler, D. (1979) 'Virum: Et tidligneolitisk bopladsfund,' *Årbøger for nordisk oldkyndighed og historie*, 11–61.

Ebbesen, K. and Petersen, E. Brinch (1973) 'Fuglebæksbanken: En jættestue på Stevns,' *Årbøger for nordisk oldkyndighed og historie*, 73–106.

Eggers, H.-J. (1950) 'Lübzow, ein germanischer Fürstensitz der älteren Kaiserzeit,' *Prähistorische Zeitschrift*, XXXIV/XXXV, 58–111.

Eggers, H.-J. (1951) *Der römische Import im Freien Germanien*, Hamburg.

Eggers, H.-J. (1955) 'Zur absoluten Chronologie der römischen Kaiserzeit im Freien Germanien,' *Jahrbuch des römisch germanischen Zentralmuseums Mainz*, II.

Ehrlich, P.R. and Holdren, J.P. (1971) 'Impact of Population Growth,' *Science*, CLXXI, 1212–17.

Ekholm, G. (1956) 'Orientalische Gläser in Skandinavien während der Kaiser- und frühen Merowingerzeit,' *Acta Archaeologica*, XXVII, 35–59.

Ekholm, G. (1958) 'Westeuropäische Gläser in Skandinavien während der Kaiser- und frühen Merowingerzeit,' *Acta Archaeologica*, XXIX, 21–50.

Ekholm, K. (1972) *Power and Prestige: the Rise and Fall of the Kongo Kingdom*, Uppsala.

Ellmers, D. (1972) *Frühmittelalterliche Handelsschiffahrt in Mittel- und Nordeuropa*, Neumünster.

Ember, M. (1967) 'The Emergence of Neolocal Residence,' *Transactions of the New York Academy of Sciences*, XXX, 291ff.

Ember, C. and Ember, M. (1973) *Cultural Anthropology*, Englewood Cliffs, N.J.

Ember, M. and Ember, C. (1971) 'The Conditions Favoring Matrilocal versus Patrilocal Residence,' *American Anthropologist*, LXXIII, 571ff.

Engelhardt, C. (1863) *Thorsbjerg mosefund*, Copenhagen.

Engelhardt, C. (1865) *Nydam mosefund*, Copenhagen.
Engelhardt, C. (1867) *Kragehul mosefund*, Copenhagen.
Engelhardt, C. (1869) *Vimosefundet*, Copenhagen.
Engelhardt, C. (1970) *Nydam Fundet*, Ørsnes, M. *(ed.) Sønderjyske Mosefund*, II, reprinted, Copenhagen.
Eriksen, P. and Thorsen, S. (1980) 'Begravet langdysse,' *Skalk* 1980/2, 29.
Es, W.A. van (1967) *Wijster: A Native Village beyond the Imperial Frontier, 125–450 AD*, Groeningen.

Faber, O. (1976) 'Hus eller grav? Et anlæg fra yngre stenalder ved Vejle,' *Mark og Montre*, 5–11.
Fischer, A. (1978) På sporet af overgangen mellem palæolitikum og mesolitikum i Sydskandinavien,' *Hikuin*, IV, 27–50.
Fischer, Chr. (1975) 'Tidlig neolitiske anlæg ved Rustrup,' *Kuml*, 29–72.
Fischer, Chr. (1979) 'Moseligene fra Bjældeskovdal,' *Kuml*, 7–44.
Flannery, K.V. and F. Hole (1969) 'Origins and Ecological Effect of Early Domestication in Iran and the Near East,' in Ucko, P.J. and Dimbleby, D.W. (eds) *The Domestication and Exploitation of Plants and Animals*, London.
Fleming, A. (1972) 'The Genesis of Pastoralism in European Prehistory,' *World Archaeology*, IV.
Fleming, A. (1973) 'Models of the Development of the Wessex Culture,' in Renfrew, C. (ed.) *The Explanation of Culture Change: Models in Prehistory*, London.
Forssander, J.E. (1936) *Der ostskandinavische Norden während der ältesten Metallzeit Europas*, Lund.
Frankenstein, S. and Rowlands, M.J. (1978) 'The Internal Structure and Regional Context of Early Iron Age Society in South Western Germany,' *Institute of Archaeology Bulletin*, no. 15, London.
Fried, Morton H. (1960) 'On the Evolution of Social Stratification and the State,' in Diamond, S. (ed.) *Culture in History: Essays in Honor of Poul Radin*, New York.
Fried, Morton H. (1967) *The Evolution of Political Society*, New York.
Fried, Morton H. (1968) 'On the Concept of "Tribe" and "Tribal Society".' in Helm, J. (ed.) *Essays on the Problem of the Tribe*, American Ethnological Society.
Friedman, J. (1975) 'Tribes, States, and Transformations,' in Bloch M. (ed.) *Marxist Analysis and Social Anthropology: ASA Studies*, London, 161– 202.
Friedman, J. and Rowlands, M.J. (1978) 'Notes towards an Epigenetic Model of the Evolution of "Civilization",' in Friedman, J. and Rowlands M.J. (eds) *The Evolution of Social Systems*, London.

Friis, P. (1963) 'Jernaldergrave ved Gjurup med teltformede dødehuse,' *Kuml*, 42–59.

Friis, P. and Lysdahl Jensen, P. (1966) 'En jernalderhustomt med kælder på Grønhedens mark,' *Kuml*, 31–58.

Gebühr, M. (1974) 'Zur Definition älterkaiserzeitlicher Fürstengräber vom Lübzow-Typ,' *Prähistorische Zeitschrift*, XLIX, 82–128.

Geisslinger, H. (1967) 'Horte als Geschichtsquelle,' *Offa Bücher*, XIX.

Gejvall, N.-G. (1955) 'The Cremations at Vallhagar,' in *Vallhagar: A Migration Period Settlement on Gotland, Sweden*, II, 700–23.

Gejvall, N.-G. (1960) *Westerhus: Medieval Population and Church in the Light of Skeletal Remains*, Stockholm.

Gejvall, N.-G., (1968) 'Mangehøje: Ældre bronzealders gravhøje på åsen ved Kårup,' *Museet for Holbæk og omegn, årsberetning*, 15–48.

Glob, P.V. (1937) 'Neues aus Vendsyssels älterer Eisenzeit,' *Acta Archaeologica*, VIII, 186–204.

Glob, P.V. (1944) 'Studier over den jyske enkeltgravskultur,' *Årbøger for nordisk oldkyndighed og historie*, 1–282.

Glob, P.V. (1949) 'Barkær: Danmarks ældste landsby,' *Nationalmuseets arbejdsmark*, 5–16.

Glob, P.V. (1951a) *Ard og plov i Nordens oldtid*, Århus.

Glob, P.V. (1951b) 'Jyllands øde agre,' *Kuml*, 136–44.

Glob, P.V. (1965) *Mosefolket*, Copenhagen. (English edn (1969) *The Bog People: Iron-Age Man Preserved*, London.

Glob, P.V. (1967) *Danske oldtidsminder*, Copenhagen.

Glob, P.V. (1969) *Helleristninger i Danmark*, Copenhagen.

Glob, P.V. (1970) *Højfolket*, Copenhagen.

Glob, P.V. (1975) 'De dødes lange huse,' *Skalk*, 1975/6.

Godelier, M. (1977) *Perspectives in Marxist Anthropology*, Cambridge.

Granlund, E. (1932) 'De svenska högmossernas geologi,' *Sv. Geol. Unders.*, ser. C, no. 373.

Gräslund, B. (1973) 'Äring, näring, pest och salt,' *Tor*, 274–93.

Gräslund, B. (1974a) 'Befolkning-bosättning-miljö,' *Fornvännen*, 3–13.

Gräslund, B. (1974b) 'Relativ datering: Om kronologisk metod i nordisk arkeologi,' *Tor*, XVI.

Grierson, P. (1959) 'Commerce in the Dark Ages,' *Transactions of the Royal Historical Society*, 5th ser, IX.

Grierson, P. (1977) 'The Origins of Money,' *The Creighton Lecture in History, University of London*.

Groenmann-van Wateringe, W. (1979) 'Nogle aspekter af jernalderens landbrug i Holland og Nordvesttyskland,' *Skrifter fra Historisk Institut, Odense Universitet*, XXVII.

Haarnagel, W. (1961) 'Zur Grabung auf der Feddersen Wierde 1955–59,' *Germania*, 42–69.

Haarnagel, W. (1963) 'Die Ergebnisse der Grabung Feddersen Wierde im Jahre 1961,' *Germania*, 280–317.

Haarnagel, W. (1969) 'Die Ergebnisse der Grabung auf der ältereisenzeitlichen Siedlung Boomborg/Hatzum in den Jahren 1965 bis 1967,' *Neue Ausgrabungen und Forschungen in Niedersachsen*, IV.

Hachmann, R. (1957a) 'Zur Gesellschaftsordnung der Germanen in der Zeit um Christi Geburt,' *Archaeologica Geographica*, V/VI.

Hachmann, R. (1957b) 'Die frühe Bronzezeit im westlichen Ostseegebiet und ihre mittel- und südosteurapäischen Beziehungen,' *6th Beiheft zum Atlas der Urgeschichte*, Hamburg.

Hagberg, U.E. (1967) *The Archaeology of Skedemosse*, I–II, Stockholm.

Hansen, H.O. (1969) 'Experimental Ploughing with a Døstrup Ard Replica,' *Tools and Tillage*, I, 2.

Hansen, U.L. (1969) 'Kvarmløsefundet- en analyse af Söstalastilen og dens forudsætninger,' *Årbøger for nordisk oldkyndighed og historie*, 63–102.

Hansen, U.L. (1972a) 'A Mesolithic Grave from Melby in Zealand, Denmark,' *Acta Archaeologica*, XLIII, 239–49.

Hansen, U.L. (1972b) 'Mellem-neolitiske jorddgrave fra Vindinge på Sjælland,' *Årbøger for nordisk oldkyndighed og historie*, 5–70.

Hansen, U.L. (1976) 'Das Gräberfeld bei Harpelev, Seeland,' *Acta Archaeologica*, XLVII, 91–160.

Hansen, U.L. (1978a) 'Himlingøje-gravpladsens høje,' *Antikvariske Studier*, II, 47–80.

Hansen, U.L. (1978b) 'International stormagt kontra randområder: Handel i romersk og ældre germansk jernalder,' *XV Nordiske arkeologmötet, Förtryck av mötesföredrag*.

Hansen, U.L. (1980) 'Zur jüngeren römischen Kaiserzeit auf Seeland unter besonderer Berücksichtigung chronologischer Probleme der Grabbeigaben,' *Studien zur Sachsenforschung*, II, 261–73, Hildesheim.

Harner, M.J. (1970) 'Population Pressure and the Social Evolution of Agriculturalists,' *Southwestern Journal of Anthropology*, XXVI, 67–86.

Hatt, G. (1935) 'Jernalderbopladser ved Ginderup i Thy,' *Nationalmuseets arbejdsmark*, 37–51.

Hatt, G. (1937) *Landbrug i Danmarks oldtid*, Copenhagen.

Hatt, G. (1938) 'Jernalders bopladser i Himmerland,' *Årbøger for nordisk oldkyndighed og historie*, 119–266.

Hatt, G. (1949) 'Oldtidsagre,' *Videnskabernes selskab, arkæologisk kunsthistoriske skrifter*, II, 1.

Hatt, G. (1953) 'An Early Roman Iron Age Dwelling Site in Holmsland,

West Jutland,' *Acta Archaeologica*, xxiv, 1–25.

Hatt, G. (1957) 'Nørre Fjand: An Early Iron Age Village Site in West Jutland,' *Videnskabernes selskab, arkæologisk kunsthistoriske skrifter*, ii, 2.

Hatt, G. (1958) 'A Dwelling Site of Early Migration Period at Oxbøl, Southwest Jutland,' *Acta Archaeologica*, xxiv, 142–54.

Hatt, G. (1960) 'The Roman Iron Age Dwelling Site at Mariesminde, Vestervig,' *Acta Archaeologica*, xxxi, 31–85.

Hayden, B. (1972) 'Population Control among Hunter–Gatherers,' *World Archaeology*, iv, 205–21.

Hedager, L. (1978a) 'Bebyggelse, social struktur og politisk organisation i Østdanmark i ældre og yngre romertid,' *Fortid og Nutid*, xxvii, 246–58.

Hedager, L. (1978b) 'Processes towards State Formation in Early Iron Age Denmark,' *Studies in Scandinavian Prehistory and Early History*, i, 217–23.

Hedager, L. (1978c) 'A Quantitative Analysis of Roman Imports in Europe North of the Limes (0–400 AD), and the Question of Roman–Germanic Exchange,' *Studies in Scandinavian Prehistory and Early History*, i, 191–216.

Hedager, L. (1980) 'Besiedlung, soziale Struktur und politische Organization in der älteren und jüngeren römischen Kaiserzeit Ostdänemarks,' *Prähistorische Zeitschrift*, lv, 38–109.

Helbæk, H. (1951) 'Ukrudtsfrø som næringsmiddel i førromersk jernalder,' *Kuml*, 65–73.

Helbæk, H. (1954) 'Prehistoric Plants and Weeds in Denmark,' *Danmarks Geologiske Undersøgelse*, ii, 80.

Helbæk, H. (1958) 'Grauballemandens sidste måltid,' *Kuml*, 83–116.

Helbæk, H. (1970) 'Da rugen kom til Danmark,' *Kuml*, 279–96.

Helle, K. (1964) *Norge blir en stat*, Oslo.

Henriksen, B.B. (1976) *Sværdborg I. (Excavations 1943–44) – A Settlement of the Later Maglemose-Culture in South Zealand*, Copenhagen.

Higham, C.F.W. (1967) 'Stock Rearing as a Cultural Factor in Prehistoric Europe,' *Proceedings of the Prehistoric Society*, 84–103.

Higham, C.F.W. (1968) 'The Economy of Iron Age Vejleby (Denmark),' *Acta Archaeologica*, xxxviii, 222–41.

Higham, C.F.W. (1969) 'The Economic Basis of the Danish Funnel-Necked Beaker (TRB) Culture,' *Acta Archaeologica*, xl, 200–9.

Hingst, H. (1971) 'Eine befestigte jungsteinzeitliche Siedlung in Büdelsdorf,' *Offa*, xxviii, 90–3.

Hodges, R. (1978) 'State Formation and the Role of Trade in Middle Saxon England,' *British Archaeological Reports, International Series (Supplementary)*, xlvii, 439–55.

Hole, F. Flannery K.V. and Neely, J.A. (1969) *Prehistory and Human Ecology of the Deh Luran Plain*, Ann Arbor.

Holmqvist W. (1976) 'Die Ergebnisse der Grabungen auf Helgö,' *Prähistorische Zeitschrift*, LI, 127–77.

Horst, F. (1971) 'Hallstattimporte und -einflüsse im Elb-Havel-Gebiet,' *Zeitschrift für Archäologie*, V, 192–214.

Hundt, H.-J. (1955) 'Versuch zur Deutung der Depotfunde der nordischen jüngeren Bronzezeit,' *Jahrbuch des römischgermanischen Zentralmuseums Mainz*, II.

Hvass, L. (1980) *Jernalderen*, I-II, Copenhagen.

Hvass, S. (1973) 'Hodde: En vestjysk jernalderlandsby med social deling,' *Mark og Montre, Fra sydvestjyske museer*, 10–21.

Hvass, S. (1975) 'Hodde: Et 2000-årigt landsbysamfund i Vestjylland,' *Nationalmuseets arbejdsmark*, 75–85.

Hvass, S. (1976) 'Das eisenzeitliche Dorf bei Hodde, Westjütland,' *Acta Archaeologica*, XLVI, 142–58.

Hvass, S. (1977a) 'Udgravningerne i Vorbasse,' *Fra Ribe amt*, 345–86.

Hvass, S. (1977b) 'Jernalderlandsbyens udvikling i Hodde og Vorbasse,' *Skrifter fra Institut for historie og samfundsvidenskab, Odense Universitet*, XXII, 39–48.

Hvass, S. (1978) 'Die völkerwanderungszeitliche Siedlung Vorbasse, Mitteljütland,' *Acta Archaeologica*, XLIX, 61–111.

Hvass, S. (1980) 'Die Struktur einer Siedlung der Zeit von Christi Geburt bis ins 5. Jahrhundert nach Christus,' *Studien zure Sachsenforschung*, II, 161–80.

Højlund, F. (1974) 'Stridsøksekulturens flintøkser og -mejsler,' *Kuml*, 179–96.

Højlund, F. (1979) 'Stenøkser i Ny Guineas højland: Betydningen af prestigesymboler for reproduktionen af et stammesamfund,' *Hikuin*, 31–48.

Ilkjær, J. (1973) 'Tilbage til ådalen,' *Skalk*, 1973/3, 14–15.

Ilkjær, J. (1975a) 'Et bundt våben fra Vimose,' *Kuml*, 117–56.

Ilkjær, J. (1975b) 'Nye udgravninger i Illerup ådal,' *Kuml*, 99–116.

Ilkjær, J. (1977) 'Illerup ådal: Udgravningen 1976,' *Kuml*, 105–17.

Iversen, J. (1937) 'Undersøgelser over Litorinatransgressionerne i Danmark,' *Meddelelser fra Dansk Geologisk Forening*, VII, 223–32.

Iversen, J. (1941) 'Landnam i Danmarks stenalder,' *Danmarks geologiske undersøgelse*, II, 66.

Iversen, J. (1949) 'The Influence of Prehistoric Man on Vegetation,' *Danmarks geologiske undersøgelse*, IV, 3.

Iversen, J. (1954) 'The Late Glacial Flora of Denmark and its Relation to

Climate and Soil,' *Danmarks geologiske undersøgelse*, II, 80.

Iversen, J. (1967) 'Naturens udvikling siden sidste istid,' *Danmarks Natur*, I, 345–448.

Iversen, J. (1969) 'Retrogressive Development of a Forest Ecosystem Demonstrated by Pollen Diagrams from Fossil Moor,' *Oikos. Acta Oecologica Scandinavica, supplementum*, XII, 35–49.

Iversen, J. (1973) 'The Development of Denmark's Nature since the Last Glacial,' *Geol. Survey of Denmark*, V, series no. 7-C.

Jacob-Friesen, G. (1967) 'Bronzezeitliche Lanzenspitzen Norddeutschlands und Skandinaviens,' *Veröffentl. d. urgesch. Sammlungen d. Landesmuseums zu Hannover*, XVII, Hildesheim.

Jakobsen, B. (1973) *Skovens betydning for landbrugets udvikling i Danmark indtil 1300*, Copenhagen.

Jacobsen, J.A. (1979) 'Bruneborg, en tidlig førromersk boplads med jernudvinding,' *Skrifter fra Historisk Institut, Odense Universitet*, XXVII, 4–14.

Jankuhn, H. (1952) 'Klima, Besiedlung und Wirtschaft in der älteren Eisenzeit im westlichen Ostseebecken,' *Archaeologia Geographica*, III, 28ff.

Jankuhn, H. (1953) 'Der fränkisch-friesische Handel zum Ostseegebiet im frühen Mittelalter,' *Zeitschrift für Sozial-und Wirtschaftsgeschichte*, XL, 193ff.

Jankuhn, H. (1969) 'Vor- und Frühgeschichte vom Neolitikum bis zur Völkerwanderungszeit,' in *Deutsche Agrargeschichte*, I, Stuttgart.

Jankuhn, H. (1972) 'Haitabu,' *Ein Handelsplatz der Wikingerzeit*, Neumünster.

Jazdzewski, K. (1973) 'The Relations between Kujawian Barrows in Poland and Megalithic Tombs in Northern Germany, Denmark, and Western European Countries,' in Daniel, G. and Kjærum, P. (eds) *Megalithic Graves and Ritual*, Copenhagen.

Jensen, J. (1965) 'Bernsteinfunde und Bernsteinhandel der jüngeren Bronzezeit Dänemarks,' *Acta Archaeologica*, XXXVI, 43–86.

Jensen, J. (1966a) 'Griffzungenschwerter der späten nordischen Bronzezeit,' *Acta Archaeologica*, XXXVII, 25–51.

Jensen, J. (1966b) 'Arkæologi og kulturforskning,' *Historisk Tidsskrift*, 1–30.

Jensen, J. (1967a) 'Voldtofte-fundet: Bopladsproblemer i yngre bronzealder i Danmark,' *Årbøger for nordisk oldkyndighed og historie*, 91–154.

Jensen, J. (1967b) 'Zwei Abfallgruben von Gevninge, Zeeland,' *Acta Archaeologica*, XXXVII, 187–202.

Jensen, J. (1968) 'Et jysk ravfund: Ravhandelen i den yngre bronzealder,'

Kuml, 93–110.

Jensen, J. (1969) 'Ein thrako-kimmerischer Goldfund aus Dänemark,' *Acta Archaeologica*, xxx, 159–84.

Jensen, J. (1970) 'Et bronzealderanlæg fra Fyrkat,' *Årbøger for nordisk oldkyndighed og historie*, 78–93.

Jensen, J. (1971) 'Rammen,' *Skalk*, 1971/5.

Jensen, J. (1972) 'Ein neues Hallstattschwert aus Dänemark: Beitrag zur Problematik der jungbronzezeitlichen Votivfunde,' *Acta Archaeologica*, XLIII, 115–64.

Jensen, J. (1979a) *Bronzealderen*, I-II, Copenhagen.

Jensen, J. (1979b) 'Oldtidens samfund: Tiden indtil 800 e. Kr.', *Dansk Socialhistorie*, I, Copenhagen.

Jensen, J. (1982) *Nordens guld*. Copenhagen.

Jensen, J., Cullberg, C. and Mikkelsen, E. (1978) 'Udvekslingssystemer i Nordens forhistorie,' *XV Nordiska arkeologmötet. Förtryck av mötesföredrag.*

Jensen, J.Å. (1972) 'Bopladsen Myrhøj: 3 hustomter med klokkebægerkeramik,' *Kuml*, 61–122.

Jensen, S. (1976a) 'Byhøjene i Thy og aspekter af samfundsudviklingen i ældre jernalder,' *Museer i Viborg Amt (MIV)*, VI, 64ff.

Jensen, S. (1976b) 'Fynsk keramik i gravfund fra sen romersk jernalder,' *Kuml*, 151–90.

Jensen, S. (1978) 'Overgangen fra romersk till germansk jernalder,' *Hikuin*, IV, 101–16.

Jensen, S. (1979) 'En nordjysk grav fra romersk jernalder: Sen romersk jernalders kronologi i Nordeuropa,' *Kuml*, 167–98.

Jensen, S. (1980) 'To sydvestjyske bopladser fra ældre germansk jernalder: Jernalderbebyggelsen i Ribeområdet,' *Mark og Montre*, 23–36.

Jeppesen, T. Grøngård (1978) 'Oldtidsbebyggelse- middelalderbebyggelse: Kontinuitet eller brud,' *Hikuin*, IV, 117–24.

Jeppesen, T. Grøngård (1979) 'Bebyggelsesflytninger på overgangen mellem vikingetid og middelalder,' *Skrifter fra Historisk Institut, Odense Universitet*, XXVII, 99–117.

Jeppesen, T. Grøngård (1981) 'Middelalderlandsbyens opståen,' *Fynske Studier*, XI, Odense.

Jessen, K. (1935) 'Archaeological Dating in the History of North Jutland's Vegetation,' *Acta Archaeologica*, V, 185–214.

Jessen, K. (1937) 'Litorinasænkningen ved Klintesø i pollenfloristisk belysning,' *Meddelelser fra Dansk geologisk forening*, IX, 2.

Jessen, K. (1938) 'Some West Baltic Pollen Diagrams,' *Quartär*, I, 129–39.

Jessen, K. (1939) 'Bundsø: En yngre stenalders boplads på Als,' *Årbøger for nordisk oldkyndighed og historie*, 65–84.

Jessen, K. (1951) 'Oldtidens korndyrkning i Danmark,' *Viking*, xv, 25–37.

Jochim, M.A. (1976) *Hunter–Gatherer Subsistence and Settlement: A Predictive Model*, New York.

Johansen, E. (1975) 'Øster Hassing huset: En hustomt fra yngre stenalder,' *Hikuin*, ii, 57–66.

Johansen, K. Friis (1917) 'Jordgrave fra Dyssetid,' *Årbøger for nordisk oldkyndighed og historie*, 131–47.

Johansen, K. Friis (1919) 'En boplads fra den ældste stenalder i Sværdborg mose,' *Årbøger for nordisk oldkyndighed og historie*, 106–235.

Johansen, K. Friis (1923) 'Hoby-fundet,' *Nordiske Fortidsminder*, ii, 3.

Johansson, A. (1964) 'Sydsjællands oldtidsbebyggelse: En foreløbig meddelelse,' *Historisk Samfund for Præstø Amt, Årbog*, 245–328.

Jones, Gwyn (1968) *A History of the Vikings*, London.

Jørgensen, E. (1968) 'Sønder Vilstrup fundet: En gravplads fra ældre jernalder,' *Årbøger for nordisk oldkyndighed og historie*, 32–80.

Jørgensen, E. (1977a) *Hagebrogård-Vroue-Koldkur: Neolitische Gräberfelder aus Nordwest Jütland*, Copenhagen.

Jørgensen, E. (1977b) 'Brændende langdysser,' *Skalk*, 1977/5.

Jørgensen, G. (1976) 'Et kornfund fra Sarup: Bidrag til belysning af Tragtbægerkulturens agerbrug,' *Kuml*, 47–64.

Jørgensen, G. (1977) 'Acorns as a Food-Source in the Later Stone Age,' *Acta Archaeologica*, xlviii, 233–8.

Jørgensen, S. (1953) 'Skovrydning med flintøkse,' *Nationalmuseets arbejdsmark*, 36–43.

Jørgensen, S. (1956) 'Kongemosen: Endnu en Åmose-boplads fra den ældste stenalder,' *Kuml*, 23–40.

Jørgensen, S. (1961) 'Zur Frage der ältesten Küstenkultur in Dänemark,' *Bericht über den V. internationalen Kongress für Vor- und Frühgeschichte, Hamburg*, 440–7.

Jørgensen, S. (1963) 'Early Postglacial in Åmosen: Geological and Pollen-Analytical Investigations of Maglemosian Settlements in the West-Zealand Bog Åmosen i-ii,' *Danmarks Geologiske Undersøgelse*, ii, 87.

Kaelas, L. (1967) 'The Megalithic Tombs in South Scandinavia: Migration or Cultural Influence?', *Palaeohistoria*, xii, 287–321.

Keely, Lawrence H. (1980) *Experimental Determination of Stone Tool Uses: A Microwear Analysis*, Prehistoric Archaeology and Ecology Series, University of Chicago.

Kjær, H. (1902) 'Et nyt fund fra Nydam mose,' *Nordiske Fortidsminder*, i, 4.

Kjær, H. (1928a) 'Oldtidshuse ved Ginderup i Thy,' *Nationalmuseets arbejdsmark*, 7–20.

Kjær, H. (1928b) 'Var Boeslunde et oldtids helligsted?,' *Årbog for Historisk Samfund Sorø.*

Kjærum, P. (1954) 'Striber på kryds og tværs: Om plovfurer under en jysk stenalderhøj,' *Kuml*, 18–29.

Kjærum, P. (1955) 'Tempelhus fra stenalderen,' *Kuml*, 7–32.

Kjærum, P. (1957) 'Storstensgrave fra Tustrup,' *Kuml*, 9–23.

Kjærum, P. (1967a) 'The Chronology of the Passage Graves in Jutland,' *Palaeohistoria*, xii, 323–33.

Kjærum, P. (1967b) 'Mortuary Houses and Funeral Rites in Denmark,' *Antiquity*, xli, 190–6.

Kjærum, P. (1969) 'Jættestuen Jordhøj,' *Kuml*, 9–66.

Kjærum, P. (1977) 'En langhøjs tilblivelse,' *Antikvariske Studier*, i, 19–26.

Klindt-Jensen, O. (1950) *Foreign Influences in Denmark's Early Iron Age*, Copenhagen.

Klindt-Jensen, O. (1957) 'Bornholm i Folkevandringstiden,' *Nationalmuseets skrifter, større beretninger*, ii.

Klindt-Jensen, O. (1959) 'To krigergrave fra Bornholms jernalder,' *Nationalmuseets arbejdsmark*, 90–100.

Köhler, R. (1975) *Untersuchungen zu Grabkomplexen der älteren römischen Kaiserzeit in Böhmen unter Aspekten der religiösen und sozialen Gliederung*, Neumünster.

Königsson, L.-K. (1969) 'Natural and Cultural Factors in the Landscape Development in Oland,' *Oikos, Acta Oecologica Scandinavica, Supplementum*, xii, 50–9.

Kossack, G. (1964) 'Trinkgeschirr als Kultgerät der Hallstattzeit,' *Varia Archaeologica, Schriften der Sektion für Vor- und Frühgeschichte d. Deutschen Akademie der Wissenschaften*, 96–105. .

Kristiansen, K. (1974) 'En kildekritisk analyse af depotfund fra Danmarks yngre bronzealder (periode iv-v): Et bidrag til arkæologisk kildekritik,' *Årbøger for nordisk oldkyndighed og historie, 119–60.*

Kristiansen, K. (1978a) 'Bebyggelse, erhvervsstrategi og arealudnyttelse i Danmarks bronzealder,' *Fortid og Nutid*, xxvii, 320–45.

Kristiansen, K. (1978b) 'The Consumption of Wealth in Bronze Age Denmark: A Study in the Dynamics of Economic Processes in Tribal Societies,' *Studies in Scandinavian Prehistory and Early History*, i, 158–190.

Kroll, H.J. (1975) *Ur-und Frühgeschichtliche Ackerbau in Archsum auf Sylt*, Kiel.

Kunwald, G. (1962) 'Broskovvejene,' *Nationalmuseets arbejdsmark*, 149–67.

Kunwald, G. (1964) 'Oldtidsveje,' *Turistforeningen for Danmarks årbog*, 18–36.

Kunwald, G. (1970) 'Der Moorfund in Rappendam auf Seeland,' *Prähistorische Zeitschrift*, XLV, 42–88.

la Cour, V. (1927) *Sjællands ældste bygder*, Copenhagen.

Larsen, K.A. (1949) 'Bornholm i ældre jernalder,' *Årbøger for nordisk oldkyndighed og historie*, 1–214.

Larsen, K.A. (1957) 'Stenalderhuse på Knardrup Galgebakke,' *Kuml*, 24–41.

Lasko, P. (1971) *The Kingdom of the Franks*, London.

Lassen, Aksel (1965) *Fald og Fremgang: Træk af befolkningsudviklingen i Danmark 1645–1960*, Århus.

Lee, R.B. (1968) 'What Hunters do for a Living, or How to Make out on Scarce Resources,' in Lee, R.B. and DeVore, I. (eds) *Man the Hunter*, Chicago.

Leeds, A. and Vayda, A.P. (1965) 'Man, Culture and Animal: The Role of Animals in Human Ecological Adjustments,' *Publications of the American Association for the Advancement of Science*, no. 78, Washington, DC.

Lévi-Strauss, C. (1962) *La pensée sauvage*, Paris.

Lichardus, J. (1976) *Rössen-Gartesleben- Baalberge: Ein Beitrag zur Chronologie des mitteldeutschen Neolitikums und zur Entstehung der Trichterbecher Kulturen*, Bonn.

Liversage, D. (1964) 'En hellekiste ved Gerdrup, Københavns amt,' *Årbøger for nordisk oldkyndighed og historie*, 32–62.

Liversage, D. (1970) 'Stendyssens forløber,' *Skalk*, 1970/1, 5–11.

Liversage, D. (1980) 'Material and Interpretation: The Archaeology of Sjælland in the Early Roman Iron Age,' *Publications of the National Museum: Archaeological Historical Series 1*, xx.

Lomborg, E. (1960) 'Donauländische Kulturbeziehungen und die relative Chronologie der frühen nordischen Bronzezeit,' *Acta Archaeologica*, XXX, 51–146.

Lomborg, E. (1963) 'Grav und fra Stubberup, Lolland: Menneskeofringer og kannibalisme i bronzealderen,' *Kuml*, 14–32.

Lomborg, E. (1964) 'Myrthue-graven: Ældre romertids jordfæstegrave i Sydvestjylland,' *Kuml*, 31–51.

Lomborg, E. (1968) 'Den tidlige bronzealders kronologi,' *Årbøger for nordisk oldkyndighed og historie*, 91–157.

Lomborg, E. (1973a) 'Die Flintdolche Dänemarks,' *Nordiske Fortidsminder*, ser. B in quarto, I.

Lomborg, E. (1973b) 'En landsby med huse og kultsted fra ældre bronzealder,' *Nationalmuseets Arbejdsmark*, 5–15.

Lomborg, E. (1975) 'Klokkebæger: og senere Beaker-indflydelser i Danmark,' *Årbøger for nordisk oldkyndighed og historie*, 20–41.

Lomborg, E. (1977) 'Udgravningerne ved Skamlebæk,' *Antikvariske Studier*, I, 123–30.

Lund, J. (1976a) 'Overbygård-landsbyen fra ældre romersk jernalder,' *Vendsyssel nu og da*, I, 53–62.

Lund, J. (1976b) 'Overbygård, en jernalderlandsby med neddybede huse,' *Kuml*, 129–50.

Lund, N. and Hørby, K. (1980) 'Samfundet i vikingetid og middelalder,' *Dansk socialhistorie* II, Copenhagen.

Lunden, K. (1972) *Økonomi og samfunn, Synspunkt på økonomisk historie*, Oslo.

Løppenthin, B. (1967) 'Danske ynglefugle i fortid og nutid,' *Acta Historica Scientarum Naturalium et Nedicinalium: Editet Bibliotheca Universitatis Hauniensis*, XIX, Copenhagen.

Mackeprang, M.B. (1943) *Kulturbeziehungen im nordischen Raum des 3.-5. Jahrhunderts*, Copenhagen.

Mackeprang, M.B. (1944) 'En bronzespand med billedfrise i en grav fra 3.århundrede,' *Nationalmuseets arbejdsmark*, 61–72.

Mackeprang, M.B. (1952) 'De nordiske guldbrakteater,' *Jysk arkæologisk selskabs skrifter*, II, Arhns.

Madsen, A.P. (1900) *Affaldsdynger fra Stenalderen i Danmark: Undersøgelser for Nationalmuseet*, Copenhagen.

Madsen, T. (1971) 'Grave med teltformet overbygning fra tidlig neolitisk tid,' *Kuml*, 127–50.

Madsen, T. (1974) 'Tidlig neolitiske anlæg ved Tolstrup,' *Kuml*, 121–54.

Madsen, T. (1975) 'Stendyngegrave ved Fjelsø,' *Kuml*, 73–82.

Madsen, T. (1977) 'Toftum ved Horsens, et "befæstet" anlæg tilhørende Tragtbægerkulturen,' *Kuml*, 161–84.

Madsen, T. (1978a) 'Bebyggelsesarkæologisk forskningsstrategi: Overvejelser i forbindelse med et projekt over Tragtbægerkulturen i Østjylland,' *Skrifter fra Historisk Institut, Odense Universitet*, XXIII, 64–76.

Madsen, T. (1978b) 'Perioder og periodeovergange i neolitikum,' *Hikuin*, 51–60.

Madsen, T. (1979a) 'Earthen Long Barrows and Timber Structures: Aspects of the Early Neolithic Mortuary Practice in Denmark,' *Proceedings of the Prehistoric Society*, XLV, 301–20.

Madsen, T. (1979b) 'En tidlig neolitisk langhøj ved Rude i Østjylland. *Kuml*, 79–108.

Malmer, M.P. (1962) *Jungneolitische Studien*, Lund.

Malmros, C. and Tauber, H. (1975) 'Kulstof-14 dateringer af dansk enkeltgravskultur,' *Årbøger for nordisk oldkyndighed og historie*, 78–95.

Marseen, O. (1959) 'Lindholm Høje,' *Kuml*, 53–68.

Marseen, O. (1960) 'Ferslevhuset,' *Kuml*, 36–55.

Mathiassen, T. (1973) 'Gudenå-kulturen,' En mesolitisk indlandsbebyggelse i Jylland,' *Årbøger for nordisk oldkyndighed og historie*, 1–186.

Mathiassen, T. (1939) 'Bundsø: En yngre stenalders boplads på Als,' *Årbøger for nordisk oldkyndighed og historie*, 1–54.

Mathiassen, T. (1940) 'Havnelev-Strandegård,' *Årbøger for nordisk oldkyndighed og historie*, 3–82.

Mathiassen, T. (1942) 'Dyrholmen: En stenalderboplads på Djursland,' *Det kongelige danske videnskabernes selskab: Arkæologisk kunsthistoriske skrifter*, I, 1.

Mathiassen, T. (1943) 'Stenalderbopladser i Åmosen,' *Nordiske Fortidsminder*, III, 3.

Mathiassen, T. (1946a) 'En senglacial boplads ved Bromme,' *Årbøger for nordisk oldkyndighed og historie*, 121–97.

Mathiassen, T. (1946b) 'En boplads fra ældre stenalder ved Vedbæk boldbaner,' *Søllerødbogen*, 19–35.

Mathiassen, T. (1948) *Studier over Vestjyllands oldtidsbebyggelse*, Copenhagen.

Mathiassen, T. (1959) *Nordvestsjællands oldtidsbebyggelse*, Copenhagen.

Mathiessen, H. (1942) *Det gamle land: Billede fra tiden før udskiftningen*, Copenhagen.

Mauss, M. (1969) *The Gift: Forms and Function of Exchange in Archaic Societies*, London.

Mellars, P. (1975) 'Ungulate Populations, Economic Patterns, and the Mesolithic Landscape,' *The Council for British Archaeology, Research Report*, no. 11.

Moberg, C.-A. (1956) 'Till frågan om samhällsstrukturen i Norden under bronsåldern,' *Fornvännen*, 65–79.

Moberg, C.-A. and Olsson, U. (1973) *Ekonomisk historisk början: Forsörjning och samhälle*, Stockholm.

Montelius, O. (1885) *Om tidsbestämning inom bronsåldern*, Stockholm.

Montelius, O. (1896) 'Den nordiske jernålders kronologi,' *Svenska Forminnesföreningens Tidsskrift*, IX.

Müller, S. (1897) *Vor Oldtid*, Copenhagen.

Müller, S. (1898) 'De jyske enkeltgrave fra stenalderen,' *Årbøger for nordisk oldkyndighed og historie*, 158–282.

Müller, S. (1904) 'Vej og bygd i sten- og bronzealderen,' *Årbøger for nordisk oldkyndighed og historie*, 1–64.

Müller, S. (1911) 'Juellinge-fundet og den romerske periode,' *Nordiske Fortidsminder*, II, 1.

Müller, S. (1912) 'Vendsyssel-studier,' *Årbøger for nordisk oldkyndighed og historie*, 83–142.

Müller, S. (1919) 'Bopladsfund fra bronzealderen,' *Årbøger for nordisk oldkyndighed og historie*, 35–105.

Müller-Karpe, H. (1968) 'Jungsteinzeit,' *Handbuch der Vorgeschichte*, II, Munich.

Müller-Wille, M. (1965) 'Eisenzeitliche Fluren in den festländischen Nordseegebieten,' *Siedlung und Landschaft in Westfalen*, V.

Müller-Wille, M. (1977) 'Bauerliche Siedlungen der Bronze- und Eisenzeit in den Nordseegebeieten,' in Jankuhn, H., Schützeichel, R. and Schwind, F. (eds) *Das Dorf der Eisenzeit und des frühen Mittelalters*, Göttingen.

Munksgaard, E. (1953) 'Collared Gold Necklets and Armlets: A Remarkable Danish Fifth Century Group,' *Acta Archaeologica*, XXIV, 67–80.

Munksgaard, E. (1955) 'Late-Antique Scrap Silver Found in Denmark: The Hardenberg, Høstentorp, and Simmersted Hoards,' *Acta Archaeologica*, XXVI, 31–67.

Myhre, B. (1975) 'Gårdshusenes konstruksjon og funksjon i jernalderen,' *Arkæologiske Skrifter, Historisk Museum, Universitetet i Bergen*, II, 73–106.

Myhre, B. (1978) 'Agrarian Development, Settlement History, and Social Organization in Southwest Norway in the Iron Age,' *Studies in Scandinavian Prehistory and Early History*, I, 224–71.

Møhl, U. (1957) 'Zoologisk gennemgang af knoglematerialet fra jernalderbopladserne Dalshøj og Sorte Muld, Bornholm,' in Klindt-Jensen, O. (ed.) *Bornholm i Folkevandringstiden*, 279–318.

Møhl, U. (1961) 'Rislevfundets dyreknogler,' *Kuml*, 96–105.

Møhl, U. (1970) 'Fangstdyrene ved de danske strande: Den zoologiske baggrund for harpunerne,' *Kuml*, 297–329.

Nash, M. (1966) *Primitive and Peasant Economic Systems*, San Francisco.

Navarro, J.M.de (1925) 'Prehistoric Routes between Northern Europe and Italy Defined by the Amber Trade,' *Geographical Journal*, LXVI, 481–507.

Neergaard, C. (1916) 'Sønderjyllands jernalder,' *Årbøger for nordisk oldkyndighed og historie*, 255–310.

Neergaard, C. (1928) 'Jernalder-gravpladsen ved Lisbjerg,' *Nationalmuseets arbejdsmark*, 21–37.

Neergaard, C. (1931) 'Nogle sønderjyske fund fra den ældre jernalder,' *Nationalmuseets arbejdsmark*, 63–80.

Neumann, H. (1953) 'Et løveglas fra Rhinlandet,' *Kuml*, 137–54.

Newell, R.R., Constandse-Westermann, T.S. and Meikeljohn, C. (1979) 'The Skeletal Remains of Mesolithic Man in Western Europe: an Evaluative Catalogue,' *Journal of Human Evolution*, VIII, 1.

Nielsen, H. (1970) 'Oldtids- og middelalderveje ved Stevns og Tryggevælde åer,' *Køge Museum 1970–73*, 27–40.

Nielsen, H. (1978) 'Det tilfældige fundstofs anvendelse i bebyggelsesarkæologien med Østsjælland som eksempel,' *Skrifter fra Historisk Institut, Odense Universitet*, XXIII.

Nielsen, H. (1979) 'Jernalderfund og stednavnetyper, en sammenligning af fynske og sjællandske forhold,' *Skrifter fra Historisk Institut, Odense Universitet*, XXVII, 87–98.

Nielsen, H. and Hansen, V. (1977) 'Oldtidens veje og vadesteder, belyst ved nye undersøgelser ved Stevns,' *Årbøger for nordisk oldkyndighed og historie*, 72–117.

Nielsen, J.L. (1975) 'Aspekter af det førromerske våbengravsmiljø i Jylland,' *Hikuin*, II, 89–96.

Nielsen, J.N. (1980) 'En jernalderboplads og -gravplads ved Sejlflod i Østhimmerland,' *Antikvariske Studier*, IV, 83–102.

Nielsen, P.O. (1977a) 'De tyknakkede flintøksers kronologi,' *Årbøger for nordisk oldkyndighed og historie*, 5–71.

Nielsen, P.O. (1977b) 'Die Flintbeile der frühen Trichterbecherkultur in Dänemark,' *Acta Archaeologica*, XLVIII, 61–138.

Nielsen, S. (1979) 'Den grubekeramiske kultur i Norden,' *Antikvariske Studier*, III, 23–48.

Nielsen, S. (1980) 'Nogle bemærkninger om de forhistoriske landbrug med særligt henblik på agerjordens beskaffenhed,' *Antikvariske Studier*, IV, 103–34.

Nielsen, V. (1970a) 'Agerlandets historie,' *Danmarks Natur*, VIII, Copenhagen.

Nielsen, V. (1970b) 'Iron Age Plough-Marks in Store Vildmose, North Jutland,' *Tools and Tillage*, I, 3, 151–72.

Nordman, C.A. (1917a) 'Jættestuer i Danmark,' *Nordiske Fortidsminder*, II, 2.

Nordman, C.A. (1917b) 'Studier öfver gånggriftkulturen i Danmark,' *Årbøger for nordisk oldkyndighed og historie*, 269–332.

Nordman, C.A. (1935) *The Megalithic Culture of Northern Europe*, Helsinki.

Norling-Christensen, H. (1945) 'Skeletgraven fra Korsør Nor: Et menneskefund fra ældre stenalder,' *Nationalmuseets arbejdsmark*, 5–17.

Norling-Christensen, H. (1949) 'Germansk jernalders bebyggelse i Norden,' *Viking*, XIII, 1–16.

Norling-Christensen, H. (1951) 'Jernaldergravpladsen ved Himlingøje,'

Nationalmuseets arbejdsmark, 39–46.

Norling-Christensen, H. (1952) 'Gravfund fra Borritshoved med romerske glas og bronzekar,' *Kuml*, 84–90.

Norling-Christensen, H. (1954) 'Katalog over ældre romersk jernalders grave i Århus amt,' *Nordiske Fortidsminder*, IV, 2.

Norling-Christensen, H. (1956) 'Haraldstedgravpladsen og ældre germansk jernalder i Danmark,' *Årbøger for nordisk oldkyndighed og historie*, 14–143.

Nylén, E. (1962) 'Bebyggelsesproblem i Norden förhistoria,' *Tor*, 169–85.

Odner, K. (1973) 'Økonomiske strukturer på Vestlandet i eldre jernalder,' *Historisk Museum, Universitetet i Bergen*.

Odner, K. (1974) 'Economic Structures in Western Norway in the Early Iron Age,' *Norwegian Archaeological Review*, VII, 104–12.

Odum, E.P. (1969) 'The Strategy of Ecosystem Development,' *Science*, CLXIV, 262–70.

Olsen, O. (1975) 'Nogle tanker i anledning af Ribes uventet høje alder,' *Fra Ribe Amt*, 225–58.

Paludan-Müller, C. (1978) 'High Atlantic Food Gathering in Northwestern Zealand: Ecological Conditions and Spatial Representation,' *Studies in Scandinavian Prehistory and Early History* I, 120–57.

Peeples, C.S. and Kus, S.M. (1977) 'Some Archaeological Correlates of Ranked Societies,' *American Antiquity*, XLII.

Petersen, C.G.J. (1922) 'Om tidsbestemmelse og ernæringsforhold i den ældre stenalder i Danmark,' *Det kongelige danske videnskabernes selskab, Biologiske meddelelser*, III, 9.

Petersen, E. Brinch (1966) 'Klosterlund–Sønder Hadsund–Bøllund: Les trois sites principaux du Maglemosien Ancien en Jutland,' *Acta Archaeologica*, XXXVII, 77–185.

Petersen, E. Brinch (1970a) 'Ølby-Lyng: En østsjællandsk kystboplads med Ertebøllekultur,' *Årbøger for nordisk oldkyndighed og historie*, 5–42.

Petersen, E. Brinch (1970b) 'Le Bromméen et le cycle de Lyngby,' *Quartär*, XXI, 93–5.

Petersen, E. Brinch (1971) 'Sværdborg II: A Maglemose Hut from Sværdborg Bog, Zealand, Denmark,' *Acta Archaeologica*, XLII, 43–77.

Petersen, E. Brinch (1973) 'A Survey of the Late Palaeolithic and the Mesolithic of Denmark,' in Kozlowski, S.K. (ed.) *The Mesolithic in Europe*, Warszawa.

Petersen, E. Brinch (1974) 'Gravene fra Dragsholm,' *Nationalmuseets arbejdsmark*, 112–20.

Petersen, E. Brinch (1976a) 'Vedbækprojektet', *Søllerødbogen*, 97–122.

Petersen, E. Brinch (1976b) 'De levede og døde ... for 7000 år siden: En undersøgelse af gravpladsen på Bøgebakken i Vedbæk,' *Nationalmuseets arbejdsmark*, 5–23.

Petersen, E. Brinch (1979) 'Vedbækprojektet,' *Søllerødbogen*, 1979.

Petersen, E. Ladewig (1980) 'Fra standssamfund til rangssamfund,' *Dansk socialhistorie*, III, Copenhagen.

Petersen, H. (1890) 'Gravpladsen fra den ældre jernalder på Nordrup Mark ved Ringsted,' *Nordiske Fortidsminder*, I, 1–14.

Phillips, A.P. (1973) 'The Evolutionary Model of Human Society and its Application to Certain Early Farming Populations of Western Europe,' in Renfrew, C. (ed.) *The Explanation of Culture Change: Models in Prehistory*, London.

Piggott, S. (1966) ' "Unchambered" Long Barrows in Neolithic Britain,' *Palaeohistoria*, XII, 381–94.

Polanyi, K. (1957) 'The Economy as Instituted Process,' in Polanyi, K., Arensberg, C.M. and Pearson, H.W. (eds) *Trade and Market in the Early Empires*, New York.

Polanyi, K. (1963) 'Ports of Trade in Early Societies,' *The Journal of Economic History*, XXII, 30–45.

Polanyi, K. (1968) 'Primitive, Archaic and Modern Economies,' in Dalton, G. (ed.) *Essays*, New York.

Polanyi, K. (1978) 'Trade, Markets, and Money in the European Early Middle Ages,' *Norwegian Archaeological Review*, II, 92–117.

Polgar, S. (ed.) (1975) 'Population, Ecology, and Social Evolution', *World Anthropology*, The Hague, Paris.

Price, B. (1978) 'Secondary State Formations: An Explanatory Model,' in Cohen, R. and Service, E.R. (eds) *Origins of the State*, Philadelphia.

Raddatz, K. (1957) 'Der Thorsberger Moorfund,' *Offa Bücher*, XIII.

Ramskou, T. (1976) *Lindholm Høje, Gravpladsen*, Copenhagen.

Randsborg, K. (1967) ' "Aegean" Bronzes in a Grave in Jutland,' *Acta Archaeologica*, XXXVIII, 1–27.

Randsborg, K. (1968) 'Von Periode II zu III,' *Acta Archaeologica*, XXXIX, 1–142.

Randsborg, K. (1970) 'Zwei Peschiera Dolche aus Südskandinavien,' *Acta Archaeologica*, XLI, 191–5.

Randsborg, K. (1972) *From Period III to Period IV: Chronological Studies of the Bronze Age in Southern Scandinavia and Northern Germany*, Copenhagen.

Randsborg, K. (1973) 'Wealth and Social Structure as Reflected in Bronze

Age Burials: A Quantitative Approach,' in Renfrew, C. (ed.) *The Explanation of Culture Change.*

Randsborg, K. (1974a) 'Befolkning og social variation i ældre bronzealders Danmark,' *Kuml*, 197–208.

Randsborg, K. (1974b) 'Social Stratification in Early Bronze Age Denmark: A Study in the Regulation of Cultural Systems,' *Prähistorische Zeitschrift*, XLIX, 38–61.

Randsborg, K. (1974c) 'Prehistoric Populations and Social Regulations: The Case of Early Bronze Age Denmark,' *Homo*, XXV, 59–67.

Randsborg, K. (1975) 'Social Dimensions of Early Neolithic Denmark,' *Proceedings of the Prehistoric Society*, 105–18.

Randsborg, K. (1979a) *The Viking Age in Denmark*, London.

Randsborg, K. (1979b) 'Resource Distribution and the Function of Copper in Early Neolithic Denmark,' in Ryan, M. (ed.) *Proceedings of the 5th Atlantic Colloquium*, Dublin, 303–18.

Rappaport, R.A. (1968) *Pigs for Ancestors*, New Haven, London.

Rasmussen, A.K. (1968) 'En byhøj i Thyland,' *Nationalmuseets arbejdsmark*, 137–44.

Rathje, W.L. (1975) 'Last Tango at Mayapan: A Tentative Trajectory of Production-distribution Systems,' in Sabloff, J. and Lamberg-Karlovsky, C.C. (eds) *Ancient Civilization and Trade*, Albuquerque, 409–48.

Redman, Charles, L. (1978) *The Rise of Civilization: From Early Farmers to Urban Society in the Ancient Near East*, San Francisco.

Renfrew, C. (1969) 'Trade and Culture Process in European Prehistory,' *Current Anthropology*, X, 151–69.

Renfrew, C. (1971) 'Europe's Creative Barbarians,' *The Listener*, LXXXV, 12–15.

Renfrew, C. (1972) *The Emergence of Civilization*, London.

Renfrew, C. (1973a) 'Monuments, Mobilization and Social Organization in Neolithic Wessex,' in Renfrew, C. (ed.) *The Explanation of Culture Change*, London.

Renfrew, C. (1973b) *Before Civilization*, London.

Renfrew, C. (1975) 'Trade as Action at a Distance: Questions of Integration and Communication,' in Sabloff, J. and Lamberg-Karlovsky, C.C. (eds) *Ancient Civilization and Trade*, Albuquerque.

Renfrew, C. (1976) 'Megalith, Territories and Populations,' in de Laet, S.J. (ed.) *Acculturation and Continuity in Atlantic Europe*, 198–220.

Renfrew, C. (1978) 'Space, Time and Polity,' in Friedman, J. and Rowlands, M.J. (eds) *The Evolution of Social Systems*, London.

Riis, P.J. (1959) 'The Danish Bronze Vessels of Greek, Early Campanian and Etruscan Manufactures, *Acta Archaeologica*, XXX, 1–50.

Rosenberg, G. (1929) 'Nye Jættestuefund,' *Årbøger for nordisk oldkyndighed og historie*, 245–62.

Rosenberg, G. (1937) 'Hjortspringfundet,' *Nordiske Fortidsminder*, III, 1.

Rostholm, H. (1977) 'Nye fund fra yngre stenalder fra Skarrild Overby og Lille Hamborg,' *Hardsyssels årbog*, 91–112.

Rowlands, M.J. (1973) 'Modes of Exchange and the Incentives for Trade with Reference to Later European Prehistory,' in Renfrew, C. (ed.) *The Explanation of Culture Change*.

Russel, J.C. (1958) 'Late Ancient and Medieval Populations,' *Transactions of the American Philosophical Society*, NS, 48, 3.

Russel, J.C. (1968) 'That Earlier Plague,' *Demography*, V.

Rust, A. (1937) *Das altsteinzeitliche Rentierlarger Meiendorf*, Neumünster.

Rust, A. (1943) *Die alt- und mittelsteinzeitlichen Funde von Stellmoor*, Neumünster.

Rønne, P. (1979) 'Høj over høj,' *Skalk*, 1979/5.

Sahlins, M.D. (1958) *Social Stratification in Polynesia*, American Ethnological Society Monograph, Seattle.

Sahlins, M.D. (1963) 'Poor Man, Rich Man, Big Man, Chief: Political Types in Melanesia and Polynesia,' *Comparative Studies in Society and History*, V, 285–303, The Hague.

Sahlins, M.D. (1965) 'On the Sociology of Primitive Exchange,' in Banton, M. (ed.) *The Relevance of Models for Social Anthropology*, New York.

Sahlins, M.D. (1968) *Tribesmen*, Foundation of Modern Anthropology Series, New York.

Sahlins, M.D. (1974) *Stone Age Economies*, Social Science Paperbacks, London.

Salmonsson, B. (1964) 'Découverte d'une habitation du Tardiglaciaire à Segebro, Scania, Suede' *Acta Archaeologia*, XXXV.

Sarauw, G.F.L. (1903) 'En stenalders boplads i Maglemose ved Mullerup sammenholdt med beslægtede fund,' *Årbøger for nordisk oldkyndighed og historie*, 148–315.

Sawyer, Peter H. (1977) 'Kings and Merchants,' in Sawyer, P.H. and Wood, I.N. (eds) *Early Medieval Kingship*, Leeds.

Scheffrahn, W. (1967) 'Paläodemograpischi Beobachtungen and den Neolitikern von Lenzburg, Kt. Aargau,' *Germania*, XLV, 34–42.

Schild, R. (1976) 'The Final Palaeolithic Settlement of the European Plain,' *Scientific American*, Feb. 1976, 88–99.

Schindler, R. (1957) 'Siedlungsprobleme im Stormarngau im Anschluss an die Ausgrabungen Hamburg-Farmsen,' *Archaeologica Geographica*, 25ff.

Schlüter, W. (1970) 'Versuch einer sozialen Differenzierung der jungkaiserzeitlichen Körpergräbergruppe von Hassleben-Leuna anhand einer Analyse der Grabfunde,' *Neue Ausgrabungen und Forschungen in Niedersachsen*, VI.

Schmid, P. and Zimmermann, W.H. (1976) 'Flögeln: Zur Struktur einer Siedlung des 1. bis 5. Jhs. n. Chr. im Küstengebiet der südlichen Nordsee,' *Probleme der Küstenforschung im südlichen Nordseegebiet*, XI, 1–77.

Schneider, H.K. (1974) *Economic Man: The Anthropology of Economics*, New York.

Schultz, C.G. (1949) 'Aggersborg, vikingelejren ved Limfjorden,' *Nationalmuseets arbejdsmark*, 91–108.

Schultz- Klinken, K.R. (1976) 'Ackerbausystem des Saatfurchen und Saatbettbaues in urgeschichtlicher und geschichtlicher Zeit sowie ihr Einfluss auf die Bodenentwicklung,' *Die Kunde*, 5–68.

Schwabedissen, H. (1967) 'Ein horizontierter Breitkeil aus Sarup und die manigfachen Kulturbeziehungen des beginnenden Neolitikums im Norden und Nordwesten,' *Palaeohistoria*, XII, 409–68.

Schwabedissen, H. (1968) 'Der Ubergang vom Mesolitikum zum Neolitikum in Schleswig Holstein,' *Führer zu vor- und frühgeschichtlichen Denkmalern*, 9, Schleswig.

Sernander, R. (1910) *Die schwedischen Torfmoore als Zeugen postglazialer Klimaschwankungen*, Stockholm.

Service, E.R. (1966) *The Hunters*, Englewood Cliffs, N.J.

Service, E.R. (1971) *Primitive Social Organization: An Evolutionary Perspective*, New York.

Service, E.R. (1975) *Origins of the State and Civilization: The Process of Cultural Evolution*, New York.

Sherratt, A.G. (1972) 'Socio-economic and Demographic Models for the Neolithic and Bronze Age of Europe,' in Clarke, D. (ed.) *Models in Archaeology*, London.

Sherratt, A.G. (1976) 'Resources, Technology, and Trade: An Essay in Early European Metallurgy,' in Sieveking, G. de G. and Wilson, K.E. (eds) *Problems in Economic and Social Archaeoloy*, London.

Sherratt, A.G. (1980) Plough and Pastoralism: Aspects of the Secondary Products Revolution,' in *Pattern of the Past: Studies in Honour of David Clarke*, Cambridge.

Skårup, J. (1973) *Hesselø-Sølager: Jagdstationen der südskandinavishen Trichterbecherkultur*, Copenhagen.

Skårup, J. (1975) *Stengade: Ein langeländischer Wohnplatz mit Hausresten aus der frühneolitischen Zeit*, Copenhagen.

Slomann, W. (1959) 'Sætrangfundet: Hjemlig tradisjon og fremmed indslag,' *Norske oldfunn*, IX 1–62, Oslo.

Slomann, W. (1968) 'The Avaldnes Find and the Possible Background for the Migration Period Finds in Southwest and West Norway,' *Norwegian Archaeological Review*, I.

Smith, C.A. (1976) 'Exchange Systems and the Spatial Distribution of Elites: The Organization and Stratification in Agrarian Societies,' in , Smith, C.A. (ed.) *Regional Analysis*, II, *Social Systems*, New York, San Francisco, London.

Smith, Ph. E.L. (1970) 'Changes in Population Pressure in Archaeological Explanation,' *World Archaeology*, II, 6–18.

Snedker, K.H. (1959) 'Naglesti bondesamfund gennem 4000 år,' *Årbog Lolland Falster*, 166–206.

Sörbom, G. (1966) 'Rutger Sernanders klimaförsämringsteori,' *Tor*, XI, 83–115.

Spooner, B. (1971) 'Report on Colloquium Entitled "Population, Resources and Technology",' *Current Anthropology*, XII, 254–55.

Spooner, B. (1972) *Population Growth: Anthropological Implications*, Cambridge, Mass.

Steensberg, A. (1943) *Ancient Harvesting Implements*, Copenhagen.

Steensberg, A. (1973) *Den danske landsby gennem 6000 år*, Copenhagen.

Steensberg, A. (1974) *Den danske bondegård*, Copenhagen.

Steensberg, A. (1979) *Draved: An Experiment in Stone Age Agriculture – Burning, Sowing and Harvesting*, Copenhagen.

Sterum, N. (1978) 'Nogle C-14-frie synspunkter på den Beckerske kontakthypothese,' *Hikuin*, IV, 61–76.

Stjernqvist, B. (1963) 'Präliminarien zu einer Untersuchung von Opferfunden,' *Meddelanden från Lunds Universitets Historiska Museum*, 5–64.

Stjernqvist, B. (1966) 'Models of Commercial Diffusion in Prehistoric Times,' *Kungl. Hum. Vetenskapssamfundet i Lund, Scripta Minora*, no. 2.

Stjernqvist, B. (1969) 'Beiträge zum Studium von bronzezeitlichen Siedlungen,' *Acta Archaeologica Lundensia*, no. 8.

Stjernqvist, B. (1970) 'Zur Frage der Siedlungskontinuität der Völkerwanderungszeit,' *Meddelanden från Lunds Universitets Historiska Museum*, 99–149.

Strömberg, M. (1961) 'Untersuchungen zur jüngeren Eisenzeit in Schonen,' *Acta Archaeologica Lundensia*, ser. in 4°, no. 4.

Strömberg, M. (1968) 'Der Dolmen Trollasten in St. Köpinge, Schonen.' *Acta Archaeologica Lundensia*, ser. in 8°, no. 7.

Strömberg, M. (1971a) 'Senneolitiske huslämningar i Skåne,' *Fornvännen*, 237–54.

Strömberg, M. (1971b) 'Die Megalithgräber von Hagestad: Zur Problematik von Grabbauten und Grabriten,' *Acta Archaeologica Lundensia*, ser. in 8°, no. 9.

Strömberg, M. (1981) *Järn i österlenska forntidsfynd*, Simrishamn.

Struever, S. (ed.) (1971) *Prehistoric Agriculture*, Garden City, N.Y.

Struve, K. W. (1955) *Die Einzelgrabkultur in Schleswig-Holstein*, Neumünster.

Sturdy, D.A. (1975) 'Some Reindeer Economies in Prehistoric Europe,' in Higgs, E.S. (ed.) *Palaeoeconomy*, Cambridge.

Stürup, B. (1965) 'En jordgrav fra tidlig-neolitisk tid,' *Kuml*, 13–22.

Suess, H.E. (1970) 'Bristle-cone Pine Calibration and the Radiocarbon Time–Space 5200 BC to the Present,' in Olsson, I.V. (ed.) *Radiocarbon Variations and Absolute Chronology*, Wiley, N.Y.

Sussmann, R. (1972) 'Child Transport, Family Size and the Increase in Human Population During the Neolithic,' *Current Anthropology*, XIII, 258–67.

Tauber, H. (1965) 'Differential Pollen Dispersal and the Interpretation of Pollen Diagrams, with a Contribution to the Interpretation of the Elm Fall,' *Danmarks geologiske undersøgelse*, II, 89.

Tauber, H. (1966) 'Copenhagen Radiocarbon Dates VII,' *Radiocarbon*, VIII, 212–34.

Tauber, H. (1970) 'The Scandinavian Varve Chronology and C-14 Dating,' in Olsson, I.U. (ed.) *Nobel Symposium 12, Radiocarbon Variations and Absolute Chronology*, Stockholm.

Tauber, H. (1972) 'Radiocarbon Chronology of the Danish Mesolithic and Neolithic,' *Antiquity*, XLVI, 106–10.

Tauber, H. (1973) 'Copenhagen Radiocarbon Dates X,' *Radiocarbon*, XV, 86–112.

Tauber, H. (1979) 'Kulstof-14 datering af moselig,' *Kuml*, 73–8.

Terray, E. (1970) *Den historiska materialismen och de 'primitiva samhällena'*, Zenithserien no. 9, Stockholm.

Thompson, E.A. (1960) 'Slavery in Early Germany,' in Finley, M.I. (ed.) *Slavery in Classical Antiquity*, Cambridge.

Thomsen, N. (1953) 'Om en vestjysk stald,' *Kuml*, 171–81.

Thomsen, N. (1959) 'Hus og kælder i romersk jernalder,' *Kuml*, 13–27.

Thomsen, N. (1964) 'Myrthue, et gårdsanlæg fra jernalder,' *Kuml*, 15–29.

Thorsen, S. (1980) 'Klokkehøj ved Bøjden: Et sydvestfynsk dyssekammer med bevaret primærgrav,' *Kuml*, 105–46.

Thorvildsen, E. (1972) 'Dankirke,' *Nationalmuseets Arbejdsmark*, 47–60.

Thorvildsen, K. (1941) 'Dyssetidens gravfund i Danmark,' *Årbøger for nordisk oldkyndighed og historie*, 22–87.

Thorvildsen, K. (1946) 'Grønhøj ved Horsens. En jættestue med offerplads', *Årbøger for nordisk oldkyndighed og historie*, 73–120.

Thrane, H. (1962) 'The Earliest Bronze Vessels in Denmark's Bronze Age,' *Acta Archaeologica*, XXXIII, 109–63.

Thrane, H. (1965) 'Dänische Funde fremder Bronzegefässe der jüngeren Bronzezeit,' *Acta Archaeologica*, XXXVI, 157–207.

Thrane, H. (1967a) 'Stenalders fladmarksgrave under en bronzealderhøj,' *Årbøger for nordisk oldkyndighed og historie*, 27–90.

Thrane, H. (1967b) 'Fornemme fund fra en jernaldergrav i Uggeløse,' *Nationalmuseets arbejdsmark*, 67–80.

Thrane, H. (1968) 'Eingeführte Bronzeschwerter aus Dänemarks jüngerer Bronzezeit,' *Acta Archaeologica*, XXXIX, 143–218.

Thrane, H. (1971) 'En bronzealderboplads ved Jyderup skov i Odsherred,' *Nationalmuseets arbejdsmark*, 141–64.

Thrane, H. (1973a) 'Urnenfeldermesser aus Dänemarks jüngerer Bronzezeit,' *Acta Archaeologica*, XLIII, 165–228.

Thrane, H. (1973b) 'Bebyggelseshistorie: En arkæologisk arbejdsopgave,' *Fortid og Nutid*, XXV, 299–321.

Thrane, H. (1975) *Europæiske forbindelser: Bidrag til studiet af fremmede forbindelser i Danmarks yngre bronzealder*, Copenhagen.

Thrane, H. (1976) 'Lusehøj ved Voldtofte,' *Fynske Minder*, 17–32.

Tischler, F. (1955) 'Das Gräberfeld Oberjersdal, Kreis Hadersleben,' 4. *Beiheft zum Atlas der Urgeschichte*, Hamburg.

Troels-Smith, J. (1942) 'Geologisk datering af Dyrholm-fundet,' in T. Mathiassen et al., *Dyrholmen: En stenalderboplads på Djursland*, Copenhagen.

Troels-Smith, J. (1953) 'Ertebøllekultur-bondekulter: Resultater af de sidste 10 års undersøgelser i Åmosen,' *Årbøger for nordisk oldkyndighed og historie*, 5–62.

Troels-Smith, J. (1955) 'Senglacialtidens jægere,' *Nationalmuseets arbejdsmark*, 129–53.

Troels-Smith, J. (1956) 'Nulevende rensdyrjægere,' *Nationalmuseets arbejdsmark*, 23–40.

Troels-Smith, J. (1957a) 'Maglemosetidens jægere og fiskere,' *Nationalmuseets arbejdsmark*, 101–33.

Troels-Smith, J. (1957b) 'Muldbjerg-bopladsen, som den så ud for 4500 år siden,' *Naturens Verden*, VII, 1–32.

Troels-Smith, J. (1959a) 'The Muldbjerg Dwelling Place,' *Annual Report of the Smithsonian Institution*, Washington, DC.

Troels-Smith, J. (1959b) 'En elmetræs-bue fra Åmosen og andre træsager fra tidlig neolitisk tid,' *Årbøger for nordisk oldkyndighed og historie*, 91–145.

Troels-Smith, J. (1960a) 'Ertebølletidens fangstfolk og jægere,' *Nationalmuseets arbejdsmark*, 95–119.

Troels-Smith, J. (1960b) 'Ivy, Misteltoe and Elm. Climate Indicators – Fodder Plants: A Contribution to the Interpretation of the Pollen Zone Border VII-VIII,' *Danmarks geologiske undersøgelse*, IV, 4.

Troels-Smith, J. (1967) 'The Ertebølle Culture and its Background,' *Palaeohistoria*, XII, 505–28.

Tromnau, G. (1975) 'Die jungpaläolitischen Fundplätze im Stellmoorer Tunneltal im Überblick,' *Hammaburg*, NF, II, 9–20.

Ussinger, H. (1975) 'Pollenanalytische und stratigraphische Unter-suchungen zn zwei Spätglazial-Vorkommen in Schleswig-Holstein,' *Mitteilungen der Arbeitsgemeinschaft Geobotanik in Schleswig-Holstein und Hamburg*, XXV, Kiel.

Vallois, H.V. (1960) 'Vital Statistics in Prehistoric Populations as Deter-mined from Archaeological Data,' in Heizer, R.F. and Cook, S.F. (eds) *The Application of Quantitative Methods in Archaeology*, Viking Fund Publications in Archaeology, XXVIII.

Vedel, E. (1886) *Bornholms oldtidsminder og oldsager*, Copenhagen.

Vedel, E. (1897) *Efterskrift til Bornholms oldtidsminder og oldsager*, Copenhagen.

Vorting, H.C. (1973) 'Endnu en bopladsforekomst fra germansk jernal-der i Esbjerg,' *Mark og montre, Fra sydvestjyske museer*, 22–7.

Voss, O. (1954) 'The Høstentorp Silver Hoard and its Period,' *Acta Archaeologica*, XXV, 171–217.

Voss, O. (1962) 'Jernudvinding i Danmark i forhistorisk tid,' *Kuml*, 7–32.

Voss, O. (1966) 'Langdysserne i Steneng ved Abterp,' *Sønderjysk Måneds-skrift*, VIII, 268–75.

Voss, O. (1971) 'Eisenproduktion und Versorgung mit Eisen in Skan-dinavien vor der Wikingerzeit,' *Antikvarisk Arkiv*, XL.

Voss, O. (1976) 'Drengsted: Et bopladsområde fra 5. årh. e. Kr. f. ved Sønderjyllands vestkyst,' *Iskos*, I, Helsingfors.

Voss, O. and Ørsnes-Christensen, M. (1948) 'Der Dollerupfund: Ein Doppelgrab aus der römischen Eisenzeit,' *Acta Archaeologica*, XIX, 209–71.

Waals, J.D. van der (1964) 'Prehistoric Disc Wheels in the Netherlands,' *Palaeohistoria*, X, Groningen.

Wallace, A. (1966) 'Religion: An Anthropological View,' New York.

Waterbolk, H.T. (1964) 'The Bronze Age Settlement of Elp,' *Helinium*, IV, 97–131.

Waterbolk, H.T. (1974) 'L'archéologie en Europe: Une réaction contre la "New Archaeology",' *Helinium*, XIV.

Watson, Patty Jo *et al.* (1971) *Explanations in Archaeology: An Explicitly Scientific Approach*, New York.

Webb, M.C. (1975) 'The Flag Follows the Trade: An Essay on the Necessary Interaction of Military and Commercial Factors in State Formation,' in Sabloff, J.A. and Lamberg-Karlovsky, C.C. (eds) *Ancient Civilization and Trade*, Albuquerque.

Welinder, S. (1977) 'Ekonomiska processer i förhistorisk expansion,' *Acta Archaeologica Lundensia*, ser. in 8°, VII.

Wells, C. (1967) *Diagnose 5000 Jahre später: Krankheiten und Heilkunst in der Frühzeit des Menschen.*

Werner, J. (1951) 'Zur Entstehung der Reihengräberzivilization,' *Archaeologica Geographica*, I.

Werner, J. (1961) 'Fernhandel und Naturalwirtschaft im östlichen Merowingerreich,' *Bericht d. Röm. Germ. Kom.*, XLII, 307–46.

Westerby, E. (1927) *Stenalderbopladser ved Klampenborg: Nogle bidrag til studiet af den mesolitiske periode*, Copenhagen.

Wielowiejski, J. (1970) *Kontakty Noricum i Pannonii z ludami Polnoçnymi*, Wroclaw, Warszawa, Krakow.

Winther, J. (1926–8) *Lindø* I-II, Rudkøbing.

Winther, J. (1935) *Troldebjerg, en bymæssig bebyggelse fra Danmarks yngre stenalder*, Rudkøbing.

Winther, J. (1943) *Blandebjerg*, Rudkøbing.

Wüstemann, H. (1974) 'Zur Sozialstruktur im Seddiner Kulturgebiet,' *Zeitschrift für Archaeologie*, VIII, 67–107.

Yellen, J. and Harpending, H. (1972) 'Hunter–Gatherer Populations and Archaeological Inference,' *World Archaeology*, IV, 2, 244–53.

Zeist, W. van (1955) 'Some Radio-Carbon Dates from the Raised Bog near Emmen, Netherlands,' *Palaeohistoria*, IV, 113–18.

Ørsnes, M. (1956a) 'Om jættestues konstruktion og brug,' *Årbøger for nordisk oldkyndighed og historie*, 221–32.

Ørsnes, M. (1956b) 'Kyndby: Ein seeländischer Grabplatz aus dem 7–8. Jahrhundert nach Christus,' *Acta Archæologica*, XXVI, 69–162.

Ørsnes, M. (1958) 'Borbjerg-fundet,' *Årbøger for nordisk oldkyndighed og historie*, 1–107.

Ørsnes, M. (1963) 'The Weapon Find in Ejsbøl Mose at Haderslev: Preliminary Report,' *Acta Archaeologica*, XXXIV, 232–47.

Ørsnes, M. (1966) *Form og Stil i Sydskandinaviens yngre germanske jernalder*, Copenhagen.

Ørsnes, M. (1968) 'Der Moorfund von Ejsbøl bei Hadersleben und die

Deutungsprobleme der grossen germanischen Waffenopferfunde,'
Vorgeschichtliche Heiligtümer und Opferplätze in Mittel- und Nordeuropa:
Abhandlungen der Akademie der Wissenschaften in Göttingen.

Ørsnes, M. (1974) 'Bejsebakken,' In *Hoops Reallexikon der germanischen Altertumskunde*, ɪɪ, 173–5.

Åkerlund, H. (1963) *Nydamskeppen*, Göteborg.

Index

DATE DUE

The Loom of Life – Unravelling Ecosystems

Menno Schilthuizen

The Loom of Life

Unravelling Ecosystems

 Springer

Menno Schilthuizen
National Museum of Natural History 'Naturalis'
P.O. Box 9517, 2300 RA Leiden
The Netherlands
e-mail: schilthuizen@naturalis.nl

ISBN: 978-3-540-68051-2   e-ISBN: 978-3-540-68058-1

DOI: 10.1007/978-3-540-68058-1

Library of Congress Control Number: 2008931032

Cover design: WMXDesign GmbH, Heidelberg

Cover Photo: View from the summit of Mount Kinabalu, Malaysian Borneo. Photo by Peter Koomen
Author portrait: Photo by Joris van Alphen (jorisvanalphen.nl)

Printed on acid-free paper

9 8 7 6 5 4 3 2 1

springer.com

When we look at the plants and bushes clothing an entangled bank, we are tempted to attribute their proportional numbers and kinds to what we call chance. But how false a view this is!

(Charles Darwin, *On the Origin of Species*, p. 74)

The science of biodiversity is not much farther along than medicine was in the Middle Ages. We are still at the stage, as it were, of cutting open bodies to find out what organs are inside.

(Stephen Hubbell,
The Unified Neutral Theory of Biodiversity and Biogeography, p. ix)

To Rachel

Preface

It is a slightly cloudy morning at the end of the rainy season in Kota Kinabalu, a city on the north coast of the island of Borneo. I am writing this on my tiny verandah overlooking the grounds of the house where I have been living for the past five years. Let me describe my garden to you. It is a crescent-shaped plot of land, perhaps 1,000 square metres, at the end of a cul-de-sac appropriately named 'Happy Garden'. The bit that I can see from the verandah is flat, with a grassy lawn and a couple of fruit trees. To my left is a pond and a compost heap where the remains of the banana tree that I sacrificed yesterday are beginning to decay, and behind that a steep retaining wall with drainage pipes sticking out. At the back of the house, the land slopes steeply upward and is covered in my own bit of secondary scrub, which I proudly cultivate to the great bewilderment of my landlord, who keeps offering to have his men cut it down.

On the door of my fridge I keep a list with all the kinds of birds that I have spotted in my garden (and the air space above it). It amounts to a grand total of 47 species, ranging from the noisy flocks of yellow-vented bulbuls that nest in the scrub on the hillslope to the lone chestnut-winged cuckoo that visits each year in October to feast on caterpillars for a few days before heading further south. Other large animals are the huge monitor lizards that sometimes unexpectedly clamber out of the gutter and scare the bejesus out of me, the black cobra that lives in one of the drainage pipes, and the plantain squirrels that frolic in the branches of the *langsat* tree every morning. Including frogs and reptiles, rats and bats, and excluding the fish that was in my pond until my dog ate it last week, there may be several tens of species of vertebrate animals residing in my garden at any one time.

Not bad, but a minuscule diversity compared with the invertebrates, which will take us up about two orders of magnitude. Peek into the water collected in the leaf axils of the 'elephant ear' aroid, and you will find a writhing assembly of mosquito larvae, nematode worms, and euconulid snails. Pore over the debris in the compost heap and many species of fruit flies, ambrosius beetles, dolichopodid flies, and ants stare you in the face. A particularly unlucky plantain squirrel may carry several species of ticks and fleas in its pelt and a mass of nematodes and flatworms in its belly. From the leaves of the fig tree, a whole entomologist's collection of ponerine ants, jewel wasps, jumping spiders, and leaf beetles could be gleaned, and any dusty corner of the garden shed will harbour ensign

wasps, the pumpkin-seed-shaped shelters of tineid caterpillars, and silverfish. I would not be surprised if my garden is home to as many as 2,000 species of insects, worms, snails, and other invertebrate animals.

And it does not stop there. From my perch I can see about 15 different species of tree, ranging from the native and ubiquitous *Dillenia* to the versatile neem tree, native to India, but planted in gardens throughout the Tropics. And I know that round the back there are at least as many more, not to mention all the woody climbers that are constantly trying to smother them. Add to that the bananas, the aroids, the algae in the pond, the grasses, the ferns, the mosses, and the many other herbs, and we can probably append at least 150 species of green plants to the growing list of Happy Garden's biodiversity.

That takes care of most animals and plants that can be seen with the naked eye, but I would not even hazard a guess as to how many species of 'microbes' inhabit this end of the street. During rainy weeks, beautiful veiled stinkhorns pop up in fungal priapism, and when I have been on a trip for a week I find that, as Tom Waits said, 'everything in my refrigerator has turned into a science project.' But the irregular appearance of their fruiting bodies is hardly a proper gauge for the actual diversity of fungi in my garden. Many more kinds are spreading invisibly through the decaying matter in the topsoil, or are living in silent symbiosis in termite nests or, as mycorrhiza, in and around the roots of my plants.

Unicellular organisms abound as well. Diatoms live in the pond, amoebae crawl micro-scopically in the wet soil, and bacteria are literally everywhere: not just free-living in the soil and the water, but as parasites or symbionts in and on each of the thousands of species of animals, plants, fungi, and protozoa, and many will be specific to their particular host. The velvety-blue *Hypolimnas bolina* butterflies that bask on the leaves of the mango tree, for example, have a *Wolbachia* bacterium in their ovaries that kills male eggs in some parts of the butterfly's range, but here in Borneo appears to be benign. And the banana aphid grows *Buchnera* bacteria in its belly that help it digest its food.

There is no way of telling exactly how many species of organisms share this minute semicircular plot of tropical suburbia, but it will definitely be several thousand. Let us say 10,000 as a very conservative guess. Now if I were to hop over the fence to the garden of the sprightly Indian lady who lives next door, would I find the same 10,000 species? Probably not, as she keeps her garden free of any incipient jungle and thus misses out on a lot of biodi-versity. Three thousand species tops, I would say. Still, there may be some species there that are missing from my garden. A paradise tree snake, for example, skulks in her backyard. That is probably accidental. Large predators are rare, and this side of the street may just be able to support one individual, which happens to live next door. But other additional biodiversity comes from habitats in the neighbour's garden that are lacking from mine. There is a coco-nut palm there, which comes with its own coconut beetles, and also a collection of orchids, which have special mycorrhizal fungi. So between us, our two gardens will have a higher biodiversity than each taken separately. But if I were to keep fence-hopping all the way down the street, continuously adding to my growing species list, how fast would the list grow? And would it keep growing forever or become complete at one point? There's a question.

Returning to the bird list on my refrigerator door, there are some species on that list that are no longer in my garden. A few years ago, startlingly blue collared kingfishers would nest in a dead branch of the mangosteen tree and feed their young with house geckos plucked off my walls. But the kingfishers seem to have disappeared. Conversely, the large-tailed nightjar only last year made its metallic-voiced entry into Happy Garden and seems to be here to stay. Until two years ago, there were huge white-winged tomb bats in my roof that would disperse at dusk with frantic clicking sounds and wildly beating wings. For some reason, the bats have left, but in their stead a yet unidentified species of rat has settled in.

The same thing with the smaller creatures. The ant fauna of my house is in continuous flux. At one point, the tiny Pharaoh ant was everywhere, travelling in six-lane highways along the walls and building their multiqueened nests in the most unlikely places, from piles of laundry to the jewel cases of CDs. But then an army of reduviid bugs and parasitic wasps began to beat them down and they became extinct, only to be replaced by the yellow crazy ant, which experi-enced a quick cycle of boom and bust, then briefly gave way to its equally nervous cousin, the black crazy ant, but finally retook the house once more. So even though the number of species in Happy Garden seems to remain constant, species become extinct and others establish them-selves all the time. Species that were rare become common, and vice versa. Why? Are there imperceptible changes in the garden's microhabitats? Or is it just random turnover, the result of accidental extinctions and immigrations? There's another question.

And let's have another look at that huge tally of 10,000 species in a piece of land barely larger than a tennis court. Does that imply my humble garden is actually an immensely complex ecosystem with that many ecological roles to play? Or not? Take those 150 species of green plants for example. Throughout the day, a deluge of photons rains down on my garden, the energy of which is tapped by the trees, ferns, herbs, and mosses and used to fuel their carbon-fixation machinery which constantly grabs carbon dioxide from the air and churns out roots, stems, leaves, flowers, and fruits. Each and every one of these plants does this; they all 'eat' carbon dioxide and absorb solar energy. But they may be different in other respects. The elephant ears, for example, grow in the soaking-wet mud beneath the retaining wall, whereas the *Melastoma* herbs prefer dry spots at the top of the wall. The *Macaranga* trees thrive in the blazing midday sun, whereas the gingers grow in the shady places underneath and survive on the flecks of light that make it through the *Macaranga* leaves. Mosses grow on the rocks, but grasses prefer flat patches of loamy soil. There may be one or two more lines by which plants delimit their ecological roles, but the question is whether there are really enough different roles to play for 150 species. If there are fewer, there must be a lot of competition between species – and yet they live happily together in my garden without driving each other to extinction. We may wonder how they do that.

The perceptive reader will already have understood where this exercise in horticultural exhibitionism has been heading. It has served to introduce the subject matter of this book, which can be broadly described as the ecology of diversity, but officially falls into such realms of science as community ecology, system ecology, and macroecology. We will now leave Happy Garden behind us and head for caves, jungles, and coral reefs, and many other natural environments besides that. We will delve into the scientific literature, visit laboratories and field experiments, and meet the brightest ecologists of this and earlier times, trying to find answers to the questions that apply to Happy Garden as much as to the whole wide world. How many species are there and where do they all live? Why are there so many species? How are ecosystems assembled? Does each species have its unique niche or are species interchangeable? Why are some species rare and others common? And we will address a few burning issues as well: How many species are going extinct and how many are newly introduced by people? And how much tampering can our ecosystems tolerate before they embark on a one-way path toward collapse?

Acknowledgements

The famous nineteenth-century American ornithologist Audubon once confided to a friend, 'God save you the trouble of ever publishing books on natural science. I would rather go without a shirt through the whole of the Florida swamps in mosquito time than labor as I have with the pen.' As people close to me can attest, I felt the same way after finishing my book on speciation, *Frogs, Flies and Dandelions*, published in 2001 by Oxford University Press. However, bitter-sweet memories have a habit of fading and transmogrifying, over surprisingly short time, into cherished ones. And it was not before long that I began to feel the urge to start work on another book. Having moved, immediately after finishing *Frogs, Flies and Dandelions*, to Universiti Malaysia Sabah (UMS) in northern Borneo, and suddenly surrounded by members of what ecologists call the 'rainforest mafia', I began to realise that, although I had a fair grasp of the evolution of species diversity, my under-standing of its maintenance and its role in ecosystems was limited. So a book project on the *ecology* of species diversity, to serve as a complement to the one on the *evolution* of species diversity, seemed like a good way of (1) teaching myself some ecology and (2) helping others who felt similarly challenged.

In the end, it was another drawn-out struggle to get from a good intention to the book you are now holding. Community ecology turned out to be quite resilient to simplifica-tion and popularisation, and I have spent many a day lying on the merbau floor of my house in Kota Kinabalu with papers and books strewn around me, grappling with species abundance curves, species–area equations, and food web stability analyses, thinking of Audubon, especially since on such occasions I was usually without a shirt and in northern Borneo it is always mosquito time. Still, that I could do so was largely thanks to the help-fulness of those around me, who allowed me to take time off, and forgave me for doing so, to write: my employers Maryati Mohamed of UMS and later Ronald van Hengstum and Dirk Houtgraaf of the museum Naturalis in Leiden; and also my children, my partner, my friends, and my colleagues.

For helping me find the relevant literature, I wish to thank the librarians of UMS and of the Danum Valley Field Centre. However, as the older literature was not always available in Borneo, I received a lot of help from trusted friends overseas who gave me access to the libraries of their institutions, and even printed and photocopied piles of obscure papers, in particular Frietson Galis of Leiden University, the Netherlands, Bronwen Scott of Victoria University, Australia, and Lounès Chikhi of the University of Toulouse, France. The Royal Society and the Sabah Foundation (by way of Glen Reynolds) arranged for me to work in Danum Valley Field Centre for a while, where bearded pigs and bearded British students were the only distractions. Marc and Isabelle Ancrenaz let me stay in their house in Sukau for a week to watch Woody Allen films and work on Chap. 3. My partner Rachel Esner tolerated me in her house in Amsterdam and her apartment in Paris as I worked feverishly on the final chapters in late 2007 and early 2008. And Stephen and Rosalind Sutton of Borneo Books were a great support, especially in the early phase, as were Annadel Cabanban, my agent Lulu Stader, and the people at Springer who made it all possible, in particular Dieter Czeschlik, Anette Lindqvist, and Isabel Ullmann.

Many friendly scientists helped me by having me interview them in person, over the phone or by e-mail, in particular Jacques van Alphen, Robert Bagchi, Suzan Benedick, Lisa Curran, Rampal Etienne, Hua Seng Lee, Andy Hector, Jef Huisman, Stephen Hubbell, Ann Krause, Irwanshah bin Mustapa, Roger Kitching, Cristian Lascu, Liew Thor Seng, Brian McGill, Nalini Nadkarni, Norman Pace, David Post, Glen Reynolds, Jonathan Silvertown, Maayke Stomp, Annette Summers Engel, Stephen Sutton, David Tilman, Geerat Vermeij, and Edward O. Wilson. Other various technical and logistic bits of help (sometimes small, but always indispensable) were provided by David Bignell, Annadel Cabanban, Charles Clarke, Laurence Cook, Paul Craze, James Cresswell, Angus Davison, John Dunbar, Lucius Eldredge, Mr. Fan, Jordi Figuerola, Edmund Gittenberger, Benoît Goossens, Georgianne Griffiths, Abbie Headon, Jane Hill, the Kinabalu Hyatt Hotel staff, Ludwig Kammesheidt, Cathy Kennedy, Hans de Kroon, Martjan Lammertink, Andrew Mitchell, Faisal bin Noor, Han Olff, Wolfgang Sand, Angelique van Til, Ed Turner, and Campbell Webb.

Several friends took the trouble of close-reading large parts of the manuscript and helping me winnow out all inconsistencies, non sequiturs, and unintelligibilities. These were Rachel Esner, Frank van Rooij, Isabel Silva, and Lulu Stader, and I thank them for their dedication.

Contents

1.1
Bottled Biotas

I just bought myself an ecosystem. Even though the promotional babble on the website says it is actually 'a work of art' that is 'carefully crafted to achieve an aesthetic, meditative beauty that can soothe any environment, including home, classroom or office', to me it is primarily an ecosystem. Ecosphere Associates of Tucson, Arizona, USA, specialises in selling little worlds in a bottle. Their Original EcoSphere® comes in various shapes and sizes. Mine is the ISS model: a clear glass sphere the size of a grapefruit, filled two thirds with seawater. Some gravel covers the bottom and a twig of dead coral provides a substrate for green algae. But the star attraction of the crystal ball is a dozen or so tiny red brine shrimp, nervously nibbling away at the algae.

The small sphere and its inhabitants may sound like a meagre sort of fishbowl for a price that could buy me a king-size fishtank with money to spare. But then EcoSphere is no ordinary aquarium. A spin-off from technology developed by NASA, the glass ball is completely isolated from the outside world. There is no way to feed the shrimp, prune the algae, or change the water. It is a self-contained ecosystem, running solely on the sunlight that flies through the glass wall and powers the photosynthesising chloroplasts in the algal cells. These split water into oxygen and hydrogen, sticking the hydrogen onto carbon dioxide molecules to build new algal tissues, and dumping the oxygen in the water. The shrimp breathe in the oxygen and eat the carbohydrates produced by the algae and in the process exhale water and new carbon dioxide for the algae to absorb. The waste products from this cycle, shrimp droppings and dead algal cells, are decomposed by bacteria in the water to provide nitrogen, phosphorus, and other nutrients for the algae. As a result, oxygen, carbon, hydrogen, and a whole bunch of other elements are continually pumped around the food cycles inside the sphere by the power of the sun. The process will not stop until all the shrimp (which do not reproduce) are dead. This, according to Ecosphere Associates, can take more than eight years.

The Loom of Life. M. Schilthuizen   1
Doi: 10.1007/978-3-540-68058-1_1, © Springer-Verlag Berlin Heidelberg 2008

Although the website of Ecosphere Associates warns one to 'be wary of inferior and lower quality imitations', the enthusiastic logbooks of people trying to make their own imitations are strewn about the Internet in great profusion. As it turns out, creating your own ecosphere can be a lot of fun for science classes and amateur ecosphereans alike. Just fill a glass bottle three quarters with pond water, stick in a few plants, shrimp, and snails, seal the bottle hermetically, and watch what happens. With a bit of luck, the system will balance itself out and continue living in its self-contained way for many years, like the one Robin Ohm built in a seven-litre glass bottle and kept running for at least two years, as he proudly proclaims on his website.

Just 60 kilometres or so north of the office of Ecosphere Associates, the managers of a somewhat more ambitious ecobubble were not so lucky. Biosphere 2, the futuristic 200,000-cubic-metre miniworld in the Arizona desert (Biosphere 1 being Earth itself), was sealed off from the outside world in September 1991. Inside were 12,700 square metres of recreated desert, thornscrub, marsh, tropical rainforest, savannah, coral reef, and agricultural ecosystems, and eight humans. The 40 metre by 40 metre rainforest ecosystem, for example, was assembled from 282 species of tropical trees, shrubs, vines, and herbs planted on a topsoil that was made from the local desert soil, mixed with compost and manure. But as soon as the key was turned, situations inside spun out of control. The bacteria thriving on the overly rich forest soil proliferated and began using up more oxygen than the plants could produce. The extra carbon dioxide these bacteria produced could have compensated for this by speeding up the plants' photosynthesis, except that the carbon dioxide was absorbed by the cement in Biosphere 2's structure. As a result, oxygen levels inside continued dropping from the normal 21% to less than 14%, and 16 months into the closure, oxygen had to be pumped in to relieve the suffering humans inside.

Despite the fact that life inside ecospheres seems destined eventually to come to a grinding halt, Biosphere 2, the Original EcoSphere®, and all other human-assembled and enclosed ecosystems are great gadgets that can be useful in science teaching and developing space technologies. But they do not qualify as realistic ecosystems. In the real world, ecosystems are open, interconnected, and not constricted in a transparent bubble (except Biosphere 1, of course). Wind, water, and the active movements of organisms constantly interchange nutrients between ecosystems. And yet, a few ecosystems seem to have been able to extract themselves from the global web of life and go it alone. Not surprisingly, such self-contained miniature worlds can only maintain their sovereignty in splendid isolation. And to find them, we have to boldly go where no man has gone before.

1.2
Not As We Know It

In 1986, geologist Cristian Lascu of the Romanian Academy of Sciences in Bucharest received a telephone call from one of Nicolae Ceaucescu's chief engineers. The country's hard-handed dictator had decided to build a new thermoelectrical power plant fuelled by low-quality coal imported from the Ukraine. The power station's planned site was in the undulating limestone hills near the town of Mangalia, three kilometres from the Black Sea coast, and the engineer was worried that the cave-riddled limestone terrain might be unstable. So he asked Lascu, an expert on caves and karst, for his advice. 'I considered that it is not a good location because there are some natural sink holes in the area. Some of them huge, like 200 metres large and 50 metres deep; it is possible that there are voids, maybe big voids, beneath,' Lascu recalls telling him. However, since the area is relatively flat and the limestone is overlain with several metres of clay, it was hard to determine whether some parts might still be suitable.

So Lascu and the engineer decided to dig six exploratory pits. When they descended into the fifth of these, drilled at a rubbish dump near a place called Movile, Lascu found, at 18-metres depth, a very narrow crack in the wall. 'I had to dig out some limestone and some clay, and after that I could squeeze into this fissure and I found a cave.' At that point, Lascu did not yet realise that he had entered into a whole different world. Armed with just a small lamp, he explored a few of the passages and, at the deepest point, came upon a small smelly sulphuric lake with some muck floating on top. Intrigued, he returned to the cave twice over the following weeks, bringing better caving and diving equipment, and several colleagues and friends, including microbiologist Serban Sarbu. 'That was the moment when we found a lot of animals on the ground there,' Lascu says. The floor of the cave was inhabited by a menagerie of 'troglobites': blind and pale animals adapted to cave life, including earthworms, millipedes, pillbugs, pseudoscorpions, spiders, beetles, and many other invertebrates. In the sulphuric lake lurked water scorpions, nematode worms, and amphipod crustaceans, to name but a few. And not just the odd individual: the animals were everywhere. 'So many animals – very, very active animals,' says Lascu. In most other caves, troglobites are forced to eke out a living on what little food reaches the inner recesses of their cave. As a result, they are scarce and their metabolism is slowed down. But the Movile troglobites were neither scarce nor slow: their abundance and their active movements suggested a rich food supply and a high metabolic rate.

As Lascu began exploring the cave, the situation grew more and more curious. Animals were crawling everywhere in great profusion, especially near the lake and in several airbells they discovered in the submerged part of the cave. But a surface-based food source could not be located. Organic debris like bat guano, dead leaves, and decaying wood, which normally filter down to the deepest corners of a cave and supply the troglobites with some sustenance, could not get in. Movile Cave consisted of just 200 metres of narrow dry passages without any natural entrance. The thick layers of clay at the surface would prevent any nutrient-rich water from percolating down via cracks, whereas the lower passages were submerged. 'We realised that the cave is well sealed; where did the food come from?' says Lascu. At a symposium in Bucharest later that same year, Lascu and Sarbu announced the inescapable conclusion that the Movile ecosystem was a unique biobubble, entirely self-sufficient, with all energy and food produced internally by some yet unknown process. 'But the scientists in Romania rejected our idea,' says Lascu.

It took until the early 1990s, after the fall of Ceaucescu, for the mystery of Movile Cave to be uncovered. Sarbu, who defected to the USA in 1987 and found a position at the University of Cincinnati, Ohio, managed to secure a grant from the National Geographic Society and returned to Movile for further work in 1990. He found that the scum floating on the sulphuric pools was actually 'microbial mats', microscopic forests made up of fungi and bacteria. Sarbu suspected that some of the microbes were not consuming food, but were in fact producing it. Limestone rocks consist of calcium carbonate, the petrified remains of corals, diatoms, molluscs, and other shell-building organisms that died in ancient seas and accumulated in sediment. Water in limestone caves thus usually carries high levels of bicarbonate ions, which form after calcium carbonate dissolves. Could these microbial mats somehow be building organic molecules from the carbon in the bicarbonate? To test this, Sarbu incubated samples of the microbes in water tainted with radioactively labelled bicarbonate. Sure enough, the radioactive carbon turned up in the microbial lipids, fatty molecules that the organisms build their cell membranes from.

So the microbial mats, which cover the surface of the water and the wet cave walls, are the staple for the whole community of troglobites. Like plants, they turn simple carbon compounds (carbon dioxide in the case of plants, bicarbonate in the case of the Movile microbes) into complex organic molecules, which can then be used by the animals in the cave as food. But where do the microbes get the energy from to run their chemical food production? Plants use sunlight, but what energy source can there be in eternal darkness 25 metres underground? The answer lies in the foul smell of the water. Besides bicarbonate, the water is rich in the rotten-egg-smell-compound hydrogen sulphide, which forms from the breakdown of sulphur-containing minerals in the rocks. And some bacteria, tongue-twistingly called 'chemolithoautotrophs' can break down hydrogen sulphide molecules and harvest the chemical energy encapsulated in their chemical bond.

A series of microbiological investigations by Sarbu, Lascu, and their collaborators have shown that the microbial mats are indeed a powerful broth of such chemolithoautotrophs, including *Thiobacillus* and *Thiothrix* (*theion* being the Greek word for 'sulphur'). The food produced by these bacteria is carried further along the food chain. Not only to the bacteria and fungi that live inside the microbial mats and feed on their chemolithoautotrophic brethren, but also to the animals that graze on the mats, and to the predators that hunt down the grazers. (The entire food web consists of an estimated 100 species, of which at least 35 were previously unknown, says Lascu.)

The definitive proof that the whole cave ecosystem does indeed depend on the chemical energy released from the hydrogen sulphide was published in 1996 ('after several years of hard work,' Lascu says) in *Science*. Sarbu and his University of Cincinnati colleagues Thomas Kane and Brian Kinkle performed a so-called stable isotope ratio analysis on the cave's food web. This technique capitalises on the fact that many biologically important elements, such as carbon and nitrogen, occur in nature in two or more stable forms. Nitrogen, for example, occurs as a light form with seven protons and seven neutrons in the atomic nucleus (^{14}N, in chemical shorthand), and a rarer, heavy form with seven protons and eight neutrons, known as – you guessed it – ^{15}N. The rates at which these two isotopes are incorporated into organic molecules depend on many factors, such as the temperature and wetness of the environment, and the kind of organism that does the incorporating. So the ratio of ^{14}N to ^{15}N in plants above ground (which get their nitrogen delivered to them by soil bacteria in the form of nitrate) would be quite a bit different from that in chemolithoautotrophic cave bacteria (which use the ammonium in the cave water). And there is another cute aspect: animals' biochemical machinery tends to include the light isotope a little bit more eagerly in its waste products, so bodies of consumers are left with a few percent more ^{15}N than was in their food source, and their predators in turn will contain even more. And roughly the same principles apply to carbon, sulphur, and other vital elements.

The researchers took samples from crucial nodes in the cave's food web: the microbial mats themselves, five species of troglobites that graze on the mats (namely an earthworm, a millipede, a shrimp, and two pill bugs), and five species of predatory troglobites (a water scorpion, a worm-sucking leech, a rove beetle, a spider, and a centipede). They also sampled some other habitats in the vicinity of Movile Cave: beetles and spiders from a 'regular' cave five kilometres away; worms, arthropods, and algae from a pond; various forest arthropods; and mussels and shrimp from the Black Sea. All samples were subjected to stable isotope ratio analysis for carbon and nitrogen.

Centre stage in the publication was given to a simple scatter graph with two axes: the vertical one for the proportion of heavy nitrogen, the horizontal one for the proportion of heavy carbon. The results were clear-cut: the Movile microbial mat samples, sitting in the bottom-left corner of the graph, had very little of the heavy isotopes of either element. The Movile grazers, just a little to the right and above the dots representing the microbial mats, had a bit more of the heavy isotopes, whereas the dots for the Movile predators were located even further off. Three interlocking oval rings, encompassing Movile's producers, grazers, and predators, nicely symbolised its food chain: the Movile predators fed on the Movile grazers, and the latter depended on the microbial mats, which ultimately kept the whole chain alive. All samples from the aboveground habitats, as well as from the other cave, held the far top right quarter of the graph, having a very different isotope signature. As suspected, the nitrogen and carbon circulating above the surface had nothing to do with the underground ecosystem! '*Science* was very happy to publish it,' says Lascu.

Meanwhile, the miracle of Movile Cave has become a speleological pilgrimage of sorts. A research station was built two kilometres away from the cave as a base for local and international researchers. One of them was geomicrobiologist Annette Engel, of Louisiana State University, who worked at the research centre as a graduate student in the second half of the 1990s. 'It has a sulphur well that feeds aquariums in the basement of the field station, so people do their experiments with the animals and microbial mats,' she says.

The cave itself now has the status of a municipal nature reserve and is also protected under national regulations. Researchers can enter, but only for two hours twice a month, and they have to wear disinfected shoes and clothes. Another protective measure is a double airlock in the cement shaft that has replaced the original pit dug by Lascu and his engineer. (Yet a further, unintentional impediment is the fact that the keys to the shaft are always being misplaced.) Engel says: 'There's a cement platform with a steel door and you slide that back and you drop about three or four metres down onto another platform. That then is where the exposed shaft is with the limestone walls. You get to the bottom of the shaft and there's an airlock. Once everybody is inside, you lock this entrance and you're sort of all in the dark at that point. And then that's when you open up the second airlock, which is just a very thick plastic cover over a very small hole. So you sort of squeeze in from this point on. So you're on your belly, and within twenty metres you can get on your knees and stand. It's pretty small.'

Yet in spite of 15 years of work, in many ways Movile Cave remains a mystery, Engel admits. Even though many of the bacteria, fungi, and animals in the cave are known, and the passage of nutrients from the microbial mats up through two layers of consumers and predators has been demonstrated, the full complexity of the food web remains elusive. In particular, it is not yet clear how the flimsy mats can support such animal diversity. 'It's a problem actually,' Engel admits. 'Either we don't understand the higher level food web or we don't understand the biomass of the microbial mats. Nobody has ever looked at all the organisms and how they all relate to each other. It's crazy that nobody has ever done that.'

1.3
A Perfect Pitcher

Although completely self-contained communities like the one in Movile Cave are very rare, there are plenty of ecosystems that are quite isolated from their surroundings. One class of such ecosystems is the species assemblages in watery habitats called phytotelmata. And I can lay claim to the dubious accomplishment of having once drunk such an ecosystem.

It was March 2004. Four friends and I had decided to climb Mount Trus Madi, the second-tallest mountain of Borneo, in the shadow of its gigantic sibling, Mount Kinabalu. The little-travelled trail had us groping through mossy lower montane forest that, the next day, gradually gave way to the stunted, gnarled trees of upper montane forest. Finally, we reached a rocky plateau at 2,300-metres altitude that was to be our base for the final ascent of the summit. What little climbing information we had had led us to believe that there would be springs around this plateau. Lured into a false sense of security we had brought just a meagre water supply, which by this time was all but exhausted. Needless to say, there was not a drop of water to be found, no matter how widely we scouted. Until our thirsty eyes fell on the peculiar vegetation.

The stocky trees that clung to the precipitous sides of the plateau were lavishly festooned with pitcher plants (Fig. 1.1). These so-called *Nepenthes* vines are among the most unusual plants of Southeast Asia. In a remarkable feat of phytoengineering, beaker-like extensions grow from the tendrils, the curly tips of their leathery leaves. The specimens growing at our rocky base camp were of the species *Nepenthes lowii*. This is considered to be one of the most bizarre species, with pitchers half a litre in volume, shaped like slightly distorted, narrow-necked decanters with hairy, upturned lids. And decant is what we did, as all the pitchers were filled to the rim with much-coveted water. We picked some of the larger bugs out, boiled many litres of the reddish-brown, sour, and slightly sickly sweet liquid and made it into *Nepenthes*-flavoured tea, *Nepenthes*-flavoured Horlicks, and *Nepenthes*-flavoured instant noodles.

Only later did we learn that our *Nepenthes*-guzzling exercise had been pre-enacted exactly 150 years before by none other than the naturalist-adventurer Alfred Russel Wallace. One of the first things Wallace did when he set foot in Southeast Asia was to climb Mount Ophir, in what is now West Malaysia. In his travelogue *The Malay Archipelago*, he writes how he came upon what must have been a former landslide, a *padang batu* (rocky field):

> [W]here it was cracked and fissured there grew a most luxuriant vegetation, among which the pitcher plants were the most remarkable . . . , their curious pitchers of various sizes and forms hanging abundantly from their leaves, and continually exciting our admiration by their size and beauty. . . . We had been told we should find water at *padang batu*, but we looked about for it in vain, as we were exceedingly thirsty. At last we turned to the pitcher plants, but the water contained in the pitchers

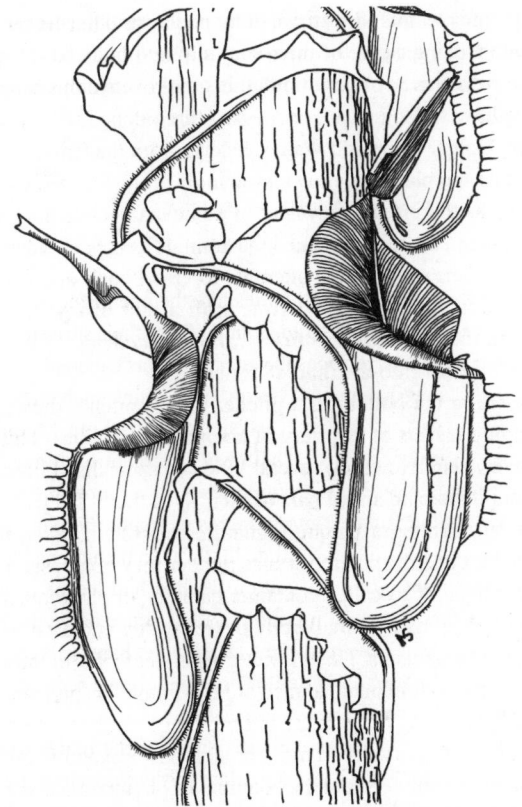

Fig. 1.1 Carnivorous pitcher plants, like this *Nepenthes veitchii*, are examples of phytotelmata, water-filled cavities that contain miniature ecosystems

(about half a pint in each) was full of insects and otherwise uninviting. On tasting it, however, we found it very palatable, ... and we all quenched our thirst from these natural jugs.

What Wallace did not know, and our climbing party on Mount Trus Madi could have known if we had done our homework, was that the water inside a pitcher plant is no rainwater. It is excreted by the plant as the pitcher grows, and is already inside before, in the final stage of growth, the pitcher's lid opens. Its pH can be as low as 1.5, acidic like vinegar. It also contains a unique enzyme called nepenthesin that can break down proteins under an unusually wide range of temperatures and degrees of acidity. And as if that weren't enough, the liquid carries high concentrations of oxygen free radicals, which also help disintegrate proteins. The noxious broth that we had gulped down so eagerly is in fact the pitcher plant's gastric juice, in which it digests dead insects and other small animals – for *Nepenthes* is a carnivorous plant.

About 70 species of *Nepenthes* are known, of which almost half occur in Borneo, and the rest are scattered throughout South and East Asia, northern Australia, and Madagascar. Like most carnivorous plants, they grow on poor soils, where they gain a competitive edge by harvesting extra nutrients (particularly nitrogen and phosphorus) from captured prey. Small animals (mostly ants) are attracted by nectar or other tempting exudate at the pitcher's edge. While feeding, some of them may slip and fall into the pitcher, where the fluid, which has the consistency of very thin glue, quickly envelops them. Even frogs and lizards are known to have fallen in, and, in one two-litre pitcher of *N. rajah*, a rat was once reported. A study by Holger Bohn and Walter Federle from the University of Würzburg in Germany revealed that the plant's trick is a system of minute ridges on the pitcher's rim, which, when wet, act as the insect equivalent of a banana peel. Bohn and Federle placed ants on the rim of *N. bicalcarata*, and filmed the animals as they skidded helplessly across the rim, fell in the pitcher, and, despite attempts to crawl back out, eventually drowned. 'In one particularly dramatic case,' they wrote with a hint of myrmecophilic sympathy in their 2004 paper in the *Proceedings of the National Academy of Sciences of the USA*, 'a *P. becarii* worker fell back into the fluid 48 times.'

The water collected at the bottom of a pitcher plant's pitcher thus usually contains a mass of dead and dying insects of a variety of taxonomic affinities. This, of course, does not qualify as an ecosystem. However, several kinds of specialised invertebrates are able to enter a *Nepenthes* pitcher and spend part of their lives there. They avoid drowning and being digested, instead forming a unique miniature ecosystem called the 'infauna' that benefits both themselves and the plant in whose pitcher they take residence. Thus, pitcher plants join a famous clique of so-called container habitats, or phytotelmata.

By definition, a phytotelma is a small body of freshwater enclosed within plant tissue, and inhabited by aquatic organisms. The rainwater-filled leaf axils of the aroid plants in my garden, for example, are phytotelmata, and so are the funnel-shaped tank bromeliads that grow in trees in South America. Water-filled internodes of bamboo stems are another good example, but the holes in tree trunks where a branch has broken off qualify just as well. One of the first ecologists to understand the potential of phytotelmata as miniature ecosystems was the great English ecologist Charles Elton. Elton founded and ran the University of Oxford's Bureau of Animal Population ('the Bureau' for short) from 1932 to 1967. He had been interested in phytotelmata since at least the 1940s, but it was only in his last year before retirement that he found a graduate student who shared his predilection for poking around in pools of stagnant water in hollow trees.

One morning in 1966, at the Bureau's legendary tea table, Elton announced that he had received a letter from a student from Imperial College London, who wanted to do his PhD dissertation on the fauna of tree holes in Elton's stomping ground, Wytham Estate near Oxford. The student was Roger Kitching. Now close to retirement age himself, the glint in Kitching's eye betrayed his undying passion for phytotelmata as I met him for breakfast on the campus of Nanyang Technological University in Singapore. We were both attending a conference there. 'It's wonderful,' he said. 'They're aquatic habitats sitting in a terrestrial milieu.'

Currently a professor of ecology at Australia's Griffith University in Brisbane, Kitching has never stopped working on phytotelms, although after completing his PhD he added more exotic waterlogged spaces to his realm of study, with Borneo's pitcher plants topping the bill. In 2000, he poured his vast knowledge into a 444-page tome entitled *Food Webs and Container Habitats: The Natural History and Ecology of Phytotelmata*. The front cover is, of course, adorned by a mean-looking *Nepenthes* pitcher. And the two spines sticking down from its lid betray that it is *N. bicalcarata*.

N. bicalcarata is probably the best-studied pitcher plant species, living in poor-soil lowland forests along Borneo's northwest coast. Kitching's student Charles Clarke spent two years in the sultanate of Brunei among its pitchers and the bestiaries that live in them. The plants are huge, with three-centimetre-thick stems snaking through the foliage for lengths of up to 20 metres, seeking support from tree stems here and there, and throwing off mug-shaped pitchers along the way, each able to hold up to a litre of water. Some of these pitchers are very long lived, actively collecting and digesting prey for up to a year before finally wilting away. Meanwhile, communities of specialised pitcher-dwellers (so-called nepenthebionts) set up in the water volume to take advantage of the food provided by the decaying mass of insect remains at the bottom.

The pitcher's bounty is fed on by four distinct groups of nepenthebionts. Recently drowned insects are eaten by the larva of a phorid fly, called *Megaselia campylonympha*, and also by the larvae of the midges *Polypedilum convexum* and a *Dasyhelea* species. The midge larvae also eat insect debris that is already fragmented and partly decayed, as do the other two groups: six different species of mosquito larvae and a species of water mite called *Zwickia*. But the complexity of the infauna does not stop there: it contains no fewer than two layers of predators. Phantom midge larvae of the genus *Corethrella* feed on the smaller midge and mosquito larvae. And they themselves are preyed on by the pitcher's top predators: larvae of three species of the giant mosquito *Toxorhynchites*. 'They look sinister – big and heavy,' Kitching says respectfully.

For the most part, the infauna is composed of species that are adapted to the pitcher plant environment. Being aquatic, they do not drown and they presumably have defences against the pitcher's acidity and digestive enzymes. Most of the 15 or so species that make up *N. calcarata*'s infauna do not live anywhere else. That is not to say that each pitcher contains the full set. On average, a pitcher will contain about six species.

Although its definition restricts a phytotelma's infauna to aquatic species, in *N. calcarata* it actually extends above the water surface. Uniquely among *Nepenthes*, the plant's tendrils are hollow where they connect with the pitcher. Soon after the formation of a pitcher, a species of ant, *Camponotus schmitzi*, will chew through the tendril wall and build its nest in the hollow space. From there, the ant workers make feeding forays. Ignoring the plant's leaves and flowers, they focus all their attention on the pitcher they live on. From a vantage point underneath the pitcher rim, they keep a close watch on the goings-on inside. As soon as a largish insect (a cockroach, for instance) slips in, two workers will climb down to the water surface, dive in (sometimes staying down for up to half a minute), and eventually drag the victim out and up to the pitcher rim. But rather than resuscitating the drowning victim, they then proceed to eat it, sloppily dropping morsels into the pitcher fluid.

Surprisingly, Kitching explains, the plant benefits from these home-grown ants. The pitcher fluid is not able to digest prey items that are too large, and pitchers that are clogged by too many big dead insects soon go putrid, a dangerous build-up of ammonia levels. In experiments where he threw large dead assassin bugs into pitchers with and without live-in ants, Clarke discovered that those with ants never went putrid, whereas those without almost always did. The ants apparently helped break up the larger food items for their *Nepenthes* host, like pitcher plant molars.

Pitcher plants' internal ecosystems still have a lot to teach us, Kitching thinks. 'You can compare replicate systems of different species, or different pitchers on the same plant. You can empty them and watch the systems reassemble.' Also, the nutrient input varies between different *Nepenthes* species in different habitats. In 1997, Clarke published a lovely book about all the pitcher plants of Borneo. *N. lowii*, the one whose content we drank on Mount Trus Madi, is also in there. It is a very interesting species, says Clarke, that does not seem to have any faculties for making insects slip in. Instead, it probably attracts sunbirds to the nectar-bearing hairs on the pitcher lid and gets its nutrients from the nitrogen-rich bird droppings that fall into the water. In fact, Clarke writes, 'the detritus found in the pitchers appears to be the excrement of birds.' Rather than a fly-trap, this pitcher plant is a toilet bowl. And my instant noodles will never taste the same again.

Leaky Buckets

2

2.1
The Boxer's Bread Knife

The little worlds we explored in the previous chapter contained a few conspicuous food chains. There was the glass ball and food chain of algae eaten by brine shrimp. Then there was a three-ring chain of chemolithoautotrophic bacteria, eaten by cave pillbugs, which were in turn eaten by cave centipedes. Finally, we have Roger Kitching's pitcher plant ecosystems, which would sometimes harbour chains of four links if we include the drowned insects. These are eaten by small midge larvae, which are in turn eaten by larger midge larvae, which finally are lunch for Kitching's 'sinister-looking' giant mosquito larvae.

Today, we are quite used to thinking of nature as made up of countless interconnected food chains. It is standard textbook stuff for most schoolchildren. But 70 years ago, when Charles Elton (the founding father of phytotelmata research whom we met in the previous chapter) first developed an ecology based on them, it was all quite novel. Elton himself, however, credits the Flemish artist Pieter Brueghel the Elder for depicting the first food chain. In one of his books, Elton reproduces the Brueghel drawing *The Big Fish Eat the Small Ones* from 1556 (Fig. 2.1), which, he says, betrays 'a rather nightmarish insight into nature.' He then goes on to describe the picture, which shows a ten-metre-long dead goldfish on a Flemish lake shore. Through its gaping mouth, a stream of smaller fish flow out, each in turn spewing out even smaller fish. As if that weren't enough, Elton explains, the giant fish's stomach contents are further exposed by 'what might well be an early ecologist carrying out a food analysis (apparently with a very large bread knife)'.

A less surrealistic image of food chains had been growing in Charles Elton's mind since he was an undergraduate student at the University of Oxford in 1921. His tutor, the evolutionary biologist Julian Huxley (grandson of Darwin's friend T.H. Huxley), invited him along on the University of Oxford's first expedition to Spitzbergen. During a summer that has been called 'one of the most important an ecologist ever spent', Elton surveyed the meagre fauna of the barren Arctic island. He watched the arctic foxes catch buntings.

The Loom of Life. M. Schilthuizen
Doi: 10.1007/978-3-540-68058-1_2, © Springer-Verlag Berlin Heidelberg 2008

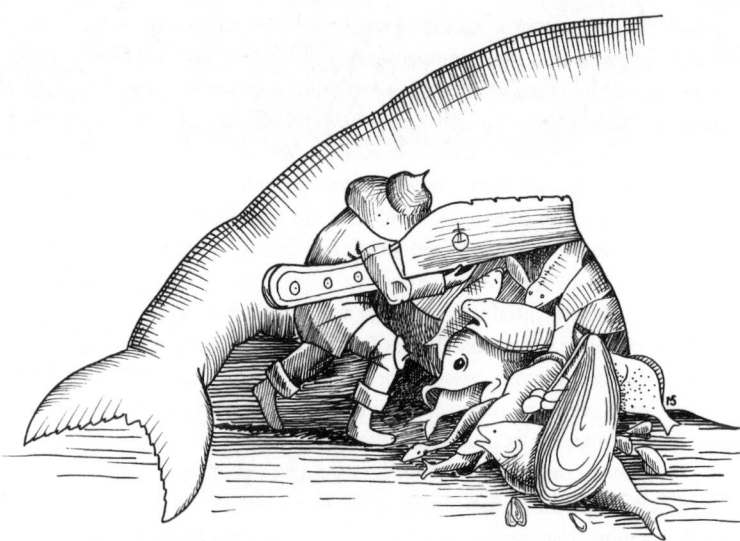

Fig. 2.1 Early Flemish insights into food chains. (Drawn after Brueghel's *The Big Fish Eat the Small Ones; detail*)

The buntings ate spiders, which themselves ate springtails, and these in turn fed on moss and algae. The entire ecosystem is contained in a little hand-drawn network of boxes and arrows in a paper he published in 1923.

By 1927, when the 26-year-old Elton wrote the classic *Animal Ecology* in a three-month flash of passion and insight, his Spitzbergen-inspired ideas about food chains had matured. Not only had he seen who ate whom, he had also pondered other characteristics of each link in the food chain, such as the organisms' body sizes and their numbers. He realised, with more clarity than anyone before him (and that includes sixteenth-century artists), that at every step higher up the food chain, the sizes of the animals would get larger. Foxes are an order of magnitude larger than the buntings they eat. Buntings are ten times larger than the spiders, and the springtails the spiders eat again are ten times smaller than their predators.

It could not be otherwise, Elton realised, with the common sense of the university boxer that he had been in his undergraduate days. 'In the animal world, fighting weight counts for as much as it does among ourselves, and a small animal can no more tackle a large one successfully than a light-weight boxer can knock out a trained man four stone heavier than himself.' Elton then went on to talk about spiders not catching elephants in their webs and students lost on the moors not able to subsist on tiny bilberries to make his point that the size of food items an animal can manage determines its level in the food chain.

And in addition to patterns in size, there was a pattern in abundance. Elton called it 'the pyramid of numbers'. Imagine yourself in an oak wood in summer, he wrote. 'You will find vast numbers of small herbivorous insects like aphids, a large number of spiders and carnivorous ground beetles, a fair number of small warblers, and only one or two hawks.' Hence, at each higher link in the food chain, animals would get less numerous. A single hawk would need a mountain of insects to support a hill of spiders, feeding a plateful of warblers. Or, as the Chinese proverb quoted by Elton would have it, 'one hill cannot shelter two tigers.'

Besides revealing his pyramid, Elton also thought he understood why it existed. 'The reason for this fact is simple enough,' he said, and then went on to explain that tiny animals, like herbivorous insects, reproduce fast and thus can build up vast populations. Larger animals, like the insects' predators, reproduce more slowly, and thus can only build up a medium-sized population, whereas the huge top predators are fewer still. But this is one of the rare instances where Elton was wrong. Even the largest and rarest of animals have astronomical reproductive potential. Charles Darwin had already pointed out that 'the fulmar lays but one egg [per nest], but it is believed to be the most numerous bird in the world.' The fact that a single hill does not shelter two tigers is not caused by a limitation of tiger reproductive output, but by a limitation of energy.

Sometimes biologists are so dazzled by the sheer complexity of nature that they cannot see the very simple and straightforward ecological principles that govern it. Perhaps it is telling that the blindingly obvious principle of energy transfer in ecosystems was belatedly discovered by a man who was blind in one eye. The short story of Raymond Lindeman is one of dedication, passion, and tragedy that, as we shall see, seems to characterise the lives of several great ecologists.

2.2
Counting Calories

Frail of health, and with the sight in one eye lost in a childhood accident, the 20-year-old Raymond Laurel Lindeman (Fig. 2.2) arrived in 1935 at the University of Minnesota's field station in Cedar Creek, to do a five-year PhD study. A portrait from that time shows a young man with a hopeless hairdo, immature cheekbones, and brittle spectacles. His sunken right eye leaves nothing but a dark shadow. But from behind the left glass of his spectacles, his other eye gazes out at the viewer with sharpness and penetration.

The title of Lindeman's thesis project was 'Ecological dynamics in a senescent lake' – the lake in question being the teardrop-shaped Cedar Bog Lake, just a few hundred metres in length. Wedged-in between patches of native prairie, oak savanna, and spruce and cedar forest, the aging lake is rich in plankton, aquatic invertebrates, and small fish. For four years, Lindeman and his wife Eleanor sampled and analysed the lake water, identifying, counting, and weighing the diatoms, water bugs, and rotifers, and charting their yearly fluctuations.

In 1937 Lindeman suffered a jaundice attack that left him very weak for a long time, during which Eleanor had to do the lifting of heavy gear and row the boat. In spite of this hardship, his ecological insight grew. And ecological insight was, at that time, a rare commodity. Although Elton's 1927 book had helped create clarity, most of ecology in the 1930s was still struggling to find a fruitful research programme. In those days people were preoccupied with classifying communities, identifying species characteristic to particular habitats, and documenting succession from 'pioneer' to 'climax' vegetation. Trying to understand the networks of interactions was not yet at the forefront of ecologists' minds.

Fig. 2.2 The founding father of food chain ecology, Raymond Lindeman. (After a photograph taken shortly before his untimely death)

Even the term 'ecosystem' itself was only coined (by the English botanist Tansley) in the year that Lindeman started his work.

What Lindeman was trying to do was measure the flow of energy through the ecosystem. When a water bug eats a diatom, the proteins and other organic molecules are burnt inside the bug's gut. Some of the fragments are used to maintain its own tissues or build its eggs, but the rest is burnt in a process called respiration. The calories released are used to power the water bug's muscles, its nerves, its cellular machinery. Some of the energy is radiated out as useless heat, and some of the molecules that cannot be broken down any further are excreted as waste. Lindeman realised that when we draw a diagram of who eats whom in a particular ecosystem, we are actually charting energy flows. He also realised that as energy is transferred upward from the lowest levels of the Eltonian pyramid to the highest, some energy gets left behind, like water carried in leaky buckets. This explains why each level is smaller. Not necessarily smaller in numbers, but smaller in the combined weight of living matter: biomass.

Lindeman was not the only person to think of ecosystems in that way. Twelve years his senior, English limnologist (freshwater biologist) Evelyn Hutchinson had been thinking very similar thoughts since he arrived at Yale University in New Haven in 1928. However, Hutchinson had never got round to writing them down properly, other than in a set of lecture notes for his students. In 1940, while he was finishing his thesis, Lindeman had started corresponding with Hutchinson about the possibility of working with him as a postdoctoral fellow. The next year, just after completing his PhD, Lindeman managed to get a scholarship and in August that year, he and Eleanor arrived at Yale University.

Lindeman brought with him the final chapter of his thesis, which he was trying to elaborate into an article with the title 'The trophic-dynamic aspect of ecology'. In it, he drew on his Cedar Bog data to measure the amounts of energy transferred and retained at each of the pyramid's levels (for which he used the term 'trophic' levels, from the Greek *trophe*, which means 'food'). At the lowest level, that of the producers (the photosynthetic algae and other water plants in the lake), the yearly energy production was 111 calories per square centimetre lake surface. Out of this, 23 calories were used in respiration for the plants' own energetic needs, three calories were released as dead, decomposing tissue, and some 15 calories were eaten by the herbivores in the lake. What remained was 70 calories' worth of standing crop or 'net productivity'. Energy values were quite a bit lower at the next trophic level. The herbivore population accumulated 14.8 calories per square centimetre per year, with 4.4, 0.3, and 3.1 calories lost to respiration, decomposition, and predation, respectively, leaving seven calories net productivity. The third level, finally, in which Lindeman combined all predators in the lake, mustered a yearly productivity of just 3.1 calories, with about half lost to respiration, and virtually nothing to decomposition and predation. The net productivity of trophic level three was thus only about 1.3 calories per square centimetre. So, each trophic level only managed to extract about 10–20% of the energy contained in the previous trophic level. This is why the biomass in each trophic level is just about one tenth of that in the level below.

Stimulated by discussions with Hutchinson, Lindeman revised his trophic-dynamic manuscript to include some of Hutchinson's ideas and publications and sent it off to the editor of the journal *Ecology* in September 1941. Hutchinson was convinced that Lindeman's creative, new viewpoint on ecology, backed up with his recent field data, would be published by such a prestigious journal as *Ecology*. Lindeman himself was less confident. To a friend he wrote, 'I'm afraid you're going to say that I've hazarded a great deal of theory on very little information, and you may be right. I have a feeling, though, that at least some of the ideas are piquing enough to start some people making ecological studies on the basis of productivity and efficiency, and that would be quite gratifying even though some of the hesitantly proposed "principles" turn out to be wrong.'

His cautious optimism was squashed, however, when in mid-November the reply came from *Ecology*. The two experts that the editor had consulted were not impressed. One wrote: 'Some of the "broad generalizations" mentioned in the paper are certainly very broad; so broad in fact that they cannot be regarded as having much value.' The other added insult to injury by saying that 'what [we need] now most of all is research of the type which yields actual significant data rather than postulations and theoretical treatments.' Consequently, the editor had decided to reject the paper, much to Lindeman's and Hutchinson's dismay.

Four days later, Hutchinson, who was a member of the journal's editorial board, wrote to *Ecology* to point out the merits of the paper, and to rebut the reviewers' criticisms. 'I believe it should be published as soon as possible,' he concluded. The editor eventually yielded, and promised to consider a revised version of the paper, which Lindeman planned to submit after Christmas. But before he could do so, his liver trouble returned, which put him in hospital for three weeks. He only managed to recover sufficiently to resubmit his paper in March 1942. After further consultation, *Ecology* finally wrote that the paper had been accepted for publication, and was scheduled for the October issue.

Lindeman never saw his most cherished paper in print. Through the spring of 1942, his condition did not improve. In April, he wrote to a friend, 'I am desperately anxious to get

2

back to my own work ... and hope to spend at least a few hours a day on it soon. The trouble is obscure – hepatic cirrhosis of unknown etiology, with a possibility that it may become progressively worse in spite of everything.' And a month later, when his health continued to deteriorate, he confided in another letter, 'there is a better than even chance I won't survive the summer.' On 29 June, two weeks after exploratory surgery, he died at the age of only 27.

His paper appeared posthumously with an addendum by Hutchinson. 'It is to the present paper that we must turn as the major contribution of one of the most creative and generous minds yet to devote itself to ecological science,' he wrote. And this, ecologists have been doing in the decades since. Lindeman's paper still stands as one of the turning points in ecology, which stimulated focused research on energetics and food chains. Even his critics eventually gave in. In 1952, Paul Welch, one of the original, critical referees of the manuscript submitted to *Ecology*, expanded a new edition of his book *Limnology* with a section to accommodate Lindeman's ideas and the new data in support of them. Even today, Lindeman's paper is still cited in dozens of scientific articles each year.

2.3
How To Build a Pyramid

Elton's pyramid of numbers (vast numbers of aphids, a large number of spiders, a fair number of small warblers, and one lone hawk) was actually a carefully chosen example of a stack of trophic levels where the numbers decrease in pyramid fashion by an order of magnitude at each higher level. If we look more closely at ecosystems, pyramids of numbers are not all we find. A pyramid of numbers will only form if consumers consume entire individuals of their prey, like a spider or a warbler. But a lot of consumers are not that voracious. Many just nibble, suck, or take a bite here and there. Hence, a patch of forest may just contain 100 trees, but the next layer (herbivores) may consist of thousands of consumers like leaf beetles and caterpillars. And the main constituents of the third layer of primary carnivores might actually be tens of thousands of tiny parasitic wasps, with one caterpillar providing enough food for dozens of those so-called parasitoids. These numbers look nothing like a pyramid. If anything, they are more like an upside-down pyramid, which is in fact quite typical for such 'parasite food chains' (caterpillars and leaf beetles being nothing less than plant parasites), since parasites tend to be much smaller than the organism they feed on, not larger. Still, if we ignore the numbers of individuals and just weigh the biomass enclosed in each trophic level, it rearranges itself nicely into a proper broad-based pyramid shape, with only a fraction of the energy enclosed in the primary producers making it to each successive trophic level higher up.

Yet, the trick of weighing organisms rather than counting their numbers does not always work to create a nice pyramid out of an ecosystem. Think of the ocean. When standing on a jetty, gazing down into the clear blue waters of the sea, we might see all kinds of trophic levels swimming and floating by: jellyfish, sea turtles, cuttlefish, large groupers, tiny shrimp, and medium-sized damselfish. Yet the lowest trophic level, that of the producers, is curiously absent. Where are the vast numbers of water plants that all these marine animals ultimately depend on? Are they growing at the bottom of the sea? Are they floating far out in the open ocean? A drop of seawater placed under a microscope will solve this conundrum. The plants that feed the oceans are actually microscopic single-celled algae, or phytoplankton, too small to see with the naked eye, yet still present in their millions in seawater. They are the food source for equally tiny zooplankton: miniature shrimp and other crustacean primary consumers that in turn feed the higher trophic levels that the jelly and damselfish sit in. Yet if we were to empty, dry, and weigh a swimming-pool-sized sample of marine habitat, we would be in for a surprise: the combined weight of the consumers exceeds the weight of the phytoplankton they consume: the biomass pyramid would still be inverted at the base. How can this be? The answer lies in the fact that phytoplankton reproduce like crazy. They continually churn out biomass that the long-lived consumers feed on, whereas the standing algal biomass, say the capital that generates the interest, is relatively small. The only way to turn this situation into a proper Lindeman-style pyramid is by calculating the amount of energy flowing from the lowest trophic level up into the next. If we do that, we will see that, indeed, the energy supplied by the sunlight to the phytoplankton is far greater than the energy taken up by the primary consumers, which is greater than the energy supplied to the secondary consumers, and so on.

There is one group of organisms for which there seems to be no place in the pyramid of energy. They are the ones lurking in my compost heap: the decomposers or detritivores. Often this trophic level is excised from the pyramid and depicted as a vertical menhir standing alongside it, absorbing scraps and morsels flying off sideways. That detritus is a combination of waste products and unconsumed bits of tissue. Throughout its lifetime, a banana tree in my garden will feed large numbers of consumers. It will have its leaves nibbled at by leaf beetles, nectar sipped from its flowers by sunbirds, some of its pollen gobbled up by ambrosius beetles. It will pay a tithe to the starlings and tree shrews in the form of banana fruits, and offer some of the sap in its leaves to cicada nymphs. Yet a lot of the energy contained it my banana tree is locked up in its heavy stem, protected against hungry insects by its sticky and bitter latex. Only after it has bloomed and its time has come will a gust of wind knock down the tree. I throw it on my compost heap and its whole dead body is up for grabs. This is when the decomposers move in. Armies of bacteria, fungi, insects, and worms will make short work of it and extract the last bit of energy from its lifeless biomass. However, before it offers its entire body to the ecosystem, the tree has already made regular down payments in the form of fallen leaves and the peels of bananas eaten by birds. It is sometimes a bit hard to say exactly where consuming ends and scavenging begins, but as a rule of thumb we may say that feeding on living tissue is consumption, while feeding on tissue that was already dead before it was acquired, or on waste products, is scavenging. Decomposers scavenge off each of the trophic levels in the energy pyramid. Dead aphids are decomposed by fungi; mites eat the shed skins of the spiders that eat the aphids. Dead spider-eating warblers are food for maggots, and the hawks that consume the warblers drop droppings on which dung beetles feast.

Yet even with the decomposers' monolith in place, additional complexities need to be added to the energy pyramid to make it more realistic. For example, I have presented the pyramid as made up of flat polished layers: primary consumers eat only producers and nothing else; secondary consumers only eat members of the primary layer and never touch a plant. Yet nature is not so neat: omnivores get their energy at several different trophic levels and it is sometimes a Clintonian judgment call whether a species has trophic relations with another species if it only occasionally consumes it. (Although officially, an omnivore is defined as a species that gets at least 5% of its energy at a trophic level different from the one it mostly feeds on.) Our own species is a good example of how sloppy some species are with the trophic role they are supposed to play. At our African dawn, we were the ultimate omnivores, feeding on nuts and grubs and fruits, spearing fish, clubbing bats, and scavenging the carrion of lion kills. Then we invented agriculture and we collectively moved down the energy pyramid, becoming almost exclusively consumers of plant material (which, incidentally, must have been one of the causes for our increased joint biomass).

Other species skip trophic levels altogether. Whales are so large that they are not eaten by anything, so they should sit in the highest marine trophic level. Yet the filter-feeding apparatus in their mouth allows them to forage in the very lowest trophic levels. Getting their food in bulk, they bypass at least two layers of trophic middlemen. And then there are species that eat their way up or down the energy pyramid as they mature. Some hydrophilid water beetles, for example, are voracious, sickle-jawed carnivores as larvae, only to turn into docile, slightly obese algae-munchers after pupating. Many fish are even more agile cat burglars, scaling the slopes of the energy pyramid as they grow. They could be primary consumers as larvae, secondary consumers as juveniles, and tertiary consumers as adults. The result could be food cycles rather than chains. Say an adult of fish species A eats a smaller fish species B. This one in turn eats an even smaller fish species C that feeds exclusively on larvae of fish species A, and the circle is closed. Cannibalism could even make trophic cycles consist of a single species, with the adults feeding on the young. Many fish do this. Such ring-shaped food chains are therefore particularly common in watery habitats. But they exist on land as well.

One of the best-studied sets of food chains in the world exists in the Coachella Valley in California. A sandy desert with just 116 millimetres of rain per year, it has been the site of the University of California Deep Canyon Desert Preserve since 1969. Many scientists have worked there over the decades and have each contributed their bit to the growth of knowledge of its ecosystem. But whereas most of them worked with species-poor groups like birds or rodents, the person to finally flesh out the entire mesh of food chains was entomologist Gary 'Scorpion Man' Polis of Vanderbilt University in Nashville. By 1990, he had clocked up a total of 4,000 hours of field work, and 4,300 'trap days' (meaning the equivalent of 43 insect traps left out for 100 days). Using his own information and 820 scientific papers on Coachella Valley and other deserts nearby, Polis was able to work out the intricacies of the desert food chains in more detail than had ever been possible for any other large ecosystem before.

In a 1991 paper in *The American Naturalist* (the world's foremost journal of highbrow ecology), Polis told his fellow ecologists what the desert had taught him. First of all, the food chains that had been appearing in journal articles' diagrams in the past had been simplified to the extent of being nothing more than caricatures. Whereas other food-chain researchers had considered cannibalism rare, with only less than 1% of all species indulging in it, Polis found that three quarters of the species in the Coachella Valley were cannibals. This included the scorpions and insects, of whom we might expect that sort of thing, but it went all the way up to the desert's large vertebrate animals, like the great horned owl, the golden eagle, and the antelope ground squirrel, all of which turned themselves into loop-shaped food chains, with the old feeding on the young. Polis also discovered that, if you look carefully, almost all species stray outside their assigned trophic level: most are omnivores to some extent. This means that trophic level may perhaps be best expressed as a continuous number if at all. Rather than, say, the Coachella clerid beetle *Phyllobaenus*, supposedly a primary carnivore, being assigned to level three, it actually sits in an average trophic level of maybe 3.76, feeding, as it does, on at least 17 species from all trophic levels. We will come back to Polis's pioneering work later in this book, when we discuss entire food webs. For the time being, however, we will pretend food chains are as simple as Polis says they are not.

2.4
The Flea Hath Smaller Fleas

In a humorous sacrifice of proper Latin pronunciation, Jonathan Swift wrote: 'So, the naturalists observe, the flea / Hath smaller fleas that on him prey / And these have smaller still to bite 'em / And so proceed, ad infinitum'. It was two centuries before Raymond Lindeman's birth and essayists cannot be expected to adhere to ecological accuracy anyway. But ecologists now know that food chains are actually quite short and do not proceed ad infinitum.

In 1986, ecologists Joel Cohen and Charles Newman of Rockefeller University in New York, and Frédéric Briand of the International Union for the Conservation of Nature in Gland, Switzerland, compiled information on as many food webs as they could find in books, articles, dissertations, and scientists' notebooks. Altogether, they delved up 113 webs for which some researcher one day had catalogued the species taking part in them and the way food flowed among them. These came from places as scattered as the Malaysian rainforest, Georgian marshland, the Antarctic pack ice zone, and a small rockpool on the coast of France. They dissected each food web into separate food chains with a beginning (a plant species) and an end (a top predator that was not eaten by anybody else in the web), and calculated the average number of trophic levels in each. They found that 90% of the webs had no more than five trophic levels. The longest individual chain, in an open sea plankton community, was ten steps long. Later, other researchers showed that long chains up to eight steps also occur in deserts and the food webs among insects living in plant galls. But the vast majority of food chains in any ecosystem are just three to five steps. That is all.

Although Cohen, Newman, and Briand were the first to provide such an abundance of proof, the shortness of food chains had been known for some time. Alfred Russel Wallace had already alluded to it in 1858. Charles Elton knew about it in 1927 and of course Evelyn Hutchinson also knew that there is an end to how infinitesimally small fleas' fleas may get. In a 1959 paper in *The American Naturalist* with the lovely title 'Homage to Santa Rosalia or: Why Are There So Many Kinds of Animals?', Hutchinson described how a visit to the cave of Saint Rosalia in Italy made him ponder the ecology of diversity. Why would the miniature ecosystem in the rock pool at the foot of Saint Rosalia's limestone-encrusted bones harbour just two species of water bugs? Why not 20 or 200?

Part of the explanation, Hutchinson realised, lies in the fact that the leaky buckets of energy transfer put a limit on food-chain lengths. Suppose that only 20% of the energy passing through one link in the food chain will be transferred to the next higher link, Hutchinson wrote. And suppose that the average body mass of the animals in a trophic level is twice as great as in the previous level. Then the animals in the sixth trophic level must be 10,000 times as rare as those in the first. Fair enough, for a large ecosystem like the open ocean. 'If, however, we wanted fifty links, starting with a protozoan or rotifer feeding on algae with a density of a million cells per millilitre,' Hutchinson wrote, 'we should need a volume of 100,000,000,000,000,000,000,000,000,000 cubic kilometres to accommodate on an average one specimen of the ultimate predator, and this is vastly greater than the volume of the world ocean.'

So there you have it: food chains are short because the energy capillaries in the highest trophic levels do not let enough energy creep up to support a population of super-top predators. You could also turn this upside down and predict that food chains that start with a lowest trophic level that is relatively energy poor cannot grow as long as those in richer habitats. And this is precisely what Swedish ecologists Lauri and Tarja Oksanen from Umeå University have found in the high latitudes of Scandinavia. For the past 20 years, they and their fellow researchers have been working in Joatka, a place in northern Norway, which is much further north than most of us would ever wish to go. There, they have been pains-takingly studying food chains along the slopes of a highland plateau. The lowland below is covered in what the team call 'typical lowland tundra with gentle hills and small lakes. … lichen heaths on the ridges and cloudberry rich vegetation in depressions. In favorable places birches are high enough to be called trees.' In this relatively benign environment with a fair amount of plant productivity, the food chains are still longish, with three trophic levels. Higher up the slopes, more than 500 metres above sea level, conditions get harsher, and the ecosystem can only manage two trophic levels. Finally, up on the highland plateau, with its 'blockfields' and 'very barren vegetation', energy input is so low that there are only plants and one or two stray ptarmigans (a species of arctic fowl). If we don't count the ptarmigans, we are left with just the basic trophic level. The few plants growing there do not provide enough energy for a population of herbivores to develop.

The energy flowing into a food chain is usually measured as the amount of carbon accumulated by a square metre per year. This is called the 'net primary production', or NPP, and since it is the starting point for all food chains, it is one of the key data known for many habitats all over the world. Gathering more information on Arctic food chains, the Oksanens found that poor ecosystems (NPP of 20–300 grams per square metre per year) tend to lose their third trophic level of primary carnivores. If the productivity drops even further, like on the blockfields of Joatka, or on the Canadian island of Devon, with an NPP of only 7.4, both herbivores and carnivores are lost.

But in spite of what goes on in the Oksanens' high Arctic ecosystems, this is by no means the whole story. NPP values differ by at least three orders of magnitude across all Earth's habitats. The poorest deserts fix just a single gram of carbon per square metre per year, whereas some tropical forests churn out more than 1,000 times as much. This would mean that such highly productive areas would have food chains with even more links than the Oksanens' Joatka lowland. Yet that does not seem to be the case. In 1993, ecologist Peter Yodzis of the University of Guelph, Canada, borrowed Cohen, Newman, and Briand's lists of 113 published food chains, reanalysed them using his own, more exact definition of trophic level, and sorted them into those dissected from ecosystems with high productivity, as opposed to those from low-productivity systems. Contrary to expectation, he found no clear correspondence between chain length (what he called 'trophodiversity') and productivity.

The majority of chains, whether they were from poor habitats or rich ones, had three levels. There was a slight, but statistically not significant tendency for the rich ecosystems to support somewhat more four-level chains, but that was all. The predicted two or three extra levels on the pyramids of rich ecosystems simply did not appear.

So food chains are not only dictated by the productivity of their environment. In fact, the longest chain in the lists compiled by Cohen, Newman, and Briand comes from the Namib Desert in Namibia, which must be one of the least productive ecosystems on the planet. At the same time, in the hot, steaming carbon factories of the tropical rainforests, ordinary three-level chains abound. What is going on?

2.5
This Food Chain Will Self-Destruct

An answer to the question of why long food chains do not appear in rich ecosystems had already been given in 1977 by two English ecologists, John Lawton of Imperial College London at Silwood Park, Ascot, and Stuart Pimm (then at Texas Tech University in Lubbock). They, too, had been struck by the fact that the expected extra-long food chains in productive ecosystems are curiously wanting. Suspecting that the answer may lie in some tendency of long food chains to be unstable, Pimm and Lawton tackled the problem mathematically by calculating the stability of imaginary food chains. Put like this, it sounds simple. But it actually involved stability analysis, which is a complex but useful field of mathematics, applied in situations where oscillations of one unit affect those of another, such as in climatology, engineering, and, indeed, ecology. Since we will come across stability analysis again later in this book when we talk about the stability of entire ecosystems, I have decided to administer a dose of mathematics. Now this may hurt just a little.

Imagine a food chain of four species. The population density of each species will depend on many factors, such as birth rate, mortality, longevity, generation time, and so on. Since most of these factors will ultimately depend on how much energy the population obtains from its food (that is, the species one step lower in the food chain), we end up with a very complicated system. If we wanted to write it mathematically, we would get an extremely convoluted differential equation, essentially describing a long wavy curve, that is too difficult to solve. This means we cannot predict with precision whether the chain will stably survive, or whether some species will sooner or later become extinct, thus breaking the chain.

But we can do something that is almost as good. Since a very short piece of that long wavy curve is not too different from a short bit of straight line, we can use the much simpler straight-line (linear) differential equations to get a rough idea of the behaviour of the system over a short bit of its life. This is the basis for so-called perturbation analysis. Let's say the system is in equilibrium and the population densities are not changing. If we artificially modify the population densities a bit, we can look at the linear differential equations to see if the system will return to the original densities, and if so, how long this will take. The key coefficients from the set of linear equations are called the 'eigenvalues' (from the German word *eigen* for 'self' or 'characteristic'). For each of the four species in our imaginary system, there is one eigenvalue.

Whether the system will return to equilibrium or not depends on the highest value among all four eigenvalues. This 'dominant eigenvalue' is of paramount importance. If it is higher than zero, the system will be unstable. If it is less than zero, the system is stable and will return to the original situation. The lower the dominant eigenvalue, the shorter the return time will be, and the more stable the system will be. So much for stability analysis. There, that was not too bad, was it?

What Pimm and Lawton did was build several computer models of food chains. In one set of tests, they compared three models. First, a linear four-species, four-level chain with each species at a higher trophic level than the previous one. Second, a four-species, three-level chain of which the last two species jointly occupied the third trophic level. And finally, a four-species, two-level chain, with the three top species all in the second trophic level. These three chains thus only differed in the number of trophic levels, not in the number of species (four) or the number of feeding relations (three).

Next, they ran each of their three computer models 2,000 times, and each time the computer selected a set of linear equations randomly from a realistic range, and calculated the return times for each system. Among the stable systems, return times were much longer for longer chains than for the shorter ones. Almost half of all two-level chains would return in fewer than five generations, whereas less than 1% of the four-level chains did so. One third of all four-level chains took more than 150 generations to return to equilibrium. So Pimm and Lawton had shown that longer chains were less stable, making it more likely that one of their component species would suffer a population crash along the way and break the chain.

To counterbalance all the mathematical onslaught, think of it this way. Imagine suspending from your fingers a chain of heavy coloured beads, strung up on a thin cotton thread. Now shake your hand a bit. If the chain is short, the beads will wobble a bit, but soon settle in their original vertical alignment. Now make the chain three times as long and do it again. Chances are that the wave travelling down the chain will give such a jolt to the bottom beads that one or two will fly off. Ergo: long chains self-destruct.

Ten years on, Pimm (by then at the University of Tennessee, Knoxville) and our old friend Roger Kitching from Chap. 1 teamed up to test this idea in Kitching's beloved phytotelmata in Australia. Kitching was using natural tree holes in southeastern Queensland's subtropical rainforest for his research and knew quite a bit about the food chains existing in these phytotelms. Pimm and Kitching suspended plastic cups from the trees in the forest and filled these with water. Then they added measured amounts of dead leaves to them, ranging from half to four times the amount normally entering tree holes. They found that, regardless of these differences in 'productivity', the same food chains with the same lengths would establish themselves in their experimental coffee cups.

Unfortunately, says ecologist David Post of Yale University, this and three more small studies are the only evidence there is for what has become known as Pimm and Lawton's 'dynamical constraints' hypothesis. In a 2002 paper in *Trends in Ecology and Evolution*, Post reviewed all the hypotheses and evidence for explaining food-chain length that had accumulated in the 40 years since Hutchinson's Santa Rosalia revelation. 'As I sat down to write it,' says Post over the telephone, 'it was just clear that we really were asking questions too simplistically. I wandered through all the text books and they all repeated the same things that had been said for years, many of which had no support. It was a fun paper to write.'

Post found that the two factors that had always been proffered as setting the limits on food-chain length, namely ecosystem productivity and dynamical constraints, have only limited applicability. Productivity only limits chain length in very poor habitats, but it is not clear exactly how poor an ecosystem needs to be to suffer the consequences on its food chain lengths. Post says the threshold lies somewhere between NPP values of one gram and 100 grams of carbon per square metre per year, but the data are not sufficient for more precision than that. Meanwhile, dynamical constraints may only really be important in small, enclosed systems.

That leaves food-chain lengths in large, productive ecosystems to be accounted for. Like Yale-men Hutchinson and Lindeman before him, Post himself has been working with food chains in freshwater lakes. But unlike his illustrious predecessors, he had the advantage of modern stable isotope techniques to measure food-chain length (see Chap. 1). As the proportion of ^{15}N increases by about 3.4% with each link in the food chain, Post was able to gauge food-chain lengths quite accurately (using a continuous, rather than a stepped figure) by measuring the ratios of ^{14}N to ^{15}N in the lakes' top predators. He also measured phosphorus concentrations, which increase with increasing primary productivity. Using these techniques, he compared 25 lakes across North America. His results, reported in *Nature* in 2000, showed that food-chain length was not at all influenced by lake productivity. But there was a strong relationship with lake volume: chain lengths increased from about 3.5 for the smallest lakes of just 100,000 cubic metres, to 5.0 for the largest and deepest lakes, holding a trillion cubic metres. Apparently, ecosystem size, and particularly lake depth, is somehow crucial for food-chain lengths.

'That strongly suggests to me that there is some component of habitat heterogeneity that is important,' says Post, 'because much of the habitat structure in a lake is vertical. Temperature profiles, oxygen profiles, and nutrient profiles are mostly much more vertical than they are horizontal.' But exactly how diversity of habitats influences food chain length is not clear yet. 'We're still trying to get our heads around that,' Post says.

The long and short of food chains is that we still do not know exactly how their lengths are determined. What is clear, though, is that they are never very long. This means that the species diversity in food webs is not so much in the vertical strands, but much more in the horizontal ones: within a single trophic level, rather than among levels. In Chap. 4 we will start disentangling that horizontal twine of ecosystem networks. But first, exactly how many species are there in those ecosystems, anyway?

3.1
Specific Issues

Dan Janzen of the University of Pennsylvania is the Don Corleone of what has been called the 'rain forest mafia'. Ever since he professionally anchored in Central America in the 1960s, he has been as all-round a tropical biologist as he possibly could. Simply studying the ecology of the 9,000 moth species of northwestern Costa Rica – and receiving the prestigious Crafoord Prize for it (the 'Nobel prize' for sciences for which there is no actual Nobel prize) – was not enough for him. Together with local conservationists, he created the 110,000-hectare Guanacaste Conservation Area, a patchwork of natural dry, rain, and cloud forest embedded in a matrix of regenerating woodland. His many successful ideas range from the profound (that the coexistence of rainforest tree species is maintained by their specialised herbivores; see Chap. 7) to the outrageous (to dump truckloads of orange peels in a nature reserve). And among his almost 500 published papers and book chapters are such intriguing titles as 'Why mountain passes are higher in the Tropics', 'Two ways to be a tropical big moth', and 'How to be a fig'.

In 1979 Janzen pioneered the training and employment of 'parataxonomists', local people with little schooling who are taught to assist biologists with sorting specimens and (at least as important) spread the gospel of conservation among their communities. Beginning with his first parataxonomist, Roberto Espinoza, Janzen has been helped by a long line of parataxonomists, volunteers, and students to set up what must be the largest inventory of tropical insects and their food plants in the world. Over the past 27 years they have meticulously collected, hand-reared, and photographed all Guanacaste butterfly and moth caterpillars they could get their hands on, and identified the plants on which they feed.

One of Janzen's butterflies is the skipper *Astraptes fulgerator*. This is a widespread species occurring throughout southern North America, Central America, and northern South America. It lives in all kinds of habitats, from the desert to the rain forest, and from the coast to the mountains, feeding on an equally broad range of food plants. It also occurs commonly in Guanacaste, and Janzen's collection boasts about 2,500 individuals reared

The Loom of Life. M. Schilthuizen
Doi: 10.1007/978-3-540-68058-1_3, © Springer-Verlag Berlin Heidelberg 2008

from caterpillars found eating from members of eight different tree families. Although the adult butterflies that emerged from the pupated caterpillars were all virtually identical, and did not show any differences in their genitals (normally a tell-tale sign to entomologists that there is a mixup of more than one species), Janzen began noticing that the caterpillars from different food plants looked subtly different. They all carried a clownish outfit of black with white or yellow bands, and had a reddish face and feet. But in those from *Inga* trees, for instance, the bands had dissolved into two crescents, whereas those from *Lonchocarpus* had disc-shaped spots on either flank. Janzen and his team began to suspect that the clown costumes cloaked more than a single butterfly species.

Recently, DNA came to the rescue, in a way that it could not have back in the late 1970s. Janzen teamed up with Paul Hebert of the University of Guelph, Canada. Hebert is sometimes called the 'father of DNA barcoding', a new initiative to register as many animal species as possible by the exact DNA base sequence (the runt of A's, C's, G's, and T's) of a chunk of a gene called cytochrome *c* oxidase I. This gene, *COI* for short, is an essential gene for almost any living being. So all animal species, whether skink, skunk, or skipper, have it. Usually, the barcodes are very similar within species, but between animal species they are different enough to identify them by their barcode alone: ideal for someone who has 2,500 subtly different butterflies on his hands. Hebert took single legs from almost 500 of Janzen's pinned specimens, extracted a tiny amount of DNA from them, and obtained their barcodes. The results, published in 2004 in the *Proceedings of the National Academy of Sciences of the USA*, showed that where previously there was thought to be one, now there appeared to exist no fewer than ten different species in Guanacaste alone, each with its own preferred food plant, forest type, and clown costume. Clearly, there are ten ways to be a tropical small skipper!

The multiple, hidden identities of *Astraptes fulgerator* illustrate some of the problems that we may encounter when we naïvely try to list and count the number of 'species' in a given area. The famous evolutionary biologist Ernst Mayr gave the world his 'biological species concept', which says that species are populations of organisms that interbreed among themselves but that do not and cannot interbreed with other such populations (which, consequently, belong to different species). But although many biologists claim to adhere to the biological species concept, few actually apply it, hard as it is to verify countless cross-breeding abilities. Instead, taxonomists use similarities in shape and size, and, more recently, DNA sequences to decide on species status. As Dan Janzen's skipper example shows, this is not always foolproof: clear genetic and life-style differences do not always translate into distinctiveness in adult body form. And vice versa: when Varaporn Kijviriya and colleagues had a closer look at 21 'species' of Asian clams, each distinguishable by its shell shape, they discovered that all were genetically identical, and presumably all belonged to a single species.

More obstacles stand in the way of the taxonomist trying to sort a bag of specimens. Except for a few large-bodied organisms like vertebrates and trees, the majority of species on Earth have not yet been described and named. Even in the best-studied quarters of the world, only a fraction of the species are known for more obscure creatures like nematode worms and mites. And the ones that do have names were often described one-and-a-half centuries ago, in a Latin one-liner without illustrations, and without a trace of surviving reference specimens. So imagine the sheer impossibility of the task a taxonomist is faced with when asked to identify, say, a bottleful of small spiders from a New Guinean rainforest floor.

He or she may be able to put names to one or two species, but the rest will remain unidentified. Yet ecologists often want to know the species richness of a certain habitat. 'Never mind the names,' they would say, 'just tell me how many species there are in that bottle.'

So taxonomists, at least the ones working on anything besides birds, mammals, and a few other well-studied groups, have (quite against their nature) taken to quick and dirty sorting into 'morphospecies'. Years of experience with gauging subtle differences in palps, eye positions, and the exact arrangement of teeth on jaws help to sort the contents of the bottle quickly to a fair approximation of the true spectrum of spider species. This method is unavoidably error-prone. The painstakingly careful comparisons that normally go into formal taxonomy are bypassed and many similar species may be lumped together under one morphospecies code. Cryptic diversities like in the Costa Rican skippers will certainly remain hidden. Or, conversely, variability within species or between sexes may be accidentally misconstrued as multiple species. And when the sorting is done by parataxonomists, the inaccuracies will be even greater. Entomologist Frank Krell of London's Natural History Museum has shown that such morphospecies sortings almost always under- or overestimate the actual species richness by more than 50%.

Some scientists, in particular barcoders like Paul Hebert, therefore advocate DNA-based taxonomy. Species of bird normally differ by at least 3% in their *COI* sequence, he says. This means that for this gene, about three in every 100 DNA bases need to be different to consider two birds as belonging to different species. If similar thresholds can be found in, for instance, spiders (and they can), then one could simply put the entire contents of a bottle of spiders in a blender, extract the DNA, and sequence all the *COI* sequences that can be found in the DNA soup. The number of barcodes differing by more than the threshold percentage then gives the number of species in the sample. This may sound slightly far-fetched and (to the traditionalist) even sacrilegeous, but for organisms that are even harder to study than spiders, such as single-celled organisms like bacteria and protozoa, or even microscopic nematode worms, DNA barcoding is already replacing culturing, petri-dishing, mounting, and identifying, and is coming up with amazing results, as we shall see shortly. But first, some old-fashioned exploration.

3.2
Alice in the Jungle

Accelerating briskly, the small Fokker 50 plane takes off from the runway of Kota Kinabalu airport in Sabah, Malaysian Borneo, and turns sharply eastward. Below, the city sprawl gives way first to the hilly country where patches of hill rice and pineapple vicariate with bits of secondary jungle, and then to the ravaged rainforest of the interior. For miles and miles, the threadbare green carpet underneath is riddled with the yellow tracks of logging operations. Yet, here and there the low-flying plane crosses swaths of pristine forest: conservation areas, concessions where logging took place so long ago that the forest has more or less recovered, or simply hills with slopes that are too steep for the heavy timber vehicles.

The appearance from the air of the canopy of undisturbed tropical rainforests has been likened to broccoli. But unlike the many heads of the vegetable, the crowns of the trees all have a slightly different hue. As we gaze down from the cabin window, we see dabs of hundreds of shades of green. Some tree crowns are a deep bluish green, others bright and fresh yellow-green. Some are emerald, some ochraceous, some pale greyish green like olive trees. The forest canopy is like an abstract painting done by an artist with a palette of cadmium yellow, ochre, ultramarine, burnt sienna, and white. Each hue, of course, represents a different species. In the Bornean forest, as many as 300 tree species can occur per hectare (100 metres by 100 metres).

But it is not just the pointillism of species-specific colouration that makes the tropical rainforest canopy so special. Together with several other 'frontier' habitats (which will be introduced later in this chapter), it harbours an amazing diversity of other organisms, which scientists are still struggling to come to terms with, let alone describe and comprehend. Ever since naturalists first entered tropical rainforests, they have been struck by the fact that very little goes on at ground level. The constant battle for access to sunlight has displaced the leafy part of the trees to a level 30 metres or more above the ground, and much of the ecosystem it supports has moved with it. In his 1964 book *The Life of Plants*, the English botanist John Corner evocatively rendered the profusion of life in a tropical treetop:

> On its canopy birds and butterflies sip nectar. On its branches orchids, aroids and parasitic mistletoes offer flowers to other birds and insects. Among them ferns creep, lichens encrust, and centipedes and scorpions lurk. In the rubble that falls among the epiphytic roots and stems, ants build nests and even earthworms and snails find homes. There is a minute munching of caterpillars and the silent sucking of plant bugs. On any of these things, plant or animal, a fungus may be growing. Through the branches spread spiders' webs.

Corner was writing from experience, because he was one of the pioneers of the now flourishing field of canopy ecology. Before becoming a professor of tropical botany at the University of Cambridge, he was an assistant director at Singapore Botanic Gardens from 1929 to 1945, and his research on the taxonomy of trees had him scrambling through the forest in desperation much of the time. Getting good botanical specimens from trees was hard. For a proper description or identification, Corner needed flowers, fruits, and leaves. And in rainforest trees, which are typically lush crowns supported by bare boles, none of these were easily available at ground level. But in 1937, Corner came up with an ingenious solution. He decided to enlist some pig-tailed macaques, cheeky monkeys that the Malays train to dislodge coconuts high up in palms. His first simian assistant, a male called Merah ('Red'), quickly understood that this master was after forest products other than coconuts. After a few weeks of training, Merah had learnt some basic Malay commands and a steady rain of fruits, flowers, twigs, and epiphytes (herbs and ferns that grow upon the branches and trunks of trees) descended upon Corner with every trip into the forest. In return, Merah could feast on whatever grub or spider or stick insect took his fancy during his foray in the tree crowns. Merah's successor Puteh ('White') was of an even greater mental agility, understanding, by Corner's reckoning, at least 24 Malay commands. With some guidance, Puteh was even able to pick the correct fruits and epiphytes from the canopy after having been shown examples.

It must have been Puteh who figured in one of Corner's tallest stories that he used to recount for his University of Cambridge undergraduate students in the 1970s. One day, while travelling along a path on a rocky ledge, Corner saw an unknown flowering liana hanging down the cliff from the path. Naturally, he commanded his monkey to go down the steep slope and get the flower for him. The monkey just tilted his head to one side and looked questioningly at his master. When the irritated botanist repeated his command, the monkey shrugged, grabbed the liana, and pulled it up hand over hand to get to the flower. Corner told his students that no human had ever, before or since, made him feel so stupid.

Although monkeys are still being used for canopy studies (a team of French researchers are using them in Sumatra), many researchers today no longer rely on animals to get samples from the canopy, but venture there personally. Referring to themselves as 'arbonauts' (Fig. 3.1), intrepid biologists have adopted a wide range of techniques to enter the fairytale world 50 metres above the forest floor.

All this is shouted into my ear by English ecologist Stephen Sutton, as the plane touches down at the minuscule airfield of Lahad Datu, and spins its propellers fiercely in reverse pitch to come to a stop just before hitting the wooden barracks that pass for arrival hall. Besides having a somewhat dubious reputation as a favourite town for pirates to raid (right up to the present day), the sleepy town on the Sulu Sea shore is well known among biologists as the gateway to the Danum Valley Field Centre, a fully equipped tropical ecology research laboratory run jointly by the Sabah government and the Royal Society (UK's academy of sciences). Situated at the edge of 438 square kilometres of undisturbed rainforest, and surrounded on all sides by logged forest, the station has been an epicentre for tropical forest ecology since it was set up in 1986. Sutton, originally with the University of Leeds but now living a retired life in Sabah, has 40 years of experience with canopy insect studies in tropical forests worldwide and was coordinator for research at Danum throughout the 1990s.

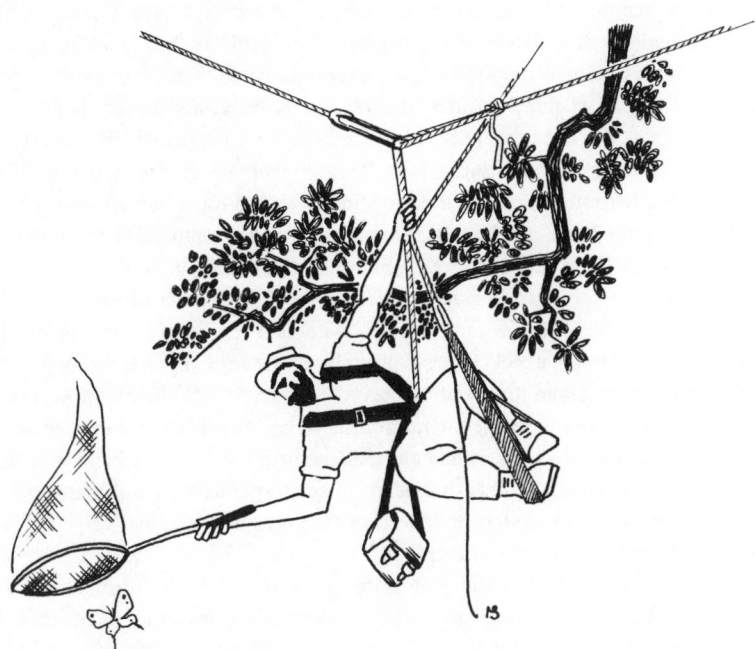

Fig. 3.1 Up in the tree tops, arbonauts boldly go where no entomologist has gone before

During the three-hour ride there, Sutton explains how canopy science, like Alice in the book, has grown up from the 'Wonderland' phase of Corner's days, when everything living up there was mysterious and exciting, to the mature scientific enterprise it is today. He begins by pointing at the 'menggaris' trees that stand along the road here and there: 80 metres tall, smooth, grey-white trunks with a majestic crown supported by massive branches. These *Koompassia excelsa* trees are among the tallest species of Borneo. Intriguingly, the trunks often bear series of regularly spaced scars all the way up to the top. Sutton explains they are the work of generations of local honey collectors, who would drive bamboo pegs into the bole to create a ladder allowing a hairy trip up to carry out the even hairier procedure of raiding the nests of the giant honey bee, *Apis dorsata*.

Like those sweet-toothed daredevils, the first scientists that ventured into the canopy to sample insects, epiphytes, or spiders used little more than their bare hands to scale trees and get to where the action is. For example, by using lumberjack techniques to climb up the stems and then descend by fixing a rope and abseiling down. Since then, the techniques have evolved and now most arbonauts use the so-called single rope technique, or SRT, a technique borrowed from cave explorers. Basically, it involves firing a thin wire over a strong branch using, for example, a crossbow. This thin wire is attached to a slightly thicker rope which can then be pulled over the branch and finally replaced by the definitive one-centimetre-thick climbing rope. The climbing rope is secured at the ground and the arbonaut climbs up from the free-dangling end of the rope.

It sounds simple, but an insiders' manual for SRT makes one's ears spin. A well-equipped SRT climber takes into the forest mysterious things like slings, climbing harnesses, maillons, carabiners, cow-tails (10.5 millimetres), chest ascenders, and a Daiwa Emblem spinning reel loaded with a Fox Pike system™ 14-kilogram line. She will be worried about whether the ropes are 'dynamic' or 'static' and what 'memory' the strings have. During climbing, there will be outlandish activities like frogging, tying girth hitches, and fixing remote belays. Most of these added complications are of course meant to increase safety. And they have paid off: in spite of three decades of SRT canopy work, and hundreds of climbers active worldwide at any one time, only a few accidents have happened. 'We had one very nasty accident on the Zaire river,' Sutton says. 'One climber managed to find himself hanging on by his hands from a rope. He tried to slide down the rope, but the friction cut his hand open right to the bone, and he fell 25 metres. He landed on the side of a termite hill, which broke his fall.' The climber survived, but was permanently injured.

One of the longest-serving arbonauts on record, Nalini Nadkarni of Evergreen College, Olympia, USA, has used SRT for three decades without a single accident. 'I learned it in 1979 and it has stood me in excellent stead ever since,' she says. She has scooted up ropes like an inchworm in the cloud forests of Monteverde, Costa Rica (a stone's throw from Dan Janzen's hangout) and in the temperate rainforests in her own Washington state so many times that the canopy is now her second home. 'Sometimes,' she says, 'when I'm sitting on this branch, and I'm making my measurements – I can forget where I am! You know, I can just eat my lunch, eat my sandwich, and then say, "Oh my gosh: yes, that's right – I'm 200 feet above the floor; I'd better remember that!"'

Her target has always been the plants that root at this high frontier. The ferns, bromeliads, orchids, mosses, liverworts, algae, lichens, and many other plants that clothe the stems, branches, twigs, and even the leaves of rainforest trees have often missed the limelight somewhat. And this is not fair, thinks Nadkarni, referring to work done by her ground-bound colleagues Grant Gentry and Craig Dodson in the 1980s. They made small plots of 0.1 hectare in several tropical forests and tallied all vascular plants (that is, plants with a dedicated water-transport system of vessels, thus excluding mosses, algae, and the like) both on the ground level and on fallen branches. The results were remarkable. In their Ecuador plot, for example, they found 365 species of plant, of which more than one third grew on freshly fallen branches. This means epiphyte diversity should not be sniffed at. And since these researchers did not climb a single tree, and ignored all the mosses and other non-vascular plants, it could even be a much greater proportion than one third.

Nadkarni has a few favourite kinds of epiphytes. Although she thinks orchids are the supreme canopy-dwelling plants, they are closely followed by a slightly less glamorous group, the bromeliads ('the pineapple is in the bromeliad family; if you can picture that: pineapples growing all over branches of tropical trees,' she explains helpfully). These do not only include those famous phytotelmata, the water-filled tank-bromeliads, but also non-tank bromeliads. These so-called atmospheric epiphytes do not gather any water, but get all their water and nutrients directly from the air. 'Really amazing plants,' Nadkarni says. Finally, the Ericaceae are also 'really neat'. In the Monteverde cloud forest these members of the heather and blueberry family come as little shrubs that grow on the branches of bigger trees. Their fruits and seeds are very important for birds and arboreal mammals, whereas their flowers provide nectar to insects.

When imagining this profusion of plants growing upon plants, it becomes clear that the epiphytes are really where all the action is: the rainforest trees just provide the framework for layers upon layers of ever-smaller epiphytes to sculpt the intricate three-dimensional garden that the canopy really is. An epiphyte growing on a tree could have another epiphyte growing on it. And then you look at that epiphyte's leaves and there are flat, miniature gardens (so-called epiphylls) of cyanobacteria, green algae, lichens, small ferns, mosses, and liverworts. Nadkarni says: 'You feel sometimes when you're sitting up there that you could spend the entire rest of your life on that one branch, figuring out who is living on who, and who is providing what for which plants. It's just fantastic!'

Still, Nadkarni, sitting in her tree, realises that SRT has its limitations: since the line will normally be shot over one of the lower branches in the canopy, it is hard to reach the very top of the tree. It is also risky to venture too far out along the branches, so the researcher's circle of activity is restricted to the area around the trunk and the lowest big branches. Soon canopy scientists began thinking of other ways to access the canopy, Sutton explains, as he and I wander the paths among the scattered buildings by the Segama river that make up the Danum Valley Field Centre. 'Aerial walkways were constructed by hanging suspension bridges high above the ground among a number of big trees,' Sutton says. 'Danum Valley has one of those. It gives the researcher a greater mobility among the treetops, but the downside is that the work is always restricted to the few trees that can be reached from the walkway.'

An improvement was the canopy crane, which began appearing in the early 1990s. These are tall cranes of the same type used in the construction of large buildings, but plonked smack in the middle of a forest. One day, tropical ecologist Alan Smith of the Smithsonian Tropical Research Institute in Panama was idly watching one constructing a building near the airport where he was waiting for a delayed plane, and realised its potential. When he got to Panama, he rented one for US $50,000 per year and it has been in use ever since. And there are now some 15 more in tropical and temperate forests worldwide. One of the largest ones is in Lambir Hills, Malaysia. It is 85 metres high, taller than the tallest tree, and has a horizontal boom 75 metres long that goes around 360 degrees, so it can cover a circle of rainforest canopy of 1.7 hectares. The scientists sit in a gondola that hangs under the boom and can go up and down as well as slide along the arm. So the researcher in the gondola has access to over a million cubic metres of forest to work in.

But for some greedy (and death-defying) arbonauts, even that is not good enough. They will settle for nothing less than independent, unlimited access to any spot among the treetops they want, explains Sutton as he leads me across a badminton field strewn with the elytra of giant beetles, victims of the resident fish owl. We go round the back of a store and stand still in front of a profusion of plastic sheeting, empty gas cylinders, and elegantly shaped, yet dented, aluminium frames. Covered in cobwebs and gecko droppings, and draped in hastily drawn tarpaulins, it looks like the hushed-up remains of an alien spaceship. And that is precisely what it is.

In 1995, Graham "Captain Fantastic" Dorrington, an aerospace engineer from Southampton University (now at the University of London), built and tested a miniature Zeppelin over Danum's forest canopy. Prozaically named the D-4, Dorrington says the machine was a 'small, mobile, lighter-than-air platform [that] could be easily used for supra-canopy exploration'. Looking down on the mangled remains, Sutton recalls chucklingly:

> He appeared at Danum with this monstrous package. Filled it up with helium and got in and discovered it would only lift one-and-a-half persons! So there was a miscalculation somewhere along the line or perhaps the helium wasn't pure enough. It was supposed to lift two people. That was absolutely critical, because you need one person to fly it and another person to do the science work. You could only operate it at dawn, because otherwise above the canopy there was just too much wind. And the thing is, he was driving it by paddle power. He had bicycle paddles connected to a propeller; a constant rain of obscenities was always coming down. It's a project that only half succeeded, but I would say that from that work you could see how you could build a lighter-than-air platform which would be tremendously valuable in getting you up close and personal with the rainforest canopy.

Dorrington reports that the D-4 is now in its second phase, with a fuel cell (rather than paddle power) for propulsion. Besides such two-person balloons, larger canopy airships have been successful since the 1980s. Most prominent has been the French Radeau des Cimes, an inflatable researchers' camp that can be dropped on top of the canopy from a hot-air balloon or a helicopter. It consists of several inflatable rings. Between them a net is strung, over which the researchers can walk and make observations and measurements at the edges. And tents provide shelter, as the 'raft', as it is called, is sometimes left for weeks in one tree.

But in many ways the most productive canopy studies are still done from the ground. Since the 1970s, impressive insights into canopy biodiversity have been gained from what can only be described as entomological overkill. Having the previous days installed pulleys in the thick branches of four tall trees and a cat's cradle of strings among the understorey below, entomologists specialising in 'fogging' gather at their study site before dawn, armed with large plastic funnels and cannon-shaped objects. Among the quiet and gloom of the predawn forest, they suspend their funnels from the strings in a predetermined spatial pattern, fill their cannon with fuel and a milky liquid, and hoist it up into the tree. Once everything is in place and dawn breaks, one of the researchers flips a switch on a radio transmitter. Fifteen metres up, the sinister object springs to life: among the noise of a small diesel engine, thick hot clouds of exhaust fumes mixed with insecticide droplets are belched out by the machine's barrel and rise through the canopy above. The scientists work quickly. After one minute of fogging, the machine is turned off and hoisted into each of the other three trees, where the process is repeated. Then, they wait in silence for the 'rain' to begin. Slight ticking sounds can be heard from the plastic funnels as thousands of dead and dying insects begin falling from the fumigated treetops. After three hours, the team unscrews the bottles with alcohol that are fitted underneath each funnel, now filled with blackish insect slush, and start leaving the scene of their crime.

One of the first people to use this fogging method was entomologist Terry Erwin of the Smithsonian Institution in Washington, DC, USA. In the late 1970s, Erwin fogged 19 trees of the same species in the forest of Panama and pulled more than 1,200 species of insects from his bottles. And this was just a single species of tree. A few years later, he took his fogging equipment to the seasonally flooded Amazon forest around Manaus, Brazil. He set up three fogging sites in each of the four main forest types in the area: dry, so-called terra firma forest, black-water inundated forest, white-water inundated forest, and mixed-water inundated forest. Even with use of only 24,350 of his sampled individuals, a small fraction of the total, it was already clear that the 1,080 species of insect species he found were not spread evenly over all four forest types. In fact, 83% of all species were only found in a single forest type, and just 1% was shared among all four types.

This shows that insect diversity in the canopy is enormous. Not just in each tree, but especially among different trees and among different sites in the same area. In the 1980s, British entomologist Nigel Stork of the London Natural History Museum (now at James Cook University in Townsville, Australia) took fogging to the Southeast Asian Tropics. In Brunei, he and his co-workers fogged ten trees belonging to five different species. Their insecticide brought down about 24,000 arthropods, belonging to more than 2,800 species. And do not think that these were all big and showy megabugs, by the way. Like everywhere else, in the Tropics most insects are tiny. Stork found that beetles one millimetre long were about 10,000 times as numerous as beetles ten millimetres in length. But in spite of these large numbers, their study mainly highlighted how much they did not manage to find: most species were represented by just a single individual. Almost 500 of the 859 species of beetle, for example, were found as just one specimen. And of the 739 chalcidoid wasp species, 437 species were such 'singletons'. This shows that much larger numbers of species must have been missed altogether.

And much more of the diversity remains hidden when just the canopy is sampled. As Nalini Nadkarni will attest to, much, if not most, of the canopy ecosystem is allocated to the world of epiphytes, rather than to the trees themselves. And epiphytes, especially if they are shaped like the giant nest fern that Stephen Sutton and I are looking up at, are hard to sample with the fogging 'knockdown' technique. We are standing at the foot of a tall *Parashorea tomentella*, a common rainforest tree along the trails around the Danum Valley Field Centre. High up, where the bole begins to branch, an enormous bunch of fern leaves sprouts up from a thick, brown 'basket' of dead leaves. It is a bird's nest fern, *Asplenium nidus*. Known among the locals as the home of the langsuir, an unattractive kind of ghost representing the upper half of a woman with her entrails tailing behind her as she flits through the forest at night, the epiphyte is famous among biologists for its more common-place inhabitants.

Bird's nest ferns are funnel-shaped and create their own patch of soil by gathering leaf litter. In it, many insects and other invertebrates find a dwelling. Given the basket shape of their epiphytic home, these animals will usually not make it to the ground after a fogging exercise. So it was always an open question how much of the canopy biodiversity was living among these and other large epiphytes. To provide an answer, a few years ago William Foster and his student Martin Ellwood of the University of Cambridge, UK, set out to dissect some of Danum's langsuir lairs.

They set up what they call a 'precision fogging' system to be able to compare the invertebrate numbers in the epiphyte with those in the tree crown above it. Using SRT, they hung sets of collecting trays directly above and directly below the nest fern of choice. Each set of trays covered the same surface area as the epiphyte itself. Then, a fogger was raised into the canopy and fog was sprayed onto the fern and into the canopy above it. After empty-ing the top trays, which collected the animals living in the canopy above the fern, and the bottom trays, which collected any animals living on the outside of the epiphyte, they cut the nest fern loose from its branch and carefully (they weigh up to 200 kilograms!) bagged it, lowered it to the floor, and took it to the laboratory. There, all invertebrates living in the fern were collected using an assembly of techniques, including cutting up the plant, the use of so-called Winkler bags (which dry the litter collected between the leaves, forc-ing out the animals inside), and several 'enthusiastic assistants armed with forceps and collecting jars'.

The results were staggering. Just five ferns yielded almost a quarter of a million individual animals, ranging from ants and earthworms to spiders and springtails. Extrapo-lating from their fogging samples to the total size of a tree crown, they concluded that the epiphytes contain about as much animal life as does the canopy above it: converted to dry weight, some four kilograms of biomass per hectare each. The study was published in *Nature* of 3 June 2004, under the title 'Doubling the estimate of invertebrate biomass in a rainforest canopy'. It forced the Field Centre to finally pop a bottle of champagne, promised many years before by Danum's senior scientist Glen Reynolds for the first Danum-based study to make the pages of the prestigious journal. Sutton says: 'Willy Foster really knows how to put a spin on a story.'

3.3
Deep Secrets, Intimate Friends

In the 1970s and early 1980s, the vast diversity of arthropods in forest canopies came as an embarrassing surprise to the all too many biologists who had been vertebrate-focused. People who had been studying insects and other invertebrates finally got some of the recognition they deserved and the more eloquent ones, like Harvard University entomologist

Edward O. Wilson, pleaded with some success for more research money and attention for the 'little things that run the world'. A case in point was Terry Erwin's work, which showed that, by extrapolation, the total biodiversity in the world must run to the tens of millions of species. But lately, yet another group of researchers, studying diversity in even smaller creatures, have stepped up. Enter microbial biodiversity and its amazing numbers.

In hindsight, the microbial revolution in biodiversity studies was bound to happen. A simple graph of body size against species richness already speaks volumes. In 1978, English ecologist Robert May provided a figure in a book chapter in which he plotted the logarithm of average body length in a taxonomic group of land animals against the logarithm of the species numbers in that group. The result was a straight line, which showed that with each decrease of body length by an order of magnitude diversity jumped up by two orders of magnitude. In other words, in the body-length category of 1,000 millimetres there are about 100 species, in the 100-millimetre class 10,000 species, and in the ten-millimetre range there are 1,000,000 species. This is not surprising: everybody knows that there are just a few giant species, and lots of small ones.

But it gets interesting when we follow the line downward, and see what happens in organisms tinier than ten millimetres long. The line, when drawn along the points for the larger animals, predicts that there should be 100 million species in the one-millimetre category, and ten billion species ten micrometres long. But when we look at the species lists that we have, this prediction does not seem to be borne out: we only know a few tens of thousands of animal species less than one millimetre, not ten billion. In his 1978 paper, May asked, and has been asking ever since, the burning question: Is the unexpected downward turn of the straight line for the smallest living things a real phenomenon or the result of our fragmentary and incomplete knowledge of microorganisms?

It now appears that the latter answer is the correct one. Taxonomists have described 4,000 species of bacteria, 5,000 species of viruses, and about 40,000 single-celled animals (Protozoa). Not numbers to be sniffed at, but a far cry from the diversities that a modern breed of DNA-barcoding microbiologists is coming up with.

It all began when, in the late 1980s, microbiologist Vigdis Torsvik took six sandwich bags to a beech forest at Seim, Norway, filled them with soil and took them back to her laboratory at the University of Bergen. Using bacterial staining techniques, she estimated each bag contained about half a trillion (500,000,000,000) individual bacteria. That is about as many as there are stars in the universe; but it is a normal bacteria abundance for forest soil samples. She and her colleagues then isolated the bacteria by centrifugation and extracted their DNA. This DNA was chopped up to smaller fragments and then heated, so that the two intertwined strands of the DNA double helices separated. Then, the temperature was lowered and the researchers monitored the mixture to see how long it took for the strands to reassemble. This length of time is a measure for how many different kinds of DNA there are in the mixture. The more bacterial species, the more different types of DNA, and the longer it takes for the matching pairs of strands to find each other again.

The researchers discovered that their 'thermal denaturation–reassociation' procedure indicated that some 5,000 species of bacteria lived in one gram of beech forest soil: more than all the known species of bacteria on Earth. Did this mean bacteria are so widespread that the entire global diversity can be found in a pinch of Scandinavian soil? No. Traditionally, the convention in microbiology has been that new species of bacteria can only be described and named if they can be kept in pure culture in the laboratory. Most bacteria (Torsvik estimates 99.5–99.9%) probably have such special requirements that they are unculturable. So it is perhaps not surprising that anywhere we look hordes of unknown bacteria will be staring us in the face. The vast majority of the bacteria in Torsvik's sandwich bags would have been new to science. In fact, when she later did the same kind of study on a sample of sediment from the Norwegian sea shore, an entirely different set of 5,000 species was found. Ten thousand species of bacteria in two grams of Norway. What does that mean for microbial diversity in entire habitats? The answers to this ominous question have been coming in over the past ten years as a series of ever louder wake-up calls.

In the same year that Torsvik's study was published, a paper by Stephen Giovannoni and colleagues from Oregon State University in Corvallis, USA, appeared in *Nature*, reporting on the diversity of bacteria in the Sargasso Sea. The Sargasso Sea is the centre of a giant oceanic whirlpool in the middle of the Atlantic. Apart from the floating seaweed that gives this swath of ocean its name, it is home to a teeming community of surface-dwelling bacteria, collectively called bacterioplankton.

Giovannoni's team used a different DNA technique from that of Torsvik to look at the bacterioplankton diversity: the polymerase chain reaction (PCR). Now a routine technique in almost any laboratory, in 1990 PCR was still newly invented. It works by separating a double-helixed DNA sample into its constituent single strands by heating it. Then, the single-stranded DNA sample is confronted with so-called primers, short stretches of single-stranded DNA that are expected to match some of the DNA in the sample; when the temperature is lowered, they will click into place. In Giovannoni's case, they used primers that fit on both ends of the *16S* gene, a runt of DNA that all bacteria carry and that is the barcode of choice for bacteria (just like the *COI* gene is for animals). During PCR, an enzyme called polymerase duplicates the piece of DNA in-between the two primers during a succession of about 30 cycles of heating and cooling. In each cycle, the copied DNA from the previous cycle is also duplicated; hence, the amount of *16S* in the sample snowballs to large quantities (well, think micrograms, which is enough to excite molecular biologists).

But of course, the PCR product is a mix of the *16S* sequences from all the bacteria in the sample, and each will have a slightly different sequence. To separate out these different *16S* sequences, the PCR-amplified *16S* is cloned. That is, it is mixed with cut 'plasmids', circular bits of DNA that are carried by many bacteria. Another enzyme (ligase) then pastes the PCR fragments into the gaps in these plasmids, after which the plasmids are mixed with *Escherichia coli* bacteria (the workhorse of molecular geneticists). The plasmids contain genes that allow the bacteria to grow on a particular growth medium, so each bacterial colony that grows is certain to contain a clone: a plasmid with one of the many *16S* sequences in it. The final step then is to keep all colonies separate, isolate their plasmids, stick them into a DNA sequencer, and look at the *16S* sequence.

When Giovannoni did this with a sample of Sargasso Sea water, he found the barcodes for a plethora of unknown bacteria. One group even belonged to an entirely new class, and is now known to contain *Pelagibacter ubique*, one of the most abundant bacterial species on the planet. Since then, hundreds of studies have appeared that used the same technique on microbial communities in a range of habitats, and it has been the same story everywhere: bacteria and other microbes are incredibly diverse in the most unlikely habitats and contain lots of groups of organisms that nobody has ever studied or even looked at before.

As an example of how this field of research is booming, in the first half of 2005 alone, five papers appeared in the top journals *Science* and *Nature*, reporting amazing new discoveries in bacterial diversity. In the first *Science* issue of the year, Paul van der Wielen of the University of Groningen in Haren, the Netherlands, looked at samples taken from hypersaline basins in the Mediterranean deep sea. These basins were formed from enormous blocks of salt, deposited when the Mediterranean was temporarily dried up around five million years ago. When the sea returned and the banks of salt dissolved, the heavy, hypersaline water did not mix everywhere with the water on top and remains as thick pools at the bottom of the sea. With salt concentrations of almost half a kilogram of magnesium chloride per litre, these basins were considered devoid of all life (magnesium chloride brines are even less hospitable than sodium chloride ones). Not so: when van der Wielen studied samples taken with advanced sampling equipment lowered from research vessels, he found that each cupful contained millions of living bacteria. And *16S* analysis showed that they belonged to a whole smorgasbord of unknown groups, unrelated to the bacteria normally found in seawater.

In two other investigations of deep-sea bacteria, both appearing in *Nature*, Axel Schippers of the German Federal Institute for Geosciences and Natural Resources in Hanover, Germany, and John Parkes of Cardiff University, UK, studied the microbes living deep in the sea floor. It had already been known for some time that sea-bottom sediments are chockfull of bacterial cells. In fact, they constitute a large fraction of all bacterial cells on Earth. But people had always assumed that all or most of them were dead. Far from it, as Parkes and Schippers found out when they studied cores drilled from the eastern tropical Pacific Ocean floor at depths of 400–5,000 metres. Schippers used techniques that specifically detect the protein-producing micromachines called ribosomes, which are only present in live cells. All sediments contained the signatures of large numbers of living bacteria (up to one million per cubic centimetre), right down to sediments more than 400 metres below the sea floor, which were buried over 16 million years ago. And Parkes's *16S* barcodes again showed great diversity, with all kinds of bacteria present, including a new division only discovered the year before.

Then, in April 2005, Jeffrey Walker of the University of Colorado in Boulder, USA, published a paper in *Nature* in which he reported 342 *16S* barcodes from the Norris Geyser Basin in Yellowstone National Park. The samples had come from a green band in the porous silica rocks that line this demonic swamp of hot sulphuric acid. Besides the algae that produced the green streak in the rock, about 40 different bacteria were present, many of which, surprisingly, were relatives of the bugs that cause leprosy and tuberculosis.

And two months later, Paul Eckburg of Stanford University took a closer look at one of our most intimate habitats: the human intestine. He generated over 13,000 *16S* barcodes from the faeces and gut interiors of three healthy people, and found altogether 396 different bacterial species, two thirds of which were new to science.

All these studies show that there are lots of unknown bacteria out there, even in the most inhospitable places. Microbiologists have been cloning and sequencing bacterial *16S* sequences from all kinds of bizarre habitats, ranging from uninviting ones like oil reservoirs and the McMurdo dry valleys of Antarctica, to unappetising ones like the 'human outer ear' and students' shower curtains. But there are so many kinds of bacteria out there that cloning and barcoding can only tell you so much. No matter how many months you let your sequencing machines churn out barcodes (and there are now about a quarter of a million *16S* sequences in the genetic databases), you will never get them all. In 2004, Craig Venter (of genome mapping fame) redid Giovannoni's Sargasso Sea analysis using ultramodern, rapid genome sequencing and found, among the more than one billion DNA bases he sequenced, 1,184 different *16S* sequences. A large number, as expected from such a titanic sequencing effort, but did it approach the true diversity?

Probably nowhere near it. There are an estimated one billion individual bacteria in every litre of seawater. That works out as about 3,600,000,000,000,000,000,000,000,000,000,000 (3.6×10^{30}) bacteria in all of the world's oceans, making up over 90% of the seas' biomass. And in the sea-floor sediments an estimated 1.3×10^{29} bacteria live. On land, the situation is no different: with 10^{16} bacteria per ton of soil, and bacteria showing up in cores drilled from hundreds of metres underground, the numbers of bacteria are probably every bit as large as in the sea. Even if we sequence many thousands of *16S* genes, it is likely that the vast majority of species will be overlooked.

So isn't there a more appropriate way to estimate the numbers of bacterial species in each habitat? Fortunately, there is. The first inroad to this was made by Vigdis Torsvik when she made her now-famous estimate of 5,000 species per gram of soil, without having to identify or sequence a single bacterium. But as Jason Gans and co-workers of the Los Alamos National Laboratory, USA, explained in a 2005 paper in *Science*, Torsvik had made the assumption that all species were equally abundant. In reality, this is never so. In any habitat, in any group of organisms (as we shall see in Chap. 7), there tend to be common species and rare species. Sometimes there are a few very common species and lots of rare ones; sometimes there are few very common ones, lots of frequent ones, and few rare ones. These are called species abundance distributions. And whatever the form of the species abundance distribution, the total number of individuals is always spread out over many more species than if all species were equally common.

To work out the correct species abundance distributions for soil bacteria, Gans compared eight different kinds of distributions, all dreamt up by previous generations of ecologists. Each would result in a different shape for the 'thermal denaturation-reassociation' curve, that is, the rate by which a mixture of DNA reassembles when the temperature is gradually lowered. Comparing the predicted curves with published data, he found that five of the eight models could be ruled out. Instead, communities of soil bacteria showed patterns of commonness and rarity that closely matched the three remaining species abundance distributions, the so-called model-free, zipf, and log-Laplace distributions, all of which are very similar. Gans then estimated the total diversity in the samples by dividing all individual bacteria over the area under the correct species abundance curve. And it turned out that Torsvik's assumption had been extremely conservative: rather than 5,000 species, one gram of soil is likely to contain about eight million species of bacteria!

Although these calculations show that Robert May was right and bacteria have more species than anything else, some microbiologists take offence at the terminology used to describe bacterial diversity. Norman Pace of the University of Colorado in Boulder, for example, has been genetically dissecting microbial communities for more than 30 years. When one innocently uses the term 'bacterial species' in his presence, he spontaneously ignites. 'You've touched a sore nerve on my part,' he says. 'In bacteria, species are in the eye of the beholder. If you didn't know that *Yersinia pestis* caused black plague, you probably wouldn't distinguish it from *Escherichia coli*, with which it is genetically almost identical.'

What Pace means is that 'species' (*excusez le mot*) in bacteria are much less static than in animals. They have short generation times and evolve fast. They also exchange bits and pieces of DNA with one another. The result is a very fluid brew of genetic types that constantly change the ecological roles they play. And on the microscopic scale on which bacteria move (the smallest ones are just 0.2 micrometres long) these roles can be chopped up incredibly finely. 'A handful of marine sediment or forest soil can contain a zillion chemical environments. And it will depend on the time of the day, or year, or eon; and whether the bison took a piss there 20 years ago,' Pace says.

Those ecological roles – niches – whether chemical and on the scale of microns, as in bacteria, or vegetational and on the scale of forest strata, as in skipper butterflies, are the subject of the next chapter.

No Niche Like Home

4

4.1
There Goes a Badger

In my garden lurk assassins. I don't see them very often, but once encountered they are hard to forget. Their bodies are sleek, clothed in bright vermilion capes. They slide stealthily among the branches on their skinny black legs, twisting their equally black heads here and there to spot potential victims. They seem to have a sinister penchant for tiny ants, which, in a surprisingly quick motion, they will spear on a long stiletto that they suddenly produce from under their cloaks. I am not afraid of them, as these assassins are just one centimetre long, and are officially termed assassin bugs or Reduviidae. Although they sometimes get lucky and run into a hapless victim by accident, their main strategy seems to be to locate the lines of ants that run up and down trees and stems of plants. Sometimes, I find such a formicine highway with several assassin bugs lined up alongside, each impaling, sucking dry, and discarding ants at leisure from the endless train. Assassins in a sushi bar.

My assassin bugs are perfect for the job. They mostly go about on foot, as this is the best way to find ants. They seem experts at locating lines of ants, for which, in the three-dimensional vastness of garden microhabitats, they must possess special chemical senses. Their dagger-like proboscis is ideally suited for its purpose and they deploy it with remarkable precision, sinking its tip with agility into an ant's minuscule abdomen, drawing the liquid parts of the prey's body up in a matter of seconds, then using their nimble forelegs to dislodge the shrivelled carcass and preparing for the next attack. If there were a prize for who is the best ant-eater in town, they would win legs down.

Not only are they perfectly adapted to finding and killing prey, they also have the right metabolism to survive in the hot corners of my garden at midday when their prey are most active. They know where and when to lay their eggs and how to survive when the ant supplies temporarily run dry. And their red-and-black colouration presumably warns of some toxicity, keeping potential predators at bay. But all this specialisation has its downsides. If they were asked to do something else, like grazing lichens off the branches like the tree snails do, or intercepting mosquitoes in mid-air like the dragonflies, or stilettoing ants

The Loom of Life. M. Schilthuizen
Doi: 10.1007/978-3-540-68058-1_4, © Springer-Verlag Berlin Heidelberg 2008

underground, they would not know where to start. Even requesting that they change target and pierce termites instead might be too much to ask. In short, assassinating walking ants in tropical secondary vegetation in Southeast Asia is the only thing they know how to do and they do it to the pinnacle of perfection. It is their profession, their hobby, their religion, their goal in life. Their night and day, their sun and moon. In short, it is their niche.

It is not entirely clear who first borrowed the word 'niche' from church architecture and appropriated it to ecology. It may have been Joseph Grinnell, who used it in 1917 to indicate what today we would call 'habitat'. But the first usage of 'niche' in what approaches the modern sense was by Elton, in his 1927 book *Animal Ecology*, which I have mentioned before. In it, he writes that ecologists need a term to describe what an animal does, not just what it looks like, 'and the term used is "niche." ' He goes on to say that the ecologist should cultivate the habit of looking at animals from this point of view. He writes: 'When an ecologist says "there goes a badger" he should include in his thoughts some definite idea of the animal's place in the community to which it belongs, just as if he had said "there goes the vicar." '

In church architecture, 'niche' denotes a recess in a church wall that contains a sculpture or an urn. In the ecological concept, the placement of species in niches is far more complicated than this unidimensional allocation of relics. My red-jacketed assassin bugs, for example, will feed on only a small section of the vast range of possible prey items. Along the church wall of prey, 'ants' are its niche. But it also has a niche along a different wall that carries all possible temperatures. And along a third wall that represents humidity, and along other walls that denote wind speed, salt concentration in the soil, amount of solar influx, presence of predators, presence of competing ant-eaters, presence of fungi and bacteria that attack its eggs, and so on and so forth. In short, a niche is the corner in a multidimensional space suspended among all the ecological 'resources' that are relevant for a species's survival and reproduction.

A species's niche, therefore, is usually so complex that scientists can only explore a limited number of all the potentially important resources. Think of a small mobile animal, like a woodlouse. Assuming that woodlice, when given a choice, tend to seek out conditions that are ideal for their survival and reproduction, we can do experiments to see where along a resource their niche exactly lies. Imagine a long tube, one end of which is at 0 C and the other is at 50 C, with a gradual change between these two extremes. When we then scatter into the tube a handful of woodlice of, say, the temperate species *Armadillidium vulgare*, they most likely will converge to a section of the tube that has their preferred temperature (perhaps around 18 C). Their niche, as far as temperature is concerned, is thus visualised as a cluster of points along a straight line.

We could then expand on this by adding a second resource. If we create a flat, square box that is cold on the left and hot on the right, and has a humidity gradient perpendicular to the temperature gradient (dry at the far side, humid at the nearer side), the scattered *A. vulgare* woodlice will all congregate in one spot where it is nicely cool and humid. They represent their own niche in temperature–humidity space as a cloud of woodlouse-shaped points huddled together in a flat plane. Add a handful of the desert woodlouse *Venezilla arizonicus* and they will form a different group somewhere in the hot and dry corner of the box. With a lot of imagination we could perhaps add a vertical third gradient (say, light intensity) to find the species's niche in a three-resource space, but that is about as far as we can go in a laboratory setting. In nature, far more than three resources determine a species's niche.

Evelyn Hutchinson expressed this notion most cogently in a 1957 paper entitled 'Concluding remarks'. It bore this curious title not because modernistic poetry had seeped into scientific writing, or because Hutchinson thus wished to bestow permanence to his notions, but simply because it was an epilogue to the proceedings of a symposium at Cold Spring Harbor. In it, Hutchinson launched his concept of the n-dimensional hyperspace alluded to above, where n stands for the number of resource axes along which a species has a slot for optimum survival and reproduction. The n slots together make up a 'hypervolume' that has since become famous as the 'Hutchinsonian niche'. And in the same year that Hutchinson's 'Concluding remarks' paper was published, a young PhD student of his put the finishing touches to what was to become a classic in the study of Hutchinsonian niches.

Robert MacArthur, who died young in 1972, after having left behind a small but unforgettable oeuvre, has been accurately called the 'James Dean of theoretical ecology'. He had a master's degree in mathematics when, in 1954, he embarked on a PhD on the ecology of warblers. Warblers are small insect-eating birds that winter in the Caribbean but nest in North America. My copy of *All the Birds of North America* says: 'More than 50 warbler species join in the migration … blanketing the entire continent. … The greatest number migrate up the eastern seaboard. … In these places, waves of warblers can overwhelm lucky birders.' There follows a 20-page smorgasbord of tiny birds in cream, buff, grey, fawn, yellow-and-black, black-and-yellow, black-white-and-green, grey-yellow-and-black, grey-buff-fawn-and-black, black-and-white, and a bunch of other subtly different palettes. I doubt how lucky a beginning birder will feel having to make sense of this profusion of colour patterns. But fortunately, the book also says, 'The place where a warbler is seen feeding can be a good clue to its identity. Some are typically high in the canopy, others feed at midlevel, and still others feed on the ground or close to it.'

Though MacArthur's legacy lives on in much more illustrious ways (as we shall see later in this book), he would no doubt have been pleased to see his doctoral work turn up in a bird guide half a century later. For MacArthur was not only a mathematician and a gifted theoretical ecologist, he was a bird enthusiast too. His thesis subject was to circumscribe accurately the niches of five warbler species (the Cape May, myrtle, black-throated green, Blackburnian, and bay-breasted warbler; Fig. 4.1) that share the same habitat: the mature spruce forests of Maine and Vermont. And this required a lot of patient birdwatching. Notebook in hand, MacArthur spent the summers of 1956 and 1957 recording in which part of the tree each of the species preferentially fed. This sounds easier than it is. Not only did he need to accurately identify a bird before he started following it, but these tiny birds flit about the branches of dense spruce trees with infuriating quickness. They pick spruce budworms off the needles, disappear into the tree's interior, and reappear elsewhere. Then they fly off to another tree. Then they fly back. And meanwhile, MacArthur had to keep track of the amount of time spent in each section of a tree. In 1957 he obtained a stopwatch, but, as he explains in the 'Methods' section of his scientific papers, in the previous year he still had to estimate seconds by saying 'thousand and one, thousand and two,…'.

Fig. 4.1 Robert MacArthur's PhD studies led him to sort out the exact niche differences between closely related warbler species all feeding on insects on spruce. The myrtle warbler (left) feeds in the lower branches, whereas the Blackburnian warbler (right) forages higher up in the spruce tree

Not surprising, then, that his two summers of field work amounted to a total of only four hours, 22 minutes and 54 seconds of reliable observations. But little as this may seem, it was sufficient to delineate accurately each species's position along some of the dimensions of the Hutchinsonian niche. The 1958 paper in the journal *Ecology* in which he describes the outcome of this study contains five schematic drawings of Christmas trees (one for each species), each subdivided into 16 sectors. For each sector, for each species, MacArthur had jotted down the proportion of time spent feeding there. It was clear that all species had their own feeding zones. The Cape May warbler fed only in the very tips of the trees, while the myrtle warbler was always in the lowest sectors. The black-throated warbler was mostly found in the central bit, whereas the other two species preferred the trees' interior, the Blackburnian warbler going higher than the bay-breasted warbler.

He also found that each species had a different hunting strategy. By counting and measuring the intervals between flights, he could show that the black-throated green warbler was more 'nervous' than the Blackburnian and the myrtle warbler, and these two were more nervous again than the Cape May and the bay-breasted warbler. The way they moved about the branches was also different. The bay-breasted and Blackburnian warblers would move along branches, the myrtle and black-throated warblers tended to hop between adjacent branches, and the Cape May warbler hopped between branches at different levels. All this reflected different hunting strategies and would affect how many caterpillars each species picked off the tips of needles and how many from underneath clumps of needles. Not only did MacArthur show very fine-grained niche differences, but, more importantly, he also showed how these five species could share the same bit of woodland without one outcompeting the other: by avoiding niche overlap, they avoided competition.

4.2
Peaceful Coexistence?

Competition is the flip side of the niche. When two species have to share their corner of n-dimensional niche space with other species, their niches will overlap to some extent; hence, they will compete for the position along the resource axes for which they overlap. In practice, this means that one species negatively affects the abundance of the other species and (usually) vice versa. This concept generated a lot of debate for much of the twentieth century. In the 1920s and 1930s, people wondered whether two species with the exact same niche could compete and yet coexist. Intuitively, one might think that this is possible as the two species would keep each other precisely in balance. However, mathematical analysis, for example by Italian mathematician Vito Volterra in 1926, showed that our intuition is wrong in this case: long-term peaceful coexistence is not the expected outcome of competition, because even the tiniest difference in population growth rate will make one species replace the other completely.

The Russian microbiologist Georgyi Frantsevitch Gause (pronounced as 'gow-zer') in 1934, at age 24, published his influential and elegantly written book *The Struggle for Existence*, in which he combined experimental proof with mathematical formulas. Gause used species of small Protozoa for his experiments: *Paramecium caudatum* and *P. aurelia*. He kept them in glass centrifuge tubes, each with five millilitres of sterilised salt solution and identical amounts of their favourite food: a suspension of *Bacillus pyocyaneus* bacteria. The tubes were stocked either with 20 individuals of one of the *Paramecium* species (the separate cultures), or with 20 of one species and 20 of the other species (the mixed cultures). Every day, Gause would spin the culture tubes in a centrifuge, which forced all the occupants to the bottom of the tube, rinse them, and replace the salt solution by fresh solution with bacteria. He also took a daily census by placing half a millilitre of culture on a microscope slide and counting how many individuals of each species he saw.

The results from the separate cultures were all very similar. Over a period of about ten days, the number of individuals would rise along an S-shaped curve to a maximum and stay there. For *P. caudatum*, this maximum (the so-called carrying capacity of their five-millilitre environment) amounted to about 2,000 individuals, and for *P. aurelia* it was roughly 5,000 individuals. But since the latter species had a body size only 40% of that of the former, the amount of biomass for both was the same. So Gause had shown that he had two species that both could live very well under the conditions that he offered; in the laboratory at least, they had the same niche. But when he then created mixed cultures, competition always drove one of the two to extinction, and it was always the same one. The two *Paramecium* species would start out by growing in unison along the S-shaped trajectory. But round about day eight, when their joint biomass almost reached the carrying capacity, the numbers of *P. caudatum* would begin to diminish, whereas those of *P. aurelia* would continue to climb until in the end *P caudatum* would be annihilated.

The upshot of these and other experiments (Gause also worked with different species of protozoa and with yeasts, and got the same results) was that two species that share a niche cannot coexist. This has become known as Gause's (or, more correctly, Volterra's and Gause's) principle of 'competitive exclusion'.

The formulation and proof of competitive exclusion provided a definitive answer to the question whether two species with the same niche could stably coexist: they could not. The corollary of this was also clear: if species coexisted, they must have different niches, no matter how similar they appeared. Take the *Nicrophorus* beetles, for example. These bulky, black-and-red beetles occur all over the world, mostly in temperate climates. In all, almost 100 species are known. And, following Elton's advice, most naturalists that come across a member of this group will think to themselves: 'There goes the undertaker.' For *Nicrophorus* are better known as 'burying beetles', and they are the most amazing insects.

When burying beetles detect a recently deceased animal of a manageable size, say a mouse or a small bird, they will loosen the soil underneath to make it sink into the earth. If it died on a rocky or otherwise unsuitable surface, they will even drag their find for metres, until they reach a more suitable spot for interment. Usually a mated pair work in unison. They dig a slanted tunnel under the corpse and use their strong legs to press it into the tunnel, meanwhile trying to knead the body into a spherical shape. Once well underground, they create a 'crypt' around the cadaver and remove all hairs or feathers from it. They also chew a little crater at the top, which soon develops into a feeding bowl filled with liquefied, decaying flesh. Meanwhile, the female deposits her eggs in a passage that leads away from the crypt. Shortly after, the male disappears, while the female stays behind to wait for the eggs to hatch.

When this happens, the hatchling larvae will orient themselves toward the crypt, where the female is making crickety sounds with a stridulatory organ on her abdomen. And then one of the most advanced kinds of insect parental care takes place. The larvae gather around the feeding crater, where the female sits and regurgitates decaying carrion. In this smelly dungeon, the larvae continue being fed in a mouth-to-mouth fashion by the female until, a week or so later, the food supply is exhausted and they are ready to pupate.

German behavioural biologist Erna Pukowski of the Zoological Institute in Frankfurt, who discovered this remarkable behaviour and described it in a classic monograph in 1933, also studied competition between different *Nicrophorus* species. And 'competition' is here meant literally. Normally, several species of burying beetle occur in the same area. A single dead vole may thus attract a mixture of individuals of different species, which will fight each other over its possession, even while the cadaver is already buried and contains larvae. Pukowski describes, in evocative German that would lose much of its splendour upon translation, how the beetles fight and injure each other until one (or one pair) remains as Lord of the Corpse. As this usually belongs to the largest-bodied species, it begs the question: How do the smaller ones manage to eke out a living?

As Pukowski found out in the vicinity of Frankfurt (and this has been confirmed in other parts of Europe, North America, and Asia), the four or five *Nicrophorus* species that normally share an area usually avoid competition by having very distinct niches. Sure, they all feed on the same food source, but they do not all frequent the same sorts of habitats, and if they do, they work in shifts. In western Europe, the large, black *Nicrophorus humator* searches for carrion in spring, in humid forests. The equally large, red-and-black *N. investigator* does so in the late summer, when *N. humator* can no longer be seen. *N. vespilloides*, a small red-and-orange species, is the only species commonly found in dry forests. *N. vespillo*, of intermediate size, frequents open fields, as does *N. vestigator*. The latter, however, flies by day, whereas all other species are nocturnal.

So, even species that share the same, highly specialised, niche of 'undertaker' of small vertebrates have sufficient niche differences along other resource axes to avoid competition and to coexist peacefully. In the 1960s, ecologists, in particular Robert MacArthur, began to express an interest in the question: How similar can two species be before they can no longer coexist peacefully anymore?

The answer to this question of so-called limiting similarity turns out to depend on how stable the environment is. Together with theoretical ecologist Robert May, MacArthur in 1972 (the year he died) published a set of computer simulations in the *Proceedings of the National Academy of Sciences of the USA*. They found that in a randomly varying environment (varying in its food supply, or in some other resource), species needed some niche differences to coexist. Still, even if their niches are very similar, and they should competitively exclude each other, extinctions in nature may not be very quick. As we shall see in Chap. 7, one ecologist in particular, Stephen Hubbell, believes that species with identical niches can coexist in the real world for much longer than Gause's *Paramecium* experiments suggested. But first, we need to have a better look at niches.

4.3
A Moveable Niche

Indispensable as it is for ecological discourse, the term 'niche' should not be trifled with. For example, it does not always mean the same, because organisms do not always get to do what they are best at. If you plonk a vicar in the middle of an all-Buddhist community in the Thai heartland, he will either starve or have to find some alternative employment, which may require a major life-style change.

It is the same for species. For example, in Europe, two common species of sparrow coexist: the house sparrow (*Passer domesticus*) and the tree sparrow (*P. montanus*). The former is a typical anthropophile: it breeds in all kinds of human constructions and descends right down to the city centre and its subway stations, where it will hop around the pavement, feeding on discarded morsels of French fries and other fast food, ignoring the busy traffic. The latter, on the other hand, is much shier and can only be found in the countryside, where it lives in groves and forest edges and breeds in hollow trees. So the two have very different niches, one would say. Yet niches are not set in stone, as the band of tree sparrows frequenting my Happy Garden demonstrate.

Borneo does not have any native sparrows, but a troupe of tree sparrows arrived as stowaways on a Hong Kong steamer in the 1960s and have since multiplied to fill the entire island. And, with no resident house sparrows already filling the role of urban pavement-hopper, tree sparrows stepped up and showed that *P. montanus* can do the job just as well. They now crowd Borneo's cities' squares and alleys, dodging stray dogs and surviving on bits of fallen noodle, but they also live in the countryside near farms and patches of secondary forest.

4

The sparrow story shows that, just like the vicar who in a different life could be a Buddhist monk, a species has what ecologists call a 'fundamental niche', which can be quite broad. Its 'realised niche', however, is the usually narrower role it gets to play in real life. In Europe, where the tree sparrow has to cope with competition from its bolder relative the house sparrow, its realised niche is contracted. In Borneo, where house sparrows are absent, the tree sparrow gets to expand its niche to something approaching its fundamental niche.

Such niche shifts normally happen under changes in competition. One scientist who has studied such niche shifts in much detail is Jared Diamond of the University of California at Los Angeles. Physiologist, ecologist, taxonomist, historian, anthropologist, and best-selling non-fiction author, Diamond is such a multifaceted gem of academia that evolutionary biologist Mark Ridley has commented that 'Jared Diamond is really a committee'. In the 1960s, when Diamond was in his late twenties and dissatisfied with just being a successful physiologist, he embarked on a parallel career in southwest Pacific ornithology and took off on a long series of bird-watching expeditions to New Guinea and surrounding islands (see also Chap. 5).

Although his work resulted in a series of high-profile publications and culminated in the 2001 monograph *The Birds of Northern Melanesia*, which he wrote with the legendary Harvard University evolutionary biologist Ernst Mayr, many of his key observations were already written down earlier, such as in a 1970 paper in the *Proceedings of the National Academy of Sciences of the USA*. In it, he describes what happens to New Guinean birds' niches upon colonisation of a smaller, and ecologically less diverse island.

On Mount Menawa on New Guinea, for example, two species of the yellow, bespectacled 'white-eyes' occur. *Zosterops atrifrons* is found from 450- to 1,050-metres elevation, whereas the related *Z. fuscicapilla* lives from 1,050 to 1,800 metres. On the island of New Britain, which has only been colonised by *Z. atrifrons*, and not by its high-altitude competitor, *Z. atrifrons* has greedily appropriated the entire niche space from sea level to 1,650-metres altitude for itself.

But niche contraction is also possible, Diamond explains. *Z. lateralis*, another white-eye, is the only species of its kind in New Zealand, and its niche is broad, feeding as it does at all strata in the forest, from the understorey right up to the treetops. However, upon colonising the small island of Espiritu Santo, *Z. lateralis* encountered a second white-eye, *Z. flavifrons*, and was forced to restrict its foraging activities in trees to the lowest four metres or so.

Niche shifts do not just involve elevation or foraging sites. They can even affect what food a bird takes. In large islands such as New Guinea and New Britain, grassland usually supported both a species of *Lonchura* finch and a species of sylviid warbler (not always the same two species, but always one representative of each). When Diamond analysed the stomach contents of these birds, he found that the finches always only ate seeds, whereas the warblers only fed on insects. But on the smaller island of Karkar, grassland only harboured one species of *Lonchura* finch, which, upon stomach analysis, turned out to feed on both seeds and insects. Conversely, on Bagabag only sylviid warblers were found and these duly ate not only their customary insects, but lots of seeds as well.

Diamond even noticed that some species would have no qualms in doing away with very basic fundaments of their behaviour. In New Zealand, for example, which has no swallows or swifts, the flycatcher *Rhipidura fuliginosa*, which normally would catch insects in brief forays from a perch, has begun to behave like an honorary swallow. '[It] may be seen spinning in the air to catch insects for long times in the air-space over ponds, a habitat which one expects to find monopolized by swifts and swallows elsewhere and where this flycatcher's behavior appears ludicrous to anyone familiar with the same species in Australia,' Diamond wrote. In all, Diamond found that about half of all colonisations had resulted in a niche shift of some kind.

Although niches are plastic, they appear to be real and all-important in determining how an ecosystem is structured and how many species can take part in it. Yet, this apparent crucial role of niches may be misleading.

4.4
Paradox of the Plankton

Zoologists like Robert MacArthur and Jared Diamond might be forgiven for being overwhelmed by the ecological importance of niches. After all, one of the first things we notice about animals is how they are all different in what kinds of food they eat, and indeed food is one of the main axes along which animal niches are separated. But it is different for plants. They lack the fine-grained trophic differentiation that so characterises animals. All plants use sunlight for energy. All of them use carbon dioxide and a few additional mineral nutrients for 'food'; all of them need water. The 422,000 plant species on Earth compete for just a handful of resources. So how do plant niches differ? Or rather, how do plants avoid competing each other to death over access to those same few resources? Carbon dioxide levels in the air are almost the same everywhere, so carbon dioxide, the plants' staple, cannot be a niche axis. Sure, some plant species grow in wet spots, and other in dry spots, some are shade tolerant, others are sun-worshippers. But is that really sufficient to explain the great plant diversity that we see?

In Borneo, 3,000 species of tree occur, and many of these live side by side: as many as 1,200 species were found in half a square kilometre of forest in Lambir Hills (where that big canopy crane is). Grassland in temperate climates can support up to 40 species of herbs in a square metre, and in the amazing 'fynbos' (pronounced as 'fain-boss') of South Africa's Cape province, 247 plant species grow on an area of only one hectare. Are we really to believe that each of those species is adapted to a particular combination of wetness, shadiness, soil acidity, and soil fertility? It hardly seems possible.

And the mystery becomes more mysterious when we look at those tiny water plants known as phytoplankton. Evelyn Hutchinson, ecologist–limnologist par excellence was already baffled by their diversity. He knew that dozens, if not hundreds, of phytoplankton species coexist in most natural waters, and yet, under constant mixing of this soup, and with just light and three or four minerals in limited supply, there were very few ways in which each species could inhabit its own niche. 'In the phytoplankton we immediately meet the paradoxical situation of an enormously complicated association of phototrophic species all living together under conditions that do not seem to permit much niche specialization,' he wrote. Hutchinson called it the 'paradox of the plankton' in a 1961 paper by that title.

Since then, the conundrum has only deepened, with the DNA-based discovery of even greater diversities of phytoplankton than previously suspected. As we saw in Chap. 3, geneticists sequencing *16S* genes from unseen microorganisms in spoonfuls of seawater are finding that known diversities are a far cry from what is really out there. And phytoplankton is no different, especially when it comes to the tiniest photosynthesising bacteria.

With such a whale of a fundamental question waiting to be answered, one would expect that fynbos, rainforests, and other rich vegetations would be crawling with field ecologists trying to measure in what way plants define their niches, and limnologists doing the same with their paradoxical plankters. Surprisingly, though, by and large ecologists have been adopting a defeatist attitude in addressing the paradox of plankton and plant diversity. Plant ecologist Jonathan Silvertown of the Open University in Milton Keynes, UK, says that between 1990 and 2005 only 13 articles were published on plant niches. He thinks this lack of interest is partly because of the fads and taboos that science sometimes seems to suffer from: of late it simply has been unfashionable to study niches. But also, he explains, 'it is very difficult. If you fail to find niches you can't reject the idea of niche separation. It can be frustrating.' However, he says, leaps forward can be made 'if you happen by chance to hit upon the right niche axis.'

Silvertown hit upon a pair of such niche axes in the late 1990s, when he was studying plants in English meadows. In a meadow near the town of Cricklade, he identified all herbs in 641 one-square-metre quadrats, randomly strewn over the 44-hectare-meadow. In each of those, he also measured two characteristics having to do with soil moisture. First, the degree of soil waterlogging, defined as the number of weeks per year that water density in the soil was more than 90%, multiplied by how much more than 90% it was in those weeks. Second, the degree of soil drought, defined as the number of weeks per year that it was so dry that roots would shut down, multiplied by how much too dry it was in those weeks. One may expect that the two factors would actually be negatively correlated, that is, that quadrats that were often waterlogged in winter would rarely experience drought in summer and vice versa. But that was not the case: all possible combinations of waterloggedness and dryness could be encountered among the hundreds of quadrats.

Then, he plotted the mean distribution of 51 species of herbs along these two soil moisture axes. Surprisingly, he found that all species were clearly separated: they all had their own tolerances for waterlogging and drought. Moreover, there was a trade-off between the two: a species could be either tolerant for strong waterlogging or tolerant for severe drought, but not both. This meant that there were no 'all-purpose' plants that could live anywhere. Hence, each would stick to its preferred corner in this two-dimensional niche space. Just like those woodlice that sought out their own niche in a flat box with all combinations of heat/cold and humid/dry conditions.

Silvertown thinks 'very, very tiny differences' in such soil moisture characteristics will be extremely important in plant niches. And he is now trying to see whether it also applies to the famously diverse fynbos. No fewer than 9,000 different plant species coexist in this South African shrubland. As Silvertown points out, walking through fynbos is like being in an ecologist's nightmare. Take the heathers (which bear the scientific name of *Erica*), for example. In Europe, a handful of species of *Erica* occur. The fynbos has 800 species. How can there possibly be 800 different ways of being a heather? As Silvertown says, 'Flying from England to South Africa involves a time difference of only one hour, so there is no jet lag, but the biodiversity lag is a killer!' In September 2005, Silvertown and colleagues from South Africa and Switzerland began mapping quadrats in fynbos vegetation. And lo and behold: the fynbos species also separate out by soil tendencies for drought and waterlogging. 'Our preliminary but very exciting results suggest that we're finding the same thing as in the meadows,' he says. 'It's really extraordinary how these things segregate out.'

Soil moisture may be important in temperate climates, but in more climatically extreme regions, plant species appear to be suspended from other niche axes. In low-productivity arctic vegetations (like the highland tundra where the Oksanens studied food chains; see Chap. 2) other things might be more important – such as nitrogen. Ecologist Robert McKane of the US Environmental Protection Agency in Corvallis, Oregon, studied impoverished 'tussock tundra', barely subsisting on a layer of peat atop permaforst at 760-metres altitude in Alaska. With a net primary productivity of just 160 grams per square metre per year (see Chap. 2), McKane and his colleagues knew that nutrients, in particular nitrogen, were of the utmost importance to the handful of plants living there.

To test whether these species coexisted by different ways of nitrogen uptake, McKane selected 12 plots where the same five plant species grew. In each plot, he injected a radioactive form of one of the three main types of nitrogen: amino acid, ammonium, and nitrate. Among the plots he also alternated injection depth (three or eight centimetres deep) and either early (June) or late (August) nitrogen application. Then, he picked all the plants and, using the radioactivity as a label, checked which species had incorporated which kind of nitrogen. The results, published in *Nature* in 2002, were quite clear: Bigelow's sedge used mainly nitrate; cottongrass and low-bush cranberry went for amino acid and ammonium, though the cranberry obtained both forms of nitrogen earlier in the summer and at a shallower depth; Labrador tea and dwarf birch, finally, relied mostly on ammonium, but differed in the timing of the uptake.

So there is more to plant niches than meets the eye, in meadows, fynbos, tundra, and, yes, even in tropical rainforests. The seemingly random scattering of rainforest trees of different species is a law of the jungle that tropical botanists had never questioned since it was first noticed by Alfred Russel Wallace in the mid-nineteenth century. But a report in *Science* of 26 May 2000 showed that things are not that simple. After having censused over 1.22 million trees in six tropical rainforests, a team of 15 researchers from seven different countries, led by Richard Condit of the Smithsonian Tropical Research Institute in Washington, DC, USA, found that the jungle is no random place after all.

To study how rainforest trees are distributed, the researchers identified each tree thicker than one centimetre in plots of 50 hectares in forests in Asia and Central America. One plot alone, in the Lambir forest, required between 50 and 60 surveyors to work for more than two years. Identifying the youngest saplings was 'a bit tricky,' says co-author Hua Seng Lee of the Sarawak Forest Department in Kuching, Malaysia, but in the end he managed to get an ID on all 366,121 trees. Other team members did similar surveys in Thailand, Peninsular Malaysia, Sri Lanka, India, and Panama. To the botanists' surprise, the distribution maps they eventually drew up did not show the expected random scatter. Instead, almost each of the species was distributed in a clumpy fashion. Certain trees grew only in gullies, while some preferred only ridge tops. The vast scale of the new study had revealed a bird's-eye view on rainforest distribution patterns that had remained hidden during earlier, smaller studies.

And a paper in the *Journal of Ecology* in 2006 explains why rainforest trees may be clumped. American forest ecologists Gary Paoli, Lisa Curran, and Donald Zak from the University of Michigan, Ann Arbor, and Yale University, New Haven, looked at the distribution of 22 members of Southeast Asia's predominant tree family, the Dipterocarpaceae, in the Gunung Palung National Park in Indonesian Borneo. They found that the presence of most of the species was related to a particular level of particular soil nutrients, such as phosphorus, magnesium, and calcium. 'Niche processes structure ... tropical tree communities,' the authors conclude. And Silvertown agrees: 'this work is very relevant,' he says.

So there you have it: plants do have niches, and they can be pretty subtle. But what about plankton? Its habitat is just as waterlogged everywhere, and nutrient availability is about the same everywhere, too. Surely it can't have much niche differentiation? Well, prepare to be surprised.

'If you take a water sample from the ocean there'll be 50, 60, 70 species of plankton in each millilitre,' says aquatic microbiologist Jef Huisman of the University of Amsterdam, the Netherlands. These do not only include diatoms and green algae, but also, as has become clear over the past decade, huge amounts of the much smaller 'picoplankton': tiny photosynthetic cyanobacteria of just a few thousandths of a millimetre in size. Like land plants, picoplankton photosynthesise with the ubiquitous chlorophyll a, but they also use a broad palette of additional photopigments, each with its characteristic sensitivity for particular chunks of the light spectrum.

Take *Synechococcus* for example. Species of *Synechococcus* come in all the colours of the rainbow. Huisman and his graduate student Maayke Stomp, a plankton ecologist, studied two closely related species, provisionally named 'BS4' and 'BS5', scooped up from the Baltic Sea in 1996 and kept in culture ever since. BS4 is blue-green in colour, because it is chockfull of phycocyanin, a protein that harvests the energy from red light, while reflecting the remaining blue and yellow wavelengths. BS5, on the other hand, is bright red, owing to its use of phycoerythrin, which, conversely, absorbs green-yellow light, and returns the other colours.

Stomp and Huisman grew BS4 and BS5 together in laboratory beakers, and found that when the picoplankters were only given red light, BS5 became extinct. When they were only given green light, BS4 kicked the bucket. But in white light, both species happily coexisted for as long as the researchers kept their experiment running. Since then, Stomp has been taking a better look at the two species in their natural habitat in the Baltic Sea and has found that, indeed, the two species are completely mixed. This means that their ability to use different chunks of the light spectrum is probably all that allows them to live side by side.

And it is not just the visible part of the light spectrum that might be an important niche axis in plankton. Just four months after Huisman and Stomp published their *Synechococcus* studies in *Nature*, Michael Kühl of the University of Copenhagen, Denmark, and his colleagues reported in the same journal their discovery that another picoplankton species, *Acaryochloris marina*, can even use infrared light by employing yet another pigment, chlorophyll d. It hides in complete darkness underneath sea squirts, where there is abundant infrared light for its clorophyll d to absorb.

Huisman thinks that the colourful niche differentiation in picoplankton, and probably also in other colour-coded groups of plankton organisms, is 'very important' in solving at least part of the paradox of the plankton. He also thinks that still other parts may be explained by fine-grained studies such as the one carried out by marine microbiologists Zackary Johnson and Erik Zinser at the Massachusetts Institute of Technology, Cambridge, USA, and published in the 24 March 2006 issue of *Science*.

In the fall of 2003, they sailed on the research vessel *James Clark Ross* from the UK to the Falkland Islands, and twice daily dipped their sample apparatus in the Atlantic waters passing underneath, taking ten samples from different depths in the upper 200 metres. Using DNA barcoding, just like Dan Janzen and his skipper butterflies, they found that their samples contained at least six (and probably more) different 'species' among what they had assumed was all one and the same picoplankter, the extremely common *Prochlorococcus marinus*.

And when they then plotted the abundance of each of these six 'species' at different latitudes and different depths, they found that, contrary to Hutchinson's original expectation, these plankters are not all just being churned around in one 'soup'. Instead, some species live in the upper layers of the water, and some live deeper. Some prefer warm water, and some prefer cold. Some like water rich in nitrogen, whereas others thrive in nitrogen-deprived seas.

Does this mean the paradox is solved? Do the herbs of the fynbos, the brave plants of the tundra, the giant trees of the rainforest, and the Technicolor plankton of the oceans coexist in such diversities because each and every one of them has its own niche? Darwin thought so, when, in *On the Origin of Species*, he wrote the famous lines, 'When we look at the plants and bushes clothing an entangled bank, we are tempted to attribute their proportional numbers and kinds to what we call chance. But how false a view this is!'

But others maintain that niches are not the answer. They think that chance events play a pre-eminent role in nature, and Darwin's entangled bank is, in fact, clothed by Fortune. As we shall see in the next two chapters, this debate between niche-dissenters and chance-chancellors touches the core of modern ecology. No surprise then, that tempers have flared up repeatedly over the past decades. The first time in what ecologist Michael Rosenzweig calls the 'glory days of species diversity work', the 1960s and 1970s, as we shall see in Chaps. 5 and 6, which are all about islands. And the second time, as Chap. 7 will show, in the first decade of the twenty-first century, which appears set to go down in ecological historiography as the epoch of the great neutrality debate.

Neutral by Nature

5.1
This Fauna Ain't Big Enough for the Two of Us

Dusk is approaching rapidly as we make our way along the rickety jetty in the harbour of Semporna, a town on the east coast of Borneo. The fishermen have come back with their catch and the jetty is strewn with the best fish for the buyers of the local restaurants to take their first pick from: large tuna, coral trout, stingrays. Zigzagging between the piles of fish, we reach the Sabah Parks boat that is going to take us to the string of islands in the distance, which together form the Semporna Islands Park, exactly at the border between the Sulu Sea and the Sulawesi Sea. Seen from the shore, only the tallest islands are visible as a line of peaks and curves that resemble, according either to local lore or to the boatman's imagination, a sleeping princess (albeit a big-nosed one). But seen from the sky, it becomes clear that the string is actually a ring, which continues under water. For the main islands of the park form the rim of a caldera, the remains of an eruption that left behind a semicircular crater of fertile volcanic rock, which now, as we see while the boat skids over the choppy waves into the amphitheatre of imposing reddish cliffs, is clad in pristine emerald forest. Around it lie mangroves and coral reefs, and, built in the shallow water, a few clusters of palm-leaf thatched shacks on tall, thin stilts: the temporary homes of the Bajau Laut or 'sea gypsies', the only nomadic seafaring people left in the world.

It is hard to imagine what the scene must have been like when the volcano erupted two and a half million years ago. The event must have wiped out all life from the volcano slopes, leaving behind the charred and sterilised islands that are now called Bodgaya, Bohey Dulang, and Tetagan. Since then, nature has repossessed the islands. Its forest, a dry and low type of coastal forest and scrub made up of some 100 species of figs, cycads, screw pines, palms, and an eclectic mix of various tree families, has reassembled itself from whatever seeds the wind and waves would bring in. And the 50 or so bird species that have been recorded from the islands are an assemblage of strong flyers such as doves and thrushes, and typical birds of islands, such as the megapodes that build large nest mounds of sand and leaves.

The Loom of Life. M. Schilthuizen
Doi: 10.1007/978-3-540-68058-1_5, © Springer-Verlag Berlin Heidelberg 2008

Even less mobile organisms have managed to arrive in sufficient numbers to build up a rich fauna. Malaysian biologist Liew Thor Seng has been studying the land snails of the islands by staking out 20 metre by 20 metre plots all over the place and collecting all snail shells he could find. And he has come up with some interesting results. Not only did he find that the snail arrivals have come from both sides of the Sulu Sea (that is, the fauna is a mixture of Bornean and Philippine species), but also that there were some puzzling distribution patterns.

The three islands are different in size. Bodgaya, at eight square kilometres, is the largest. On its eastern flank lies Bohey Dulang, three square kilometres large and separated from it by a narrow channel of just 120 metres. And on Bodgaya's western side, also less than 200 metres away, lies the small (0.3 square kilometres) islet of Tetagan. You would think that islands so close to each other and with such similar vegetation would harbour the same kinds of snail. But Liew found otherwise.

The lanky field biologist pulls out a tray with rubber-banded stacks of plastic boxes, each filled with whole and broken shells of all sizes and shapes and in various shades of white, yellow, and brown. 'On the islands are four species of large ground-dwelling snails,' he says, pulling off one of the rubber bands and taking out a conical shell with pretty brown zigzag patterning and tiny brush-like hairs. Liew says it is a yet undetermined species of *Japonia* that occurs on all three islands. He takes out two other ones, a large disc-like species with a circular, trumpet-like aperture, and a very flat lens-shaped species with a few pretty brown spiral lines along the whorls and an aperture that is turned downward: *Pterocyclos trusanensis* and *Obba marginata*, hailing from Borneo and the Philippines, respectively. 'You cannot find these on the smallest island, Tetagan,' Liew says, putting back the tray. He then dashes to another rack of specimens and produces a tray with even larger plastic boxes and shows me a handful of specimens of a bulky brown species. 'This is *Hemiplecta humphreysiana*, also a Bornean species. It is very common on Bodgaya, but I cannot find it on Bohey Dulang or Tetagan. Very strange,' he says (Fig. 5.1).

Very strange indeed. One would expect that an eight and a three square kilometre, forested island with identical habitats, separated by a shallow and narrow bit of water that does not take much sea-level drop to connect the two, would share such a common species. But they do not. It is almost as if *Hemiplecta humphreysiana* is forbidden from living on Bohey Dulang. In fact, that is how Jared Diamond would describe it. In 1975 he wrote: 'Permissible combinations [of species] resist invaders that would transform them into forbidden combinations.' It is one of seven so-called assembly rules that he wrote down in a 102-page chapter in the book *Ecology and Evolution of Communities*.

As we saw in Chap. 4, Diamond was sitting on a wealth of data on bird distributions in the archipelagoes around New Guinea. And in the 1975 paper he had a good and hard look at what his data told him about combinations of related species. By examining the bird inventory lists that he had compiled for 50 islands, he discovered peculiar patterns. For instance, certain combinations of species never coexisted on the same island. And on a small island, two particular bird species might resist invasion by a particular third species, almost as if they had formed a pact, whereas on larger islands the three would live happily side by side.

In explaining these assembly rules, Diamond invoked niches and competition for resources. Let us imagine, for example, an island harbouring a range of species of fruit trees.

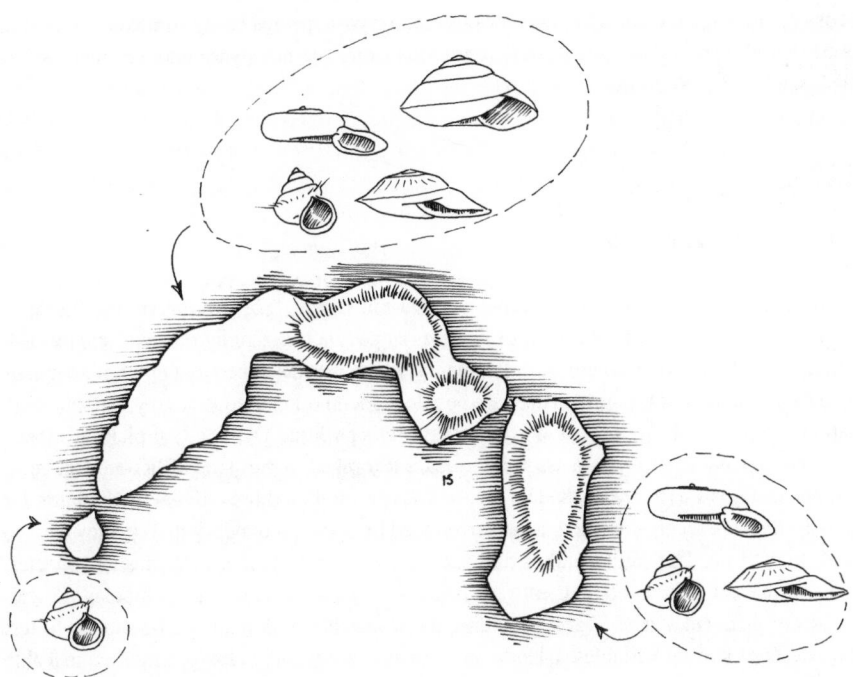

Fig. 5.1 Certain combinations of land snail species appear to be forbidden on some of the Semporna islands

In the region live three different species of fruit-eating pigeons. Let us call them Smallfruit Pigeon, Mediumfruit Pigeon, and Bigfruit Pigeon, for the size of fruits that each species is adapted to feeding upon. Now think of a small island with just one type of tree that produces medium-sized fruits. The trees on the island produce enough fruit for Mediumfruit Pigeon, and even though some fruits are a bit too small or a bit too large for Mediumfruit Pigeon, there is not enough food available on either extreme of the size range to sustain populations of Smallfruit Pigeon or Bigfruit Pigeon. Nearby is a somewhat larger island with a wider range of fruit trees, which produce enough food for either Mediumfruit Pigeon by itself or for both Smallfruit Pigeon and Bigfruit Pigeon, but not for all three, and also not for Mediumfruit Pigeon plus one of the other two. This means that if Smallfruit Pigeon invades first, Mediumfruit Pigeon can no longer invade, but Bigfruit Pigeon can. If Bigfruit Pigeon settles first, there is still enough niche space left for the invasion of Smallfruit Pigeon, but not of Mediumfruit Pigeon. Lastly, if Mediumfruit Pigeon gets there first, neither of the other two will be able to get in anymore. And things get more complicated when the range of species that vie for a place on the island gets wider and if the islands get bigger so that they can accommodate more (but not all) species. Eventually, Diamond said, the structure of ecosystems as they grow depends on the available niches and the resulting assembly rules would direct each step along the path toward a mature ecosystem. Hence, Diamond's view on the formation of ecosystems is known as 'niche-based assembly', and we will get back to it in Chap. 9. But niche-based assembly assumes that an aspiring ecosystem is surrounded by an overwhelming army of species ready to invade, and that, once settled, a species is there to stay, conditions which are not always met so nicely, as we shall see in the next section.

5.2
Far-Flung Flora and Fauna

In *Reflections on a Marine Venus*, Lawrence Durrell writes, 'Somewhere among the notebooks of Gideon I once found a list of diseases as yet unclassified by medical science, and among these there occurred the word Islomania, which was described as a rare but no means unknown affliction of the spirit. There are people, Gideon often used to say, by way of explanation, who find islands somehow irresistible.' Perhaps Jared Diamond, in picking islands to deduce his list of ecosystem assembly rules, succumbed to the same affliction. But community ecologists have always had an additional, less morbid, more rational predilection for islands: they are nicely confined areas surrounded by a sharp boundary that species need to cross to get to it. They are usually small and have a limited number of niches and species, so they are easily studied in their entirety. And it is often possible to find archipelagoes with islands of different sizes or ages, providing the researcher with natural laboratories to test the effects of several variables. Islands, in summary, are nature packaged into manageable chunks. They have the same appeal as the 'little worlds' we discussed in Chap. 1, but they are more complex, more real than those biotas in a bubble, yet not as frustratingly large and unwieldy as full-blown continental mainland ecosystems. And in fact, these aspects apply not just to conventional islands in the sea, but to all island-like environments. That is, as ecologist Michael Rosenzweig put it, 'self-contained regions whose species originate entirely by immigration from outside the region'. Besides water-ringed bits of land, such island-like regions also include lakes (which are really just the inverse of islands), isolated mountain tops, caves, patches of forest surrounded by corn fields, and many other insular fragments of life. So, the reader should bear in mind that a lot of biological phenomena that apply to conventional islands go just as well for all such other 'self-contained' habitats.

The first community ecologist *avant la lettre* who developed a penchant for islands was none other than Charles Darwin. In *On the Origin of Species*, he developed the idea that species are not independently created, but that they are related by evolutionary descent. One of his many arguments was that if species had been created by God, then why would the animals of, say, Australia, where the same range of climates, soils, and vegetation exists as in, for example, Africa, be so different? If God had created the dog then why had he divined to replace it by a marsupial wolf in Australia? Clearly dogs could survive perfectly well Down Under. His answer was, of course, that species evolve, by natural selection, from one another in one place and spread only as far as their powers of migration allow them. There are no dogs in Australia, simply because dogs never got there. And there are marsupial wolves because marsupials were the kind of animals available in Australia for evolution to mould into a dog-like species. Conversely, Darwin's evolutionary view on the distribution of life would also mean that a species on an island, if it is identical or very similar to another species on the continent, must have got there under its own steam, and was not created and placed there by the Hand of God. Hence, Darwin was under some obligation to show that many animals and plants actually do have greater powers of long-distance dispersal than one would think. And he went to great lengths to prove his point.

In the mid-1850s, long-distance dispersal was the buzzword at Down House, where Darwin lived. In April 1855, he read an article by one of his correspondents, botanist and clergyman Miles Joseph Berkeley, in the *Gardeners' Chronicle and Agricultural Gazette* on the survival of plant seeds in seawater. Spurred by this, Darwin started on a series of experiments of his own, soaking seeds of various species of plants in salt water and, after several months, checking if they would still germinate (and thus could, possibly, colonise far-flung islands). In a letter to Berkeley of 3 July 1855, he wrote:

> I report to you that the following have germinated: Beet, Rhubarb, Orache: after 65 days. … Oats, Canary Seeds, Capsicum: after 70 days. … Cress, Lettuce, Radish, Carrott: after 70 days, but only a few of each have come up. … Celery, Onion: after 85 days. – This last seems to me a very striking fact. My dear Sir / Yours very sincerely / Charles Darwin. [P.S.:] The Peas as you were so very kind to send me are growing splendidly.

In *On the Origin of Species* he tabulated the full set of results: 'To my surprise I found that out of 87 kinds, 64 germinated after an immersion of 28 days, and a few survived an immersion of 137 days.' But Darwin also noticed that fresh seeds sank quite quickly. So even if they survived, they would not be able to float on the ocean and wash ashore an uninhabited island. In *On the Origin of Species* he wrote: '[I]t occurred to me that floods might wash down plants or branches, and that these might be dried on the banks, and then by a fresh rise in the stream be washed into the sea. Hence I was led to dry stems and branches of 94 plants with ripe fruit, and to place them on sea water.' He found that the dried fruit and seeds of many of these (for example hazel, asparagus, and celery) would float for more than three months and then germinate with no problems. And after some calculations involving germination ratios and sea currents he concluded: '[We may] assume that the seeds of about 10/100 plants of a flora, after having been dried, could be floated across a space of sea 900 miles in width, and would then germinate.'

So plant colonisation of islands by seeds is possible, but will not be random. Only those plants that have seeds that float, either fresh or in a dried state, will make it over. And among those, not all species will be able to survive the seawater for long enough. The same applies to floating animals (Fig. 5.2). Canadian entomologist Stewart Peck of Carleton University in Ottawa has been studying the insect fauna of Darwin's favourite archipelago, the Galápagos Islands off Ecuador. When compared with that of the South American mainland, the Galápagos fauna is 'impoverished and unbalanced,' Peck wrote in a 1996 book chapter. For example, he says, although there are lots of beetles, flies, grasshoppers, butterflies, and moths, the islands lack other groups, such as, for example, stick insects. And even within the well-represented groups, there are curious near-absences. There are only nine species of butterfly, for example, against almost 8,000 in the rest of South-America. And there is only one species of bee. Presumably, Peck says, the islands have had to make do with what the wind and waves bring in. And some insects are just too feeble to survive wind and waves.

But Peck was not content with mere speculation. Like Darwin, he wanted to *know*. So in 1992, he rigged a boat with surface-sweeping nets and cruised the seas around the

Fig. 5.2 A grasshopper bent on accidental colonisation

islands to pick up any floating insects (what he called 'pleuston'). Trawling a total area of 130,000 square metres of sea surface, he gathered a total of 3,841 living or recently drowned insects. In spite of this respectable number, he reckons colonisation by pleuston may be a rare event. Like the soldiers at D-Day, the insects, upon arrival at a Galápagos beach, would need to run the gauntlet of hungry iguanas and birds. Instead, Peck thought dispersal through the air might be a more important means for small organisms to reach the islands. So off to his boat he went again, this time fixing a very large insect net to the mast. And after dragging his net through a volume of air measuring more than two thirds of a cubic kilometre, he had gathered no fewer than 18,251 insects and spiders.

A surprising number, perhaps (though 94% of those were taken up by just two families, whiteflies and fungus gnats), but not to those familiar with the work the Entomology Department of the Bishop Museum in Honolulu did in the late 1950s and 1960s. The department carried out a large study to investigate how easily oceanic islands such as Hawaii would be colonised by insects via the air. And like Peck, the researchers used boats to do so. For example, between May 1969 and February 1970, Eugene Holzapfel, a technician in the programme, made two cruises aboard the vessel *Argo*, one from Yokohama to Guam, the other from Tahiti to San Diego.

In front of (one imagines) the perplexed eyes of the other crew members, Holzapfel suspended ten 75-centimetre-diameter insect nets from ropes attached to the yardarms of the mainmast. He also employed three more insect-trapping methods, namely: (1) an electric suction trap, which used a blacklight to attract insects, which were then sucked into a container; (2) a moving net insect sampler, a mini-net attached to a sucker, through which a strip of sticky gauze ran automatically for two weeks, so that the time and position of the insects trapped could be recorded exactly; and (3) walking around the deck with an aspirator (a collecting bottle with a suction tube attached) and arresting every insect that would have the audacity to alight on the ship. As he describes in the 20 October 1978 issue of the journal *Pacific Insects*, a total of 1,114 insects, mites, and spiders were caught in his traps while the ship was at full sea, no doubt aided by some large storms that blew in from the continent on several occasions, and released a rain of tiny creatures as the winds subsided. But the catch showed very uneven proportions of kinds of insects and other arthropods: the vast majority were aphids, flies, and mites, whereas, for example, termites and grasshoppers were represented by just a single specimen each.

This study showed that insects did not just float in near-still air, wafted on by their lacy wings. More importantly, storms could kick up large numbers of small organisms and keep them in suspension until wind speeds had slowed down sufficiently for the propagules to fall down as a rain of so-called aeolian plankton. Just like stony particles are transported by rivers: turbulence in a fast-flowing mountain stream will keep silt, sand, and gravel in suspension until the inclination of the terrain and the river's flow speed are reduced in the lowlands and the heaviest gravel particles settle on the river bed. At even slower flow, the sand will also drop out of suspension, and finally only in the estuary do the waters stream with such a lazy motion that even the tiny-grained silt sinks to the muddy bottom. Similarly, strong winds could transport quite large animals and plant seeds in the sky over long distances, only to drop them once the wind speed has reduced.

Given this possibility, Holzapfel was not satisfied with catching insects only at sea level. In all probability, the greatest dispersal distances would be attained in the highest layers of the atmosphere, he figured. In fact, as he described in another 1978 paper in *Pacific Insects*, many anecdotal reports existed of this. Already in 1828, Commodore Perry had found aphids on the ice of the North Pole, 290 kilometres off Spitzbergen. And Charles Elton himself, when he was in Spitzbergen in the 1920s (see Chap. 2), had seen non-native black aphids and hover flies scattered over large icy areas, probably blown in from the Kola Peninsula in Norway, 1,300 kilometres away. Even Charles Lindbergh had reported collecting a mixture of pollen, volcanic ash, algae, diatoms, and insect parts on sticky slides held outside the cockpit while flying over the Atlantic at up to 3.7-kilometres altitude. So in addition to ships, the Hawaiian team turned to aircraft as well.

Improving on an earlier design, by 1966 the Bishop Museum team had rigged up an EC-121K aeroplane with a 5.5-metre-long aeolian plankton sampler. A ten-centimetre-wide inlet tube was fitted to the starboard side of the cockpit, giving way, while passing through the fuselage in an S-shaped curve, to a wider collecting chamber where all the incoming air was filtered for tiny particles, including organisms. In all, Holzapfel flew more than 1,000 hours with the machine at altitudes up to 3.2 kilometres, during which he sampled two cubic kilometres of air. Altogether, he collected 101 insects, of which most appeared to suffer little ill effect from floating at several kilometres' height, for, as he writes with a hint of regret, 'several live insects escaped from the collecting cup before they could be aspirated'. He also collected pieces of rock up to 5.4 millimetres by 2.5 millimetres, pollen grains, and spores and bits of fungus.

Just one bug per ten hours of flying seems a bit scanty. But we have to remember that there is an awful lot of air over the Pacific Ocean. Some 1.7 billion cubic kilometres, in fact, of which Holzapfel sampled two. This means that a cloud of about 85 billion insects may be looming permanently over the Pacific Ocean, and raining down on the oceanic islands that pop up here and there. And not just insects. The size of the mineral particles the machine picked up suggests that quite large seeds and snails could be carried by the air currents as well. Still, once again, the insects flying in the sky were a very unbalanced sample of the continental fauna: mostly small, light, insects with large wings. Two thirds were flies, the rest mostly small wasps and thrips, and a few beetles and moths. And four spiders, presumably lifted into the sky by the threads of silk that they release when they wish to disperse (a behaviour aptly known as ballooning).

Besides floating on water and in thin air, organisms have at least two more manners of dispersing that make one think of leisurely teenage summer holidays: rafting and hitch-hiking. Again, Darwin was one of the early experimenters to study these modes of dispersal: 'Drift timber is thrown up on most islands,' he wrote. He continued:

> [T]he natives of the coral-islands in the Pacific, procure stones for their tools, solely from the roots of drifted trees, these stones being a valuable royal tax. I find on examination, that when irregularly shaped stones are embedded in the roots of trees, small parcels of earth are very frequently enclosed in their interstices [and] out of one small portion of earth thus *completely* enclosed by wood in an oak about 50 years old, three dicotyledonous plants germinated: I am certain of the accuracy of this observation.

And many other nineteenth-century observations have confirmed Darwin's conviction that flotsam can be a very effective transporter. In his 1880 book *Island Life*, Alfred Russel Wallace writes that a large boa constrictor once floated 320 kilometres from Trinidad to the island of St. Vincent twisted round the trunk of a cedar tree 'and was so little injured by its voyage that it captured some sheep before it was killed.' And around the same time, the geologist Charles Lyell reported that not just individuals, but also entire ecosystems can raft across the oceans: in Southeast Asia, floating islands have been seen 'on which trees and shrubs were growing on a stratum of soil, which even formed a white beach round the margin of each raft.' No doubt lots of animals would be tucked away on them as well.

Besides being transported as stowaways, animals and plants can go places by hitch-hiking. As we shall see in Chap. 9, many invasive species have made their way to pastures new by hitching a ride on unsuspecting humans. But birds and other large animals can be very efficient carriers of smaller organisms too, even posthumously. Darwin, ever the intrepid experimenter, did several experiments along these lines. Peas and beans, he wrote, are killed by even a few days' immersion in seawater. But when he left a dead pigeon in seawater for 30 days and then took out the peas and beans that were still in its crop, to his surprise, they all germinated. He also realised that dispersal may begin two trophic layers beneath the surface. He wrote:

> Freshwater fish, I find, eat seeds of many land and water plants: fish are frequently devoured by birds, and thus the seeds might be transported from place to place. I forced many kinds of seeds into the stomachs of dead fish, and then gave their bodies to fishing-eagles, storks, and pelicans; these birds after an interval of many hours, either rejected the seeds in pellets or passed them in their excrement; and several of these seeds retained their power of germination.

And if that weren't enough Victorian blank-faced experimentation, Darwin also admits how, over a period of two months, he picked up bird poo in his garden and managed to grow plants from some of the seeds he picked out. A much larger study of the same unhesitating kind was carried out more recently. In the 1998 and 1999 migrating season, Spanish ornithologist Jordi Figuerola and his colleagues impinged on flocks of ducks and other birds in the Doñana wetlands in southern Spain, an important stopover for birds migrating between Europe and Africa. After a group of birds had left, the team went in to collect what the birds had left behind. Sifting through more than 400 droppings with fine-meshed sieves, they discovered that two thirds of the samples contained hundreds of live water flea eggs, bryozoan statoblasts, and even fragile water bug eggs. The microscopic resting stages must be regularly swallowed by birds mucking about in the lake bottom, and probably derive from their previous resting place, more than 1,300 kilometres to the north. So the inside of a duck's intestine may not win any prizes for passenger satisfaction, but for freshwater fauna, it is the long-haul carrier of choice.

Some animals even take the concept of hitch-hiking to its literal extreme. As Japanese entomologist Katsuya Ichinose discovered, when the winged virgin kings and queens of leaf-cutter ants get ready to leave their nests for their so-called nuptial flight, the *Attacobius* spiders that live in their nests cling on to their thoraxes to hitch a ride. In mid-air, they let go and float down to what may be a better place. And, in yet another creative attempt to show that birds are important transporters of small aquatic animals, Darwin described how he suspended a pair of duck feet (after first having removed their owner) in an aquarium with juvenile snails in it and he wrote: 'I found that numbers of the extremely minute and just hatched shells crawled on the feet, and clung to them so firmly that when taken out of the water they could not be jarred off, though at a somewhat more advanced age they would voluntarily drop off.'

Speaking of snails, we started out this islomanic foray with Liew Thor Seng and his volcanic islands full of snails. Contrary to what one might expect, there is hardly an island in the world that does not have a good representation of land snails. In fact, Wallace remarked that 'more species of land shells are found on the islands than on the continents'. And yet these animals must be doubly challenged in the dispersal department. Not only are they proverbially among the slowest moving animals known, but their abhorrence of salt would also mean that they cannot survive in seawater. So are all snail colonisations due to the improbable event of their accidentally attaching to duck's feet to cross great swathes of open ocean? Again, Darwin was the first who tried to answer this question by placing the large escargot *Helix pomatia* in seawater and discovering that, after having spent 20 days floating in it, it 'perfectly recovered'. Presumably, the air bubble inside the shell prevents salt water from creeping in.

And modern research confirms that snails, despite appearances, are unflinching mariners. Systematic zoologist Edmund Gittenberger of the National Museum of Natural History 'Naturalis' in Leiden, the Netherlands, has had a life-long passion for so-called Clausiliidae, a family of tree- and rock-dwelling snails with pretty spindle-shaped shells. Several endemic species from this family, all belonging to the genus *Balea*, have been discovered in the archipelago of Tristan da Cunha and Gough, literally in the middle of nowhere. The islands lie smack in the centre of the southern Atlantic Ocean, some 3,000 kilometres away from either the African or the South American coast, and some 8,500 kilometres from the European mainland, where all the other *Balea* species occur.

To find out how the snails got there, and making use of some specimens of the Tristan da Cunha/Gough species he had obtained from his colleague Richard Preece, Gittenberger asked his students Dick Groenenberg and Bas Kokshoorn to take a look at the snails' DNA barcodes. The team compared their barcodes with those of three European species and two species from the Azores and Madeira, also Atlantic islands but directly west of Europe. The evolutionary family tree they constructed on the basis of these DNA data showed that the *Balea* snails had indeed travelled far and wide. An ancestral species had first migrated to the Azores, split in two, one of which then made it all the way south to Tristan da Cunha and Gough. There, it gave rise to a whole bunch of endemic species. Meanwhile, one of the Azorean species migrated to Madeira (another 1,000-kilometre leg), and from there back again to the European homeland. Wading birds, says Gittenberger, regularly travel between all these islands, so he reckons that at some points in time they must have engaged in some serious *Balea* trafficking. No wonder they entitled their paper in the 26 January 2006 issue of *Nature* 'Molecular trails from hitch-hiking snails'.

5.3
Dying by Random Numbers

Jared Diamond's niche-based assembly rules assumed that islands are exposed to a rich and varied barrage of suitable species, more than willing to fill any vacant niches. But in the previous section we saw that this barrage may be a very uneven sample from the range of possible species. There might very well be stick-insect niches on the Galápagos, but these niches either remain unfilled, or are filled by other, underqualified species, simply because no stick insect ever survived the journey there. Similarly, the available freshwater species that manage to colonise the streams and pools on an island are limited to those that are particularly good at adhering to duck's feet. So, ecosystem assembly might just as well be modulated by the availability of suitable immigrants: it would, at least to some extent, be 'dispersal-based'. And even if a wide variety of immigrants announce themselves on the island's shores, there is no guarantee that each immigrant will also manage to establish a population. Far from it, as we shall see in this section.

First of all, it takes two to tango one's way into an island's incipient ecosystem. Wallace's castaway boa constrictor, despite finding its sheep-killing niche upon arrival, may only have been the ancestor of a snake population in its new home if it just happened to be a gravid female, or if a second individual of the opposite sex washed ashore within its lifetime. And population size is a crucial aspect of a species's success at invading anyway. Even if there are two, or 20, or 200 individuals, this is no guarantee of survival. Enter the stochastic behaviour of populations.

Consider *Mammuthus primigenius*. By 9,500 years ago, the woolly mammoth had become extinct from the European and Asian continent with its rapidly ameliorating climate, which did not leave any suitable tundra steppes for the hairy beasts to roam. But in one place, both the tundra and the mammoth survived. Eight-thousand-square-kilometre Wrangel Island, now a UNESCO World Heritage Site for its rich tundra vegetation, lies in the Arctic Ocean, 140 kilometres off the Siberian mainland. Having remained unglaciated throughout the last ice age, it has maintained a vegetation of 417 tundra plant species, twice the number normally found on a patch of Arctic land of that size. As far as mammals go, it has the dubious honour of sporting the highest density of polar bears, and, of course, lots of mammoth bones, tusks, skin, and even almost complete animals beautifully preserved in the permafrost.

It was those fresh-looking mammoth bones that attracted the attention of Russian researcher Sergei Vartanyan of the Wrangel Island State Reserve, in the early 1990s. Together with colleagues from the Russian Academy of Sciences, he did radiocarbon dating on the bones and tusks to determine their age. Their results showed that on Wrangel mammoths had hung on right up till classical times: their most recent sample, from an eight-centimetre-thick tusk from the bed of the lower Neozhydannaya River, proved to be just 3,730 years old, meaning it had walked around Wrangel not long before the first Egyptian dynasty.

But the interesting thing is not that this is so recent, but that the mammoth is not there anymore. Since 4,000 years ago, the climate and vegetation on Wrangel have not changed much, and also are not currently different from the climate and vegetation that existed at the time when large herds of mammoths still roamed the Eurasian continent. So why did they not survive on Wrangel? Unlike most other recent extinctions, humans are not to blame in this case, because they only settled on Wrangel in the twentieth century. The question will never be answered, of course, but it might just have been a matter of bad luck.

Mammoths are large animals, living on tough tundra grass, and anybody who has ever seen how its closest relative, the Indian elephant, makes short work with the 200 kilograms of food it needs per day can understand that the population on the 100 kilometre by 80 kilometre island can never have been very large. Add to that the low primary productivity at such a high latitude (see Chap. 2), and one can imagine that the island simply cannot have supported a very great number of mammoths. And this is where population stochasticity comes in. Populations are never completely stable, because the yearly number of births will never exactly equal that of deaths, and the difference will be positive or negative, and smaller or larger every year as well. Compare it with your yearly financial accounts. You win some, you lose some. Some years will be good, others bad, depending on a whole range of unpredictable factors. If the population (or your bank balance) is very large, this does not matter much. Unless there is an ongoing decline, small increases and decreases can be cushioned by the reserves. But when the population is very small, as it must have been on Wrangel, a few years of many deaths and no births could drive the population down to almost zero, just like a few big expenses can bring your bank account into the red if you do not have much in the way of reserves.

So the Wrangel mammoths, which colonised the island some 20,000 years ago (for that is the radiocarbon date attached to the oldest teeth found on the island), may simply have been victims of a small population size that happened to hit rock bottom at the time that recolonisation from the mainland was no longer possible. If it hadn't, mammoths might still have been with us today.

In the 1960s, Kenneth Crowell of Saint Lawrence University in Canton, USA, did an experiment on small islands off the coast of Maine to show such vagaries of demography in the field, using a somewhat smaller mammal than the mammoth. He sought out nine islets (ranging in size from 0.3 to six hectares) that were free of the regionally common *Peromyscus* and *Clethrionomys* mice, and released individuals of these rodents on them, with the numbers ranging between one and eight pairs of colonists. After following the populations for several years, he found that chances of successful establishment of the new mice were just 30% when he had only introduced a single pair, whereas between three and eight pairs boosted the success rate to almost 100%. Again, demographic stochasticity had wreaked havoc on the smallest clutches of colonists.

5

Data on stochastic dispersal and colonisation have been used as a warning flag to niche-assembly community ecologists who believe that ecosystems are assembled faithfully along lines of the available niches. Au contraire, dispersal-assemblists think that niche assembly may just be a pipe dream. Even if the niches are there, they say, the unpredictability of dispersal and population boom and bust upon colonisation will mean that islands' ecosystems may be assembled from castaway species in the same way that a beachcomber builds his shack. With a chunk of surfboard for a door, a discarded fishing net for a window, and a block of Styrofoam for a doorstep, none of the parts of the building has been made from materials designed for that particular niche. But fall to pieces it does not.

In Splendid Isolation

6

6.1
A Bug's Life

The first time I met Edward O. Wilson was in an Amsterdam hotel. Slumped in a sofa in the lobby, he allows himself, somewhat reluctantly, to be interviewed. Reluctantly, because, he says, he is very tired. He has just flown in from Harvard University, where he is in the middle of teaching a major course, to be awarded an honorary membership of the Netherlands Entomological Society. He has also just delivered a long lecture on ants. And as if the éminence grise of myrmecology needs any more excuses for making a somewhat fatigued impression after all that, he adds that he has just put the finishing touches to the definitive monograph of the American species of the ant genus *Pheidole*: 606 species, more than half of which Wilson himself discovered, illustrated with over 5,000 line drawings of his own hand. Anyway, he says, fixing me with his one good eye and an off-centre smile, 'Why don't you just ask me your first question, and then we'll see when I collapse.'

I hesitate. Born in 1929, Edward Osborne Wilson has had a series of interconnected careers, each of which highly successful in its own right. World-class entomological taxonomist, leading rainforest ecologist, sociobiologist, activist and lobbyist for biodiversity conservation, Harvard University professor for four decades, winner of the prestigious Crafoord Prize, the National Medal of Science, two-time winner of the Pulitzer prize (for his books *On Human Nature* and *The Ants*). ... Not knowing where to start, I stupidly ask: 'What first got you started on ants?' Despite the fatigue, and despite the fact that hundreds of people before me must have asked him this obvious question, a twinkle appears in Wilson's left eye, he sits up a bit straighter, and says: 'When I was nine years old, I had what we call in America, a bug period. All children have a bug period – and I never grew out of mine.'

It is one of the most-quoted lines from his 1994 biography *Naturalist*, on the cover of which Wilson appears while peering through a hand lens at what must be a specimen of *Camponotus gigas*, one of the world's largest ant species. 'I have vision only in one eye,' Wilson says, referring to the freak childhood accident when, while fishing, he yanked his fishing rod too hard and a fish with long spines on its fins flew straight into his face and perforated his right eye. 'But it is a very sharp vision – sharper than average. So it seemed natural that I study insects.' Wilson, who grew up a precocious introverted boy in Alabama and spent a large part of his childhood in solitary outdoor pleasures (ranging from netting butterflies to wrangling snakes), first thought he'd study flies. But at the time, right after the Second World War, the supply of insect pins, which mostly came from Eastern Europe, had dried up, and Wilson was forced to study a group of insects that can be preserved in vials of alcohol, rather than pinned and dried. So ants it was to be. And he has never regretted it since.

Already armed with a wealth of entomological knowledge, he made his way, via the University of Alabama and the University of Tennessee, to Harvard University's graduate programme, where he had access to the largest collection of ant specimens in the world. And in 1953, when he joined a Harvard University graduate course in tropical botany in Cuba, he finally made it to the tropics – the eventual destiny of all entomologists for hosting the pinnacle of insect abundance, diversity, and exuberance. He was hooked. The next year, he had the opportunity to collect ants on a ten-month solitary expedition to the islands of the South Pacific, and, despite the fact that he had just got engaged, did not waver for long. As his plane touched down among the emerald archipelago of Fiji, his first destination, he immediately realised that the South Pacific was to be the natural laboratory he had been looking for. As he writes in *Naturalist*, willy-nilly he began expanding from ant systematics to broader and deeper interests in ecology: '[I]f well equipped, [a field naturalist] can gather information swiftly while continuously thinking, every working hour, What patterns do the data form? What is the meaning of the patterns? What is the question they answer? What is the story I can tell?'

And as he collected ants in Fiji, New Caledonia, the New Hebrides, New Guinea, Australia, and all the smaller and larger islands in these areas that he could reach, the story that he was about to tell was forming in his mind. After returning to Harvard University and obtaining an assistant professorship there shortly after, Wilson spent several years sorting, identifying, and describing the ants from his tropical field trips, and analysing what the data meant. In a 1961 article in *The American Naturalist*, he laid it all down. In this paper, Wilson combined all his data on the ponerine and cerapachyine ants from Melanesia and the Moluccas – ponerines and cerapachyines being two particularly well-studied ant subfamilies. Centre stage took a graph in which Wilson plotted the numbers of species of these two groups of ants against the size of each of the 26 islands on which he had collected them. Or rather, he plotted the logarithms, meaning that with every equidistant tick on the two axes, species number and area were multiplied by ten. The result was a cluster of dots roughly scattered along a straight line, ranging from the tiny island of Ternate (25 square kilometres, five species) in the bottom left-hand corner to the second-largest island of the world, New Guinea (800,000 square kilometres, some 200 species) in the top-right corner. It was the start of what was to be Wilson's greatest contribution to ecology: the theory of island biogeography.

Not that nobody had noticed before the linear relationship between the logarithms of species number and area size. Wilson himself credited his advisor Philip Darlington, who, in his 1957 book *Zoogeography*, had written that in the reptiles and amphibians of the islands of the West Indies, with each tenfold increase in island area, the number of species doubles. But already in the early 1920s, botanist Olof Arrhenius reported that he had discovered that the number of species of plants in small bits of Sweden followed the simple equation $S = cA^z$, in which S is the total number of species in an area, A is the size of that area, and c and z are constants, which does not mean that they can never change, but it means that they are fixed numbers within a particular system of species and areas. And the Arrhenius equation produces a straight line in a log–log plot, of which the inclination (the slope) is set by z. So what was new?

Well, first of all, as Wilson eventually was to discover, the species–area relationship is not really one relationship. It is composed of at least three separate phenomena. The first is a simple consequence of sampling. In larger areas, there is space for more individuals. If we stake out a ten centimetre by ten centimetre patch of turf, we can count and identify every individual plant. And there can never be more species in that patch than there are plants. Obviously, when we then demarcate a 100 centimetre by 100 centimetre plot and again identify all the plants, there will be 100 times as many individual plants, among which in most cases there will be more species than in the ten centimetre by ten centimetre plot. It is not hard to find out what kind of graph you get under this situation. Thirty years ago, theoretical biologist Robert May (whom you may remember from Chap. 3) did it for us. He let his computer generate a virtual vegetation made up of a set number of species that differed in commonness but were otherwise spread out evenly, and then took larger and larger samples from this flora. The species–area curve he got showed a straight line with only a slight inclination: the z value (which tells us how steeply species number rises with area increase) was only about 0.05, whereas graphs from real data usually have z values above 0.15. So on top of this simple sampling effect, real biological phenomena are stacked.

The first of these is that the larger the area we investigate, the more habitats we are likely to be sampling. And as most species have specific niches in preferred habitats, this will increase the number of species we find. As we shall see in Chap. 9, this is indeed the explanation for the species–area relationship on the mainland, like in Arrhenius plots of Swedish vegetation, for example. But Wilson's ant data were not from different areas staked out on the mainland. They were from real islands with a fixed boundary. And, as Wilson began to suspect, the processes responsible for the island species–area relationship called for a radically different explanation. But he lacked the mathematical insight to find it. He needed a friend who understood both field ecology and algebraic formulas.

6.2
The Coffee Table of Science

When Wilson was working on his Melanesian ant papers, it was not an easy time for him. As the only ecologist in Harvard University's Biological Laboratories, he found himself surrounded by geneticists, biochemists, and microbiologists, who were openly hostile toward ecologists and other 'old-fashioned' breeds of biologist. One of them, James Watson, of DNA fame, told him condescendingly: 'anyone who would hire an ecologist is out of his mind.' As Wilson wrote in *Naturalist*: 'I was physically trapped in the Biological Laboratories among the molecular and cellular biologists, who seemed to be multiplying like the *E. coli* … on which their finest work had come to be based.' Feeling isolated within his own department, Wilson began to look around for like-minded souls elsewhere.

In 1961, during a seminar break at the meeting of the American Association for the Advancement of Science, Wilson's University of Michigan colleague Larry Slobodkin, with whom he was planning to write a textbook on population biology, told him that there was someone he had to meet – a potential third author for the book. 'It's Robert MacArthur,' Slobodkin said. 'And he's a real theoretician – very bright.' A few years earlier, MacArthur had finished his PhD on warbler niches (see Chap. 4). After that, he had spent some time doing theoretical work on niche structure, including developing his famous 'broken stick model', which will make its appearance in Chap. 7. But by 1961, having recently been appointed assistant professor at the University of Pennsylvania, MacArthur was ready for a new challenge. Though perhaps not on that particular day. He was, as Wilson recalls: 'a thin, diffident young man who spoke with an American accent but in the British style of cautious understatement. … The book is an attractive idea, he said. We should explore it further. He had a headache. He wanted to go home. We shook hands, and he left.'

It was not a very promising beginning for a collaboration that was to culminate in a milestone of twentieth-century biology. MacArthur went back to Pennsylvania, Wilson went on a field trip to Trinidad, and it was almost a year before the two met again, during a one-day meeting at Harvard University where they discussed the future of their planned book with Slobodkin. But then, despite the fact that MacArthur was an addition to the original Wilson–Slobodkin team, Wilson hit it off with MacArthur more than he had with Slobodkin. On the surface, Wilson seemed to be everything MacArthur was not: the former a classical field biologist with maths anxiety, the latter a thinker whose greatest work was done while scribbling graphs and profusions of algebraic formulas. But the differences did not run deep. 'I felt a strong personal attraction to MacArthur,' Wilson says. Like himself, MacArthur was an outdoor person, infatuated not with insects but with birds. They shared a passion for 'discovering beautiful true-life patterns'. And MacArthur also loved the trop-ics. 'We became close friends,' Wilson writes, recalling MacArthur's pleasant demeanour: '[H]e met you with a disarming smile and widening of eyes. He spoke with a thin baritone voice in complete sentences and paragraphs, signaling his more important utterances by tilting his head slightly upward and swallowing.' Meanwhile, relationships between Slobodkin and MacArthur soured because the former became less and less enthused about the merits of theoretical ecology. Eventually, Slobodkin pulled out of the book project, and the historic MacArthur–Wilson partnership was born.

Wilson sent MacArthur his graphs of ant diversities on islands; he brushed up on his calculus to be able to follow MacArthur's high-brow theoretical ecology. They sat by MacArthur's fireplace, papers and notes fanned out before them on the coffee table. Wilson infected MacArthur with his islomania, arguing that island biogeography could be nurtured from a collection of anecdotes into a mature scientific theory, provided somebody (nudge) could do the maths. He showed him his lists of ponerine and cerapachyine ants, which demonstrated, Wilson thought, that when a species settles on a new island, it tends to eliminate an earlier species. MacArthur reciprocated with his knowledge of bird species on Indonesian islands. Wilson cautiously talked to MacArthur about his notion that species numbers on an island might somehow be held in a balance. Ah, MacArthur said, his mathematical mind piqued, an equilibrium!

On 21 April 1962, MacArthur sent Wilson a letter, hastily scribbled as he was about to set off on a trip, in which he wrote, 'I did want to tell you my ideas about a model of number of species so that you can improve it while I am away.' And underneath it he had drawn the first version of a now-famous graph with two lines, one sloping downward, the other curving upward. Where the two lines crossed, MacArthur had drawn a dashed vertical line and written 'equilibrium no. of species' where it hit the x-axis.

In almost unaltered form, this graph still makes standard appearances in ecology textbooks. It represents the trajectories of immigration and extinction on an island. The downsloping curve is immigration of new species. When a vacant island appears, species begin to colonise it, using the haphazard modes at their disposal (see chap. 5). The rate of new immigrants appearing declines over time (that is why the line slopes downward) for the simple reason that the more species that are already there, the fewer *new* ones will be among the immigrants. At the same time, extinction goes up, mostly because as more species are there, more are also available to become extinct, but also because there will be increased competition for space and resources. Over time, with the rate of new immigrants declining, and the rate of extinction increasing, the number of species on the island will build up more and more slowly, until a moment is reached when the number of new immigrant species arriving each year equals the number of species becoming extinct in that year. At that time, a species equilibrium is reached. And from then on, the number of species present on the island stays more or less constant, although their exact identities are continually changing, because immigration and extinction continue to take place unabated.

The one-page letter of MacArthur held the key to understanding species diversity on an island as a so-called dynamic equilibrium (where the kinds of species present change steadily, but the gross number of species remains the same). With this model in hand, it became obvious what would happen if an island were to get smaller. With less space, hence smaller populations (think of those mammoths on Wrangel from Chap. 5), the extinction curve would be raised, and the crossing point moved to the left: toward a lower species equilibrium. Wilson called this the area effect. And MacArthur's mathematical models showed that under these conditions the species equilibrium would indeed relate to the island size as the $S = cA^z$ equation of Arrhenius! And what about distance? An island close to the mainland would 'catch' more immigrants than an equal-sized island out in the ocean, so its immigration curve would be raised, while extinction would not be affected. The result would be that the point where the two lines cross would be moved to the right, leading to a higher species equilibrium; the so-called distance effect. Thus, the theory predicted that far-away islands would hold fewer species than islands of the same size close to a mainland that could act as a source of immigrants.

MacArthur and Wilson knew they were on to something good. A theory that explained and predicted the numbers of species on islands, composed of just two processes, immigration and extinction, both of which could be framed mathematically. They quickly drew up their main findings, and published them as an article in the December 1963 issue of *Evolution*. It did not attract much attention. Over the next few years, however, the duo began preparing a book on the same subject, expanding and refining the mathematical models. They gathered more data from island floras and faunas. They showed that the area effect held, leading to z values that typically lay between 0.20 and 0.35, and that the greater the degree of isolation, the higher the z value (and, thus, the steeper the curve for the species–area relationship). And they explored the implications of their theory for as many nooks and crannies of ecology as possible. The book appeared in 1967 as *The Theory of Island Biogeography* and was an instant classic. Still, theory was one thing, proof was another. To confirm that the species–area relationship really set itself up as a result of the processes identified by MacArthur and Wilson, a whole new field of ecology, a kind of 'experimental island bio-geography' had to emerge. And emerge it did, quite literally.

6.3
Earth Sinks in the Sea

It was the morning of 14 November 1963, and Robert M. MacArthur and Edward O. Wilson were, one imagines, in eager anticipation to see their island biogeography paper in print, scheduled for the December issue of *Evolution*. On the other side of the Atlantic, however, some 40 kilometres south of Iceland, the crew of the fishing boat *Isleifur II* were as far removed from caring about island biogeography as possible. Or were they? They had just paid out their lines, when the cook, who was on watch, suddenly drew attention to a cloud of black smoke rising from the surface of the sea, not far astern. When the skip-per steered the boat closer, the seamen noticed that the waters were getting rougher and warmer and that particles of rock appeared to be thrown up in the smoke. As the skipper realised with a shudder, the phenomenon was nothing less than the eruption of a submarine volcano. Soon, there was no more doubt: the smoke and steam column had risen high up into the sky, drawing bolts of lightning from the clouds, while showers of ash and pumice were constantly being spewed out from underneath the water.

The next day, it became clear to the Icelandic authorities that a small expansion of their territory was afoot. From the bottom of the sea, 130 metres below the surface, a volcanic cone had risen which, over the following six months, built up and cooled down to form a brand-new island complete with hills, lava flows, cliffs, and pumice-boulder-strewn beaches. It measured 1.6 kilometres by 2.0 kilometres, and reached a height of 174 metres above sea level. It was christened Surtsey, or Surtur's island, after Surtur the Black, the fire giant of Norse mythology of whom is sung in the tenth-century poem *Völuspá*: 'Surtur fares from the South / With the scourge of branches / The sun turns black / Earth sinks in the sea / The hot stars down / From heaven are whirled / Fierce grows the steam / And the life-feeding flame / Till fire leaps high / About Heaven itself.'

Aptly named, and cooled down sufficiently for life to settle, the island soon attracted Icelandic and foreign biologists, who realised that here was a unique chance to work in a natural laboratory of island biogeography. A virgin island ready to be settled by a haphaz-ard collection of immigrants that eventually would form an ecosystem, and modern sci-ence was there to watch it all happen. The Surtsey Research Society was founded, which strictly controlled entry of scientists to the island, making sure that no plants or animals were brought there by other than natural means. Foremost among them was botanist Sturla Fridriksson, who has been studying the arrival and spread of plants on Surtsey since the very start up till the present day.

The first time Fridriksson set foot on the barely cooled down shore of Surtsey, on 14 May 1964, he found among the flotsam, as Darwin had predicted, some seeds and living bits of coastal plants, such as lyme grass (*Elymus arenarius*) and sea mayweed (*Matricaria maritima*), but no living plant had yet dared root among the black volcanic rocks. The island was still a very hostile place. Fridriksson describes how the scientists had to walk fast to prevent the soles of their rubber boots from melting. 'And if a rucksack was carelessly left behind it might start to melt in the uprush of hot air.' But the next year, conditions had ameliorated, and plant colonisation had taken place, albeit on a very hesitant scale: all told, Fridriksson found 23 individuals of the arctic sea rocket, *Cakile arctica*, and nothing else. Still, he had been an eyewitness of an island-biogeographic event: 'When walking along the coast of the virgin island, it was an amazing sight to see the first leaves of a sprouting seedling like a small green star on the black basaltic sand,' he wrote in his 1975 book *Surtsey*.

The ensuing years brought more and more green colonists. *Cakile arctica* held on for three years, after that reappearing and disappearing again five more times. In 1966 it was joined by the lyme grass, which barely survived in vanishingly small numbers for 20 years, until in the mid-1980s its numbers suddenly sky-rocketed. Sea mayweed arrived in 1967, disappeared again the next year, and came back for good in 1972. The same year saw the first individuals of sea sandwort, *Honkenya peploides*, which by the early 1980s was present in its hundreds of thousands. And so the vegetation built up. One species in 1965, two in 1966, four in the years 1967–1970, then six in 1971, reaching 11 in 1972. But from then on for 15 years the number of species hovered around 12 or so. Apparently, an equilibrium had been reached. And, as predicted by MacArthur and Wilson, it was a dynamic equilibrium: in 1972, common chickweed became extinct, only to be replaced the following year by red fescue. And in the early 1980s, fragile fern was lost, but smooth meadowgrass was gained. Of the 11 species of plant that were present in both 1972 and 1984, only seven were the same.

A time window of just 20 years or so is of course short by comparison with the aeons that are normally involved in the geological roller coaster of island ecosystem assembly, maturation, and turnover. But fortunately, palaeontologists have also picked up on the relevance of their work for bolstering the theory of island biogeography. Sediments from the atoll of Aldabra in the Indian Ocean, for example, show a succession of sediments that were laid down in a marine environment (with fossil corals and sea shells in them) and terrestrial sediments (with giant tortoises and land snail shells). A study by John Taylor and co-workers from the Natural History Museum in London on the land snail fossils showed that the atoll has been completely submerged at least two times over the past few hundred thousand years. Each time the island re-emerged, a dynamic equilibrium had to be re-established in the snail fauna. And as expected from a dynamic equilibrium, which is to a large extent a random game (it cannot be predicted which species will happen to be blown to the island, nor which ones will survive and which ones won't), the London researchers found that each time the re-established fauna was a different one.

But hang on – then what about the assembly rules we talked about in Chap. 4? Hadn't Jared Diamond said that island ecosystems are assembled along strict rules dictating which species can and which cannot share the same habitat? So shouldn't that mean that species compositions cannot change by the whims of MacArthurian–Wilsonian processes? Well, yes.

And MacArthur and Wilson did not dispute this. The kinds and numbers of species that can partake in any equilibrium, dynamic or otherwise, depend to a certain extent on the niches available on an island. For example, in the mid-1980s, when plant diversity at Surtsey was stuck at 11 species, a breeding colony of herring and lesser black-backed gulls began to form on the southern tip of Surtsey. Soon, the plant diversity began to increase, partly because new, high-nutrient niches became available in and around the colony. The dynamic balance that had been maintained at around 11 species since the early 1970s, shot up to almost 50 species during the 1990s. So the numbers of available niches are important for the shape of the extinction curve. If there are more niches, fewer species will become extinct, so the extinction curve will be lower, leading to a species equilibrium that is pushed toward the higher end.

But the randomness of immigration and demographic collapses mean that in reality stochastic events may be even more important than the kinds and numbers of available niches. Moreover, those niches are flexible, as Diamond himself has pointed out. And some species may have the same niche, so they are redundant, replaceable. *And* competition may not always be as strong. In 1978, Daniel Simberloff, a former PhD student of Wilson's (see Sect. 6.4), wrote a paper in *The American Naturalist* in which he showed that Diamond's bird data were actually too limited to say anything about assembly rules, since with only 50 islands of various sizes, there really were not enough islands of the same size to get any patterns that would show fauna assembly was based on species' niches. In other words, Simberloff was saying, to really get a handle on island biogeography, the field has to go experimental. Wise words from somebody who was in the know. For if anybody knew about experimental island biogeography, it was Dan Simberloff.

6.4
Chainsaws and Methyl Bromide

History does not record whether MacArthur and Wilson at the time of writing their 1967 book were aware of the possibilities Surtsey offered. They do not mention the island in it. They do dwell at length, however, on Krakatau, the Indonesian island that was fragmented and cauterised by a volcanic eruption in 1889, the recolonisation of which has been recorded, albeit somewhat more anecdotally than for Surtsey, by biologists since the early twentieth century. Either way, new volcanic islands that were born once a century did not offer what Wilson required for a true natural laboratory of island biogeography. They were too rare, too big, too unreplicated. What Wilson set out to find, shortly after MacArthur and he had published their *Evolution* paper, was a collection of miniature-Surtseys that could be emptied and refilled by colonisation at will.

As Wilson recalls, he spent a long time poring over maps of the North American coastline, looking for archipelagoes where such work could be done (his earlier plans of making the South Pacific his field laboratory had to be re-evaluated now that he had a family and a full-time teaching job at Harvard University). 'How in the world could I explore an island wilderness while staying close to home? And if I found such a place, how could I turn it into a laboratory?' he wondered desperately. And then, the solution came to him: '*miniaturize* the system!' As soon as he had made this decision, his eye rested on the sprinkling of land at the very tip of the Florida peninsula: the myriads of mangrove islands among the Florida Keys. Rather than working with Surtsey-sized islands, he would seek out tiny islands of square metres, rather than kilometres. Sure, there would be no mammals or birds on those islands, but island biogeography could just as easily be done with smaller creatures: spiders, beetles, bugs, millipedes… *ants*! Wilson had come back to his roots.

The following summer, he spent many weeks in a small boat inside the 150-kilometre-long labyrinth of small mangrove keys between Key Largo and Key West. The field naturalist in him was reawakened: 'My spirits soared. I was back where I was meant to be!' Despite the rumble of the nearby US Route 1, he was as happy as he had been in Melanesia. 'The swamps and islets were pristine, a virgin wilderness. Mangrove wood has little commercial value. No one but a naturalist or escaped convict would choose to traverse the gluelike mudflats and climb through the tangled prop roots and trunks of the mangrove trees. So I had it all to myself: one more time, a world I knew so well, more complex and beautiful than anything contrived by human enterprise.'

But Wilson did not forget he had an ulterior motive above mere kinaesthetic pleasure. He quickly saw that the islets were indeed ideal for his purpose. The smallest ones were just clumps of a few trees, but even they hosted a complete ecosystem of dozens of species of small invertebrates and the occasional lizard. A dedicated field biologist could collect and identify every animal in a matter of days. Still, it was not yet clear to Wilson how he could do real experimental work. For that, it would be necessary to completely empty islets of all animal life, and watch them be recolonised over time.

Wilson was still pondering this quandary when he was back at Harvard University after the 1965 summer break. Then, into his office stepped a young graduate student looking for a PhD project. It was Daniel Simberloff. Wilson looked him up and down and figured he would be perfect for the Florida project. His hawkish features and a solid muscular body suggested that he could handle the field work. There was just one snag: Simberloff had majored in mathematics, and while he had decided to move into biology, he had as yet little field experience. But that proved not to be a problem. With some tutoring by Wilson, Simberloff soon learned to recognise all the major arthropod groups. At the same time, the brilliant, though somewhat drastic, solution to the island-emptying problem came to Wilson: they would select tiny islands, take full censuses of the animal life, and then kill everything with a quick-acting pesticide that would not persist and would not harm the plant life. Then, they would observe how the islands were repopulated. Perhaps surprisingly, the National Parks Service agreed to the audacious plan, and it was decided that while Simberloff busied himself with selecting islands, Wilson would persuade a pest control company to take on an unorthodox assignment.

The latter proved easier than expected. After having the phone put down on him twice, Wilson hit upon the director of a pest control company in Miami, National Exterminators, who thought he could do the job. Meanwhile, Simberloff had selected nine suitable islands, all of which were about 15 metres in diameter, but differed in their distance to the mainland: the nearest one was just two metres away, the furthest one was more than a kilometre out in the sea. In the summer of 1966, they started the work in earnest. First, Simberloff and Wilson collected and identified all the arthropods they could find on each of the islands. There were spiders, insects, millipedes, centipedes, scorpions, pseudoscorpions, and isopods. To be on the safe side, they excluded strong flying insects that were probably just roaming the area and alighting briefly on an island, such as butterflies, dragonflies, and large cicadas. On all islands, this left a resident fauna of between 20 and 43 species, and there was, as predicted by the distance effect, a strong correlation between species number and distance to the mainland. After censusing, they kept two islands as controls: these were left as they were. On the remaining seven islands, National Exterminators was set loose to do what Wilson and Simberloff euphemistically called 'defaunation'.

The exterminators treated the islands as they did Miami homes that needed fumigating. They erected scaffolding on the island, covered it all in a tent of black plastic, and pumped methyl bromide in. After two hours, the tent was removed and, with all animal life belly-up, the defaunation was complete. Then, the tedious process started of paying regular visits to see whether recolonisation would happen, and, more importantly, by which and by how many species. This was Simberloff's task, though Wilson came down from Harvard University to join him as often as possible. 'Within weeks it was apparent that the project was going to be a success,' Wilson wrote. 'Moths, bark lice, and other flying insects appeared early. ... Winged ant queens, newly inseminated during their nuptial flights, landed, shed their wings, and started colonies. Spiders came early in abundance, some were wolf spiders the size of silver dollars.' Simberloff even watched how a floating cricket arrived on one of his islands by grabbing and ascending a mangrove root and then disappearing into the foliage.

Simberloff kept visiting each of the islands every two or three weeks, dedicatedly keeping track of the comings and goings of species. Within eight months, all but the most distant islands had regained their original species numbers. Island E1, for example, had had 26 species before defaunation; eight months after defaunation it had 22. Island E2 had 43 before, and 44 after, island E3 had 31 before and 33, and island ST2 had 29 both before and after. The results almost seemed too good to be true. And not only were the original species richnesses exactly restored, the species turnover as predicted by MacArthur and Wilson was also there in all its stochastic glory. Simberloff's biweekly tallies showed exactly how species arrived, hung on for a few months, then disappeared, only to be replaced by new immigrants. On average, the 'turnover rate' amounted to about one species every ten days. As a result, most species after the first eight months were not the same ones as had been there at defaunation. In fact, just about a quarter of them were. This meant that after defaunation, ecosystems had been established on the islands that were completely different from those that had been there before. And this also showed that the island miniature ecosystems, even when not tampered with by ecologists, were highly unstable to begin with: constantly rearranged by incoming and outgoing species, like small companies with poor employment fidelity.

The work, by now a classic study in ecology and still one of the best field demonstrations of island biogeography, earned Simberloff his PhD in 1968. Wilson and he went on to publish their results in a series of prominent papers in *Ecology* in 1969 and 1970. And while Wilson moved on to other things, Simberloff took a job at Florida State University and continued working in the Keys. From this new base, much closer to his now much-beloved field site, he took experimental island biogeography to the next level. In 1969 he selected nine islands that were about five times bigger than the ones he and Wilson had worked at a few years earlier, and did something almost as drastic as fumigating them: he cut off parts. After taking full censuses of the invertebrates on the islands (much more work with these larger mangrove patches, the largest of which were over 1,000 square metres), in 1970 he had some workmen with chainsaws remove parts of the vegetation. (Mangrove islands consist of little more than a tangled network of prop roots rising above the water; so cutting the trees effectively removed the island surface.) Eight of the nine islands were about halved in size, and the next year four of them were halved again.

Of course, this experiment was meant to see if species numbers would drop after the area had been reduced. Sure enough, they did. All islands lost the expected number of species within a year after being made smaller. Island G1, for example, held 74 species when it was still 343 square metres. The next year, having lost two thirds of its size to the chainsaws, its species numbers dropped to 65. And when Simberloff's men then cut away yet another 50% of the remaining island, it lost three more species. Simberloff published these amazing results in *Ecology* in 1976. It must have been an odd realisation: 15 years ago, the theory of island biogeography did not even exist yet, and now people were experimenting by creating their own archipelagoes.

6.5
Lubricant Biogeography

Since Daniel Simberloff introduced his particularly ruthless brand of chainsaw ecology in the 1970s, the theory of island biogeography has continued to expand its reach. It has found far-reaching applications in conservation biology and the management of nature reserves, as we shall see later. It also has been the basis for a new theory that has begun to revolutionise ecology (Chap. 7). And it has been found to be effective in settings less and less like the traditional animals-on-islands situations. Take, for example, this study of bugs on roundabouts.

In July 2002, Alvin Helden of University College Dublin, Ireland, and Imperial College London's applied ecologist Simon Leather realised that roundabouts with vegetated central islands are ideal settings for a bit of urban island biogeography, given that they are surrounded by a traffic-infested dispersal barrier that is every bit as deadly as seawater. They selected 14 road islands in the town of Bracknell in southeast England and used a modified vacuum cleaner to sample the vegetation on each for the plant-feeding insect order Hemiptera (which includes things like shield bugs, cicadas, aphids, and scale insects). Bracknell's traffic system being generously supplied with large and complex roundabouts, there was no shortage of 'island' sizes available to the researchers: the roundabouts ranged in size from 400 square metres to more than 6,000 square metres (Fig. 6.1). And, as they report in a 2004 paper in *Basic and Applied Ecology*, there was a clear species–area relationship between roundabout size and number of species of hemipterans living on them.

Even more exotic is the work that microbiologist Christopher van der Gast of the University of Oxford has been doing. Van der Gast studies bacteria in island-like habitats. In the pools of water in hollow trees, for example, and also in man-made environments, such as in the metal-cutting fluids in the sump tanks of engineering equipment. I'll let that sink in for a second.

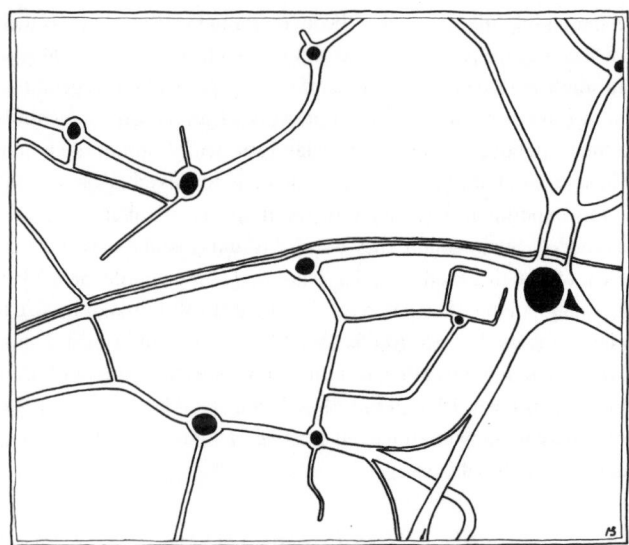

Fig. 6.1 Bracknell's town planners have created an archipelago of road islands in a sea of traffic

In 2005, van der Gast published a study in the journal *Environmental Microbiology* entitled 'Island size and bacterial diversity in an archipelago of engineering machines'. He had gone down to the University of Oxford's Engineering Science Department's metal workshop, where a veritable arsenal of lathes and mills is kept for cutting, bending, and sawing metal. For cooling and lubrication, these machines use cutting fluid, a mixture of water and soluble oils, which is kept in a sump tank. The smallest machine had a nine-litre sump tank, whereas the largest, the impressively sounding Bostomatic 405 CNC mill, carried 181 litres in its tank. Perhaps surprisingly, in these cutting fluids several species of bacteria live, which use the organic compounds as food (in fact, these bacteria are a well-known cause of infected skin wounds in metal workshop machinists). So, on a hunch, van der Gast thought the variably sized oil tanks in this machine park might represent an island-biogeographical archipelago to the bacteria.

He took 100-millilitre samples from the cutting fluid of 15 different machines and used *16S* DNA sequences (see Chap. 3) to estimate the number of different species of bacteria in the tanks. As it turned out, even in this highly artificial environment, with organisms that were, in size and ecology, as far removed from ants, birds, and plants as possible, MacArthur and Wilson ruled supreme: van der Gast found a perfect species–area relationship with ten species of bacteria living in the smallest sump tanks, and up to 25 in the largest. 'This study is a demonstration that the species–area relationship of island biogeography is applicable to bacterial populations and communities,' van der Gast wrote, incidentally offering a sweet revenge to Wilson by showing that the molecular microbiologists that made his life so miserable in the 1960s have now embraced his theories in their work.

Still, the roundabout and sump tank studies highlight the main current point of dispute in island biogeography: Do larger islands have larger numbers of species because, as MacArthur and Wilson would have it in their original version of the theory, they hold larger, more extinction-resistant populations, or, as some ecologists since then have argued, because larger islands provide more habitats? In the roundabout study, the researchers found that the number of different tree species planted on a roundabout was actually a better indicator of the numbers of Hemiptera than the size of the roundabout itself. This suggested that it was indeed the available habitats that made the difference.

In the sump tank study, however, it is hardly imaginable that a 180-litre tank provides more bacterial habitats than a nine-litre tank, especially when we realise that the fluid is constantly churned about. On the other hand, greater extinction-proneness in the smaller 'islands' is hard to believe as well. Population sizes of bacteria, as we saw in Chap. 3, are astronomic: van der Gast did microscope counts of bacterial cells in the sump tank samples and estimates that there are about ten million bacteria in every millilitre of cutting fluid. This means that extinction of microbe species due to small population size is hardly plausible even in the smallest tanks.

So some mysteries in the laws of island biogeography remain. As Michael Rosenzweig wrote in his book *Species Diversity in Space and Time*, '[W]e must ask what effects of area actually generate the species–area curve on islands. Is it habitats? Is it population size? Is it both?' Rosenzweig reviewed 15 separate studies where people had looked at the effects of habitat diversity on an island and island size separately. He came up with mixed results. Sometimes, such as in the case of the plants of the Galápagos Islands, the size of the island did not appear to predict species number at all, but the number of available habitats did. In other cases, such as the plants of islands in Swedish Lake Hjälmaren, the numbers of habitats had no effect on the numbers of species, and island size explained it all. Overall, Rosenzweig concluded that the strong species–area relationship in island biogeography is the result of less extinction *and* more habitats on larger islands. Which of the two effects is the strongest depends on the part of the world we are in, the kinds of organisms we are looking at, and the sizes and degrees of isolation of the islands (on archipelagoes of very small or very faraway islands, extinction is likely to be the more important factor).

So island biogeography has now turned out to be a little more complex than it appeared when the theory was first launched back in 1967. Still, that does not diminish its relevance. Rosenzweig sums it up very nicely: 'The theory of island biogeography sparked a revolution in ecology. It did so, not because people cared so much ..., but precisely because they did not care. ... [B]ecause species got to islands by accident, they assumed ... there was no science to discover, only history to recount.' Wilson and MacArthur showed them how wrong that assumption was.

Unfortunately, only Wilson lived to see the success of the theory. Robert MacArthur died from renal cancer in 1972, at age 42. But his brainchild, the view of species diversity as a simple balance between immigration and extinction, lives on in many ways. Not least, as we shall see in the next chapter, as the foundation for a new and even more all-encompassing ecological theory that was born in the early twenty-first century.

Ecology of Wildcards

7

7.1
Guild by Association

In the final paragraph of *On the Origin of Species*, Darwin sums up his thoughts and feelings on what today we would call ecology and evolution. His phrases are so beautiful and the meaning so profound that this little piece of text has been mined for mottos, quotes, and titles almost to exhaustion by hundreds of authors since. The title of American paleontologist Stephen Jay Gould's famous long-running column *This View Of Life* in the magazine *Natural History* was taken from the very last sentence in the paragraph where Darwin says, on the mechanistic world view he has just become the flagbearer of: 'There is grandeur in this view of life, with its several powers, having been originally breathed into a few forms or into one; and that, whilst this planet has gone cycling on according to the fixed law of gravity, from so simple a beginning endless forms most beautiful and most wonderful have been, and are being, evolved.' Snippets from the same sentence have been used, for example, for the evolution books *Endless Forms* and *Endless Forms Most Beautiful*. And 'evolved' of course gave rise to the term 'evolution' itself, a word that Darwin did not use.

But the paragraph's most prolific quote-generator has indubitably been its opening sentence, where Darwin says: 'It is interesting to contemplate an entangled bank, clothed with many plants of many kinds, with birds singing on the bushes, with various insects flitting about, and with worms crawling through the damp earth, and to reflect that these elaborately constructed forms, so different from each other, and dependent on each other in so complex a manner, have all been produced by laws acting around us.' Although this is the more famous sentence, the same entangled bank already made its appearance earlier in Darwin's book, where he doubts that chance has anything to do with the numbers and relative proportions of species living on it, as we saw at the end of Chap. 4.

The 'entangled bank' (or 'tangled bank') has been appropriated by at least two books by that title, a science blog carnival, countless websites, one conference, numerous scientific articles, one linguistic theory, and one theory on the evolution of sex. It has become such a popular phrase metaphor for the struggle for life that it came as a surprise a few years

Doi: 10.1007/978-3-540-68058-1_7, © Springer-Verlag Berlin Heidelberg 2008

ago that Darwin's great-great-grandson Randal Keynes, while preparing a new biography of his famous ancestor, announced that the entangled bank had actually existed. Mapping Darwin's daily forays around his home in Kent, Keynes became convinced that the densely vegetated slope that Darwin referred to must have been what his family and he called Orchis Bank, for the 11 species of orchids growing there. Now known as Downe Bank, it is a protected piece of chalk grassland still full of rare orchids and plants such as toothwort, adders tongue, and false oxlip.

It is not hard to imagine Charles Darwin strolling across this bank in spring, enjoying the profusion of common plants and the chance encounters with rare ones and wondering about 'their proportional numbers and kinds'. After all, proportional numbers and kinds are what countless naturalists and ecologists have since concerned themselves with, attempting to get at a universal formula for 'species abundance distributions'.

After species richness, the relative species abundance is probably what has fascinated naturalists most, traditionally at least. The *Heukels' Flora*, the venerable plant identification book that has been used by generations of schoolchildren and students in the Netherlands since 1883, for example, uses a system of six terms to indicate the rarity and commonness of plant species: *zeer algemeen* (very common), *algemeen* (common), *vrij algemeen* (fairly common), *vrij zeldzaam* (fairly rare), *zeldzaam* (rare), and *zeer zeldzaam* (very rare). Picking a random sample of 225 species from the book, for the six categories, I find, arranged from very common to very rare, 10, 52, 77, 22, 29, and 25 species. So there are few very common ones, lots of moderately common ones, and a long tail of rare ones.

It is a familiar pattern for ecologists who have studied species abundance distributions more exactly and in more detail. In the late 1930s, English entomologist Steven Corbet spent two years in Malaya collecting butterflies. In all, he got 620 species, and for each he kept track of exactly how many specimens he had captured: a much more exact measure of commonness or rarity than placing them in a limited number of abundance categories. Upon returning to England, Corbet showed his data to the famed theoretical biologist Ronald Fisher, who recognised that Corbet's butterfly abundances seemed to follow a mathematical function, called the log-series. In a log-series, if the species are arranged from the commonest to the rarest, each species has an abundance that is a fixed proportion from that of the next commonest species. For example, let us say there are 600 individuals of the commonest species, 300 of the next commonest one, 150 of number three in line, 75 of the fourth commonest one, and so on, until the species get so rare that there is less than one individual of them.

In this example, if we were to construct a bar graph, each species bar would be half as tall as the bar of the commoner species on its left and twice as tall as the rarer species on its right. If we drew a line through the tops of those bars, we would get a line that begins high on the left, drops quickly to medium levels, and then gently slopes down to imperceptible levels on the right. And if we were to choose a proportion of increasing rarity of, say, 0.1, rather than the 0.5 from the example, the bars would drop in height more gradually, but the general shape of the line would not change. The mathematical formula for describing such a line involves a natural logarithm, hence the term 'logarithmic series', or log-series for short.

But the generality of the log-series as a proper description of species abundance curves in nature was not convincing to everybody. One person who had his doubts was an independent researcher named Frank Preston, working from the Preston Laboratories of Butler,

Pennsylvania. Over the 60 years of his professional life, Preston made a number of very significant contributions to ecology, yet he was no biologist and the Preston Laboratories were no biological research institution either.

Born in Leicester, England, in 1897, Preston came from a poor family background, but had the good fortune to have an encouraging father. He got a scholarship to secondary school and initially qualified to enter the University of Oxford. However, because his family could not afford the university, he went into apprenticeship with a civil engineer and at the age of 20, without attending any classes but on the basis of examination and papers, got a BSc degree in engineering from the University of London. This was the height of the First World War and his knowledge of optics and the physical properties of glass was in great demand for designing lenses for aerial photography. After the war, he moved to the USA and set up his own consulting firm (the Preston Laboratories) for the glass industry, eventually employing a large staff of scientists and engineers and being granted dozens of industrial patents.

So how did the owner of American Glass Research (as the Preston Laboratories were also known) get to write a series of classic papers on relative species abundance in the journal *Ecology*? When Preston died in 1989, one of the obituaries called him an 'authentic genius' who 'illuminated whatever he touched'. And glass was not the only thing he touched. Blessed with an insatiable curiosity about the natural world and an analytical mind (early in life, he once said to want to make a career dealing with 'things rather than people'), he was a passionate bird-watcher, entomologist, and botanist (as well as a musician, polyglot, marksman, conservationist, geologist, and travel-writer) and raised to world-class level almost every interest he took up. So when he started collecting moths and recording birds on the 36-hectare grounds of the Preston Laboratories together with ornithologist Russell Norris (Preston's official justification for the hiring of whom was to stimulate the cross-fertilisation of ideas among his team of scientists and engineers), he did not stop at ticking species in his field guides.

Instead, Preston became interested in relative species abundances. He read Fisher's papers and realised that something was wrong. First of all, data such as those collected by Corbet were likely to be a non-random sample of the fauna, because (as he knew from experience), collectors tend to target rare species and ignore the common ones. Second, Fisher's log-series did not fit Corbet's data all that well. And finally, as he wrote in his 1948 paper in *Ecology* entitled 'The commonness, and rarity of species', it would be better to work with octaves.

In music, of course, octaves are intervals between two tones in which the pitch of the second is double that of the first. Preston realised that species' commonness and rarity fit an octave scale better than a linear scale. The 'very common' species in *Heukels' Flora* are not found five times as frequently as the 'very rare' species five intervals down the line. Instead, the abundances are more likely to differ by several orders of magnitude. So Preston introduced octaves of commonness and rarity. At each octave, the abundance doubles. So octave A runs from abundances of between one and two individuals, octave B from two to four individuals, octave C from four to eight individuals, octave D from eight to 16, and so on. And in contrast to Fisher, who drew the abundance along the *y*-axis, Preston drew his octaves along the abscissa, and the number of species falling into each octave along the ordinate (Fig. 7.1.).

Fig. 7.1 Like notes at octave intervals, Frank Preston envisaged octaves of abundance, with the animal species in each higher octave twice as abundant as the ones in the previous octave

And this graphical representation clearly revealed the inadequacy of the log-series. Using Fisher's formula would give a row of bars all of the same height: each octave would be populated with the same number of species. As Preston showed, using his bird and moth counts as well as some of the counts used by Fisher, real data showed a different pattern, with the bars starting low on the left (few species in the 'very rare' octaves), rising to a maximum in the middle (many species in the octaves of intermediate rarity and commonness), and then dropping again on the right (few species in the 'very common' octaves). In other words, the bars would show the familiar symmetrical pattern that mathematicians call a 'normal' or 'Gaussian' curve, but that everybody else calls a 'bell curve'. Because the normal curve was projected onto the logarithmic octave axis, Preston called his relative species abundance curve the 'log-normal'.

Preston also realised that it would be impossible for any field survey to capture the entire bell curve: the rarest octaves would always remain hidden, so curves based on real data would always be 'decapitated' at the left. The border between the real bell curve and the right-hand part that was shown in a sample is what Preston called the 'veil line'. As samples became larger and larger, more and more of the left hand side of the real log-normal distribution would be revealed. And lots of subsequent ecologists have proved Preston right: real life is log-normal, and does not fit the log-series.

But there was one snag marring the success of the log-normal: it did not have any ecological basis. Why would real species in real ecosystems follow the log-normal distribution rather than the log-series or any of the almost 30 alternative species abundance formulas that ecologists have dreamt up? It should come as no surprise that Robert MacArthur was one of the ecologists who attempted to explain the log-normal in an ecological framework. In 1957, MacArthur had just finished his thesis on warbler niches and was of course primed to see every pattern in ecology as driven by niches and resources. Let us suppose, he wrote in a paper in the *Proceedings of the National Academy of Sciences of the USA* of 15 March of that year, that we have a bunch of species in the same trophic level, sharing the same resource. Say insect-eating birds or leaf-beetles. What ecologists call a guild. Let us imagine the resource as a long stick, which is then randomly broken into bits, and each species gets handed out such a portion of the total resource. Since the commonness of a species will correspond to the amount of the resource it is apportioned, the distribution of stick lengths would be reflected in relative species abundances, MacArthur argued. Sure enough, his 'broken-stick hypothesis' resulted in a curve that looked similar to the log-normal bell. But, it was too flat: common species were not common enough, and rare species were too common. The ubiquity of Preston's log-normal remained unexplained.

7.2
Registry of Births and Deaths

This is where the American tropical forest biologist Stephen Hubbell comes in. Hubbell, although he wrote his first scientific paper at the age of 18 on a satyr butterfly, initially wanted to become a biochemist. But after a trip to Honduras he changed his mind and became an ecologist instead. A decision that has probably left a bigger mark on the latter than on the former discipline. For Hubbell, born 1942, is now one of the world's most influential ecologists. Starting off modestly in the 1960s and 1970s, when he busied himself with the niches of pillbugs, competition in microbes, and the ecology of tropical bees in Costa Rica, he found his footing in the late 1970s. Having become interested in the mysteries of tropical forest tree biodiversity during his work in Costa Rica, he and colleague Robin Foster in 1979 approached the Smithsonian Tropical Research Institute (STRI) with an unusual plan.

Since the 1940s, the STRI had been in charge of research on Barro Colorado Island (BCI), a 15-square-kilometre patch of land left in the middle of the artificial lake that has connected the Atlantic and Pacific arms of the Panama Canal since it opened in 1923. What Hubbell and Foster suggested was to stake out a 50-hectare (0.5-square-kilometre) plot of forest smack in the middle of the island, tag and identify all trees thicker than one centimetre at breast height (breast height being the forest ecologist's standard height of reference), ban all other research activities in the plot, and follow the fate of the trees by five-yearly censuses into perpetuity. Surprisingly, the STRI agreed to their audacious proposal and the 50-hectare plot has since become the mother of all tropical forest research sites, having spurned 17 (and counting) similar plots worldwide, including the one in Lambir (see Chaps. 3, 4).

The BCI plot was supposed to generate lots of data on the way tropical forests change over time, and it has done so in a multitude of ways, some of which were unanticipated when the plot was set up. But one of the explicit reasons why Hubbell wanted to be able to keep regular censuses of births, deaths, and migration in a swath of tropical forest was that it would be a test case for a relative species abundance model that he had just thrown at the feet of ecologists in a paper in *Science* in 1979. Unlike most previous relative species abundance models, Hubbell's used real ecological events, rather than mathematical but biologically meaningless properties of curves and graphs. To do so, he made use of the rationale of MacArthur and Wilson's theory of island biogeography, which, as we saw in the previous chapter, explained biodiversity as a balance between immigration and extinction. But where MacArthur and Wilson had mainly been interested in species richness, and had all but ignored relative species abundances, Hubbell realised that their theory could just as well be used for that purpose.

Let us suppose, Hubbell had said, that a particular guild in a certain area is 'saturated', that is, all available slots in the habitat are taken. In the tropical rainforest, this is not hard to imagine: tree species (which can be considered a 'guild' because they use the same resource, i.e. light) compete for a sunlit spot in the forest canopy, which results in a tight filling of all the canopy space. Each time an existing tree falls over, it is replaced by a young tree drawn from the bank of seedlings of existing trees (with commoner species having a proportionately higher chance of providing a seedling) or by a recent immigrant. This process repeats itself over and over again. Gaps in the canopy are created, filled, and the composition of the patchwork that makes up the canopy is in constant flux. Using computer simulations, Hubbell showed that the result of this process is a near-perfect log-normal pattern of species abundances. For the first time, somebody had shown that simple biological processes such as birth, death, and migration could yield Preston's bell curve. In Hubbell's words, the curve could be 'derived from first principles'.

By today, the BCI plot has been censused six times, cumulating researchers' encounters with more than 350,000 individual trees belonging to over 300 species. Already by the late 1990s, these censuses had begun generating sufficient data for Hubbell to start using them to test and elaborate on his model. In 1997, he published a paper in the journal *Coral Reefs* in which he did exactly that. It may seem strange that he used a coral journal as the platform to launch a modern version of his 1979 theory, but, as Hubbell reminded his readers, his model would work for all guilds that play a so-called zero-sum game: a community that uses up all the available space, so that a new individual can only settle once an older one has keeled over. And this does not only apply to trees, but also, for example, to corals on a reef.

Whereas in his 1979 paper Hubbell had only used words to convince his audience, he supported his argument with a whole lot of formulas in the paper in *Coral Reefs*. And he had also expanded his model by including evolution: each time a new individual would settle in the community, there was a tiny chance for this to become a speciation event, that is, for it to be the founder of a newly evolved species. In spite of all the algebraic sophistication, Hubbell's model was surprisingly simple: it only depended on the number of individuals in the community, the rate by which new individuals migrate in and out, and a parameter that Hubbell called theta, or 'the fundamental biodiversity number'; theta being the product of, first, the size of the 'source population' from which migrants would come in, and, second, the speciation rate.

As Hubbell's calculations showed, the shape of the species abundance curve would depend strongly on theta. With theta close to zero, that is, very little immigration, and very little speciation, the community would eventually gravitate toward a situation with just one or a few species. With theta close to infinity (lots of immigration and/or lots of speciation), each new arrival would either already belong to a new species or evolve into one upon arrival, leading to a hyperdiverse situation with just a single individual for each species. Most realistic values for theta, though, would produce a species abundance curve that Hubbell called the 'zero-sum multinomial': a bell curve very similar to the log-normal, but with one important difference. In the zero-sum multinomial the level of the flare on the left side of the bell would be somewhat higher than on the right: a relative excess of species in the rarest-species' octaves.

Since these rarest categories are also the hardest to find (they often sit beyond Preston's veil line), Hubbell needed very large and accurate data sets to test whether his model indeed described nature better than did the log-normal. And the BCI plot provided such data, as did some similar tropical rainforest plots that had sprung up in other places, such as in Pasoh, on the Malaysian Peninsula. In the *Coral Reefs* paper, Hubbell presented the species abundance curves for both Pasoh and BCI and on them superimposed the traditional log-normal curve. Reading from right (the commonest species) to left, the two curves nicely overlap until the rare-species octaves are reached, with fewer than ten individuals per species. Here, the log-normal begins to fall further and further below the actual data curve: indeed an excess of rare species exists in the wild. And when Hubbell then plotted his zero-sum multinomial, with theta and migration rate tweaked to fit the right-hand side of the curve as accurately as possible, he showed that it did not diverge from the real data around the lower octaves: instead, it exactly predicted the relative abundances of the rarest species.

In the conclusion to his paper, Hubbell wrote: 'Of course, real species are not identical, and they have niches. But the success of the present theory suggests that most of the detail about niche structure ... becomes ineffective at controlling community structure.' In other words, he had used real species doing real things like being born, dying, immigrating, and evolving, and produced eerily exact species abundance curves without at any time taking the species' niches into account. Once again, like in MacArthur and Wilson's work, ecological patterns could be understood without any involvement of niches. A neutral revolution was in the air.

7.3
Maintaining Neutrality

Hubbell, in his *Coral Reefs* paper, repeatedly (in fact, 14 times) cited an upcoming publication by himself from that very same year: 'Hubbell, 1997'. Looking this up in the bibliography at the end of the paper, one finds the following entry for a yet unpublished book: 'Hubbell SP (1997) *A Unified Theory of Biogeography and Relative Species Abundance*. Princeton University Press, Princeton, NJ (in press)'. Hubbell evidently hoped his big book, of which the *Coral Reefs* paper was just a very concise abstract, would be finished that year. But in the end, it took four more years before the book finally came off the press. And by then its title had changed too: *The Unified Theory of Biodiversity and Biogeography* appeared in 2001 as number 32 in Princeton University Press's illustrious series of *Monographs in Population Biology*.

The first volume in this series had, of course, been Robert MacArthur and Edward O. Wilson's landmark publication *The Theory of Island Biogeography*, and it was very fitting that Hubbell's book was to appear in the same series. Not only because it built upon the work of MacArthur and Wilson, but also because it was set to make as big a splash as had its predecessor.

In essence, the book said the same things as had the *Coral Reefs* paper four years earlier. But where the paper had been cited just a dozen or so times in the years after it appeared, the book immediately generated much more interest. By now, it has been cited a staggering 850 times in other scientific publications ('I have been enjoying the rollercoaster ride,' Hubbell confides). This was perhaps partly due to Hubbell's by then impressive status:

at age 59, he was a Distinguished Research Professor at the University of Georgia, Senior Staff Scientist at the Smithsonian Tropical Research Institute, Fellow of the American Association for the Advancement of Science, nominee for the Crafoord Prize, and author of four articles in *Science* (and one ecological board game). But more importantly, *The Unified Neutral Theory of Biodiversity* (as it has become known) simply is a very clever and well-written book. 'Hubbell's model is mathematically very elegant,' says theoretical ecologist Brian McGill of McGill University (no relation) in Montreal, Canada, although Hubbell himself is more modest: 'I am a sundry mathematician – the maths in the book are about as far as I get.' Nowadays he works with a few very good mathematicians to do all the hard sums, he says.

The book centres, of course, around his new model and the zero-sum multinomial. But unlike the rather brief and technical 1997 paper, it offers so much more. To begin with, the new theory is placed in the context of the biodiversity crisis. In the preface, Hubbell makes a heart-felt plea for better biodiversity science and then goes on to blame some of his colleagues for feeling that the search for a general theory of biodiversity was 'a quixotic waste of time'. Even ten years later, as I meet him at an ecology conference in the Netherlands, he fulminates about the way ecologists eschew building comprehensive theories: 'We are all postmodernists,' he says. 'I'll tell you my little narrative and you tell me yours – and we leave it at that. My physicist friends are appalled by the way we ecologists work. If Galileo had been an ecologist, they say, he would have written 40 volumes of observations of the ways different kinds of objects can be dropped from the tower of Pisa without ever coming up with the theory of gravity.'

In his book, he recounts the story of how his unified theory developed from the germ originally laid in the 1979 *Science* paper. 'At some point now lost to memory,' he recalls, 'while teaching ..., I wondered what would happen if a process of speciation were incorporated in the theory.' He tells how, by the mid-1990s, after he had done the maths, a surprise was in stall for him: 'I was completely unprepared for what happened next. Adding speciation unexpectedly resulted in a unification of the theories of island biogeography and relative species abundance – theories that heretofore have had almost completely separate intellectual histories.' He tells about the emergence of theta, 'a truly remarkable dimensionless number' that connects all aspects of his theory, and that, for its ubiquity, centrality, and practicality, he christened the '*fundamental biodiversity number*', using italics to add typographical emphasis to his palpable excitement. And then there are some personal notes. A dedication to the memory of his father, who had been the director of the Museum of Zoology at the University of Michigan, and whom Hubbell lovingly describes as the 'entomologist and evolutionary biologist *extraordinaire*' who took him on field trips throughout North, Central, and South America and introduced him to biodiversity before it was called such. And a dedication to the memory of his wife, 'scientist, scholar, artist, teacher, mother, and lover', who died in the years that he was working on the book.

In developing the 375-page tome, Hubbell realised his unified theory could be applied not only to local species abundance distributions and species richness, but also to larger-scale and even global patterns of biodiversity and biogeography. 'Writing the book was a voyage of discovery,' he recalls. 'With each chapter the scope widened.' He was also aware that by building a nicheless, neutral ecological theory, he was taking a leap of faith that many of his colleagues would be unwilling to take. Still, that did not deter him.

'I have never been shy,' he says. 'I always say what I feel.' And in the book he writes, 'It is … an unabashedly neutral theory.' And then hastens to explain what he means. Of course, 'the notion of complete neutrality is patently false.' Species have niches and are ecologically different, especially when viewing them at small spatial scales. But at the same time, communities are often thrown together largely by chance, history, and random dispersal: whether a species manages to colonise a piece of habitat often depends more on accident (are there vacant spots, has the species had a bloom nearby, is the wind in the right direction) than on the presence of the neatly circumscribed species's niche. All Hubbell was setting out to do, he explained, was investigate whether it was possible to mimic and predict real, broad-brush biodiversity patterns while ignoring the niches that undeniably existed. A bit like trying to understand economic boom and bust without referring to individual people's personalities.

Hubbell spent quite a few pages of his book explaining what he meant by neutrality and reassuring his readers (many of the more vocal and knowledgeable of whom he undoubtedly knew personally) of his honourable intentions. But no matter how Hubbell made provisos and quid pro quos, and no matter how he propped up his theory with mathematical struts and how well his diligently assembled data supported his theory, it was unavoidable that the ecological community, having spent the better part of the twentieth century on niches and their importance, was bound to kneejerk in unison.

7.4
Algebraic Kneejerks

And kneejerk they did. Although, scientists being what they are, they would shroud their kneejerks in scholarly discourse. And it did not take long after the appearance of *The Unified Neutral Theory of Biodiversity* for the first throats to be cleared. Among those was Brian McGill's (see Sect. 7.3), then still with the University of Arizona in Tucson, USA. McGill recalls that when he first read Hubbell's book and saw the good fit between the tropical forest species abundances and the zero-sum multinomial, his first thought was: 'That is outrageous! It can't be true!' Then, he realised that Hubbell had only hand-drawn the curves. And although the zero-sum multinomial *seemed* to match the data better than the log-normal, Hubbell had not actually done the statistics to prove that it did. 'I thought: hold on… he didn't test it,' McGill says.

So McGill got hold of two data sets, the BCI data of Hubbell himself, and also data from North American breeding bird surveys. He then used large numbers of estimations for theta and the migration rate to test whether the difference between the best-fitting zero-sum multinomial had a smaller overall difference with the actual species abundance curve than did Preston's bell curve, the log-normal distribution. The results, which appeared in the 24 April 2003 issue of *Nature*, showed that, in fact, they did not: the regular log-normal performed better throughout. Understandably, McGill did not mince his words. In the article's conclusion, he wrote: '[T]he central empirical test of the [theory] is in fact not true. [W]e may well not wish to favour any distribution derived from a complex theory until it is shown to perform better than the log-normal. Moreover, the [theory] starts with assumptions that are known to be wrong: the competitive equivalence of species.' In other words, McGill said: I cannot prove that Hubbell's niche-less theory produces a more realistic species abundance distribution, so let us not get overexcited about this new and, frankly, fairly shaky theory.

It did not take Hubbell long to retort. Four months later that same year, he and three even more mathematically inclined colleagues published a paper in *Nature* in which they presented a so-called analytical solution of the zero-sum multinomial. This means Hubbell now had an exact algebraic formula for the curve, rather than the estimations he had used in his book. And of course they immediately used it to check whether McGill had been right or not. So once again the by now dog-eared BCI data were unearthed and put to the test. And lo and behold, they found that the zero-sum multinomial did actually follow the real data significantly closer than did the log-normal. No wonder, they said in their paper, because McGill had used computer simulations, and had had no way of knowing when his simulations had reached the desired degree of accuracy. Moreover, they reminded the reader that it was time to stop fitting curves to data and get some real work done: 'Such fitting exercises in and of themselves … do not constitute an adequate test of the underlying theory.'

Still, McGill was not deterred. In a 2006 paper in *Ecology*, he and two colleagues reviewed all the tests carried out so far and concluded that 'there is a current overwhelming weight of evidence against neutral theory'. However, at the same time, they pointed out that there was at least one flaw in each and every one of the tests. As far as Hubbell is concerned, testing whether one model has a slightly better fit to real data than the other is of limited relevance anyway. He even admits that the log-normal does slightly better than the neutral theory for the data from the Pasoh forest in Peninsular Malaysia, but adds that, with sufficient tweaking of parameters, several models are likely to offer a near-perfect fit.

Others emphasise that the neutral model may be useful, but only for those guilds that play this 'zero-sum game'. Trees in a forest and corals in a reef and perhaps things like barnacles on a humpback's skin are tightly packed and space-limited: a new individual can only settle when a spot has been vacated. But this does not apply to many other guilds. In the cloud of phytophagous insects enveloping a forest, there is always space to scootch and make place for a bunch of new arrivals. The neutral theory is not meant to be able to deal with such non-zero-sum situations. Ecologist Jacques van Alphen of Leiden University, the Netherlands, says: 'The neutral literature is beginning to get contaminated with examples that are beside the point, like guilds of moths or fish. It is nonsense to try and apply Hubbell's theory to those.' But Dutch ecologist Rampal Etienne of the University of Groningen has recently discovered that the zero-sum condition is not so strict after all. In fact, the heaps of mathematics that he poured into a 2007 paper in *The Journal of Theoretical Biology* show that the zero-sum multinomial also appears in unaltered form when the guild is playing a non-zero-sum game. Hence, he suggests changing the name to the 'dispersal-limited multinomial' instead (dispersal being the main factor determining the species abundance distribution).

So, in spite of some misgivings of niche-chauvinists, the neutral theory has held up quite well in the first few years of its life and, overall, most ecologists are happy that the theory is here to stay. Van Alphen says: 'Hubbell's book has stimulated me tremendously to start thinking hard.' And Etienne thinks that the theory is a wonderful null model, and 'has fostered a rich debate about community structure. … It has inspired and will continue to inspire further developments.' He adds: 'People worry that all their old work on niches is now shunted as irrelevant. But all that the neutral theory has done is change the framework. At the spatial scale of host plants and their herbivorous insects you shouldn't try to apply the neutral theory. Of course niches are the most important factor at that scale.' It is a bit like in physics, he explains. Thermodynamics assumes hypothetical ideal gases, which works fine as an approximation, but breaks down at the scale of individual molecules.

And theoretical ecologist George Sugihara of the University of Oxford, UK, who is one of the few ecologists who have managed to derive log-normal species abundance distributions from data on the niches species occupy, is even more lucid. In a 2003 paper, he writes: 'Although the mechanisms in niche ordering and dispersal may appear different and are potentially operating on very different time scales, the models are not mutually exclusive.' In other words, his advice is throw in one or two further realistic bits of ecology, and we might really have a unified (more or less neutral) theory of biodiversity. And that, as we shall see in the final section of this chapter, is exactly what is happening.

7.5
Pest Control

Forestry in the Amazon of Brazil is synonymous with mahogany. The famed neotropical hardwood, of which the timber can fetch thousands of dollars per cubic metre, is by far the most-sought-after tropical rainforest tree in the region. It is also characteristically rare, growing at densities of less than one per hectare. Teams of airborne and bulldozer-bound prospectors scan vast areas of forest on the lookout for mahogany trees. Once a tree has been located from the air, a ground-based prospector will drive his bulldozer through the dense forest, clearing an improvised logging road and dragging away the felled tree, and all vines and neighbouring trees that came down with it. No wonder the 800,000-square-kilometre belt where mahogany is found is also known as the 'deforestation belt'.

The strategy used by mahogany loggers is typical for any timber operation that relies on a single kind of tropical rainforest tree. For, as we have seen before, despite some niche-based clustering (see Chap. 4), almost all species of rainforest tree are rare and widely dispersed. But rarity begets diversity, because this pattern of dispersion also translates into great numbers of tree species in small areas. According to Hubbell's neutral model, the tree diversity pattern in a tropical forest can be explained largely in terms of immigration, extinction, and speciation. However, on top of that, some older, more subtle explanations still seem to retain some validity as well.

Returning to mahogany, ecologist Julian Norghauer from the University of Toronto has been studying the tree's natural enemies in Southeastern Amazonia. He found that seedlings of *Sweetenia macrophylla*, as is the species's scientific name, are under severe attack from caterpillars and other herbivorous insects. Most importantly, he discovered that the older the parent tree the seedlings were growing under, the more they suffered from having their leaves nibbled at by insects, and this effect was particularly striking for insects that feed specifically on mahogany, such as the miniature moth *Steniscadia poliophaea*. Also, seeds germinated better if they were placed further away from the parent tree. Apparently, the longer a tree has been established in a certain place, the less hospitable the ground under its branches becomes for its offspring. So for some reason, juvenile mahogany trees only have a chance if they flee mummy's sphere of influence and seek their fortune far away – which would explain the fact that mahogany trees are, much to loggers' frustration, few and far between.

Norghauer and his colleagues published their findings as support for the so-called Janzen–Connell hypothesis. In 1970, Dan Janzen and Joseph Connell, both budding capos of the rainforest mafia, had been talking about the roles that plant natural enemies play in determining where trees can grow and where they cannot. Janzen (see Chap. 3) had been working in the Central American rainforest, and Jo Connell (of the University of California at Santa Barbara) had been running a rainforest research project in northern Australia since the early 1960s, and both agreed on the patterns they saw in their respective areas. That year, Janzen published his version of their joint ideas in a paper in *The American Naturalist*, and Connell did the same the next year in a book chapter. Since then, this fruit of their shared rainforest experience has been known as the Janzen–Connell hypothesis.

As Janzen explained in his paper, the offspring of tropical rainforest trees are threatened by a great many trials of life, and many of those come on one, two, or three pairs of legs. While he was at it, he introduced a new vocabulary for animals eating plants: in analogy to the enemies of animals, he called those feeding on (but not killing) a living plant a 'plant parasite', whereas the terms he used for those eating (and killing) a seed or a seedling were 'seed predator' and 'plant predator', respectively. Seed predators, he said, can take their toll while the seeds are still on the tree: birds, bats, monkeys, and other vertebrates do so. Once fallen to the ground, the seeds fall prey to hogs, rats, mice, squirrels, and lots of other mammals, as well as seed-eating insects. But the real onslaught only happens after germination: a veritable cloud of plant parasites will descend on the fresh green in the form of insects that tax the new leaves of the seedlings. And on top of that there are plant predators like deer who will eat the entire seedling.

Now many of those parasites and predators would be host-specific, because plants tend to contain such unique cocktails of chemical compounds to make themselves unpalatable, that most herbivores can evolve to cope with the defences of just one or a few different food plants. 'From 1963 to 1970 I have reared insects from the seeds of better than 300 lowland Central American plant species. Almost without exception, a given insect species reproduces on only a small subset (one to three species) of the hundreds of potential host species available,' Janzen wrote. And he gave some other examples for the plant parasites. Mammals and birds may not be so host-specific, he admitted, but they would congregate around trees that are fruiting, and would actively seek out trees of a particular species if that species is in its fruiting season. So at least for a short duration, they, too, would behave host-specifically.

This would mean, reasoned Janzen and Connell independently, that an old tree of a particular species would be a source of all the pestilences that may befall that species. It would attract seed predators from afar, and populations of insect seed predators and plant parasites would build up and be sustained around its trunk, subsisting on the regularly descending manna of seeds and seedlings. As a result, those seedlings that happen to grow up quite far away from their parent would have a better chance in life. And, most significantly, this would also mean that the soil around a tree, thus made relatively unsuitable for its own offspring, would be available for seedlings of other species, similarly forced to flee their parents, to germinate and grow up in. In essence, Janzen and Connell said host-specific herbivores prevent trees of the same species from growing close to each other. This prevents competition and allows a larger number of tree species to share the same patch of forest. It also meant that rare species have a certain advantage owing to the fact that they hide from their predators and parasites.

Over the years, quite some evidence has accumulated indicating that Janzen–Connell effects do take place in forests. Connell himself has been studying several patches of pristine rainforest in the Atherton Tablelands of Australia's tropical North Queensland since 1963 (Fig. 7.2). In this highland area south of Cairns, snippets of the original rainforest of the Australian wet tropics still survive in gullies and on slopes among the dairy farms, improbable retailers, and badly decorated pubs. Each year, the proprietor of the Golden Leaf Motel in Mareeba (the very finest in concrete block accommodation) would let a section of the establishment to Connell and his students, who would then descend with their measuring tapes, notebooks, bottles and vials, dissection microscopes, and crown densiometers, and obligingly be the laughing stock to the pub's regulars for a few weeks.

From this lab in a pub, Connell and his students worked at a site in Davies Creek National Park. Situated at about 850 metres above sea level, the cool, everwet, evergreen rainforest is of the so-called mesophyll type. Superficially, with its buttressed emergents, its vines and palms, and dusky-leaved understorey herbs, this forest looks not much different from hill forest in nearby Indonesia, but to a botanist it is like peering into the past. For it carries a relictary collection of tree species, from families that date back to the Jurassic times when Australia, Africa, India, Antarctica, and South-America were still joined together in one land mass known as Gondwana, and ancient vegetation covered this area, which was replaced by more modern plants in most continents and subcontinents

Fig. 7.2 The Atheton Tablelands in Australia's tropical North Queensland, where Joseph Connell discovered the effect that later got to bear his and Dan Janzen's names

that constituted Gondwana. Remnants of the ancient flora survive in South Africa's fynbos (see Chap. 4) and in Australia.

The site at Davies Creek, Connell says, is presumably one of the few bits of Australian rainforest that have never been touched by human hands. Australian aborigines had no interest in clearing forest for agriculture, and logging only started when the white man began cultivating the area in the nineteenth century. And the fact that centuries-old specimens of the most-prized timber species still thrive in Davies Creek suggests that this patch somehow escaped attention until it was eventually set aside as a conservation area and later even obtained World Heritage Status.

Counting and identifying seedlings and doing experiments with seeds placed on the ground under a wire mesh cage to keep out the possums, Connell and his team performed a 20-year series of censuses and tests in this ancient woodland to see whether seedlings grew and germinated better if they were close to or far away from a conspecific adult tree. They found that, indeed, seedlings under an adult tree of the same species grew about 50% slower and died about 20% more frequently than those that sprouted underneath a tree of a different species. And the same applied to seed germination. In one experiment the researchers had taken sackloads of seeds of a species of *Chrysophyllum* tree, and planted these in batches of 98 each under four adult trees of the same species and four adults of different species. After three years, about 40% of the seeds under *Chrysophyllum* trees had germinated, but of the seeds planted in the protective environment of different trees, more than 70% had grown into seedlings.

Other evidence for the Janzen–Connell hypothesis has come not from tropical forests but from North American woodland. And not involving plant parasites or seed predators, but microscopic germs living in the soil. Alissa Packer and Keith Clay of Indiana University studied six black cherry (*Prunus serotina*) trees in Griffy Lake Nature Reserve just outside Bloomington, Indiana. Starting from the trunk of each of their trees, they scoured a 30-metre-long pie-wedge of forest for cherry seedlings, tagged them, and censused them again the next year. They found that the survival rate of seedlings, no more than 40% around the cherry tree, steadily climbed to almost 90% toward the edge of the pie-wedge. Suspecting that some soil-borne cherry disease may lie at the root of the poor survival near the parent tree, the researchers took soil from the foot of a cherry tree and soil from some distance away, and planted each pot with seedlings. Sure enough, the seedlings in pots of cherry-derived soil did very poorly, especially when planted at a high density. Those in neutral soil did well, as did those planted by way of a control in sterilised soil, regardless of its origin. In a final coup de grâce, the researchers managed to isolate the likely culprit from the roots of dying seedlings: a fungus known as *Pythium*.

So the Janzen–Connell model rules supreme in forests the world over, it seems. And, with some imagination, it is possible that its sphere of influence is not limited to trees either: many organisms are bound to a greater or lesser extent to a particular place, and their specific enemies will congregate there as well. However, just like niches may be of limited importance (see in several of the previous chapters), this does not necessarily mean than Janzen–Connell effects are instrumental in maintaining high species diversity. People have objected that its effects may be too small-scale: the experiments of Connell and others have revealed its workings on scales of tens of metres. Would this create enough of a pest-free patchwork to explain the great biodiversity on the scale of entire forests? And what about host-specificity? Janzen had claimed that most plant parasites and predators, especially in the tropics and at least where insects are concerned, are very host-specific, but some ecologists doubt that we have enough information to be sure of that. And finally it is known that many species of tree have in fact evolved mechanisms to deal with the 'death zones' underneath their branches. Rather than fruiting regularly and independently, in many forests, all trees, even those belonging to unrelated species, fruit massively in particular years. During these so-called mast years, a forest produces so many seeds and seedlings that its resident plant predators and parasites are completely overwhelmed, and the trees thus escape from Janzen–Connell tyranny.

Still, it is generally accepted that the Janzen–Connell effect does play some role in explaining species abundance distributions. So in 2005, Igor Volkov of Pennsylvania State University, together with several other authors, published a paper in *Nature* in which they used the tree species abundance distributions from BCI, Lambir, Pasoh, and other famous rainforest plots, and showed that the Janzen–Connell model explains the data no better than does the neutral model. Again, this proves the value of Hubbell's theory as a null model: if a model based on ecological observations (such as niche differences or Janzen–Connell effects) does not explain the species abundance distributions any better than does the neutral model, we can do without them if we want to acquire a broad-brush understanding of biodiversity. Again, this does not mean that niches or predator/parasite-free zones do not play an important role in the brass tacks of species interactions. It just means that, to a truly unified theory of biodiversity, they are embellishments, rather than essence.

The Loom Of Life

8

8.1
Weft and Warp

In Greek mythology, the course of a man's life is determined by three goddesses, the Moirae, who work the Loom of Life. Clotho, 'the spinner', spins the threads. Lachesis, 'the disposer of lots', ordains the manner in which the tapestry of life is woven. And Atropos, 'the inevitable', finally, holds the shears of death with which life's threads are eventually severed.

In the past seven chapters, we have looked at the workings of an ecological version of the loom of life. We have followed many of the strands that are woven together to construct ecosystems. In Chap. 1, we checked out miniature ecosystems to get some idea of the basics of their weave. Moving on to Chap. 2, we examined the warp, by looking at energy pyramids and trophic levels, and we discovered that energy in ecosystems quickly runs out as it filters upward, and that even the richest ecosystems support only a few trophic levels. In fact, most of an ecotapestry's richness turned out to be contained in the 'horizontal' yarns: the many different species in 'guilds' that occupy the same trophic level. In Chap. 3, we tried to get an idea of these dazzling diversities that can be found in ecosystems' weft. In Chap. 4, we then looked at the different ecological roles that the species in guilds play: their niches, or, if you will, the colours of the weft threads. And, to carry on our weaving metaphor, in Chaps. 5–7, we looked at the way nature works this loom: how random processes such as dispersal and extinction determine which strands and how many of them are strung together, and which pattern they produce.

But despite our now detailed knowledge of the workings of this loom of life, we have not yet had a chance to view the end product as a whole. How does the tapestry, thus woven, behave? How easily does it stretch, tear, or fray? Does it matter how tightly woven it is and from how many yarns or does its resilience depend only on a few extra-strong threads? In other words, what properties does an ecosystem have and how does its functioning and stability depend on these properties? Are simple, species-poor systems for example, more stable than complex ones? Does an ecosystem work as one big machine or is it subdivided into more or less independent compartments? Are ecosystems regulated more by what

The Loom of Life. M. Schilthuizen   97
Doi: 10.1007/978-3-540-68058-1_8, © Springer-Verlag Berlin Heidelberg 2008

happens in the higher trophic levels or by events in the primary production department? Are simple ecosystems less productive than complex ones or does the biodiversity contained in an ecosystem tell us little about the amount of carbon that goes around in it?

These are not idle academic questions. Everywhere on Earth, environmental upheaval is making changes to ecosystems. The weave of species is being messed up: species become extinct, biodiversity declines, common species become rare and sometimes vice versa, alien species are inserted with or without their original parasites, pathogens, and predators. As ecologist Kevin McCann warned ominously in an article in *Nature* in 2000: 'We are, in a very real sense, deconstructing the Earth under the implicit assumption that ecosystems have evolved the ability to withstand such assault without collapse.' And ecology is not at all certain that this assumption is justified. Spurned by possible environmental imminence, scientists are racing to understand and, ideally, predict the changes that take place. And with good reason: as it stands, humans appropriate fully one quarter of Earth's primary plant production, so we ourselves are an integral part of many of the world's ecosystems, whether we like it or not. Consequently, for our survival, we depend on the 'services' that the ecosystems of which we are a part provide us with. These services include anything from the provision of clean air and water, the pollination of the fruits we eat, and the aesthetic pleasure that a natural habitat offers, to breakdown of our wastes, the prevention of diseases, and staple food production.

In this and the next chapter, we will be looking at some of the properties of ecosystems and how these properties – and in particular those properties that have to do with the biodiversity contained in them – influence ecosystems' stability: their ability to withstand change and, once perturbed, to return to their original state. We will be hearing of the experiments that scientists have carried out to obtain answers to these questions. We will also be hearing of unplanned experiments: where ecosystems have been exposed inadvertently to drastic changes in their composition by extinction or the introduction of exotic species with all the ensuing reverberations. And we will hear of experiments that nature herself has carried out in her distant past. But first, a game of Jenga.

The textile metaphor that I have used so exhaustively in the previous few paragraphs to explain the weft and warp of an ecosystem, is just one of the many that have been used to write about ecosystems. A machine metaphor, for example, is also commonly used: rather than a carefully woven tapestry of biodiversity, an ecosystem can be seen as a giant biological apparatus, in which each species is an essential cog that plays a small but vital role. Remove a species and the whole system may come to a grinding halt. Sure, some species may be more essential to an ecosystem's functioning than others, but by and large, each species sits where it should, plays the role it is supposed to and does its bit to keep the system running. Yet another metaphor often used is that of an arched vault: each stone (i.e. species) sits in the right place where it helps support the great ensemble weight. A few stones, placed strategically where multiple stresses converge, play a crucial role: remove such a 'keystone' and the whole arch comes tumbling down.

The big cats that used to live in the forest of Barro Colorado Island before it became an island in the Panama Canal in 1923 (see Chap. 7) were such keystone species. When the island was formed, it proved too small to sustain populations of pumas and jaguars, and the two top predators disappeared from its ecosystem. The result was a fourfold increase of coatis, agoutis, and other small mammals on which the cats used to feed. This superabundance in turn created a greater predation pressure on the large seeds of some rainforest trees that these animals eat. As a result, the trees that produce smaller seeds gained the edge and have since increased in number in the forest. And consequently, the entire suite of herbivores that feed on these small-seeded trees have become commoner. So, the neatly stacked rainforest ecosystem was shaken up when just two of its keystone species were removed.

Yet ecologists nowadays are beginning to feel less and less comfortable with a view of ecosystems as static, preordained structures (arches, cogwheels, woven webs) that come apart as soon as they are tampered with. We have seen that the importance of niches may be limited, so a view of species as essential cogs in a machine may not be appropriate, if species are redundant or replaceable by other species. Also, as we shall see, ecologists are beginning to borrow methods and insights from other fields of science that focus on the stability of networks, such as information and communication technology or social science. And with these new tools, too, they are beginning to recognise that ecosystems are more pliable and dynamic than they had seemed before, and the brittle stone arch, the tightly woven cloth, or the vulnerable neatly balanced machine no longer seem proper metaphors. In 2005, ecosystems theorist Peter de Ruiter of the University of Utrecht in the Netherlands wrote in an opinion article in *Science*: '[It] might better be replaced with the metaphor of the structures built during … the game Jenga. … A Jenga structure is constantly changing, with additions and deletions of stones and its stability at any moment depends on the importance of a given ingoing or outgoing stone's contribution to the structure.' Ecosystems, he says, are 'open and flexible Jenga-like systems that can change in species attributes, composition, and dynamics.'

This change in perspective from viewing ecosystems as relatively static frameworks like a stone arch to seeing them as fluid, ever-changing superorganisms is best illustrated by following the twists and turns of the 'diversity–stability debate' over the past 50 years. Brace yourself: this is going to be a complicated story. But we start on familiar ground: with our old friend Charles Elton.

8.2
The More the Merrier?

In 1958, Charles Elton (see Chaps. 1, 2, 4) wrote a book entitled *The Ecology of Invasions by Animals and Plants*. We will have a better look at this landmark publication when we start discussing invasive species in the next chapter, but here I would just like to turn your attention to Elton's final chapter, in which he states that 'the balance of relatively simple communities of plants and animals is more easily upset than that of richer ones; that is, more subject to destructive oscillations in populations … and more vulnerable to invasions.' To Elton and some of his fellow ecologists in the mid-twentieth century, such a diversity–stability relationship was common knowledge that derived both from observations and from theory.

The observations seemed irrefutable: who had not heard of those simple arctic ecosystems periodically overrun with lemmings, or boreal pine forests ravaged by caterpillar outbreaks? Similar horror stories were never reported for rich, tropical ecosystems containing numbers of species that were orders of magnitude larger. Moreover, since the late 1940s, mathematical evidence had accumulated that also supported the notion that species richness in a system bestowed stability on it. Unexpectedly, this evidence derived not from ecology but from the burgeoning field of telecommunications. In the 1940s, telephone engineers of Bell Systems's laboratories developed a theory that explained how messages are best sent down complicated networks of telephone lines. One of the people involved was the famous engineer and mathematician Claude Shannon. Shannon's legacy to ecology is twofold: first, he developed a measure for network diversity that nowadays is also used for expressing biodiversity: the Shannon index. And second, he was one of the scientists at Bell Systems who discovered that the greater the Shannon index of a set of information channels, the greater the stability of the flow of information through that system, because any blockage in one node is compensated for by many other nodes.

Then, a series of unfortunate misunderstandings quickly infused ecology with the notion that diversity necessarily begets stability. First, Robert MacArthur published a short paper in 1955 in which he adopted Shannon's formula as a possible link between ecosystem stability and diversity. And though he did not say that such a link actually existed, a few years later, in his *Santa Rosalia* paper (see Chap. 2), Evelyn Hutchinson took MacArthur's formula to mean that he had. A few more influential ecologists embellished the story even further and by the mid-1960s it was considered an established fact, much referred to by environmentalists.

But as ecologist Paul Colinvaux writes in his gem of a book *Why Big Fierce Animals Are Rare*, ecology was caught in a snare, 'for the mathematics never said what ecologists came to think it said.' Food webs, after all, differ fundamentally from telephone networks, in that organisms want to keep as much of the energy flowing through it for themselves, rather than pass all of it on to the next node in the network. Also, when tropical ecology came off the ground in the 1970s, the myth that rich, tropical ecosystems are stable was exposed: in 1978, Robin Foster (see Chap. 7) discovered that a particular tree species in the South American rainforest could be completely defoliated from time to time by the caterpillar of the moth *Zunacetha annulata*; and in subsequent years, people like Stephen Hubbell and Dan Janzen reported frequently in the ecological journals of similar herbivorous insects booming unexpectedly smack in the middle of a supposedly stable and well-balanced tropical forest ecosystem. And, also in the 1970s, ecological theory finally caught up with the popular diversity–stability notion as well.

In 1972, theoretician Robert May (whom you may remember from Chaps. 3, 6) published a paper in *Nature* entitled 'Will a large complex system be stable?' It highlighted the main results from a study that he published the year after as the book *Stability and Complexity in Model Ecosystems*. May had carried out large series of computer simulations with hypothetical food webs and, using the same kind of stability analysis that Pimm and Lawton had also applied to food chains (see Chap. 2), examined what would increase or decrease their stability. To his surprise, he found that his results refuted the diversity–stability hypothesis. In fact, the most complex systems, at least in his computer, were the least stable! A conundrum that since has become known as 'May's Paradox'.

May's work, and also an influential 1975 paper in *The Quarterly Review of Biology* by Daniel Goodman, did much to bury the diversity–stability hypothesis, at least until recently. As Dan Simberloff wrote in a 2000 foreword to a republication of Elton's 1958 book, '[The hypothesis] was quite discredited by 1980, though it lives on among much of the public and has recently recrudesced, somewhat transmogrified, in a widespread (and controversial) attempt to show that "healthier" function of ecosystems is inevitably fostered by increased numbers of species.' We shall hear more about this more recent incarnation of the hypothesis at the end of this chapter. And that it lives on in environmentalist circles is clear from such websites as the one of the Common Sense Environmental Fund, which, in support of their biodiversity policy, states, 'The higher the diversity, the greater the stability.' But Simberloff may be a bit too categorical in stating that science has done away with the diversity–stability hypothesis. For although it is clear that diversity per se does not induce stability, in recent years, as we shall see later, scientists have come to understand that in diversity's wake may come some other properties that sometimes *do* stabilise ecosystems.

And even if May's work has discredited the hypothesis in its crudest form, it also begs some new questions. For May's computer simulations did not show that simple and complex systems are equally stable; they showed that the more complex a system, the *less stable* it would be. And that clearly cannot be true: in the real world, ecosystems are often extremely complex and yet they do not collapse all the time. So there must be something about real ecosystems that May did not replicate *in silico*. And in the next sections, we shall see what that something might be. Cut to a bunch of shivering scientists at the South Pole.

8.3
Six Degrees of Separation

In the austral winters of 1991–1994, sociologist Jeremy Johnson of East Carolina University studied the social interactions among the groups of scientists, technicians, and support staff overwintering at the Scott–Amundsen research station in Antarctica. He observed each member of the group, asked them to fill out questionnaires, and recorded who hung out with whom, how various peoples' habits and daily routines made them interact, and watched how the social position of each would evolve over the duration of a winter. From the data, using a computer program called MAGE, he created graphs that showed how those South Pole social networks developed over time. One graph, for example, showed 20 little blue spheres clustered tightly in space. Each blue sphere represented one of the station's inhabitants and his or her social position relative to the others in March of one year, shortly after this batch of residents had newly arrived. Superimposed on this blue network was a much more scattered collection of brown spheres, showing the social network among the same people, but seven months later, after a long winter full of irritation, depression, hardship, but also camaraderie and support. The resulting network was much more dispersed, with some tightly knit subgroups, but also some outliers: group members who, over the long dark winter, had become socially isolated from the rest.

Because of the kind of research he was doing, and because food-web ecologist Joseph Luczkovich lived next door in the Biology Department of the same university, Johnson became one of the social scientists who, in the late 1990s, realised that the questions asked by sociology in studying the structure and stability of social networks were very similar to those asked by ecologists studying food webs. In 2001, Johnson and Luczkovich jointly wrote a paper published in the *Journal of Social Structure* in which they pointed out many similarities between these two, seemingly very different fields. They also showed how methods developed in the one discipline, could be put to good use by the other. And it was not long before such an adoption took place: in November 2003, Ann Krause of the University of Michigan, East Lansing and colleagues published a paper in *Nature* in which they used a sociological method to settle a long-standing debate in food-web ecology: compartmentalisation.

The issue of compartmentalisation was first brought forward by Robert May as a possible solution for the paradox that he had revealed (see Sect. 8.2). His diverse, complex, but highly unstable food webs had been randomly assembled in a computer. In reality, he thought they might be subdivided into many smaller, more or less independent 'blocks'. Each of those blocks would behave as a simple and more stable subsystem and together these subsystems thus might help stabilise the entire ecosystem to which they belong.

Imagine, for example, the food web in my garden, as sketched in the Preface. The thousands of species living there are all interconnected by energy-transfer relationships. But not every species is connected with every other species. In fact, most species will be connected chiefly among little groups that interact within the same miniature habitat. The *Macaranga* tree, its mealybugs, weaver ants, and jumping spiders probably form one compartment of species, as do the algae, water bugs, and dragonflies in my pond. Both compartments may be part of the rest of the garden ecosystem solely by virtue of the yellow-vented bulbul, which eats both the dragonflies that sit at the pond surface and the jumping spiders on the *Macaranga* leaves. In all probability, real ecosystems are also composed of many such loosely interconnected compartments. And it is easy to imagine how this would enhance stability: when things go awry in one compartment, the mess would be more or less contained within that compartment and not necessarily contaminate the rest of the system.

Since May's papers, ecologists had been trying to find proof that ecosystems are indeed compartmentalised. But this proved more difficult than it seems, because, says Krause, previous studies tended to put species together in a compartment if they had similar predators or prey – and the researchers often did not check whether these species were indeed strongly or frequently interacting. But Krause and her colleagues found a way around this. They took Johnson and Luczkovich's advice and used a sociological method developed in the 1990s to detect subgroups in human societies. Like food webs, societies are known to be stabilised and made more durable by the existence of cliques – tightly knit groups of people that interact much more intensively than they do with members of other such groups. And such cliques are interconnected by a relatively small number of people who, like the omnivorous bulbuls in my garden, have connections within each of many different cliques. (It is these well-connected persons who, despite this fragmentation, famously ensure that each of us is separated from everybody else by on average no more than six degrees of separation.) To apply the method in sociological research, sociologists use statistical software called KliqueFinder. They feed the program with data on the network of interactions among people in a society. Then, the software calculates and maps the various cliques that can be discerned and also determines whether or not these cliques can be explained by chance.

But instead of using information on person-to-person interactions, Krause and her colleagues fed KliqueFinder with data taken from the ecological literature. They had found five ecosystems for which the food web was quite complex (between 33 and 181 species involved) and had been studied in sufficient detail: the Ythan Estuary, Little Rock Lake in Arkansas, St. Martin Island in the Caribbean, Chesapeake Bay, and a cypress wetland. For most of the plant–herbivore or prey–predator interactions in these ecosystems, they had information on either the frequency of feeding or the amount of carbon transferred, which they used in place of the social interaction data in the original sociological application of the method. The result was that they found evidence for distinct compartmentalisation in three out of the five ecosystems. Only for St. Martin Island and the Ythan Estuary did the program not come up with any ecological cliques.

In Chesapeake Bay, for example, the researchers clearly recognised two separate compartments. Compartment A with 28 species or groups of species in it, and compartment B with 17. The members of compartment A turned out to be mostly 'pelagic' species, that is organisms living in the water itself, whereas compartment B was filled with organisms that are 'benthic', feeding on the seafloor and the shore. Some animals in compartment A were benthic in the sense that they lived on the seafloor, such as the soft-shelled clam and the oyster, but because these species feed mostly on plankton and bacteria from the water, rather than on other benthic organisms, they were grouped in the pelagic compartment. The analysis also revealed the core interactions of each compartment. For the pelagic network, for example, the food chain – phytoplankton eaten by the copepod shrimp *Acartia tonsa*, eaten by zooplankton – was central to the compartment, because almost all other species interacted with this food chain.

So real food webs are to some extent chopped up into smaller, more or less independently operating 'cells', or compartments. And this could partly help solve May's Paradox. But there is more. Interestingly, ecologists have come to realise that the stretchability of a food web also depends on the kinds of interactions between species; more specifically, on bottom-up effects, weak links, and trophic loops. Sounds intriguing? Let me tell you about bottom-up and top-down first.

8.4
Top-Down or Bottom-Up?

In the previous sections, we have come across two examples of ecosystems that differ in how they are controlled. In Chesapeake Bay, the core of the system was the consumption of phytoplankton eaten by a copepod shrimp. Should the balance of this food chain change, for example during a phytoplankton bloom or die-out, the whole system would change dramatically. Chesapeake Bay is thus an example of a bottom-up controlled ecosystem, where nutrients and primary production are calling the shots. On Barro Colorado Island, however, the ecosystem appeared to be controlled from the top down: the disappearance of two members of the highest trophic level sent a wave of ecological changes cascading down through the entire forest ecosystem.

These two cases exemplify two different views on how ecosystems are governed: more by top-down effects (predation and consumption) or more by bottom-up effects (the available light and nutrients for the primary producers). The bottom-up view is that the basic resources in ecosystems are limited and that changes in the amount of food powering the system will have major effects: in Chesapeake Bay, the amount of nutrients supporting the population of phytoplankton is limited, and the whole system dances to the tunes of waxing and waning primary production. The top-down view, on the other hand, holds that populations of primary producers are kept in check by consumption and predation from the top, no matter how many nutrients or how much light is actually available to them (Fig. 8.1).

The argument dates back to 1960 when three authors, Nelson Hairston, Frederick Smith, and Larry Slobodkin (see Chap. 6 for the latter) published a paper in *The American Naturalist* entitled 'Community structure, population control, and competition'. In it, they drew attention to the undeniable fact (at least where land-based ecosystems were concerned) that 'the world is green': apparently, not all plants are eaten up by herbivores. Herbivores, therefore, must be held in check by their predators. Top-down, that is.

Surprisingly, the paper's at first sight rather innocuous statement unleashed an acrimonious debate among ecologists about top-down versus bottom-up control. Stephen Fretwell, for example, pointed out that large parts of, say, Kansas, are not green at all. And this was less facetious than it may seem: Fretwell meant to say that the number of trophic layers was important. In a three-layer system, indeed, predators would keep herbivores in check and this would allow the world they live in to remain a lush green. But with two trophic levels, the herbivores could respond to plant availability unhindered by any predation, and may defoliate their habitat. And in ecosystems with four trophic levels, the predators themselves would be regulated by their own predators, which would release the pressure on the herbivores. The interesting corollary was that ecosystems with odd numbers of trophic levels would be green, whereas systems with even numbers of trophic levels would not be.

But other ecologists pointed out that, since each ecosystem is ultimately driven by the food produced by the lowest trophic level, all are ultimately bottom-up-controlled. In the

Fig. 8.1 In bottom-up controlled ecosystems, the producers hold the consumers in check. In top-down control, the tables are turned

end, as is so often the case in such polarised debates, ecologists had to concede that all eco-systems contain a bottom-up/top-down duality. It is just the relative conspicuousness of each that determines whether we view an ecosystem as one or the other. Still, as we shall see in the next two sections, it is important to keep in mind a sense of the difference between these two ecosystem properties, especially when trying to understand environmental upheaval. For example, in 1998, James Estes and colleagues reported on a top-down environmental upheaval if there ever was one. And it all centred around *Enhydra lutris*: the sea otter.

Sea otters are among the cutest marine mammals around: floating on their backs among the kelp, they absentmindedly whack a sea urchin over the periproct with a rock, meanwhile staring around happily, completely oblivious to their role as a keystone species to the northeast Pacific ecosystem. By the early twentieth century, the likeable creatures were almost extinct as a result of overhunting by fur traders, and the marine ecosystem off the western coast of Alaska in which they lived had been effectively reduced to a top-down-controlled two-trophic-layer system, with the once-vast forests of long heavy kelp leaves having been reduced to barren underwater deserts by astronomic numbers of grazing sea urchins. A ban on overhunting helped the otters rebound and by the 1970s they had recovered in most areas. But not in all: in some areas the otters did not recover. By comparing kelp ecosystems with otters with those without, researchers were able to establish the otter's role as a keystone species: in areas where the otters had resettled, sea urchin populations crashed, kelp forests grew back, and other algae moved back in, along with squid, crustaceans, fish, and most of the other original inhabitants, including grey whales that fed on the now plentiful plankton. And all that because of a medium-sized mammal with a quizzical expression on its face.

But in the last decade of the twentieth century, history repeated itself, and the kelp ecosystem once again came crashing down, because of its top-down manner of regulation. And once again the implosion was sparked by the disappearance of the keystone species the sea otter. But this time man was responsible in a more indirect way. As Estes described in *Science*, otter populations began to decline in 1990 for no apparent reason. Whereas the otter population around the Aleutians had amounted to 53,000 in the 1970s, it had dropped to just 6,000 in 1997. A first inkling of what was happening was got in 1991 when Estes saw a killer whale eat an otter. Orcas are not supposed to eat sea otters; they feed on much meatier prey like seals and sea lions. But with these bigger marine mammals in decline, the whales began to attack otters as well. As one of Estes's colleagues said, 'they're eating popcorn instead of steaks.'

Although Estes was at first sceptical that the orca attacks could be solely responsible for the otter decline, experiments and computer modelling removed those doubts. First of all, deaths of radio-tracked otters in lagoons where orcas did not go were much lower than those in the open water. And his computer simulations showed that, indeed, as few as four otter-eating orcas could wipe out the entire sea otter population along the 3,300-kilometre western Alaskan coastline. But that then begged the question why the orcas' favourite food, seals and sea lions, was declining. The cause was, said Estes, overfishing. But in 2005, Canadian marine biologists Daniel Ware of the University of British Columbia in Vancouver and Richard Thomson of the University of Victoria reported in *Science* that fish stocks in the northeast Pacific appear to be dependent on bottom-up processes, and not primarily on the pressure from fishing.

Ware and Thomson had obtained data on fish stocks, zooplankton, and remote-sensing satellite measurements of chlorophyll (which represented the amount of phytoplankton in the water) along the coastline from the western tip of Alaska down to southern California. They found very strong correlations between all: areas with high productivity (that is, high chlorophyll concentration) had greater zooplankton counts, and consequently more fish. This meant that fish stocks were mostly under – literally as well as trophically – bottom-up control.

The decline in fish stocks since the 1980s, which Ware and Thomson had also noticed, may thus not be the result of overfishing, as Estes thought, but also, at least partially, a result of a change in phytoplankton availability. And this could be linked to a change in climate which warmed up the sea surface waters in the mid-1970s, with a concomitant drop in plankton density. They were all somewhat circumstantial data, but Ware and Thomson said it looked as if climate change had, in a bottom-up fashion, reduced the productivity of the northern Pacific. This would have reduced the amount of zooplankton, which then would have impacted the fish stocks and, consequently, the sea lion and seal populations. At the top of the food pyramid, the effects were then felt by the orcas, who changed their diets by starting to eat sea otters, and because of that the ecological cascade changed direction and began hurtling top-down again in the direction of desertified and depauperated kelp forests.

This story, riveting as it may be, so far has not helped us much in our search for what determines stability in ecosystems. But we are getting there. The crucial thing to keep in mind is that species in a food web exert both top-down and bottom-up forces on one another. Next: the importance of being weak.

8.5
The Weakest Link

Where the waves of the Pacific Ocean lap the cold shores of Tatoosh Island, just off the northwestern coast of Washington state, a typical temperate-region intertidal community clings on to the rocks and boulders. It has all the usual occupants: most space just above the low water line is hogged by California mussels, sitting shoulder to shoulder. Here and there, a gap in the mussel cover appears where plants, acorn barnacles, blue mussels, and goose barnacles eagerly take up the vacant spots. In addition to this collection of sedentary residents, which all feed on plankton during high water, are several mobile mollusc species: herbivorous limpets, for example, and carnivorous dogwhelks. And then there are the birds: gulls, oystercatchers, and crows regularly descend on the defenceless intertidal creatures and gobble up large numbers of the dogwhelks, goose barnacles, and mussels. Finally, a small seastar gropes about, here and there snacking on a dogwhelk or an acorn barnacle.

It is a fairly simple compartment of an ecosystem with a limited number of interactions. Yet it took ecologist Timothy Wootton of the University of Washington in Seattle his entire PhD studies and quite a few changes of clothes to figure out the exact shape of the food web. After obtaining permission from the local Macaw tribe, who own the island, Wootton carried out a series of experiments on the rocky shores by systematically excluding the effects of one of the species from the system. The remote island is ideal for this purpose, he says, because 'it's often challenging to find a place where the general public doesn't mess up your experiments'. Suitably unharassed on the desolate shore, Wootton studied the effects of birds, for example, by stringing rectangular wire baskets (the kind used as "IN" and "OUT" trays on office desks) to some rocks so the birds could not get to the molluscs and barnacles. And he studied the effects of the dogwhelks by removing them by hand, one by one, from marked patches of rock.

The letter-basket experiments, for example, showed how, over the course of a year, the space underneath the basket, where bird beaks could not reach, filled to the brim with goose barnacles – obviously the species that profited most from being protected from the predators. But this would also mean that, indirectly, the birds interact with the mussels and acorn barnacles, because the latter two compete for space with the goose barnacles. So experiment by experiment, Wootton revealed parts of the entire web of interactions. A web that, as it turned out, was dominated by a few strong interactions and many weak ones. (Roughly speaking, interactions are considered strong if the population size of one species has a relatively great effect on that of another, by providing food, by competing with it, or by preying on it.) The strong ones were, for example, the feeding of birds on goose barnacles, the feeding of dogwhelks on acorn barnacles, and competition for space between goose barnacles on the one hand and acorn barnacles and mussels on the other. Many other arrows in the web of shoreline interactions were very weak, such as the feeding of birds on mussels and dogwhelks, or the feeding of dogwhelks on goose barnacles.

Picking up on Wootton's finding, ecologist Peter 'Jenga' de Ruiter (then at the Research Institute for Agrobiology and Soil Fertility in the Netherlands) and his colleagues looked at how such strong and weak interactions were distributed in entire ecosystems and whether perhaps this distribution pattern had anything to say about stability. A few years earlier, de Ruiter had been studying the soil ecosystem on a farm in the Dutch Flevopolder as it made the transition from conventional crop farming to ecological farming. He had worked out the food web in much detail, including all bacteria, fungi, bacterium-, plant-, and fungus-eating nematode worms, pot worms, springtails, fungus- and nematode-eating mites, amoebae, nematode-eating nematodes, and mite-eating mites, and the exact flows of energy among them, just like Raymond Lindeman had done in Cedar Bog Lake (see Chap. 2). This allowed him to calculate the exact interaction strengths throughout the web. Remember, interaction strength indicates the effect that one species has on a species with which it interacts. This means that the interaction between two species, say, a predator and its prey, usually has two components: a top-down interaction (the effect of predator on prey), as well as a bottom-up interaction (the effect of prey on predator).

As de Ruiter and his team reported in *Science* in 1995, like Wootton, they had found (in their experimental farm as well as in three other soil food webs) that interaction strengths were not randomly distributed: they found some very strong interactions, but also many weak ones. Focusing on the strong ones, these were mainly bottom-up in the higher trophic levels, whereas in the lower trophic level top-down effects dominated. Having thus confirmed Wootton's finding of a few strong interactions embedded in a web of weak ones, de Ruiter did a stability analysis, similar to the one May had done 20 years earlier, to see which interactions were the ones that most stabilised the system.

Surprisingly, he found that there was no relationship between the strength of an interaction and its impact on the entire system. The extremely weak interaction between predatory nematodes and the mites that eat them, for example, turned out to have a major effect on the stability of the web. At the same time, the strong interaction between amoebae and the flagellates (a collection of single-celled Protozoa that move about by means of a whip-like flagella) that they eat had no effect on the system whatsoever! What he did find, though, was that the distribution of interaction strengths (a few strong top-down effects at the bottom of the trophic pyramid, some strong bottom-up effects in the top layers, and lots of weak interactions interspersed) was crucial: when he created artificial food webs in the computer and rearranged the interaction strengths randomly throughout the pyramid, his mock ecosystems would collapse in no time. Only if they mimicked the distribution of interaction strengths found in natural ecosystems would they be stable.

A few years later, theoretical ecologist Kevin McCann threw a wheelbarrow full of mathematical formulas at food webs to explain why ecosystems worked the way de Ruiter had found they did. The key, McCann discovered, was in the weak interactions, which prevent strong interaction from throwing an ecosystem out of whack. Aptly but somewhat uninventively named 'the weak-interaction effect' by McCann, it works like this.

Imagine two prey species, say the goose barnacle and the mussel, both competing for space and both eaten by gulls on the rocky shores of Wootton's Tatoosh Island. There is a strong interaction between the gulls and the goose barnacles, but a weak interaction between the birds and the mussels (that is, gulls prefer goose barnacles over mussels). In this three-species food web, the mussels and the goose barnacles compete with one another via the gulls' stomachs: when there are many birds, these eat up a lot of goose barnacles, which allows the mussels to flourish because they can take up the space vacated by the eaten goose barnacles; and because of the weak interaction, the high gull density does not bother the mussels so much. Since there is such a strong interaction between gulls and goose barnacles, if left to themselves, the two would exterminate one another: lots of gulls lead to the near extinction of goose barnacles, which in turn would drive the gulls to the edge of disappearance, which would result in a rebound for the goose barnacles, etc., until one day either species would crash irrevocably. But the weak interaction between gulls and mussels dampens these potentially disastrous oscillations in the food web: when goose barnacle populations decline because the gulls have eaten almost all of them, the mussels will expand and at a certain point the gulls will begin eating those instead. This allows the goose barnacles to recover to such a level that the gulls switch their attention back to them again. The result: the weak interaction between gulls and their not-so-preferred mussels saves the day.

A final refinement to the role of weak links as mediators in ecosystem crises appeared in *Science* in 2002, when one of de Ruiter's PhD students, ecosystems theorist Anje-Margriet Neutel of the University of Utrecht, published her study of loops. Trophic loops that is, in food webs. A trophic loop is a closed chain of interactions; a feature of food webs that is particularly common when there are many omnivores around, feeding, as they do, on more than one trophic level (and remember from Gary Polis's work in Chap. 2 that omnivores are omnipresent). In Wootton's rocky shore ecosystem, this would, for example, be the trio gulls, dogwhelks, and goose barnacles (dogwhelks feed on goose barnacles, the omnivorous gulls feed on both). Remember, we are talking interactions, not one-way feeding relationships. So there would be two three-step loops among them: one composed of two top-down effects (from gulls on dogwhelks and from dogwhelks on goose barnacles) plus a bottom-up effect (from goose barnacles on gulls), and another loop composed of one top-down effect (from gulls on goose barnacles) and two bottom-up effects (from goose barnacles on dogwhelks and from dogwhelks on gulls).

Now what Neutel was interested in was the 'weight' of loops and their effect on ecosystem stability. She defined weight by taking the average over the interaction strengths in each loop. Then, she examined several real food webs, including the farm soil ecosystem of de Ruiter, but also, for example, the food web in the soil of the Central Plains Experimental Range of the University of Northern Colorado. For each system, she made a table of all the loop lengths and their weights, and also calculated, using stability analysis, the stability of the system. Then, she let her computer mess up the food webs by exchanging interaction strengths from different species pairs and watched what happened to the loop weights and the stability.

It turned out that in the artificial, rearranged systems, longer loops were also heavier, whereas in the real systems, loops were always light, no matter how long they were (and some were up to six steps long). This was due to the fact that loops in the real systems contained relatively many weak interactions. We can understand this by looking again at the gulls–dogwhelks–goose barnacles loop. The gull top predators are omnivorous, feeding at two trophic levels at the same time: the goose barnacles are primary consumers, whereas the dogwhelks are predators of the primary consumers, so they sit in a higher trophic level. Since we know that energy and biomass are reduced by about 90% at each higher trophic level (see Chap. 2), the gulls get most of their energy from the goose barnacles, which sit in a lower trophic level than the dogwhelks. As a result, the top-down effect of gulls on goose barnacles will be much greater than on dogwhelks. So the loop 'gulls to goose barnacles to dogwhelks to gulls' contains just one strong interaction and two weak ones. Also, the loop 'gulls to dogwhelks to goose barnacles to gulls' contains one strong top-down interaction (from dogwhelks to goose barnacles) and two weak ones. Neither of the loops could have two strong interactions in it. So there you have it: both loops will be light, forced by the energy pyramid.

In the artificial, rearranged ecosystems, interaction strengths were randomly assigned by the computer, which did not care about any energy pyramid. So that is why the loops in the artificial webs were not always light. And, moreover: the artificial webs were also much less stable than the real webs with all their weak-interaction loops.

Okay, enough about that; I hope you have not gone completely loopy. Time to let it all sink in and then recap: what do all these compartments, loops, strong and weak, top-down and bottom-up interactions tell us? Take a break, have some trophic interactions of your own and meet me in 15 minutes in the next section.

8.6
Elton Revisited

Now I have a confession to make. Until now, I have glossed over an important difference in terminology used. Unforgivably, these terms lie at the heart of this chapter, nay of this book itself. My only defence is that many top-notch ecologists have done the same in many of the studies that I have introduced to you in this chapter. But now it is time to come clean: ecosystem diversity and ecosystem complexity are not the same.

So far, I have treated the number of species in an ecosystem (species richness or diversity, although some sticklers will maintain there is a difference even between those two terms: see Notes) as a measure for complexity. But strictly speaking, diversity is not the same as complexity. Imagine two hypothetical ecosystems, both with 100 species in them. In the one ecosystem, there are 98 plant species, one generalist bug that feeds on all the plants, and one bird that eats the bugs. Unlikely, but possible. The other ecosystem contains 20 plant species, fed on by a mixture of 50 specialist and generalist herbivores, which in turn are preyed on by 20 different predatory insects, some specialists, some generalists, and, to top it all off, ten bird species (some of which feed on the herbivores, some on the predators, and some are omnivores, feeding on all trophic levels). Now, would we consider both 100-species ecosystems equally diverse? Yes, because they have the same number of species in them. But would we say they are equally complex? No, we would not, because in the first ecosystem, there are only as many feeding links in the food web as there are species, whereas in the second there are many more; so the first would be considered simple, the second would be complex.

Ecologists who care passionately about terminology would prefer to use the word 'complexity' only when they mean the combination between the number of species on the one hand, and the number of connections between them on the other. And May's Paradox should be seen in this light. The fact that May found that more complex ecosystems are the least stable has to do as much with the fact that they contain more species as with the fact that these species have many connections among them. When some species interaction begins to fluctuate dangerously somewhere in a highly interconnected web (and the more species there are the more likely it is that there will be a problem somewhere) the crisis is not easily contained. That is why May thought that compartments may help. When a food web is subdivided into compartments, it means that connections are missing between groups of species. In other words, a compartmentalised ecosystem has fewer connections overall than an equally diverse uncompartmentalised ecosystem. That is, it is less complex. So frankly, compartmentalisation does not really solve May's Paradox at all, because a compartmentalised 100-species ecosystem is not equally complex as a 100-species ecosystem that is not compartmentalised: it is less complex, hence more stable.

So compartments do not resolve the paradox. But as we saw in the previous section, the pattern of interaction strengths does. Weak interactions, especially when arranged in loops, are safety devices that defuse crises in the web. So this may explain why complex ecosystems in the real world do not collapse, whereas randomly constructed in the computer, they do.

Still, solving May's Paradox does not answer the question whether complex ecosystems are actually *more* stable than simple ones, as Charles Elton would have it. We know that diversity and complexity per se do not increase stability. But perhaps if diversity increases, so do the properties that stabilise an ecosystem. So, after Elton's idea was initially debunked by May's analyses and by the fact that plagues and pestilences turn out to befall complex ecosystems just as well as simple ones, and despite Simberloff's misgivings, it might be time for a reappraisal of the idea. And over the past few years, the problem has been approached in two different ways: by looking at succession in soil ecosystems and by supersizing ecological experimentation. We will have a look at the latter first.

Although these days the resolution of satellite images is so great that you could probably use them to read a newspaper on a Paris café table, it still speaks to the imagination when we hear of something man-made that can be seen from space. And David Tilman's prairie grassland experiment in Cedar Creek, the same University of Minnesota field station where Raymond Lindeman did his research (see Chap. 2), certainly fits that description. Virtually swooping in on the area via Google Earth, the geometric patchwork of experimental fields already becomes visible before even Lindeman's Cedar Bog Lake reveals its teardrop-like shape. Like an invitation to extraterrestrials to come and play a game of Chinese checkers, the 168 neatly arranged nine metre by nine metre plots certainly look impressive. And they should: established in May 1995, the site, designed to study the effects of plant diversity on the functioning of ecosystems, has yielded over two dozen research papers in top journals like *Nature* and *Science*. And Tilman does not hide his gratitude to the prairie habitat that has been so beneficial to his career: 'Grasslands are wonderful ecosystems in their own right; I love them. And they are so readily amenable to experimentation and results can be obtained relatively quickly,' he says.

One of the latest fruits Tilman picked from his prairie plots was a paper he published in *Nature* on 1 June 2006 entitled 'Biodiversity and ecosystem stability in a decade-long grassland experiment'. In it, Tilman describes how he and his team had sown the 168 plots with different combinations of one, two, four, eight, or 16 species of wild prairie plants, and had meticulously maintained the mix of species over the ten years since the site had been established by weeding out all other plants a few times per year. The fate of the plots was monitored regularly: each year, they would clip, dry, sort to species, and weigh one strip from each plot to see how much biomass had been produced for each plant species separately.

Taken over a decade, the results were intriguing: the biomass production (the primary productivity) of the plots increased with diversity, almost doubling when the 16-species plots were compared with the one-species plots. So indeed, the functioning of the nine metre by nine metre ecosystems, measured by the amount of carbon they churned out yearly, was increased as diversity increased. This is nothing new, really, because in 1859 Darwin already wrote that 'It has been experimentally proved that if a plot of ground be sown with one species of grass, and a similar plot be sown with several distinct genera of grasses, a greater number of plants and a greater weight of dry herbage can thus be raised.' His visionary claim was based on the work done in the experimental garden of Woburn Abbey in the early nineteenth century, as British ecologist Andy Hector of Imperial College London at Silwood Park, UK, found out. Hector, now at the University of Zurich, Switzerland, together with University of California, Santa Barbara, ecologist Brad Cardinale and six other authors, in 2007 published an overview of all 44 studies they could find, and discovered that, overall, they showed the same result: productivity goes up as biodiversity goes up.

It is this set of consistent results which Simberloff referred to when he lamented about the recent recrudescence of the diversity–stability hypothesis. Simberloff's scepticism is understandable: of course, productivity is not the same as stability. But it could be caused by stability, could it not? An ecosystem running stationary might, in the long run, produce more biomass than one that has to reset itself all the time. Unfortunately, the cause for the effect of diversity on plant productivity (and, in fact, also the productivity in other trophic layers, as Cardinale and his team reported in another article) is a little mysterious. Some people have said that it was the result of plants having somewhat complementary niches. So a single plant may only be able to get at a part of all the nutrients and light and carbon dioxide available in the plot, whereas a mix of plants with diverse niches would be able to exploit those resources in a more complete and efficient way. But, says Hector, others have argued that the results are just a statistical quirk: some plant species are just very good at

8

producing biomass under the conditions present. And the more species are sown in a plot, the greater the chance that one or more of those superplants will be found among them: the so-called sampling effect.

A close-up look at (or rather, an advanced statistical analysis of) all the 44 experiments that Cardinale and Hector scrutinised, revealed that the answer was, as so often, a little bit of both. 'The effect is due to about 2/3 complementarity effects and about 1/3 sampling effects,' he says, comparing it a bit to the way a soccer team works: 'Teams are composed of both star players and supporting players. You probably can't win many games if you lose your top striker because she or he is the most productive player and can dominate a game. But strikers cannot win games by themselves. They need great passes from supporting players and solid goal-tending if the team is going to be successful as a whole.' So diverse ecosystems are winning teams: they churn out a lot of biomass because they contain many species, each somewhat specialised on their own niche, and on top of that, purely by chance, they contain a few superplants that bring home the bulk of the bacon.

But Tilman's latest grassland data show that the relationship between increased productivity and stability is not that straightforward. Indeed, as he also reported in the 2006 *Nature* paper, the species-rich plots not only are the most productive, but their productivity also varies much less from year to year than in the species-poor plots. But at the same time, species stability declines with increasing diversity: the species-rich plots varied much more in relative abundance of each species than the species-poor ones. So that means that the stable biomass output was maintained not *because* of a steadily, stably running ecosystem, but rather *despite* a very unstable, dynamic ecosystem in which 'soccer players' were constantly hired and fired. Indeed, a Jenga-like ecosystem.

But I still have one card up my sleeve. All the studies mentioned so far in this section have been done at a single trophic layer, mostly that of the primary producers. Moreover, their diversities have been established and maintained very artificially: by sowing and weeding. Understandably, people have said that we can only be really sure of what goes on in nature by observing nature itself, rather than a checkerboard of man-made horticultural plots. And to look at all trophic levels rather than just one. And that is precisely what Anje-Margriet Neutel and co-workers did in a study published in *Nature* on 4 October 2007.

They went to two areas of sand dunes in the Netherlands: coastal dunes on the island of Schiermonnikoog and inland dunes on the Veluwe, a hilly landscape of rocky and pebbly moraines left behind when the land ice of the penultimate glacial period retreated, some 120,000 years ago, and then covered by sand during the sandstorms of the next ice age. In some places of the otherwise forested Veluwe, this sand is still being moved about occasionally by the wind. At the edges of recently formed dunes, the team picked sites that represented four consecutive stages in succession of the vegetation: recently deposited bare sand (zero years old), sand with a few loose plants (five to ten years old), sand with a thick layer of vegetation of mosses and lichens (five to 25 years old), and sandy soil with shrub and tree saplings (50 to 100 years old).

For each of the eight sites, they took soil samples and, like they had done on their experimental farm, extracted all the bacteria, fungi, protozoa, nematodes, mites, and springtails, weighed them, mapped the feeding relations and drew a good approximation of the soil food web with all the interaction strengths. As expected, the older the habitats were, the more diverse, the more complex (in the strict sense), and also the more productive they were. But when they then did a stability analysis, they did not find a clear relationship between stability on the one hand and age, diversity, or complexity of the ecosystems on the other.

Then Neutel, with her predilection for trophic loops, mapped the loop weights in each of the systems, and a beautifully consistent relationship was revealed: the heavier the heaviest loop was, the less stable the system was. This maximum loop weight was not related to food-web complexity or diversity. Instead, it seemed that as trophic layers were added to ecosystems as they self-assembled, they went through stages of instability. As a trophic layer filled up, the increased biomass up there would create heavier and heavier loops, destabilising the system, until a new top predator arrived to mop up some of this biomass, reduce the loop weights, and reinstate stability. Indeed, Neutel found that stability was highest in the first successional stage, then reduced when the next stage was reached, then increased again in stage three and finally decreased again. So Neutel's analysis showed two things: (1) the heaviest loop is the Achilles heel of an ecosystem – that we already knew; (2) systems do not get more stable as they get more complex – rather, they ride a rollercoaster of more and less stable states.

Well, you will be more than forgiven for being confused by all this. Ecologists themselves are confused too. And that is not surprising: ecosystems are very complex things and it is hard to make sense of all the conflicting processes that we see happening in them. In many ways, advanced ecosystems science is still in its infancy. But I think this chapter has shown us a few things. First, natural ecosystems are more stable than you would think, but it is a dynamic stability: quite a lot of changes and turnover take place in the way they are built up and these changes do not, by themselves, put the systems at risk of folding. Also, stability does not depend on how many species there are in a natural ecosystem and in how complex a way they are arranged. But it does seem to depend on the amounts of energy being pushed around in cycles in the web structure. Meanwhile, the diversity of a system, though it does not need to affect its stability, does seem to affect the biomass produced by it: both the amount of biomass and the stability of its production.

Going back to a sociological analogy, ecosystems thus are a bit like companies. Big companies produce more and do so in a more consistent way, despite the fact that they may be hiring and firing employees all the time. This does not mean that big firms are more stable: like ecosystems and Jenga towers, they too can collapse under mismanagement. And mismanagement – ecological mismanagement, that is – is what we will talk about in the final chapter.

The Age of Atropos

9

9.1
Ecosystems Unravelled

The Moirae of nature, who weave the intricate and colourful ecological tapestries of tropical rainforests, arctic tundras, limestone caves, freshwater lakes, rocky shores, and all the other ecosystems that we have come across in this book, are by now quite familiar to us. Using sophisticated ecology, we have unravelled the workings of natural ecosystems and understood the characters of their Moirae. Nature's Clotho governs the numerous species and their idiosyncratic niches. Life's Lachesis is a whimsical creature, rarely abiding by rules other than those of trophic relations, and mostly working her loom with whatever threads in Clotho's grabbag take her fancy. That nevertheless the tapestry she weaves strikes us as cleverly designed may just be an illusion. And the ecological incarnation of Atropos, finally, may not wield just a pair of shears but rather a collection of needlework tools with which she tampers with the craft of her two sisters. Testing the strength of the trophic interactions, she may or may not succeed in unravelling the ecosystem.

Whereas in the past, the ecological Atropos would normally come in the guise of natural disasters (floods, lightning strikes, fire, hurricanes, volcanic eruptions), these days more often than not, she takes a human form. And the tools we use to ply her trade, the implements we use so clumsily to make ecosystems unravel inadvertently, are all too familiar. Fishermen with their trawl nets remove the big fish, the upper trophic levels in coral reefs and other marine systems. Timber loggers use their axes and chainsaws to cut away the giant energy-producing legs from underneath rainforests. Well-intentioned wildlife managers insert foreign twine into the tapestry by introducing alien species. And on a much larger scale, intercontinental cargo vessels do the same. Finally, the giant, blunt wedges of agriculture, road and water works, mining, hydroelectrical projects, and all other 'land use change' cut ecosystems to tatters.

In this final chapter, we will use our knowledge of ecosystems' workings to understand how human actions may, wittingly or unwittingly, create upheaval in them. Conversely, large-scale human tampering with real ecosystems, as undesirable as it may be, can as a

The Loom of Life. M. Schilthuizen
Doi: 10.1007/978-3-540-68058-1_9, © Springer-Verlag Berlin Heidelberg 2008

9

collateral benefit also provide us with the natural experiments so badly needed to test our ecosystem theories at the scale that matters. So we will also have a fair amount of reciprocal illumination. In the following sections, I will parade the three chief tools of our ecological Atropos, the main types of ecosystem interventions that humans are particularly good at: removing species, adding species, and cutting them up.

9.2
The Shears of Extinction

In *On the Origin of Species*, Charles Darwin writes, 'so profound is our ignorance, and so high our presumption, that we marvel when we hear of the extinction of an organic being.' Indeed, in Darwin's days, animal extinctions were still rare and conspicuous events. The dodo had been gone for more than one and a half centuries and was already used proverbially as the archetypical goner. The three-metre elephant bird of Madagascar and the giant moa of New Zealand presumably had also kicked the bucket as early as the seventeenth century, while the cape lion, the great auk, and the quagga expired around the time Darwin's book was published. Still, by and large, most people in the mid-nineteenth century shared Darwin's naiveté where extinction was concerned.

Today, we are no longer so innocent. Species are keeling over all over the place. A Google Earth glimpse of a small area west of the city of Kuantan in West Malaysia shows that the Panching limestone hill, the world's only place where the weird miniature snail *Opisthostoma sciaphilum* lived, has recently been levelled for a housing estate. Exit *O. sciaphilum*. When the last surviving Californian condors were trapped for a captive breeding programme, the bird species was saved, but its condor-specific feather louse *Colpocephalum californici* went extinct when the well-meaning but ill-informed conservationists deloused the birds as they were brought in. And in 2007, the famous Chinese baiji dolphin, endemic to the Yangtze river and sole-surviving member of the family Lipotidae, was declared extinct owing to hunting and accidental killings by fishing gear. It does not even survive in captivity.

Such individual speciecide and specieslaughter are commonplace and are not likely to let up any time soon, as clashes between wildlife and the still expanding human population intensify. However, sad as the death of each species may be, they remain incidental, and pale in comparison with the wilful, intentional genocide waged against biodiversity in the name of the human appetite for wild species. And I do not mean bushmeat, which is a relatively minor problem. I am talking of hardwood and seafood, the global, legalised, and largely accepted driving to the brink of extinction of wild species. Globally, these are the two human enterprises that continue to shave, deliberately and unsustainably, entire layers off the Eltonian pyramid.

Let us have a look at what is happening at the bottom of the pyramid first. And where better to look than in Borneo, hardest hit among all the tropical regions in the world that are targeted by timber companies. The island, twice the size of Germany, has been haemorrhaging more wild-harvested hardwood in the past 20 years than Africa and Latin America combined. For Malaysian Borneo alone, the total annual value of legally exported wood is US \$2.5 billion. This is not surprising: the world's consumption of tropical hardwood is still on the increase, and Borneo has some of the best species on offer. Its forests are dominated by the tree family Dipterocarpaceae, many members of which make fine timber for construction. But even more prized are species like Borneo ironwood or 'belian' (*Eusideroxylon zwageri*, a member of the laurel family), untreated beams of which are virtually indestructible (and hence the wood of choice for the traditional Borneo longhouse). Other highly valued trees are the *Agathis* and *Shorea* species, 'merbau' (*Intsia palembanica*), and 'ramin' (*Gonystylus bancanus*). Some of these tree species have almost been logged to extinction and are listed on the Red List of endangered species.

Since so many trees in Borneo's forests are valuable, loggers will not spurn many when they begin harvesting a concession. The forests are, however, usually not clearfelled; instead, the desirable trees are pulled out one by one. With the exception of a few bits of exemplarily logged and conserved forests, the average Borneo lowland rainforest has suffered several rounds of such logging since the 1960s, and looks suitably bedraggled. Often, only gnarled trees, young, thin ones, and those belonging to undesirable species have been left standing. Giant pits have been etched in the canopy, overgrown with vines and fast-growing pioneer species. And the logging roads, baring the laterite soils, snake like orange tentacles between.

With official timber concessions depleted, even the network of nature reserves in Indonesian Borneo (Kalimantan) is no longer safe, says tropical ecologist Lisa Curran of Yale University, New Haven, USA. As Curran reported in a 2004 paper in *Science*, by 1999, loggers had already ravaged most of the ten-kilometre-wide buffer zone around the 2,700-square-kilometre Gunung Palung National Park. Since then, with government supervision diminished after the country's administrative revolution of 1998, forest in the park itself fell prey to them and has been disappearing at a rate of 10% per year. Curran says that similar hollowing-out of so-called protected areas takes place throughout Kalimantan. Next to using satellite images and flyovers in small planes, Curran obtained a lot of intelligence in the logging camps that she worked from for most of the 1990s. On how she found out that most timber cartels are now targeting protected areas, she says, 'I speak the language – know the forest and logging extremely well, can tell crude logging jokes and am not judgemental with anybody from local labourer to general manager. Also, I do not publicly rant on anyone.' Fortunately, in recent years, with the park under new management, illegal logging is under control again.

Given so many things that are wrong with logging practices in Borneo, it is almost perversely clinical to point out what timber extraction means within an ecosystem framework. The energy pyramid of a snippet of tropical rainforest is supported by a highly productive bottom layer, composed of thousands of plant species, which together fix more than one kilogram of carbon per year per square metre (see Chap. 2). Much of this biomass sits in the huge, up to 80-metre-tall emergent trees. A timber operation breaches this layer by uprooting a large number of the most productive species in one go. The loss of these species from the lowest trophic layer is likely to have repercussions higher up in the pyramid.

As we saw in the previous chapter, the disappearance of a keystone species can send shock waves throughout the food web. Such shock waves are called 'cascades', and usually they are considered to ripple top-down from the higher trophic levels to the lower ones.

But, as two ecologists wrote in a 1992 paper in *Ecology*, the term 'cascading upward', though an oxymoron, can be used to indicate that in food webs effects can flow upward as well as downward, 'as in Escher paintings'. (In fact, as we saw in the sea otter cascade of Chap. 8, the original disturbance probably was an event in the phytoplankton, all the way down in the lowest trophic level.) The removal by lumberjacks of a whole cohort of biomass producers from a rainforest ecosystem may thus be expected to cause cascades penetrating the rest of the food web from below.

Such bottom-up cascades are surprisingly hard to spot within the mind-bogglingly complex web of rainforest interactions, with its hundreds of thousands of species. This is even despite the river of ink that ecologists have caused to flow in the name of the impact of logging on biodiversity. Large investigations have mostly shown that animal biodiversity drops in logged forests. But whether such effects are the direct consequence of messing with the bottom rung of the food web is often not clear. At least nowhere near as clear as the tsunami-like marine top-down cascades that will feature in the remainder of this section. But one example of a bottom-up cascade that might illustrate the kind of thing we could expect as logging removes the largest trees is provided by work done by University of Amsterdam PhD student Martjan Lammertink in the same Gunung Palung reserve that Lisa Curran worked at.

Now, Lammertink is no ordinary PhD student. In the preface to his thesis he writes, 'I had grown up following a small population of banded Black Woodpeckers in a coastal nature reserve in the Netherlands'. Not the kind of experience many people would claim as their overriding childhood memory. But Lammertink clearly was born with woodpeckers on his mind. Besides his formative Dutch woodpecker experiences, all his working life seems to have been devoted to these admittedly lovely birds. He had searched for the presumed-extinct ivory-billed woodpecker in Cuba and Arkansas (and famously found it, as part of the Cornell University team, in the latter site). He had done his MSc studies on the extinction of the imperial woodpecker of Mexico. And, in fact, when you meet him in real life, his crest of reddish blond hair, high forehead and sharp, low-set nose, do remind you of....

Still, despite admitting that woodpecker research has an 'engrained lure' to him, he had to think twice before accepting a PhD project on woodpeckers in Borneo. 'Asian woodpeckers did not look all that appealing,' he writes. 'There was for instance the ungainly Great Slaty Woodpecker with a drab grey coloration and a ridiculous thin neck.' But he went, and was pleasantly surprised: '[The woodpeckers] were splendid. The drab, thin-necked Great Slaty Woodpeckers in real life turned out to be very fun animals to watch. They would hang around in small noisy flocks, constantly uttering giggling calls as if they were a group of happy schoolgirls.' And after a while he had to admit that they were very beautiful too, 'with their ochre throats, rounded heads, long bills, and big, soulful brown eyes' (Fig. 9.1).

What Lammertink did was monitor woodpeckers in logged and (yet) unlogged parts of Gunung Palung. He outlined eight four-kilometre trails and walked these up and down for a total of 88 hours each, counting woodpeckers as he went along. He also measured the average diameter of the trees that had been cut there. He found clear differences: woodpeckers were much more numerous in the unlogged parts of the forest. Not surprising for a group of animals that require a lot of dead branches on standing trees to find their food.

Fig. 9.1 Great slaty woodpeckers ('with their soulful brown eyes') are one of the species that have taken the brunt of a bottom-up cascade in Southeast Asian lowland rainforests

Using a perhaps odd biometric unit, he found unlogged forest to support three kilograms of woodpecker per hectare, which declined to just one kilogram for the most severely logged forest. Among the 14 species of woodpecker that he saw, the great slaty woodpecker clearly responded most strongly to logging: whereas in pristine forest he would see an average of six birds per square kilometre, in logged forest there was just one.

Lammertink suspects that this has to do with the species' foraging habits. The great slaty woodpecker forages in groups of three to six birds. They scour the thickest rainforest trees for nests of termites, stingless bees, and ants and, once they have located them, collectively work the quarry. Lammertink thinks that group hunting might be particularly suited for what appears to be their favourite food: stingless bees. These tiny bees build very complex nest systems out of resin and wax inside large hollow trees, often with multiple entrances spread over surfaces of many square metres. By attacking a nest in a gang, the woodpeckers may be able to cover all possible escape routes. The species is thus adapted to foraging in the fattest of rainforest trees. Once logged out, the remainder of the vegetation simply won't do for these birds.

So, this woodpecker story is one example of the many tiny ripples that will pass bottom-up through logged forests. Not a trophic ripple, in this case, because the emergent trees do not provide food to the stingless bees but provide nesting space; but a ripple nonetheless.

Top-down cascades, trophic cascades, of an entirely different order of magnitude can be found in the sea. Just like rainforest timber, seafood is a huge resource for humans that is still for a very large part taken directly from wild species out in nature. And at the moment, many seafood species are hurtling toward extinction.

As we saw in Chap.2, the photosynthesisers of the sea are very small. Forced to live in the sunlit top layers of the water, and unable to take root, they mostly take the shape of the microscopic, single-celled green organisms that we call phytoplankton. Since phytoplankton is tiny, so is the herbivorous zooplankton that eats it: minuscule shrimp and other invertebrates. Most zooplankton-eaters by necessity also do not get very large, and it is only above the third trophic level that marine animals begin to get big enough for humans to be interested in them. The fish we fish with our hooks and nets mostly sit high up in the food chain. This means we are shaving the very tip off the marine energy pyramid. And thus it takes very little for fishing to become overfishing.

In 1998, in a paper in *Science*, a team led by fisheries biologist Daniel Pauly of the University of British Columbia, Vancouver, Canada, compiled Food and Agriculture Organisation data on landings from 1950 to 1994. Their lists included 220 seafood species caught by fishermen world-wide. For each year, for each part of the oceans, they calculated the average trophic level of the animals being caught. And their graphs show precisely the kind of patterns you would expect from the overexploitation of the tip of a food pyramid. Over the whole period, in all seas, the average trophic level of the fish that fishermen catch has gone down from more than 3.3 to less than 3.1, meaning that the ocean's fishermen are slowly working their way down the food pyramid.

But a set of graphs in which the average trophic level was plotted against the annual tonnage of catch reveals much better what is going on. Rather than a slow descent into lower levels of the food pyramid, with concomitant catch increase, the graphs show abrupt shifts. Fisheries would fish at a high trophic level, with catches rising for several years on end, and then suddenly shift to a lower trophic level, be sustained at that level for a while, and then again drop further. In fact, what we are seeing is the removal of layer by layer off the top of the pyramid. Once the largest top predators have been fished to near extinction, attention shifts to the next level down, and so on.

Take sharks, for instance. Many of the 350 species of this ancient group of cartilaginous fishes take an apical position in the food pyramid. Even the smaller species of shark, such as the Atlantic sharpnose shark (*Rhizoprionodon terraenovae*) that grows over one metre in length, are so large that they are only eaten by other sharks, such as the dusky shark (*Carcharinus obscurus*; up to four metres long) and the tiger shark (*Galeocerda cuvier*; up to seven).

Sharks have been around for 350 million years, they passed unscathed through the mass extinction 65 million years ago that finished off the dinosaurs, only to be brought to the brink of extinction by humans over just the past few decades. Since 1970, demand for shark has risen sharply, largely fuelled by the popularity of sharkfin in Asia. With Asian economies booming, this delicacy is now financially within reach for ever-larger numbers of people, and no wedding party is complete without copious amounts of sharkfin soup. The result has been a precipitous decline of the populations of these long-lived predators. The numbers of bull and dusky sharks as well as scalloped hammerheads, for example, have plummeted by a staggering 99% in just 30 years. The real impact is probably even greater, because fishermen primarily target the largest individuals, so all that remains are probably immature ones, too young to reproduce. Effectively, these species are extinct. More than one third of all shark species are now considered endangered.

In a 2007 paper in *Science*, researchers from Dalhousie University in Halifax, Canada, investigated what impact the near extinction of the largest of sharks has on the marine ecosystem. Expecting a reduced top-down impact on the smaller sharks that are eaten by the larger ones, they scoured fisheries data from the coast off North Carolina, and indeed found that all smaller shark species preyed on by bigger ones had increased. The most conspicuous response was actually not in a shark but in a relative, the cownose ray (*Rhinoptera bonasus*), which had increased tenfold since the mid-1970s. This upsurge in turn meant the death knell for the North Carolina bay scallop fishery. The rays consumed these shells with such abandon that the century-old scallop fishery had to close down in 2004. And do not be tricked into thinking this is just a local tragedy. When trophic cascades brought about by East Asian wedding menus can make a bivalve population on the other side of the world collapse, it is a sign that the ecosystem is in the throes of trophic cascades. And the cascade that hit North Carolina is not the only one. Shark overfishing has also been implicated in the Caribbean coral catastrophe.

The staghorn coral forests of the Caribbean, though much less biodiverse than the ones of the Indo-Pacific, are well known, among other reasons because they were where much of the early modern coral reef ecologists did their scuba-diving in the 1960s and 1970s. But even they were not prepared for the disaster that befell their playground unexpectedly in the late 1970s. First, the reefs' dominant coral species, the staghorn *Acropora cervicornis*, suffered a massive die-off due to a combination of storm damage and an epidemic of the infectious white-band disease (possibly caused by a bacterium). In the same period, the two main groups of algae-eating animals on the reef, parrotfish and the sea urchin *Diadema antillarum*, traded places: the number of parrotfish went down, the number of sea urchins went up. Until, that is, *Diadema* reached such high densities (with more than ten individuals per square metre) that when a sea urchin disease struck in 1983, it spread throughout the population like wildfire and virtually wiped them out. With the parrotfish still dwindling and all sea urchins gone, algae saw their chance and in no time covered the surviving coral stands, smothering them to death. Today, the reefs are just greenish-brown algae-covered fields of rubble with up to 98% of the original corals dead. Little of their erstwhile glory that so impressed Jacques Cousteau and others remains.

In hindsight, says coral reef ecologist David Bellwood of James Cook University in Townsville, Australia, many signs of what was going to happen were already there in the 1970s: a diverse mix of algae-feeding fish was being replaced by just a single species of sea urchin – a risky situation if a species-specific disease should strike. And these sea urchins are much less careful eaters than parrotfish. Whereas the fish, with their parrot-like beaks, gently graze the surface of the coral, *Diadema* burrow into the coral as they feed and can make coral lose over ten kilograms of 'body weight' per square metre per year.

But the real cause may have lain much higher up the food pyramid, according to a 2005 study published in the *Proceedings of the National Academy of Sciences of the USA* by a team of Spanish and American researchers. They compiled all the literature on the Caribbean coral reef and drew out its food web: 250 species and groups of species, with 3,313 interactions connecting them. Using data from stomach contents from 5,526 fish belonging to 212 species, they worked out the exact interaction strengths, at least for the interactions that involved fish. Then, using methods similar to the ones used by Neutel and others, they figured out how stable the food web would be to disturbances – in this case overfishing. They found that if fish were netted randomly, the system was pretty resilient, thanks to many light interaction loops (which, as we saw in Chap. 8, helps stabilise a food web). But as they point out, fisheries are anything but random. Fishermen work their way through a food web from the top down. And if this is done, the team's calculations show, things do not look so pretty. Ten heavily fished top predators are sharks, which together account for half of all the strong interactions in the web. With these removed, the remaining set of interactions proved less stable. Trophic cascades after the disappearance of the top predators would allow smaller predatory fish, like groupers, to expand and eat up all the parrotfish, with all the ensuing effects on sea urchins, algae, and coral that we have seen. 'It appears that ecosystems such as Caribbean coral reefs need sharks to ensure the stability of the entire system,' the authors say.

These examples are particularly troubling because they do confirm, in real-life settings, that the size and complexity of an ecosystem do not say much about how likely they are to fall victim to trophic cascades. Ecosystem theorists believe that stability relies on the manner in which interaction strengths are arranged throughout the food web, not on diversity or complexity per se. Life-sized, unplanned experiments such as a fleet of fishing vessels removing all top predators from a species-rich tropical or warm-temperate coastal marine ecosystem sadly prove the theorists right: the ecological Atropos can bring any ecosystem to its knees with a few well-placed snips of her shears of extinction.

9.3
The Awl of Invasion

At the beginning of this book, when I described the biodiversity in my garden in Borneo for you, I may have hinted at the fact that not all of those species are native Borneans. In fact, many aren't. The tree sparrows (that have shifted their niche to that of house sparrows – see Chap. 4) are from Europe. The *Macrochlamys indica* snails that munch on fallen bananas are from India, while the banana itself hails from China. The pharaoh ants that travel in throngs along my walls were African in a previous life, and the Siam weed (*Chromolaema odorata*) that crops up everywhere was introduced from South and Central America and is a pest throughout tropical Asia, Africa, and Melanesia. And then there are giant African snails, of course, and *Rattus norvegicus*, which is not actually from Norway but probably from northern China, and lots of other aliens. Sitting on my verandah, overlooking the ecosystem that is my garden, I am faced with a surprising number of animal expats and foreign flora.

Not that surprising, really. The sparrows and the rats came as stowaways on ships. The snails hitched a ride with agricultural crops. Siam weed was planted intentionally as an ornamental plant. And the tiny pharaoh ants could have hidden anywhere, even in the clothes of a traveller. Humans have been similarly responsible for the insertion of species from one place into the ecosystem of another place on thousands of occasions and in hundreds of ways. And when such an exotic species unexpectedly expands explosively in its new home and causes ecological, economic, or medical mayhem, it is recast as 'invasive'. In 1983, for example, the Oceanographic Museum in Monaco dumped a bit of wastewater from one of its aquariums, containing the Pacific seaweed *Caulerpa taxifolia*, into the Mediterranean. The next year, the plants covered a one-square-metre area in the sea in front of the museum. Five years later, they had expanded to a one-hectare area. Today, the entire Mediterranean is covered, leading to the disappearance of many a native seafloor-dwelling plant.

And while the Monaco museum may throw its hands in the air and claim ignorance, since it were not aware that the weed was in its wastewater, the same plea of innocence cannot be made by the authorities that intentionally released the smallmouth bass (*Micropterus dolomiae*) and rock bass (*Ambloplites rupestris*), two predatory freshwater fish from temperate parts of North America, into lakes and rivers in Canada as game fish. At the moment, the two species are invading pristine lakes in the transition zone between Canada's northern hardwood forest and its boreal forest. The lakes' native top predator is the lake trout, *Salvelinus namaycush*. As researchers from McGill University discovered, upon invasion, the bass species starts feeding on the trout's main prey, small shore-dwelling fish. As a consequence (and the researchers showed this by stable isotope analysis – see Chaps. 1, 2), the food web changed: the native trout was forced to a lower trophic level. While in uninvaded lakes it fed at trophic level 3.9, in lakes with bass, where its preferred prey, the smaller fish, were all taken by the bass, it started eating zooplankton and dropped to trophic level 3.3.

But of far greater importance than intentional or accidental transfers of single species are the transports of entire ecosystems. As soon as people began moving stuff around in boats, they became wonderful agents of dispersal. Not only because sometimes the cargo consisted of live animals or plants, but also because of the use of ballast. A boat that has emptied its cargo in a port suddenly sits very high and unstably on the water. To increase stability for the journey home, seafarers have used all kinds of ballast. In the early days of maritime navigation, it was mostly rocks or soil. The vessels of the early European colonial powers, upon unloading their cargo of exotic produce in European ports, would return to their colonies filled with soil or bricks. This explains the large heaps of soil near seaports in Southeast Asia and Australia and the fact that many seventeenth-century fortresses in present-day Indonesia are built from bricks of Dutch clay. It also explains how some European plant and invertebrate species found their way to the soils of Australia and Southeast Asia.

With the invention of the electric pump, water was instead used for ballast. Today, great tanker ships imbibe over 200,000 cubic metres of water from the port where they have unloaded their cargo and then spew it out again when they reach their next destination. And although it is called ballast 'water' it is actually a chunk of marine ecosystem that is gulped up, barnacles and all. Phytoplankton, zooplankton, crustaceans, molluscs, fish, and all manner of other marine life are included. If the port is shallow, silt and benthic organisms are also sucked up and deposited on the bottom of the ship's hull. As invasive-species expert Lucius Eldredge of the Bishop Museum in Hawaii says, 'ballast water contains complete schools of fish, and ballast sediment can sometimes contain entire marine benthic communities.' And all these are then deposited at the next port of call, a risky practice that ecologists call 'ecological Russian roulette'.

One of the more notorious examples of invasive species carried in ballast water is *Mnemiopsis leidyi*. The natural home of this ten-centimetre long comb jelly (a group of invertebrates distantly related to regular jellyfish, but with rows of iridescent hairs or plates along their transparent bodies with which they propel themselves) is the western Atlantic. It hitched a ride in ballast water and turned up in 1982 in the Black Sea, where it found a rich source of zooplankton to feed on. Within seven years it had occupied the entire Black Sea, reaching densities of 400 jellies per cubic metre of water, and outcompeted many other local zooplanktivores, including the anchovy on which the local fisheries depended. These fisheries duly collapsed. Since then, *Mnemiopsis* populations have declined thanks to the arrival of another ballast-water stowaway, another Atlantic comb jelly called *Beroe ovata*, which feeds on *Mnemiopsis*. However, in the mid-1990s, probably again via ballast water, *Mnemiopsis* turned up in the Caspian Sea, and in 2006 in the North Sea and the Baltic. In all these places it seems to be spreading.

Despite these recent horror stories and the many similar ones that grab headlines with ever-increasing frequency, the invasion of exotic species is not a recent thing. The West Asian pheasant (*Phasianus colchicus*) was introduced into western Europe in Roman times, the rabbit in the thirteenth century, and the European soft-shell clam *Mya arenaria* probably arrived on the North American east coast with Icelandic Vikings in the Middle Ages too. With the 'official' discovery of the Americas in 1492, many more species were accidentally and intentionally introduced across the Atlantic in both directions. By Columbus personally on his second voyage, in 1493, when he tried to introduce chickpeas, grape vines, melons, cattle, chickens, dogs, and goats into Hispaniola. And the conquistadores then added human pathogens, horses, and pigs, while maize, turkeys, Muskovy ducks, sand fleas, and syphilis crossed the ocean in the opposite direction.

But only in recent times, with travel and transport expanding and intensifying globally, have dispersal barriers between continents really begun to crumble. Graphs of the numbers of new exotic species reported each year show exponential increase for all parts of the world. Not all exotics successfully insert themselves into their new surroundings, though. Ecologists often quote the 'tens rule', which says that at each step in the series of obstacles a would-be invader has to conquer (import, escape into the wild, settlement, and developing into a pest), only about one in ten species succeeds. The tens rule was first introduced by Mark Williamson in his 1997 book *Biological Invasions*, and he used data on the introduced plants of Britain to prove it. The total number of plant species ever imported into Britain is 12,507. Out of those, 1,642 managed to escape, and of those 210 were able to develop into a locally settled population. Finally, only 14 of them became serious pest species and truly qualify as invasive (indeed about 10% success at each step). But in 2005, Jonathan Jeschke and David Strayer of the Institute of Ecosystem Studies in Millbrook, USA, found that the tens rule does not apply generally. They compiled data on introductions of vertebrate animals from Europe into North America and vice versa, and found a 50% success rate at each step.

Invasive species are a great concern for many of us. They create unanticipated upheaval in native ecosystems and are a scourge for aesthetic, economic, agricultural, or medical reasons. But they also provide us with natural experiments that might provide answers to many major questions that prey on ecologists' minds. What determines whether a colonising species will spread or not? Does it require a vacant niche or is it enough that some of its predators and parasites are absent? How quickly will a food web rearrange itself to accommodate the newcomer, if at all? And are such rearrangements predictable or random? And, most importantly, are more complex ecosystems more resistant against invaders?

An invaded ecosystem that certainly was not complex before it was invaded is the remote island of Ascension in the tropical south Atlantic. Some 2,000 kilometres from the nearest continent, it never received many visitors, so it was particularly lucky to have got such an esteemed visitor as Charles Darwin himself, who briefly landed in July 1836, homeward bound on the *Beagle*. Darwin was not taken by the place, though. In his diary, he wrote, 'The island is entirely destitute of trees' and agreed with what the inhabitants of the nearby island of St. Helena jokingly say, namely: 'We know we live on a rock, but the poor people of Ascension live on a cinder'. Indeed, at the time of Darwin's visit, Ascension sported just between 25 and 30 plant species, most of them ferns, which made for a very boring biota.

A few years later, British botanist Joseph Hooker also dropped by and was asked by the Royal Navy officer who commanded a garrison on the island how the place might be improved. Hooker thought for a while and then sketched out an elaborate plan of planting trees and shrubs to stimulate rainfall and form the nucleus of a richer, greener, lusher vegetation on a thicker soil. Alas, he wrote, 'The consequences to the native vegetation ... will, I fear, be fatal.' After he left, the zealous sailors set to their task with gusto. Seeds and seedlings were brought in by naval cargo ships from Argentina, from the South African Cape Botanic Gardens, and from Kew Gardens near London. It turned out that Hooker had been correct. In two decades, after having been started off by the trees and shrubs planted by the navy around their barracks, the barren island was transformed into a richly vegetated, much wetter environment, and its erstwhile rocky peak, now enveloped in clouds, was renamed 'Green Mountain'.

Today, Green Mountain is covered in a diverse, complex, all-invasive cloud forest vegetation. Its slopes are clothed in guava, banana, and gingers, African *Clerodendrum*, periwinkle from Madagascar, Norfolk Island pine, and Australian eucalyptus. On its summit a bamboo forest grows. It has aptly been called an 'accidental rainforest'. Most of the native species, however, as Hooker had expected, have gone. In their stead has come a forest ecosystem thrown together from species deriving from all over the world, evolved to suit niches that likely are not present on Ascension. And yet it is there. And it seems to work.

What does Ascension teach us about invasion, ecosystems, and biodiversity? First of all, it has not told us as much as it could, because ecologists have tended to look down their noses at it, dismissing it as just an 'artificial ecosystem' and preferring to study nearby St. Helena, which has a much more varied native flora. Consequently, we know very little of how the novel food web works, which animals play a role in it, and where they come from. But clearly it shows that complex rainforest ecosystems are not necessarily delicately balanced species assemblages evolved over millions of years. They could also be a grabbag of odds and ends of plant life introduced by humans. In a way, it proves Hubbell right, that rainforests may be dispersal-assembled. It also proves MacArthur and Wilson right, that island ecosystems' biodiversity depends on a balance between immigration and extinction. The island could have supported a much richer biota, if only immigration had been sufficiently heavy. Only when given a helping hand by humans did the island show its real potential. Whether the same introduced species would have been successful had Ascension already sported a rich ecosystem is debatable, though. With just a handful of plants present, much niche space apparently was not yet filled, and many of the invaders took up vacant spaces in the open weave of its ecological tapestry.

But other habitats in the world where invasion has made an indelible mark were ecologically less depauperate. The San Francisco Bay and Delta, for example, is a temperate, nutrient-rich estuarine habitat of 1,500 square kilometres on North America's west coast. It is also an area of intense human activity, and has been so for the past 150 years. So it is not surprising that it has accumulated a total of almost 250 exotic species (plants, protozoa, invertebrates, fish) over that period, with rates of invasion still rising. In addition, some 125 'cryptogenic' species occur there, which may or may not have been introduced. The proportion of invaders is so great that most of the region's ecosystem compartments are dominated by them. The food webs in and on the muddy bay bottom, the so-called fouling communities of snails, crabs, starfish, sea urchins, and worms living on docks and jetties, the zooplankton in brackish water, and the fish guilds in the fresh water… in each of them, invasives account for 40–100% of the species. Next to Ascension, the San Francisco estuary may be the most invaded ecosystem in the world, made up almost entirely of exotic species. There is a difference, however: unlike Ascension, the estuary was not devoid of native residents. And still the invaders managed to squeeze them out. In this case, at least, biodiversity did not offer enough protection against invasion (and more about that later).

To understand what happens when the awl of invasion rearranges a native food web, it is not sufficient to look at invasion overkill as has happened on Ascension and in San Francisco Bay. Instead, we need to follow the fate of individual invasions. For instance, when two gall flies, *Urophora quadrifasciata* and *U. affinis*, were introduced from Europe into western North America to control the (also invasive) spotted knapweed (*Centaurea maculosa*), they had an unexpected effect on rodents. The larvae of the flies, which live in galls that they induce in the knapweed flower heads, turned out to be a nutritious source of food for the local deer mice (*Peromyscus maniculatus*), which climbed the plants' stems to get to the larvae. It transpired that areas with high knapweed densities also supported high mouse densities. And the cramped mouse populations, in turn, induced a higher prevalence of the Sin Nombre virus, which causes a human lung disease and uses rodents as its wild reservoir (Fig. 9.2). So adding species, just like removing them, can cause unanticipated ecosystem ripples that eventually can hit humans too. However, as the introduction of another kind of gall-forming insect showed, sometimes the consequences may not be unanticipated. In fact, they may be completely anticipated.

In the late 1950s, the gall wasp *Andricus quercuscalicis* reached Britain from the European continent. The wasp lays its eggs in oak leaves and acorns and there induces the formation of large, walnut-shaped galls ("knopper galls") in which the larvae develop. The galls attract parasitic wasps, which lay their eggs in the gall wasp larvae, but also so-called inquilines, tiny 'illegal squatter' wasps that use the gall to construct their own little chambers for their larvae to develop in. Only by 1980, a community of parasitic and inquiline wasps began to form around British knopper galls, and by the late 1990s consisted of 13 native British species. Surprisingly, as was discovered by Karsten Schönrogge and colleagues at Imperial College London at Silwood Park, UK, this community is almost identical to the community that attacks *A. quercuscalicis* in its native continental Europe, where all these

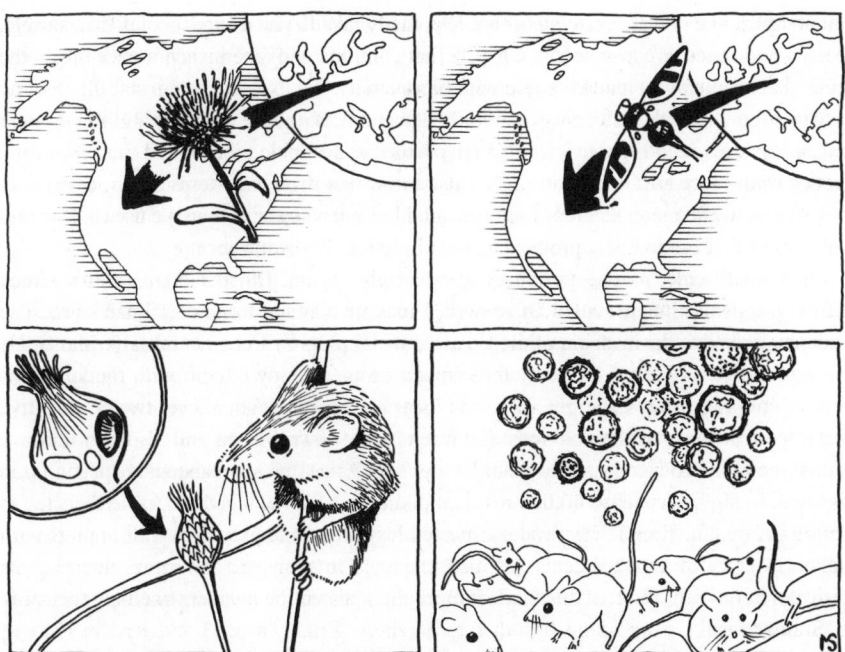

Fig. 9.2 The unexpected effects of an introduced species. European gall flies were introduced to control the invasive knapweed (also from Europe). The local deer mice feed on the gall fly larvae, which boosts their populations, thereby increasing transmission of the Sin Nombre virus, a human pathogen

13 species also occur. In other words, an introduced species, upon insertion into a new ecosystem, recruited the same species for its immediate interaction network as it had in the old place. So in this case, the ecosystem effects of a species introduction were predictable. But since all the main players were the same as in the new species's original habitat, perhaps this is not so surprising. And perhaps it is also the reason why *A. quercuscalicis* never developed into a pest, for the fact that invaded areas are enemy-free safe havens is one of the suspected reasons for their becoming invasive in the first place.

In support of this so-called enemy-release hypothesis, two papers published back-to-back in *Nature* in 2003 reported that 26 invasive animal species (molluscs, crustaceans, and vertebrates) and 473 invasive plant species had about half as many parasites and pathogens as related native species that they shared their habitat with. Further investigations showed that of the parasites that they had, they had brought half with them from their original area of distribution, and had newly acquired the other half in their new home. So that may explain, at least in part, why introduced species behave so aggressively when they invade a new ecosystem and why they can have such a far-reaching impact.

That leaves the matter of invasibility and biodiversity to be dealt with. As we saw in Chap. 8, Charles Elton, in *The Ecology of Invasions by Animals and Plants*, proclaimed

9

that complex and diverse ecosystems are less easily invaded by exotic species than simple, species-poor ones. We also saw in Chap. 8 that complex and diverse is not necessarily the same, that productivity tended to rise with biodiversity, but that ecosystem stability had no easy relation with either diversity or complexity. But how about invasibility? Elton thought that ecosystems with high species diversity had few available niches, and thus incoming exotics would face stiff competition. We also know that diverse systems are more productive, so that would mean that less food is available for new species to make use of. It would make sense that biodiversity protects against invasion, but is it true?

On a small scale, it appears that Elton was right. Again, David Tilman's Cedar Creek prairie grassland plots provided an answer. Theodore Kennedy, one of Tilman's graduate students, looked at the invasion of their experimental plots by Eurasian invasive plants. He had established 147 three metre by three metre plots, and sown them with random mixtures of one, two, four, six, eight, 12, or 24 local herb species. Then, over two consecutive years, he kept track of the positions and sizes of the sown plants, and also any invasive plants (mostly introduced species from Europe and Asia) that spontaneously sprung up in his plots. In all, he censused 40,000 resident plants and 13,000 invaders. As he reported in *Nature* in 2002, he found that invaders invaded less often, and grew less well in plots with higher diversity of native species. He also managed to show that the more diverse plots were more crowded, and that this made it more difficult for the invaders to elbow their way in. Similar results were found by other researchers. Erika Zavaleta and Kristin Hulvey, for instance, found a similar result when they looked at the invasion by an exotic thistle in patches in which they had reconstructed naturally occurring vegetation types: the more biodiverse the patch, the less likely the thistle was to insert itself.

But on a larger scale, the pattern seems reversed. Globally, the areas with the greatest biodiversity also have the greatest numbers of invasive species. This so-called invasion paradox is still not resolved, although it seems that, just like in the niche-neutrality debate, it centres around the scale at which niches are relevant. On a small spatial scale, available niches determine whether a species can invade, whereas on a larger spatial scale, island biogeography becomes important: the areas with the greatest biodiversity may be the ones where immigration is high and extinction is low. And whatever causes high immigration will also result in high invasion.

The awl of invasion is therefore Atropos' most curious instrument. With it, she inserts new threads into the weave of life, either as individual twine or as whole bunches of yarn. This may cause the tapestry to go to tatters. It may cause the tapestry to be slightly rearranged, but otherwise continue to function as before. But it may also cause a new, strong tapestry to be formed for the old one.

9.4
The Ecosystem Ripper

Remember Daniel Simberloff and his chainsaw from Chap. 6? The researcher who cut up mangrove islands to see how species numbers would drop, as predicted by the theory of island biogeography? At the time, it sounded like a particularly drastic brand of ecological experimentation. But, again, real life provides natural experiments that are far more ruthless. Habitats are fragmented all over the world. And at a much larger scale, with much farther-reaching effects than Simberloff could accomplish on his own on a 0.1-hectare islet. By chainsaws and channels, draglines and dams, highways and housing projects, once continuous natural habitats are cut up into smaller, disjointed bits.

Take tropical lowland rainforests, for example. Besides logging, which is bad enough in itself, they also fall prey to clearfelling for conversion to farmland, plantations, pastures, and other land uses that require flat land. When one drives the potholed, 200-kilometre road from the sleepy town of Ranau at the foot of Mount Kinabalu to the city of Sandakan on the north coast of Borneo, the fragmentation of natural habitats is evident. Until the 1950s, this area was uninterrupted lowland rainforest. Now, it is uninterrupted oil palm plantation with here and there a postage-stamp-sized forest reserve, visible as a ragged treeline peeking out from among the geometrically arranged rows of palms. Labuk forest reserve, for example, is just about 120 hectares. Ulu Sapa Payau is 725 hectares, while Lungmanis is 3,390 hectares. These forest fragments are different-sized samples, punch-holed from what once was an undulating, uninterrupted forest that reached as far as the eye could see.

With the same fate befalling rainforests and other habitats all over the world, ecologists and conservationists alike have been asking the question: If you went into each of these fragments, would you still find the same biodiversity as had been there when the habitat was still in one piece? To begin answering that question, we have to realise that, even before the forest was cut up, you would not have found the same biodiversity in bounded plots of 120, 725, and 3,390 hectares. Let me remind you that in Chap. 6 we saw that even in mainland areas we find a species–area relationship. If you recall, back in the 1920s, Arrhenius discovered that if you sample ever-larger pieces of an area (in his case Swedish vegetation), you will find ever more species. This is simply because of statistics (larger areas have more individuals, and if your sample is larger, you are more likely to find rare species), and also because larger areas contain more different habitats, and you will run into more habitat-specialist species if you cover a larger area. These two things make for enough predictability to be captured in a species–area relationship that forms a straight, climbing line in a logarithmic graph of species number against area. In mainland areas, the rate by which the line goes up (the z value) is around 0.15.

Now let us go back to those forest fragments in Borneo. In 2002 and 2003, two Malaysian PhD students, Suzan Benedick and Nazirah Mustaffa, working with English entomologist Jane Hill of the University of York, went into ten of these forest reserves, armed with strange-looking cylinders made out of mosquito netting and, somewhat disturbingly, copious amounts of rotting bananas. The bananas went into the mosquito-net butterfly traps (for that is what they were), which were then suspended from branches in the forest in a standard pattern and for a fixed duration. Each day, they conscientiously checked their traps and identified which species of fruit-feeding butterflies of the family Nymphalidae had flown in. Over their study period, they collected almost 7,000 butterflies belonging to 83 species. As expected, the largest fragments yielded many species (over 50), whereas the smallest ones contained fewer (just 20 or so). But when they then plotted their data as a graph and extracted the species–area relationship, they found a z value not of 0.15, but of around 0.25. A small but crucial difference.

Crucial, because where have we heard of such a high z value before? Right: in MacArthur and Wilson's theory of island biogeography (Chap. 6 again). Islands separated by the sea, forced by the unswerving edicts of immigration and extinction, tend to converge to a species–area relationship in which z typically lies between 0.20 and 0.35. The results of Benedick and Nazirah suggested that the fragments of forest no longer behaved as if they were part of a once-connected greater forest. They behaved like islands. Islands of nymphalid-friendly habitat surrounded by an ocean of monotonous oil palm trees.

In the 1970s, when ecologists and conservationists began asking those pressing questions on the fate of biodiversity in fragmented habitats, data such as those on Bornean butterflies in forest islands were still very scarce. And what there was, was equivocal. One of the people annoyed by this lack of knowledge was Tom Lovejoy, then working at the World Wildlife Fund in Washington, DC, USA. A former graduate student of Evelyn Hutchinson, steeped in ecological theory, Lovejoy found himself in the unenviable position of needing to make decisions on the disbursement of grants to conservation projects, without any scientific knowledge to base those decisions on. Where should conservation areas be situated? And how big should they be? Would it be better to have one large reserve or several small ones? Especially where tropical forests were concerned, there were no data to back up his decisions with. Meanwhile, deforestation carried on relentlessly. So Lovejoy took it upon himself to generate the data himself. But how? Enveloping mangrove islands in black plastic or cutting them up with a chainsaw was one thing, but experimentally fragmenting an entire rainforest was definitely not within the realm of ecologists' possibilities. Then, in 1976, during a workshop with other biologists (among whom was also Simberloff, whose chainsaw paper had just been published in *Ecology* a few months earlier), the answer was conceived, germinated, grew, and came to fruition in Lovejoy's head, just like that, between coffee and lunch.

Lovejoy was aware of a development project taking place at that moment in Brazil. Eighty kilometres north of the city of Manaus, at the confluence of the Amazon and the Rio Negro, in an area that had suffered an economic downturn due to the collapse of the rubber market, the Brazilian government was stimulating the clearfelling of rainforest for cattle ranching. Following presidential decree MP2.166–67, however, the government stipulated that each rancher left 50% of the forest in the concession untouched (today, 80% is mandatory). This would mean that, within this so-called Manaus Free Zone, forest islands would be created within a sea of pasture. Perhaps, Lovejoy reckoned, with some diplomacy from the World Wildlife Fund, the Manaus project could be turned into a giant island biogeography experiment.

To make a long story short, Lovejoy and his newly hired field director Rob Bierregaard managed to persuade both the authorities and the ranchers to let their chainsaws and bulldozers be guided by the rules for proper scientific experimentation: reproducibility, replication, and experimental controls. Aerial photographs strewn in front of them, they sat down with the officials and outlined five blocks of one hectare, four of ten hectares, and two of 100 hectares. These square chunks would be left standing as the surrounding forest would be felled in the years to come. Twelve more blocks of one, ten, 100, and even 1,000 hectares were outlined in continuous forest and would serve as control plots. Then, with Bierregaard handling things in Brazil, and Lovejoy in Washington overseeing the project and generating financing, they set to work. First, the plots were demarcated on the ground. A number of rapid biodiversity assessments were carried out in them. The ones set to become isolated were fenced off. Then, the woodsmen moved in and as hell and mayhem broke out around them, Lovejoy's fragments remained standing, future time capsules to preserve – or not – the forest's erstwhile glory.

Over the years to follow, the Biological Dynamics of Forest Fragments Project, as it became known, grew to involve hundreds of scientists, students, technicians, and volunteers. It set up an office in Manaus, eight base camps in the Manaus Free Zone, and a fleet of four-wheel drive vehicles. But more importantly, it generated almost 500 publications and over 100 graduate dissertations, all of them in some way or another related to the forest fragments' island biogeographical character. With the fragments isolated from one another, MacArthur and Wilson processes would now reign supreme in them. The smaller fragments would have fewer species to begin with, and would begin to lose those species for which population sizes were so small that demographic stochasticity would kill them off. At the same time, their small size would prevent them from catching many immigrants from the 'continents' of continuous forest further afield. At least, that was the expectation.

Indeed, some groups adhered nicely to island biogeography's tenets. Insect-eating ground-dwelling birds, for example. In the one-, ten-, and 100-hectare fragments lived on average zero, two, and six species, respectively. In similarly sized control plots in the continuous forest, those numbers were two, five, and nine. The latter three figures show the expected diversities for these birds in undisturbed Arrhenius plots of increasing size, whereas the reduced numbers in the fragments show the impoverishing effects of island life.

A much larger study shows the same is true for all birds. In 2003, Bierregaard, Lovejoy, and four co-authors (among whom was also food-chain ecologist Stuart Pimm, whom you may remember from Chap. 2) published a paper in the *Proceedings of the National Academy of Sciences of the USA* in which they compiled data on all 21,600 individual birds captured in mist-nets over a 13-year period. In all, the birders got 164 species, mostly from the families of tyrant flycatchers, antbirds, ovenbirds, and brush-finches. When tabulated over the years, for each fragment, the bird diversities show a tell-tale pattern. Perhaps surprisingly, in some plots, numbers went up, not down, during the first one or two years after isolation. This was probably because rather than losing birds, the forest islands briefly absorbed refugees from the intervening, now clearfelled forest. In any case, the surge did not last long: two years after isolation numbers were back to normal. And then they began to plunge. Ten-hectare fragment '1202' went down from over 80 species before isolation to about half that in 1986, five years after the fragment was isolated. Larger fragments, like the 100-hectare '3304', as expected, did not decline as rapidly (100 species before isolation, around 80 nine years on). But the one-hectare ones were hardest hit: '2107', for example, crashed from 50 species to 20 in a matter of two years.

Similar results were also found by project scientists studying the monkeys, dung beetles, termites, and butterflies. But the detailed data sets, painstakingly assembled by mud-trampling researchers, also revealed that to portray the fragmentation as a simple extinction–immigration balance was really a travesty of what actually happened in the fragments' ecosystems.

Army ants, for example, have such large colonies (up to two million individuals), and cover such large areas (up to 100 hectares) during their raids that they, though individually tiny, require large areas to survive. Within six months after isolation, the army ants became extinct in the one-hectare fragments, and soon thereafter also on the larger fragments. And with them went a whole suite of birds called 'ant-followers'. These birds are adapted to feeding in the wake of a passing front of army ants, foraging on all the insects and other creatures that try to flee the marauding troops. The white-plumed antbird (*Pithys albifrons*) and the rufous-throated antbird (*Gymnopithys rufigula*) were among such secondary extinctions. Other ant-followers, such as *Myrmornis torquata*, had other problems as well. Normally, this species looks for insects attempting to flee an oncoming ant army, by flipping over leaves on the forest floor. But with the forest edges exposed to the outside world, pioneer tree species began to invade the fragments. In some areas, the forest became dominated with such a pioneer tree, *Cecropia*; this sheds leaves that are so large and heavy that the dainty antbird species cannot handle them.

The intrusion of *Cecropia* is an example of one of the many so-called edge-effects that began penetrating the forest fragments. With the surrounding forest matrix removed, what happened at the newly formed borders revealed how narrow the tolerance of a rainforest actually is. The increased sunlight, heat, and drought at the forest edge brought down the magnificent and seemingly indestructible rainforest trees in no time. They dropped their leaves, died, and keeled over, their roots unable to support their whitened corpses in the shallow soil. After a few years, the smallest, one-hectare fragments by and large collapsed inward and were overgrown with vines and thickets. But also the larger fragments suffered from edge effects. Wind speeds increased up to 400 metres away from the edge. Tree mortality was significantly raised up to 300 metres into the forest. And within 100 metres from the forest edge, a whole Pandora's box of ill edge-effects were felt: drier soils, greater litter fall, invasion of weeds, frogs, and insects from the pastures, fewer fungi, and so on. All these things also had their effect on the forest ecosystem.

With so many species disappearing from the forest fragments, with new species invading, and with species abundances changing, the effects on the food web were also obvious. The top layers of the food pyramid largely disappeared from the fragments: the fragments did not provide enough food for populations of large herbivores such as the monkeys, the paca, and the white-lipped peccary to be sustained and they disappeared. With them, their predators, the pumas, jaguars, and margay cats, walked out as well. Among the birds, the numbers of insect-eating ones went down, whereas the numbers of omnivores and the ones feeding on nectar, such as hummingbirds, actually went up (the latter presumably because the increase in gaps and edge vegetation provided plenty flowering vines). Insect biodiversity changed too. Among the termite fauna, for example, there was a shift toward species that feed on leaf litter – the result from the increased leaf fall near the forest edges. On the other hand, with the large dung- and carrion-providing mammals now missing, the number of dung beetles declined.

Farther-reaching effects can only be guessed at. The absence of orchid bees, for example, which disappeared for unknown reasons, will undoubtedly affect the survival of the orchids that they pollinate. With the numbers of insect-eating birds declining, insect populations may boom, which will result in defoliation for some of the trees. And the lack of dung beetles will reduce germination of seeds (that normally sit in the mammal droppings that dung beetles bury).

And so on. The list of actual, likely, plausible, possible, and potential consequences, one, two, or more steps further down the food chains is sheer endless. The ecosystem ripper is a blunt instrument that will tear up the weave of an ecosystem. When applied by Atropos with too much indifference, she will leave us with scattered, useless fragments of carpet, insufficient to clothe our planet with.

9.5
Coda

Once again, I sit on my verandah in Happy Garden, watching the sun set over the South China Sea. The bats have just woken up and emerge, one by one, from the roof tiles of my neighbour's house. They hardly take the time to stretch their wings, but immediately start feasting eagerly on the moths that circle the street lights. Tumbling chaotically through the air, they are silhouetted against a purplish red sky that, veined with vermillion, merges to violet higher up. Some dark clouds are gathering on the horizon: the weather forecast says that a tropical storm is brewing over the Philippines and is likely to pass over Borneo as well. Better close the shutters tonight.

Reliable weather forecasting is considered one of the triumphs of modern science. With supercomputers, weather satellites, weather stations all over the world, and highly detailed simulation models of wind, evaporation, and air pressure and all their interdependencies, meteorologists can predict weather many days ahead with a fair degree of accuracy. That seems a respectable accomplishment, but when set against ecology, it is of a laughable simplicity. Meteorology deals with a handful of different molecules, that are affected by a handful of physical processes. Compare that with the complexities ecology has to put up with. Scientists have currently described about 1.8 million species. But when we extrapolate from the numbers of species of specialised herbivorous insects that rain down from a rainforest tree after a 'fogging' exercise, or from the numbers of different DNA barcodes that we can generate from a pinch of garden soil, we have to admit that we probably know just a few percent of all the species that there are on this planet. Even in well-studied areas, vast deficits in our knowledge exist when species become too small to see with the naked eye. We don't know what there is, what it looks like, and what we should call it, let alone what it does. The food-web models that I have written about in Chaps. 8 and 9 are, let's face it, little more than caricatures. Can a web with 250 species really claim to represent the Caribbean coral reef ecosystem when we know that the real number of species in that ecosystem must be several orders of magnitude larger? Almost all of the food webs ever disentangled have just a single node that says 'bacteria', whereas we saw in Chap. 3 that one gram of forest soil is likely to hold about eight million species of bacteria, each with a different chemical niche.

Of course we cannot hold these shortcomings against hardworking ecologists. After two centuries of biodiversity studies, they are just beginning to unravel the complexities of life's tapestry, the colours of its threads, and the way the threads are held together. And perhaps we do not need to know all species and all the details of their interactions with pin-point precision to understand the workings of ecosystems. Perhaps we can simplify. We just don't know. The problem is that we have so little time. We need ecological weather forecasts now. Even if we cannot slow down Atropos' awl, shears, and ripper, at least we should be able to prepare for the impact they will have on our lives. We need to know what to expect.

But if this book has taught us anything, it is that, without good ecological knowledge, we can only expect the unexpected. The golden sunset that illuminates my hands as I write this comes courtesy of forest fires in Indonesia, which throw up vast amounts of soot into the air that refract the sun's rays in such a picturesque manner. The fires are started to aid in the clearing of logged-over rainforest for the planting of six million hectares of oil palm. Some of the areas studied by Lisa Curran around the Gunung Palung national park are among them. In the process, species guilds will be hollowed out, the energy pyramid will be altered, and the ripples of trophic cascades will sooner or later lap our human shores.

Seen against a geological backdrop, it is tempting to adopt a Zen-like attitude toward all ecological upheaval. The awl of invasion is nothing new. When the Isthmus of Panama was formed several millions of years ago, species from North America became invasive species in South America and vice versa: more than 90% of the South American plants have invaded from the north, presumably extirpating many natives. The shears of extinction is old hat. Mass extinctions have taken place at all scales of space and time and ecosystems have always reassembled. The ecosystem ripper? We've seen it before: pollen from the ice ages shows that the familiar species abundance distributions in temperate and boreal forests have held up throughout the habitat fragmentations wreaked by the ice-ages. The world will not end. Life will not be extinguished. Ecological change is just that: ecological change. There is no good or bad in ecosystems.

True enough. But the fact remains that we are at a really unique position in the history of Earth. Never before has a single species appropriated such a large portion of the world's primary productivity as we do today. Whether we like it or not, we are an integral and crucial part of the world's ecosystems. We ourselves are a keystone species. And Atropos' toolkit is in our hands.

Notes

Preface

The male-killing *Wolbachia* endosymbiont in *Hypolimnas bolina* ('Bolly' for friends) is described in Dyson et al. (2002) and Charlat et al. (2005). More on the *Buchnera* symbiont of aphids may be found in Baumann et al. (1997).

Acknowledgements

The Audubon quote is from Ford (1957), cited by Rosenzweig (1995).

Chapter 1   Little Worlds

1.1
Bottled Biotas

I was first shown an Ecosphere by my former professor in geophysiology at Leiden University, Peter Westbroek. It also figures prominently in his book *Life as a Geological Force* (Westbroek 1991). The quotes are taken from the website of Ecosphere Associates at http://www.eco-sphere.com. Robin Ohm's website, with links to resources on home-built ecospheres is at http://www.euronet.nl/users/rkohm/biosphere/. The information on Biosphere 2 was based on Severinghaus et al. (1994), Marino and Odum (1999), Leigh et al. (1999), and Zabel et al. (1999).

1.2
Not As We Know It

The ecosystem in the Movile Cave is described in Sarbu et al. (1996), Sarbu (2000), Rohwerder et al. (2003), and on the website of the Mangalia Field Center, http://www.geocities.com/rainforest/vines/5771/. The quotes by Cristian Lascu and Annette Summers Engel are taken from telephone interviews I had with them on 27 and 1 February 2005, respectively, and e-mail correspondence during the same period. A good introduction to stable isotope techniques in ecology can be found in Peterson and Fry (1987). A few other self-supporting ecosystems like Movile exist in the world. For example the famous deep-sea vents, where specialised communities of clams, worms, crabs, and fish feed on the food provided by bacteria that, just like in Movile, oxidise the sulphides in the scalding water spewed from the bottom of the sea (van Dover 2000). And another might, just might, lurk under four kilometres of ice off the South Pole. Lake Vostok, a huge bell of freshwater the size of Lake Ontario, could be the only body of water on Earth devoid of life. Or it could be the most exotic ecosystem ever discovered. The lake, wedged between bedrock and glacial ice, has been locked away from sunlight and the atmosphere, and immersed in freezing cold and unimaginable pressures for 15 million years. As I write this, a Russian–French team of researchers are inching their way toward the boundary between frozen lake ice and liquid lake water, which they hope to punch through about two years from now. In 1999, microbes were found in the lake ice, which suggests that an ecosystem, perhaps driven by processes similar to the ones that keep Movile and deep-sea vents alive, could be present in Vostok (Jouzel et al. 1999; Karl et al. 1999; Priscu et al. 1999; Bulat et al. 2004; George 2004).

1.3
A Perfect Pitcher

Most of the general information in this section was taken from Clarke and Kitching (1993), Clarke (1997), Cresswell (2000), and an interview I had with Roger Kitching in Singapore on 8 December 2004. A comprehensive overview of the phytotelmata is Kitching (2000). The digestive activities of nepenthin and free radicals in the pitchers are described in Athauda et al. (2004) and Chia et al. (2004), respectively, whereas the physics of the slippery pitcher rim is detailed in Bohn and Federle (2004); the gluey properties of the pitcher fluid were recently elucidated in Gaume and Forterre (2007). Wallace's quote was taken from Wallace (1869). The details on Charles Elton, Roger Kitching, and their phytotelmata were taken from Crowcroft (1991) and from a conversation I had with Stephen Sutton on 15 January 2005.

Chapter 2   Leaky Buckets

2.1
The Boxer's Pyramid

Elton (1958) presents Brueghel's art in his book *The Ecology of Invasions by Animals and Plants*. The quote on the value of Elton's summer in Spitzbergen is from Colinvaux (1978). The Spitzbergen food chains were first published in Summerhayes and Elton (1923). Elton's other quotes are all from *Animal Ecology* (Elton 1927). Darwin's fulmar example is in Darwin (1859).

2.2
Counting Calories

The history of Raymond Lindeman and his classic *Ecology* paper (Lindeman 1942) are described in Cook (1977) and Morrison (2000). The term 'ecosystem' was first coined by Tansley (1935). The current citation frequency of Lindeman's paper can be found at ISI Web of Knowledge. The book by Welch is Welch (1952).

2.3
How To Build a Pyramid

Insights into the trophic pyramids in marine ecosystems were taken from Colinvaux (1978) and Wilson (1992). The changes in trophic level for humans were already mentioned by Elton (1927). The discussion on trophic cycles was based on Pimm (2002). The paper in which Gary Polis describes scorpion trophic cycles is Polis (1991). His nickname 'Scorpion Man' comes from the children's book with same title by Pringle (1994).

2.4
The Flea Hath Smaller Fleas

The papers by Cohen, Newman, and Briand are Cohen et al. (1986) and Briand and Cohen (1987) and Wallace's allusion to food chain length is in Wallace (1858). The paper that contains food-chain lengths in gall insects is Schoenly et al. (1991). Hutchinson's 1959 paper is Hutchinson (1959). The work on trophic levels at Joatka and elsewhere in the Arctic is summarised in Oksanen et al. (1995). The quotes on Joatka were taken from the research group's website at http://www.emg.umu.se/research/joatka/?.

Regarding NPP, there are actually two versions of this measure: ANPP, which limits it-self to the easily measurable above-ground NPP, and the more biologically relevant total NPP (TNPP), which includes roots and tubers. A map of world-wide NPP measurements is found in Zheng et al. (2003) and also at htpp://daacl.esd.ornl.gov/npq/GPPDI/Com-bined_GPPDI_des.html. Yodzis's study of food-chain lengths in rich and poor ecosys-tems is in Yodzis (1993). His definition of trophic level differs from Cohen et al.'s in that the latter used the maximum trophic level at which a species gets its food (maximum length), whereas Yodzis used the minimum level. Since species are more likely to get most of their food at the lowest of all the levels at which they forage, Yodzis's definition is probably the more realistic one (Rosenzweig 1995).

2.5
This Food Chain Will Self-Destruct

The mathematics of stability analysis was taken from Rosenzweig (1995) and Pimm and Lawton (1977). Pimm's phytotelma studies were described in Pimm and Kitching (1987). David Post's comments were taken from a telephone interview I had with him on 8 June 2005. His review of food-chain length is Post (2002), and his stable isotope study on eco-system size and food-chain length is Post et al. (2000). Three other, similar studies are van der Zanden et al. (1999a, b), and Lake et al. (2001).

Chapter 3   Hidden Riches

3.1
Specific Issues

The term 'rain forest mafia' was coined by E.O. Wilson (1994). I took some informa-tion on Janzen's career from Thomson (2003) and on the Guanacaste Conservation Area from http://janzen.sas.upenn.edu and http://www.guanacaste.ac.cr. The Janzen–Connell hypothesis of rainforest tree coexistence is discussed in Chap. 7, whereas the orange peel story was told by Janzen at a lecture in Patras, Greece, in August 2002 (the orange peels were meant to help regenerate woodland). The three papers with intriguing titles are Janzen (1967, 1979, 1984). The quote on the first parataxonomist is from the acknowledgements page of http://janzen.sas.upenn.edu, whereas the entire database is correctly cited as Janzen and Hallwachs (2005). The *Proceedings of the National Academy of Sciences of the USA* paper is Hebert et al. (2004a). More in-depth discussions of species and speciation may be found in Mallet (1995) and Schilthuizen (2000, 2001). Mayr's biological species concept is developed in Mayr (1942). The clam paper is Kijviriya et al. (1991). Krell's critique of morphospecies sorting is Krell (2004). Besides the *Astraptes* paper, a few other DNA-barcoding papers are Hebert et al. (2003, 2004b).

3.2
Alice in the Jungle

A reference to the tree diversity in a one-hectare plot in Borneo is Small et al. (2004). Corner's quote was taken from Corner (1964). The story of Corner and his monkeys is told by Vines (2002), whereas the anecdote of the monkey that was cleverer than its master was added by Wallingford (2003). Current use of monkeys in canopy studies is described by Trichon (2002). Stephen Sutton and I discussed canopy science on many occasions since 2000. He first showed me around Danum Valley Field Centre in March 2000, whereas some of the quotes have been taken from a telephone conversation I had with him on 29 July 2005. Details on the menggaris tree can be found in Whitmore (1998) and Anonymous (1997). Tree-climbing techniques are explained in detail in Barker and Standridge (2002) and Ellwood and Foster (2002). The quotes by Nalini Nadkarni are from a telephone conversation I had with her on 31 August 2005. Some of her work is described in Nadkarni (1994, 1995) and Nadkarni et al. (2001). The Ecuador epiphyte diversity is mentioned in Gentry and Dodson (1987). The general information on canopy cranes was taken from Sutton (2001), from my interview with Nalini Nadkarni, and from a public lecture by Andrew Mitchell in Kota Kinabalu, Malaysia, on 7 December 2005. The measurements of the Lambir canopy crane are from Sakai et al. (2002) and Harrison and Ashton (2003). The details on Dorrington's D-4 are based on the interview with Stephen Sutton on 29 July 2005, on Dorrington (2002), and on Graham Dorrington's homepage http://www.eng.qmul.ac.uk/people/dorrington.htm. The fogging procedure described is the one described by Erwin (1983). His Manaus results are also reported in this paper, whereas the Panama study can be found in Erwin and Scott (1980) and Erwin (1982). The figures of the Brunei fogging studies are from Morse et al. (1988) and Stork (1988). General information on nest-shaped epiphytes was taken from Whitmore (1998). The Danum nest fern study was reported in Ellwood and Foster (2002, 2004). The quote about the enthusiastic assistants is from the latter reference.

3.3
Deep Secrets, Intimate Friends

Following convention (e.g. Curtis et al. 2002), when I refer to bacteria (with a small b) here and elsewhere, I mean to indicate all prokaryotes, both Archaea and Bacteria (with a capital B). However, when I speak of microbes, this may also include microscopic eukaryotes, such as protists and Fungi. Wilson's slogan is the title of Wilson (1987). May's graph of body length versus species richness is in May (1978, 1988). The results of Torsvik's forest soil study are in Torsvik et al. (1990), while the outcome of her marine sediment sampling is mentioned by Wilson (1992). Some details of the ecology of the Sargasso Sea are mentioned in Colinvaux (1978), while the study of its bacterioplankton is published as Giovannoni et al. (1990). The details on *Pelagibacter ubique* were taken from Giovannoni's website, http://www.cgrb.orst.edu/faculty/giovannoni/. The study of microbes in hypersaline basins in the Mediterranean is described in van der Wielen et al. (2005); it is part of the BIODEEP project (http://www.geo.unimib.it/BioDeep/Project.html). Schippers's study is in Schippers et al. (2005). Parkes's study is in Parkes et al. (2005); the fact that sub-seafloor sediments contain more than half of all bacterial cells on Earth is mentioned in Whitman et al. (1998). The Yellowstone paper is Walker et al. (2005) and the human gut study is Eckburg et al. (2005). The studies on the microbial diversities of the McMurdo valleys, oil reservoirs, the human ear, and shower curtains are, respectively, de la Torre et al. (2003), Jeanthnon et al. (1995), Frank et al. (2003), and Kelley et al. (2004). The number of known bacterial *16S* sequences is based on my 10 November 2005 search for "16S" and "Prokaryota" in Genbank (http://www.ncbi.nlm.nih.gov). The latest Sargasso Sea bacterioplankton sequencing is in Venter et al. (2004). The estimates of the numbers of bacteria in the sea are from the webpages of the International Census of Marine Microbes (http://www.coml.org/descrip/icomm.htm). The one of the numbers of bacteria in deep sea sediments is in Schippers et al. (2005). The numbers of bacteria on land are mentioned in Gans et al. (2005), Curtis and Sloan (2005), and Fliermand and Balkwill (1989). The reanalyses of DNA reassociation data are in Gans et al. (2005) and Curtis and Sloan (2005). Norman Pace's quotes are taken from a telephone conversation I had with him on 3 November 2005.

Chapter 4   No Niche Like Home

4.1
There Goes a Badger

The experiments on woodlice as described were actually carried out in a 'preferendum apparatus' by, e.g., Gromysz-Kalkowska and Oder (1983). Hutchinson's 'Concluding remarks' paper is Hutchinson (1957). The qualification of Robert MacArthur as 'the James Dean of theoretical ecology' is by Quammen (1996). The bird guide that I quote from is Griggs (1997). The other information on Robert MacArthur and his PhD work is taken from Colinvaux (1978), Quammen (1996), Wilson (1994), and MacArthur (1958).

4.2
Peaceful Coexistence?

The history of the concept of interspecific competition and competitive exclusion is based on Volterra (1926), Gause (1934), Colinvaux (1978), and Rosenzweig (1995). Hutchinson (1957) called Gause's principle the Volterra–Gause principle. The account on the ecology and behaviour of burying beetles (*Nicrophorus*) is based on Pukowski (1933)[1], Milne and Milne (1976), Henderson (1986), and Schilthuizen and Vallenduuk (1998). Some of the many Web-based resources for general information on burying beetles (*Nicrophorus*) are http://www.digimorph.org/specimens/Nicrophorus_americanus/, where a *Nicrophorus* specimen can be virtually examined in 3D, *Nicrophorus* Central, http://collections2.eeb.uconn.edu/nicroweb/nicrophorus.htm, and http://www.beetlelady.com/?page_id=6. Field experiments

---

[1]   A (poor) translation into English can be found at http://collections2.eeb.uconn.edu/nicroweb/nicrophorus.htm.

on competition are reviewed in Schoener (1983). Papers discussing limiting similarity are May and MacArthur (1972) and Hubbell and Foster (1986).

4.3
A Moveable Niche

Information on the settlement of Borneo by the tree sparrow can be found in Smythies and Davison (1999). A biography of Jared Diamond can be found at http://www.evowiki. org/wiki.phtml?title=Jared_Diamond. His paper on niche shifts in New Guinean birds is Diamond (1970). Additional information can be found in Mayr and Diamond (2001).

4.4
Paradox of the Plankton

The number of 422,000 plant species on Earth is taken from Bramwell (2002). The tree diversity in Sarawak is mentioned in Condit et al. (2000) and Wills et al. (2006), whereas the figure on diversity in fynbos comes from Latimer et al. (2005). Overviews of the literature on plant niches are given in Silvertown (2004, 2005). The quotes by Jonathan Silvertown are from a telephone interview I had with him on 14 March 2006, and also from his website: http://www.demonsineden.com/ff.htm. His paper on the hydrology of plant niche space is Silvertown et al. (1999). A good introduction to the Cape flora is Goldblatt and Manning (2002). Examples of studies on niches in rainforest trees are Condit et al. (2000) and Paoli et al. (2006), whereas the paper on tundra plants is McKane et al. (2002). The text on Condit et al.'s (2000) study is based on a news item that I wrote earlier for *ScienceNOW* (http://sciencenow.sciencemag.org/cgi/content/full/2000/526/2). Hutchinson's 'paradox of the plankton' was first outlined by him in Hutchinson (1961), although the quotes come from Hutchinson (1965). The quotes by Jef Huisman and Maayke Stomp are from a telephone interview I had with them on 20 March 2006. The study on *Synechococcus* species BS4 and BS5 is described in Stomp et al. (2004), whereas Kühl et al. (2005) reported on the infrared-harvesting picoplankton. Johnson et al. (2006) describe the *Prochlorococcus* differentiation by various other resources.

Chapter 5   Neutral by Nature

5.1
This Fauna Ain't Big Enough for the Two of Us

The description of the Tun Sakaran marine park and its land snail fauna was based on a field trip there in April–May 2005 (made possible by Irwanshah bin Mustapa, Annadel Cabanban, and the Sabah Parks staff), interviews with Liew Thor Seng in August 2007, and unpublished work by Liew and Schilthuizen. More information on the park may be found at http://www.sempornaislandsproject.com and http://www.sabahparks.org.my/pages/news.html?Body=sip.html.

Diamond's groundbreaking paper on assembly rules is Diamond (1975). Concise explanations of assembly rules can be found in Wilson (1992) and Fox (2001).

5.2
Far-Flung Flora and Fauna

I acknowledge Peake (1981) for the quote by Durrell (1953). I have used pages 358–387 from Darwin (1859) as a guideline for this section. Further details on his dispersal experiments and his correspondence with Berkeley were taken from the Darwin Correspondence Project (http://www.darwinproject.ac.uk/). The dispersal modes by which the Galápagos Islands were colonised are reviewed in Peck (1996); his papers on aerial and oceanic dispersal in the Galápagos are Peck (1994a, b), whereas the earlier, larger studies across the Pacific are in Holzapfel (1978) and Holzapfel et al. (1978). The record of a 5.4 millimetre by 2.5 millimetre particle taken from aeroplane sampling over the Pacific at 3,000-metres altitude was found in Peake (1981) and, since Peake did not give a reference, tentatively attributed here to the Bishop Museum studies. All quotes of Wallace in this section are from Wallace (1880). Hitch-hiking as seen in migratory birds is described by Figuerola et al. (2003); this paragraph is taken nearly verbatim from a story I wrote about this subject for *ScienceNOW* (http://sciencenow. sciencemag.org/cgi/content/full/2003/916/2). Hitch-hiking by spiders on ants is described by Ichinose et al. (2004) and long-distance dispersal in *Balea* snails is discussed in Gittenberger et al. (2006).

5.3
Dying by Random Numbers

The information on the mammoths of Wrangel island was taken from Rosenzweig (1995), Vartanyan et al. (1993, 1995), and the Wrangel Island pages at http://en.wikipedia.org and http://whc.unesco.org, whereas the Maine experiments are in Crowell (1973).

Chapter 6   In Splendid Isolation

6.1
A Bug's Life

Direct quotes of Wilson are from interviews I had with him on 14 October 1995 and 23 May 2006, both times in Amsterdam. Newspaper articles based on these interviews appeared in *Intermediair* (27 October 1995) and *Bionieuws* (26 May 2006). Further biographical information on Wilson is taken from Wilson (1994) and Quammen (1996). The brief history of the species–area relationship is from Rosenzweig (1995) and Quammen (1996), the book by Darlington (1957), and the papers by Arrhenius (1921), Preston (1960), and May (1975).

6.2
The Coffee Table of Science

The quotes in this section are all from Wilson (1994), whereas the two major island bioge-ography publications of the two authors are MacArthur and Wilson (1963, 1967).

6.3
Earth Sinks in the Sea

Information on Surtsey is taken from Fridriksson (1975, 2000) and from the Surtsey Re-search Society's website: http://www.surtsey.is/. The repeated extinction and reconstitution of the fauna of Aldabra is described in Taylor et al. (1979) and Peake (1981). Simberloff's discussion of Diamond's niche-based assembly is Simberloff (1978).

6.4
Chainsaws and Methyl Bromide

The information on the history of the Florida Keys experiments was taken from Wilson (1992, 1994) and Quammen (1996), whereas the key papers are Wilson and Simberloff (1969), Simberloff and Wilson (1969, 1970), and Simberloff (1976, 1978). I also used Rosenzweig (1995).

6.5
Lubricant Biogeography

The work on bugs on British roundabouts was published as Helden and Leather (2004). The study on bacteria in machine oil tanks is van der Gast et al. (2005). Information on the medical importance of these bacteria was taken from http://psc.che.tamu.edu/wp-content/uploads/bacteria-in-lathe-cutting-fluid.pdf. The review by Rosenzweig is in Rosenzweig (1995). The two studies mentioned, of Galápagos plants and Lake Hjälmaren plants, are Hamilton et al. (1963) and Rydin and Borgegård (1988), respectively.

Chapter 7   Ecology of Wildcards

7.1
Guild by Association

The two books *Endless Forms* and *Endless Forms Most Beautiful* are Howard and Ber-locher (1998) and Carroll (2005), respectively. The story on the reality of Darwin's bank is in Thorpe (2000). The Downe area and its bid to become a World Heritage Site are showcased at http://www.darwinatdowne.co.uk. The most recent edition of *Heukels' Flora* is van der Meijden (2005), although I collected the data on commonness and rarity from the online database http://soortenbank.nl. Corbet's butterfly data are in Corbet (1941) and Fisher et al. (1943). For my overview of the main types of species abundance curves, I have relied on Rosenzweig (1995) and Hubbell (2001). I took information on Frank Preston's life mostly from Mayfield's (1989) obituary, from which source I have also quoted, and Quammen (1996). Preston's most important papers on relative species abundance are Preston (1948, 1960, 1962a, b). The figure of 30 for the number of published species abundance models is from McGill (2003). MacArthur's papers on relative species abundance are MacArthur (1957, 1960), and the inferiority of his broken-stick model compared with the log-normal is in Hubbell (2001).

7.2
Registry of Births and Deaths

Biographical information on Stephen Hubbell is based on his curriculum vitae as available from the University of Georgia's website, http://www.plantbio.uga.edu/shubbell/CVs/ steve_cv.pdf, from Hubbell (2001), and from *The New York Times'* article on Hubbell's involvement in the Barro Colorado Research (6 June 2006). Information on BCI itself is mostly based on the website of the STRI: http://www.stri.org. The details of Hubbell's zero-sum multinomial are taken from Hubbell (1979, 1997, 2001). The quote that the bell curve could be 'derived from first principles' is taken from Hubbell (1997). More exactly, theta (θ) was defined as $2J_M\nu$, where J_M is the number of individuals in the 'meta-community' and ν equals the speciation rate (Hubbell 1997, 2001). Etienne et al. (2007b) investigated the impact on the model's behaviour of the kind of speciation process assumed. They found that Hubbell's original assumption, namely that an individual has a fixed chance to speciate, regardless of the abundance of its species, fits the data best.

7.3
Maintaining Neutrality

Quotes by Hubbell in this section were taken, unless stated otherwise, from an interview I had with him in Lunteren, the Netherlands, on 13 February 2008. The number of citations of Hubbell's book was taken from the Web of Science, 2 July 2007. Brian McGill's quotes are from a telephone interview I had with him on 17 May 2006. The board game Hubbell created is Extinction. A good, independent development of neutral ecology is Bell (2001), and popular accounts of the niche versus neutrality debate are Whitfield (2002) and Gewin (2006).

7.4
Algebraic Kneejerks

The debate between Hubbell and McGill centres around the following publications: McGill (2003), Volkov et al. (2003), and McGill et al. (2006). A paper on the application of the neutral theory on fynbos, mathematical corrections on that, and a review of merits of the neutral theory are, respectively, Latimer et al. (2005), Etienne et al. (2006), and Alonso et al. (2006). The quotes by Jacques van Alphen are based on a telephone interview held in May 2006, as are the quotes by Etienne, and the paper in which the zero-sum condition is lifted is Etienne et al. (2007a). In the final paragraph, reference is made to the following 2003 paper: Sugihara et al. (2003).

7.5
Pest Control

The information on mahogany and its herbivores was taken from Norghauer et al. (2006a, b). I also benefited from conversations with Rob Bagchi and from Silvertown (2005) in preparing this section. The Janzen–Connell hypothesis was first published in Janzen (1970) and Connell (1971). It and other mechanisms that explain coexistence are reviewed by Wright (2002). Eye-witness accounts of Connell's field work in Queensland that led, among many other things, to the paper by Connell et al. (1984) were given to me by Bronwen Scott, who drove me around the Atherton tablelands and told me all there is to know about the area and more. The cherry tree work is described in Packer and Clay (2000) and van der Putten (2000). The paper in which the rare species advantage is compared with the neutral theory is Volkov et al. (2005). Finally, the quotes in the last few paragraphs are from Gewin (2006).

Chapter 8   The Loom of Life

In this chapter, I use the terms 'richness' and 'diversity' somewhat interchangeably, although some ecologists (but not others, e.g. Rosenzweig 1995) use strict definitions in which richness is the total number of species in a habitat, whereas diversity is a combination of the richness and the relative abundances of each species. I also use the term 'stability', for which at least six different definitions exist (Neutel et al. 2007; McCann 2000), although they tend to fall into two categories: resilience (ability to return to the original state) and inertia (resistance to change), which are not exactly the same thing, although in most of this book, I pretend that they are.

8.1
Weft and Warp

The keystone species concept is described in Wilson (1992) as are the events that ensued when pumas and jaguars became extinct on Barro Colorado Island. The latter is described in more detail in Terborgh (1988). The quote by McCann is from McCann (2000). Recent estimates for the amount of global primary production that humans appropriate are, e.g., Haber et al. (2007) and Imhoff et al. (2004). The Jenga metaphor is in de Ruiter et al. (2005).

8.2
The More the Merrier?

General overviews of the diversity–stability debate are (in chronological order) Goodman (1975), Colinvaux (1978), Shrader-Frechette and McCoy (1993), Simberloff (2000), and McCann (2000). Elton's quote is from Elton (1958, p. 145), although it should be noted here that the same conclusion was reached independently by Odum (1953) a few years earlier. Data on defoliation by insects in tropical forests are in Wong et al. (1990) and references therein. May's *Nature* paper is May (1972) and his book on food webs is May (1973). The term 'May's Paradox' is found in, e.g., Neutel et al. (2007). The quotes by the Common Sense Environmental Fund on the relationship between biodiversity and ecosystem stability are at http://www.csshome.com/biodiversity.htm.

8.3
Six Degrees of Separation

The social network study of scientists at the South Pole is in Palinkas et al. (1998) and McMahon et al. (2001). Johnson's application of social structure methods to food webs is in Johnson et al. (2001), and the groundbreaking *Nature* paper is Krause et al. (2003). Ann Krause also helped me by clarifying some points in her paper by e-mail on 2 January 2008. May's *Nature* paper is May (1972) and his book on food webs is May (1973).

8.4
Top-Down or Bottom-Up?

This section is largely based on the papers in *Ecology*'s 1992 special feature on the top-down and bottom-up debate, in particular Power (1992) and Menge (1992). The original 'the world is green' paper is Hairston et al. (1960). The paper on bottom-up control of fish production in the Northeast Pacific is Ware and Thomson (2005), whereas the sea otter/killer whale references are Wilson (1992), Estes et al. (1998), and Kaiser (1998).

8.5
The Weakest Link

This section is based largely on Paine (1992), Wootton (1994), de Ruiter et al. (1995, 2005), McCann et al. (1998), McCann (2000), and Neutel et al. (2002). Information on Tatoosh Island and Timothy Wootton's research was also taken from the video clip at http://ib.berkeley.edu/labs/power/lab_people/lab_alumni.html, which is where Wootton's quote was taken from as well. The various definitions of interaction strength are discussed in Laska and Wootton (1998).

8.6
Elton Revisited

The discussions on the exact meaning of complexity are largely based on Neutel et al. (2007) and McCann (2000). The information on the Cedar Creek experiments was taken from Tilman et al. (2001, 2006), the Cedar Creek website (http://www.cedarcreek.umn.edu), and a telephone interview I had with Tilman on 3 June 2003. Reviews of biodiversity/productivity experiments are in Cardinale et al. (2006, 2007) and Hector and Bagchi (2007). Darwin's quotes on greater productivity of more diverse turf are in Darwin (1859, p. 185); the role of this insight in Darwin's speciation theory is elaborated in Schilthuizen (2000, 2001). The story of the Woburn Abbey garden, which Darwin's observations derived from, is told by Hector and Hooper (2002). Hector's quotes are from a telephone conversation I had with him on 3 June 2003, and from an e-mail from him of 5 November 2007. Tilman's results on stable ecosystem functioning despite instability in the species composition were confirmed by van Ruijven and Berendse (2007). And criticisms of the artificiality of Tilman and others' studies have been waged by Bezemer and van der Puten (2007). Information on the sand dunes of the Veluwe was taken from Borman (1984) and Oosterloo and van Soest (1977).

Chapter 9   The Age of Atropos

9.1
Ecosystems Unravelled

The mythology of the three Moirae was taken from Hamilton (1942) and Richardson (2007).

9.2
The Shears of Extinction

Darwin's quote is in Darwin (1859, p. 73). The extinctions that took place during and before Darwin's time were compiled from Wilson (1992) and Quammen (1996). The examples of current extinctions are referenced as follows: *Opisthostoma sciaphilum* (Schilthuizen and Clements 2008); *Colpocephalum californici* (the Natural History Museum, London, press release accompanying Koh et al. 2004); *Lipotes vexillifer* (baiji) (Adams and Carwardine 1990; Wu et al. 2003; Carwardine 2007[2]). The section on the ecosystem effects of tropical forest logging was mostly based on Schilthuizen (2006a), Curran et al. (2004), the IUCN Red List (http://www.redlist.org), Lammertink (2004, 2007), Kagata and Ohgushi (2006), Hunter and Price (1992), Lawton et al. (1998), and a telephone interview and subsequent e-mail correspondence with Lisa Curran in the first half of February 2004, originally used for a story in

---

[2]   An obituary in *New Scientist* under the title *So Long, and Thanks for All the Fish* by Carwardine, who documented the dwindling species with science-fiction author Douglas Adams in the 1980s.

ScienceNOW (Schilthuizen 2004), as well as e-mail correspondence with her in March 2008. The section on general overfishing was based on Pauly et al. (1998, 2003). The one on shark overfishing was based on Wilson (1992), Fishbase (http://www.fishbase.org), and Myers et al. (2007), whereas the one on Caribbean coral reef collapse was based on Wapnick et al. (2004), Bellwood et al. (2004), Hoegh-Guldberg (2006), and Bascompte et al. (2005). The quote at the end of the section comes from a Scripps Institute press release that accompanied the *Proceedings of the National Academy of Sciences of the USA* paper.

9.3
The Awl of Invasion

The information on species introductions (both accidental and intentional; both incidental and in bulk) is mostly taken from Elton (1958), van der Weijden et al. (2007), and from a conversation with Lucius Eldredge in Singapore on 7 December, 2004. The example of two introduced bass species is taken from van der Zanden et al. (1999b). The tens rule was introduced by Williamson (1997), whereas the data on vertebrate introductions that do not show the tens rule are presented in Jeschke and Strayer (2005). The story of Ascension is based on Wilkinson (2004) and Pearce (2004), and the one on the San Francisco Bay area on Cohen and Carlton (1998). The knapweed story is in Pearson and Callaway (2006), whereas the knopper gall one is told by Schönrogge et al. (1996). The two papers in *Nature* are Torchin et al. (2003) and Mitchell and Power (2003). The invasion–diversity experiments mentioned were published as Kennedy et al. (2002) and Zavaleta and Hulvey (2004).

9.4
The Ecosystem Ripper

The study by Suzan Benedick and Nazirah Mustaffa was published as Benedick et al. (2006); the z value of 0.25 is not actually in that paper, but I derived it from its Fig. 3. For the references for island biogeography theory I refer to the notes that go with Chap. 6. The history of Lovejoy and his Forest Fragments Project were mostly taken from Quammen (1996); other details on the research project are from Pimm (1998) and Laurance et al. (2002). The bird data were published in Stratford and Stouffer (1999) and Ferraz et al. (2003).

9.5
Coda

Information on the oil palm crisis in Southeast Asia was obtained from a variety of sources compiled in a Dutch-language article (Schilthuizen 2006b). A good Web-based source is http://www.rspo.org. The invasions after the closing of the Isthmus of Panama are mentioned in Vermeij (1991). The pollen data on stability of forest diversity are reported by Clark and McLachlan (2003).

References

Adams D, Carwardine M (1990) Last chance to see. Ballantine Books, New York

Alonso D, Etienne RS, McKane AJ (2006) The merits of neutral theory. Trends Ecol Evol 21: 451–457

Anonymous (1997) A nature trail in primary forest. Sabah Foundation and WWF Malaysia, Kota Kinabalu

Arrhenius O (1921) Species and area. J Ecol 9:95–99

Athauda SBP, Matsumoto K, Rajapakshe S, Kuribayashi M, Kojima M, Kubomura-Yoshida N, Iwamatsu A, Shibata C, Inoue H, Takahashi K (2004) Enzymic and structural characterization of nepenthesin, a unique member of a novel subfamily of aspartic proteinases. Biochem J 381:295–306

Barker M, Standridge N (2002) Ropes as a mechanism for canopy access. In: Mitchell AW, Secoy K, Jackson T (eds) Global canopy handbook; techniques of access and study in the forest roof. Global Canopy Programme, Oxford, pp 13–23

Bascompte J, Melián CJ, Sala E (2005) Interaction strength combinations and the overfishing of a marine food web. Proc Natl Acad Sci USA 102:5443–5447

Baumann P, Moran NA, Baumann L (1997) The evolution and genetics of aphid endosymbionts. Bioscience 47:12–20

Bell G (2001) Macroecology's neutrality. Science 293:2413–2418

Bellwood DR, Hughes TP, Folke C, Nyström M (2004) Confronting the coral reef crisis. Nature 429:827–833

Benedick S, Hill JK, Mustaffa N, Chey VK, Maryati M, Searle JB, Schilthuizen M, Hamer KC (2006) Impact of rain forest fragmentation of butterflies in northern Borneo: species richness, turnover and the value of small fragments. J Appl Ecol 43:967–977

Bezemer TM, van der Putten WH (2007) Diversity and stability in plant communities. Nature 446: E6–E7

Bohn HF, Federle W (2004) Insect aquaplaning: *Nepenthes* pitcher plants capture prey with the peristome, a fully wettable water-lubricated anisotropic surface. Proc Natl Acad Sci USA 101:14138–14143

Borman R (1984) De geologische hoofdtijdperken. In: Borman R, Willemsen G, Stapert D (eds) De IJstijden in Nederland. Terra, Zutphen, pp 7–24

Bramwell D (2002) How many plant species are there? Plant Talk 28:32

Briand F, Cohen JE (1987) Environmental correlates of food chain length. Science 238:956–960

Bulat SA, Alekhina IA, Blot M, Petit JR, de Angelis M, Wagenbach D, Lipenkov VY, Vasilyeva LP, Wloch DM, Raynaud D, Lukin VV (2004) DNA signature of thermophilic bacteria from the aged accretion ice of Lake Vostok, Antarctica: implications for searching for life in extreme icy environments. Int J Astrobiol 3:1–12

Cardinale BJ, Srivastava DS, Duffy JE, Wright JP, Downing AL, Sankaran M, Jouseau C (2006) Effects of biodiversity on the functioning of trophic groups and ecosystems. Nature 443:989–992

Cardinale BJ, Wright JP, Cadotte MW, Caroll IT, Hector A, Srivastava DS, Loreau M, Weis JJ (2007) Impacts of plant diversity on biomass production increase through time because of species complementarity: a meta-analysis. Proc Natl Acad Sci USA 104:18123–18128

Carroll SB (2005) Endless forms most beautiful: the new science of Evo Devo and the making of the animal kingdom. Norton, New York

Carwardine M (2007) So long, and thanks for all the fish. New Sci 195(2621):50–53

Charlat S, Hornett EA, Dyson EA, Ho PHY, Loc NT, Schilthuizen M, Davies N, Roderick GK, Hurst GDD (2005) Is extreme male-killer prevalence a local or common event in the butterfly *Hypolimnas bolina*? A survey across Indo-Pacific populations. Mol Ecol 14:3525–3530

Chia TF, Aung HH, Osipov AN, Goh NK, Chia LS (2004) Carnivorous pitcher plant uses free radicals in the digestion of prey. Redox Rep 9:255–261

Clark JS, McLachlan JS (2003) Stability of forest biodiversity. Nature 423:635–638

Clarke CM (1997) Nepenthes of Borneo. Natural History Publications (Borneo), Kota Kinabalu

Clarke CM, Kitching RL (1993) The metazoan food webs from six Bornean *Nepenthes* species. Ecol Entomol 18:7–16

Cohen AN, Carlton JT (1998) Accelated invasion rate in a highly invaded estuary. Science 279:555–558

Cohen JE, Briand F, Newman CM (1986) A stochastic theory of community food webs: III. Predicted and observed lengths of food chains. Proc R Soc Lond Ser B 228:317–353

Colinvaux PA (1978) Why big fierce animals are rare – an ecologist's perspective. Princeton University Press, Princeton

Condit R, Ashton PS, Baker P, Bunyavejchewin S, Gunatilleke S, Gunatilleke N, Hubbell SP, Foster RB, Itoh A, LaFrankie JV, Lee HS, Losos E, Manokaran N, Sukumar R, Yamakura T (2000) Spatial patterns in the distribution of tropical tree species. Science 288:1414–1418

Connell JH (1971) On the role of natural enemies in preventing competitive exclusion in some marine animals and in rain forest trees. In: den Boer PJ, Gradwell GR (eds) Dynamics of populations. Centre for Agricultural Publishing and Documentation, Wageningen, pp 298–313

Connell JH, Tracey JG, Webb LJ (1984) Compensatory recruitment, growth, and mortality as factors maintaining rain forest tree diversity. Ecol Monogr 54:141–164

Cook RE (1977) Raymond Lindeman and the trophic-dynamic concept in ecology. Science 198:22–26

Corbet AS (1941) The distribution of butterflies in the Malay Peninsula. Proc R Soc Lond Ser A 16:101–116

Corner EJH (1964) The life of plants. Wiedenfeld and Nicolson, London

Cresswell JE (2000) Resource input and the community structure of larval infaunas of an eastern tropical pitcher plant *Nepenthes bicalcarata*. Ecol Entomol 25:362–366

Crowcroft P (1991) Elton's ecologists; a history of the Bureau of Animal Population. University of Chicago Press, Chicago

Crowell KL (1973) Experimental zoogeography: introductions of mice to small islands. Am Nat 107:535–558

Curran LM, Trigg SN, McDonald AK, Astiani D, Hardiono YM, Siregar P, Caniago I, Kasischke E (2004) Lowland forest loss in protected areas of Indonesian Borneo. Science 303:1000–1003

Curtis TP, Sloan WT (2005) Exploring microbial diversity – a vast below. Science 309:1331–1333

Curtis TP, Sloan WT, Scannell JW (2002) Estimating prokaryotic diversity and its limits. Proc Natl Acad Sci USA 99:10494–10499

Darlington PJ (1957) Zoogeography. Wiley, New York

Darwin C (1859) On the origin of species, by means of natural selection or the preservation of favoured races in the struggle for life. Murray, London

de la Torre JR, Goebel BM, Friedmann EI, Pace NR (2003) Microbial diversity of cryptoendolithic communities from the McMurdo dry valleys in Antarctica. Appl Environ Microbiol 69: 3858–3867

de Ruiter PC,. Neutel A-M, Moore JC (1995) Energetics, patterns of interaction strengths, and stability in real ecosystems. Science 269:1257–1260

de Ruiter PC, Wolters V, Moore JC, Winemiller KO (2005) Food web ecology: playing Jenga and beyond. Science 309:68–71

Diamond JM (1970) Ecological consequences of island colonization by Southwest Pacific birds, I. types of niche shifts. Proc Natl Acad Sci USA 67:529–536

Diamond JM (1975) The assembly of species commnities. In: Cody ML, Diamond JM (eds) Ecology and evolution of communities. Harvard University Press, Cambridge, pp 342–444

Dorrington G (2002) "Project Hornbill" and future lighter than air platforms. In: Mitchell AW, Secoy K, Jackson T (eds) Global canopy handbook; techniques of access and study in the forest roof. Global Canopy Programme, Oxford, pp 103–105

Durrell L (1953) Reflections on a marine Venus: a companion to the landscape of Rhodes. Faber & Faber, London

Dyson EA, Kamath MK, Hurst GDD (2002) *Wolbachia* infection associated with all-female broods in *Hypolimnas bolina* (Lepidoptera: Nymphalidae): evidence for horizontal transmission in a butterfly male killer. Heredity 88:166–171

Eckburg PB, Bik EM, Bernstein CN, Purdom E, Dethlefsen L, Sargent M, Gill SR, Nelson KE, Relman DA (2005) Diversity of the human intestinal microbial flora. Science 308:1635–1638

Ellwood MF, Foster WA (2002) Techniques for inserting and positioning lines in forest canopies. In: Mitchell AW, Secoy K, Jackson T (eds) Global canopy handbook; techniques of access and study in the forest roof. Global Canopy Programme, Oxford, pp 24–28

Ellwood MDF, Foster WA (2004) Doubling the estimate of invertebrate biomass in a rainforest canopy. Nature 429:549–551

Elton CS (1927) Animal ecology. Macmillan, London

Elton CS (1958) The ecology of invasions by animals and plants. Methuen, London

Erwin TL (1982) Tropical forests: their richness in Coleoptera and other arthropod species. Coleopt Bull 36:74–75

Erwin TL (1983) Beetles and other insects of tropical forest canopies at Manaus, Brazil, sampled by insecticidal fogging. In: Sutton SL, Whitmore TC, Chadwick AC (eds) Tropical rain forest: ecology and management. Blackwell, Oxford, pp 59–75

Erwin TL, Scott JC (1980) Seasonal and size patterns, trophic structure, and richness of Coleoptera in the tropical arboreal ecosystem: the fauna of the tree *Luehia seemannii* Triana and Planch in the Canal zone of Panama. Coleopt Bull 34:305–322

Estes JA, Tinker MT, Williams TM, Doak DF (1998) Killer whale predation on sea otters linking oceanic and near-shore ecosystems. Science 282:473–477

Etienne RS, Latimer AM, Silander JA, Cowling RM (2006) Comment on "Neutral ecological theory reveals isolation and rapid speciation in a biodiversity hot spot". Science 311:610

Etienne RS, Alonso D, McKane AJ (2007a) The zero-sum assumption in neutral biodiversity theory. J Theor Biol. doi:10.1016/j.jtbi.2007.06.010

Etienne RS, Apol MEF, Olff H, Weissing FJ (2007b) Modes of speciation and the neutral theory of biodiversity. Oikos 116: 241–258

Ferraz G, Russell GJ, Stouffer PC, Bierregaard RO, Pimm SL, Lovejoy TE (2003) Rates of species loss from Amazonian forest fragments. Proc Natl Acad Sci USA 100:14069–14073

Figuerola J, Green AJ, Santamaría L (2003) Passive internal transport of aquatic organisms by water-fowl in Doñana, southwest Spain. Glob Ecol Biogeogr 12:427–436

Fisher RA, Corbet AS, Williams CB (1943) The relation between the number of species and the number of individuals in a random sample of an animal population. J Anim Ecol 12:42–58

Fliermans CB, Balkwill DL (1989) Microbial life in deep terrestrial subsurfaces. Bioscience 39:370–377

Ford A (1957) The bird biographies of John James Audubon. Macmillan, New York

Fox BJ (2001) The genesis and development of guild assembly rules. In: Weiher E, Keddy P (eds) Ecological assembly rules: perspectives, advances, retreats. Cambridge University Press, Cambridge, pp 23–57

Frank DN, Spiegelman GB, Davis W, Wagner E, Lyons E, Pace NR (2003) Culture-independent molecular analysis of microbial constituents of the healthy human outer ear. J Clin Microbiol 41:295–303

Fridriksson S (1975) Surtsey. Wiley, New York

Fridriksson S (2000) Vascular plants on Surtsey, Iceland 1991–1998. Surtsey Rese 11:21–28

Gans J, Wolinsky M, Dunbar J (2005) Computational improvements reveal great bacterial diversity and high metal toxicity in soil. Science 309:1387–1390

Gaume L, Forterre Y (2007) A viscoelastic deadly fluid in carnivorous pitcher plants. PLoS One 2:e1185

Gause GF (1934) The struggle for existence. Williams & Wilkins, Baltimore. http://www.ggause.com/Contgau.htm

Gentry AH, Dodson CH (1987) The contribution of non-trees to tropical forest species richness. Biotropica 19:145–156

George A (2004) Lifeless lake or exotic ecosystem? New Sci 183(2459):6–7

Gewin V (2006) Beyond neutrality – ecology finds its niche. PLoS Biol 4:e278

Giovannoni SJ, Britschgi TB, Moyer CL, Field KG (1990) Genetic diversity in Sargasso Sea bacterioplankton. Nature 345:60–63

Gittenberger E, Groenenberg DSJ, Kokshoorn B, Preece RC (2006) Molecular trails from hitch-hiking snails. Nature 439:409

Goldblatt P, Manning JC (2002) Plant diversity of the Cape region of southern Africa. Ann Mo Bot Gard 89:281–302

Goodman D (1975) The theory of diversity-stability relationships in ecology. Q Rev Biol 50:237–266

Griggs JL (1997) American bird conservancy's guide to all the birds of North America: a revolutionary system based on feeding behaviors and field-recognizable features. HarperCollins, New York

Gromysz-Kalkowska K, Oder M (1983) Humidity, light, and thermal preferendum of some terrestrial isopods. Fol Biol 31:279–295

Haber H, Erb KH, Krausmann F, Gaube V, Bondeau A, Plutzar C, Gingrich S, Lucht W, Fischer-Kowalski M (2007) Quantifying and mapping the human appropriation of net primary production in earth's terrestrial ecosystems. Proc Natl Acad Sci USA 104:12942–12947. doi:10.1073/pnas.0704243104

Hairston NG, Smith FE, Slobodkin LB (1960) Community structure, population control, and competition. Am Nat 94:421–424

Hamilton E (1942) Mythology; timeless tales of gods and heroes. Penguin, New York

Hamilton TH, Rubinoff I, Barth RH, Bush GL (1963) Species abundance: natural regulation of insular variation. Science 142:1575–1577

Harrison RD, Ashton PS (2003) Sarawak's best kept secret. Malays Nat 57:12–23

Hebert PDN, Cywinska A, Ball SL, DeWaard JR (2003) Biological identification through DNA barcodes. Proc R Soc Lond Ser B 270:313–321

Hebert PDN, Penton EH, Burns JM, Janzen DH, Hallwachs W (2004a). Ten species in one: DNA barcoding reveals cryptic species in the neotropical skipper butterfly *Astraptes fulgerator*. Proc Natl Acad Sci USA 101:14812–14817

Hebert PDN, Stoeckle MY, Zemlak TS, Francis CM (2004b). Identification of birds through DNA barcodes. PLoS Biol 2:e312

Hector A, Bagchi R (2007) Biodiversity and ecosystem multifunctionality. Nature 448:188–190

Hector A, Hooper R (2002) Darwin and the first ecological experiment. Science 295:639–641

Helden AJ, Leather SR (2004) Biodiversity on urban roundabouts – Hemiptera, management and the species-area relationship. Basic Appl Ecol 5:367–377

Henderson MK (1986) Some recent work on burying beetles: a review. AES Bull 45:44–49

Hoegh-Guldberg O (2006) Complexities of coral reef recovery. Science 311:43–44

Holzapfel EP (1978) Transoceanic airplane sampling for organisms and particles. Pac Insects 18:169–189

Holzapfel EP, Clagg HB, Goff ML (1978) Trapping of air-borne insects on ships in the Pacific, part 9. Pac Insects 19:65–90

Howard DJ, Berlocher SH (1998) Endless forms – species and speciation. Oxford University Press, Oxford

Hubbell SP (1979) Tree dispersion, abundance, and diversity in a tropical dry forest. Science 203:1299–1309

Hubbell SP (1997) A unified theory of biogeography and relative species abundance and its application to tropical rainforests and coral reefs. Coral Reefs 16:S9–S21

Hubbell SP (2001) The unified neutral theory of biodiversity and biogeography. Princeton University Press, Princeton

Hubbell SP, Foster RB (1986) Biology, chance, and history and the structure of tropical rain forest tree communities. In: Diamond J, Case TJ (eds) Community ecology. Harper and Row, New York, pp 314–329

Hunter MD, Price PW (1992) Playing chutes and ladders: heterogeneity and the relative roles of bottom-up and top-down forces in natural communities. Ecology 73:724–732

Hutchinson GE (1957) Concluding remarks. Cold Spring Harb Symp Quant Biol 22:415–427

Hutchinson GE (1959) Homage to Santa Rosalia, or: Why are there so many kinds of animals? Am Nat 93:145–159

Hutchinson GE (1961) The paradox of the plankton. Am Nat 95:137–145

Hutchinson GE (1965) The ecological theater and the evolutionary play. Yale University Press, New Haven

Ichinose K, Rinaldi I, Forti LC (2004) Winged leaf-cutting ants on nuptial flights used as transport by *Attacobius* spiders for dispersal. Ecol Entomol 29:628–631

Imhoff ML, Bounoua L, Ricketts T, Loucks C, Harriss R, Lawrence WT (2004) Global patterns in human consumption of net primary production. Nature 429:870–873

Janzen DH (1967) Why mountain passes are higher in the Tropics. Am Nat 101:233–249

Janzen DH (1970) Herbivores and the number of tree species in tropical forests. Am Nat 104:501–528

Janzen DH (1979) How to be a fig. Annu Rev Ecol Syst 10:13–51

Janzen DH (1984) Two ways to be a tropical big moth: Santa Rosa saturniids and sphingids. Oxf Surv Evol Biol 1:85–140

Janzen DH, Hallwachs W (2005) Dynamic database for an inventory of the macrocaterpillar fauna, and its food plants and parasitoids, of the Area de Conservacion Guanacaste (ACG), northwestern Costa Rica. http://janzen.sas.upenn.edu

Jeanthnon C, Reysenbach A-L, Haridon S, Gambacorta A, Pace NR, Glenat P, Prieur D (1995) *Thermotoga subterranea* sp. nov., a new thermophilic bacterium isolated from a continental oil reservoir. Arch Microbiol 164:91–97

Jeschke JM, Strayer DL (2005) Invasion success of vertebrates in Europe and North America. Proc Natl Acad Sci USA 102:7198–7202

Johnson JC, Borgatti SP, Luczkovich JJ, Everett MG (2001) Network role analysis in the study of food webs: an application of regular role coloration. J Soc Struct 2. http://www.cmu.edu/joss/content/articles/volume2/JohnsonBorgatti.html

Johnson ZI, Zinser ER, Coe A, McNulty NP, Woodward EMS, Chisholm SW (2006) Niche partitioning among *Prochlorococcus* ecotypes along ocean-scale environmental gradients. Science 311:1737–1740

Jouzel J, Petit JR, Souchez R, Barkov NI, Lipenkov VY, Raynaud D, Stievenard M, Vassiliev NI, Verbeke V, Vimeux F (1999). More than 200 meters of lake ice above subglacial Lake Vostok, Antarctica. Science 286:2138–2141

Kagata H, Ohgushi T (2006) Bottom-up trophic cascades and material transfer in terrestrial food webs. Ecol Res 21:26–34

Kaiser J (1998) Sea otter declines blamed on hungry killers. Science 282:390–391

Karl DM, Bird DF, Björkman K, Houlihan T, Shackleford R, Tupas L (1999) Microorganisms in the accreted ice of Lake Vostok, Antarctica. Science 286:2144–2147

Kelley ST, Theisen U, Angenent LT, St Amand A, Pace NR (2004) Molecular analysis of shower curtain biofilm microbes. Appl Environ Microbiol 70:4187–4192

Kennedy TA, Naeem S, Howe KM, Knops JMH, Tilman D, Reich P (2002) Biodiversity as a barrier to ecological invasion. Nature 417:636–638

Kijviriya V, Viyanat ESUV, Woodruff DS (1991) Genetic studies of Asiatic clams, *Corbicula*, in Thailand: allozymes of 21 nominal species are identical. Am Malacol Bull 8 97–106

Kitching RL (2000) Food webs and container habitats: the natural history and ecology of phytotelmata. Cambridge University Press, Cambridge

Koh LP, Dunn RR, Sodhi NS, Colwell RK, Proctor HC, Smith VS (2004) Species coextinctions and the biodiversity crisis. Science 305:1632–1634

Krause AE, Frank KA, Mason DM, Ulanowicz RE, Taylor WW (2003) Compartments revealed in food-web structure. Nature 426:282–285

Krell F-T (2004) Parataxonomy vs. taxonomy in biodiversity studies – pitfalls and applicability of 'morphospecies' sorting. Biodivers Conserv 13:795–812

Kühl M, Chen M, Ralph PJ, Schreibers U, Larkum AWD (2005) A niche for cyanobacteria containing chlorophyll *d*. Nature 433:820

Lake JL et al (2001) Stable nitrogen isotopes as indicators of anthropogenic activities in small freshwater systems. Can J Fish Aquat Sci 58:870–878

Lammertink M (2004) A multiple-site comparison of woodpecker communities in Bornean lowland and hill forests. Conserv Biol 18:746–757

Lammertink M (2007) Community ecology and logging responses of Southeast Asian woodpeckers (*Picidae*, *Aves*). PhD thesis, University of Amsterdam, Amsterdam

Laska MS, Wootton JT (1998) Theoretical concepts and empirical approaches to measuring interaction strength. Ecology 79:461–476

Laurance WF, Lovejoy TE, Vasconcelos HL, Bruna EM, Didham RK, Stouffer PC, Gascon C, Bierregaard RO, Laurance SG, Sampaio E (2002) Ecosystem decay of Amazonian forest fragments: a 22-year investigation. Conserv Biol 16:605–618

Latimer AM, Silander JA Jr, Cowling RM (2005) Neutral ecological theory reveals isolation and rapid speciation in a biodiversity hotspot. Science 309:1722–1725

Lawton JH, Bignell DE, Bolton B, Bloemers GF, Eggleton P, Hammond PM, Hodda M, Holt RD, Larsen TB, Mawdsley NA, Stork NE, Srivastava DS, Watt AD (1998) Biodiversity inventories, indicator taxa and effects of habitat modification in tropical forest. Nature 391:71–76

Leigh LS, Burgess T, Marino BDV, Wei YD (1999) Tropical rainforest biome of Biosphere 2: structure, composition and results of the first 2 years of operation. Ecol Eng 13:65–93

Lindeman RL (1942) The trophic-dynamic concept of ecology. Ecol 23:399–417

MacArthur RA (1957) On the relative abundance of bird species. Proc Natl Acad Sci USA 43:293–295

MacArthur RA (1958) Population ecology of some warblers of Northeastern coniferous forests. Ecology 39:599–619

MacArthur RA (1960) On the relative abundance of species. Am Nat 94:25–36

MacArthur RA, Wilson EO (1963) An equilibrium theory of insular zoogeography. Evolution 17:373–387

MacArthur RA, Wilson EO (1967) The theory of island biogeography. Princeton University Press, Princeton

Mallet J (1995) A species definition for the modern synthesis. Trends Ecol Evol 10:294–299

Marino BDV, Odum HT (1999) Biosphere 2: introduction and research progress. Ecol Eng 13:3–14

May RM (1972) Will a large complex system be stable? Nature 238:413–414

May RM (1973) Stability and complexity in model ecosystems. Princeton University Press, Princeton

May RM (1975) Patterns of species abundance and diversity. In: Cody ML, Diamond JM (eds) Ecology and evolution of communities. Belknap Press of Harvard University Press, Cambridge, pp 81–120

May RM (1978) The dynamics and diversity of insect faunas. In: Mound LA, Waloff N (eds) Diversity of insect faunas. Blackwell, Oxford, pp 188–204

May RM (1988) How many species are there on earth? Science 240:1441–1449

May RM, MacArthur RH (1972) Niche overlap as a function of environmental variability. Proc Natl Acad Sci USA 69:1109–1113

Mayfield HF (1989) In memoriam: Frank W. Preston. Auk 106:714–717

Mayr E (1942) Systematics and the origin of species. Columbia University Press, New York

Mayr E, Diamond JM (2001) The birds of northern Melanesia. Speciation, ecology, and biogeography. Oxford University Press, Oxford

McCann KS (2000) The diversity-stability debate. Nature 405:228–233

McCann KS, Hastings A, Huxel GR (1998) Weak trophic interactions and the balance of nature. Nature 395:794–798

McGill BJ (2003) A test of the unified neutral theory of biodiversity. Nature 422:881–885

McGill BJ, Maurer BA, Weiser MD (2006) Empirical evaluation of neutral theory. Ecology 87:1411–1423

McKane RB, Johnson LC, Shaver GR, Nadelhoffer KJ, Rastetter EB, Fry B, Giblin AE, Kielland K, Kwiatkowski BL, Laundre JA, Murray G (2002) Resource-based niches provide a basis for plant species diversity and dominance in arctic tundra. Nature 415:68–71

McMahon SM, Miller KH, Drake J (2001) Networking tips for social scientists and ecologists. Science 293:1604–1605

Menge BA (1992) Community regulation: under what conditions are bottom-up factors important on rocky shores? Ecology 73:755–765

Milne LJ, Milne MJ (1976) The social behavior of burying beetles. Sci Am 235(2):84–89

Mitchell CE, Power AG (2003) Release of invasive plants from fungal and viral pathogens. Nature 421:625–627

Morrison D (2000) A creek runs through it. Front Ma Coll Biol Sci Univ Minn 3(1):6. http://cbs. umn.edu/main/aboutcbs/frontiers/fall2000.pdf

Morse DR, Stork NE, Lawton JH (1988) Species number, species abundance and body length relationships of arboreal beetles in Bornean lowland rain forest trees. Ecol Entomol 13:25–37

Myers RA, Baum JK, Shepherd TD, Powers SP, Peterson CH (2007) Cascading effects of the loss of apex predatory sharks from a coastal ocean. Science 315:1846–1850

Nadkarni NM (1994) Diversity of species and interactions in the upper tree canopy of forest ecosystems. Am Zool 34:70–78

Nadkarni NM (1995) Good-bye Tarzan. Sciences 35:28–33

Nadkarni NM, Merwin MC, Nieder J (2001) Forest canopies: plant diversity. In: Levin S (ed) Encyclopedia of biodiversity. Academic, San Diego, pp 27–40

Neutel A-M, Heesterbeek JAP, de Ruiter PC (2002) Stability in real food webs: weak links in long loops. Science 296:1120–1123

Neutel A-M, Heesterbeek JAP, van de Koppel J, Hoenderboom G, Vos A, Kaldeway C, Berendse F, de Ruiter CP (2007) Reconciling complexity with stability in naturally assembling food webs. Nature 449:599–602

Norghauer JN, Malcolm JR, Zimmerman BL (2006a) Juvenile mortality and attacks by a specialist herbivore increase with conspecific adult basal area of Amazonian *Swietenia macrophylla* (Meliaceae). J Trop Ecol 22:451–460

Norghauer JN, Malcolm JR, Zimmerman BL, Felfili JM (2006b) An experimental test of density- and distant-dependent recruitment of mahogany (*Swietenia macrophylla*) in southeastern Amazonia. Oecologia 148:437–446

Odum EP (1953) Fundam Ecol. Saunders, Philadelphia

Oksanen L, Oksanen T, Ekerholm P, Moen J, Lundber P, Bondestad L, Schneider M, Aruoja V, Armulik T (1995) Structure and dynamics of arctic-subarctic grazing webs in relation to primary productivity. In: Polis GA, Winemiller K (eds) Food webs: integration of patterns and dynamics. Chapman and Hall, London, pp 141–232

Oosterloo H, van Soest J (1977) Leuvenumse Bos en Hulshorster Zand. In: Coops A, Maas FW, Scheygrond A (eds) Natuurmonumenten in Nederland. Luitingh, Laren, pp 49–52

Packer A, Clay K (2000) Soil pathogens and spatial patterns of seedling mortality in a temperate tree. Nature 404:278–281

Paine RT (1992) Food-web analysis through field measurement of per capita interaction strength. Nature 355:73–75

Palinkas LA, Johnson JC, Boster JS, Houseal M (1998) Longitudinal studies of behavior and performance during a winter at the South Pole. Aviat Space Environ Med 69:73–77

Paoli GD, Curran LM, Zak DR (2006) Soil nutrients and beta diversity in the Bornean Dipterocarpaceae: evidence for niche partitioning by tropical rain forest trees. J Ecol 94:157–170

Parkes RJ, Webster G, Cragg BA, Weightman AJ, Newberry CJ, Ferdelman TG, Kallmeyer J, Jørgensen BB, Aiello IW, Fry JC (2005) Deep sub-seafloor prokaryotes stimulated at interfaces over geological time. Nature 436:390–394

Pauly D, Christensen V, Dalsgaard J, Froese R, Torres F (1998) Fishing down marine food webs. Science 279:860–863

Pauly D, Alder J, Bennett E, Christensen V, Tyedmers P, Watson R (2003) The future of fisheries. Science 302:1359–1361

Peake JF (1981) The land snails of islands – a dispersalist's viewpoint. In: Forey PL (ed) The evolving biosphere. British Museum (Natural History), London, and Cambridge University Press, Cambridge, pp 247–263

Pearce F (2004) The accidental rainforest. New Sci 183:(2465):44–45

Pearson DE, Callaway RM (2006) Biological control agents elevate hantavirus by subsidizing deer mouse populations. Ecol Lett 9:443–450

Peck SB (1994a) Aerial dispersal of insects between and to islands in the Galápagos Archipelago, Ecuador. Ann Entomol Soc Am 87:218–224

Peck SB (1994b) Sea-surface (pleuston) transport of insects between islands in the Galápagos Archipelago, Ecuador. Ann Entomol Soc Am 87:576–582

Peck SB (1996) Origin and development of an insect fauna on a remote archipelago: the Galápagos Islands, Ecuador. In: Keast A, Miller SE (eds) The origin and evolution of Pacific island biotas, New Guinea to eastern Polynesia: patterns and processes. SPB, Amsterdam, pp 91–122

Peterson BJ, Fry B (1987) Stable isotopes in ecosystem studies. Ann Rev Ecol Syst 18:293–320

Pimm SL (1998) The forest fragment classic. Nature 393:23–24

Pimm SL (2002) Foreword. In: Pimm ST (ed) Food webs, reprinted. University of Chicago Press, Chicago, pp xiii–xxxix

Pimm SL, Kitching RL (1987) The determinants of food chain lengths. Oikos 50:302–307

Pimm SL, Lawton JH (1977) The number of trophic levels in ecological communities. Nature 268:329–331

Polis GA (1991) Complex desert food webs: an empirical critique of food web theory. Am Nat 138:123–155

Post DM (2002) The long and short of food-chain length. Trends Ecol Evol 17:269–277

Post DM, Pace ML, Hairston NG (2000) Ecosystem size determines food-chain length in lakes. Nature 405:1047–1049

Power M.E (1992) Top-down and bottom-up forces in food-webs: do plants have primacy? Ecology 73:733–746

Preston FW (1948) The commonness, and rarity, of species. Ecology 29:254–283

Preston FW (1960) Time and space and the variation of species. Ecology 41:611–627

Preston FW (1962a) The canonical distribution of commonness and rarity: part I. Ecology 43:185–215

Preston FW (1962b) The canonical distribution of commonness and rarity: part II. Ecology 43:410–432

Pringle L (1994) Scorpion Man: exploring the world of scorpions. Scribner's, New York

Priscu JC, Adams EE, Lyons WB, Voytek MA, Mogk DW, Brown RL, McKay CP, Takacs CD, Welch KA, Wolf CF, Kirshtein JD, Avci A (1999) Geomicrobiology of subglacial ice above Lake Vostok, Antarctica. Science 286:2141–2144

Pukowski E (1933) Ökologische Untersuchungen an *Necrophorus* F. Z Morphol Okol Tiere 27:518–586

Quammen D (1996) The song of the dodo; island biogeography in an age of extinctions. Pimlico, London

Richardson AL (2007) The role of scientist, narrator, mother, Pandora, nursemaid, therapist, and Baucis in Mary Zimmerman's Metamorphoses: a production thesis in acting. MA thesis, Louisiana State University, Baton Rouge

Rohwerder T, Sand W, Lascu C (2003) Preliminary evidence for a sulphur cycle in Movile Cave, Romania. Acta Biotechnol 23:101–107

Rosenzweig ML (1995) Species diversity in space and time. Cambridge University Press, Cambridge

Rydin H, Borgegård SO (1988) Plant species richness on islands over a century of primary succession: Lake Hjälmaren. Ecology 69:916–927

Sakai S, Nakashizuka T, Ichie T, Nomura M, Chong L (2002) Lambir Hills canopy crane, Malaysia. In: Mitchell AW, Secoy K, Jackson T (eds) Global canopy handbook; techniques of access and study in the forest roof. Global Canopy Programme, Oxford, pp 77–79

Sarbu SM (2000) Movile Cave: a chemoautotrophically based groundwater ecosystem. In: Wilkens H, Culver DC, Humphries WF (eds) Subterranean ecosystems. Elsevier, Amsterdam, pp 319–343

Sarbu SM, Kane TC, Kinkle BK (1996) A chemoautotrophically based cave ecosystem. Science 272:1953–1955

Schilthuizen M (2000) Dualism and conflicts in understanding speciation. BioEssays 22:1134–1141

Schilthuizen M (2001) Frogs, flies, and dandelions; the making of species. Oxford University Press, Oxford

Schilthuizen M (2004) Caribbean coral catastrophe. ScienceNOW. http://sciencenow.sciencemag.org/cgi/content/full/2004/326/3

Schilthuizen M (2006a) Biodiscoveries; Borneo's botanical secret. WWF-Indonesia, Jakarta. http://assets.panda.org/downloads/biodiscoveriesborneosbotanicalsecret.pdf

Schilthuizen M (2006b) Wuivende palmen en orangoetanhoofden. Bionieuws 17 Feb 2006, pp 8–9

Schilthuizen M, Clements R (2008) Tracking land snail extinctions from space. Tentacle 16:8–9. http://www.hawaii.edu/cowielab/Tentacle/

Schilthuizen M, Vallenduuk HJ (1998) Kevers op kadavers. KKNV, Utrecht

Schippers A, Neretin LN, Kallmeyer J, Ferdelman TG, Cragg BA, Parkes RJ, Jørgensen BB (2005) Prokaryotic cells of the deep sub-seafloor biosphere identified as living bacteria. Nature 433:861–864

Schoener TW (1983) Field experiments on interspecific competition. Am Nat 122:240–285

Schoenly K, Beaver RA, Heumier TA (1991) On the trophic relations of insects: a food-web approach. Am Nat 137:597–638

Schönrogge K, Stone GN, Crawley MJ (1996) Alien herbivores and native parasitoids: rapid developments and structure of the parasitoid and inquiline complex in an invading gall wasp *Andricus quercuscalicis* (Hymenoptera: Cynipidae). Ecol Entomol 21:71–80

Severinghaus JP, Broecker WS, Dempster WF, MacCallum T, Wahlen M (1994) Oxygen loss in Biosphere 2. Eos Trans Am Geophys Union 75:33

Shrader-Frechette KS, McCoy ED (1993) Method in ecology; strategies for conservation. Cambridge University Press, Cambridge

Silvertown J (2004) Plant coexistence and the niche. Trends Ecol Evol 19:605–611

Silvertown J (2005) Demons in Eden; the paradox of plant diversity. Chicago University Press, Chicago

Silvertown J, Dodd ME, Gowing DJG, Mountford JO (1999). Hydrologically defined niches reveal a basis for species richness in plant communities. Nature 400:61–63

Simberloff DS (1976) Experimental zoogeography of islands: effects of island size. Ecology 57:629–648

Simberloff DS (1978) Using island biogeographic distributions to determine if colonization is stochastic. Am Nat 112:713–726

Simberloff DS, Wilson EO (1969) Experimental zoogeography of islands: the colonization of empty islands. Ecology 50:278–296

Simberloff DS, Wilson EO (1970) Experimental zoogeography of islands: a two-year record of colonization. Ecology 51:934–937

Simberloff DS (2000) Foreword. In: Elton CS The ecology of invasions by animals and plants. University of Chicago Press, Chicago, pp vii–xiv

Small A, Martin TG, Kitching RL, Wong KM (2004) Contribution of tree species to the biodiversity of a 1 ha Old World rainforest in Brunei, Borneo. Biodivers Conserv 13:2067–2088

Smythies BE, Davison GWH (1999) The birds of Borneo, 4th edn. Natural History Publications (Borneo) and Sabah Society, Kota Kinabalu

Stomp M, Huisman J, de Jongh F, Veraart AJ, Gerla D, Rijkeboer M, Ibelings BW, Wolenzien UIA, Stal LJ (2004) Adaptive divergence in pigment composition promotes phytoplankton biodiversity. Nature 432:104–107

Stork NE (1988) Insect diversity: facts, fiction and speculation. Biol J Linn Soc 35:321–337

Stratford JA, Stouffer PC (1999) Local extinctions of terrestrial insectivorous birds in a fragmented landscape near Manaus, Brazil. Conserv Biol 13:1416–1423

Sugihara G, Bersier L, Southwood TRE, Pimm SL, May RM (2003) Predicted correspondence between species abundances and dendrograms of niche similarities. Proc Natl Acad Sci USA 100:5246–5251

Summerhayes VS, Elton CS (1923) Contributions to the ecology of Spitsbergen and Bear Island. J Ecol 11:214–286

Sutton S.L (2001). Alice grows up: canopy science in transition from Wonderland to reality. Plant Ecol 153:13–21

Tansley AG (1935) The use and abuse of vegetational concepts and terms. Ecology 16:284–307

Taylor JD, Braithwaite CJR, Peake JF, Arnold EF (1979) Terrestrial faunas and habitats of Aldabra during the Late Pleistocene. Philos Trans R Soc Lond Ser B 286:47–66

Terborgh J (1988) The big things that run the world – a sequel to E. O. Wilson. Conserv Biol 2:402–403

Thomson JN (2003) James Thomson's tribute to sesquicentennial lecturer Daniel Janzen. Zoonews, Newsletter of the Zoology Department, University of Toronto, October 2003

Thorpe V (2000) Darwin's theory was inspired by a hillock. Observer 22 Oct. http://www.guardian.co.uk/uk/2000/oct/22/booksnews.peopleinscience

Tilman D, Reich PB, Knops JMH, Wedin D, Mielke T, Lehman C (2001) Diversity and productivity in a long-term grassland experiment. Science 294:843–845

Tilman D, Reich PB, Knops JMH (2006) Biodiversity and ecosystem stability in a decade-long grassland experiment. Nature 441:629–632

Torchin ME, Lafferty KD, Dobson AP, McKenzie VJ, Kuris AM (2003) Introduced species and their missing parasites. Nature 421:628–630

Torsvik V, Goksøyr J, Daae FL (1990) High diversity in DNA of soil bacteria. Appl Environ Microbiol 56:782–787

Trichon V (2002) Monkeys as canopy collectors. In: Mitchell AW, Secoy K, Jackson T (eds) Global canopy handbook; techniques of access and study in the forest roof. Global Canopy Programme, Oxford, pp 11–12

van der Meijden R (2005) Heukels' flora van Nederland, 23rd edn. Wolters-Noordhoff, Groningen

van der Gast CJ, Lilley AK, Ager D, Thompson IP (2005) Island size and bacterial diversity in an archipelago of engineering machines. Environ Microbiol 7:1220–1226

van der Putten WH (2000) Pathogen-driven forest diversity. Nature 404:232–233

van der Wielen PWJJ et al (2005) The enigma of prokaryotic life in deep hypersaline anoxic basins. Science 307:121–123

van der Weijden WJ, Leewis R, Bol P (2007) Biological globalisation; bio-invasions and their impacts on nature, the economy, and public health. KNNV, Utrecht

van der Zanden MJ et al (1999a) Patterns of food chain length in lakes: a stable isotope study. Am Nat 154:406–416

van der Zanden MJ et al (1999b) Stable isotope evidence for the food web consequences of species invasions in lakes. Nature 401:464–467

van Dover CL (2000) The ecology of deep-sea hydrothermal vents. Princeton University Press, Princeton van Ruijven J, Berendse F (2007) Contrasting effects of diversity on the temporal stability of plant populations. Oikos 116:1323–1330

Vartanyan SL, Garutt VE, Sher AV (1993) Holocene dwarf mammoths from Wrangel Island in the Siberian Arctic. Nature 362:337–340

Vartanyan SL, Arslanov KA, Tertychnaya TV, Chernov SB (1995) Radiocarbon dating evidence for mammoths on Wrangel island, Arctic Ocean, until 2000 BC. Radiocarbon 37:1–6

Venter JC et al (2004) Environmental genome shotgun sequencing of the Sargasso Sea. Science 304:66–74

Vermeij GJ (1991) When biotas meet: understanding biotic interchange. Science 253:1099–1104

Vines G (2002) King of the canopy. New Sci 176(2374):72

Volkov I, Banaver JR, Hubbell SP, Maritan A (2003) Neutral theory and relative species abundance in ecology. Nature 424:1035–1037

Volkov I, Banavar JR, He F, Hubbell SP, Maritan A (2005) Density dependence explains tree species abundance and diversity in tropical forests. Nature 438:658–661

Volterra V (1926) Variazioni e fluttuazioni del numero d'individui in specie animali conviventi. Mem R Accad Linceai Ser 6 2:1–36

Walker JJ, Spear JR, Pace NR (2005) Geobiology of a microbial endolithic community in the Yellowstone geothermal environment. Nature 434:1011–1014

Wallace AR (1858) On the tendency of varieties to depart indefinitely from the original type. J Proc Linn Soc (Zool) 3:53–62

Wallace AR (1869) The Malay Archipelago; the land of the orang-utan and the bird of paradise; a narrative of travel with studies of man and nature. Macmillan, London

Wallace AR (1880) Island life. Macmillan, London

Wallingford SH (2003) Monkey sense. New Sci 177(2379):27

Wapnick CM, Precht WF, Aronson RB (2004) Millennial-scale dynamics of staghorn corals in Discovery Bay, Jamaica. Ecol Lett 7:354–361

Ware DM, Thomson RE (2005) Bottom-up ecosystem trophic dynamics determine fish production in the Northeast Pacific. Science 308:1280–1284

Welch P (1952) Limnology, 2nd edn. McGraw-Hill, New York

Westbroek P (1991) Life as a geological force; dynamics of the Earth. Norton, New York

Whitfield J (2002) Neutrality versus the niche. Nature 417:480–481

Whitman WB, Coleman DC, Wiebe WJ (1998) Prokaryotes: the unseen majority. Proc Natl Acad Sci USA 95:6578–6583

Whitmore TC (1998) An introduction to tropical rain forests, 2nd edn. Oxford University Press, Oxford

Wilkinson DM (2004) The parable of Green Mountain: Ascension Island, ecosystem construction and ecological fitting. J Biogeogr 31:1–4

Williamson M (1997) Biological invasions. Chapman and Hall, London

Wills C et al (2006) Nonrandom processes maintain diversity in tropical forests. Science 311:527–531

Wilson EO (1987) The little things that run the world (the importance and conservation of invertebrates). Conserv Biol 1:344–346

Wilson EO (1992) The diversity of life. Penguin, London

Wilson EO (1994) Naturalist. Island, Washington

Wilson EO, Simberloff DS (1969) Experimental zoogeography of islands: defaunation and monitoring techniques. Ecology 50:267–278

Wong M, Wright SJ, Hubbell SP, Foster RB (1990) The spatial pattern and reproductive consequences of outbreak defoliation in *Quararibea asterolepis*, a tropical tree. J Ecol 78:579–588

Wootton JT (1994) Predicting direct and indirect effects: an integrated approach using experiments and path analysis. Ecology 75:151–165

Wright SJ (2002) Plant diversity in tropical forests: a review of mechanisms of species coexistence. Oecologia 130:1–14

Wu J, Huang J, Han X, Xie Z, Gao X (2003) Three-Gorges Dam: experiment in habitat fragmentation? Science 300:1239–1240

Yodzis P (1993) Environment and trophodiversity. In: Ricklefs R, Schluter D (eds) Species diversity in ecological communities: historical and geographical perspectives. University of Chicago Press, Chicago, pp 26–38

Zabel B, Hawes P, Stuart H, Marino BDV (1999) Construction and engineering of a created environment: overview of the Biosphere 2 closed system. Ecol Eng 13:43–63

Zavaleta ES, Hulvey KB (2004) Realistic species losses disproportionately reduce grassland resistance to biological invaders. Science 306:1175–1177

Zheng D, Prince S, Wright R (2003) Terrestrial net primary production estimates for 0.5° grid cells from field observations – a contribution to global biogeochemical modeling. Glob Change Biol 9:46–64

Index

Printing: Krips bv, Meppel, The Netherlands
Binding: Stürtz, Würzburg, Germany